Politics in the
American States

Politics in the American States

A COMPARATIVE ANALYSIS

TENTH EDITION

Editors

VIRGINIA GRAY, *University of North Carolina at Chapel Hill*

RUSSELL L. HANSON, *Indiana University Bloomington*

THAD KOUSSER, *University of California, San Diego*

Los Angeles | London | New Delhi
Singapore | Washington DC

Los Angeles | London | New Delhi
Singapore | Washington DC

FOR INFORMATION:

CQ Press
An Imprint of SAGE Publications, Inc.
2455 Teller Road
Thousand Oaks, California 91320
E-mail: order@sagepub.com

SAGE Publications Ltd.
1 Oliver's Yard
55 City Road
London, EC1Y 1SP
United Kingdom

SAGE Publications India Pvt. Ltd.
B 1/I 1 Mohan Cooperative Industrial Area
Mathura Road, New Delhi 110 044
India

SAGE Publications Asia-Pacific Pte. Ltd.
33 Pekin Street #02-01
Far East Square
Singapore 048763

Acquisitions Editor: Charisse Kiino
Production Editor: Gwenda Larsen
Marketing Manager: Jonathan Mason
Typesetter: C&M Digitals (P) Ltd.
Cover Designer: Mike Pottman, M Design & Print

Printed in the United States of America

Library of Congress Cataloging-in-Publication Data

Politics in the American states: a comparative analysis/editors,
Virginia Gray, Russell L. Hanson, Thad Kousser.—10th ed.

p. cm.

Includes bibliographical references and indexes.

ISBN 978-1-60871-998-3 (pbk. : alk. paper)

1. State governments—United States. I. Gray, Virginia, II. Hanson,
Russell L., III. Kousser, Thad,

JK2408.P64 2013

320.973—dc23

2011048562

This book is printed on acid-free paper.

12 13 14 15 16 10 9 8 7 6 5 4 3 2 1

Contents

Tables, Figures, and Boxes

FIGURES

Preface

U.S. Supreme Court Justice Louis D. Brandeis famously referred to the American states as laboratories of democracy because a "single courageous state may, if its citizens choose, serve as a laboratory and try novel social and economic experiments without risk to the rest of the country." Some of these experiments fail, but others succeed and become models for other states to emulate. A few even provide templates for new federal programs that serve the entire nation. In this way, states pioneer solutions to the social, economic, and political problems facing the United States.

Brandeis's political insight is widely appreciated, but it is also true that states function as laboratories in another sense: their governments and policies permit comparisons that enable social scientists and others to identify the basic political processes at work in all or most of the states. Because states are similar in many important respects, it is possible to identify differences in geography, population, and economy that account for differences in their political institutions and that help explain why states differ in the policies they enact. These systematic comparisons are the social science equivalent of the controlled experiments undertaken in natural science laboratories; they yield important findings that account for the election results or policy decisions reported in newspapers and on radio, television, and news Web sites.

Understanding these political processes is especially important today. The Great Recession of 2007–2009 was broader, deeper, and longer than any economic downturn since the 1930s. Unemployment rates reached double digits in several states and remained high, even after the recession ended officially. Incomes fell, the number of mortgage foreclosures and personal bankruptcies spiked, and poverty gripped millions—some 15 percent of the population. Governments felt the pain as well. Revenues from sales and income taxes plunged, and states had great difficulty balancing their budgets, even with massive assistance in the form of a federal stimulus package.

The economic strains facing policymakers were exacerbated by political developments. The 2010 midterm elections left Republicans in complete control of the governments of twenty states; Democrats held only eleven states. The two parties split control in eighteen states, where it was correspondingly harder to reach compromises on spending reductions and tax increases. Minnesota's government actually shut down on July 1, 2011, when the Democratic governor and Republican legislature could not agree on a budget for the next year. But even in states under the control of a single party, the level of conflict was high. Wisconsin Democrats, who were in the minority, left the state for part of the 2011 legislative session to protest Republican plans to reduce benefits and collective bargaining rights for state workers. Indiana Democrats did the same thing, and extracted some concessions in exchange for returning in time to pass a new budget.

This pattern is likely to persist. State revenues are slowly recovering, but they have not yet returned to pre-recession levels. The stimulus funds are exhausted, and other federal grants to states are being reduced or eliminated. Overall, then, the financial situation of states is grim, and partisan differences are being reinforced by Tea Party activists, who are pressing for smaller government all around. None of these factors shows any sign of abating; if anything, conflict will intensify as retrenchment occurs at the federal level and spending cuts trickle down to state and local governments. In short, the country has achieved a "new normal" in state politics in which austerity, not prosperity, is the overarching theme.

One aspect of the new normal deserves special mention. As Congress cuts domestic spending, the national government will forfeit considerable leverage over state policymakers, who currently must comply with federal mandates in order to qualify for grants-in-aid. Thus, although less money will be flowing from Washington, governors and state legislators will have more freedom to pursue their own goals, albeit at their own expense. States will use this freedom differently, in part because some are more self-sufficient than others. Also, policies will likely diverge as public officials respond to the concerns and values of the citizens of their respective states. Therefore, Texas and California, which are located at different ends of the political spectrum, will take different paths in educational, environmental, and social policy, with less direction from the nation's capital.

Federalism permits policies to vary across the states, and indeed encourages it. People in each state can chart their own course in matters on which there is no national consensus. Federalism encourages variation by creating incentives for political leaders to craft innovative solutions to important problems. Governors who, for example, succeed in reforming education will win reelection. They may then parlay this success into approval at the national level, propounding their signature policies as nostrums for what ails the nation. The number of governors who were seeking the Republican Party's presidential nomination in 2012 was testimony to their reliance on their accomplishments as reformers in moving up the political ladder.

But federalism is not just about states' rights; it imposes some limits on states as well. Those limits are tighter in some policy areas than others. The fundamental rights of individuals are now uniform across the nation, though there is considerable debate over which rights are fundamental and therefore beyond the control of states (as the disputes surrounding same-sex marriage illustrate). Some entitlements are national as well, and more will be if the Patient Protection and Affordable Care Act is upheld by the U.S. Supreme Court. Key elements of environmental policy are most efficiently addressed at the national level, but state and local governments do play an important role in the implementation of national policy and actually dominate natural resource management and the regulation of land use. Meanwhile, criminal justice, education, and economic development are the province of state and local governments, and the policy choices in these areas differ greatly.

Policy variations across the states reflect the growing diversity of American society. Demographic trends are reconstituting the nation and its states, as are immigration and the mobility of populations within the United States. These changes affect state politics in many ways, because political leaders must address the competing—and sometimes conflicting—demands of longtime residents and newcomers with different needs and preferences. Managing this tension is the responsibility of state policymakers, who are themselves divided over the best way to meet the challenge. The conflict over immigration policy is a case in point; within each state and across the country some leaders welcome the changes and others resist them.

As state populations become more diverse, so does their political leadership. An important theme in this volume is the growing involvement of women and racial minorities in the political process. Historically, these groups have been underrepresented in the institutions of state government, but that is changing. Several chapters in this book document gains that have been made by women, African Americans, and Hispanic Americans in the legislative, executive, and judicial branches of state government. Our contributors also identify obstacles to further gains and consider how the changing pattern of representation affects policy choices in the states that are diversifying the fastest.

Understanding these developments is the goal of this new edition of *Politics in the American States*. The contributors to this volume, building on their own research and the work of scholars in the field, seek to advance the knowledge of state politics. In that sense, this volume is a handbook for academicians, administrators, policymakers, consultants, and other experts in state politics. At the same time, *Politics in the American States* provides teachers with instructional resources that students can grasp, appreciate, and use for their own purposes. Our contributors address both audiences: they appeal to students' curiosity about their own states as well as professionals' interest in generalizations. Thus each chapter provides nuanced treatments of individual states in the context of rigorous analyses of the fifty states as a whole. On that basis, readers can make systematic comparisons of states, while remaining sensitive to the diversity and subtlety of political life at the state level.

We are very pleased to welcome Thad Kousser to the team of volume editors for this tenth edition of *Politics in the American States*. Thad is associate professor of political science at the University of California, San Diego; author of *Term Limits and the Dismantling of State Legislative Professionalism*; and a former coeditor of *State Politics and Policy Quarterly*. His expertise and editorial experience have been invaluable in revising our book, and we look forward to his own contribution to the next edition of this long-running volume.

Twelve chapters from the previous edition have been revised, updated, and streamlined for this edition. In Chapter 1, Virginia Gray describes the current socioeconomic and political context of states, drawing on the latest information from the U.S. Census Bureau. In Chapter 2, Russell L. Hanson reviews the intergovernmental context of state governments, highlighting emerging trends. With Raymond J. La Raja, Thomas M. Holbrook analyzes in Chapter 3 parties and elections in the states, including the results of the 2010 contests. In Chapter 4, a new coauthor, Adam J. Newmark, joins Anthony J. Nownes in assessing the contemporary role of interest groups in state politics, and in Chapter 5 Shaun Bowler and Todd Donovan gauge the impact of initiatives and referendums on state politics and policymaking.

Each branch of state government is treated at length in a separate chapter. Keith E. Hamm and Gary F. Moncrief explore legislative politics in the fifty states in Chapter 6. In Chapter 7, Margaret Ferguson covers the governors and executive branch. And in Chapter 8 Melinda Gann Hall analyzes state judiciaries and their impact on controversial policy questions such as same-sex marriage, the right to die, and capital punishment.

Following coverage of the courts, John Wooldredge examines in Chapter 9 corrections policy in the fifty states in light of the ongoing movement to get tough on criminals. In Chapter 10, Robert C. Lowry compares fiscal policies in the states, and Mark Carl Rom turns in Chapter 11 to health and welfare policy in view of the impending reforms. Finally, in Chapter 16 Martin Saiz and Susan E. Clarke reprise their assessment of economic development and infrastructure policy under the pressure of globalization.

This tenth edition of *Politics in the American States* also includes four new chapters. Chapter 12, by Michael B. Berkman and Eric Plutzer, looks at the politics of education. In Chapter 13, Alisa Hicklin Fryar and Robert C. Lowry analyze the politics of higher education. Justin H. Phillips examines in Chapter 14 policies on moral issues in the context of public opinion in the states. And in Chapter 15 David M. Konisky and Neal D. Woods cover environmental policy in the American states.

To assist readers, all of our contributors offer clear road maps to their chapters at the outset and summaries at the end. Throughout the volume, key terms appear in boldface and are listed at the end of the chapter in which they are introduced.

At the end of the volume is a glossary of short definitions of these terms, along with detailed indexes with page listings and cross-references.

In association with the printed volume, CQ Press has established an instructor's resources Web site at http://college.cqpress.com/grayhanson. Every table, figure, and illustration in the printed volume is reproduced at that site and may be downloaded for use in class. The data underlying many of the tables are also available so that instructors can explore patterns in state politics and policymaking with their students. The data enable readers to investigate the relationship between political institutions and their environments and to test hypotheses about the causes and consequences of different policies in the American states. Instructors can download the datasets and assign them to their students.

For help in preparing this edition, we thank the following reviewers, who provided valuable insight and recommendations: Brian Adams, San Diego State University; Gerald Benjamin, SUNY New Paltz; Brian DiSarro, California State University, Sacramento; Gary Halter, Texas A&M University; Susan Hansen, University of Pittsburgh; John Klemanski, Oakland University; Suzanne Leland, UNC Charlotte; Charles Matzke, Michigan State University; John McGlennon, College of William & Mary; David Peterson, Iowa State University; James Riddlesperger, Texas Christian University; and James Stoutenborough, Texas A&M University. We also thank the following staff at CQ Press: Charisse Kiino, our sponsoring editor; Nancy Loh, our development editor; and Gwenda Larsen, our production editor. Freelancer Sabra Bissette Ledent copyedited the text. Each of them made important contributions to this volume, and it was our pleasure to work with such dedicated and skilled professionals. We are very grateful for their guidance and support.

Virginia Gray
Russell L. Hanson
Thad Kousser

Contributors

MICHAEL B. BERKMAN is professor of political science at Penn State University. With Eric Plutzer, he is the author of two books on education policy, *Ten Thousand Democracies* (2005) and *Evolution, Creationism, and the Battle to Control America's Classrooms* (2010). In addition to his research on education policy, his research on state politics and policy has appeared in the *American Political Science Review, American Journal of Political Science, Political Research Quarterly,* and *Social Science Quarterly.*

SHAUN BOWLER is professor of political science at the University of California, Riverside, and is a member of the Board of Scholars of the Initiative and Referendum Institute. He is the author of many articles on direct democracy and is the author or coeditor of several books, including *Demanding Choices: Opinion Voting and Direct Democracy* (1998) and *Citizens as Legislators: Direct Democracy in the United States* (1998).

SUSAN E. CLARKE is professor of political science at the University of Colorado at Boulder and the faculty director of the SEEDS (Social Entrepreneurship, Equitable Development, Sustainability) Residential Academic Program. She is a coeditor of *Urban Affairs Review,* and her research currently centers on economic development policies, neighborhood regeneration strategies, and border security policies. She is coauthor, with Gary L. Gaile, of *The Work of Cities* (1998) and, with Rodney Hero, Mara Sidney, Luis Fraga, and Bari Erlichson, of *Multiethnic Moments: The Politics of Urban Education Reform* (2006).

TODD DONOVAN is professor of political science at Western Washington University and a member of the Board of Scholars of the Initiative and Referendum Institute. He is the author of many articles on direct democracy and is the coauthor or coeditor of several books, including *Demanding Choices: Opinion, Voting, and Direct Democracy* (1998), *Citizens as Legislators: Direct Democracy in the United States* (1998), *Why Iowa? How Caucuses and Sequential Elections Improve the Presidential Nominating Process* (2010), and *State and Local Politics: Institutions and Reform* (2012).

MARGARET FERGUSON is associate professor and chair of political science at Indiana University–Purdue University Indianapolis. Her research interests include governorships, legislatures, and lawmaking in the states; executive branch politics; and leadership and personality. She teaches courses on state politics, southern politics, and the presidency. Her articles have been published in the *Journal of Politics, Women and Politics, Publius: The Journal of Federalism, Political Psychology, Public Administration Review,* and *State Politics and Policy Quarterly.* She is the editor of *The Executive Branch of State Government: People, Process, and Politics* (2006).

ALISA HICKLIN FRYAR is an assistant professor of political science at the University of Oklahoma. Her scholarly work has appeared in numerous peer-reviewed journals, including *Journal of Politics, Journal of Public Administration Research and Theory, Public Administration Review,* and *Policy Studies Journal.* Her research interests include higher education policy, state politics, immigration policy, and public management.

VIRGINIA GRAY is the Robert Watson Winston Distinguished Professor of Political Science at the University of North Carolina at Chapel Hill. She teaches and conducts research on state politics, public policy, and interest groups. She has published numerous articles and books on these topics, including *The Population Ecology of Interest Representation* (with David Lowery). In 2007 Gray received the APSA State Politics and Policy Career Achievement Award, which is awarded annually to a political scientist who has made a significant lifetime contribution to the study of politics and public policy in the American states.

MELINDA GANN HALL is distinguished professor of political science at Michigan State University, where she specializes in judicial politics. Her research has appeared in the *American Political Science Review, American Journal of Political Science, Journal of Politics, Political Research Quarterly, Social Science Quarterly, American Politics Quarterly, State Politics and Policy Quarterly* (*SPPQ*), and other journals, law reviews, and edited volumes. She also is coauthor of *In Defense of Judicial Elections* (2009). For her research on judicial elections, she received both the American Judicature Society Award and the McGraw-Hill Award from the Law and Courts Section of the American Political Science Association and the *SPPQ* Award from the State Politics and Policy Section. She is formerly the chair of the Law and Courts Section of the American Political Science Association, president of the State Politics and Policy Section, and vice president of the Midwest Political Science Association.

KEITH E. HAMM holds the Thomas Cook and Marty Elizabeth Edwards Memorial Chair in American Government at Rice University. In 2006 he was a Fulbright research scholar at the Center on North American Politics and Society at Carleton

University (Canada). Hamm has spent the better part of the past decade studying issues related to state legislative elections and campaign finance. Among his publications are *101 Chambers: Congress, State Legislatures, and the Future of Legislative Studies* (2005), coauthored with Peverill Squire.

RUSSELL L. HANSON is professor of political science at Indiana University Bloomington, where he has taught since 1980. He is interested in American federalism and has published articles on political culture, economic development, and social policy in the American states. Among his edited books are *Reconsidering the Democratic Public* (1993) and *Governing Partners: State-Local Relations in the United States* (1998). His articles have appeared in the *Journal of Politics, American Journal of Political Science, Political Research Quarterly,* and *State Politics and Policy Quarterly.* He also writes on American political thought.

THOMAS M. HOLBROOK is the Wilder Crane Professor of Government at the University of Wisconsin–Milwaukee. He is author of *Do Campaigns Matter?* (1996) and has published extensively on state politics and presidential campaigns. He is currently working on a long-term project on voting behavior in urban mayoral elections.

DAVID M. KONISKY is assistant professor of public policy at Georgetown University. His research focuses on American politics and public policy, with particular emphasis on environmental politics and policy, state politics, and public opinion. His articles on environmental politics and policy have been published in numerous journals, including the *American Journal of Political Science, Journal of Policy Analysis and Management, Political Research Quarterly, Public Opinion Quarterly,* and *State Politics and Policy Quarterly.*

THAD KOUSSER is associate professor of political science at the University of California, San Diego, and director of the California Constitutional Reform Project at Stanford University's Lane Center for the West. He has served as a legislative aide in the California, New Mexico, and U.S. Senates. He is the author of *Term Limits and the Dismantling of State Legislative Professionalism,* coauthor of *The Logic of American Politics,* and coeditor of *The New Political Geography of California.* Kousser has been awarded the UCSD Academic Senate's Distinguished Teaching Award and has served as coeditor of the journal *State Politics and Policy Quarterly.*

RAYMOND J. LA RAJA is associate professor of political science at the University of Massachusetts, Amherst, and editor of *The Forum,* an electronic journal of applied research in contemporary American politics. He has published articles on political parties, interest groups, and electoral reform. He is the author of *Small Change: Money, Political Parties, and Campaign Finance Reform* (2008) and serves on the Academic Advisory Board of the Campaign Finance Institute in Washington, D.C.

ROBERT C. LOWRY is professor of political science in the School of Economic, Political and Policy Sciences at the University of Texas at Dallas. His scholarly work has appeared in numerous peer-reviewed journals, including the *American Political Science Review, American Journal of Political Science, Journal of Politics, Economics and Politics, Economics of Education Review*, and *State Politics and Policy Quarterly*. His research interests include state fiscal policy and institutions, the political economy of higher education, political and civic organizations, and campaign finance.

GARY F. MONCRIEF is University Distinguished Professor of Political Science at Boise State University, where he teaches courses on state politics, legislative politics, and campaigns and elections. He is the coauthor, with Peverill Squire, of *State Legislatures Today* (2010) and the editor of *Reapportionment and Redistricting in the West* (2012). He has published numerous books, book chapters, and research articles on legislatures, and he is a frequent speaker at various meetings of state legislators.

ADAM J. NEWMARK is associate professor of political science at Appalachian State University. His teaching and research interests include state politics, interest groups and lobbying, and public policy. His research has appeared in a number of edited volumes and academic journals, including *Journal of Politics, State Politics and Policy Quarterly, Social Science Quarterly*, and *Legislative Studies Quarterly*.

ANTHONY J. NOWNES is professor of political science at the University of Tennessee, Knoxville. His work has appeared in numerous political science journals and edited volumes. His most recent book, *Total Lobbying: What Lobbyists Want (and How They Try to Get It)*, was published in 2006.

JUSTIN H. PHILLIPS is associate professor of political science at Columbia University. He studies American state and urban politics and public opinion, and has published articles in the *American Journal of Political Science, Legislative Studies Quarterly*, and *Journal of Law, Economics, and Organization*. His current research projects include analyzing the effects of public opinion on subnational policymaking and evaluating the power of state governors in negotiations with legislatures.

ERIC PLUTZER is professor of political science and academic director of the Survey Research Center at Penn State University. With Michael B. Berkman, he is the author of two books on education policy, *Ten Thousand Democracies: Politics and Public Opinion in American* (2005) and *Evolution, Creationism, and the Battle to Control America's Classrooms* (2010). His research on public opinion, turnout, and voting has appeared in the *American Political Science Review, American Sociological Review, Journal of Politics*, and *American Journal of Political Science*.

MARK CARL ROM is an associate professor of government and public policy at Georgetown University. He has published books and articles on state health and welfare policy as well as other topics in American public policy, including *Welfare Magnets* (1990), *Public Spirit in the Thrift Tragedy* (1996), and *Fatal Extraction* (1997). Recent and forthcoming works include a review of state health and welfare policies in the *Oxford Handbook of State and Local Government*, the chapter "President Obama's Health Care Reform: The Impossible Inevitable" in *Obama's Presidency: Change and Continuity*, and the chapter "Below the (Bible) Belt: Religion and Sexuality in American Public Schools" in *Curriculum and the Culture Wars: When and Where Is Religion Appropriate in the Public Schools?*

MARTIN SAIZ is a professor of political science at California State University, Northridge. He was a community activist in Denver, Colorado, where he served two terms as a planning commissioner. He is a coeditor of *Local Parties in Political and Organizational Perspective* (1999), which analyzes relations between political party systems and local communities in the United States and several other nations. His articles on issues of urban politics, local political parties, economic development, and the effects of voting turnout on public policy have been published in the *Journal of Politics*, *Urban Affairs Review*, *Political Research Quarterly*, *Policy Studies Journal*, and *Economic Development Quarterly*, as well as other books and journals.

NEAL D. WOODS is associate professor of political science at the University of South Carolina. His research focuses on public policy, federalism, and state politics. His work on state environmental policy has appeared in numerous journals, including *Political Research Quarterly*, *Social Science Quarterly*, *State Politics and Policy Quarterly*, *Publius: The Journal of Federalism*, and *Journal of Public Administration Research and Theory*.

JOHN WOOLDREDGE is a professor in the School of Criminal Justice at the University of Cincinnati. His research and publications focus on institutional corrections (crowding, inmate violence, and inmate adaptation) and criminal case processing (sentencing and recidivism, extralegal disparities in case processing and outcomes). He is currently involved in research on the impact of a defendant's race on court decisions ranging from pretrial release through sentencing (in Cleveland, Ohio), and research on the effects of both inmate and prison characteristics on the odds of being victimized by violence during incarceration (in Kentucky and Ohio prisons). His work has most recently appeared in *Criminology*, *Journal of Empirical Legal Studies*, and *Justice Quarterly*. He is now working on the *Oxford University Handbook on Prisons*, which is part of Oxford University Press's *Handbook* series edited by Michael Tonry.

CHAPTER 1

The Socioeconomic and Political Context of States

VIRGINIA GRAY

In November 2010, the nation elected a Republican House of Representatives. At the state level, Republicans gained control of twenty-nine of the fifty governorships and twenty-five of the state legislatures. Meanwhile, both levels of government faced a fourth year of fiscal crisis, unprecedented strains on safety net programs such as unemployment insurance and Medicaid, and, for the states, a dramatic fall-off in national stimulus dollars in 2012. Many issues high on the Republicans' national legislative agenda dovetailed with issues on the states' agendas where those issues had a greater chance of enactment because of Republicans' greater degree of party control. Many Republican governors, and a few Democratic ones, argued for cutting taxes despite budget deficits, and especially slashing corporate taxes. Streamlining government—consolidating and reorganizing agencies—was in vogue in both parties at all levels of government. Squeezing money out of the public employee workforce was also popular: President Barack Obama froze the wages of federal workers for two years beginning in 2011, and state policymakers from both parties proposed reducing the size and cost of their public sector workforces, including their health care costs and their pensions. Some Republican governors and legislatures such as Wisconsin's even eliminated collective bargaining rights for unionized employees. Thus at times the policy issues facing society have a contemporaneous effect on both levels of government (Baumgartner, Gray, and Lowery 2009)—an effect that is magnified if one party controls both levels of government or significant parts of both levels.

Another way in which the agendas of national and state governments are linked is when policies are pursued at different levels of government in a sequential fashion. Indeed, state policymakers often frame their attention to problems as a response to federal inaction, or a substitute for federal action. Perhaps the best current example is illegal immigration. The U.S. Congress considered a comprehensive immigration policy in 2006 but failed to pass it. That year, the states considered more than 570 bills related to immigration and passed seventy-two of them (National Conference of State Legislatures 2006). Those numbers nearly tripled in 2007 when 1,562 bills were introduced and 178 were enacted. The number of bill introductions continued at roughly that pace through 2011 (National Conference of State Legislatures 2011). The most (in)famous of these state laws is Arizona's, which requires immigrants to carry "alien" registration documents at all times and which orders police officers to determine the immigration status of a person during any lawful stop where reasonable suspicion exists that the person is an "alien." The 2010 law also forbids illegal immigrants from accepting jobs. The law is, however, being challenged in federal court by the Obama administration and by a coalition of Latino civil rights organizations.

A third way in which national and state policy agendas may be connected is that laws passed in Washington, D.C., may stimulate further state lawmaking. Take, for example, President Obama's "Race to the Top," in which grants totaling $4.3 billion were offered to states for implementing educational reforms favored by his administration. During 2010, state legislatures were busy reforming their school systems in order to compete for these federal dollars. Thirty-six states adopted a common academic curriculum in order to boost their application chances; other states lifted caps on the number of charter schools authorized; still others changed teacher pay systems to merit-based systems. In the two rounds of the contest, eleven states were announced as winners and received varying amounts of federal money. The other states were left with reformed school systems but no federal money.

Of course, many topics on state policy agendas have nothing to do with the federal government at all; they are strictly related to the states themselves. Sometimes, proposed solutions to state problems are borrowed from other states. Policies adopted via this diffusion process include the lottery, renewable energy programs, bans on smoking in public places, the AMBER Alert System, charter schools, "lemon" laws, and no-fault divorce. Many issues on state policy agendas are either routine or unique to that particular state such as the safety of the trans-Alaska oil pipeline, mining in Montana, and annual flood preparation along the Red River in North Dakota. The unique bills often deal with the state's major industries, many of which will ask state government at some point for financial support or tax or regulatory relief. The routine items all states deal with are spending and revenue bills, bonding bills, transportation bills, and enacting many bills about local governments.

At the time preparation of this edition of this book was under way, the fifty states were in the worst financial shape since the Great Depression. The culprit was the national recession that began at the end of 2007. Although the recession officially ended in 2009, the high rate of home foreclosures in many parts of the country and the nationwide unemployment rate of 10 percent substantially reduced state government tax collections. The same economic problems made it difficult for many states to increase their tax rates or impose new taxes, with the result that they slashed government services, exhausted "rainy day" funds, and increased various forms of debt. As a consequence, on state government agendas the topic of cutting old programs replaced that of starting new programs.

The purpose of this book is to help you understand why state governments make the decisions they do in good economic times and bad. The authors of this volume compare the fifty states in terms of their policy differences and explain these differences using the methods of political science. We find these political differences both fascinating and intriguing to analyze. The social and economic differences among states are also significant. This chapter will make you aware of some of the differences among states in population, natural resources, and wealth—differences that affect what policymakers can do, the sorts of problems they face, and what kinds of solutions they may place on the agenda.

DIFFERENCES AMONG THE STATES

Differences among the states abound. If you pay close attention to the news, you will notice that different states have different problems, and different solutions to them. California often leads the way on the environment; in 2006 it enacted the nation's first greenhouse gas legislation. The California Global Warming Solutions Act aims to cut carbon emissions to 1990 levels by 2020; it includes a cap-and-trade program and other related measures overseen by a state board for monitoring and enforcement. The act was sponsored by Assembly Speaker Fabian Núñez (prodded by his fourteen-year-old daughter). This Democrat was enthusiastically supported by Republican governor Arnold Schwarzenegger, who had already declared, "The debate is over. We have the science. We see the threat. And we know the time for action is now!" (Mieszkowski 2005).

Small states can lead as well. In 2003 the state of Maine was the first among the current boomlet of states to adopt universal health care coverage; its program was called Dirigo—Latin for "I lead."[1] By 2011 universal health care programs had been enacted in Vermont and Massachusetts, and the individual mandate in the latter state served as a prototype for the national health care plan adopted in 2010.

A more systematic way to see the policy differences among states is to look at the rankings of the states on various quantitative policy indicators. For this purpose, political scientists often select issues on which liberals and conservatives differ and then rate the states as to whether they have liberal or conservative policies on these issues. We have done this on five policies and summed and averaged the scores to produce an index of overall policy liberalism. Table 1-1 presents state rankings on

---

1. In June 2011, Maine Republicans ended the state's experiment in universal care. The program was slated to end at the beginning of 2014.

Table 1-1 State Rank on Policy Liberalism Index, 2011, and Its Components

State	Policy liberalism	Gun law index	Abortion index	TANF index	Tax progressivity
California	1	1	1	1	3
New York	2	6	12	8	1
New Jersey	3	2	9	18	5
Vermont	4	29	8	3	2
Connecticut	5	4	3	22	25
Hawaii	6	8	4	7	33
Maryland	7	5	5	35	14
Rhode Island	8	7	24	4	22
Oregon	9	14	6	14	7
Maine	10	21	7	13	4
Massachusetts	11	3	17	25	24
Minnesota	12	18	20	10	8
Wisconsin	13	23	23	5	13
Montana	14	37	12	16	11
Washington	15	14	2	6	50
New Mexico	16	37	11	11	35
West Virginia	17	37	16	26	16
Illinois	18	9	18	23	39
New Hampshire	19	26	15	9	41
Alaska	20	44	14	2	43
Delaware	21	12	20	43	9
Michigan	22	11	32	32	19
Colorado	23	18	22	24	30
Pennsylvania	24	10	40	12	38
Iowa	25	20	19	20	21
Kentucky	26	44	45	19	20
Missouri	27	37	46	28	23
Ohio	28	21	41	36	27
Kansas	29	33	31	33	12
North Carolina	30	13	25	49	15
Nevada	31	26	9	30	45
Georgia	32	29	27	39	28
Nebraska	33	29	43	31	18
South Carolina	34	23	35	45	6
Indiana	35	34	34	48	37
Virginia	36	14	38	46	17
Utah	37	50	43	27	26
Arizona	38	44	27	29	42
Tennessee	39	29	30	21	46
North Dakota	40	37	49	17	31
Alabama	41	17	36	34	40
Idaho	42	44	38	47	10
Oklahoma	43	44	33	38	34
South Dakota	44	37	41	15	47
Wyoming	45	23	26	37	48
Florida	46	34	29	40	49
Mississippi	47	34	48	41	29
Texas	48	26	37	42	44
Louisiana	49	44	50	44	36
Arkansas	50	37	46	50	32

SOURCES: Constructed by the author from data from the Brady Campaign to Prevent Gun Violence (gun law index, 2009 data), NARAL Pro-Choice America (abortion index, 2011 data), Urban Institute (TANF index, 2008 data), and Institute on Taxation and Economic Policy (tax progressivity, 2007 data).

Table 1-1 *(Continued)*

NOTES: Each index is ranked as follows: 1 = most liberal, 50 = most conservative. The policy liberalism index also includes right-to-work laws that are not included in this table because the law is a binary variable. The gun law index is derived from the 2009 Brady Campaign State Scorecard (www.bradycampaign.org/xshare/bcam/stategunlaws/scorecard/StateRatings.pdf). It was constructed by standardizing the Brady Campaign's score for each state. The abortion index is derived from the 2011 NARAL Pro-Choice American Report Card on Women's Reproductive Rights (www.prochoiceamerica.org/government-and-you/who-decides/who-decides-2011-report-card.pdf). It was constructed by first converting the letter grade given to each state into a numerical score according to the following scale: A+ = 4, A = 3.67, A– = 3.33, B+ = 3, B = 2.67, B– = 2.33, C+ = 2, C = 1.67, C– = 1.33, D+ = 1, D = 0.67, D– = 0.33, F = 0. This measure was then standardized. Finally, the average of the standardized letter grade and NARAL's state ranking was computed and standardized to produce the index. The TANF (Temporary Assistance to Needy Families) index is derived from the 2008 data of the Urban Institute (www.urban.org/welfare/tanf.cfm). The first step in its computation was summing the number of conditions associated with receiving benefits, such as whether a job search is required or whether food stamp use counts as income. Then four continuous measures were standardized: the percentage reduction in benefits after the first sanction, the months of assistance guaranteed before the first time limit, the maximum benefit, and the maximum income to remain eligible for benefits. The average of these four standardized measures and the summation of conditions was then computed and standardized to produce the index. The tax progressivity index is derived from the 2007 data of the Institute on Taxation and Economic Policy (www.itepnet.org/wp2009/statespecific.html). It was constructed by first calculating the average tax as a percentage of income after the federal deduction offset for the top 5 percent and for the bottom 40 percent of income earners (sales/excise, property, and income tax). Then the ratio of these two averages (top 5 percent/bottom 40 percent) was calculated and standardized to produce the index. Information on right-to-work laws comes from the 2011 data of the National Right to Work Legal Defense Foundation (www.nrtw.org/rtws.htm). The policy liberalism index was constructed by computing the average of the standardized version of the five indicators.

this index in 2011 on which California ranks first and Arkansas last (see the first column).[2] The index makes intuitive sense: other liberal states joining California are New York, New Jersey, Vermont, and Connecticut. Clustering at the bottom are the traditionally conservative southern states such as Louisiana, Texas, and Florida, and the smaller western or plains states such as Wyoming and South Dakota.

The policy liberalism index is based on five policy indicators measured between 2007 and 2011: gun control policies, coded from strictest to loosest; a scale of abortion laws, coded from most facilitative to most restrictive; conditions for receiving benefits under Temporary Assistance to Needy Families (TANF), coded from those most expanding eligibility to the most restrictive; and tax progressivity (the extent to which the tax burden falls on the top 5 percent of earners as compared with the lowest 40 percent), ranging from those systems that tax the rich the most heavily to those that burden the working poor the most heavily. The fifth component of the index has to do with unionization: whether a state has laws that facilitate collective bargaining or whether it has a "right-to-work" law that impedes unionization. Because this is a simple binary variable (1 or 0), it is not presented in a column, although the data are incorporated into the policy liberalism index.

The sharp-eyed reader will notice that a specific state is not necessarily liberal (or conservative) in every category. The best way to see this is to select a state and look at its overall policy liberalism ranking and then see how it ranks on each component. For example, I live in North Carolina, which ranks thirtieth overall on the policy liberalism scale, or slightly conservative. It is most liberal on its gun laws and

---

2. I would like to thank Jeff Harden for his research assistance on this chapter, and especially for his help in constructing the policy liberalism index.

its tax policies, ranking thirteenth and fifteenth, respectively, and is right at the average on the abortion law index. But it is exceeded only by Arkansas in the tightness of its welfare eligibility conditions and has a right-to-work law, both of which move it in the conservative direction. Thus my state averages out at thirtieth on policy liberalism. States have a general tendency toward a conservative or liberal or middle-of-the-road position, but their degree of liberalism or conservatism does not play out exactly the same on each policy.

The next questions are: Why do some states make liberal policy choices while others make conservative ones? What factors distinguish California, New York, and other liberal states from Arkansas, Louisiana, and other conservative states? These are the types of questions the authors pursue in this book and in the field of state politics. I will return to these questions later in the chapter.

EXPLAINING POLICY DIFFERENCES

The second half of this book focuses on a state government's many activities. These outputs of a government's activities are called **public policies**, which can be defined as means to governmental ends. The public policies reviewed in this book deal with taxation, health and welfare, K–12 education, higher education, corrections, the environment, economic development, morality, and infrastructure.

Scholars have spent years investigating the differences among states' public policies and the reasons for those differences. The intellectual task is to explain interstate patterns—that is, what conditions or characteristics of states lead to a generous educational expenditure, a low welfare expenditure, or innovation in health policy? In general, these investigations focus on two broad sets of variables: political characteristics and socioeconomic factors. Among a state's political variables, researchers have found the following to be important: political party control and interparty competition, interest group balance and strength, gubernatorial power, professionalism of the legislature and bureaucracy, and public and elite opinion. Many of these factors will be examined in the chapters that follow.

In this chapter I look at a set of socioeconomic factors that affect patterns of state policy. Included in these factors are the following: population size and composition; immigration; physical characteristics and natural resources; and types of economic activities stemming from a state's physical endowments, wealth, and regional economic forces. These factors structure a state government's problems and affect a state government's ability to deal with them. I also explore the broader political context that affects state governments, such as political culture, other states' actions, and national political forces.

Understanding the magnitude of state differences also helps those trying to understand the existence of federalism. The states are so different that it is hard to imagine they would get along within a single government. Only federalism could accommodate the cultural distance between, say, clean-living Utah and gambling mecca Nevada. Federalism allows these differences to flourish, and fester.

THE PEOPLE

The first state resource I examine is the human resource. What kinds of people live where? How does the movement of people back and forth affect states? Why are trends in population growth and economic competition important for a state's future?

Population Size and Growth

A fundamental fact influencing a state's policies is its population. The largest state, California, had 37.25 million residents as of 2010. In fact, California's population is slightly larger than Canada's, and California's provision for education, highways, hospitals, and housing is on the same scale as that of many large nations. The second-largest state, Texas, has 25.1 million residents. There are also some sparsely populated states, and again, size has its consequences. Alaska and Wyoming are among the least populated states, but they are huge in number of square miles. Thus their unit cost of building highways and providing other services is high. Neither state, but especially Alaska, can achieve economies of scale in many of its public programs. Smaller democracies, then, have difficulties and opportunities not found in California and Texas.

Whatever the population size, a state's leaders must cope with it. More difficult to manage in the short run are changes in population. States experiencing sudden population growth have difficulty providing the schools, roads, bridges, waste management, and law enforcement needed for an expanding population. By contrast, states experiencing a decline in population have a different set of concerns. As people leave the state and businesses die, the tax base erodes. But if a state government adjusts by raising taxes, more people may leave, thereby initiating a vicious cycle. Obviously, states would rather be growing than shrinking.

Changes in population between 2000 and 2010 are shown in Figure 1-1. Growth in this decade declined from the previous decade, in part because of the recession of 2007–2009. During the worst of the recession Americans recorded the lowest mobility rates since the late 1940s. At the same time, immigration from other countries, especially Mexico, also declined. Often the influx of immigrants cushioned the out-migration of domestic migrants to other states—this happened in the metropolitan New York area and in Los Angeles (Frey 2009). Nevertheless, during the first decade of this century Nevada grew by more than 35 percent; next were Arizona, Utah, Texas, and Idaho, all of which experienced growth of over 20 percent. Thus high growth was a southwestern and mountain west phenomenon. These states in those regions have to race to build enough schools, highways, hospitals, prisons, and other public infrastructure to keep pace with their expanding populations. In the same period, one state lost population: Michigan shrank by –0.6 percent. Michigan's population flight mainly stemmed from its economic problems related to a declining auto industry and the resulting high unemployment. In the

Figure 1-1 Population Change, 2000–2010

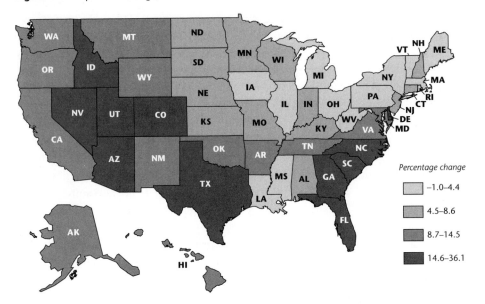

SOURCES: Map constructed by the author from calculations conducted on U.S. Census data for 2000 and 2010.

barely perceptible growth category were the states of Rhode Island, which gained only 0.4 percent over the decade; Louisiana, which gained 1.4 percent; and Ohio, which had a gain of 1.6 percent. Louisiana lost more than 200,000 people in just one year because of Hurricane Katrina and the accompanying devastation.

Population shifts among states are a result of differential fertility rates and different rates of net migration (in other words, the difference in the number of people moving into a state and the number moving out of that state). Migration patterns in turn are a function of economic opportunities: people usually move to find better jobs and a better quality of life. State leaders therefore strive for economic growth and full employment as a means of retaining old citizens and attracting new ones.

Population Composition

States also differ in the composition of their populations—that is, in the demographic groups that make up their populations. States vary in the proportion of old people to young people, in the number of foreign-born people, and in the number of minorities. The increasingly diverse population presents challenges to government and often provides a basis for political conflict.

Age. The U.S. population as a whole is aging because many "baby boomers" are now entering the sixty-five and older age cohort. Some people refer to this boomlet as the coming "silver tsunami": 79 million baby boomers will exit the workforce over the next twenty years and become dependent on Medicare and Social Security (Johnson and Kasarda 2011, 7–8). And yet the number and concentration of seniors are quite variable at the state and local levels. The Midwest and Northeast have large elderly populations because of "aging in place" and the out-migration of younger persons, whereas retirement magnets in the South and West attract relatively affluent retirees. In 2010 Florida had the highest percentage (17.3 percent) of people aged sixty-five and over (U.S. Census Bureau 2011a). Not surprising, then, according to the economic impact reports, Florida's senior population is the state's second-largest economic sector: the senior community contributes an annual $2.8 billion net tax benefit to the state's coffers (Aging and Disability Resource Center of Broward County 2010).

In three states—West Virginia, Pennsylvania, and Maine—over 15 percent of their populations were sixty-five and over, which ranked them right after Florida. These states are illustrative of aging in place (U.S. Census Bureau 2011a). They will face an increasing demand for nursing homes, doctors, mass transportation, and senior centers that will be more difficult to meet because their labor forces will grow more slowly and their tax bases will diminish. Even so, studies reported in Pittsburgh newspapers focused on the positive economic impact of seniors: the pensions and medical insurance of Pennsylvania seniors cushioned the impact of the 2007–2009 recession compared with the situations in other states because the state's seniors spent a lot of money and used more medical care, which increased the number of jobs in the health care industry (Miller 2010).

In youth-gaining states and metro areas, younger immigrants and domestic migrants dampen the demographic impact of aging. All states want to attract young college graduates with the skills, talent, and creativity to forge a twenty-first-century economy, one directed at high-tech industries rather than traditional manufacturing. In his 2002 article "The Economic Geography of Talent," Richard Florida argued that talented people are attracted to locales with high diversity and cultural "coolness." The comingling of talent, diversity, and coolness is associated with high-tech industries, and together they generate higher regional incomes. Professor Florida's ideas have attracted a following in the state and local economic development community. By the end of the 2000s, even the state of Florida was attempting to rebrand itself, shifting from retirement mecca to haven for young adults looking for good jobs and affordable housing. Policymakers in the Sunshine State talked up the pristine beaches as well as "cool cities" such as Tampa, where street life buzzes amid the surrounding cafes, concerts, art exhibits, major-league sports teams, and plenty of partying (RIS Media 2011).

Nevertheless, it is inevitable that the desires of young families for schools and day care will compete with the demands of the elderly for senior services and adult day care, and public officials will have to allocate scarce resources among these priorities (Frey 2011). In the near term, the baby boomers hold the political power, but in the long term the future lies with the youth, and so these needs must be balanced.

Foreign-Born. The United States is a nation formed by immigrants. Much of the nation's history can be told by reviewing the arrival of the different waves of immigrants—the Italians, the Irish, the Scandinavians, and so forth. Indeed, the entry of these ethnic groups into the political system formed the basis of many political cleavages. Overall, immigrants numbered nearly 37 million or 11 percent of the population in 2009 (U.S. Census Bureau 2011d). Today, more than half of immigrants are from Latin America, about one-quarter from Asia, and the rest from other countries (calculated from Table 3 in Pew Hispanic Center 2011a). The pace of immigration slowed with the onset of the recession in 2007, possibly because of enhanced border enforcement by federal and state authorities and by the passage of stricter state laws that signaled an anti-immigrant stance. In addition, some immigrants left the United States to return to their home countries during this period of economic hardship. The result is that since 2007 the number of illegal immigrants has actually declined by nearly a million people, from a high of 12 million in 2007 to 11.2 million in 2010 (Pew Hispanic Center 2011b). By the summer of 2011, the flood of Mexicans crossing the U.S. border illegally had slowed to something more like a trickle because of the expanding economic and educational opportunities and shrinking family size in Mexico juxtaposed with the already noted factors on the U.S. side, plus expanded legal immigration under temporary agricultural work visas (Cave 2011).

In the long run, the country will reap substantial benefits from the arrival of today's immigrants, just as it did from those who arrived earlier. But in the short run, the states attracting the most refugees, "regular" immigrants (those who are not fleeing to this country for political asylum), and illegal immigrants will experience difficulties in absorbing them. Immigrants still tend to arrive in just six states—California, Florida, Illinois, New Jersey, New York, and Texas—but since 2000 the proportion of total national immigration has dropped in these states, from 70 percent of the immigration stream to 63 percent, and not all of them are remaining in the gateway states (Pew Hispanic Center 2011a). Since 2000, immigrants have increasingly moved into second-tier states in the Southeast, such as Georgia and North Carolina, and into other states such as Massachusetts and Washington, where a quarter of them have settled since 2000 (Lyman 2006).

The set of states experiencing the greatest percentage growth in foreign-born between 2000 and 2010 included racially homogeneous states such as New Hampshire (58.0 percent increase) and Montana (60.9 percent), where small numbers of new immigrants added to a tiny base yield high percentage increases, plus southern and border states such as South Carolina (76.6 percent) and Kentucky (73.9), where the numerical base is not as minuscule. In Georgia, both the numbers of foreign-born and the percentage increase (59.5 percent) are impressive contributors to the

Peach State's overall strong increase in population growth. The correlation between overall population growth and foreign-born growth in the first decade of the twenty-first century is a positive 0.32, showing that it is difficult for a state to grow if it relies only on domestic migration.

There is a general consensus among economic researchers that the U.S. economy gains in the long run from immigration because it boosts the supply of skills in the workforce, increases the supply of low-cost services, and contributes to innovation (*Economic Report of the President* 2007, chap. 9; Peri 2010, 6). Legal immigrants pay taxes and contribute to Social Security, and many illegal immigrants do as well (50 percent compliance is assumed by most economic studies). However, an oft-asked question is whether the costs of government services for immigrants exceed the benefits? This is a difficult question to answer because a proper study would compare the stream of costs and benefits over a lifetime for both natives and non-natives and because data on illegal immigrants are especially difficult to obtain. But a few answers are available. Both immigrants and the native-born pay most of their taxes to the federal government. Illegal immigrants are not eligible for any federal welfare and health benefits, and legal immigrants must wait five years to apply for programs such as SNAP (Food Stamps), TANF, SSI (Supplemental Security Income), Medicaid, or SCHIP (State Children's Health Insurance Program). So we can reason that the taxes immigrants pay to the *federal* government probably exceed the services received.

Immigrants (and the native-born) pay less in taxes to state and local governments, but it is these governments that pick up more of the costs of immigrants than does the federal government. Thus if there is a negative cost-benefit ratio to be found, it will more likely be at the state and local level. Nevertheless, the few state reports on the economic impacts of immigrants conclude that immigrants pay more in state taxes than they receive in state benefits. In *The Economic Impact of Immigrants in Minnesota*, Fennelly and Huart (2009) summarize (in Appendix A) the existing state analyses of the fiscal impacts of immigrants, and all the analyses that report a summary conclusion cite a positive net gain for the state.[3] The National Conference of State Legislatures (2009b) has summarized additional studies that focused only on *illegal immigrants*. In Missouri and New Mexico, unauthorized immigrants were estimated to have paid more in taxes than they received in educational services, whereas in Colorado their tax payments were estimated to have covered 70–86 percent of federally mandated services for illegal immigrants.

The magnitude, geographic concentration, and type of immigration have affected many state governments, primarily in the areas of education, health care, and law enforcement, and have provoked a backlash in some states. One obvious impact is that many new arrivals do not speak English, or do not speak it well.

3. The reports were from Arizona, Arkansas, Florida, Iowa, Nebraska, and Texas, and all were written since late 2006.

A political movement touched off by the prevalence of non-English speakers has succeeded in getting more than half the states to enact laws making English the official language. It is unclear what practical effect such laws have because most immigrants want to learn English anyway; classes in English as a second language are full almost everywhere, and the waiting lists are often several months long.

The task of teaching English to children falls to the public schools, particularly to the large urban school districts. Most of the cost of English instruction is met by state and local coffers; the federal government provides relatively little funding. In 2007–2008, Nevada and California were the states with the highest proportions of English language learners (ELLs)—31.3 percent and 24.3 percent, respectively (Migration Policy Institute 2010). In California, efforts to teach English quickly became a divisive political issue, culminating in the adoption in 1998 of Proposition 227, which ended bilingual instruction in the public schools. Arizona voters adopted a similar proposition in 2000, and Massachusetts followed in 2002. The ideological battle over bilingual instruction versus immersion in English continues today in muted form.

Language proficiency also affects immigrants' ability to access health care. Under an executive order issued by President Bill Clinton in 2000, all federal agencies that fund nonfederal entities must ensure "meaningful access" to those entities for people with limited English proficiency. This order means that state, county, and local health and welfare agencies; hospitals, emergency rooms, and clinics; managed care organizations; nursing homes and senior centers; and mental health centers must provide translation of written materials and free interpreter services to patients. Some federal financial help is available through Medicaid and other funds, but much of the money has to come from state governments and private medical practices.

Minorities. Because of immigration and differential birthrates among groups, the United States has gradually evolved from a largely white, European society to an increasingly diverse one; today more than one in three Americans is a member of a racial or ethnic minority. By 2042, minorities will surpass the majority. This has already happened in California, New Mexico, and Texas, where minorities constitute over half the population, and in Hawaii, where whites have long been in the minority. Hispanics or Latinos are the country's largest minority group (over 50 million) and are growing very fast: they increased by 43 percent between 2000 and 2010 (U.S. Census Bureau 2011a).[4] Hispanic families tend to be large, with twice as many children under eighteen as compared with non-Hispanic families (Cook 2011). Asians grew at an equally rapid pace from 2000 to 2010, but are a much

---

4. Hispanics are an ethnic group, not a racial group; Hispanics can be white, black, or of mixed race. The term *Hispanic* is a U.S. Census Bureau label that applies to all people from Spanish-speaking countries—that is, from Spain or Latin America. Many Hispanics born in the United States prefer to be called Latino, which refers to people of Latin American descent living in the United States. Or they prefer to be known by their national origin—for example, Cuban or Mexican.

smaller population (nearly 15 million). Blacks or African Americans, who are nearly 39 million strong, grew by 12.3 percent and whites by 5.7 percent over the same period. Native Americans and Alaskan Natives are the smallest minority group at 2.9 million, and they increased by 10 percent over the decade.

As the previous discussion of immigration would suggest, each minority population tends to be concentrated in certain states. Historically, the politics of individual southern states have varied according to the proportion of blacks. The Deep South states—Alabama, Georgia, Louisiana, Mississippi, and South Carolina—which had the highest concentrations of blacks, were much more conservative politically than the peripheral South—Arkansas, Florida, North Carolina, Tennessee, Texas, and Virginia. Political behavior varied because where there were more blacks, whites were more likely to unite behind racial conservatism and exercise racially exclusionary practices that enhanced their political strength (Key 1949, chap. 24). Today, blacks constitute from a quarter to over a third of the population in those five Deep South states, as well as in Maryland (U.S. Census Bureau 2011e).

Latinos, by contrast, have been concentrated primarily in the Southwest, totaling 46 percent of the population of New Mexico in 2010 and 38 percent of the populations of California and Texas (U.S. Census Bureau 2011e). There is also a significant Latino presence in Arizona (30 percent) and Nevada (27 percent) to round out the top five states. But the big story of the 2010 census was the increasing and dramatic dispersion of Latinos across the country: dramatic gains in their population share emerged in unexpected locales such as Connecticut, Iowa, Kansas, Nebraska, New Jersey, Ohio, and Rhode Island (Brownstein 2011, 21). Like blacks, Latinos are a disadvantaged minority, but unlike blacks many Latinos lack fluency in English, which provides an additional obstacle in finding jobs. And for those who are here illegally, their unauthorized status is a serious impediment to obtaining both higher education and jobs.

Asian Americans tend to live along the coasts, especially in Hawaii, where they constituted 39 percent of the population in 2010, or in California, where they made up 13 percent. Other states with notable proportions of Asians are New Jersey (8 percent) and New York, Nevada, and Washington, each at 7 percent. In Hawaii, Asian Americans are joined by the 10 percent of the population that is native Hawaiian Islanders, so that whites are a minority of the total population. Hawaii has enjoyed successful race relations for a long time and may provide a model for other states.

Native Americans primarily reside in the Southwest and West, especially New Mexico, South Dakota, Oklahoma, and Montana. There, their proportions ranged from 6 to 9 percent of the population in 2010. About half live on tribal lands and about half are urbanites. In their state, Alaskan Natives constitute about 15 percent of the population.

Finally, an increasing number of Americans are taking advantage of a new option on the U.S. Census to state that they are of more than one race: 9 million people or 2.9 percent of the population identified themselves as multiracial on the 2010 census (Saulny 2011), an increase of more than 30 percent since 2000. The growth was greatest in the South and parts of the Midwest.

In this description I have emphasized the spatial concentration of minorities, but it is also important to point out that the minority share of the population increased in every state; indeed, even extremely homogeneous states are becoming more diverse. As of 2010, minorities represented more than 20 percent of Utah's population, nearly 17 percent of Minnesota's, and 15 percent of South Dakota's, just to take a few examples (Brownstein 2011, 21). Also it is noteworthy that by 2010, 46.5 percent of people under eighteen were minorities, a dramatic jump from 2000 (Brownstein 2011, 21). At this rate, by 2015 minorities will constitute a majority of children in the United States. The minority status of the younger population has significant implications for politics into the future. Minorities are likely to give priority to public schools, health care, and infrastructure as the keys to economic progress. By contrast, the mostly white senior population may be reluctant to fund such services through their taxes (Brownstein 2011, 21). This intergenerational racial and ethnic conflict over priorities has the potential to be a long-standing divide.

The rapid growth of minorities has increased their political clout in the electorate, although they are still underrepresented among elected officials. Thus far, Latinos have achieved the governorships in Florida, Arizona, New Mexico, and Nevada. African Americans have been elected to this office only in Virginia and Massachusetts.[5] Greater inroads have been made in state legislatures: in 2009 blacks held 8.1 percent of the seats nationwide (National Conference of State Legislatures 2009a), which was below their 12.9 percent population share. The six states with the most African American residents all had legislatures with 20 percent or more black legislators. Latinos held only 2.9 percent of legislative seats (National Conference of State Legislatures 2009a), well below their 15.8 percent population share in 2009. In the top five states for Latino population, New Mexico's legislature was over 40 percent Latino in 2009, and California's and Texas's over 20 percent. By contrast, Arizona's House was only 7 percent, and Nevada's Senate was a mere 5 percent and its House 10 percent. Native Americans are represented in notable numbers only in Alaska (Native Alaskans) and in Oklahoma. Asians, who made up 4.6 percent of the U.S. population in 2009, are the least well represented. They do well electorally in Hawaii and make a dent in Washington (5 percent of state legislators in 2009), but otherwise are not elected to state legislatures in numbers large enough to note. The close proximity of minority groups sometimes creates racial tensions over political issues. Several states have faced legal challenges to congressional districts drawn along racial lines, and the U.S.

5. David Paterson also attained the office of governor of New York, but it was by succession from the office of lieutenant governor, not election.

Supreme Court has dealt with a series of such "affirmative gerrymandering" cases. Chapter 6 describes in more detail the racial issues involved in legislative reapportionment. In California, a white backlash erupted in 1996 in the form of Proposition 209. Adopted by the voters, it says that state government cannot use racial quotas or preferences in education, contracting, and employment. In 2006 Michigan voters enacted a ban on the use of race in the provision of public services, including education, thereby vitiating the Supreme Court ruling *Grutter v. Bollinger,* 539 U.S. 306 (2003), which had allowed the University of Michigan Law School to take race into account in admissions. Chapter 5 examines these and other states' use of the initiative vis-à-vis minorities.

Overall, diversity in the composition of state populations—whether racial, ethnic, age, or country of origin—leads to political diversity. Political parties in California are likely to be different from those in Iowa because of population diversity or the lack thereof. State parties will differ in their political cleavages and citizens' opinions about public policy needs. To take one example, there are likely to be more groups representing a wider spectrum of interests in Florida than in Mississippi. Subsequent chapters will describe some of the political consequences of states' population diversities.

THE PLACE

States also differ in their physical characteristics. Some of these attributes are fixed and cannot be changed, such as land area, location, and climate. State leaders can try to compensate for the effects of a remote location, a cold or unpleasant climate, or small geographic size, but for the most part they are constrained by nature. Similarly, states are constrained by their natural resource endowments: some states have rich soil; others cannot grow much. Some states have plenty of water, forests, minerals, oil, or coal; others have to get their water from other states or must rely on imported oil and coal. The net effect of the uneven distribution of natural resources is that states vary in the types of economic activities that can be conducted in them. The overall wealth of states in turn depends on the vigor of their economies—and the wealth of states affects the policy choices they make.

Land

States vary enormously in land area. Alaska is more than twice the size of Texas, the second-largest state. In fact, twenty-two of the smallest states would have to be combined to reach an area as large as Alaska's. The two smallest states, Delaware and Rhode Island, together would fit comfortably within Los Angeles County.

What difference does its geographic size make to a state? First, it affects a state's political style, leading to distinct differences among the states. In the larger states, legislative districts are by necessity quite large. In wide-ranging districts, it is hard for legislators to keep in touch with constituents; airplanes are frequently used for campaigning in Alaska, for example. In rural Texas, the districts are vast. Moreover, legislators must travel hundreds of miles from their homes and jobs to Austin, the state capital. The travel burden, then, is a factor in who can serve in the legislature—only those who can afford it.

In smaller states such as New Hampshire and Vermont, districts are small and compact. Legislators can run personal, almost one-on-one campaigns. Vermont's former Speaker, Ralph Wright, said that all he needed to start campaigning was a list of eligible voters, which cost $50, and a map of the town of Bennington, which was free (Wright 2005). His district was only six miles end to end, so he was able to walk it nine times, going door-to-door. Once in office, these legislators can commute to the capital every day, while remaining in their regular occupations. The result is politics with a somewhat amateur, small-town flavor.

Second, geographic size has policy implications. In the provision of highways, for example, geographic area and population density determine expense. Alaska, Montana, and Wyoming are large, sparsely populated states, and so their per capita highway expenditures are among the highest in the nation. Rhode Island is a small state with a compact population; its expenditure on highways is among the lowest. A state's size affects the delivery of services in many other policy areas as well.

Third, land can be the basis of political conflict. Among the most divisive issues in the western states is that the federal government owns much of the land. Eighty-two percent of Nevada is held by the federal government; more than 60 percent of Alaska, Idaho, and Utah is federal domain. Thus vast areas of the West are not under state jurisdiction; this land can be put only to the uses allowed by the federal government. Chapter 2 explores this issue in more detail.

Natural Resources

Natural resources such as soil, water, minerals, and energy sources are attached to the land. The distribution of natural resources has great economic consequences: it allows states blessed with abundant water and rich topsoil to concentrate on crop production. Less fortunate states must import their water and some of their food. Some states receive income from the coal, oil, and minerals extracted from the land. Not only do these states have access to nonrenewable resources, but they also derive tax revenue from the companies that mine the coal or pump the oil and natural gas. Those companies then refine the natural resources and sell them to customers at prices sufficient to cover the tax and make a profit. In essence, resource-rich states can shift some of their tax burden onto the citizens of other states, as long as there is a demand for oil, coal, and natural gas.

In agriculture, California was the top farm producer in 2008 as measured by value of agriculture production; it was followed by Iowa, Texas, Nebraska, and Minnesota (U.S. Census Bureau 2011c). Most of the other states in the Midwest rank fairly high, and the New England states rank low because their state economies produce few agricultural products. Unlike in earlier times, however, in no state is agriculture the largest sector of the state's **gross state product (GSP)**.[6] But agriculture looms large in other ways. In the rural states, there is a sense of pride and identification with the land. Iowa, for example, had on its billboards for a time the slogan "Iowa, a Place to Grow," suggesting simultaneously the growth of sturdy crops as well as sturdy children.

In addition to fertile topsoil, agriculture requires a reliable supply of water. The Midwest is blessed with sufficient water, but the West is not. Nowhere is water a more important issue than in the Southwest and West. On the wall of the Colorado state capitol is an inscription that reads, "Here is the land where life is written in water." The battle over the use of water from the Colorado River continues to be a major issue in seven western states. Chapter 2 describes the interstate compact governing the water's usage among states; within states the water conflicts are among agriculture, energy projects, and economic development.

Finally, nonrenewable natural resources are unevenly distributed across the states. Coal is found in large quantities in Kentucky, Pennsylvania, West Virginia, and the surrounding states, and in the West, particularly in New Mexico and Wyoming. Oil is located in the South and Southwest, primarily Louisiana, Oklahoma, and Texas, and in Alaska. The unequal distribution of minerals and other natural resources has major consequences for state governments. One favorable consequence for a state that has such resources is that it can levy a **severance tax** on these resources.

The states in which the severance tax looms largest are Alaska, North Dakota, and Wyoming. Wyoming has no income tax; interest from a mineral trust fund and severance taxes on natural gas, coal, and oil furnished 34 percent of 2010 tax collections.[7] North Dakota, which does have an income tax and a sales tax, collected 43 percent of its tax revenues from the severance tax on oil and coal. In fact, the oil boom presented its policymakers with a $1 billion surplus in the 2009–2011 biennium. Alaska is even more dependent upon its oil reserves: three-fourths of its state tax revenues in 2010 were from severance taxes on oil and natural gas. The state has no individual income tax or general sales tax and has even been able to grant each citizen an annual dividend, amounting to $1,281 in 2010.

Reliance on the severance tax to the exclusion of other taxes has drawbacks, however. Wyoming has found natural gas prices to be rather volatile and tax revenue difficult to predict. Alaska dipped into its reserve fund in the early 2000s, and state officials expect that someday soon the severance tax's revenues will no longer be adequate (Barrett and Greene 2005, 39). Today, however, high oil prices have restocked the state's treasury and removed fiscal pressures for the moment.

---

6. The GSP is the gross market value of the goods and services attributable to the labor and property located in a state. It is the state equivalent of the gross domestic product (GDP).

7. Calculated from data provided by the U.S. Census Bureau (2011b).

THE ECONOMIC CONTEXT

The economic performance of a state depends on its natural resources, available human capital, and national and international economic trends.

State Economic Activities

The land and its natural resources initially determine the type of economic activities that will prosper in different regions of the country. Because of regions' different resource bases, they concentrate on different economic activities, and they enjoy different levels of prosperity. As measured by GSP, in 2010 California had by far the largest economy at $1.9 trillion, followed by Texas, New York, Florida, and Illinois (U.S. Bureau of Economic Analysis 2011). Florida's economy, the fourth-largest, was not quite half the size of California's. Vermont had the smallest state economy at $25.6 billion.

State economies vary not only in size, they also vary in which economic sector is most important and in the major goods or services produced. Many of these variations result from the natural resources of each state—that is, minerals, timber, soil, and access to waterways. Over time, however, the sectors of the economy based on natural resources have declined in dollar value and in employment relative to the rest of the economy. Indeed, in 2005, for the first time, the services sector of the private economy was larger than the goods sector in all states (each of these broad sectors contains many different industries). By 2010, in twenty-three states manufacturing was still the largest single industry within the goods sector, even though it was no longer as dominant as in the past (calculated from data in U.S. Bureau of Economic Analysis 2011). Meanwhile, mining is still the leading industry in three states: Wyoming, West Virginia, and Alaska.

As noted earlier, the services sector is now larger than the goods sector in all states. One example of a service industry is the real estate, rental, and leasing industry, which ranks as the largest industry in eighteen states, including large economies such as California and Florida. The finance and insurance industry is tops in four states, including the financial capitals of New York and nearby Connecticut and in the popular business havens of Delaware and South Dakota. Because the latter states offer especially favorable regulatory conditions for the banking and insurance industries, banks locate their subsidiary operations there. Nevada seems to be in a service category of its own: accommodation and food services, which seem to be another name for the hotel and casino business. And Virginia, adjacent to the District of Columbia, was the only state to have professional services as its leading industry in 2010.

The shift from a goods-based economy to a services-based economy is just one example of the larger changes in the national and international economies. Because of the **globalization of capitalism,** states are increasingly feeling the effects of surges and declines in prices, labor markets, and exchange rates thousands of miles away. States' economic fortunes in a global economy depend on their abilities to export products and their capacities to attract direct foreign investment. Chapter 16 describes states' efforts to attract foreign as well as domestic investors and highlights the political salience of exports in a global economy.

International trade—the import and export of goods and services—is an important and integral part of the economy today. In 2009 export-related manufacturing employment accounted for nearly 5 percent of all private sector employment, but states varied in their success in finding export markets for their products. The state of Washington ranked first, with 8.7 percent of its employment related to export-related manufacturing (U.S. Census Bureau 2009), probably because Boeing aircraft were Washington's number one export. In the next four states, 7.4–8.6 percent of private sector employment was generated by export-related manufacturing: Kansas (civilian aircraft was also its number one export), South Carolina (passenger vehicles), Alabama (passenger vehicles), and Indiana (pharmaceuticals and medical devices). These facts are revealing: amid the political discussion of U.S. jobs lost to cheap foreign labor, those created by the manufacture of exports for foreign markets are often overlooked. Many state economies depend in part on the buying power of consumers far away.

Because of the globalized economy, export industries are a source of higher wages, and state leaders actively seek international trading opportunities. Recognizing that international trade agreements can have profound impacts on their economies, states are working together to influence U.S. trade policy and especially the actions of the U.S. trade representative. The state of Washington has its own state trade representative to represent it in trade negotiations. And Maine has a Citizen Trade Policy Commission, established by law in 2004, to assess the effects of international trade policies and agreements on the state's laws, working conditions, and business climate.

States along the borders of Mexico and Canada have special ties to the international economy. As explained further in Chapter 2, trade relations among all three countries are governed to some extent by the North American Free Trade Agreement (NAFTA). A series of other international agreements attempt to coordinate border policies on pollution, wildlife, fishing, treatment of disease, law enforcement, and so on. Mexico is particularly important to Texas; after a new governor is elected in Texas, he or she usually visits Mexico even before visiting Washington, D.C. Florida's economy is buoyed by foreign investment and merchandise trade with Latin America. In fact, Miami is often said to be the economic and commercial capital of Latin America (Barone 2009, 339).

State Personal Income

The net effect of states' natural resources, national and international economic trends, and the flow of federal funds is reflected in states' wealth, usually measured by **per capita personal income**. Because this figure includes an individual's income from all sources, a state's growth in personal income is a good index of how well its economy is doing. The states vary significantly in personal income. Connecticut, the top state at $56,001, is significantly ahead of last-place Mississippi at $31,186. Personal income is an important constraint on state programs because wealth determines what a state can afford to do on its own to meet its people's needs. States such as Mississippi do not have a lot of taxable income. States at the top of the income ranking, such as Connecticut, have a larger tax base and can afford to offer their citizens more generous benefits. The irony is, of course, that Mississippi's needs are greater than Connecticut's. But, as described in Chapter 2, federal aid reduces these interstate disparities to some extent.

State leaders do not simply "convert" economic wealth into expenditures for public programs. Indeed, there are too many anomalies in state wealth and expenditure rankings for simple conversion to be a convincing explanation for state expenditure and policy differences. Moreover, the economic performances of states change over time. Some develop new fiscal capacities that might be tapped by government; the fiscal capacities of others shrink, leaving them with overdeveloped public sectors in the eyes of many of today's conservatives. Politics shapes how economic resources will be translated into public policies. In the next section, I introduce some of the political dimensions that structure how states use their economic resources.

THE POLITICAL CONTEXT

The broader political context that influences state policymaking includes long-standing historical and cultural patterns, contemporary public opinion and ideology, and national political trends.

Historical Differences

Many of the political differences in states today—differences in voter turnout and party competition, for example—are long-standing ones. The South in particular has had a different political history than the rest of the country, and not just since 1865. Some of the South's differences from other regions of the country are rooted in distinct economic interests. But another important historical difference is the South's political culture. It shapes the habits, perspectives, and attitudes that influence present-day political life.

Daniel Elazar (1984) has written extensively on how state political cultures have shaped the operations of state political systems. He has argued that the United States shares a general political culture that is in turn a synthesis of three major subcultures—individualist, moralist, and traditionalist. The values of each subculture were brought to this country by the early settlers and spread unevenly across the country as various ethnic and religious groups moved westward. Along the way, these migration streams deposited their political values, much like the Ice Age left permanent geological traces on the Earth. Today's differences, according to Elazar, can be traced to the bedrock political values and perspectives of the earliest settlers, who, among other things, created the original state constitutions.

The **individualist political culture** emphasizes the marketplace. Government has a limited role, primarily to keep the marketplace working properly. Bureaucracy is viewed negatively as a deterrent to the spoils system. Corruption in office is tolerated because politics is thought to be a dirty business. Political competition tends to be partisan and oriented toward gaining office rather than toward dealing with issues.

In distinct contrast is the **moralist political culture,** which emphasizes the commonwealth. In this view, government's role is to advance the public interest or the good of the commonwealth. Thus government is a positive force in the lives of citizens. Politics revolves around issues; corruption is not tolerated. Politics is a matter of concern to all citizens; it is therefore a citizen's duty to participate in elections.

The third subculture, the **traditionalist political culture**, is rooted in an ambivalent attitude toward the marketplace and the commonwealth. The purpose of government under this philosophy is to maintain the existing social and economic hierarchy. Politicians hail from society's elite, who have almost a familial obligation to govern. Ordinary citizens are not expected to participate in political affairs or even to vote.

Elazar's cultural theory has intuitive appeal because it is consistent with general impressions about state differences in political values, style, and tone and provides a historical explanation for differences. More than a hundred studies have tested his predictions about political and policy differences among the three subcultures and found some support for them. Internal migration patterns between regions may either reinforce or override the cultural base laid by the first settlers. If the population influx is quite large, the cultural base may be transformed into a different one. Florida, for example, was first transformed by northerners moving there to retire, and now by immigrants from Cuba and other countries in Latin America. Only pockets of traditionalism remain in Florida today. States with stable populations, such as North Dakota, remain relatively pure examples of their subcultures.

Contemporary Differences

Others argue that historical cultural differences are not as important as contemporary differences in explaining public policy. Rodney Hero and Caroline Tolbert (1996; Hero 1998, 2007) argue that present-day patterns of racial and ethnic diversity are more influential than political subcultures derived from settlement patterns of the past. They show that states vary in their policy choices according to the heterogeneity of their populations. Joel Lieske (2010) combines the ideas of both Elazar and Hero and Tolbert; he uses multiple measures of racial and ethnic origins, religious affiliations, and social structure in 2000 to classify all U.S. counties into

Figure 1-2 Regional Political Subcultures by County, 2000

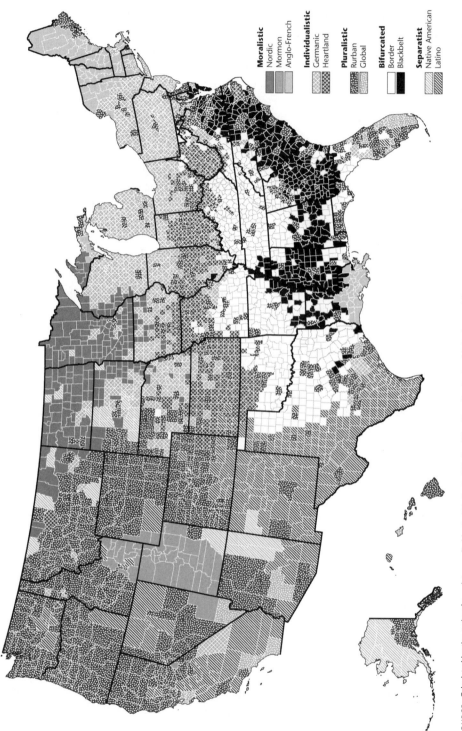

SOURCE: Calculated by the author from data supplied by Joel Lieske. Joel Lieske, "The Changing Regional Subcultures of the American States and the Utility of a New Cultural Measure," *Political Research Quarterly* 63 (2010): 538–552.

eleven subcultural categories. He then uses these categories to predict social and political behavior and state performance in various areas, making claims for their predictive superiority over the measures of previous researchers. As shown in Figure 1-2, Lieske groups his eleven subcultures into five larger categories used by Elazar and Hero. He places three subcultures—the Nordic, Mormon, and Anglo-French—under the Moralist category used by Elazar that mostly arose out of a core Puritan culture. His Individualist category, similar to that of Elazar, embraces two relatively homogeneous subcultures—the Germanic and Heartland—that represent the geographic extensions of German and Dutch settlers. The Pluralistic category includes two culturally diverse subcultures—the Rurban and Global—that represent the outgrowth of internal migratory streams and the arrival of a third global wave of immigration since 1965. His Bifurcated category (one of Hero's categories) encompasses two culturally diverse subcultures—the Border and Black-belt—that represent the geographic extensions of early waves of British immigration and the subsequent migration of their African slaves to the Upland South. Finally, the Separatist category includes two other bifurcated subcultures—the Native American and Latino—that have been the most protective of their native language and cultural traditions.

Another contemporary difference in states' political makeup is public opinion. Public opinion encompasses the attitudes of individual citizens toward public issues: Should their state spend more on welfare? Allow same-sex marriages? Establish a lottery? The cultural thesis outlined previously suggests that public opinion on these and other issues should vary by state, and indeed it does. An even more important question is whether state policy differences are related to (or caused by) differences in public opinion (see Chapter 14 for a fuller discussion of public opinion).

Erikson, Wright, and McIver in *Statehouse Democracy* (1993) pioneered a method for comparing public opinion across states by pooling CBS News/*New York Times* telephone surveys from 1976 to 1988 to obtain measures of citizen ideology and party identification by state. I use a similar and more recent citizen ideology measure constructed from the 2008 Cooperative Congressional Election Study (CCES) by Thomas Carsey and Jeffrey Harden (2010) to predict policy differences among the states. Recall the policy liberalism index presented in Table 1-1 earlier in the chapter. The index is constructed so that 1 indicates the state making the most liberal choices (California) and 50 indicates the state making the most conservative policy choices (Arkansas). Given the direction of the two scales, one might expect citizen ideology and the policy liberalism index to be positively correlated.

Figure 1-3 reveals that indeed there is a positive relation between the two measures: as states increase in liberal ideology (move to the right along the x-axis), they make more liberal policy choices (move upward along the y-axis). The correlation between the two scales is 0.81, almost the same as the 0.82 correlation reported by

Figure 1-3 Citizen Ideology and Policy Liberalism in the States

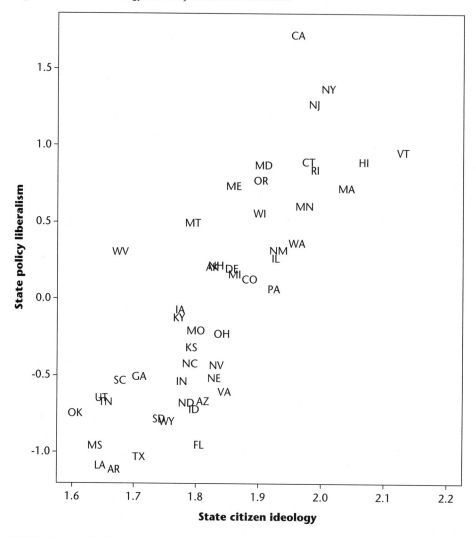

SOURCE: Constructed by the author. Policy liberalism index is taken from Table 1-1. Citizen ideology is taken from Thomas M. Carsey and Jeffrey J. Harden, "New Measures of Partisanship, Ideology, and Policy Mood in the American States," *State Politics and Policy Quarterly* 10 (2010): 136–156.

Erikson, Wright, and McIver (1993) for a different policy index measured in the 1980s. Of course, other factors besides public opinion must be included in a properly specified model, but the measure of citizen ideology holds up quite well statistically against other variables (Gray et al. 2004).

In addition to public opinion, states' political organizations are crucial to policymaking. This book examines in detail two types of organizations: political parties, treated in Chapter 3, and interest groups, discussed in Chapter 4. The chapter authors describe how parties and groups function and how they differ from state to state.

National Forces

The states' political contexts are also conditioned by national political trends. These external forces have an effect on the linkages between politics and policy within states. A classic article by John Chubb (1988) found that presidential and senatorial coattails, voter turnout surges and declines, and national economic conditions have all affected the outcomes of state legislative races since 1940. For example, in 2006 when voters showed their wrath over the Iraq War by turning the Republican Congress out of office in Washington, D.C., they also looked favorably upon Democrats at the state level. Governors were elected in thirty-six states: fifteen Republicans and twenty-one Democrats. Republican-controlled legislatures fell to fifteen. In an analysis of those gubernatorial elections, Adam Brown (2010) found that Democratic voters whose governor was a Democrat approved of their governor's performance and blamed the unemployment problem on President George W. Bush. Republican voters in the same state blamed the state's Democratic governor, not President Bush, for putting people out of work. Brown called this attribution of blame "divided federalism." Thus national political trends may indirectly affect state government through their impact on state elections.

Interest organizations sometimes try to coordinate multistate campaigns in order to achieve their legislative or electoral objectives, perhaps by placing statutory initiatives or constitutional amendments on state electoral ballots. After the Massachusetts Supreme Court ruled in early 2004 that the state's ban on same-sex marriage violated the state constitution, the pro-family movement sought to rewrite state constitutions so that state judges could not find a right to same-sex marriage in state fundamental documents, even if state statutes had already defined marriage in traditional terms. By summer 2011, thirty states had defined marriage in their constitutions so as to preclude same-sex marriage.

Besides these forces, other national political factors may affect the states. One such factor is the hierarchy of national offices that exists in the United States. As Schlesinger (1966, 1991) has documented, there is a regular career progression from state legislative and other entry-level offices to the governorship to Washington-based positions such as senator, vice president, and president. Most people who achieve high office in Washington have "worked their way up" through this office hierarchy. Former governors Ronald Reagan, Jimmy Carter, Bill Clinton, and George W. Bush are four examples of this phenomenon, which Chapter 7 describes in more detail.

These are but a few of the ways in which national political trends may affect state politics. Together with the historical and contemporary political differences among states, they structure how states handle their problems. Fiscal resources offer only the opportunity to solve problems; political leadership must still be used to confront the problems.

GOVERNING IN AUSTERITY

Today, the fifty states face a number of challenges, the most daunting of which is prolonged financial austerity. However, leaders differ in their assessments of how those challenges ought to be met. In the twenty states in which Republicans enjoyed party control of the legislature and the governorship in 2011, they honored campaign pledges not to raise taxes by enacting deep spending cuts to balance budgets. These cuts hit health care (especially Medicaid), unemployment benefits, higher education, and even K–12 education, a previously sacrosanct budgetary item (Gramlich 2011). A particular target was the public workforce, including teachers; at least three states—Indiana, Ohio, and Wisconsin—passed laws to limit collective bargaining rights in the public sector. Republican-controlled states enacted a number of social policy measures, including antiabortion laws and anti-immigration statutes. By the same token, the effects of party control could also be seen in the eleven states held completely by Democrats in 2011. Vermont's Democrats enacted the nation's first single-payer health care system, while Connecticut's Democrats increased taxes and required private companies to provide sick leave for workers, a first in the nation. Thus the impact of party control was very clear in the 2011 legislative sessions.

Only one of the states under split party control—Minnesota—shut down its government. It happened on July 1, 2011, because party leaders could not reach an agreement on the budget. In the other seventeen states in this group, leaders were able to reach across party lines and make compromises to enact a budget. In that sense, the states seemed better able to handle the challenge of austerity than the federal government, which was also split between the two political parties. By taking a close look at smaller political systems such as the American states, this book will reveal how politics in America operates.

KEY TERMS

globalization of capitalism, 18
gross state product (GSP), 17
individualist political culture, 21
moralist political culture, 21

per capita personal income, 20
public policies, 6
severance tax, 17
traditionalist political culture, 21

REFERENCES

Aging and Disability Resource Center of Broward County, 2010. "The Economic Impact of Florida's Seniors." www.adrcbroward.org/economicimpact.php.

Barone, Michael. 2009. *The Almanac of American Politics 2010*. With Richard E. Cohen. Washington, D.C.: National Journal Group.

Barrett, Katherine, and Richard Greene. 2005. "Grading the States '05: A Management Report Card." *Governing,* February, 24–95.

Baumgartner, Frank R., Virginia Gray, and David Lowery. 2009. "Federal Policy Activity and the Mobilization of State Lobbying Organizations." *Political Research Quarterly* 62: 552–567.

Brown, Adam R. 2010. "Are Governors Responsible for the State Economy? Partisanship, Blame, and Divided Federalism." *Journal of Politics* 72: 605–615.

Brownstein, Ronald. 2011. "The Next America." *National Journal,* April 2, 19–23.

Carsey, Thomas M., and Jeffrey J. Harden. 2010. "New Measures of Partisanship, Ideology, and Policy Mood in the American States." *State Politics and Policy Quarterly* 10: 136–156.

Cave, Damien. 2011. "Better Lives for Mexicans Cut Allure of Going North." *New York Times,* July 6. www.nytimes.com/interactive/2011/07/06/world/americas/immigration.html?pagewanted=print.

Chubb, John. 1988. "Institutions, the Economy, and the Dynamics of State Elections." *American Political Science Review* 82: 133–154.

Cook, Nancy. 2011. "A (Uni) Vision for Life after a Mass Market." *National Journal Special Supplement on the Next Economy,* Summer, 7.

Economic Report of the President. 2007. Washington, D.C.: Government Printing Office. www.gpoaccess.gov/eop/2007/2007_erp.pdf.

Elazar, Daniel J. 1984. *American Federalism: A View from the States,* 3d ed. New York: Harper and Row.

Erikson, Robert S., Gerald C. Wright, and John P. McIver. 1993. *Statehouse Democracy: Public Opinion and Policy in the American States.* Cambridge, U.K.: Cambridge University Press.

Fennelly, Katherine, and Anne Huart. 2009. *The Economic Impact of Immigrants in Minnesota.* www.hhh.umn.edu/people/kfennelly/pdf/eco_impacts_report_2010.pdf.

Florida, Richard. 2002. "The Economic Geography of Talent." *Annals of the Association of American Geographers* 92: 743–755.

Frey, William H. 2009. *The Great American Migration Slowdown: Regional and Metropolitan Dimensions.* Washington, D.C.: Brookings. www.brookings.edu/~/media/Files/rc/reports/2009/1209_migration_frey/1209_migration_frey.pdf.

———. 2011. *The Uneven Aging and "Younging" of America: State and Metropolitan Trends in the 2010 Census.* Washington, D.C.: Brookings. http://www.brookings.edu/papers/2011/0628_census_age_frey.aspx.

Gramlich, John. 2011. "In an Era of One-Party Rule, Republicans Pass a Sweeping State Agenda." www.stateline.org/live/details/story?contentId=580741.

Gray, Virginia, David Lowery, Matthew Fellowes, and Andrea McAtee. 2004. "Public Opinion, Public Policy, and Organized Interests in the American States." *Political Research Quarterly* 57: 411–420.

Hero, Rodney E. 1998. *Faces of Inequality: Social Diversity in American Politics.* New York: Oxford University Press.

———. 2007. *Racial Diversity and Social Capital: Equality and Community in America.* New York: Cambridge University Press.

Hero, Rodney E., and Caroline J. Tolbert. 1996. "A Racial/Ethnic Diversity Interpretation of Politics and Policy in the States of the U.S." *American Journal of Political Science* 40: 851–871.

Johnson, James H., Jr., and John D. Kasarda. 2011. "Six Disruptive Demographic Trends: What Census 2010 Will Reveal." Frank Hawkins Kenan Institute of Private Enterprise, University of North Carolina, Chapel Hill. www.kenan-flagler.unc.edu/ki/documents/UNC_Kenan Institute_2010Census.pdf.

Key, V. O., Jr. 1949. *Southern Politics in State and Nation.* New York: Random House.

Lieske, Joel. 2010. "The Changing Regional Subcultures of the American States and the Utility of a New Cultural Measure." *Political Research Quarterly* 63: 538–552.

Lyman, Rick. 2006. "New Data Shows Immigrants' Growth and Reach." *New York Times,* August 15, sec. A.

Mieszkowski, Katharine. 2005. "Arnold Goes Green." Salon.com. http://dir.salon.com/story/news/feature/2005/06/02/green_arnold/index.html.

Migration Policy Institute. 2010. "States and Districts with the Highest Number and Share of English Language Learners." ELL Information Center Fact Sheet Series, No. 2. www.migrationinformation.org/ellinfo/FactSheet_ELL2.pdf.

Miller, Harold D. 2010. "Regional Insights: The Impact of Seniors' Spending." Post-Gazette.Com. www.post-gazette.com/pg/10339/1108108–432.stm.

National Conference of State Legislatures. 2006. "Immigrant Policy: 2006 State Legislation Related to Immigration: Enacted and Vetoed." www.ncsl.org.

———. 2009a. "Legislator Demographics." www.ncsl.org/default.aspx?tabid=14850.

———. 2009b. "A Summary of State Studies on Fiscal Impacts of Immigrants." www.ncsl.org/default.aspx?tabid=16867.

———. 2011. "Immigrant Policy Project: State Laws Related to Immigration and Immigrants." www.ncsl.org/default.aspx?tabid=19897#Introduction.

Peri, Giovanni. 2010. "The Impact of Immigrants in Recession and Economic Expansion." Migration Policy Institute. www.migrationpolicy.org/pubs/Peri-June2010.pdf.

Pew Hispanic Center. 2011a. "Statistical Portrait of the Foreign-Born Population in the United States, 2009." http://pewhispanic.org/files/factsheets/foreignborn2009.

———. 2011b. "Unauthorized Immigrant Population: National and State Trends, 2010." http://pewhispanic.org/reports/report.php?ReportID=133.

RIS Media. 2011. "Sunshine State Rebranding Attempts to Attract New Residents." http://rismedia.com/2011–02–05/sunshine-state-rebranding-attempts-to-attract-new-residents/print/.

Saulny, Susan. 2011. "Census Data Presents Rise in Multiracial Population of Youths." *New York Times,* March 24. www.nytimes.com/2011/03/25/us/25race.html?_r=1&sq=Susan%20Saulny&st=cse&scp=2&pagewanted=print.

Schlesinger, Joseph A. 1966. *Ambition and Politics.* Chicago: Rand McNally.

———. 1991. *Political Parties and the Winning of Office.* Ann Arbor: University of Michigan Press.

U.S. Bureau of Economic Analysis. 2011. "Gross Domestic Product by State, 2010." www.bea.gov/iTable/print.cfm?fid=E047CFD6602C76A3984A19D434CD21C4FDA28BF478F BCA9519C3ECC3AF48E00811E0F42090E6943132810C8222D3D46E7E4FCBA019 75148F5F6BDDCF1F226E12.

U.S. Census Bureau. 2009. "Table 1. Employment Related to Manufactured Exports by Major Economic Sector for States: 2009." www.census.gov/mcd/exports/.

———. 2011a. "Age and Sex Composition, 2010." www.census.gov/prod/cen2010/briefs/c2010br-03.pdf.

———. 2011b. "Annual Survey of State Government Tax Collection." www.census.gov/govs/statetax/.

———. 2011c. "Farm Output, Income, and Government Payments by State." *2011 U.S. Statistical Abstract.*   www.census.gov/compendia/statab/cats/agriculture/farm_income_and_balance_sheet.html.

———. 2011d. "Nation's Foreign-Born Population Nears 37 Million." www.census.gov/newsroom/releases/archives/foreignborn_population/cb10–159.html.

———. 2011e. "Overview of Race and Hispanic Origin, 2010." www.census.gov/prod/cen2010/briefs/c2010br-02.pdf.

Wright, Ralph. 2005. *Inside the Statehouse: Lessons from the Speaker.* Washington, D.C.: CQ Press.

SUGGESTED READINGS

Print

Barone, Michael, and Chuck McCutcheon. *The Almanac of American Politics 2012.* Chicago: University of Chicago Press, 2011. An annual publication that offers a brief description of each state's political history and current issues and a profile of each state's governor, senators, and members of Congress.

Lieske, Joel. "The Changing Regional Subcultures of the American States and the Utility of a New Cultural Measure." *Political Research Quarterly* 63 (2010): 538–552. Offers new political subculture categories based on 2000 census data.

U.S. Census Bureau. *Statistical Abstract of the United States: 2012.* Washington, D.C.: Government Printing Office, 2011. The official source of statistics on many aspects of state demography, economy, and policy. Online editions are available at www.census.gov/compendia/statab/.

Wright, Ralph. *Inside the Statehouse: Lessons from the Speaker.* Washington, D.C.: CQ Press, 2005. A first-hand account of what life in the legislature is really like.

Internet

Governing. www.governing.com/. The site for *Governing* magazine; provides a variety of other state politics content, including a daily blog and newsletter.

Newspaper Association of America. http://newspaperlinks.com/home.cfm. A source of links to all machine-readable newspapers in the country, organized by state.

Pew Hispanic Center. http://pewhispanic.org/. A center that archives surveys, statistics, and other research information on Latinos, especially immigrants and their attitudes and politics.

Stateline.org. www.stateline.org. Funded by the Pew Charitable Trusts, Stateline.org provides in-depth coverage of state government and public policy. The content, which is organized by state and by policy topic, is updated daily.

CHAPTER 2

Intergovernmental Relations

RUSSELL L. HANSON

Americans' confidence in their political institutions plunged during a deep recession that officially ended in June 2009. It sank even lower when the economy failed to rebound quickly, despite vigorous government efforts to "prime the pump." A year into the anemic recovery a poll reported that a whopping 81 percent of respondents considered the U.S. system of government broken, though they also thought it could be fixed.[1] The poll did not ask what reforms people generally favored, however.

Another survey supplies clues on that score. Americans seem to prefer a system in which each level of government has discrete responsibilities. Domestically, the public believes the national government should champion civil rights, provide Social Security and health care for the elderly, and protect the environment. State governments should promote economic development, build roads and other public works, and oversee education. Local governments should concentrate on public safety and urban development (Schneider, Jacoby, and Lewis 2011).

This tidy image of responsibilities is sharply at odds with existing arrangements. Most public goods and services in the United States are provided through partnerships involving multiple levels of government. Even public education, once the exclusive preserve of local school boards, is now delivered within a framework of

1. CNN/Opinion Research Corporation Poll, February 12–15, 2010. $N = 1,023$ adults nationwide. Margin of error is ±3.

state regulations and is subject to evaluation in terms of national performance standards. A similar pattern of "intergovernmentalization" is evident in many other policies covered in this volume. The exact division of labor varies by policy area, as does the level of cooperation among national, state, and local agencies, but the interdependence is pervasive.

The interdependence of American governments makes it difficult for citizens to hold policymakers accountable. Most voters know little about the intricacies of intergovernmental policymaking. Even if they were better informed, though, voters would be hard-pressed to assign responsibility for policy outcomes (Wlezien and Soroka 2011). When programs succeed, each of the governing partners is quick to claim full credit for their combined efforts. When policies fail, each blames the others for the outcome. Obviously, this is convenient for elected officials, but not for voters who prefer a system with clear lines of accountability (Nicholson-Crotty and Theobald 2011).

Issues of accountability aside, there are some advantages to intergovernmental policymaking. Today's social and economic problems span local, state, and national boundaries, defying solution by any single level of government. Such problems cannot be ameliorated by one-size-fits-all policies implemented from the top. Nor can they be solved at the local level without significant financial, technical, and legal assistance from above. Complex systems of governance offer flexibility in meeting challenges insofar as they produce general policies that can be adapted to fit local circumstances, assuming governments cooperate.

The political dynamics of this system of intergovernmental relations in the United States is the subject of this chapter. **Federalism** is the most obvious feature of the U.S. system of governance; it refers to the division of responsibility between the national government in Washington, D.C., and state governments. It also describes the relation between the national government and tribal governments on Native American reservations. Although different, both types of relations involve the division of authority that is characteristic of multilevel systems of governance.

Relations between states are not federal. They are **confederal**, to use an older terminology that is still useful in conveying the importance of sovereignty in these interactions. As constitutionally recognized entities, states are on equal footing; none has a higher status than any other in the Union. There are differences in political power and influence, but the symmetry of constitutional authority means that state governments must negotiate their differences or rely on national agencies such as the Supreme Court of the United States to resolve them.

Relations between states and their local units of government are **unitary**. Localities do not enjoy sovereignty; they are creatures of state government. This asymmetry of constitutional power is seldom displayed openly. Rather, it forms the backdrop for political relations that are much more balanced. The states vary tremendously in the powers they delegate to different units of local government, and so this aspect of intergovernmental relations is further distinguished by diversity within and across states.

States also manage communications between national and local governments, carrying the goals and concerns of one to the other, while adding the preferences of governors and legislators to the mix. Similarly, states increasingly regulate interactions among local governments, adjudicating conflicts and creating regional agencies to coordinate the actions of neighboring localities (Andrew 2009). Thus state governments are at the center of an elaborate web of **intergovernmental relations** that continues to expand.

The behavior of government agencies is shaped by the system of governance in which they operate, and state governments are no exception. Their central location exposes them to pressures from above, below, and even from the side (as a result of interacting with other states and foreign actors). But that same location permits states to influence all prospective partners, and groups of states even have the capacity to reshape the system in which they operate. That is what makes them critical to the success of the U.S. political system in the face of a rapidly changing environment.

CONFEDERALISM

States were sovereign under the Articles of Confederation (1781–1788), and in certain respects they still behave like sovereigns under the Constitution. For example, state governments frequently interact with other nations (Frye 1998). Under the Great Lakes–St. Lawrence River Water Resources Compact, American states and Canadian provinces manage the world's largest surface freshwater system. Along the Rio Grande, U.S. and Mexican states jointly monitor the spread of tuberculosis across the border, regulate the international trucking industry, and allocate water resources.

States also develop economic ties with other countries. In fact, every state now devotes considerable attention to foreign trade. States actively promote overseas markets, providing information and technical assistance to exporting firms and capitalizing their activities. At least thirty-seven states now maintain trade offices abroad; further details are in Chapter 16 of this volume.

States interact with each other as well (Zimmerman 2011). Conflicts arise over natural boundaries that shift over time, or when a state is harmed by pollution or some externality generated elsewhere. Competition occurs when states bid against each other for businesses seeking subsidies or exemptions from taxes and environmental regulations. There is also competition to shed those who depend on state services. In the past, some states gave free bus tickets to welfare recipients willing to relocate to states with more generous benefits. Now states tighten law enforcement to stem an influx of immigrants.

To promote cooperation, regulate competition, and resolve conflicts, states enter into **interstate compacts**, which are like treaties between states. Before 1920, only three dozen compacts were signed by states and approved by Congress. Most were bilateral agreements involving the location of boundaries. Since then, more than 150 compacts have been established—100 of them since World War II. The average state is now a member of twenty-five compacts, some of them regional or national in scope (National Center for Interstate Compacts 2011).

Modern compacts cover a host of issues: conservation and resource management, pollution control, transportation, navigation on interstate waterways, law enforcement, and emergency assistance, to name a few. Some compacts include agencies of the national government as parties to the agreement, but most do not. Such compacts exemplify what Elazar (1984) called "federalism without Washington." The Delaware River Compact and the Colorado River Compact are two instances in which states make regional allocations of water without federal direction. In fact, upper-basin states in the Colorado River agreement have their own compact within a compact to allocate water from the Colorado River (Lord and Kenney 1993).

Compacts are not the only means of ensuring interstate cooperation. Ten states have pioneered a Regional Greenhouse Gas Initiative to reduce emissions in the Northeast. The states agreed to a regional cap on CO_2 emissions from power plants and now require power plants to obtain an allowance for each ton of CO_2 they emit. A limited number of allowances are bought and sold in certain markets, as Chapter 15 notes. Some tout this "cap-and-trade" scheme as a model for the nation in the time-honored tradition of states functioning as "laboratories of democracy."

Many states have reciprocity agreements with other states. A state's public universities may offer in-state tuition to residents of adjacent states in exchange for similar discounts in their schools. Licensure of teachers, real estate agents, and other professions may be covered by reciprocal agreements. Many states now permit individuals to carry concealed weapons, and these permits are recognized by other states.

States also cooperate routinely in less formal ways. In recent years, states have joined forces in challenging powerful corporations. For example, state attorneys general won an estimated $246 billion settlement from tobacco companies in 1998. In 2002 they won modest regulatory relief in antitrust litigation against Microsoft. State officials are now seeking relief and damages for homeowners victimized by mortgage lenders and foreclosure agents. States have also formed cooperatives to buy and distribute pharmaceuticals in order to reduce the costs of Medicaid and other public health programs.

State officials communicate with each other, monitoring issues and political developments in Washington. Associations of state officials lobby on behalf of subnational governments. The National Governors Association, National Conference of State Legislatures, National League of Cities, U.S. Conference of Mayors, and National Association of Counties zealously oppose national encroachments on "states' rights" and "local autonomy." Such complaints make Congress more attentive to the concerns of state politicians and occasionally lead to the defeat of regulations that states find objectionable.

Derthick (2009) provides a good example of the power of intergovernmental lobbies in Washington. In the wake of Hurricane Katrina in 2005, President George W. Bush, a Republican, sought control of the Louisiana National Guard as part of the effort to coordinate relief, but Gov. Kathleen Blanco, a Democrat, refused to cede command. Bush subsequently requested amendments to the Insurrection Act of 1807 permitting presidents to federalize the Guard when state authorities seem incapable of maintaining public order after a natural disaster, public health emergency, or terrorist attack. Every governor opposed the change, as did the National Conference of State Legislatures, but a Republican Congress sided with the president in 2006. In 2008, however, the governors and National Guard leaders persuaded Congress to rescind the change and restore state control over the Guard. Such struggles are inevitable under federalism, and they are a vital sign of democratic politics.

FEDERALISM

In the United States, the formal allocation of power between state and national governments is prescribed in the Constitution, which delegates some powers primarily or exclusively to the national government. Other powers are reserved to the states or the people under the Ninth and Tenth Amendments. Then there are powers concurrently exercised by national and state governments, including the authority to tax, borrow money, and make laws and enforce them. Within this group of concurrent powers are some that must be exercised jointly—for example, the power to conduct federal elections and amend the Constitution.

The allocation of specific powers is imprecise and subject to change over time. All politicians want to control policies of vital interest to their constituencies. Frequently, this leads to a tug of war between state and national officials, each of whom wants to dictate policy and claim credit for the results. The ensuing political contest is refereed by the Supreme Court, which plays a critical role in defining relations between national and state governments.

National Power and States' Rights

During the nineteenth century, the doctrine of **dual federalism** prescribed a sharp division of responsibilities between governments. Defense and foreign policy, regulation of currency, and, to a lesser extent, interstate trade were the responsibility of the national government. Property laws, civil rights, and basic services were the province of the state governments and, through them, local communities. The two spheres of responsibility were considered distinct, and conflicts between governments over the right to make policy in specific instances were decided in favor of one or the other by the Supreme Court.

By the middle of the twentieth century, however, power was gravitating toward the national level. This shift occurred with the blessing of the Supreme Court, which expanded both the power of Congress to regulate interstate transactions, particularly those related to commerce, and the domestic powers of the president. The Supreme Court even allowed some degree of national control over local affairs, especially in matters pertaining to civil rights and public employment. Bowman and Krause (2003) measure the gradual, albeit uneven, progress of centralization during this period.

The trend moderated in the 1990s, when Chief Justice William H. Rehnquist delivered several opinions upholding states' rights (Walker 2000). *United States v. Lopez,* 514 U.S. 549 (1995), overturned a federal law outlawing possession of a firearm within a thousand feet of a school, setting a limit to Congress's power to regulate interstate commerce for the first time since 1937. Two years later, the Court challenged the expansion of congressional power under the necessary and proper clause of the Constitution. In *Printz v. United States,* 521 U.S. 98 (1997), a majority ruled that Congress could not require state and local police to check the background of prospective handgun buyers as the act mandated.

In other cases, the Supreme Court immunized state governments from federal legislation. *Seminole Tribe of Fla. v. Florida,* 517 U.S. 44 (1996), shielded states from lawsuits filed in federal court, based on Eleventh Amendment guarantees of **sovereign immunity**. Applying this precedent, the Supreme Court ruled in *Kimel v. Florida Board of Regents,* 120 S. Ct. 631 (2000), that states could not be sued in federal court by state employees claiming to be victims of age discrimination that was outlawed by Congress in 1967. Nor can states be sued in their own courts for violating federal laws: *Alden v. Maine,* 527 U.S. 706 (1999), exempted states from the Fair Labor Standards Act of 1938, and *Board of Trustees of the University of Alabama v. Garrett,* 531 U.S. 356 (2001), spared states from challenges under the Americans with Disabilities Act.

Not all of the decisions favored states' rights. Conlan and Dudley (2005) point to the Rehnquist Court's acquiescence in congressional preemptions of state laws under Article VI of the Constitution. The Supreme Court also limited the powers of state judges over criminals. *Apprendi v. New Jersey,* 530 U.S. 466 (2000), held that juries, not judges, must decide whether to extend a guilty person's sentence because of aggravating factors. Finally, *Ring v. Arizona,* 536 U.S. 584 (2002), ruled that juries must decide the sentence of persons convicted of crimes for which the penalty is death.

Under Chief Justice John G. Roberts Jr., the Supreme Court has declined to overturn state laws that conflict with federal statutes, unless those statutes expressly preempt state action or a state egregiously violates a person's civil rights or liberties. Thus in *Chamber of Commerce v. Whiting,* 563 U.S. ___ (2011), the Court upheld an Arizona law punishing employers who hire undocumented workers because such laws were not preempted by the Immigration Reform and Control Act.

Another Arizona law requiring police to detain persons suspected of being in the United States illegally may not fare so well; in *Bond v. United States,* 564 U.S. ___ (2011), a unanimous Court concluded that state sovereignty, no less than federal authority, must respect the fundamental liberties of individuals. Thus *Brown v. Plata,* 564 U.S. ___ (2011), held that California's overcrowded prisons violated Eighth Amendment prohibitions on "cruel and unusual punishment."

Two cases heading to the Supreme Court have major implications for federalism however they are decided. One involves Proposition 8, California's ban on same-sex marriage, which is being challenged under the Fourteenth Amendment guarantee of equal protection. The Court will either uphold the status quo, in which each state decides the issue for itself, or the justices may insist that same-sex marriages are legal everywhere in the United States, the contrary opinions of Congress and state legislatures notwithstanding.

The second federalism case could further limit the powers of Congress in relation to the states. In 2009 Congress enacted sweeping health care reforms, including a requirement that persons not insured by their employers or government programs must purchase insurance by 2014. Poor people will receive a subsidy for this purpose, but anyone who remains uninsured must pay a tax that increases over time. This "individual mandate" has been challenged as an intrusion upon states' rights and an invasion of personal liberty. It has been defended as "necessary and proper" for executing an enumerated power of Congress, the authority to regulate interstate commerce. Twenty-seven (mostly Republican) attorneys general are challenging the constitutionality of the Patient Protection and Affordable Health Care Act in federal court. At stake is not only the fiscal viability of the act, but also the balance of power between nation and states in domestic policymaking (Joondeph 2011).

Fiscal Federalism

In policy areas where it is constitutionally supreme, the national government can mandate compliance with its objectives. More often, it secures the cooperation of state and local governments by offering grants-in-aid for programs that benefit citizens. Participation in such programs is voluntary, but the goals are popular and the amount of assistance is sufficient to induce widespread involvement by subnational governments. Cho and Wright (2007) report that three-quarters of all state agencies now receive grants from national agencies, and more than a quarter depend on those grants for more than half of their revenues.

By authorizing an income tax, the Sixteenth Amendment made it easier for Congress to finance grants-in-aid and spend directly on programs such as Social Security and Medicare. This is evident in the historical patterns of government spending. Figure 2-1 shows domestic spending as a proportion of gross domestic product (GDP) by national, state, and local governments in selected years from 1927 to 2012.

Figure 2-1 Direct Federal, State, and Local Domestic Spending as a Percentage of GDP, 1927–2012

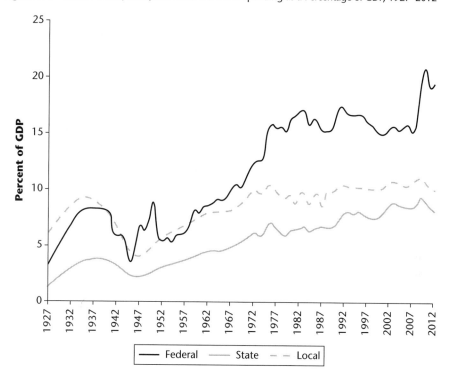

SOURCES: Author's calculations based on data from U.S. Advisory Commission on Intergovernmental Relations, *Significant Features of Fiscal Federalism* (Washington, D.C.: Government Printing Office, 1993); Executive Office of the President, *Budget of the United States Government: Historical Tables, Fiscal Year 2011* (Washington, D.C.: Government Printing Office, 2011); and U.S. Bureau of the Census, *State and Local Government Finances* (Washington, D.C.: Government Printing Office, annual issues).

NOTE: Spending is estimated for 2010–2012. To facilitate comparisons with state and local spending, only spending on domestic programs by the national government is shown. It is calculated by subtracting outlays for defense and foreign aid from the total national outlays. Only direct spending is shown; it does not include grants-in-aid from one government to another.

Before 1927, local governments spent more on public goods and services than the state and national governments combined. During the Great Depression, spending by the national government accelerated rapidly. Social Security, unemployment insurance, and public assistance were established at that time. Massive public works projects were undertaken, with the national government subsidizing the construction of roads, dams, and public buildings by state and local governments. The attendant mixing of responsibilities and resources replaced the "layer cake" of dual federalism with a "marble cake" of swirls around grant-in-aid programs (Grodzins 1966).

The intergovernmental partnership deepened after World War II as veterans' benefits were added to income security programs and new public works, such as the interstate highway system, were constructed. The 1960s War on Poverty was a period of "creative federalism," with many new grant programs stimulating action by state and local governments. By 1970 spending by the national government out-paced spending by state and local governments. Even the presidency of Republican Ronald Reagan, characterized by reductions in the scope of federal regulation, saw a burst of spending unmatched by any corresponding increase in the pace of spending by state and local governments. Still another sharp upturn occurred in 1990, when the "peace dividend" was used to finance new programs in health and education after the cold war ended.

National spending surged in 2008 with passage of the Toxic Assets Relief Program (TARP) to stabilize the financial industry. The "bailout" was quickly followed by passage of the American Recovery and Reinvestment Act (ARRA), more familiarly known as the "stimulus package," which injected more than $814 billion into the economy over a two-year period. Domestic spending by the national government now exceeds the combined spending of state and local governments.

In fact, the spending disparity is understated in Figure 2-1, which does not include expenditures for more than 1,100 grants to state and local governments. At least a dozen were created by the stimulus package alone, which included an additional $87 billion subsidy for Medicaid, the single largest item in most state budgets; $80 billion for unemployment benefits and other assistance programs; $54 billion for education via a new State Fiscal Stabilization Fund; and $48 billion for transportation improvements. Overall, a third of the stimulus funds flowed to, or through, state governments (tax breaks for individuals and corporations accounted for another third).

Federal grants did not fully offset a $430 billion decline in state tax revenues during the recession (McNichol, Oliff, and Johnson 2011). The remaining budget shortfalls led state and local governments to lay off 500,000 workers between March 2008 and March 2011, including at least 100,000 (and perhaps as many as 300,000) teachers. In the absence of the stimulus, much bigger layoffs would have been required. As it is, about 14.6 million full-time-equivalent civilian employees still work for local governments in the United States; another 5.1 million work for state governments, and a mere 2.8 million work for national agencies. Most public goods and services are still provided by state and local employees, though the national government subsidizes much of their work.

Politics of Grants-in-Aid

Grants encourage state governments to enact programs and policies designed to achieve national objectives. Typically, they are the product of **vertical coalitions**, geographically dispersed individuals and groups who form political alliances to gain a favorable hearing in Congress (Anton 1989). The coalitions succeed by sublimating policy differences under general, unobjectionable goals, while leaving details of program design and implementation to the discretion of state and local policymakers. Once formed, these grant programs are highly resistant to attack; the clients who receive services, the government employees who provide them, the administrators who oversee programs, and the politicians who claim credit for action lobby to continue grants. Even in the face of rising deficits, created in part by the successes of many vertical coalitions, Congress and the president are reluctant to eliminate grant programs.

National policymakers prefer categorical project grants because they maximize control over state and local governments. Categorical grants may be used only for narrow purposes approved by Congress. Project grants are awarded on a competitive basis to governmental units that submit proposals for review and funding by an agency of the national government. A categorical project grant, then, allows a national agency to determine which governments will receive money and for which purposes.

State and local policymakers prefer block formula grants, which come with fewer strings attached. Block grants permit recipients to determine how grants are used, within broad limits. Formula grants are awarded on the basis of population, need, or some other objective consideration; conditions—not agencies in Washington—dictate which applicants will receive funds. When block grants are awarded according to a congressionally approved formula, national influence is minimized, and state and local discretion is correspondingly enhanced.

The national government annually funds about $654 billion worth of grants-in-aid to state and local governments, which is just a little less than it budgets for defense. More than half of the grant money is for medical assistance, social services, cash assistance, food stamps, and housing subsidies for disadvantaged populations. The remainder is for agriculture, education, transportation, law enforcement, and homeland security.

Federal grants-in-aid represent 32 percent of the general revenue of state governments, but some states are more dependent on these grants than others. Less than 20 percent of Nevada's revenue is from national grants, but Louisiana and Mississippi receive almost 50 percent of their general revenue from Washington. States pass most of this money to local governments, adding matching funds as required by Congress. States also provide their own grants-in-aid to local governments to equalize school funding and further other goals of state legislators and governors. The bottom line, then, is that local governments receive more than one-third of their revenue from higher levels of government, although in some states the level of local financial dependency approaches 50 percent.

The proliferation of grants-in-aid results in policy fragmentation at the national level. It gives rise to "picket fence federalism," with each grant program representing a vertical tie between local, state, and national agencies (Wright 1988). State and local officeholders are often frustrated by these bureaucratic systems because they make it harder to control their own employees, who fall under the sway of financial patrons in national agencies (Cho and Wright 2007).

Distribution and Impact of Grants

The grant-in-aid system is not geographically neutral. It diverts more resources to states and localities with great needs but few resources of their own, as determined by legislative formulas. Under these formulas, some states reap especially large shares of financial assistance from the national government, and other states receive smaller shares. Redistribution also occurs when the national government spends more for its own purposes—for example, Social Security and defense—in some states than it does in others.

The extent of redistribution by the national government for 2009 is shown in Figure 2-2. The length of each state's bar represents the amount of national spending in that state for every dollar of national tax collected there. Thus for every national tax dollar collected in Hawaii the national government spent $3.65, making the Aloha State a big winner in the exchange. Only twelve states received less than their taxpayers gave, although the number would have been higher except for deficit spending by Congress.

Generally speaking, poor rural states benefited from redistribution, as did those with extensive military bases and large numbers of retirees. Ironically, many political leaders from these states are staunch defenders of states' rights and sharp critics of spending by the national government. Some advocate a balanced budget amendment to the U.S. Constitution, which, if enacted, would require massive reductions in grants to states and smaller national payments to individuals. The latter would depress revenues from taxes and make it extremely difficult to balance state budgets. The fact that a balanced budget amendment to the Constitution is unlikely to be ratified makes it easier for state officials to endorse it, however.

Most of the redistribution is the result of national spending in the form of payments to individuals, vendors, and corporations (represented by the gray portion of the bars in Figure 2-2). But there are clear differences in states' success in obtaining grants-in-aid (the dark portion of the bars). Some states—for example, Alaska, New Mexico, and Mississippi—qualify for more grants than others, whereas states such as Delaware, Minnesota, and New Jersey prefer to remain independent (and are financially able to do so).

Given the scale of redistribution, it is hardly surprising that donor states complain. This unhappiness gives rise to pitched battles over formulas for distributing aid. Representatives from states with divergent interests, each supplied with statistical analyses of the estimated impact of alternative formulas, must then resolve their differences. Even the U.S. Census Bureau's methods for estimating population at the state level are a matter of contention in Congress because different statistical techniques yield different population estimates and therefore different grant allocations.

The budgetary impact of grants-in-aid does not always depend on their size; even small reductions make a big difference at the margin of agency budgets. Most grants require matching funds from states, and, depending on the stringency of

Figure 2-2   Federal Expenditures per Dollar of Federal Tax Collected, by State, FY2009

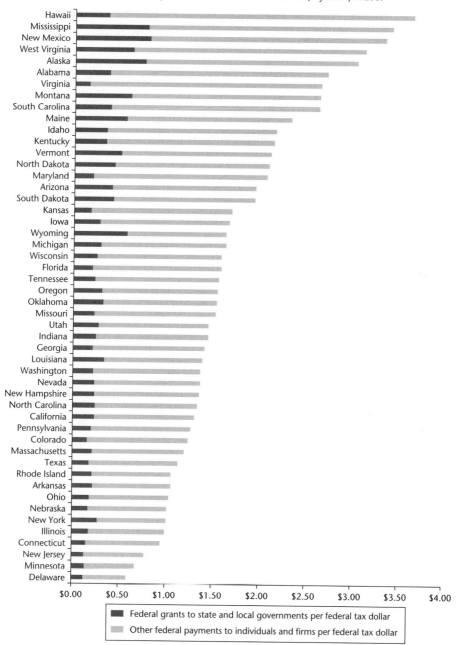

SOURCES: Author's calculations based on data from *Federal Tax Collections, 2009* (Washington, D.C.: Internal Revenue Service, 2010), and *Consolidated Federal Funds Report for Fiscal Year 2009* (Washington, D.C.: U.S. Census Bureau, 2010).

NOTE: Total federal expenditures in a state are divided by total federal tax collections, yielding the return per dollar of federal tax collected. This return is apportioned between intergovernmental grants and payments by calculating the ratio of total expenditures for grants to state and local governments to total federal expenditures, and multiplying the return by that number. This is the share of the return for intergovernmental grants; the share for other payments is obtained by subtraction.

these requirements, states may have to commit a substantial portion of their own revenues to purposes served by the grants. The reverse is also true: when states cut spending in order to balance budgets, they may forfeit federal funds, doubling or tripling the impact of the reduction.

This is what Congress intends, but grant programs skew the priorities of state policymakers who concentrate on obtaining grants with low matching-fund requirements (Cho and Wright 2007). These programs give a bigger "bang for the buck" than programs with high matching-fund requirements or policies for which there are no national funds. In addition, clever state officials sometimes attempt to substitute national dollars for their own or those of local governments in order to avoid tax increases.

"Maintenance-of-effort" provisions are Congress's response to the strategy of substituting national dollars for state outlays. New grant programs often require state and local governments to continue spending at existing levels in order to qualify for assistance from the national government. In this way, the politics of grants are like a chess game, with each side trying to anticipate and block the other's moves.

South Carolina, for example, was entitled to receive $140 million under the formula for distributing grants provided under the Education Jobs Fund, which was established in 2010 to minimize teacher layoffs. However, the U.S. Department of Education refused to release funds when the state violated a maintenance-of-effort provision by slashing appropriations for higher education. Texas was also denied $830 million because it would not promise to maintain K–12 funding. The Lone Star State subsequently obtained the funds when Republicans gained control of the U.S. House of Representatives and amended the statute to exempt Texas. A Democratic Senate and president were forced to accept the amendment because Republicans made it a condition for avoiding a government shutdown in the spring of 2011.

Regulatory Federalism

In some policy areas, Congress is able to impose its will on subnational governments. **Mandates** are the chief mechanism of this "coercion," as some call it. States resist mandates, especially if they are unfunded, whereas they embrace monetary incentives provided under grant programs (Gormley 2006). That is why Congress has established so many grant programs; members of the House and Senate want to please elected officials and constituents in the states they represent.

When national budgets are tight and money is not available for new grants, Congress uses mandates to achieve its objectives. Different kinds of mandates have been employed by Congress (and the executive branch). A direct order may be issued in policy areas where national power is well established under the supremacy clause of the Constitution. Subnational governments must abide by the Equal Employment Opportunity Act and the Occupational Safety and Health

Act, for example, and they risk civil and criminal sanctions if they do not respond to orders of compliance.

Cross-cutting regulations affect all or most federal assistance programs. They prohibit the use of funds from any national source in programs that discriminate on the basis of race, ethnicity, gender, or religious practice, for example. Another familiar cross-cutting regulation requires the preparation of an environmental impact statement for any construction project involving national funds. State and local governments must provide evidence of compliance with these regulations, and they incur administrative costs for preparing the necessary scientific and technical reports.

National officials may terminate or reduce assistance in one program if state and local officials do not comply with the requirements of another grant-in-aid program. This is a cross-over sanction. National highway funds are often used in this way to pressure states into adopting policies preferred by Congress. A recent act required states to adopt 0.08 blood alcohol content laws to combat drunk driving or lose 2 percent of their national highway funds each year, up to a maximum of 8 percent.

Subnational government officials strongly resent mandates. They gained some relief after passage of the Unfunded Mandates Reform Act in 1995. The law did not rescind any previous mandates, but it did modify subsequent mandates, which are less sweeping, less expensive, and less heavy-handed than before (U.S. Congressional Budget Office 2011). Passage of the act also deterred lawmakers from proposing mandates that are popular only with some interest groups and congressional constituencies (Posner 1998).

Agencies of the executive branch are also bound by the Unfunded Mandates Reform Act if their regulations impose heavy costs on state and local governments. Many of these regulations fall below the threshold, however. Still others impose new conditions on existing grants-in-aid and are not considered unfunded mandates under the law; the No Child Left Behind Act is a prime example of this. Congress shows little inclination to close this loophole. Evidently, it wants to preserve the option of coercion by regulation when legislative mandates are politically risky.

Mandates compel states to perform acts prescribed in national laws and regulations. **Preemption** does the opposite. Complete preemption prevents states from enacting new laws and sets aside existing laws when they conflict with national policy. Partial preemption limits what states can do, and so defines what they must not do, in matters of concern to national policymakers. Both types of preemption rest on the supremacy clause of Article VI, which resolves conflicts between national and state laws in favor of Congress so long as it is exercising a constitutionally delegated power.

Regulation of commerce is the usual vehicle for preempting state laws. The Constitution gives Congress the sole power to regulate commerce with other nations, and the United States has entered into free trade agreements with many nations.

State officials welcome these overseas markets for goods and services produced in their states, but they also support "Buy American" programs and other protectionist measures that insulate their economies from foreign competition. Article 105 of the North American Free Trade Agreement (NAFTA) requires the national governments of the United States, Canada, and Mexico to ensure that states and provinces comply with treaty obligations and international law.[2]

Once uncommon, preemption became popular in Congress after 1965. Democrats especially favored this approach to policymaking, but Republican Congresses also continued the practice after 1994, albeit less intensively. Republicans were responding to pressure from business organizations, which preferred uniform regulations to the patchwork of regulations in the fifty states (Zimmerman 2005). Automakers, for example, favor national standards of fuel efficiency, which are set by the Environmental Protection Agency (EPA). Under President George W. Bush, the EPA preempted California laws requiring new cars to meet more stringent standards. By contrast, President Barack Obama pressed Congress and the EPA to permit states to exceed the national standards, overcoming the objections of automakers. Obama has pursued a policy of partial preemption in a wide range of agencies, indicating his desire to pursue national goals in cooperation with states (Conlan and Posner 2011).

Some states have pressed for stiffer laws on immigration, but Congress has been unable to agree on a comprehensive policy. In 2010 the Arizona legislature took matters into its own hands, broadening the powers of police to identify, prosecute, and deport illegal immigrants. Several other states followed suit in 2011, when state legislatures considered more than 1,500 immigration bills (National Conference of State Legislatures 2011). Most called for stricter enforcement of existing laws and stronger documentation of immigrants' legal status. Others sought to reserve access to public services, including Medicaid and public universities, for people with valid documentation. Alabama and Georgia went even further, making it illegal to knowingly transport or harbor an illegal immigrant. In the summer of 2011, Georgia's law deterred so many migrant laborers that farmers faced a severe labor shortage during the harvest season.

Critics of Arizona's law, including President Obama, are asking the federal courts to declare that Congress alone has the power to make and enforce laws defining the status of immigrants, thereby preempting enforcement measures in some states. The Utah Compact, though, avoids preemption by accepting the supremacy of national law in matters of enforcement. Acknowledging the importance of migrant workers in agriculture and the building trades, Utah is proposing an experimental guest workers' program for individuals who qualify. The program would operate

---

2. On the other hand, in *Leal Garcia v. Texas*, 564 U.S. ___ (2011), the U.S. Supreme Court declined to stay the execution of a foreign national convicted of murder, even though he was denied rights ensured him under international treaties signed by the United States. Congress had not yet acted to enforce the treaty rights in question.

under a waiver from the national government, and does not challenge the authority of Congress.

FEDERAL LANDS

Relations between state and national governments dominate federalism but do not exhaust this field of intergovernmental relations. The national government controls vast tracts of land in the United States, and control of that land is routinely challenged by states and Native American tribal governments. These conflicts over land use raise questions of sovereignty and are an important, though often overlooked, aspect of American federalism.

The Public Domain

The United States originally consisted of thirteen states. During the next 170 years, Congress admitted thirty-seven more states, each created from territory claimed by the nation or ceded to it. Some of the territory was retained for national use, even after a state was admitted. The cumulative amount of land reserved for the public domain exceeds 650 million acres, roughly twice the land area of Alaska, which is by far the largest state in the United States.

Figure 2-3 shows the distribution of public lands, which are heavily concentrated in western states. The Department of the Interior's Bureau of Land Management controls more than a quarter-million acres, most of which are leased to mining companies, ranchers, and farmers. The Department of Agriculture's Forest Service manages national forests and park lands. The Department of Defense operates military bases and testing ranges, while Native American tribes control reservations with oversight by the Bureau of Indian Affairs.

More than half of the land within the states of Alaska, Nevada, Utah, Idaho, and Oregon is in the public domain and not subject to control by state government. The same is true for one-third to one-half of the land in California, Arizona, New Mexico, Colorado, and Wyoming. Only negligible proportions of land in states east of the Mississippi River are in the public domain, and it is reserved for the use of Native tribes.

National agencies' control over the vast acreage in western states is politically contentious. The residents of those states, historically accustomed to unfettered access, chafe under land use restrictions imposed by "bureaucrats in Washington." The latter in turn are pressured by environmental organizations seeking to preserve the public domain. The conflict exploded during the late 1970s and early 1980s when resentment of the national regulation of public lands peaked in the western states. The Sagebrush Rebellion, as it was known, culminated in Ronald Reagan's appointment of Colorado's James Watt as Secretary of the Interior. Since then, every secretary of the Department of the Interior has come from a western state, and national policy has become more responsive to state and local sentiments.

Figure 2-3   Federal Lands in Western States

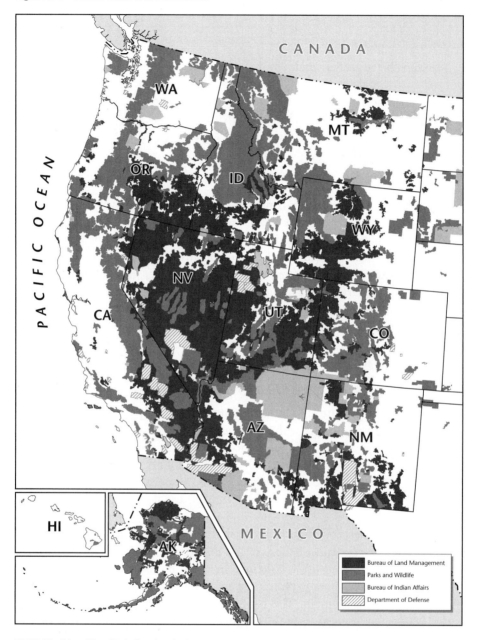

SOURCE: Adapted from "Federal Lands and Indian Reservations," in *National Atlas of the United States of America* (Washington, D.C.: U.S. Department of the Interior), http://www.nationalatlas.gov/printable/images/pdf/fedlands/fedlands3.pdf.

Tribal Governments

Native American tribes in the United States enjoy powers of self-determination, though not as many as state governments. In *Cherokee Nation v. Georgia,* 30 U.S. (5 Pet.) 1 (1831), Chief Justice John Marshall characterized tribes as "dependent domestic nations." The tribes are "nations" insofar as they were once sovereign, "domestic" insofar as they have been absorbed into the Union, and "dependent" insofar as the U.S. government is entrusted with the protection of indigenous peoples and their ways of life. In practice, this means that tribes are semisovereign entities, subject to the will of Congress, but relatively independent of governments in the states where reservations are located.

The national government officially recognizes 564 of the more than 600 tribes in the United States, many of them in the upper Midwest and western states. Most of the recognized tribes operate under written constitutions delineating the powers, responsibilities, structure, and composition of tribal governments. These governments pass civil and criminal laws, which are enforced by tribal police and adjudicated in tribal courts. To finance these activities, tribal governments impose taxes on Indians and non-Indians living or doing business on reservation lands. People on the reservation are not subject to most state laws or regulations, however, nor do they pay state taxes on property, sales, or income earned from activities conducted on the reservation.

States have little control over reservation affairs, but the states are well represented in Congress—and Congress exercises plenary power over tribal governments. At the behest of states, Congress previously used its power to abrogate treaties, dilute tribal ownership of lands, and regulate tribal governance. More recently, Congress limited the jurisdiction of tribal courts in criminal matters. Non-Indians accused of committing crimes on reservation lands can be prosecuted only under state or federal laws based on *Oliphant v. Suquamish Indian Tribe,* 435 U.S. 191 (1978). Major crimes committed by Indians on reservations are tried in U.S. courts, and Indians tried in tribal courts for lesser crimes are protected by the Indian Civil Rights Act, which affords guarantees similar to those in the Bill of Rights and Fourteenth Amendment.

The pattern is different in civil matters, where tribal governments enjoy sovereign immunity. Tribal governments may not be sued by states or their citizens for breaching state laws. Nor are tribal members subject to state regulations such as those governing the use and operation of motor vehicles on the reservation. In fact, tribes may impose their own regulations, with one important limitation. In *Montana v. United States,* 450 U.S. 544 (1981), the Supreme Court ruled that in the absence of any congressional authorization Indian tribes lack authority over the conduct of non-Indians on privately owned land within a reservation, unless nonmembers have entered into consensual agreements with a tribe or their conduct threatens the tribe's political integrity, economic security, or welfare.

State governments are sometimes frustrated by the autonomy of tribal governments. For example, tensions have grown over tribes' development of gambling enterprises. Until states rescinded laws against gambling, only reservations could offer Class II gambling, including bingo, lotto, and pull tabs. But the stakes were raised in 1988 when Congress passed the Indian Gaming Regulatory Act, which preserved tribes' right to offer Class II games on reservations and opened the door for Class III gaming (slot machines, casino gambling, and pari-mutuel betting). States that did not explicitly prohibit Class III games were required to enter into good-faith negotiations with tribes seeking to expand their operations by offering Class III games.

The negotiations produced compacts between state and tribal governments defining the conditions under which Class III gaming may be offered and specifying the state's share of the proceeds from such gambling. Tribes view compacts as an infringement on their sovereignty and resent having to share profits from an industry they developed—and it is an industry. There are now 419 Class III gaming operations in twenty-eight states. These operations employ more than 300,000 people (only a quarter of whom are Indians) and gross over $26 billion annually, or more than one-quarter of all legal gaming revenues in the United States (National Indian Gaming Association 2011).

The Seneca Nation made such a compact with the state of New York in 2002. The nation agreed to give the state 25 percent of the revenue from slot machines in exchange for an exclusive franchise on slot machine gambling in western New York. The state kept most of this revenue for its own purposes, but shared 25 percent with Buffalo, Niagara Falls, and Salamanca, where Seneca casinos were located. For several years, the nation made payments to the state, but it withheld $228 million in payments for 2009 and 2010, arguing that New York violated the exclusivity provision of the compact by allowing video lottery terminals at racetracks in Hamburg, Batavia, and the Finger Lakes. The state disagreed, saying that lottery terminals are a legitimate source of revenue for state government because they are not slot machines.

Some state legislators from western New York sided with the Seneca Nation, which offered to share slot machine revenues directly with local communities instead of routing them through the state. To protect its revenues, the state declined, and the dispute is now in arbitration. Deprived of their share of slot revenues, the cities of Buffalo, Niagara Falls, and Salamanca are trimming budgets, laying off workers, and deferring maintenance and construction on public works. Leaders in these communities complain they have become hostages in the standoff between the Seneca Nation and the state of New York.

Another dimension of this standoff is cigarettes. Since 1988, the state has threatened to collect taxes on cigarettes sold on Native lands in New York. To avoid a $4.35 tax on each pack of cigarettes, smokers visit stores on the reservations, which are not subject to state law and do not collect sales tax. As a result, the state loses an estimated $500,000 a day in sales taxes on cigarettes.

Soon after his inauguration in January 2011, New York governor Andrew Cuomo vowed to impose a sales tax on wholesale distributors who supplied brand-name cigarettes to stores on Native lands. The distributors are subject to state law and were expected to raise wholesale prices on cigarettes bound for Native stores, equalizing retail prices across the state and eliminating smokers' incentives to evade the sales tax. The Seneca Nation sued in state court, claiming that a tax aimed at cigarettes bound for Native stores was a violation of tribal sovereignty. But they lost and are appealing the decision.

Even if the tax is upheld, the state may not achieve its goal. The Seneca Nation may plow its proceeds from casinos into factories on Native lands that would produce new brands of cigarettes, which would be exempt from sales taxes. Smokers might very well switch to the Native brands, because they would cost about half of the name-brand cigarettes on which taxes are paid. That would frustrate state policymakers and vindicate tribal assertions of sovereignty.

STATE CONSTITUTIONS AND LOCAL GOVERNMENTS

Except on tribal reservations and national lands, state governments wield power in accordance with their constitutions. Each state constitution identifies the rights of persons residing in that state, including privileges and immunities beyond those guaranteed in the U.S. Constitution. (The right to an equal public education is a common example.) Each state constitution also prescribes the structure of state government, the terms and qualifications for holding various state offices, and suffrage requirements. Some state constitutions establish local governments or processes for creating different types of local government; others leave such matters to the legislature (Tarr 2000).

Many state constitutions include policy pronouncements. Several preserve traditional fishing, hunting, and trapping privileges. Dominant interests also may be protected in a state constitution—for example, the South Dakota state legislature is required to provide farmers with hail insurance. Traditional values inform recent amendments to ban same-sex marriage, abortion, affirmative action, union organization, and gun control. In fact, Alabama's current constitution—its sixth—has been amended 854 times; it is now thirty times longer than the U.S. Constitution with its twenty-seven amendments. That is exceptional, however; the typical state constitution is only four times the length of the U.S. Constitution.

State constitutions may be amended in a variety of ways (Dinan 2009). Delaware's constitution may be altered by supermajorities in two sessions of the legislature separated by a general election. Everywhere else, voters must approve amendments. Proposals may be presented to voters by a constitutional convention summoned by the legislature or called in a popular referendum. Fourteen states actually present the option of a convention to voters at mandatory intervals, and several others allow the people to issue a call at will. A somewhat easier method is available in sixteen states that permit citizens to vote on ballot initiatives to amend their constitution. But most amendments originate in state legislatures, albeit in different ways, as shown in Table 2-1.

Table 2-1 State Constitutional Amendment Procedures and Success Rates, as of January 1, 2010

State	Origin of proposal		Legislature		Ratification vote required	Overall success, all routes		
	Convention	Initiative	Vote required[d]	Consideration by two sessions?		No. submitted[x]	No. adopted[x]	Approval rate
Nebraska	Yes	Yes	Majority	No	Majority vote on amendment[r,s]	350	228	0.65
Arizona	Yes	Yes	Majority	No	Majority vote on amendment	266	147	0.55
Arkansas	No	Yes	Majority	No	Majority vote on amendment	196	98	0.50
Minnesota	Yes		Majority	No	Majority vote in election	215	120	0.56
Missouri	Yes	Yes	Majority	No	Majority vote on amendment	175	114	0.65
New Mexico	Yes	No	Majority[e]	No	Majority vote on amendment[e]	293	160	0.55
North Dakota	No	Yes	Majority	No	Majority vote on amendment	265	150	0.57
Oklahoma	Yes	Yes	Majority	No	Majority vote on amendment	354	187	0.53
Oregon	Yes	Yes	f	No	Majority vote on amendment[n]	490	249	0.51
Rhode Island	Yes	Yes	Majority	No	Majority vote on amendment	12	10	0.83
South Dakota	Yes	Yes	Majority	No	Majority vote on amendment	229	215	0.94
Alabama	Yes	No	3/5	No	Majority vote on amendment	1,179	854	0.72
Florida	Yes	Yes	3/5	No	3/5 vote on amendment[t]	154	118	0.77
Illinois	Yes	No[a]	3/5	No	Majority vote on amendment[u]	18	12	0.67
Kentucky	Yes	No	3/5	No	Majority vote on amendment	75	41	0.55
Maryland	Yes	No	3/5	No	Majority vote on amendment	261	225	0.86
New Hampshire	Yes	No	3/5	No	2/3 vote on amendment	287	145	0.51
New Jersey	No	No	g	No	Majority vote on amendment	79	44	0.56
North Carolina	Yes	No	3/5	No	Majority vote on amendment	43	35	0.81
Ohio	Yes	Yes	3/5	No	Majority vote on amendment	284	171	0.60
Alaska	Yes	No	2/3	No	Majority vote on amendment	42	29	0.69
California	Yes	Yes	2/3	No	Majority vote on amendment	891	525	0.59
Colorado	Yes	Yes	2/3[h]	No	Majority vote on amendment	336	155	0.46
Connecticut	Yes	No	i	No	Majority vote on amendment	31	30	0.97
Georgia	Yes	No	2/3	No	Majority vote on amendment	94	71	0.76
Hawaii	Yes	No	j	No	Majority vote on amendment[t]	131	110	0.84
Idaho	Yes	No	2/3	No	Majority vote on amendment[f]	210	123	0.59
Kansas	Yes	No	2/3	No	Majority vote on amendment	125	95	0.76
Louisiana	Yes	No	2/3	No	Majority vote on amendment[v]	233	164	0.70
Maine	Yes	Yes	2/3[k]	No	Majority vote on amendment	204	171	0.84
Michigan	Yes	Yes	2/3	No	Majority vote on amendment	68	30	0.44
Mississippi	No	No[b]	2/3[l]	No	Majority vote on amendment[s]	158	123	0.78
Montana	Yes	Yes	2/3[k]	No	Majority vote on amendment	56	31	0.55
Texas	No	No	2/3	No	Majority vote on amendment	642	467	0.73
Utah	Yes	No	2/3	No	Majority vote on amendment	167	115	0.69

Washington	Yes	2/3	No	Majority vote on amendment	176	103	0.59
West Virginia	Yes	2/3	No	Majority vote on amendment	121	71	0.59
Wyoming	Yes	2/3	No	Majority vote in election	125	98	0.78
Indiana	No	Majority	No	Majority vote on amendment	79	47	0.59
Iowa	Yes	Majority	Yes	Majority vote on amendment	59	54	0.92
Massachusetts	No[c]	Majority[m]	Yes	Majority vote on amendment[s]	148	120	0.81
Nevada	Yes	Majority	Yes	Majority vote on amendment	232	136	0.59
New York	Yes	Majority	Yes	Majority vote on amendment	295	220	0.75
Pennsylvania	No	Majority[n]	Yes[n]	Majority vote on amendment	36	30	0.83
Virginia	Yes	Majority	Yes	Majority vote on amendment	54	46	0.85
Wisconsin	Yes	Majority	Yes	Majority vote on amendment	194	145	0.75
Vermont	No	[o]	Yes[p]	Majority vote on amendment	212	54	0.25
Tennessee	Yes	[p]	Yes	Majority vote in election[w]	62	39	0.63
Delaware	Yes	2/3	Yes	Not required	n/a	141	n/a
South Carolina	Yes	2/3[q]	Yes[q]	Majority vote on amendment	686	497	0.72

SOURCES: Surveys conducted in previous years by Janice May and updated by John Dinan in 2005–2010. *The Book of the States 2011* (Lexington, Ky.: Council of State Governments, 2011).

NOTE: n/a = not applicable.

a. Only Article IV, the Legislature Article, may be amended by initiative petition.

b. Before being submitted to the electorate, initiated measures are sent to the legislature, which has the option of submitting an amended or alternative measure alongside the original measure.

c. Before being submitted to the electorate for ratification, initiative measures must be approved at two sessions of a successively elected legislature by not less than one-fourth of all members elected, sitting in joint session.

d. In all states not otherwise noted, the figures shown in this column refer to the proportion of elected members in each house required for approval of proposed constitutional amendments.

e. Amendments concerning certain elective franchise and education matters require a three-fourths vote of members elected and approval by three-fourths of electors voting in the state and two-thirds of those voting in each county.

f. Majority vote to amend constitution, two-thirds to revise ("revise" includes all or a part of the constitution).

g. Three-fifths of all members of each house at one session, or majority of all members of each house at two successive sessions.

h. Legislature may not propose amendments to more than six articles of the constitution in the same legislative session.

i. Three-fourths vote in each house at one session, or majority vote in each house at two sessions between which an election has intervened.

j. Two-thirds vote in each house at one session, or majority vote in each house at two sessions.

k. Two-thirds of both houses.

l. The two-thirds must include not less than a majority elected to each house.

m. Majority of members elected sitting in joint session.

n. Emergency amendments may be passed by two-thirds vote of each house, followed by ratification by majority vote of electors in election held at least one month after legislative approval. There is an exception for an amendment containing a supermajority voting requirement, which must be ratified by an equal supermajority.

o. Two-thirds vote senate, majority vote house, first passage; majority both houses, second passage. As of 1974, amendments may be submitted only every four years.

p. Majority of members elected to both houses, first passage; two-thirds of members elected to both houses, second passage.

q. Two-thirds of members of each house, first passage; majority of members of each house after popular ratification.

r. Majority vote on amendment must be at least 50 percent of the total votes cast at the election, or, at a special election, a majority of the votes tallied, which must be at least 30 percent of the total number of registered voters.

s. For initiative amendments, majority must be at least 30 percent of total votes in Massachusetts, 40 percent in Mississippi, and 35 percent in Nebraska.

t. Three-fifths vote on amendment, except that an amendment for "new state tax or fee" not in effect on November 7, 1994, requires two-thirds of voters in the election.

u. Majority voting in election, or three-fifths voting on amendment.

v. If five or fewer political subdivisions of the state are affected, a majority in a state as a whole and also in affected subdivisions is required.

w. Majority of all citizens voting for governor.

x. Consult *The Book of the States* for explanatory notes associated with these counts.

Table 2-1 lists states according to the difficulty of enacting amendments. The process is particularly daunting in states near the bottom of the table; they require approval by a lengthy sequence of supermajorities. States near the top of the table permit simple majorities to propose and approve amendments. Generally speaking, proposals emanating from the legislature have the greatest chance of succeeding, but opponents of abortion and same-sex marriage have relied on the initiative where it is available.

Constitutional Status of Local Governments

State governments are often viewed as smaller versions of the national government in the United States, but there is an important constitutional difference. The authority of the national government is defined positively; Congress and the president can exercise only the powers conferred upon them under the Constitution. State governments, by contrast, enjoy **plenary powers**, which are negatively expressed: states have the power to enact laws and promulgate policy unless their constitutions prohibit it.

The point is essential for understanding relations between state and local governments. Constitutionally speaking, local governments are creatures of the state; their terms of existence are spelled out in laws or in the state constitution itself. The structure, powers, and responsibilities of local governments may be modified by the legislature in the course of exercising its plenary powers. In states where constitutions provide for local governments, amendments may alter the very terms of their existence.

The extent of this relation is evident in Table 2-2, which lists the numbers of different types of local units in each state in 2007. There are 89,476 independent local governments in the United States. More than half are special districts responsible for providing a single service: libraries, schools, hospitals, mass transit, fire protection, water and sewer services, and the like. Township, municipal, and county-area governments account for the remainder; they are general-purpose governments, providing a variety of public goods and services to residents. General and **special-purpose governments** have overlapping boundaries, so the average citizen is subject to the authority of several local governments at once. Property owners are keenly aware of this, because most special governments levy taxes on private property within their jurisdiction.

The number of local governments varies across the states, and the differences are not merely a reflection of the size of a state or its population. Some populous states such as Florida have relatively few governments, whereas less populous states such as Kansas and Minnesota have many. Higher numbers mean that states devote more time, energy, and resources to interactions with the local governments subject to their control. This requires some capacity to manage relations with subordinate entities and an ability to withstand pressure from a large number of local officials pleading their cases to the legislature.

Table 2-2   States Ranked by Number of Local Governments, 2007

State	Local governments, total	County governments	Municipal governments	Town governments	Special districts	School districts
Illinois	6,994	102	1,299	1,432	3,249	912
Pennsylvania	4,871	66	1,016	1,546	1,728	515
Texas	4,835	254	1,209	0	2,291	1,082
California	4,344	57	478	0	2,765	1,102
Kansas	3,931	104	627	1,353	1,531	316
Missouri	3,723	114	952	312	1,809	536
Ohio	3,702	88	938	1,308	700	668
Minnesota	3,526	87	854	1,788	456	341
New York	3,403	57	618	929	1,119	716
Indiana	3,231	91	567	1,008	1,272	293
Wisconsin	3,120	72	592	1,259	756	444
Michigan	2,893	83	533	1,242	456	730
North Dakota	2,699	53	357	1,320	771	198
Nebraska	2,659	93	530	454	1,294	288
Colorado	2,416	62	270	0	1,904	180
South Dakota	1,983	66	309	916	526	166
Iowa	1,954	99	947	0	528	380
Oklahoma	1,880	77	594	0	642	567
Washington	1,845	39	281	0	1,229	296
Florida	1,623	66	411	0	1,051	95
Arkansas	1,548	75	502	0	724	247
Oregon	1,546	36	242	0	1,034	234
Georgia	1,439	154	535	0	570	180
New Jersey	1,383	21	324	242	247	625
Kentucky	1,346	118	419	0	634	175
Montana	1,273	54	129	0	758	332
Idaho	1,240	44	200	0	880	116
Alabama	1,185	67	458	0	529	131
Mississippi	1,000	82	296	0	458	167
North Carolina	963	100	548	0	315	173
Tennessee	928	92	347	0	475	136
New Mexico	863	33	101	0	633	96
Massachusetts	861	5	45	306	423	332
Maine	850	16	22	466	248	299
Vermont	733	14	45	237	144	293
Wyoming	726	23	99	0	549	55
South Carolina	698	46	268	0	299	85
West Virginia	663	55	232	0	321	55
Connecticut	649	0	30	149	453	166
Arizona	645	15	90	0	301	253
Utah	599	29	242	0	288	40
New Hampshire	545	10	13	221	137	174
Louisiana	526	60	303	0	95	69
Virginia	511	95	229	0	186	135
Delaware	338	3	57	0	259	19
Maryland	256	23	157	0	76	39
Nevada	198	16	19	0	146	17
Alaska	177	14	148	0	15	54
Rhode Island	134	0	8	31	91	36
Hawaii	19	3	1	0	15	1
United States	89,476	3,033	19,492	16,519	37,381	14,561

SOURCE: Adapted from U.S. Census Bureau, *2007 Census of Governments: Government Organization* (Washington, D.C.: Government Printing Office, 2007).

NOTE: 1,510 school districts operated by local governments are not included in the total column to avoid double-counting.

Perhaps more important, states must coordinate relations among the numerous units of local government (Krueger and Bernick 2010). Much of the activity consists of refereeing disputes, or setting rules for the incorporation of new governments, annexation of unorganized areas, consolidation of existing governments, or creation of legal frameworks for service contracts between local governments. Then there are the rules for shrinking governments: separation of an area from an existing unit of government, voluntary disincorporation of a previously organized entity, and the abolition of superfluous local units. Immediately after World War II, many state governments eliminated small schools in rural areas and transferred their students to consolidated districts in order to provide education more efficiently. The number of school districts nationwide fell from 67,355 in 1952 to 14,561 in 2007, even though two new states were added to the Union and the number of children enrolled in public elementary and secondary schools climbed more than 40 percent during this same period. Today, a declining rural population could trigger another round of school consolidation in some sparsely settled states.

Political Relations between State and Local Governments

The constitutional dependence of local governments is mitigated by political considerations. A commitment to local determination is central to Americans' political heritage. In the Northeast, state constitutions were adopted after the Declaration of Independence, when local governments were already a hundred years old or older. Other areas of the country were settled, and towns established, before territories became states. In these states, communities are legally powerless to prevent states from invading their powers, but they enjoy a large measure of independence because tradition favors delegation of authority to the local level. Once delegated, this authority is difficult for states to recover, except when national standards are imposed or fiscal problems arise.

The same forces that make Congress responsive to states also make states responsive to local government. Representation in the legislature is by locale, and elected representatives often have prior experience in local affairs. They are sensitive to the desire of local policymakers for autonomy, and they learn of opposition to pending legislation from lobbyists employed by individual local governments, not to mention associations of local governments, mayors, law enforcement officers, and school superintendents. These associations are powerful lobbies in the state capital. They routinely defend local governments from unwanted legislation and occasionally succeed in obtaining laws advocated by local governments.

The major political consideration, therefore, is not whether states will be responsive to local governments but rather to which set of local governments they will be most responsive. Historically, the malapportionment of state legislatures gave rural counties a disproportionate say in state policymaking. Reapportionment strengthened the representation of urban areas in state legislatures in the 1970s and 1980s.

Now suburbs and exurbs are growing faster than cities; their representation is swelling in state legislatures and big cities are losing influence.

Certain locales enjoy greater independence from state government. Municipal governments in forty-eight states qualify for **home rule** charters offering some degree of self-determination. County governments do, too, in thirty-seven states. The degree of autonomy under home rule varies from state to state and is subject to change by legislatures (Krane, Rigos, and Hill 2000). In most cases, though, general-purpose governments operating under home rule choose their form of government from options defined by the state. They also enjoy independent taxing and spending powers.

Another area of discretion involves the range of functions local units may undertake. The greatest discretion exists in states that devolve authority to local governments, which enjoy powers not specifically denied to them by the legislature or the constitution. At the other extreme are **Dillon's Rule** states, which enumerate the powers and functions of local governments; powers not explicitly given are denied, although the legal understanding of granted powers may be fairly liberal. More subtle ways of affecting the level and kind of services provided by local governments are restricting revenues, earmarking the use of funds, and establishing performance standards.

Although garbage collection, fire protection, and even elementary education can be provided through contractual arrangements with private concerns, they are most often supplied by public employees, and the conditions of employment by local government are stipulated in detail by state government. The most important requirements concern the extent to which merit informs hiring, promoting, and firing decisions. States may also establish training, licensing, and certification standards for employees; define collective bargaining rights and compulsory arbitration rules; control hours of employment and working conditions; regulate disability benefits; and mandate retirement programs. In 2011 several newly elected Republican governors and legislatures sought reductions in the benefits and collective bargaining rights of public employees, including local teachers, public safety officers, inspectors, and other municipal and county workers.

The exercise of local discretion may be limited by fiscal regulations (Berman 2010). Cities in Arizona, Illinois, Maine, and Texas have substantial latitude in fiscal matters, but local units elsewhere do not. In most states, the constitution or legislature determines which taxes may be levied by local units, which methods of assessment must be employed, and what sorts of exemptions must be granted. In addition, the magnitude of local tax increases is often restricted by constitutional amendments enacted in response to "taxpayer revolts." Local borrowing is tightly regulated in most states; overall debt loads are limited; and the type of debts that may be incurred, as well as the interest rates that may be paid on bonds, are typically controlled by the legislature. Similar restrictions affect spending practices, and in New Mexico cities and counties must submit their entire budgets to an agency of the state government for approval.

State governments routinely audit local finances, and they occasionally take over local units that become insolvent. The receivership is temporary but may result in restructuring the government in question. For example, three cities in Michigan— Benton Harbor, Pontiac, and Ecorse—are currently controlled by emergency financial managers appointed by the governor. A parallel process exists for school systems that are declared "academically bankrupt" by a state department of education. This deeply unpopular action has become more frequent with passage of the No Child Left Behind Act, which requires annual improvement in schools' effectiveness, measured by gains in students' performance on standardized tests.

Bowman and Kearney (2011) catalog variations in the autonomy of local governments across the states. The differences are the result of many factors. The political culture of a state shapes beliefs about the most appropriate relation between state and local government. The length of legislative sessions and the number of local governments in a state have an effect as well. Legislatures cannot closely supervise a large number of local units when state representatives meet infrequently and for short periods of time.

Finally, actions of Congress can affect the power local governments enjoy in their states. When Congress appropriated $286 billion for highways and mass transit in 2005, it also provided funds for training employees of county highway departments and city street departments, making them more effective partners with state departments in planning processes.

Fiscal Relations between State and Local Governments

Although their discretionary powers have increased in recent years, many local governments lack the resources to promote economic development, finance infrastructural improvements, protect the environment, and upgrade public services, including education. To meet the needs of constituents, and to comply with mandates from higher levels of government, local leaders lobby state leaders for assistance. As a result, policymaking is becoming more centralized at the subnational level in these policy areas.

The degree of centralization varies from state to state and across policy areas within the same state. States generally take the lead in constructing highways, maintaining correctional institutions and mental health hospitals, and regulating the use of land and natural resources, including wetlands, shorelines, and wildlife. States also organize health and welfare services, although some devolve responsibility for them to counties now that national controls over public assistance have been relaxed. Municipal governments typically provide public safety, sanitation, and sewage disposal, and school districts manage educational services. Yet even these locally provided services are heavily influenced by state actions insofar as many state governments provide huge sums of money to the responsible local units.

From 1980 to 2008, total state aid to local governments increased from $82.8 billion to $467 billion—about twice the rate of inflation over the same period. States became the principal financiers of many public services, even those provided by local governments. In the process, new legal requirements and general policy guidelines were imposed by state officials seeking greater accountability from local governments. State governments now control or strongly influence areas of policymaking long dominated by local governments, education being the most prominent example.

State aid is only one aspect of policy centralization, however. States achieve the same result by providing goods and services directly, without involving local governments. This necessitates substantial outlays by state governments, but it does ensure control over the formulation and implementation of public policy. Under this method, no intermediaries are needed—or rather, the intermediaries are agencies and employees of state government, whose actions are easier to regulate than those of local government officials.

States differ in the extent to which they rely on direct or indirect methods of centralizing control over the provision of public goods and services. Hawaii gives local governments almost no state aid, but it fully funds the state's one public school district from the state treasury. Because education is the most expensive service provided by state and local governments, the state ranks high on measures of fiscal centralization.

New Mexico, by contrast, augments direct spending with a significant amount of state aid, mostly for local school systems. The use of money is the same as in Hawaii, but the method of financing is indirect. In New Mexico, the importance of state aid in funding education gives the state government substantial control over this vital service. Other states, including Vermont and New Hampshire, are moving in this direction as they comply with court orders to equalize school funding (see Chapter 12 of this volume).

State aid is politically important in large states such as California, Michigan, and New York. In simple terms, it represents a determination to work through local governments in providing basic services. In part, this approach reflects the fact that local governments are powerful enough to persuade legislatures in these states to assist them financially. But many of these governments are also capable policymakers, with long histories of service provision and relatively high levels of citizen satisfaction with local government. The idea of a partnership between state and local governments is particularly strong in such states.

Local governments' dependence on state aid makes them vulnerable to cutbacks imposed by state legislatures facing budget problems of their own. When the Texas legislature convened in the spring of 2011, revenues were down and stimulus funds were nearly exhausted. The state faced a $27 billion deficit, but Gov. Rick Perry pledged to balance the budget without raising taxes or tapping the state's $9 billion rainy day fund. As the session wore on, the governor agreed to use $3.2 billion of the rainy day fund to narrow the gap, but insisted that cuts in spending cover the remainder. Eventually, a $4 billion reduction in formula funding for public schools was adopted in a special session of the legislature, along with another $1 billion reduction in discretionary grants for preschool, dropout prevention, and bonus pay for teachers.

Because of this "deficit sharing," the Texas State Teachers Association predicts that another 65,000 teachers will lose their jobs. Governor Perry, however, denies responsibility, arguing that the local school districts decide who to hire and fire. Districts that do not wish to fire teachers can ask local citizens for an increase in property taxes to offset the reduction in state funding. Inevitably, though, some school referenda will succeed and others will fail. As a result, spending in some districts will greatly exceed spending in other districts, potentially running afoul of the state constitution. According to the Texas Supreme Court, that constitution requires school districts to have substantially equal access to similar revenues per pupil at similar levels of tax effort. Legal challenges to the budget cuts are already under way.

State Mandates and Preemptions

Aid is the carrot used by state officials to influence local decision making. Mandates are the stick. States resent mandates from Congress, and they have the capacity to resist national policymakers who depend on them for policy implementation. But local governments are administrative conveniences of the state, and they are vulnerable to state officials who insist on having their way. Consequently, local governments labor under hundreds or even thousands of mandates from state governments, much to their political consternation and financial distress.

Local opposition to state mandating is intense, and it is expressed in the legislature, where localities are well represented. All states require fiscal notes, or estimates of the cost of mandates imposed by states on local units of government. Some states have statutes prohibiting mandates unless the state legislature provides funding for the activity in question, reimburses local governments for the cost of mandates, or provides them with a new source of funding to cover the costs. In California, Proposition 1A permits local governments to stop providing a mandated service if the state does not reimburse localities in a timely manner. Maine has a much stronger protection for local governments. A 1992 constitutional amendment requires the state to pay 90 percent of the estimated costs of mandates. There is an escape clause, however: the payment may be set aside by a two-thirds vote in each chamber of the legislature. There are ways around mandate restrictions, and many state legislators would rather mandate than raise state taxes and face the wrath of voters, particularly during a deep recession.

States routinely preempt local ordinances. Several states recently enacted laws that either prohibit antismoking ordinances altogether or establish statewide regulations much weaker than those preferred by some municipal and county policymakers. The National Rifle Association lobbied state legislatures to limit local gun controls and bar localities from suing firearms manufacturers who market handguns used in crimes. Many states passed limitations on local powers of eminent domain after the widely criticized U.S. Supreme Court decision *Kelo v. City of New London,* 545 U.S. 469 (2005), which allowed a Connecticut city to compel a homeowner to sell property needed for redevelopment. In all of these instances, state policymakers exercised sovereignty over local governments, just as Congress exercises its powers over states—and with the same political result. Those who must obey mandates complain about paying the bills while those who issue the mandates claim credit for solving problems.

CHALLENGES TO INTERGOVERNMENTAL RELATIONS

One hundred years ago, national, state, and local governments had separate and distinct responsibilities in the United States. Now they interact extensively in most areas of domestic policy and service provision. Local governments are the providers of public education, but they operate under mandates from state governments responding to national legislation. State governments are the principal regulators of social conduct and economic behavior, but they do so under constraints imposed by the U.S. Supreme Court, and they rely on local authorities to enforce state laws. Even the national government now depends on state and local governments to implement its policies in exchange for grants-in-aid.

Precisely because they are effective partners in the delivery of goods and services, state and local authorities dislike requirements that accompany grants from the national government. Their resentment festered as state and local governments became more dependent on grants during the economic recession of 2007–2009 and its aftermath. By 2010 Republican governors, legislators, and attorneys general began to challenge the assertive federalism of President Obama. They revived the idea that a state may nullify national laws it deems unconstitutional, although the Constitution reserves the power of judicial review to the U.S. Supreme Court. There was even talk of secession in the Republic of Texas, which nevertheless took full advantage of the stimulus package enacted by Congress.

A reassertion of states' rights was to be expected because of the national government's decision to stimulate the economy by means of grants that required states to comply with national guidelines. Now that the stimulus funding has run its course, national outlays for grants-in-aid will shrink. As that happens, states will recover some of their fiscal independence; how much they recover depends on the size of spending cuts enacted by Congress. If fiscal conservatives have their way, domestic discretionary spending by the national government—including grants-in-aid—will be sharply curtailed.

At that point, states will have to decide which programs they want to maintain at their own expense. Some states will continue to spend heavily and tax accordingly.

Others will tax lightly and provide fewer goods and services. The range of variation in policies will expand as the redistributive effect of the current grant system decreases. Differences in capacity will then play a larger role in determining a state's policies than they do now, and voters will know whom to reward or punish for this outcome.

KEY TERMS

confederal, 31

Dillon's Rule, 55

dual federalism, 34

federalism, 31

home rule, 55

intergovernmental relations, 32

interstate compact, 32

mandate, 42

plenary power, 52

preemption, 43

sovereign immunity, 35

special-purpose governments, 52

unitary, 31

vertical coalitions, 38

REFERENCES

Andrew, Simon A. 2009. "Recent Developments in the Study of Interjurisdictional Agreements: An Overview and Assessment." *State and Local Government Review* 41: 133–142.

Anton, Thomas J. 1989. *American Federalism and Public Policy: How the System Works.* New York: Random House.

Berman, David R. 2010. "State-Local Relations: Authority and Finances." *The Municipal Yearbook* 77: 41–59.

Bowman, Ann O'M., and Richard C. Kearney. 2011. "Second-Order Devolution: Data and Doubt." *Publius: The Journal of Federalism* 41: 563–585.

Bowman, Ann O'M., and George A. Krause. 2003. "Power Shift: Measuring Policy Centralization in U.S. Intergovernmental Relations, 1947–1998." *American Politics Research* 31: 301–325.

Cho, Chung-Lae, and Deil S. Wright. 2007. "Perceptions of Federal Aid Impacts on State Agencies: Patterns, Trends, and Variations across the 20th Century." *Publius: The Journal of Federalism* 37: 103–130.

Conlan, Timothy J., and Robert L. Dudley. 2005. "Janus-Faced Federalism: State Sovereignty and Federal Preemption in the Rehnquist Court." *PS: Political Science and Politics* 38: 363–366.

Conlan, Timothy J., and Paul L. Posner. 2011. "Inflection Point? Federalism and the Obama Administration." *Publius: The Journal of Federalism* 41: 421–446.

Derthick, Martha. 2009. "The Transformation That Fell Short: Bush, Federalism, and Emergency Management." Nelson A. Rockefeller Institute of Government, State University of New York.

Dinan, John J. 2009. *The American State Constitutional Tradition.* Lawrence: University Press of Kansas.

Elazar, Daniel J. 1984. *American Federalism: A View from the States,* 3d ed. New York: Harper and Row.

Frye, Earl H. 1998. *The Expanding Role of State and Local Governments in U.S. Foreign Affairs.* Washington, D.C.: Council on Foreign Relations Press.

Gormley, William T., Jr. 2006. "Money and Mandates: The Politics of Intergovernment Conflict." *Publius: The Journal of Federalism* 36: 523–540.

Grodzins, Morton. 1966. *The American Political System.* Chicago: Rand-McNally.

Joondeph, Bradley W. 2011. "Federalism and Health Care Reform: Understanding the States' Challenges to the Patient Protection and Affordable Care Act." *Publius: The Journal of Federalism* 41: 447–470.

Krane, Dale, Platon N. Rigos, and Melvin Hill. 2000. *Home Rule in America: A Fifty-State Handbook.* Washington, D.C.: CQ Press.

Krueger, Skip, and Ethan M. Bernick. 2010. "State Rules and Local Governance Choices." *Publius: The Journal of Federalism* 40: 697–718.

Lord, William B., and Douglas S. Kenney. 1993. "Resolving Interstate Water Conflicts: The Compact Approach." *Intergovernmental Perspective* 19: 19–23.

McNichol, Elizabeth, Phil Oliff, and Nicholas Johnson. 2011. "States Continue to Feel Recession's Impact." Center on Budget and Policy Priorities, Washington, D.C., March 9.

National Center for Interstate Compacts. 2011. "Fact Sheet," "Frequently Asked Questions," and database. www.csg.org/programs/policyprograms/NCIC.aspx.

National Conference of State Legislatures. 2011. "2011 Immigration-Related Laws, Bills, and Resolutions in the States." www.ncsl.org/default.aspx?tabid=13114.

National Indian Gaming Association. 2011. *The Economic Impact of Indian Gaming.* www .indiangaming.org.

Nicholson-Crotty, Sean, and Nick Theobald. 2011. "Claiming Credit in the U.S. Federal System: Testing a Model of Competitive Federalism." *Publius: The Journal of Federalism* 41: 231–256.

Posner, Paul L. 1998. *The Politics of Unfunded Mandates Reform: Whither Federalism?* Washington, D.C.: Georgetown University Press.

Schneider, Saundra K., William G. Jacoby, and Daniel C. Lewis. 2011. "Public Opinion toward Intergovernmental Policy Responsibilities." *Publius: The Journal of Federalism* 41: 1–30.

Tarr, G. Alan. 2000. *Understanding State Constitutions.* Princeton, N.J.: Princeton University Press.

U.S. Congressional Budget Office. 2011. "A Review of CBO's Activities in 2010 under the Unfunded Mandates Reform Act." March. www.cbo.gov/ftpdocs/121xx/doc12117/03-31-UMRA.pdf.

Walker, David. 2000. *The Rebirth of American Federalism: Slouching toward Washington.* New York: Chatham House.

Wlezien, Christopher, and Stuart N. Soroka. 2011. "Federalism and Public Responsiveness to Policy." *Publius: The Journal of Federalism* 41: 431–453.

Wright, Deil S. 1988. *Understanding Intergovernmental Relations,* 3d ed. Pacific Grove, Calif.: Brooks/Cole.

Zimmerman, Joseph F. 2005. *Congressional Preemption: Regulatory Federalism.* Albany, N.Y.: State University of New York Press.

———. 2011. *Horizontal Federalism: Interstate Relations.* Albany, N.Y.: State University of New York Press.

SUGGESTED READINGS

Print

The Book of the States. Lexington, Ky.: Council of State Governments. This annual publication contains a wealth of comparative data and information about state governments.

Publius: The Journal of Federalism. A quarterly journal devoted to research on federalism, with a special issue each year on the current state of American federalism.

Stephens, G. Ross, and Nelson Wikstrom. *American Intergovernmental Relations: A Fragmented Federal Polity.* New York: Oxford University Press, 2007. Surveys the development of intergovernmental relations in the United States in a global context.

Internet

Council of State Governments. www.csg.org/. Reports on trends and policy concerns of state officials.

Federal, State, and Local Governments (U.S. Census Bureau). www.census.gov/govs/www/index .html. Information about state and local government finance, employment, and government organization.

National Conference of State Legislatures. www.ncsl.org/. Reports on legislative developments in state capitals.

Rockefeller Institute of Government. www.rockinst.org/. Publishes the latest research on intergovernmental policymaking, with a focus on state governments.

CHAPTER 3

 Parties and Elections

THOMAS M. HOLBROOK AND
RAYMOND J. LA RAJA

Political parties permeate every aspect of state governments. Political scientists have long stressed their crucial role in acting as agents of political socialization, aggregating and mobilizing the interests of vast numbers of citizens, organizing the decision-making institutions of government, and enhancing voters' capacities to hold public officials accountable. In many ways, parties have become resurgent in recent decades after having been buffeted by a succession of threatening challenges. These challenges include the loss of patronage traditionally used to sustain their organizations; the surrender of control over nominations as states have adopted primary elections to choose candidates; and the competition from interest groups, candidates' personal organizations, and campaign consultants. Despite these challenges, parties have demonstrated amazing adaptability and durability. They have found their niche in the current candidate-centered era as institutions that serve their candidates by providing resources to meet the rising campaign costs and to compete for partisan control of government (Aldrich 1995, 269–274). At the same time, the coherence of party policies has increased as partisan activists use their influence to shape the outcome of primary nominations and hold governing elites accountable for passing programmatic legislation (Masket 2009). Overall, recent trends suggest a strengthened role for the party in shaping who runs for and wins office.

STATE PUBLIC POLICY TOWARD PARTIES

In most Western democracies, political parties are considered to be private associations. As such, they are permitted to transact business in private, largely unregulated by government. American political parties, however, are heavily regulated by state laws. They function in a manner similar to public utilities in that they provide essential public services (such as nominating candidates, contesting elections, organizing the government) that have sufficient impact on the public to justify governmental regulation (Epstein 1986, 157).

State regulation of parties was encouraged by the introduction in the 1890s of the Australian ballot: secret general election ballots provided by the government with candidates designated by party labels. By granting official recognition to political parties on government-provided ballots, the states acquired a legal justification for engaging in the regulation of parties (Epstein 1986, 152–167).

Ballot Access and Form

State laws define what constitutes an officially recognized political party eligible for a line on the general election ballot. The requirements for parties retaining automatic ballot access normally involve winning a specified percentage of the vote for any statewide race in the last election (the percentage ranges from 20 percent in Alabama to half of 1 percent in states such as Michigan and New Mexico). The median test for the fifty states is a vote of 2 percent in the previous election. In Vermont, Mississippi, and Florida, a party can stay on the ballot indefinitely as long as it informs the state of its party officers. New parties or independent candidates seeking ballot access must secure signatures from a designated percentage of the voters. Whatever specific form the statutes governing ballot access may take, their general effect is to protect the dominant status of the two major parties and serve as barriers to independent candidacies and the emergence of third-party movements (Winger 1997, 165–172). Thus in the sixty-eight-year history of Georgia's ballot access law, which requires a minor-party candidate to secure the signatures of 5 percent of the registered voters on a petition, no minor-party candidate for the U.S. House has ever been able to comply with the petition requirement and qualify for a place on the ballot (Richard Winger, editor, *Ballot Access News,* interview with author, April 13, 2011).

Through their regulation of the form of the ballot, states may either encourage straight-ticket party voting through use of the party column ballot or encourage voters to engage in split-ticket voting by using the office bloc ballot. Party column ballots list candidates together by party, whereas office bloc ballots sort candidates by the elective office they seek, which makes it easier for voters to select candidates from different parties for different offices. The trend since the 1960s has been for states to switch from the party column ballot to the office bloc form of ballot. As a result, only a bare majority of states still use the party column ballot. A companion trend that eliminates the ability of citizens to vote for all of a party's candidates with a single action in the polling booth further encourages a candidate-centered style of politics. In 2011 only fourteen states retained a ballot form containing a provision for expedited straight-ticket voting (Winger 2011).

The importance of state regulation and administration of elections was dramatically demonstrated by the postelection vote-counting controversies that swirled around the 2000 presidential election in Florida. The confusion was created by Palm Beach County's so-called butterfly ballot, which appeared to cause some voters to cast their votes for a candidate other than the one intended. However, it was but one of the many sources of controversy. There were also disputes over counting punch-card ballots with "hanging chads" and absentee ballots from overseas; allegations that persons were denied the right to vote; and issues concerning the proper role of the secretary of state (Florida's chief election officer), the state legislature, and courts in determining whether George W. Bush or Al Gore won the state's electoral votes. Indeed, the outcome of the national election hinged on Florida.

As a consequence of the 2000 election administration controversies in Florida and other states, Congress passed in 2002 the Help America Vote Act, an election reform that authorized $3.86 billion to upgrade voting equipment, improve election administration, and train poll workers. The act also mandated that states prepare computerized voter registration lists, provide provisional ballots to voters whose names did not appear on voter lists, and make voting machines accessible to the handicapped. As of 2010, the states had received more than $3 billion through the act (U.S. Electoral Assistance Commission 2010). One challenge is that states must implement the federal requirements in a political context that has traditionally given considerable discretion to localities (including counties or, in some states, cities or townships) in determining voting procedures.

Eased Procedures for Voting

In recent decades, states have eased the process of voting through more liberal absentee ballot rules, early voting, and mail-in ballots—all of which have made the political parties' function of mobilizing voters more complicated, time-consuming, and crucial. Currently, thirty states and the District of Columbia give absentee ballots to any voter who simply requests that option. In addition, thirty-two states and the District of Columbia allow early voting at an election official's office or, in some states, at other satellite voting locations with the same voting equipment in place for the regular election. Early voting is most often available during a period of ten to fourteen days before an election (National Conference of State Legislatures 2011a). Oregon, which pioneered mail-in ballots, and Washington (in a 2011 law) have eliminated the polling booth altogether, holding elections only through the mail. Meanwhile, a growing number of states are allowing vote-by-mail in state and local races. With these developments, early voting rates (the national percentage of votes cast before election day) increased from 21 percent in 2004 to 30 percent in

2008 (McDonald 2010). The trend toward easing the voting process is dramatically changing the timetable under which parties operate and is forcing them to reexamine their strategies.

Organizational Structure

State regulations frequently extend to matters of internal party organization such as procedures for selecting officers, composition of party committees, dates and locations of meetings, and powers of party units. In each of the states, the two major parties have state central committees headed by a state chair. The state committees are normally composed of members elected by county committees, state and congressional district conventions, or party primaries. The state committee's duties vary from state to state but normally include calling the state convention, adopting party policies, fund-raising, assisting with campaigns, aiding local party units, and serving as a party public relations agency. Most state parties have vested an executive committee with the same powers as the parent state central committee and authorized it to act for the party between the infrequent meetings of the central body.

More than three-quarters (77 percent) of state party chairs are elected for two-year terms, and 23 percent have four-year terms. Turnover, however, is high. The average tenure of state party chairs is roughly two years, with Republicans serving on average 2.3 years and Democrats 1.6 years (Aldrich 2000, 656). State chairs or the party executive directors act as the operational heads of state party organizations responsible for fund-raising, candidate recruitment, campaign activities, party publicity, and coordinating with local and national party organizations and internally elected officials. Both Republican and Democratic state chairs serve on their parties' national committees. State chairs are frequently handpicked by their party's governor and therefore are expected to advance and protect gubernatorial interests within the party. For the party out of power—that is, the one that does not control the governor's office—the state chair may be the real party leader and its principal spokesperson.

The state party committee is an umbrella organization for numerous local parties, including those at the level of the congressional district, legislative district, county, city, ward, and precinct. Each level of party organization is controlled by a committee that is headed by an elected leader. Although local parties have proved to be effective in influencing elections and campaigns, many tend to be weak or inactive. Indeed, it is often difficult for party leaders to find partisans willing to serve as officers of local parties.

In reality, the state party organization is much more encompassing than this description would suggest. The party can be viewed as a network of individuals and organizations with an array of resources upon which party candidates can draw. Included in this network are allied interest groups (for example, unions, teachers, trial lawyers, and environmental groups for the Democrats; business groups and evangelical Christians for the GOP), political action committees (PACs), fund-raisers, candidates' personal campaign organizations, political consultants, and the state legislative campaign committees controlled by legislative leaders.

Campaign Finance

States have long set at least some minimal limits on campaign spending and activities. Most ban election day expenditures; all prohibit bribery and vote buying; and each imposes some form of public disclosure and reporting of campaign receipts and expenditures. Since the Watergate scandal of the 1970s, campaign finance legislation has been the most rapidly growing body of election law. Just four states place no limits on the amount or sources of contributions. Thirty-seven states have imposed some limits on individual contributions, the constitutionality of which was upheld by the U.S. Supreme Court in 2000 (*Nixon v. Shrink Missouri Government PAC*, 93 U.S. 963). However, in 2006 the Supreme Court struck down the relatively low expenditure and contribution limits in Vermont for being too restrictive (*Randall v. Sorrell*, 382 F. 3d 91, reversed and remanded).

Currently, all but four states (Missouri, Oregon, Utah, and Virginia) have prohibited or placed limits on corporate contributions—twenty-four states have limits on the amounts corporations can contribute to candidates, and twenty-two states prohibit *any* corporate contributions. Meanwhile, all but seven states (Alabama, Iowa, Mississippi, Missouri, Oregon, Utah, and Virginia) have put restrictions on labor unions—twenty-eight have limits on how much they can contribute, and fifteen ban contributions directly from unions (National Conference of State Legislatures 2010). The Supreme Court's ruling in *Citizens United v. Federal Election Commission*, 558 U.S. ___ (2010), will have considerable indirect effects on how states regulate election spending by corporations and unions. In that decision, the Court declared that the federal government may not prohibit corporations and unions from spending funds to help defeat or elect a candidate. Because twenty-four states have laws that restrict corporate spending, labor union spending, or both, it is likely that such laws will be repealed or revised. The loosening of restrictions on corporate and union political spending will likely strengthen the election-eering influence of these groups relative to the political parties (La Raja 2008).

One approach to reducing the influence of private money in elections is to provide public subsidies to defray the cost of campaigns. Almost half the states provide some form of state financing of elections that channels public funds to candidates, political parties, or both. In the past, most state funding was inadequate for financing campaigns at a level commensurate with candidates' needs. Arizona, Maine, and Connecticut have implemented "clean elections" programs that allow legislative candidates to receive generous subsidies as long as they promise to forgo private financing. Other states, such as New Jersey, have pilot projects in a limited number of local races to evaluate such programs before expanding them statewide. Some analysis indicates that these programs somewhat enhance political competition

(Malhotra 2008), but there has been little research to assess whether public subsidies help increase the number and diversity of candidates, or improve levels of public trust in candidates and officeholders who no longer accept private contributions.

The diffusion of clean election reforms to additional states is doubtful because of recent court decisions declaring aspects of these programs unconstitutional. In Connecticut, the Second Circuit Court sided with plaintiffs from the Green Party and others not aligned with the two major parties who argued that the allocation of public funds unfairly discriminated against third parties and independent candidates—see *Green Party of Connecticut v. Garfield*, 2010 U.S. App. LEXIS 14248 (2d Cir. Conn. July 13, 2010). The appeals court also struck down the so-called trigger provisions in which publicly financed candidates receive additional funds beyond the initial subsidy when they are outspent by privately funded candidates or independent groups opposing their candidacy. In Arizona, a similar challenge to the trigger provision was upheld in a 5–4 decision by the Supreme Court in *McComish v. Bennett*, 564 U.S. ___ (2011). At issue in both *Green Party* and *McComish* is whether the trigger provision violates the free speech rights of privately financed candidates when the government gives additional funds to publicly financed candidates. The plaintiffs argue that privately financed candidates feel compelled to limit campaign activity when presented with a situation in which the government gives additional funds to their opponents. The trigger provision was intended as an inducement for candidates to participate in public financing and to discourage privately financed candidates from trying to outspend them. The courts, however, do not view government actions to level the playing field as a compelling government interest that would allow infringements on free speech rights. For these reasons, it remains to be seen whether clean election programs will survive in their current form. More likely, states that desire to subsidize elections may move toward programs like those used in the cities of New York and Los Angeles, in which the government provides a matching public subsidy for each small, private contribution raised by the candidates. To be sure, such cities will be under pressure to reduce these programs if they face ongoing financial shortfalls.

Despite the abundance of state campaign finance laws, the effectiveness of state regulation is severely limited by the fact that most enforcement agencies are understaffed and have inadequate resources. States have made great strides, however, in making campaign finance data accessible to the public on the Internet, although the quality of public disclosure remains mixed (Campaign Disclosure Project 2008).

The Changing Legal Status of State Parties

State statutes have given parties legal standing and special benefits (for example, ballot access and public funding), stipulated the functions they will perform, and regulated how those functions will be carried out. As a result, the parties have become quasi-public agencies. As adjuncts of state government, their existence has been practically mandated by state law and their continued existence virtually assured. The legal status of parties is, however, undergoing modification in the face of a series of U.S. Supreme Court decisions. These decisions have extended First and Fourteenth Amendment freedom of association rights to political parties and struck down a series of state-imposed restrictions on parties.

In *Tashjian v. Connecticut,* 479 U.S. 20 (1986), the Court held that Connecticut could not prevent voters registered as independents from voting in a Republican primary if the state GOP wanted to permit independents as well as registered Republicans to vote in its primaries. Although this decision had potentially important long-term implications for constraining the states' regulatory power over parties, its short-term effects were limited because only a few states used the Court-granted power to open their primaries to independents. It was not until California enacted a 1996 blanket primary law that state parties sought to use the *Tashjian* precedent to close rather than open their primaries. The blanket primary law permitted voters to participate in any party's primary and to vote in different party primaries as long as they voted for only one candidate per office. It was challenged on First and Fourteenth Amendment grounds by the parties in California, and in 2000 the U.S. Supreme Court in *Democratic Party v. Jones,* 530 U.S. 567 (2000), declared California's blanket primary unconstitutional as a "stark repudiation of political association" that denied parties the ability to control their own nomination processes and define their own identities. Because two dissenting justices asserted that the decision cast serious doubt upon the constitutionality of various forms of open primaries, the California case left open the question of whether open primaries are constitutional. However, it is not at all clear that the states, parties, or the Court are prepared to throw out traditional open primary systems that have become established parts of the states' political culture.

In another instance of asserting the freedom of association rights of state parties to limit state regulatory power over parties, the Supreme Court in *Eu v. San Francisco Democratic Central Committee,* 49 U.S. 214 (1989), threw out a California law that banned parties from endorsing candidates in primaries, limited the length of state chairs' terms, and called for rotating the position between northern and southern California every two years.

Although the Court has stated clearly that there are limits on the extent of regulation that states may impose on political parties, it has also demonstrated a willingness to allow the states considerable leeway in determining the nature of their electoral and party systems. Thus in 1997 it held in *Timmons v. Twin Cities New Party,* 520 U.S. 351 (1997), that although parties have an unquestioned right to nominate their own candidates, the states also have the constitutional right to regulate elections and prevent manipulations of the ballot and factionalism among the voters. The Court therefore ruled that Minnesota had the power to prevent the left-leaning New Party from engaging in the practice of "cross-filing" or "fusion" by nominating a candidate for the state legislature who had already accepted the

Democratic nomination. This decision, of course, struck a severe blow against a struggling third party and in effect gave the Court's blessing to state efforts to promote a two-party system.

STATE PARTY ORGANIZATIONS: INSTITUTIONALIZED SERVICE AGENCIES

Although state party organizations have gone through a resurgence since the early 1980s, they bear scant resemblance to the traditional party organizations that dominated state politics, particularly in the Mid-Atlantic, New England, and lower Great Lakes states of the early twentieth century (Mayhew 1986). These patronage-based organizations, which controlled nominations and ran their candidates' campaigns, had largely passed from the scene by the mid-1980s (Reichley 1992, 383–384). Patronage as a basis for building party organizations was severely weakened by civil service laws, stronger public employee unions, and a critical public. In the 1970s, the Supreme Court threw its might into the anti-patronage movement. In a series of cases, the Court hit at the heart of large-scale patronage operations run by both Democrats and Republicans in Illinois. It ruled in *Elrod v. Burns,* 427 U.S. 347 (1976), that the Cook County Democratic organization could no longer fire people on the basis of their party affiliations, and it followed this decision with one in *Rutan v. Republican Party,* 488 U.S. 1872 (1990), declaring that the state GOP could not use "party affiliations and support" as a basis for filling state jobs unless party affiliation was an "appropriate requirement" for filling the position. In this once patronage-rich state, the Democratic chair observed that "the party no longer functions as an employment agency. More and more we must rely on the spirit of volunteerism" (Reichley 1992, 385).

Even though patronage jobs no longer provide an important basis for party workers and money, other forms of governmental preferment remain important. Gubernatorial appointments to state boards and commissions that control professional licensing, gambling, higher education, hospitals, state investments, environmental and recreation policy, and cultural activities are assignments that are much sought after by persons seeking policy influence and recognition. Partisan considerations can also affect state decisions regarding state contracts, bank deposits, economic development, and purchase of legal and consulting services. However, these types of preferments are useful primarily for fund-raising and do not provide campaign workers in the same way that patronage jobs once did (Reichley 1992, 385).

Lacking material incentives to offer potential party workers, many party organizations became moribund through midcentury. In the 1950s, the leading student of American political parties, V. O. Key Jr. (1956, 287), gave the following dismal assessment of state parties: "The general impression that most . . . [state party committees] are virtually dead is probably not far from wrong." During the 1960s and 1970s, prominent observers of American politics continued to express concern for the state of the parties. Yet state party organizations have become since the 1980s increasingly professional and stronger in the sense that most can provide campaign services to their candidates and assistance to their local affiliates. The once highly autonomous state party organizations are also now closely integrated with the national party organizations, which use them to implement their campaign strategies in presidential, senatorial, and congressional campaigns (La Raja 2008). The national party committees have even become a significant source of financing and campaign services in close gubernatorial races and state legislative contests in which party control of legislative chambers is at stake.

The institutionalization of state parties as campaign service organizations parallels the resurgence of the national party organizations, where a massive fund-raising capacity has transformed the once weak Republican and Democratic National Committees into major service agencies to candidates and state and local party organizations. There are also parallels between the substantial campaign roles being played by the parties' senatorial and congressional campaign committees at the national level with the emergence of state legislative campaign committees as an important party-based campaign resource for legislative candidates. Most state parties now have permanent headquarters, professional leadership and staffing, and robust budgets to maintain the organization and support candidates (Cotter et al. 1984; Appleton and Ward 1997; Aldrich 2000; La Raja 2008).

Party Activities: Organization Building and Candidate Support

Enjoying larger and more professional staffs as well as adequate financial resources, state parties have expanded their activities in the areas of candidate support and party building, especially (since the early 1980s) financial support of candidates. More than 80 percent of state parties contribute to gubernatorial, state constitutional, congressional, and state legislative candidates (Aldrich 2000, 656). Parties also aid their nominees by matching them up with the appropriate PAC donors so that the organized groups become partners with the party. Political consultants frequently assist the party by providing an array of campaign services such as polling, fund-raising assistance, media consulting, research, and campaign seminars (Aldrich 2000; La Raja 2008). Because their resources are limited, however, state parties must be selective in the services they offer, and they have tended to engage in labor-intensive voter mobilization programs that have the potential to benefit party candidates up and down the ballot.

Although state parties have been strengthened in terms of their abilities to provide services to their candidates, their role is to supplement the activities of the candidates' own personal campaign organizations principally in the areas of voter mobilization and fund-raising. In assuming this restricted campaign role, the parties are adapting to the candidate-centered nature of state electoral politics in which candidates rely primarily on their own organizations, set up personal headquarters, and depend on nonparty groups to provide campaign assistance. The candidates also often hire campaign consultants to work exclusively on their behalf. The relative autonomy of candidates from political parties in organizing their campaigns is unique to the United States and accounts in part for the weakness of American parties compared with those in other nations.

Although the role of party organizations is to supplement the candidates' own personal organizations, the level of party organizational strength can affect elections. Southern Republican parties, for example, were initially unable to take advantage of the inroads made by GOP presidential candidates in the 1950s and 1960s because their organizations were weak. However, the spectacular gains by Republican candidates for congressional, state, and local office in more recent years are in large measure a product of much stronger Republican organization (Jewell and Morehouse 2001, 99). The real significance of party organizational strength is not so much its impact in any given year, but rather that such strength provides the infrastructure for candidates and activists to continue to compete in the face of short-term defeats and even long-term minority status and to take advantage of favorable conditions when they occur (for example, scandal, an opposition incumbent's retirement, divisiveness within the other party, or a shift in the public mood).

Demographic changes also encourage state parties to be proactive in their electoral activities. Both major parties hope to incorporate Hispanic voters, the largest immigrant group, into their coalitions. In Texas, Gov. George W. Bush achieved some success courting Mexican American voters for the Republican Party based on appeals to the conservative social values espoused by Mexican American Catholics and evangelicals. He also appointed Mexican Americans to highly visible political positions. In California, by contrast, Mexican Americans have trended toward the Democratic Party dating back to a 1994 ballot initiative, supported strongly by a Republican governor, that was perceived to be anti-immigrant. In spite of President Bush's efforts to replicate his success in Texas at the national level, Republicans appear to have hurt their image with Hispanic voters by pushing in Congress for immigration legislation that is widely perceived as being unfriendly to Hispanic immigrants.

As Hispanic populations grow throughout the nation, particularly in the Southwest, their impact on state politics will become critical. Hispanics comprise almost half of the population of New Mexico and 37 percent of that of both California and Texas. An additional six states—Arizona, Colorado, Florida, Illinois, New Jersey, and New York—have more than a million Hispanic residents (U.S. Census Bureau 2011). Party organizations and their allied groups in these states have been trying to register and mobilize these voters—not always with much success—in statewide races where they might be essential to electoral victory.

There is no doubt that the political power of Hispanics has been rising steadily, as evidenced by their growing presence in statehouses. Between 1984 and 2010, the ranks of Hispanic representatives in state legislatures rose from 106 to 245. Although this sum is only 3 percent of all state legislative seats in the nation, the numbers are rather significant in large and influential states. In California, for example, Hispanics occupy one in four seats in the legislature, and in Texas they hold one in five seats. Hispanics in other major states, such as New York and Florida, hold roughly one in ten seats. Research demonstrates that at a certain threshold of population growth the incorporation of Hispanics through such institutional representation has an important positive impact on policy for Hispanic communities in these states (Preuhs 2007).

Party Differences and the Heightened Involvement of Party-Allied Groups

Studies of state central committees have generally revealed that Republicans are stronger organizationally than their Democratic counterparts (Aldrich 2000, 655; Cotter et al. 1984; La Raja 2008). This finding reflects a key difference between the parties: Republican state organizations tend to be a more important source of campaign support than do Democratic Party organizations. This difference does not mean that Democratic candidates are necessarily lacking or unequal in resources, but it does mean that Democrats tend to rely more heavily for assistance on allied nonparty groups such as labor unions, teachers, abortion rights advocates, environmentalists, and trial lawyers to help supply money, workers, media advertising, and in-kind services. Democratic state parties thus tend to be more labor-intensive than the more capital-intensive GOP organizations.

The use of party-allied groups appears to be growing for both major parties. This growth is linked in part to both federal and state laws that place greater restrictions on the financing of parties than that of nonparty committees. For example, the federal Bipartisan Campaign Reform Act of 2002 bans contributions of soft money (those with no limits on their size or source) to political parties, but partisans may establish so-called **"527" or "501c4" organizations** to funnel soft money into elections. These organizations derive their numerical names from sections of the tax code. Even though 527 groups must report donors to the IRS, they face far fewer restrictions than parties or political action committees, which are regulated closely by the Federal Election Commission. Registered as civic or social welfare organizations, 510c4 groups do not have to disclose donors at all, as long as political spending constitutes less than half of organizational expenses. Because of the high stakes for taking control of state legislatures or Congress, partisans have felt compelled to use nonparty organizations to raise large sums quickly and spend them on broadcast advertising and grassroots efforts. In the 2010 midterms, Karl Rove, a former political adviser to President George W. Bush, and Ed Gillespie, the former chair of the RNC, inaugurated "American Crossroads" (a 527 organization) and "Crossroads GPS" (a 501c4). Together these organizations spent more than $50 million to support Republican congressional candidates throughout the nation (Rutenberg 2010). Democrats will attempt to compete with Republicans in 2012 through a 527 organization called "Priorities USA Action," and a 510c4 called "Priorities USA." Generally, these groups work in parallel with the candidates and party organizations, although campaign finance laws typically forbid allied organizations from formally coordinating their campaign activity.

Party-allied group activity is also pervasive in state elections, with important implications for political influence within the party. One scholar attributes the growing ideological gap between the parties in California to the ability of ideological activists in the major parties to control significant campaign resources for winning elections (Masket 2009). These "informal" party organizations help put more ideologically pure candidates (liberal Democrats and conservative Republicans) into office at the expense of moderates in each party. The use that state parties and their candidates make of allied group assistance—indeed, oftentimes their dependence on it—demonstrates the need to view parties in an inclusive and comprehensive manner that encompasses more than the formal, legally sanctioned organizational structure. The state party organization is actually a network that includes the regular party structure, candidate organizations, party-allied groups, fund-raisers, campaign consultants, and the army of staffers of incumbent legislators, who are frequently and heavily involved in advancing their bosses' electoral interests as well as those of the party. The decentralized nature of a partisan organization in which fund-raising and campaigning often occur outside the formal party structure may give advantages to the ideological factions in the party that have the wherewithal to organize electoral machinery.

The *Citizens United* decision, which prevents the government from restricting corporate or labor union political spending, has the potential to shape how different groups participate in elections. The conventional wisdom is that corporations will exploit the Court decision to increase the amounts they spend to influence elections. A comparison of states with and without a ban on corporate spending in the election cycle before the Court's decision indicates that there is some basis for this claim (La Raja 2010). Table 3-1 looks at a sample of eight states for which data exist on independent spending (campaign activities performed directly by groups without coordinating with candidates). In states without a ban, business interests tend to have the greatest amount of independent expenditures, typically approaching 50 percent of the total. By contrast, states that ban corporate spending tend to have elections in which labor unions spend the most independently. Interestingly, political parties tend to play a greater role in states with no ban on corporate spending, perhaps because these states also allow corporations (and unions) to make political contributions to the parties, a practice that appears to carve out a larger role for the formal party organization.

Parties as Networks of Issue-Oriented Activists

An emerging feature of American parties is that they are increasingly networks of "issue based participatory activists" (Shafer 1996, 35). The sources for this trend are found in a complex set of interacting forces: the development of a postindustrial society in which noneconomic social-cultural issues have gained heightened

Table 3-1   Independent Expenditures by Type of Organization in States with and without Corporate Spending Bans, 2008 Legislative Elections

State	Independent expenditure per eligible voter	Percentage by type of organization			
		Advocacy	Party	Labor	Business
States with a ban on corporate spending					
Colorado	$1.39	22%	5%	56%	17%
Minnesota	1.26	12	71	7	10
Arizona	0.81	17	7	66	10
Massachusetts	0.13	1	0	99	0
States with no ban on corporate spending					
Washington	$0.49	6%	40%	7%	46%
Idaho	0.21	26	27	0	47
Maine	0.61	6	84	0	10
California	0.67	4	2	43	51

S O U R C E : Secretary of State Web sites. Note that the constitutionality of state bans on corporate spending has been called into question by the U.S. Supreme Court's 2010 decision in *Citizens United v. Federal Election Commission.*

salience (for example, abortion, environmentalism, crime, gun control, women's rights, and gay rights); sociological and economic change that has resulted in higher educational attainment, less blue-collar employment, and an expanding white-collar workforce; and a decline in the availability of patronage as an incentive for political participation. Changes in the rules governing presidential nominating politics that have diminished the influence of party leaders have also enhanced the role of issue-oriented activists.

Surveys of national and state convention delegates, financial contributors, campaign workers, and candidates have demonstrated that party activists are more ideologically motivated than in the past, and that activists are from the extremes of opinion distribution (Layman, Carsey, and Horowitz 2006). Thus even though the rank-and-file voters are largely moderates comfortable with compromises and trade-offs, many activists are hard-liners who are not willing to compromise their strongly held views (Fiorina, Abrams, and Pope 2005). These "true believers" with their advocacy style of politics have now become deeply ensconced in state and local organizational structures (Bruce, Clark, and Kessel 1991). For example, *Campaigns and Elections* reported in the mid-1990s that eighteen Republican state organizations were dominated by the Christian Right and that it had substantial influence in thirteen more (Wilcox and Larson 2006, 89–91).

As significant as the Christian Right's involvement in GOP politics is in several states such as Texas and Virginia, an in-depth analysis has shown that its influence is not as great as its enemies, such as People for the American Way, fear or one of its leaders, Rev. Pat Robertson, claims. Its power varies widely across the states (Conger 2010), and it faces internal party opposition (Green, Guth, and Wilcox 1999, 133). The Christian Right, which reflects a social movement against rising

secularism, confronts the dilemma of working through American political institutions such as political parties, which are built around compromise and bargaining.
The movement, however, is fueled by ardent believers in religious doctrines who
tend to view compromise with elements of the secular culture—including moderate Republicans—as inherently immoral. For this reason, party infighting has
played itself out at the state level over selection of candidates and party platforms.
To push for the Ten Commandments to be displayed in government buildings in
Alabama, for example, Christian Coalition activists sought to nominate candidates to run against Republican incumbents in judicial contests and in the
governor's race (Baxter 2004). However, research shows that the Christian Right's
influence rests largely on the political context in a given state—that is, its strength
depends considerably on whether residents share conservative values that are
supportive of the movement's goals (Conger 2010). The emergence in the 2010
elections of the Tea Party movement, whose supporters appear to be primarily
antigovernment populists rather than religious conservatives (Jacobson 2011),
suggests that the Christian Right will continue to be challenged for control over
the direction of the GOP.

The Democrats, too, have been affected by an issue-oriented group influence
that has made it difficult to maintain the support of rank-and-file voters. An analysis of Democratic Party–interest group relations concluded that "many of the post-
material issues advocated by liberal citizen groups and Democratic candidates are
peripheral to the lives of middle-class Americans. . . . The Democrats' preoccupa-
tion with civil rights, women's rights, environmentalism, and other causes has
surely contributed to the Democrats' gender gap with white males" (Berry and
Schildkraut 1998, 155). Democrats became the advocates of these causes because
they were lobbied effectively by groups engaged in traditional political organizing,
just as the Republicans have been subjected to intense organizing efforts by conservative groups. Indeed, the drift to extremes by officeholders has been driven, in
part, by networks of issue activists who operate like informal party organizations
(Masket 2009). These activists coordinate their campaign work to influence the
nomination of preferred candidates in low turnout primaries. By virtually controlling nominations, these activists can groom and select candidates for public office,
as well as challenge officeholders who do not toe the line on policy. Because most
districts are not competitive in the general election, the winner of the primary typically wins the seat, even though he or she probably tilts heavily to the ideological
left or right of the median in the district.

The mounting involvement in party-like activity by individuals and groups
whose motivation to participate is based not on material rewards such as patronage
but rather on issue-based concerns is creating conflicts between the rank-and-file
party voters and the activists. It is also causing rifts between officeholders and party
organizations. Indeed, in some states an almost schizophrenic party structure has
developed: elected officials who need broad-based electoral support to win must

exist side by side with a growing body of organizational activists mainly concerned about ideology and principles. For this reason, some elected officials have pushed for reforming the nomination process in their state to diminish the influence of ideological activists. In California, for example, Gov. Arnold Schwarzenegger pushed successfully for passage of Proposition 14, which creates a primary in which the top two vote-getters, regardless of their party affiliations, face a run-off election. The hope is that this institutional reform will weaken the ability of ideological elements in either party to control the nomination, which would enhance the prospects for moderate candidates to win office.

To the extent that state parties increasingly become networks of issue-oriented activists, elected officials' conflicts with party organizational and allied-group activists are likely to proliferate. In addition, the growing influence of issue-oriented activists within the parties and on their candidates will in all likelihood widen the policy differences between the parties. In the 2010 midterm elections, for example, conservative activists took advantage of the enthusiasm generated by the Tea Party movement to challenge the party's establishment candidates for Senate contests in states such as Alaska, Delaware, Nevada, and Utah. In at least two of these states, the Republican Party likely lost a Senate seat because the candidate supported by the Tea Party enthusiasts in the nomination was seen as too extreme by general election voters (Courser 2010). Thus the traditional conception of parties as "vote maximizers" appears to require some revision. Like interest groups, parties now contain an enlarged element that is mainly interested in achieving policy objectives—that is, the party structures are heavily influenced by "policy maximizers."

STATE LEGISLATIVE CAMPAIGN COMMITTEES

As is the case at the national level, the state party organizational structure is decentralized, with a variety of organizations focusing on different offices and activities. The state central committees tend to concentrate on the statewide races, and the state legislative campaign committees focus their resources exclusively on legislative races and have emerged as the major source of party assistance to legislative candidates. The legislative campaign committees, which are composed of incumbent legislators in both chambers and are usually headed by legislative party leaders, tend to operate independently of their parties' state central committees. These committees emerged in response to intensifying partisan competition for control of legislative chambers, rising campaign costs ($500,000 expenditures in targeted races are no longer unusual in many states), growing uncertainty about election outcomes, and the inability of many state central committees in the 1970s to provide meaningful assistance to legislative candidates (Gierzynski and Breaux 1992, 11–14). In addition, the development of strong legislative campaign committees is linked to greater legislative professionalism—full-time legislators who are paid a reasonable salary and are backed by ample staff (Squire and Moncrief 2010). Professionalism increases the value of legislative service, especially when accompanied by majority-party status. Legislative leaders therefore created campaign committees to protect and further their own and their party colleagues' interests.

Legislative campaign committees began as mechanisms to raise and distribute funds to candidates, but they have developed into full-service operations for individual candidates, particularly in states with professionalized legislatures. The committees' involvement in candidate recruitment is particularly crucial. Recruitment of high-quality candidates is directly related to being able to raise campaign dollars, gain volunteer workers, and run truly competitive races for legislative seats. Although candidates in the United States are often self-starters, meaning they choose when to run and they organize their own campaigns, research shows that being asked to run by party leaders matters a great deal (Moncrief, Squire, and Jewell 2001). This seems especially true for women, who continue to face more institutional and social obstacles to candidacy than men (Lawless and Fox 2005; Sanbonmatsu 2006). Women legislative candidates, for example, are more likely to rate political parties and other groups as critical for their success in raising campaign funds, which suggests they must work harder because they have fewer social ties than men to wealthy individuals who can contribute money (Jenkins 2007).

Women candidates have made substantial progress, however. Since 1969, the number of women serving in the fifty state legislatures has increased from just a few hundred to more than 1,728, or 23 percent of all seats (National Conference of State Legislatures 2011b). Roughly 60 percent are Democrats, and the number of Republican women legislators is declining. Legislatures in Colorado and Vermont have the highest percentage of women legislators at 41 percent and 37.8 percent, respectively. States in the West, especially Arizona, Hawaii, and Washington, also tend to have more women legislators than other states (typically in the range of 25–34 percent). By comparison, states in the South—Alabama, Mississippi, Oklahoma, and South Carolina—have legislatures in which women occupy less than 15 percent of the seats. The reasons for the low rates in some states are not entirely clear, but they likely reflect the state political culture and the important role of traditional "gatekeepers" within the parties who do not necessarily see women as being able to win office (Conway 2001).

PARTY NATIONALIZATION AND HEIGHTENED INTRAPARTY INTEGRATION

Until the 1970s, political scientists emphasized the decentralized and confederate nature of American party organizations. The Republican National Committee (RNC) and the Democratic National Committee (DNC) were thought to be so lacking in influence that a landmark study even characterized them as "politics without power" (Cotter and Hennessy 1964). Power within the party structure resided with state and local organizations, and the national committees were heavily dependent on the state organizations for their funds. The national committees, which once existed in a state of dependency on their state affiliates, have now been transformed into large-scale, well-heeled enterprises housed in party-owned modern office buildings. Through their abilities to raise massive amounts of money, the national committees have been transformed into institutions capable of playing a major role in providing significant assistance to candidates and to their state affiliates. The larger resources and influence of the national party organizations have been accompanied by heightened integration and interdependence between national and state party organizations.

Centralizing Power through National Party Rule Enforcement

Since 1968, the national Democratic Party organization has intensified efforts begun in 1948 to use its rule-making authority, as well as its financial leverage, to ensure the loyalty of state party organizations to the national ticket. Starting with the McGovern-Fraser Commission (1969–1972), promulgated in the wake of the tumultuous 1968 nominating convention, the national party has developed elaborate rules that state parties are required to follow in the selection of national convention delegates. In addition, the National Democratic Charter, adopted in 1974, contains stipulations about the organization and operation of state parties. The national party's authority has been backed up by two Supreme Court decisions—*Cousins v. Wigoda*, 419 U.S. 450 (1975), and *Democratic Party of the U.S. v. Ex rel. La Follette*, 450 U.S. 107 (1981)—that ruled that national party rules governing delegate selection take precedence over state party rules and state statutes.

Unlike the Democrats, the national GOP has not sought to gain influence over its state affiliates through tough rule enforcement. Instead, it has maintained the confederate legal structure of the party, and the RNC has assumed a relatively passive role in delegate selection and internal party organization.

National Party Assistance Programs to State Parties and the Shift of Intraparty Influence to National Organizations

The Republican Party was the first to use its ability to raise massive amounts of money to institute programs of financial, technical, and staff assistance designed to strengthen its state affiliates during the 1960s and 1970s. By the 1980s, the Democratic Party was quite consciously copying the RNC's state party assistance programs. Among the programs provided to state parties by the national committees are cash grants, professional staff, consulting services for organizational development, data processing, fund-raising, campaigning, media communications, and redistricting. Both parties operate special programs to assist state legislative candidates, and there have been major investments of money and personnel in the development and maintenance of voter lists and efforts to get out the vote. The RNC has a more extensive array of programs than the DNC, which has sought to make up for this deficiency by encouraging state parties, state-level candidates, and allied interest groups (particularly organized labor) to pool resources with the national party and engage in **coordinated campaigns.**

By providing an array of services to their state and local party organizations, the national committees have gained intraparty influence and leverage. These assistance programs operate in a manner similar to that of the federal grant-in-aid programs for the states; before the state parties can receive aid they frequently have to accept conditions—albeit usually quite flexible ones—imposed by the national party. Through these national-to-state party aid programs, the state parties have gained campaign assets—professionalized staffs, money, current voter lists and telephone banks for get-out-the-vote operations, computers and smart phones, and micro-targeting databases.

Implications of the Bipartisan Campaign Reform Act

National-state party relations were put into flux by the passage of the **Bipartisan Campaign Reform Act of 2002** (BCRA, also known as the McCain-Feingold reforms). Previously, the national parties had transferred soft money to their parties in battleground states to pay for "issue advertisements" (ads that did not explicitly ask voters to support or oppose a candidate) prepared by the national party. Under the 2002 BCRA, however, the national parties could no longer raise and spend **soft money** (unrestricted funds raised outside of the contribution limits of the Federal Election Campaign Act). The consequences of reform have been felt especially by the Republican Party. In presidential election years in the post-BCRA era, the national Republican committees transferred substantially less to their state parties than previously. As Table 3-2 shows, the national committees of the Republican Party transferred $56 million in the 2004 presidential election and just $46 million in 2008 compared with $112 million in 2000 (these figures include only funds for grassroots efforts and party building and not transfers for advertising, which have no lasting benefit for state parties). In the 2008 elections, Democrats recovered from BCRA's initial negative impact on national party transfers in 2004. The DNC chair, Howard Dean, pursued a "50-state strategy" by distributing significant funds to all state parties, even those that were not critical to winning the electoral college vote. In the 2008 election, national party transfers from the DNC accounted for 43 percent of state spending in elections. Dean was able to pursue this strategy because the party's presidential candidate, Barack Obama, raised the remarkable sum of $800 million for both his primary and general election campaigns. Thus the Obama campaign did not need to rely that much on DNC campaign support. By contrast, the Republican candidate, John McCain, was highly dependent on the RNC because McCain participated in a public funding program that limited his general election expenditures to just $85 million. Thus the RNC

Table 3-2 State Parties and National Party Support (adjusted 2008 U.S. dollars, millions)

	1992	*1996*	*2000*	*2004*	*2008*
Republicans					
State party expenditures	$63	$101	$184	$224	$208
Transfers from national party	12	59	112	56	46
Median transfer	n/a	0.878	1.383	0.511	0.050
% from national party	20%	58%	61%	25%	22%
Democrats					
State party expenditures	$78	$109	$238	$200	$272
Transfers from national party	11	26	111	72	116
Median transfer	n/a	0.784	0.509	0.174	0.415
% from national party	14%	24%	47%	36%	43%

SOURCE: Federal Election Commission data compiled by the authors.

NOTES: Does not include funds or transfers spent on issue ads. n/a = not applicable.

became, de facto, the major source of campaign support and did not have a surplus of funds to distribute to state parties, particularly in states that were not important for winning the electoral college vote. Table 3-2 shows that the median transfer of national party funds to Republican state party committees plummeted in the 2008 elections to just $50,000 compared to as much as $1.3 million in the 2000 elections (pre-BCRA). That year, RNC transfers accounted for 22 percent of state party spending—far less than before the implementation of BCRA when the RNC accounted for roughly 60 percent in both 1996 and 2000 (La Raja 2010).

The full impact of BCRA on the parties is not yet clear, particularly because recent court decisions have rendered parts of the legislation unconstitutional. Indeed, these court decisions have weakened aspects of BRCA in ways that tend to benefit interest groups at the expense of political parties. Although the ban on soft money was upheld by the U.S. Supreme Court in *McConnell v. Federal Election Commission*, 540 U.S. 93 (2003), the Court loosened its restrictions on interest groups. In *Wisconsin Right to Life, Inc. v. Federal Election Commission*, 551 U.S. 449 (2007), the Supreme Court declared that interest organizations have a constitutional right to advertise on issues without restrictions, even close to an election. Moreover, the decision in *Citizens United v. Federal Election Commission*, 558 U.S. 08-205 (2010), extends this right to both corporations and labor unions, which were previously restricted from electioneering in federal elections and in twenty-four states. It is likely that nonparty groups will use these decisions to influence both state and federal elections. Although many of these groups are allied with the political parties and thus will support their candidates, the increasing flow of resources outside the channels of the formal party organizations may sap efforts to strengthen the parties' electoral machinery and reduce their influence relative to those of various interest factions with the ability to raise and spend money with few constraints.

PARTY NOMINATIONS

The nomination process is crucial for parties because quality candidates can bring victory on election day, whereas weak nominees can doom the party to defeat. In addition, control of the party is at stake because nominations go a long way in determining which party factions will gain ascendancy, who receives the rewards that elected officials bestow on their supporters, and what shape a party's policy orientation will take.

In most Western democracies, party candidates are selected by leaders of the party organization, who operate largely without government regulation, and who do not have to withstand any appeal of their decisions to the voters. Rank-and-file voters participate only in the general election—a contest between parties—and not in the intraparty contests to select nominees. By contrast, the widespread use of the **direct primary election** in the American states involves in the nomination process not only party activists but also ordinary voters. Because it gives rank-and-file voters a deciding voice in nominations, the direct primary has weakened the capacity of party hierarchies to control candidate selection. Among the nomination methods used by Western democracies, the American direct primary is unique not only for the amount of popular participation it permits but also for the wide variety and extent of state-level regulation that accompanies it.

Early in the twentieth century, the direct primary gradually replaced nominations by party conventions and caucuses as a part of the Progressive Era reform movement, whose leaders decried bossism and corrupt party machines and believed that ordinary voters should have a direct say in selecting party candidates. The absence of real two-party competition in much of the country also furthered the spread of the direct primary. In one-party states, nomination by leaders of the dominant party was tantamount to election. As a result, instituting primary elections to nominate candidates constituted a means of ensuring meaningful popular participation in elections and "an escape from one-partyism" (Key 1956, 81).

Just as the progressive reformers had hoped, the direct primary has undercut the influence and control that parties can exert over nominations. With nominations ultimately in the hands of voters, party organizations cannot unilaterally designate party nominees. Primaries therefore encourage a candidate-centered style of politics, because without parties capable of controlling nominations candidates have an incentive to set up their own personal campaign organizations.

Although direct primaries have succeeded in breaking the party organizations' grip on the selection of nominees, they have never fulfilled all the expectations of their reform-minded sponsors. Voter turnout is typically much lower than in general elections. In addition, the extent of vigorous competition in primaries has been limited because incumbents run either unopposed or with only token opposition. More than 90 percent of incumbent governors and U.S. representatives win renomination, and turnover in the statehouses is less than 25 percent (which includes retirements as well). Contests occur most often within the party that has the greatest opportunity of winning the general election and when there is no incumbent seeking renomination.

Types of Direct Primaries

The constitutional principle of federalism gives the states wide latitude in regulating the nomination process. They can specify the circumstances under which a primary must be used and the type of primary to be used for a party's candidates to secure a slot on the general election ballot. Thus the state laws regulating party nomination procedures vary significantly in terms of the degree of public disclosure of party preference required of voters (see Table 3-3).

Table 3-3 Party Affiliation Requirements for Voting in State Direct Primaries (nonpresidential)

Closed	Semiclosed	Semiopen	Open	Top-two	Blanket
Connecticut[a]	Arizona	Alabama[h]	Hawaii	California[d]	Alaska[d]
Delaware	Colorado[e]	Arkansas[h]	Michigan	Louisiana[i]	
Florida	Idaho[g]	Georgia[h]	Minnesota	Washington[j]	
Kentucky	Iowa	Illinois[h]	Missouri		
Maryland[d]	Kansas[c]	Indiana[h]	Montana		
Nevada	Maine	Mississippi[h]	North Dakota		
New Mexico	Massachusetts	Ohio[h]	Vermont		
New York	Nebraska[a]	South Carolina[h]	Wisconsin		
Oklahoma	New Hampshire[c]	Tennessee			
Oregon[d]	New Jersey	Texas			
Pennsylvania	North Carolina	Virginia[h]			
South Dakota	Rhode Island[c]				
	Utah[f]				
	West Virginia[g]				
	Wyoming[b]				

SOURCES: Federal Election Commission, "Party Affiliation and Primary Voting 2000," Washington, D.C., 2001; Richard Winger, editor of *Ballot Access News*, e-mail exchange with the authors, April 23, 2011.

NOTES: *Closed:* party registration required; changes permitted within a fixed time period. *Semiclosed:* unaffiliated voters permitted to vote in a party primary. *Semiopen:* voters must publicly declare their choice or party ballot at polling place on election day. *Open:* voter decides in which party primary to vote in privacy of voting booth. *Top-two:* top two primary vote-getters, regardless of party, are advanced to the general election. *Blanket:* voter may vote in more than one party's primary, but may only support one candidate per office.

a. At present, unaffiliated voters may not participate, but parties can adopt rules to permit participation by unaffiliated voters by party rule.

b. Same-day registration permits any voter to declare or change party affiliation at the polls and reverse the change after voting.

c. Independent voters may choose either party ballot, which registers them with that party. The exception is Kansas, where Democrats only allow voters to retain their independent status.

d. Unaffiliated voters may vote in primaries, if permitted by party rule. In Alaska, the Republican Party holds a semiclosed primary, while the Democratic, Libertarian, and Alaskan Independence Parties hold a blanket primary, which is allowed if parties do not object (but which the U.S. Supreme Court's 2000 decision in *California Democratic Party v. Jones,* 530 U.S. 567, declared to be unconstitutional if a party objects).

e. Voters may declare party affiliation at the polls, which enrolls them with that party.

f. No public record is kept of independent voters' choice of party primary.

g. Independents may vote in Republican primary only in West Virginia. Independents may vote in Democratic primary only in Idaho.

h. Voter's choice of party is recorded and parties have access to the lists.

i. Louisiana has semiclosed primaries for congressional elections, but nonpartisan elections with party labels for state and local office. The presidential primary is closed.

j. No public record is kept of voter choice of party primary.

Open Primary Systems. Nine states have an open primary system. In this system, a public declaration of party preference is not required to vote in primaries. Voters typically receive a ballot containing the names of all parties' candidates and then decide in the secrecy of the voting booth in which party's primary they wish to vote. Once they choose a party, voters must take part in that party's primary for all offices on the ballot.

In eleven mainly southern states, a semiopen system is used in which voters do not have to register with a party to vote but are required to declare openly at the polls in which party's primary they wish to vote. This system is only slightly less restrictive than the open primary.

Closed Primaries. Twelve states operate closed primary systems. In this system, voters must be registered as party affiliates to vote in partisan primaries. They are permitted to vote only in the primary of the party in which they are registered. A voter who wishes to switch party registration must typically do so in advance of the primary, normally twenty to thirty days before the primary. As shown in Table 3-3, fifteen states permit unaffiliated voters to vote in a party primary so long as they choose to participate in one party primary, usually in the privacy of the voting booth or by registering with a party on election day. For this reason, these states are considered semiclosed. Several states permit unaffiliated voters to participate in party primaries either by statute or by state party rule. These arrangements tend to turn these states' primaries into virtually open primaries for unaffiliated voters.

Top-Two Primaries and Blanket Primaries. In top-two primaries, all of the candidates for each office are placed on the ballot, and each candidate's party affiliation is listed on the ballot. If a candidate receives a majority of the votes cast in the primary, that candidate is elected then and there. If no candidate receives a majority of the primary votes, the two top finishers, regardless of party, must face each other in the general election. Louisiana was the first state to implement this system. In recent years, California and Washington changed to a slightly different form of the top-two primary after the Supreme Court declared they could not use "blanket primaries" (described earlier) if any of the parties objected (which they did). Unlike the blanket primary, in which candidates with the most votes from each party— including qualifying minor parties—advance to the general election, the top-two primary allows candidates from the same party to advance to the general election. In Washington and California, there is a guaranteed run-off between the top two candidates in the primary, with the run-off occurring as part of the general election in November.

Effects of Different Primary Rules. Open primary systems encourage crossover voting—partisans of one party voting in the primary of the other party—whereas closed primary systems largely preclude this type of behavior. Crossover voting tends to occur in the party's primary in which there is a meaningful nomination contest, and those voters who cross over typically are engaging in sincere rather than strategic crossover voting—that is, they are voting for their most preferred candidate in that party rather than crossing over to "spoil" the opposition party's primary by voting for its weakest candidate. Because sincere crossover voting can affect primary outcomes, the candidates with policy positions closest to the median voter's views are more likely to be selected in open primary systems than in closed primaries (Gerber and Morton 1998).

In closed primary systems, voters who participate in their party's nominations tend to be more ideological than the median voter, which may result in greater ideological extremism of elected officials (Gerber and Morton 1998; Grofman and Brunell 2001). Because the turnout in primaries is typically low, ideological elements in either party have been able to use their informal organization and resources to help nominate candidates who are more ideological than rank-and-file party voters. These candidates then win the general election because districts typically favor one party (Masket 2009). For this reason, moderate politicians have tried to move their states from closed to open or top-two primaries. As mentioned earlier, California governor Arnold Schwarzenegger, a centrist Republican, pushed successfully for Proposition 14, a ballot initiative to amend the state constitution to include a top-two primary, which Californians adopted in 2010.

Runoff Primaries. Usually the candidate who receives the most votes (a **plurality**) in the primary gains the nomination, even if that individual receives less than a majority of total votes cast. In eleven southern and border states, plus South Dakota, a majority of the vote in the primary is required for nomination (40 percent in North Carolina). If no candidate receives a majority, then a second, or runoff, primary is held between the top two finishers in the first primary. This system was instituted in the South when the Democratic Party was so dominant that winning its primary was equivalent to being elected. To ensure that the person nominated in the Democratic primary and therefore "elected" had the support of a majority of Democrats, the runoff primary was instituted.

Nominating Conventions and Preprimary Endorsements

Although the direct primary is the predominant method of nomination, thirteen states either permit or require conventions for the nomination process. Four states—Alabama, Georgia, South Carolina, and Virginia—permit parties to nominate by either party convention or primary. Seven states—Colorado, Connecticut, New Mexico, New York, North Dakota, Rhode Island, and Utah—by law provide for preprimary endorsements by party conventions. In New Mexico, New York, and Utah, primaries are not mandatory and are held if two or more candidates receive a specified share of the delegate vote (40 percent in Utah, 25 percent in New York, and 20 percent in New Mexico). A Connecticut law that required candidates to receive 15 percent of the votes at a party-endorsing convention in order to qualify for a place on the primary ballot was declared unconstitutional by the U.S. Supreme Court on the grounds that it imposed undue burdens on party members seeking to participate in the nomination process. In Utah, the convention designates for each office two candidates whose names are placed on the primary ballot, although if one receives 70 percent of the convention vote that person is automatically declared the nominee. Colorado law makes it possible for a candidate to become the nominee and avoid a primary by receiving the support of 50 percent of the convention delegates. In several of the states with statutorily required preprimary conventions, candidates may also get on the ballot by securing a requisite number of signatures on a petition.

Some state party organizations use informal or extralegal preprimary endorsements in an effort to influence the selection of nominees. For example, in Massachusetts and Minnesota both parties regularly endorse candidates at state party conventions, and in New Jersey county party committees endorse gubernatorial candidates in an effort to influence who will enter and win the primary. Behind the scenes, it is not at all unusual for party leaders to assist favored and experienced candidates and discourage others from entering the race. The various methods that party organizations may use to influence primaries demonstrate that parties can be a critical factor in the nomination process. A frequent pattern in states that by law require preprimary conventions is for non-endorsed candidates to drop out of the race. However, the trend since the 1980s has been one of declining primary victories for party-endorsed candidates. Thus, although 89 percent of endorsed candidates for governor won contested nominations between 1960 and 1980, successful endorsees dropped to 53 percent between 1982 and 1998 (Jewell and Morehouse 2001, 109–110).

Although preprimary endorsements appear to have declined in influence in recent years, preprimary endorsements in gubernatorial races appear to reduce the likelihood of having contested primaries (Bardwell 2002). When a primary is contested, such endorsements also reduce the impact of money on the outcome of primary contests for governor. Candidates who succeed in securing party convention endorsements normally become as well known as their challengers because the endorsement process requires them to engage in face-to-face meetings with about a thousand party activist delegates from across the state (Morehouse 1998). The public visibility achieved in the endorsement process helps to compensate for any campaign spending advantage their challengers may have. Further offsetting the impact of campaign spending in gubernatorial primaries are the resources of time and effort that parties confer on endorsed candidates. By contrast, in states that do not use preprimary endorsing conventions, candidate spending has been the overwhelming predictor of the outcome of primary contests for governor (Morehouse 1998, 121, 199).

Implications of the Primary for the General Election

The outcome of the primary, of course, has implications for the general election. In addition to narrowing the field of candidates and choices available to voters, the primary results can enhance or demolish a party's general election prospects, depending on which candidates are victorious. Party leaders frequently strive to avoid contested primaries on the assumption that divisive primaries will undermine the party's prospects in the general election. In the 2010 elections, this is precisely what happened in the Delaware contest for the Republican U.S. Senate nomination when the Tea Party movement inspired voters to pick the more conservative but weaker candidate, Christine O'Donnell, over the establishment candidate, former governor Michael Castle. Polls indicated that Castle would have won the general election handily, but instead the Democratic candidate beat O'Donnell in a landslide. And yet there is no consistent pattern demonstrating that contested primaries are necessarily damaging (Kenney 1988). Indeed, nominees emerging from contested primaries tend to do better in the general election than nominees who had no primary opposition (Hogan 2003). This is partly because primary contests more often occur in the electorally stronger party. In addition, contested primaries tend to produce seasoned candidates with battle-tested organizations as well as much-needed candidate publicity and momentum.

POLITICAL COMPETITION

Since V. O. Key's seminal work on state politics in the South (1949), scholars have recognized the importance political competition can have on the nature of politics in the states. First, it is generally recognized that competition can affect state public policy, with competitive states tending to spend more on social programs than states with weak interparty competition. Second, strong interparty competition is associated with higher levels of voter turnout. Because political participation is a valued good in a democratic society, the connection between competition and voter turnout highlights the importance of competition to a functioning democracy.

Competition for Control of Government

A measure of interparty competition developed by Austin Ranney (1976, 59–60) is a widely used and long-standing indicator of competition for control of government. The **Ranney index** has several components: proportion of success, duration of success, and frequency of divided control. Ranney used these three dimensions to calculate his index of interparty competition, which we updated for 2007–2011.[1]

---

1. We calculated the average percentage of the popular vote won by Democratic gubernatorial candidates; the average percentage of seats held by Democrats in the state senate, in all legislative sessions; the average percentage of seats held by Democrats in the state house of representatives, in all sessions; and the percentage of all gubernatorial, senate, and house terms controlled by the Democrats. For each state, we averaged these four percentages to create an index value representing the degree of interparty competition. Because of its use of nonpartisan state legislative elections, no index value was calculated for Nebraska.

The index is actually a measure of control of government, with a score of 0 indicating complete Republican control and a score of 1 indicating absolute Democratic control. At its midpoint (0.5), control of government is evenly split between the two parties, indicating a highly competitive environment.

The values of the Ranney party control index calculated for the period 2007–2011 are presented in Table 3-4, where two important patterns emerge. First, the relative strength of the parties is fairly balanced, though with a slight tilt toward Republican control: the vast majority of the states are competitive two-party states, the number of modified Republican states (twelve) is more than twice the number of modified Democratic states (five), and there are no

Table 3-4   States Classified According to Party Control and by Degree of Interparty Competition, 2007–2011

State	Ranney party control index	Ranney competition index	State	Ranney party control index	Ranney competition index
Modified one-party Democratic					
Massachusetts	0.758	0.742	Hawaii	0.717	0.783
West Virginia	0.722	0.778	Maryland	0.701	0.799
Arkansas	0.717	0.783			
Two-party competition					
Washington	0.644	0.742	Montana	0.540	0.960
Delaware	0.640	0.860	Wisconsin	0.532	0.968
New Mexico	0.621	0.879	Maine	0.523	0.977
Rhode Island	0.620	0.880	Kentucky	0.523	0.977
New York	0.620	0.880	Alabama	0.512	0.988
Colorado	0.620	0.880	Mississippi	0.500	1.000
Illinois	0.615	0.885	Nevada	0.484	0.984
New Hampshire	0.609	0.891	Pennsylvania	0.475	0.975
Oregon	0.605	0.895	Michigan	0.470	0.970
North Carolina	0.602	0.898	Louisiana	0.437	0.937
Connecticut	0.602	0.898	Virginia	0.435	0.935
New Jersey	0.589	0.911	Ohio	0.426	0.926
Iowa	0.588	0.912	Tennessee	0.413	0.913
Vermont	0.583	0.917	Oklahoma	0.377	0.877
California	0.579	0.921	Indiana	0.371	0.871
Minnesota	0.551	0.949	Missouri	0.370	0.870
Modified one-party Republican					
Arizona	0.339	0.839	South Dakota	0.263	0.763
South Carolina	0.324	0.824	Nebraska	0.261	0.761
Alaska	0.322	0.822	North Dakota	0.248	0.748
Texas	0.311	0.811	Wyoming	0.246	0.746
Georgia	0.304	0.804	Utah	0.199	0.699
Kansas	0.295	0.795	Idaho	0.194	0.694
Florida	0.292	0.792			
Fifty-state mean	0.486	0.868			

SOURCE: Calculated by the authors.

one-party states.[2] Historically speaking, this finding reflects an important evolution in the balance of power in American politics. Before the early 1990s, the Democrats consistently held a distinct advantage over the Republicans, an advantage that was largely surrendered in the 1994 elections. Second, there has been an important regional transformation in party control of state governments. Whereas the Democratic Party strength was until recently concentrated in the South and the Northeast and Republicans tended to dominate the Mountain West, the current alignment shows the Democrats holding onto the Northeast and solidifying the West Coast but ceding much of the South to the Republican Party. Indeed, Republican gains in the control of state government during the period 2007–2011 were greatest primarily in the southern and border states (Louisiana, Tennessee, Oklahoma, and Alabama) and also in some Democratic-friendly states (Maine and New Jersey). The Democrats saw their largest gains in New Hampshire and Delaware. It should be noted, however, that for most states the gains or losses experienced by the parties are relatively small. In fact, the correlation between the Ranney party control index from 2007 to 2011 and the same index from 2003 to 2006 is 0.87.

The Ranney index can be recalculated to indicate the level of competition between the parties for control of government rather than the degree of Democratic or Republican control.[3] Consider the most competitive state in Table 3-4—Mississippi—which has a Ranney party control index value of 0.50. As one moves away from Mississippi in both directions, the states are less and less competitive. For example, even though Vermont and Tennessee display different partisan leanings, their party control values (0.583 and 0.413, respectively) make them nearly equally competitive: Vermont is 0.083 units above and Tennessee is 0.087 units below the point of equal party strength, 0.500, held by Mississippi. The Ranney competition index is derived from the original Ranney index and represents how close the states are to perfect competition between the parties for control of government.[4] The Ranney competition index ranges from 0.500 (no competition) to 1.000 (perfect competition). The data in Table 3-4 indicate that although the least competitive states are somewhat concentrated in the South and in the plains states, many of the most competitive states are also southern states, thereby making the regional pattern much weaker than it has been in the past.

Although interparty competition is a long-term phenomenon and so should be relatively stable, the nature of competition for control of government has changed significantly over time. The changes from 1948 to 2011 in the mean level of Democratic control, as measured in Table 3-4, and the mean level of interparty competition, based on the Ranney competition index, are presented in Table 3-5. These two

2. See Bibby and Holbrook (2004) for the traditional party control cut-points of the Ranney index.

3. In the professional literature, this is called the **folded Ranney index**.

4. The formula for the Ranney competition index is $1 - |(0.5 - \text{Ranney})|$. This index measures how close a state's level of interparty competition is to "perfect" competition on the Ranney index.

Table 3-5   Changes in the Ranney Indexes of Party Control and Interparty Competition, 1948–2011

	1948–1960	1962–1973	1974–1980	1981–1988	1989–1994	1995–1998	1999–2003	2004–2006	2007–2011
Mean level of Democratic control (range: 0–1)	0.56	0.58	0.64	0.60	0.55	0.49	0.49	0.51	0.49
Mean level of interparty competition (range: 0.5–1)	0.78	0.83	0.81	0.84	0.87	0.86	0.87	0.86	0.87

SOURCES: Compiled from data in Samuel Patterson and Gregory Caldeira, "Etiology of Partisan Competition," *American Political Science Review* 78 (1984): 691–707; John F. Bibby, Cornelius P. Cotter, James L. Gibson, and Robert J. Huckshorn, "Parties in State Politics," in *Politics in the American States,* 5th ed., ed. Virginia Gray, Herbert Jacob, and Robert B. Albritton (Glenview, Ill.: Scott, Foresman, 1990); John F. Bibby and Thomas M. Holbrook, "Parties and Elections," in *Politics in the American States,* 6th, 7th, and 8th eds. (Washington, D.C.: CQ Press, 1996, 1999, 2004); Thomas M. Holbrook and Raymond J. La Raja, "Parties and Elections," in *Politics in the American States,* 9th ed. (Washington, D.C.: CQ Press, 2008); and Table 3-4.

measures show signs of both stability and change. First, the mean score of Democratic control in the Ranney index tilted toward the Democratic side throughout most of the period but has been at near parity since 1995. Second, despite the Republican gains noted previously from 2007 to 2011, party control is still very evenly split. Much of the decline in Democratic strength in the 1980s and 1990s has occurred in southern states, where Republicans have made significant inroads. Third, in terms of the level of competition for control of government, the least competitive period was from 1948 to 1960, and the most competitive period has been since 1995. Again, in large part Republican gains in southern states account for the increase in competition in recent years.

Many of the recent changes in party control and interparty competition shown in Table 3-5 reflect the impact of the 1994 elections. Before those elections, Democrats controlled twenty-five state legislatures and Republicans controlled eight. After those elections, Democrats controlled eighteen legislatures and Republicans controlled nineteen. (In the remainder of the states, each party controlled one house of the bicameral legislatures, a surprisingly frequent occurrence in the states.) A similar change occurred in governorships: Democrats went into the 1994 elections with a twenty-nine to nineteen advantage in governorships and came out with nineteen governorships to Republicans' thirty (the rest of the governorships were formally independent). Thus the 1994 elections represented a true reversal of fortunes for the two major parties. The picture has whip-sawed a bit since then. After the 2006 elections, Democrats controlled twenty-two state legislatures to Republicans' fifteen, and twenty-eight governorships to Republicans' twenty-two. However, instead of representing a long-term shift in the equilibrium level of party support in the states, the 2006 outcome was largely reversed by the 2010 midterm elections. After those elections, Republicans controlled twenty-five legislatures to sixteen for Democrats, and twenty-nine governorships to Democrats' twenty. It is important to note that the current measurement of the Ranney index includes the outcomes of the 2010 elections but assigns more weight to the 2006 and 2008 elections.

Electoral Competition

One of the limitations of the Ranney index is that because it is based on control of government, it is not an ideal measure of electoral competition. This is especially disconcerting because many of the hypotheses on the effect of competition on state politics are about how electoral competition affects state politics and policymaking. In the early 1990s, Holbrook and Van Dunk (1993) developed a measure of electoral competition based on district-level state legislative election outcomes from 1982 to 1986. Although the two are conceptually distinct, the relationship between the Ranney competition index from the late 1980s and the original Holbrook–Van Dunk index is moderately strong ($r = 0.68$; Bibby and Holbrook 1996).

Consequences of Competition. It is widely expected that competition has an influence on public policy and voter turnout. Specifically, it is expected that competitive states will produce more liberal public policies and have higher rates of voter turnout than noncompetitive states. The line of reasoning on liberal policy outcomes dates back to Key (1949), who argued that competitive elections put pressure on parties to support redistributive policies that benefit the "have-nots" in society. These redistributive policies are typically characterized as liberal. And turnout is expected to be higher in competitive contests because candidates and parties have a greater incentive to mobilize supporters (Holbrook and Van Dunk 1993; Powell 1986).

To a large extent, the data bear out these propositions, especially for the Holbrook–Van Dunk index. Recent research on the impact of competition has blended the concepts of party control and electoral competition. Barrilleaux, Holbrook, and Langer (2002) examined welfare spending in the states from 1973 to 1992 and found that in states with low levels of electoral competition, party control of the legislature had relatively little impact on welfare spending. In states with a high level of electoral competition, however, there were sizable differences in welfare spending between Republican-controlled states and states in which Democrats controlled the legislatures.

Determinants of Competition. As we pointed out earlier, competition has tended to follow a regional pattern. Historically, southern states have been among the least competitive—in part a long-lasting effect of the Civil War and Reconstruction—and this pattern was still very apparent into the 1970s and 1980s. However, the regional patterns are less distinct today, because Republicans have made significant inroads in the South and in fact now hold a firm grip on the governments of some southern states such as Florida, Georgia, South Carolina, and Texas.

Beyond the effects of region, several other variables help explain state differences in competition. First, states with diverse populations have more competitive political systems than states with homogeneous populations (Patterson and Caldeira 1984; Barrilleaux 1986). Second, some states have lower levels of competition because they have higher levels of partisan bias in the electorate. If a state's electorate is overwhelmingly Democratic, then it makes sense that Democrats would face little competition at the polls and would be able to establish control of state government (Barrilleaux 1986). Finally, incumbency and the use of multimember districts have been found to suppress electoral competition, and large (in terms of population) legislative districts have been found to enhance electoral competition (Van Dunk and Weber 1997).

POLITICAL PARTICIPATION

Political participation in the United States takes many different forms: contributing to campaigns, attending rallies or protests, writing letters to elected representatives, working for a campaign or community cause, attending town meetings or school board meetings, and, of course, voting in elections. Although voting is the most commonly practiced form of political participation, the degree to which citizens across the states take advantage of their right to vote varies widely.

Patterns of Turnout across the States

For a variety of reasons, many people decide not to take advantage of their right to vote in elections. Although individual attributes have a lot to do with whether a person votes, turnout rates can also be affected by the type of election being held and by certain aspects of the state political environment. The traditional way of measuring turnout has been to take the total number of votes cast as a percentage of the voting-age population in the state. However, the voting-age population of a state includes significant numbers of people who are not eligible to vote because they are not citizens or they are institutionalized in correctional or mental health facilities. McDonald (2002) calculates a measure of the voting-eligible electorate by accounting for the number of noncitizens and ineligible felons living in states, neither of which is reflected in the standard voting-age population measure of turnout. McDonald finds that reliance on the voting-age population tends to underestimate the true turnout rate in states, sometimes by an especially large margin in states with large noncitizen populations and with prohibitions against convicted felons voting. For example, California and Texas, both of which have large noncitizen populations and prohibit voting by convicted felons, had voting-eligible population turnout rates that were 9 and 7 percentage points higher, respectively, than their voting-age population turnout rates. McDonald (2002) makes a strong argument in favor of calculating turnout as the total votes cast as a percentage of the voting-eligible electorate, a point supported by Holbrook and Heidbreder's recent analysis (2010) of turnout models using alternative measures of the dependent variable.

In order to maintain some continuity with earlier editions of this book and still incorporate McDonald's innovation, we present in Table 3-6 both the voting-age and voting-eligible turnout in all states for presidential, gubernatorial, and congressional elections for 2007–2010. The states are sorted by voting-age population in the "overall" column, which presents the average rate of turnout across all four

Table 3-6 Average Rates of Voter Turnout in the States, by Office, 2007–2010

State	Overall VAP	Overall VEP	President VAP	President VEP	Governors VAP	Governors VEP	U.S. Senate VAP	U.S. Senate VEP	U.S. House of Representatives VAP	U.S. House of Representatives VEP
Minnesota	64.7	68.8	73.3	77.7	52.0	55.5	72.5	77.1	61.1	64.9
Maine	63.6	64.5	70.0	70.9	54.4	55.5	69.3	70.2	60.6	61.5
Montana	62.6	63.7	65.6	66.9	65.1	66.3	63.9	65.1	55.7	56.5
New Hampshire	58.5	60.2	69.2	71.1	55.0	56.7	55.5	57.2	54.3	56.0
Iowa	57.3	59.8	67.4	69.7	48.5	50.5	57.0	59.2	56.4	59.6
North Dakota	57.1	58.1	63.5	64.6	63.2	64.2	46.9	48.1	54.7	55.7
Wisconsin	56.1	58.5	69.2	72.1	49.2	51.4	49.5	51.7	56.5	59.0
Michigan	56.0	58.5	65.7	68.5	42.3	44.3	63.7	66.3	52.4	54.7
Alaska	56.0	59.3	64.3	67.7	48.8	51.9	55.5	58.9	55.4	58.5
Vermont	55.9	56.8	66.0	67.2	56.5	57.5	47.1	47.6	54.1	55.0
Delaware	55.8	60.5	61.6	66.5	58.8	63.7	51.9	56.4	51.0	55.3
Missouri	55.6	57.8	64.7	67.3	63.5	66.1	42.2	43.8	52.1	54.1
Wyoming	55.5	57.4	63.1	64.5	44.5	46.4	61.4	63.2	53.0	55.4
Washington	55.3	61.0	60.6	66.9	59.6	65.8	48.2	53.1	52.9	58.1
South Dakota	55.1	56.6	63.0	64.1	51.0	52.8	49.6	50.9	56.9	58.4
North Carolina	54.9	59.0	61.5	66.1	60.7	65.5	48.7	52.4	48.5	52.0
Oregon	54.5	58.8	62.8	67.5	48.3	52.3	54.2	58.6	52.6	56.7
Colorado	54.4	59.3	64.5	70.2	45.9	50.0	53.9	58.9	53.3	58.0
Massachusetts	53.3	58.3	60.8	65.9	43.9	48.0	58.0	64.1	50.3	55.0
Virginia	50.9	55.1	62.5	67.5	33.2	36.0	60.9	66.0	47.1	50.9
Ohio	50.8	52.3	64.9	66.9	43.4	44.6	43.0	44.2	52.1	53.5
Nebraska	50.5	53.5	60.1	63.4	35.9	38.4	59.3	62.7	46.9	49.7
Rhode Island	49.6	53.9	57.3	61.9	41.2	45.3	53.2	57.5	46.8	50.9
Mississippi	49.5	51.2	59.4	61.4	34.2	35.4	57.3	59.4	47.0	48.6
New Mexico	49.3	54.4	56.1	61.7	38.5	43.1	55.4	61.2	47.1	51.6
Idaho	48.8	53.0	58.9	64.0	39.5	43.0	48.5	52.7	48.2	52.2
Indiana	48.8	50.6	57.4	59.5	56.2	58.3	35.7	37.3	45.8	47.5
Kansas	48.7	51.7	58.9	62.1	39.3	42.0	48.4	51.3	48.4	51.2
Maryland	48.7	54.0	61.2	67.4	42.2	47.1	41.6	46.5	49.7	55.1
Connecticut	48.5	53.2	61.3	67.4	41.8	45.7	42.1	46.0	49.0	53.8
Pennsylvania	47.7	49.4	61.5	63.8	40.2	41.7	40.1	41.6	48.8	50.6
Alabama	47.4	49.4	59.2	61.4	41.3	43.2	49.5	51.6	39.8	41.4
New Jersey	47.4	54.5	58.5	67.4	36.6	42.1	52.6	60.5	41.8	48.1
West Virginia	47.2	48.0	50.0	50.8	49.4	50.2	49.1	49.9	40.4	41.1
Illinois	46.9	51.7	57.2	63.2	37.9	41.8	46.4	51.2	45.9	50.7
South Carolina	46.5	48.7	56.0	58.5	37.9	39.8	45.7	48.0	46.2	48.4
Kentucky	45.7	47.5	55.8	57.9	32.2	33.4	47.8	49.7	47.0	48.9
Tennessee	44.7	46.6	54.7	57.1	32.8	34.3	50.9	53.2	40.2	42.0
Florida	43.8	50.2	58.5	67.1	36.6	41.8	36.9	42.2	43.3	49.6
Louisiana	43.8	45.6	58.9	61.1	38.5	40.2	46.9	49.0	30.8	32.2
Oklahoma	42.8	45.3	53.4	56.3	36.8	39.0	42.6	45.1	38.6	40.7
Georgia	42.7	47.9	55.0	61.6	34.8	39.1	43.4	48.8	37.6	42.1
Utah	41.4	44.5	50.7	54.8	41.5	44.5	32.2	34.4	41.2	44.2
Nevada	40.8	48.0	49.9	58.6	36.0	42.3	36.2	42.6	41.0	48.3
Arkansas	40.5	43.0	50.3	52.6	35.5	37.6	41.0	43.3	35.3	38.5
California	40.1	49.2	49.9	61.3	36.0	44.1	35.7	43.7	39.0	47.7
Hawaii	40.1	44.1	45.7	50.5	37.7	41.1	36.5	39.8	40.6	44.8
Arizona	39.0	44.8	48.0	55.3	34.8	39.9	34.5	39.5	38.8	44.5
Texas	38.2	45.3	46.1	54.5	27.1	32.3	44.8	53.3	34.8	41.2
New York	38.1	43.5	51.4	58.3	30.5	34.9	30.1	34.4	40.4	46.3
Fifty-state mean	49.8	53.3	59.3	63.4	43.8	46.9	48.7	52.2	47.4	50.8

SOURCES: Dave Leip's *Atlas of U.S. Presidential Elections*, www.uselectionatlas.org/; U.S. Census Bureau, *Statistical Abstract of the United States*, www.census.gov/compendia/statab; United States Election Project, http://elections.gmu.edu/; *New York Times* Election Results 2010, http://elections.nytimes.com/2010/results.

NOTES: VAP = turnout as a percentage of the voting-age population; VEP = turnout as a percentage of the voting-eligible population.

types of elections for each state. Here, a familiar regional pattern emerges: eight out of the fifteen lowest-turnout states are southern or border states. At the other end of the scale the regional pattern is not as clear, but most of the highest-turnout states are small, sparsely populated states.

Besides differences across the states, another difference is apparent across election types: the voting-eligible turnout is always higher than the voting-age turnout, which is expected because the denominator for calculating turnout is always smaller for the voting-eligible calculations. In addition, there are substantial differences in turnout in different types of elections. The best way to examine differences across offices is to look at individual years because most gubernatorial elections are held at the midterm, when typical turnout is lower. As the data in Table 3-7 illustrate, turnout tends to be highest (controlling for year) in gubernatorial and presidential elections. U.S. Senate elections follow, and turnout is lowest in U.S. House elections. Table 3-7 also illustrates that turnout is always higher in presidential election years. Turnout has been roughly 15 percentage points higher for all offices in the presidential years than in the midterm election years because presidential elections are highly visible events that generate a lot of interest and bring out many voters who do not normally turn out for elections for lower offices during midterm election years.

Table 3-7 Mean Percentage of Voter Turnout (VAP) in the States, by Year and Office, 1990–2010

Year	President	Governor	U.S. Senate	U.S. House of Representatives
1990	—	40.9[a]	38.6	37.8
1992	58.3	59.2	55.2	54.3
1994	—	41.4[b]	41.8	40.2
1996	50.8	52.6	51.5	48.9
1998	—	39.3[c]	38.8	35.6
2000	53.9	55.9	52.0	50.5
2002	—	42.9[d]	42.2	40.4
2004	58.0	56.2	59.5	54.5
2006	—	40.9[e]	40.3	38.0
2008	59.3	59.8	58.0	55.7
2010	—	40.2[f]	40.2	39.1
Presidential-year increase		15.8	14.9	14.3

SOURCES: Turnout of voting-age population calculated from Table 3-6; John F. Bibby, Cornelius P. Cotter, James L. Gibson, and Robert J. Huckshorn, "Parties in State Politics," in *Politics in the American States*, 5th ed., ed. Virginia Gray, Herbert Jacob, and Robert B. Albritton (Glenview, Ill.: Scott, Foresman, 1990); John F. Bibby and Thomas M. Holbrook, "Parties and Elections," in *Politics in the American States*, 6th, 7th, and 8th eds. (Washington, D.C.: CQ Press, 1996, 1999, 2004); and Thomas M. Holbrook and Raymond J. La Raja , "Parties and Elections," in *Politics in the American States*, 9th ed. (Washington, D.C.: CQ Press, 2008).

NOTE: VAP = voting-age population.

a. Includes turnout rates for the 1989 and 1991 gubernatorial elections.

b. Includes turnout rates for the 1993 and 1995 gubernatorial elections.

c. Includes turnout rates for the 1997 and 1999 gubernatorial elections.

d. Includes turnout rates for the 2001 and 2003 gubernatorial elections.

e. Includes turnout rates for the 2005 gubernatorial elections.

f. Includes turnout rates for the 2007 and 2009 gubernatorial elections.

What Determines Turnout?

Many factors help explain differences in voter turnout across states and individuals. For the individual voter, a variety of important demographic and attitudinal variables are related to turnout (Wolfinger and Rosenstone 1980; Rosenstone and Hansen 1993). For example, middle-aged people with high levels of income and education have a high probability of voting. People with a strong sense of political efficacy and strong ties to political parties are also very likely to vote. Many of these variables also help explain the pattern of turnout in the states. Socioeconomic differences across the states, for example, are strongly related to differences in voter turnout; wealthy states and states with well-educated citizens generally have the highest rates of voter turnout.

But state politics also have an effect on voter turnout. First, turnout is higher in states with high levels of electoral competition (Holbrook and Van Dunk 1993). In noncompetitive environments, the elections are less likely to generate much interest and voters are less likely to vote. Turnout can also be influenced by the level of campaign spending in particular races (Jackson 1997). As more money is spent in a campaign, voters are provided with more information about the candidates, which increases the likelihood that they will vote. In addition, during presidential election years there is a significant relationship between presidential campaign activities and voter turnout (Holbrook and Heidbreder 2010).

Another important determinant of turnout is the stringency of state voter registration laws (Wolfinger and Rosenstone 1980). In states in which it is difficult for voters to register or to stay registered, fewer people register, and voter turnout tends to be lower than it would be if registration laws made it easier to register. One example of such a law is the closing date for registration, or the number of days before the election that one must register to vote. The closing date ranges from zero (election day registration or, in North Dakota, no voter registration) to thirty or more days before the election. The correlation between the number of days registration closes before the election and voting-age turnout in the 2008 presidential election was –0.52 (–0.46 for voting-eligible turnout). The difference in turnout in the 2008 presidential election (Table 3-6) between states with a closing date of ten or fewer days before the election and states with a closing date of thirty or more days before the election illustrates the effects that registration laws can have: the average overall rate of turnout in states with the shorter closing period is 66.8 percent as opposed to 57.2 percent for states with the longer period.

The **National Voter Registration Act of 1993** (NVRA) was an attempt by the national government to ease the burden of voter registration in the states. It placed limits on the purging of nonvoters and required states to register voters or renew voter registration as part of the driver's license application and renewal process (motor-voter registration), to make mail-in registration available, and to make voter registration materials available at other state agency (primarily welfare and social services) offices. It is difficult to judge the full impact of the NVRA because the existing research has produced mixed results. Martinez and Hill (1999) found that the NVRA had little discernible impact on overall state turnout rates and may even have contributed to slightly higher class and racial inequalities in the active electorate. In a similar vein, Wolfinger and Hoffman (2001) found that the motor-voter component of the law made registration easier for those who might already be inclined to register and to vote, whereas the agency registration component tended to be used by those who were not inclined to vote. More to the point, Wolfinger and Hoffman found that those who registered to vote at an agency site were less likely to vote than those who registered at a motor-voter site, and those who registered at a motor-voter site were less likely to vote than those who registered via more traditional means. Fitzgerald's comprehensive analysis of the impact of states' efforts to ease the voting process found very little evidence that voting reforms have paid many dividends, although there are some hints of effectiveness (Fitzgerald 2005). Although early voting, unrestricted absentee voting, and mail registration had no impact on voter turnout, Fitzgerald found that moving to same-day registration and adoption of motor-voter registration practices did increase turnout.

Class Bias in Turnout

One avenue of research on voter turnout has focused on the role of class bias in shaping public policies for the poor (Hill and Leighley 1992; Hill, Leighley, and Hinton-Anderson 1995; Avery and Peffley 2005). Class bias is defined in this research as the extent of overrepresentation (or underrepresentation) of higher (or lower) socioeconomic status voters in the electorate. The results of this research indicate that there is wide variation in the extent of class bias in state electorates and that this bias is related to the provision of policies for the poor. Specifically, states in which the level of upper-class bias is relatively low (the poor are better represented in the electorate) tend to provide more generous welfare benefits than do states in which the level of class bias is more severe. This research also found that class bias tends to be most extreme in poor, racially diverse states (Hill and Leighley 1994). The findings of Martinez and Hill (1999) and Wolfinger and Hoffman (2001) suggest that class bias might actually increase as a result of government attempts to improve the position of low-income voters via the NVRA. Holbrook and Heidbreder (2007) examined changes in class bias over time in the states and found that the adoption of mail registration and motor vehicle registration practices mandated by the NVRA led to lower levels of class bias, though adoption of early voting and no-excuse absentee balloting had no effect. More recently, Rugeley and Jackson (2009) found that implementation of the NVRA attenuated the influence of socioeconomic characteristics on turnout, thereby potentially reducing class bias. At the same time, Brown and Wedeking (2006) found that by making it easier for low-income citizens to vote, and thereby reducing class bias in registration, the NVRA acts to weaken the relationship between voter registration and voter turnout. These results, along with those cited earlier, indicate that voting reforms have somewhat limited effects on political participation and class bias in the electorate.

Turnout-Related Controversies

Several simmering controversies related to who is allowed to vote and what they should be required to do to vote have important partisan implications. As noted earlier, the definition of the voting-eligible electorate excludes felons who are prohibited by state law from voting. According to data gathered by McDonald (2011), more than 4 million voting-age residents were ineligible to vote in the 2010 elections because of their felon status. Although this was only 2.17 percent of the national voting-age population, there is wide variation among the states, ranging from relatively high levels in Georgia (6.4 percent), Idaho (5.3 percent), and Texas (3.8 percent), to nul in Maine and Vermont, where there are no prohibitions on felons voting (and where even inmates are allowed to vote).

In addition to important issues of representation and the reintegration of felons into society, important political consequences are associated with **felon disenfranchisement** laws. Because the felon population is disproportionately poor and composed of racial minorities—both important constituency groups for the Democratic Party—it is likely that restrictive felon voting laws benefit Republican candidates on election day. However, because of their relatively small proportion of the potential electorate and the likely low turnout rate for felons, the political impact may be rather small (Haselswert 2009; Miles 2004). Still, even with these considerations, research by Uggen and Manza (2002) indicates that since 1978 seven closely decided races for the U.S. Senate won by Republicans would have gone to the Democratic candidates if felons had been allowed to vote. Uggen and Manza also found that Democratic presidential candidate Al Gore would have carried Florida by 31,000–84,000 votes had felons voted. More recently, Bowers and Preuhs (2009) found evidence of "collateral" effects, whereby turnout among nonfelon African Americans was negatively affected by felon disenfranchisement laws.

Another important related issue is the push by the Republican Party to pass stricter laws governing the type of identification voters must present at the polls as a means of combating voter fraud. Voter fraud has become a bit of a rallying cry for the national and state Republican parties. Democrats, of course, see Republican efforts to impose stricter voter identification regulations as an effort to suppress likely Democratic constituency groups such as racial minorities and the poor. The federal Help America Vote Act (HAVA) mandates the use of voter identification in all states for first-time voters who did not provide identification when registering. But twenty-nine states have passed laws requiring all voters to provide some type of identification at the polls, including ten states (Florida, Georgia, Hawaii, Idaho, Indiana, Kansas, Louisiana, Michigan, South Dakota, and Wisconsin) that require some kind of photo identification card (National Conference of State Legislatures

2007). Unfortunately, little research exists on the extent of voter fraud or the impact of strict voter identification laws on either turnout or election fraud. Minnite (2007), in a report for Project Vote, found claims of widespread voter fraud to be greatly exaggerated and pointed to the fact that from 2002 to 2005 there were only thirty-eight federal prosecutions for voter fraud, and only twenty-four of those cases ended with a conviction or guilty plea. Other work by Minnite (2010) and Piven, Minnite, and Groarke (2009) provide additional evidence of the relative infrequency of electoral fraud and lay the vote fraud fervor of the Republican Party squarely at the feet of efforts to suppress minority turnout. Vercellotti and Anderson (2006) found that requiring voters to produce identification at the polls lowers turnout, especially among racial and ethnic minority groups, although the additional burden of producing a photo ID does not have the same effect. At the same time, Alvarez, Bailey, and Katz (2007) found no aggregate effect from photo ID regulations but did find significant negative individual-level effects from the strictest regulations, effects that were most pronounced among the poor and the uneducated. By contrast, Mycoff, Wagner, and Wilson (2009) found no relationship between voter ID laws and the turnout rates of specific demographic groups. The potential for such effects are, however, a very real possibility, based on recent work by Barreto, Nuno, and Sanchez (2009), who found that minorities and other Democratic-aligned groups were the least likely to possess the types of identification required by voter ID laws.

The partisan nature of the debate over voter fraud and voter identification laws is illustrated by suggestions that the prosecution of voter fraud cases in key states was a high priority for the Bush administration prior to the 2006 elections and that failure to pursue such cases may have played a role in the dismissal of several U.S. attorneys (Eggen and Goldstein 2007). In addition, Yoshinaka and Grose (2005) found that the repeal of existing felon disenfranchisement laws is most likely to take place when Democrats have unified control of state government. Both parties view these issues as having important political consequences, and so the issues are likely to continue to play a prominent role in both the state and national parties.

PARTY ADAPTABILITY AND DURABILITY IN AN ERA OF CANDIDATE-CENTERED POLITICS

The theme of change runs consistently through this survey of state political parties and elections. Since the 1960s and 1970s, state party organizations have developed into increasingly professional service agencies assisting candidates and local parties. State parties have also come into the orbit of the national party organizations, which, through massive transfers of funds plus supplies of personnel and expertise, now use the state parties to implement national campaign strategies. This nationalization of the parties, with its heightened national–state party integration, has brought organizational benefits to the state parties but also some loss of traditional state party autonomy.

Within the states, autonomous state legislative campaign committees have emerged as major-party support agencies for legislative candidates. Campaign costs have escalated as candidates have sought to take advantage of the latest techniques and technologies. However, state regulation of campaign finance is in flux, with several recent Supreme Court decisions that appear to make it easier for interest groups to raise and spend money, while making it somewhat more difficult to finance elections with public subsidies. Candidates continue to rely primarily on their own personal campaign organizations rather than the party machinery, but they can gain considerable campaign support or face blistering opposition from partisan interest groups operating in an environment with few restrictions on "independent" campaign activity.

Parties, however, remain a major force in state electoral politics. Interparty competition has intensified since the 1970s as hard-fought battles rage for control of legislative chambers and governorships. On election day, partisanship continues to be a major determinant of voter choice. In the face of an increasingly candidate-centered style of politics, both state central committees and legislative campaign committees have become more sophisticated and capable of providing an array of services to their clienteles. The story of state parties since World War II is thus an impressive one of adaptability and durability. Although state parties neither control nominations nor run campaigns, they nevertheless remain the principal agencies for making nominations, contesting elections, recruiting leaders, and providing a link between citizens and their government.

KEY TERMS

"527" (or "501c4") organizations, 73
Bipartisan Campaign Reform Act of
    2002 (BCRA), 80
coordinated campaigns, 80
direct primary election, 82
felon disenfranchisement, 97

folded Ranney index, 89
National Voter Registration Act of
    1993, 95
plurality, 85
Ranney index, 87
soft money, 80

REFERENCES

Aldrich, John H. 1995. *Why Parties? The Origin and Transformation of Party Politics in America.* Chicago: University of Chicago Press.
———. 2000. "Southern Parties in State and Nation." *Journal of Politics* 62: 643–670.
Alvarez, R. Michael, Delia Bailey, and Jonathan Katz. 2007. "The Effect of Voter Identification Laws on Turnout." Social Science Working Paper 1267, California Institute of Technology. http://jkatz.caltech.edu/research/files/wp1267.pdf.
Appleton, Andrew M., and Daniel S. Ward, eds. 1997. *State Party Profiles: A 50 State Guide to Development, Organization, and Resources.* Washington, D.C.: CQ Press.
Avery, James M., and Mark Peffley. 2005. "Voter Registration Requirements, Voter Turnout, and Welfare Eligibility Policy: Class Bias Matters." *State Politics and Policy Quarterly* 5: 47–67.

Bardwell, Kedron. 2002. "Money and Challenger Emergence in Gubernatorial Primaries." *Political Research Quarterly* 55: 653–668.

Barreto, Matt A., Stephen A. Nuno, and Gabriel R. Sanchez. 2009. "The Disproportionate Impact of Voter-ID Requirements on the Electorate—New Evidence from Indiana." *PS: Political Science and Politics* 42: 111–116.

Barrilleaux, Charles. 1986. "A Dynamic Model of Partisan Competition in the American States." *American Journal of Political Science* 30: 822–840.

Barrilleaux, Charles, Thomas Holbrook, and Laura Langer. 2002. "Electoral Competition, Legislative Balance, and State Welfare Policy." *American Journal of Political Science* 46: 415–427.

Baxter, Tom. 2004. "Ousted Judge Fails to Sway Alabama Vote." Cox News Service, June 1.

Berry, Jeffrey, and Deborah Schildkraut. 1998. "Citizen Groups, Political Parties, and Electoral Coalitions." In *Social Movements and American Political Institutions,* ed. Anne N. Costain and Andrew S. McFarland, 136–158. Lanham, Md.: Rowman and Littlefield.

Bibby, John F., and Thomas M. Holbrook. 1996. "Parties and Elections." In *Politics in the American States,* 6th ed., ed. Virginia Gray and Herbert Jacob, 78–121. Washington, D.C.: CQ Press.

———. 2004. "Parties and Elections." In *Politics in the American States,* 8th ed., ed. Virginia Gray and Russell Hanson. Washington, D.C.: CQ Press.

Bowers, Melanie, and Robert R. Preuhs. 2009. "Collateral Consequences of a Collateral Penalty: The Negative Effect of Felon Disenfranchisement Laws on the Political Participation of Nonfelons." *Social Science Quarterly* 90: 722–743.

Brown, Robert D., and Justin Wedeking. 2006. "People Who Have Their Tickets but Do Not Use Them: 'Motor Voter,' Registration, and Turnout Revisited." *American Politics Research* 34: 479–504.

Bruce, John M., John A. Clark, and John H. Kessel. 1991. "Advocacy Politics in Presidential Parties." *American Political Science Review* 85: 1089–1105.

Bullock, Charles S., III, and Loch K. Johnson. 1992. *Runoff Elections in the United States.* Chapel Hill: University of North Carolina Press.

Campaign Disclosure Project. 2008. UCLA School of Law, Center for Governmental Studies, and California Voter Foundation. www.campaigndisclosure.org/gradingstate/index.html.

Conger, Kimberly H. 2010. "A Matter of Context: Christian Right Influence in U.S. State Republican Politics." *State Politics and Policy Quarterly* 10: 248–269.

Conway, Margaret M. 2001. "Women and Political Participation." *PS: Political Science and Politics* 34: 231–233.

Cotter, Cornelius P., James L. Gibson, John F. Bibby, and Robert J. Huckshorn. 1984. *Party Organizations in American Politics.* New York: Praeger.

Cotter, Cornelius P., and Bernard Hennessy. 1964. *Politics without Power: National Party Committees.* New York: Atherton.

Courser, Zachary. 2010. "The Tea Party at the Election." *The Forum.* http://www.bepress.com/forum/vol8/iss4/art5/. DOI: 10.2202/1540-8884.1410.

Eggen, Dan, and Amy Goldstein. 2007. "Voter-Fraud Complaints Drove Dismissals." *Washington Post,* May 14, sec. A.

Epstein, Leon D. 1986. *Political Parties in the American Mold.* Madison: University of Wisconsin Press.

Fiorina, Morris P., Samuel J. Abrams, and Jeremy Pope. *Culture War? The Myth of a Polarized America.* New York: Pearson Longman, 2005.

Fitzgerald, Mary. 2005. "Greater Convenience but Not Greater Turnout." *American Politics Research* 33: 842–867.

Gerber, Elisabeth R., and Rebecca B. Morton. 1998. "Primary Election Systems and Representation." *Journal of Law, Economics, and Organization* 14: 304–324.

Gierzynski, Anthony, and David A. Breaux. 1992. *Legislative Party Campaign Committees in the American States.* Lexington: University of Kentucky Press.

Green, John C., James L. Guth, and Clyde Wilcox. 1999. "Less than Conquerors: The Christian Right in State Republican Parties." In *Social Movements and American Political Institutions,* ed. Anne N. Costain and Andrew S. McFarland, 117–135. Lanham, Md.: Rowman and Littlefield.

Grofman, Bernard, and Thomas L. Brunell. 2001. "Explaining the Ideological Differences between the Two U.S. Senators Elected from the Same State: An Institutional Effects Model." In *Congressional Primaries and the Politics of Representation,* ed. Peter F. Galderisi, Marni Ezra, and Michael Lyons, 132–142. Lanham, Md.: Rowman and Littlefield.

Haselswerdt, Michael V. 2009. "Con Job: An Estimate of Ex-Felon Voter Turnout Using Document-Based Data." *Social Science Quarterly* 90: 262–273.

Hill, Kim, and Jan Leighley. 1992. "The Policy Consequences of Class Bias in State Electorates." *American Journal of Political Science* 36: 351–365.

———. 1994. "Mobilizing Institutions and Class Representation in the U.S. State Electorates." *Political Research Quarterly* 47: 137–150.

Hill, Kim, Jan Leighley, and Angela Hinton-Anderson. 1995. "Lower-Class Mobilization and Policy Linkage in the U.S. States." *American Journal of Political Science* 39: 75–86.

Hogan, Robert E. 2003. "The Effects of Primary Divisiveness on General Election Outcomes." *American Political Research* 31: 27–47.

Holbrook, Thomas M., and Brianne Heidbreder. 2007. "The Etiology of Class Bias in the American States." Paper presented at the 2007 Conference on State Politics and Policy, Austin, Texas, February 23–24.

———. 2010. "Does Measurement Matter? The Case of VAP and VEP in Models of Voter Turnout in the United States." *State Politics and Policy Quarterly* 10: 157–179.

Holbrook, Thomas M., and Raymond J. La Raja. 2008. "Parties and Elections." In *Politics in the American States: A Comparative Analysis,* 9th ed., ed. Virginia Gray and Russell L. Hanson. Washington, D.C.: CQ Press.

Holbrook, Thomas M., and Emily Van Dunk. 1993. "Electoral Competition in the American States." *American Political Science Review* 87: 955–962.

Jackson, Robert. 1997. "The Mobilization of the U.S. State Electorates in the 1988 and 1990 Elections." *Journal of Politics* 59: 520–537.

Jacobson, Gary C. 2011. "The President, the Tea Party, and Voting Behavior in 2010: Insights from the Cooperative Congressional Election Study." Paper prepared for delivery at the 2011 annual meeting of the American Political Science Association, Seattle, Wash., September 1–4.

Jenkins, Shannon. 2007. "A Woman's Work Is Never Done? Fund-Raising Perception and Effort among Female State Legislative Candidates." *Political Research Quarterly* 60: 230–239.

Jewell, Malcolm E., and Sarah M. Morehouse. 2001. *Political Parties and Elections in American States,* 4th ed. Washington, D.C.: CQ Press.

Kenney, Patrick J. 1988. "Sorting Out the Effects of Primary Divisiveness in Congressional and Senatorial Elections." *Western Political Quarterly* 41: 756–777.

Key, V. O., Jr. 1949. *Southern Politics in State and Nation.* New York: Knopf.

———. 1956. *American State Politics: An Introduction.* New York: Knopf.

La Raja, Raymond J. 2008. *Small Change: Money, Political Parties, and Campaign Finance Reform.* Ann Arbor: University of Michigan Press.

———. 2010. "Back to the Future? Campaign-Finance Reform and the Declining Importance of the National Party Organization." In *The State of the Parties: The Changing Role of Contemporary American Parties,* ed. John C. Green and Rick Farmer. Lanham, Md.: Rowman and Littlefield.

————. 2011. "Will *Citizens United v. FEC* Give More Political Power to Corporations?" Paper prepared for presentation at the 2011 meetings of the Midwest Political Science Association, Chicago, March 31–April 3.

Lawless, Jennifer L., and Richard L. Fox. 2005. *It Takes a Candidate: Why Women Don't Run for Office.* Cambridge, U.K.: Cambridge University Press.

Layman, Geoffrey C., Thomas M. Carsey, and Juliana Menasce Horowitz. 2006. "Party Polarization in American Politics: Characteristics, Causes, and Consequences." *Annual Review of Political Science* 9: 83–110.

Malhotra, Neil. 2008. "The Impact of Public Financing on Electoral Competition: Evidence from Arizona and Maine." *State Politics and Policy Quarterly* 8: 263–281.

Martinez, Michael D., and David Hill. 1999. "Did Motor Voter Work?" *American Politics Quarterly* 27: 296–315.

Masket, Seth E. 2009. *No Middle Ground: How Informal Party Organizations Control Nominations and Polarize Legislatures.* Ann Arbor: University of Michigan Press.

Mayhew, David R. 1986. *Placing Parties in American Politics.* Princeton, N.J.: Princeton University Press.

McDonald, Michael P. 2002. "The Turnout Rate among Eligible Voters in the States, 1980–2000." *State Politics and Policy Quarterly* 2: 199–212.

————. 2005. United States Elections Project. http://elections.gmu.edu/Voter_Turnout_2004.htm.

————. 2010. "2010 Early Voting." November 2. http://elections.gmu.edu/early_vote_2010.html.

————. 2011. "2010 General Election Turnout Rates." United States Elections Project. http://elections.gmu.edu/.

Miles, Thomas J. 2004. "Felon Disenfranchisement and Voter Turnout." *Journal of Legal Studies* 33: 85–129.

Miller, Gary, and Norman Schofield. 2008. "The Transformation of the Republican and Democratic Party Coalitions in the U.S." *Perspectives on Politics* 6: 433–450.

Minnite, Lorraine C. 2007. "The Politics of Voter Fraud." Report prepared for Project Vote. http://projectvote.org/fileadmin/ProjectVote/Publications/Politics_of_Voter_Fraud_Final.pdf.

————. 2010. *The Myth of Voter Fraud.* Ithaca, N.Y.: Cornell University Press.

Moncrief, Gary F., Peverill Squire, and Malcolm E. Jewell. 2001. *Who Runs for the Legislature?* Upper Saddle River, N.J.: Prentice Hall.

Morehouse, Sarah McCally. 1998. *The Governor as Party Leader: Campaigning and Governing.* Ann Arbor: University of Michigan Press.

Mycoff, Jason D., Michael W. Wagner, and David C. Wilson. 2009. "The Empirical Effects of Voter-ID Laws: Present or Absent?" *PS: Political Science and Politics* 42: 121–126.

National Conference of State Legislatures. 2007. "Voter Identification Requirements." www.ncsl.org/default.aspx?tabid=16602#State_Reqs.

————. 2010. "State Limits on Contributions to Candidates." www.ncsl.org/Portals/1/documents/legismgt/limits_candidates.pdf.

————. 2011a. "Absentee and Early Voting." April 22. www.ncsl.org/default.aspx?tabid=16604.

————. 2011b. "Women in State Legislatures: 2011 Legislative Session." April 18. www.ncsl.org/LegislaturesElections/WomensNetwork/WomeninStateLegislatures2011/tabid/21606/Default.aspx.

Patterson, Samuel, and Gregory Caldeira. 1984. "Etiology of Partisan Competition." *American Political Science Review* 78: 691–707.

Piven, Frances Fox, Lorraine C. Minnite, and Margaret Groarke. 2009. *Keeping Down the Black Vote: Race and the Demobilization of American Voters.* New York: New Press.

Powell, G. Bingham. 1986. "American Voter Turnout in a Comparative Perspective." *American Political Science Review* 80: 17–44.

Preuhs, Robert R. 2007. "Descriptive Representation as a Mechanism to Mitigate Policy Backlash." *Political Research Quarterly* 60: 277–292.

Ranney, Austin. 1976. "Parties in State Politics." In *Politics in the American States: A Comparative Analysis,* 3d ed., ed. Herbert Jacob and Kenneth Vines. Boston: Little, Brown.

Reichley, A. James. 1992. *The Life of the Parties: A History of American Political Parties.* New York: Free Press.

Rosenstone, Steven J., and John Mark Hansen. 1993. *Mobilization, Participation, and Democracy in America.* New York: Macmillan.

Rugeley, Cynthia, and Robert A. Jackson. 2009. "Getting on the Rolls: Analyzing the Effects of Lowered Barriers on Voter Registration." *State Politics and Policy Quarterly* 9: 56–78.

Rutenberg, Jim. 2010. "Conservative Donor Groups Lay a Base for 2012." *New York Times,* October 31.

Sanbonmatsu, Kira. 2006. *Where Women Run: Gender and Party in the American States.* Ann Arbor: University of Michigan Press.

Shafer, Byron E. 1996. "The United States." In *Postwar Politics in the G-7: Order and Eras in Comparative Perspective,* ed. Byron E. Shafer, 12–46. Madison: University of Wisconsin Press.

Squire, Peverill, and Gary F. Moncrief. 2010. *State Legislatures Today: Politics under the Domes.* New York: Longman/Pearson.

Uggen, Christopher, and Jeff Manza. 2002. "Democratic Contraction: Political Consequences of Felon Disenfranchisement." *American Sociological Review* 67: 777–803.

U.S. Census Bureau. 2011. "2011 Statistical Abstract: Resident Population by Race, Hispanic Origin, and State: 2009." April 27. www.census.gov/compendia/statab/cats/population.html.

U.S. Electoral Assistance Commission. 2010. "Strengthening the Electoral System One Grant at a Time: A Retrospective of Grants Awarded by EAC, April 2003–December 2010." www.eac.gov/assets/1/Documents/FY2010%20Grants%20Report%20FINAL.pdf.

Van Dunk, Emily, and Ronald Weber. 1997. "Constituency-Level Competition in the U.S. States: A Pooled Analysis." *Legislative Studies Quarterly* 22: 141–159.

Vercellotti, Timothy, and David Anderson. 2006. "Protecting the Franchise, or Restricting It? The Effects of Voter Identification Requirements on Turnout." Paper presented at the 2006 annual meeting of the American Political Science Association, Philadelphia, August 31–September 3.

Wilcox, Clyde, and Carin Larson. 2006. *Onward Christian Soldiers: The Religious Right in American Politics.* 3d ed. Boulder, Colo.: Westview Press.

Winger, Richard. 1997. "Institutional Obstacles to a Multiparty System." In *Multiparty Politics in America,* ed. Paul S. Herrnson and John C. Green, 159–172. Lanham, Md.: Rowman and Littlefield.

Wolfinger, Raymond E., and Jonathan Hoffman. 2001. "Registering and Voting with Motor Voter." *PS: Political Science and Politics* 34: 85–92.

Wolfinger, Raymond E., and Steven J. Rosenstone. 1980. *Who Votes?* New Haven, Conn.: Yale University Press.

Yoshinaka, Antoine, and Christian R. Grose. 2005. "Partisan Politics and Electoral Design: The Enfranchisement of Felons and Ex-Felons in the United States, 1960–99." *State and Local Government Review* 37: 49–60.

SUGGESTED READINGS

Print

Berinsky, Adam. "The Perverse Consequences of Electoral Reform in the United States." *American Politics Research* 33 (2005): 471–491. A review essay that synthesizes existing research on electoral reform and citizen participation.

Epstein, Leon D. *Political Parties in the American Mold.* Madison: University of Wisconsin Press, 1986. A comprehensive treatise on American parties by a distinguished scholar, with significant insights in Chapters 5 and 6 on state parties.

McDonald, Michael P., and Samuel L. Popkin. "The Myth of the Vanishing Voter." *American Political Science Review* 95 (2001): 963–974. An important demonstration of the consequences of measuring voter turnout with the *voting-eligible* rather than *voting-age* electorate as the denominator.

Morehouse, Sarah M., and Malcolm E. Jewell. *State Politics, Parties, and Policy.* Lanham, Md.: Rowman and Littlefield, 2003. A survey of state politics by leading authorities in the field.

Internet

Federal Election Commission. www.fec.gov/. This site provides information about party finances in federal elections.

National Institute on Money in State Politics. www.followthemoney.org/. Details of party finances in state elections are provided here.

Project Vote Smart. www.vote-smart.org/index.htm. Lists state party Web sites.

United States Elections Project. http://elections.gmu.edu/. This site offers detailed information on voter turnout in the states.

CHAPTER 4

 Interest Groups in the States

ANTHONY J. NOWNES AND
ADAM J. NEWMARK

Organized interests (also known as interest groups) and their lobbyists are active at all levels of government, but they are particularly active at the state level. Historically, some interest groups—such as the Southern Pacific Railroad in California and Standard Oil in Pennsylvania—virtually dominated politics in their states. To this day, in some states one or a few groups exercise an inordinate amount of influence in state politics. In Nevada, for example, gaming interests are influential players in state politics. Indeed, during the 2010 state elections, two of the top three contributors to campaigns were gaming companies (National Institute on Money in State Politics 2011d). Similarly, coal companies continue to loom large in West Virginia politics. Lobbyists for coal companies actually wrote portions of a 1986 bill that "restructured coal mine safety and environmental enforcement" in the state, and were part of a group that drafted the state's workers' compensation reform legislation in 2005 (Brisbin et al. 2008, 67–68). Clearly, then, interest groups are powerful players in state politics.

To understand state politics fully, one must understand interest group politics. In this chapter, we provide a brief but inclusive overview of interest group politics in the states. We begin by defining key terms and concepts and presenting an overview of the types of interest groups active in the states. Next, we examine some recent trends in state interest group politics. From there, we examine variations in state interest group systems, followed by a look at lobbyists and the ways they attempt to affect government decisions in the states. We then examine interest group power in the states by asking: How powerful are interest groups in state politics? A brief look at how states regulate the behavior of interest groups and to what effect follows. We conclude with a few general observations about interest group politics in the states.

THE BASICS: TERMS AND CONCEPTS

There is no single, agreed-on definition of **interest group**. Some studies of state politics define the term narrowly to include only those groups required to register under state interest group registration laws. Yet, many organizations that engage in lobbying are not required to register under state law. Among the most important are those representing the various levels and agencies of government. Many states do not require public officials at any level of government to register as lobbyists. In light of all this, a broad definition of the term *interest group* is clearly appropriate: an interest group is an association of individuals or organizations or a public or private institution that attempts to influence government decisions.

Types of Interest Groups

Traditional membership groups are groups made up of individuals promoting economic, social, or political concerns (or some combination thereof) such as anti-tax advocates, environmentalists, farmers, schoolteachers, and senior citizens. Among the types of traditional membership groups active in the states are citizen groups (groups that any citizen can join such as environmental groups), labor unions (such as state teachers' unions), and professional associations (such as state bar associations) that consist of individuals active in a specific profession.

Associations are organizational interests that are composed not of individuals but of organizations such as businesses or labor unions. Among the types of associations active in the states are trade associations (groups of business firms such as state chambers of commerce) and coalitions of labor unions such as the AFL-CIO.

Finally, there are **institutional interests,** which are not really groups at all, but rather nonmembership organizations such as business firms, local governments, state and federal agencies, think tanks, and universities and colleges. As interest group scholars Virginia Gray and David Lowery (2001b) have noted, most interests active in the states are institutional interests.

Lobbying and the Concept of the State Interest Group System

Interest groups operate in the state political process by **lobbying,** which is defined as attempting to influence current government decisions or creating a relationship conducive to shaping future government decisions. Thus a **lobbyist** is a person who represents an interest group while lobbying. The decisions most often targeted by interest groups and their lobbyists are those concerning public policies, but they also include other types of decisions, such as those about who is elected, who is appointed to make those policies, what state governments purchase, and from whom. Lobbyists include not only those required to register by law but also those who are not required to register. Some states have laws that do not require lobbyists for state agencies to register, but such people are still considered lobbyists.

Finally, there is the concept of the **state interest group system**. This is the array of organizations and the lobbyists representing them who work to affect government decisions within a state. It includes a multitude of political actors such as the lawmakers with whom lobbyists must interact and the restrictions that the state places on these interactions. The characteristics of an interest group system—its size, development, composition, methods of operating, and so on—affect a state's political power structure, the public policies that are pursued, and the nature of representation and democracy.

DEVELOPMENTS IN STATE INTEREST GROUP POLITICS

States have always been home to interest group activity, but state interest group politics has changed a great deal since the beginning of the Republic, and especially over the last thirty years (Thomas and Hrebenar 1991). The most obvious change has been a proliferation in both the number and types of interests lobbying in the states. Some 15,000 lobbyists were registered in the states in 1980 (Laskow 2006), but by 2009 that number had more than doubled, to 37,401 (National Institute on Money in State Politics 2011b). Along with this growth, there has been an increase in the specialization of interests and in the number of single-issue groups. For example, in Georgia the Medical Association of Georgia represents the multitude of interests of physicians across numerous specialties, whereas the Association of Black Cardiologists deals with the much more specific issue of racial disparities related to heart disease. The states have also seen an increase in the number of politically active institutions (typically businesses and government agencies), political action committees (PACs), and citizen groups. Lobbying has become more sophisticated as well, and in many states large contract firms represent a multitude of clients.

Changes

To understand why changes have occurred in state lobbying and interest group activity, it is important to consider some of the concepts addressed in Chapter 2. As power was gradually returned to the states through devolution from the federal government in the 1970s and 1980s, the states became much more active in delivering services and administering programs. Because the states began to handle what once were federal government responsibilities, interest groups began increasingly to target the states. For example, as the responsibility for administering welfare programs became a state-level function, and particularly as the Temporary

Assistance for Needy Families (TANF) program replaced Aid to Families with Dependent Children (AFDC) in 1996, state lobbying in this policy area became increasingly important. Interests have also fragmented in recent years. In some respects, fragmentation has been both a cause of the changes that have occurred in state interest group activity as well as a consequence of them. In 2005 the AFL-CIO, which represents labor interests, split because of divergent interests within the organization. And then there are the many new interests that have emerged from social, political, economic, and technological developments. As medical research expanded in controversial areas such as stem cell research, new interests developed or existing interests increased their lobbying activity. At the national level, the George W. Bush administration opposed stem cell research; however, states such as California supported it. Numerous interests on both sides of the issue lobbied prior to the passage of Proposition 71 in California, which created the California Institute for Regenerative Medicine and provided $3 billion in bonds for stem cell research (MSNBC 2004).

Finally, a greater number of corporate entities began to target the states because many of their business activities take place there and because the states are responsible for many regulatory activities. Although major corporations such as AT&T and Coca-Cola are concerned with national legislation and therefore target Washington, they also operate within the states and, accordingly, lobby state governments. Indeed, because the states regulate the environment, transportation, utilities, and labor, it makes sense for corporations to lobby state governments. This practice has led to what some scholars have called the "nationalization of state lobbying." In other words, state lobbying has become a lot like national lobbying, and many interests lobby in a variety of states (Thomas and Hrebenar 1991, 1999). However, most interest groups that lobby at the state level do so in only one or two states (Wolak et al. 2002).

Money

Another major change in state politics is the massive increase in the amount of money spent by political action committees and other types of groups in state elections. According to the National Institute on Money in State Politics, over $3 billion was spent in the states by campaigns and PACs in 2010 (National Institute on Money in State Politics 2011c). As one might expect, the campaign expenditures by lobbyists and interest groups tend to be larger in the larger states. In 2010 almost $715 million was spent in California and $332 million in Florida (National Institute on Money in State Politics 2011c). Levels of electoral spending vary widely across states. For example, in Colorado about $30 million was spent in 2010 (National Institute on Money in State Politics 2011a), and in South Dakota the total was $10.4 million (National Institute on Money in State Politics 2011e).

VARIATIONS IN STATE INTEREST GROUP NUMBERS

All fifty states have a variety of active interest groups, and all states regulate interest group activity to some extent. Nevertheless, state interest group systems differ in important ways. In fact, no two state interest group systems are exactly alike. In this section, we examine one important variable on which interest group systems differ—size.

Differences in Group Numbers

Table 4-1 reports the numbers of interest groups registered in each of the fifty states in 2009. One thing is very clear: some states have far more interest groups than others. For example, New York had a whopping 3,161 registered groups in 2009, while Hawaii had only 274 (National Institute on Money in State Politics 2011b). What explains the vast differences in numbers across states? It is tempting to conclude that population is all that matters—that is, to conclude that populous states such as Texas and New York will have more interest groups than less populated states such as Hawaii and Alaska. But this conclusion is facile. It cannot explain why, for example, Missouri, which is a medium-populated state, has so many interest groups, or why South Carolina, which is also a medium-populated state, has relatively few interest groups. It turns out that size is not the only thing that matters; there are other important determinants of group numbers.

The ESA Model. Interest group scholars Virginia Gray and David Lowery have created the **energy-stability-area (ESA) model** to explain variations in group numbers across states (Gray and Lowery 1996—see also Gray and Lowery 2001a; Lowery and Gray 1993). At its core, the model (which borrows from population ecology) holds that the number of interest groups in a given state is a function of its energy, area, and stability. We will now briefly examine each of the terms in the model—energy, area, and stability.

What provides *energy* for interest groups? One answer, according to Gray and Lowery, is policy issues. The ESA theory holds that as a state government actively considers issues of a certain kind, it provides energy for the groups that deal with these issues. For example, if a state government is actively addressing gun issues, it is providing energy for pro- and anti-gun control groups to use to recruit new members. If a state government ignores gun-related issues for a couple of years, it is starving gun-related groups of the energy they need to thrive. In short, Gray and Lowery conclude that energy in the form of government attention to policy issues affects the number of interest groups in a state. In other words, the number of interest groups in a state is partially determined by the size of the state government's agenda. States with large, activist governments involved in lots of issue areas will have more interest groups than states with smaller, less active governments that ignore lots of issue areas.

Table 4-1 Number of Interest Groups Registered by State, 2009

State	Number of interest groups
1. New York	3,161
2. Texas	2,953
3. Missouri	2,718
4. Florida	2,714
5. Illinois	2,341
6. California	2,267
7. Georgia	2,256
8. Pennsylvania	2,175
9. New Jersey	1,916
10. Ohio	1,436
11. Arizona	1,400
12. Minnesota	1,368
13. Michigan	1,350
14. Connecticut	1,278
15. Louisiana	1,185
16. Washington	1,128
17. Colorado	1,094
18. Nevada	1,029
19. Massachusetts	996
20. Virginia	884
21. New Mexico	859
22. Oregon	853
23. Maryland	828
24. Iowa	816
25. Alabama	741
26. North Carolina	724
27. Utah	722
28. Oklahoma	720
29. Indiana	715
30. Kansas	709
31. Arkansas	676
32. Wisconsin	658
33. Kentucky	656
34. Tennessee	643
35. Mississippi	612
36. Nebraska	516
37. New Hampshire	498
38. South Carolina	496
39. Idaho	474
40. West Virginia	472
41. Delaware	446
42. Montana	435
43. North Dakota	421
44. Wyoming	390
45. South Dakota	384
46. Maine	357
47. Vermont	354
48. Rhode Island	337
49. Alaska	277
50. Hawaii	274

SOURCE: National Institute on Money in State Politics, "Lobbyist Map, Total Lobbyists for 2009." www.follow themoney.org/database/graphs/lobbyistlink/lobby map.phtml?p=0&y=2009&l=0 (accessed July 14, 2011).

N O T E : These numbers are based on the number of "clients" represented by lobbyists in each state.

Another aspect of energy that affects group numbers is the probability of policy change. Gray and Lowery argue that groups will have relatively good luck attracting supporters if they can convince people that their interests are threatened by potential changes in government policy. Using our previous example, if there is a high probability of changes in gun policy, gun-related groups can appeal to potential members by arguing they must join to ensure that the changes to existing policy do not hurt them. Gray and Lowery argue that the higher the level of party competition, the more likely there will be policy changes. It follows, then, that states with relatively high levels of party competition have more interest groups than states with relatively low levels of party competition. In summary, ESA theory predicts that a larger state government agenda (more issues) and more party competition (a higher probability of policy change) will create more energy, which in turn will lead to a greater number of interest groups.

We turn next to *area*. Gray and Lowery define *area* as where interest groups live. Interest groups, they point out, rely on members and supporters to survive. Thus there are likely to be more interest groups in areas in which there are more potential members and supporters with different interests. Similarly, associations of organizations depend upon the existence of constituents such as businesses, health plans, dairies, nonprofits, hospitals, and others that want to join together to lobby collectively for their industry or sector. The ESA model holds that states with more developed economic sectors should yield more interests, which helps to explain why California and New York have more interest groups than Wyoming and Idaho. But this is not the whole story. One of the more important insights of the ESA model is that increases in area (that is, in the size of the state's economy and its population) lead to increases in group numbers only up to a point. At some point (which varies from state to state, primarily depending on the nature of the economy), a state will become saturated with interest groups, and competition between existing groups will leave few resources for new groups to form. Each state, the ESA model holds, has an interest group carrying capacity, and thus there is a limit to the number of groups each state can support.

Finally, we turn to *stability*. Gray and Lowery say that, in practice, stability is not all that important in determining the number of groups in a state because since the Civil War state boundaries and governments have been remarkably stable. In theory, instability—for example, some calamitous event that destroys the very foundation of a state's governmental system—could have a profound effect on the number of interest groups in a state. But because stability in all fifty states has been the norm for 140 years, the stability term of the ESA model is relatively inconsequential in practice.

Other Factors That Affect Group Numbers. Studies show that other factors such as political culture are important as well. State interest group experts Ronald Hrebenar and Clive Thomas conducted a fifty-state study of interest groups during the 1980s and 1990s and found that political culture profoundly affects state interest group numbers (Hrebenar and Thomas 1987, 1992, 1993a, 1993b). Political culture expert Daniel Elazar (1984) maintains that New York, for example, has a combination of individualistic and moralistic political cultures. This combination explains in part why so many interest groups are active in New York state politics—citizen participation is viewed by many as legitimate, and all sorts of citizens join interest groups. By contrast, South Carolina has a traditionalist political culture that typically discourages participation, and this factor explains a great deal about the low number of groups in the state.

Another factor that affects the number of groups in a state is the nature of direct democracy. Interest group scholar Frederick Boehmke (2002) has found that, other things being equal, states with an initiative process have more interest groups than states without an initiative process. Scholars Daniel Smith and Caroline Tolbert (2004) also cite the importance of direct democracy, arguing that when controlling for other factors, states in which the initiative process is used frequently—such as California and Florida—tend to have more interest groups than states in which the initiative process is used sparingly. In relation to the ESA theory, the initiative process appears to produce energy, which leads to more interest groups.

Why Care?

Why do researchers and others care about the differences in group numbers across states? The answer is that the numbers appear to affect state policymaking. First, there is credible research showing that the higher the numbers of interest groups, the greater the chances for legislative gridlock (Gray and Lowery 1995, 1996). However, the relationship is not straightforward. Bowling and Ferguson (2001) have shown that the greater the number of interest groups, the higher the levels of gridlock in policy areas that typically exhibit partisan conflict, but the lower the levels of gridlock in policy areas that typically do not exhibit partisan conflict. Second, recent research suggests that states with more interest groups enter into more interstate compacts than states with fewer interest groups (Bowman and Woods 2010). Why? In crowded interest group systems, groups look beyond the confines of the state to fulfill their goals. Finally, Yackee (2009) has found that increased group competition—which may result from increases in group numbers—can lead to policy outcomes that are more reflective of the public's wishes.

LOBBYING AND LOBBYISTS IN THE STATES

Interest groups and lobbyists are political actors who seek to affect what state government does. How do interest groups attempt to affect state government decisions? And who are state lobbyists, and what do they do?

Techniques of Lobbying

If there is one thing we have learned about lobbying in the states, it is that lobbyists have a large number of techniques at their disposal. State lobbyists employ four main types of lobbying techniques: **direct techniques**, which utilize direct contact between a lobbyist and government officials such as testifying before the legislature or meeting with bureaucrats; **indirect techniques**, which target citizens rather than government officials; electoral techniques, which are designed to affect electoral outcomes; and direct-democracy techniques, which are designed to affect the outcome of direct-democracy campaigns or elections (see Chapter 5 for more explanation of direct democracy).

Table 4-2, which is based on three studies of state lobbyists, reveals that five of the top six most commonly used lobbying techniques are direct lobbying techniques: meeting personally with executive agency personnel, meeting personally with members of the governor's staff, meeting personally with state legislators, meeting personally with state legislative staff, and testifying at legislative committee hearings. The other technique used by almost all state lobbyists is entering into coalitions with other state lobbyists or interest groups, which is not classified as direct, indirect, direct democracy, or electoral. Several other commonly used techniques are direct techniques, including doing favors for officials who need assistance, engaging in informal contacts with state government officials, meeting personally with the governor, serving on advisory boards or commissions, and submitting written comments on proposed rules or regulations.

As for indirect techniques, Table 4-2 shows that several are used quite often by state lobbyists. Among the most commonly used indirect techniques are holding

Table 4-2 Lobbying Techniques Used by Lobbyists in the States

Technique	Type
Techniques used by almost all state lobbyists	
Entering into coalitions with other lobbyists or interest groups	a
Meeting personally with executive agency personnel	Direct
Meeting personally with members of the governor's staff	Direct
Meeting personally with state legislative staff	Direct
Meeting personally with state legislators	Direct
Testifying at legislative committee hearings	Direct
Techniques used by most state lobbyists	
Campaigning for or against a state initiative or referendum (if applicable)	Direct democracy
Doing favors for state government officials who need assistance	Direct
Engaging in informal contacts (such as wining and dining) with state government officials	Direct
Holding press conferences	Indirect/media
Inspiring letter-writing, telephone, or e-mail campaigns to executive agencies	Indirect
Inspiring letter-writing, telephone, or e-mail campaigns to state legislators	Indirect
Making personal monetary contributions to candidates for office	Electoral
Making personal monetary contributions to political parties	Electoral
Meeting personally with the governor	Direct
Serving on advisory committees or boards	Direct
Submitting written comments on proposed rules or regulations	Direct
Submitting written testimony to legislative committees	Direct
Talking with people from the media	Indirect/media
Working on campaigns for candidates	Electoral
Techniques used sparingly by state lobbyists	
Engaging in protests or demonstrations	Indirect
Filing suit or otherwise engaging in litigation	Direct
Giving gifts to state government officials	Direct
Providing travel for state government officials	Direct
Running advertisements in the media	Indirect/media
Seeking to put a measure on the ballot as an initiative	Direct democracy

SOURCES: Coding for this table was done by the authors based primarily on the following studies: Anthony J. Nownes and Krissy Walker DeAlejandro, "Lobbying in the New Millennium: Evidence of Continuity and Change in Three States," *State Politics and Policy Quarterly* 9 (2009): 429–455; Anthony J. Nownes and Patricia K. Freeman, "Female Lobbyists: Women in the World of 'Good Ol' Boys,' " *Journal of Politics* 60 (1998): 1181–1201; and Alan Rosenthal, *The Third House: Lobbyists and Lobbying in the States*, 2d ed. (Washington, D.C.: CQ Press, 2001).

NOTE: This table does not contain every possible technique that state lobbyists use, only those about which we can make reasonable estimates about their frequency of use based on previous studies.

a. This technique does not fit into any of the categories we describe in the text.

press conferences; inspiring letter-writing, telephone, or e-mail campaigns to executive agencies or state legislators; and talking to media representatives.

Several electoral lobbying techniques appear to be used by most state lobbyists, including making personal monetary contributions to candidates for office. Here we distinguish between making a personal contribution to a candidate or a party and delivering a PAC contribution to a candidate or party. Money, although not the primary weapon in the lobbyist's arsenal, is still an important one. It is not exactly clear what money buys a lobbyist, but the fact that contributing money is so common suggests that it does indeed buy something. Working on campaigns for candidates is also a relatively common electoral lobbying technique, as is making personal monetary contributions to political parties.

Rise of Indirect and Media Lobbying. For many years, it was the conventional wisdom that direct techniques dominated the state lobbying business. In fact, it is fair to say that until well into the 1970s many state lobbyists relied almost exclusively on direct techniques. Moreover, lobbyists often utilized many informal strategies, including wining and dining lawmakers that are now more heavily regulated (Rosenthal 2001). Although the use of direct lobbying techniques is still more widespread than the use of indirect techniques, it is clear that indirect techniques are now part and parcel of the typical state lobbyist's tool kit.

Indirect techniques that have long been a part of national politics are now common in the states as well. Among these techniques are inspiring letter-writing, telephone, or e-mail campaigns to state legislators, or to state agency officials. Less common but not unheard of is engaging in protests or demonstrations. Media techniques—indirect lobbying techniques that involve the news media—are also now very common. Studies suggest that well over half of state lobbyists engage in some form of media lobbying, whether it be holding press conferences, running advertisements in the media, or talking with people from the media (Nownes and Freeman 1998b; Nownes and DeAlejando 2009). Although state lobbying used to be limited primarily to direct "inside" techniques, it is now a highly variegated phenomenon made up of many indirect and media techniques.

Relevance and Value of Personal Connections. Despite the prevalence and growth of indirect and media lobbying, state lobbying remains an intensely personal business. The essence of the art of lobbying is still interpersonal communication. Studies of lobbying suggest that even with the rise of indirect lobbying techniques, lobbyists believe that meeting personally with government officials is still the most effective way to influence government decisions (Rosenthal 2001; Nownes 2006, 201–202).

Three important general points can be made about the influence techniques used by state lobbyists. First, state lobbyists lobby all three branches of state government as well as the public. Although most people think of lobbyists as focusing their efforts on the legislature, lobbyists also lobby the executive branch, the judicial branch, and the public. Second, monetary contributions to candidates (and political parties) are less common than many people think. The extant studies indicate that, although many state lobbyists do indeed contribute money to elected officials and political parties, monetary contributions are not all that important to most lobbyists. Contributing money to candidates is far less common than a slew of other, more mundane and less controversial lobbying techniques. Finally, the typical lobbyist does not specialize in one or a few lobbying techniques. Instead, he or she tends to use literally dozens of lobbying techniques to get the job done (Nownes and Freeman 1998a, 93; Newmark 2008b). This means using a variety of different techniques and meeting with a variety of government officials (and perhaps citizens).

Who Are the Lobbyists?

Thus far we have said little about the actual people who lobby state government. There are various types and categories of state lobbyists, and so they bring different assets and liabilities to the table and are perceived differently by state government officials and the public at large. These perceptions affect the extent of a lobbyist's ability to affect government decisions as well as the way a lobbyist accomplishes the job. Here, we divide lobbyists into five categories: contract, in-house, volunteer, government, and private individuals (see Hrebenar and Thomas 1987, 1992, 1993a, 1993b).

Contract Lobbyists. These are the "hired guns," lobbyists who "are not employees of a single organization, but instead have a number of clients" (Rosenthal 2001, 18). Contract lobbyists are the types of lobbyists about whom the public hears the most, primarily because their high salaries, cultivated connections, and presumed ability to influence government make good copy for news organizations. Some contract lobbyists are independent agents; others work for public relations firms, law firms, or consulting firms. Although contract lobbyists tend to receive more attention than other types of lobbyists, we estimate that they typically account for 15–20 percent of the lobbyist community in most states.

In-house Lobbyists. These lobbyists work for a specific organization. Many in-house lobbyists have duties and responsibilities "that extend beyond lobbying" (Rosenthal 2001, 18). In the ranks of in-house lobbyists are the executive directors, presidents, and employees of a plethora of organizations, including environmental groups, school board associations, state chambers of commerce, trade associations, state bar associations, and business firms. Today, in-house lobbyists account for as much as 45–50 percent of the lobbyist community (Thomas 2004b, 152–153). Because the term *lobbyist* has negative connotations, in-house lobbyists often go by other honorific labels such as agent, government affairs specialist, executive director, or government relations specialist.

Volunteer Lobbyists. These lobbyists are often referred to as citizen lobbyists or cause lobbyists. They are usually ordinary citizens who represent single-issue, service provision, charitable, social welfare, or community groups on a not-for-pay basis. Many groups use volunteer lobbyists because they cannot afford professional in-house or contract lobbyists. Many others use volunteer lobbyists in addition to professional lobbyists, hoping that ordinary citizens can bring a certain legitimacy and immediacy to their interests and goals. We estimate that 10–15 percent of state lobbyists are volunteer lobbyists.

Government Lobbyists. Government lobbyists are employees of state, local, or federal agencies or entities who, as part of or all of their jobs, represent their agency or entity before state government. They often lobby to ensure that their agency or entity receives its "fair share" of the state budget. Examples of government lobbyists are the head of a state agency, the "legislative liaison" who works for a public university, or the mayor of a city or county. Technically, virtually all government lobbyists are in-house lobbyists, but we give them their own category here because they are unique among lobbyists—they represent one part or entity of government before some other part or entity of government. These lobbyists constitute about a quarter or less of state lobbyists.

Private-Individual Lobbyists. These lobbyists act on their own behalf, not on behalf of an organization as an official representative. Many political scientists do not consider private-individual lobbyists to be lobbyists at all. We mention them here because they are active and occasionally influential in the states. Private-individual lobbyists generally lobby for pet projects or direct personal benefits, or for or against a specific policy proposal of particular interest to them. Private-individual lobbyists probably make up about 5 percent or less of state lobbyists.

Lobbyists' Skills and Roles

Research suggests that different types of lobbyists have different skill sets. Typical contract lobbyists, for example, possess specialized knowledge about certain parts or processes of government (such as the budget process or the inner workings of a specific state agency), maintain close personal connections with state government officials, or have several areas of expertise (Rosenthal 2001, chap. 2). Many contract lobbyists are former government officials who learned about the political system and developed close ties with government officials while they were serving in government (Rosenthal 2001, chap. 2). Most contract lobbyists are facilitators of dialogue between their clients and public officials. And they often have considerable influence over how their clients disburse campaign funds. In fact, many contract lobbyists organize fund-raisers for candidates and work on behalf of candidates during election season.

The major political asset of most in-house lobbyists is an unequaled knowledge of a particular issue. An in-house lobbyist for a telecommunications firm, for example, may not be particularly well-connected politically and may not know the rules of the state legislature inside and out, but he or she probably knows more about the telecommunications industry and state telecommunications law than almost anyone else in the state capital. Like contract lobbyists, in-house lobbyists often make monetary contributions to candidates for state office. They also (if they represent membership organizations such as citizens' groups or professional associations) mobilize their members whenever possible to put pressure on government officials.

Government lobbyists are uniquely situated in state politics. They are often well connected (as government employees), have specialized knowledge of the government (especially the part of government in which they work), and possess tremendous knowledge of the policy area(s) in which they work. A lobbyist who works for a state university, for example, may know many state government officials personally, may know a great deal about how state education policy is made, and may have an encyclopedic knowledge of state higher education policies. Government lobbyists also often use their constituent groups to their advantage. For example, a lobbyist for the state department of education may work (unofficially) with state parent-teacher groups and other client groups (such as those representing handicapped or gifted children) to secure increased funding for public education. Utilizing constituents in this way helps government lobbyists overcome the disadvantage of not being able to rely on campaign contributions to help them get what they want.

Volunteer lobbyists usually rely upon moral persuasion, coupled with the mobilization of their membership, to sell their causes. For example, a volunteer lobbyist for an antiabortion group may meet with state legislators and argue that abortion is a sin. This volunteer may also encourage the group's members to send e-mails or letters to the same state legislators stating their opposition to abortion. Volunteers generally lack the insider status of the government lobbyist, the connections and inside knowledge of the political process of the contract lobbyist, and the technical expertise of the in-house lobbyist. Volunteer lobbyists do, however, have a certain amount of legitimacy compared with other types of lobbyists, and they may be able to make up for some of these deficiencies with hard work and perseverance.

Finally, private-individual lobbyists, unless they are state bigwigs (celebrities or moguls), have few assets at their disposal. Sometimes termed the "hobbyist," the private-individual lobbyist must rely primarily on perseverance and powers of persuasion.

Lobbyists' Personal Characteristics

Few studies take a close look at the makeup of the lobbyist universe in the states, but it seems clear that the typical state lobbyist is a white male in his forties or fifties, with government experience. We do not have particularly reliable estimates, but the evidence suggests that less than 25 percent of state lobbyists are women (see Nownes and Freeman 1998a), and very few (probably fewer than 10 percent) are nonwhite. In addition, the typical state lobbyist is well educated and well paid.

In short, in all fifty states people who are not white, not male, not particularly well educated, and who do not have government experience are profoundly underrepresented in state lobbyist communities. Many critical observers of state politics see this as a problem. An elite, monolithic lobbyist community, they maintain, is bound to underrepresent the views of large numbers of people, especially people who are already disadvantaged in society. This, in the end, might bias public policy toward the interests of well-off white men. Less critical observers argue that lobbying is like most other highly professional occupations—it is dominated by well-educated, affluent, ambitious individuals. Moreover, some observers maintain that well-educated and affluent Americans are not precluded from representing the interests of people who are not like them—poor people, for example.

The Bottom Line on Lobbying: Lobbying = Information

Despite considerable variation in both lobbying and lobbyists, there is one thing that virtually all state lobbyists have in common: they rely primarily on information to make their cases. A lobbyist's stock in trade is information. In other words, a lobbyist at work—whether lobbying a government official or the public—almost always provides information to the target of the lobbying, and the information is designed to convince the recipient that the lobbyist is right. The assumption that lobbyists are primarily information providers is at the center of political scientist John R. Wright's **communications theory of lobbying** (Wright 1996; see also Esterling 2004).

Wright (1996, 82) assumes that legislators have three goals. The first goal is reelection because a legislator who is not reelected to office cannot achieve any additional goals. Second, legislators want to make good public policy that benefits the people they serve. The third goal of legislators is to exercise influence within the legislature. Legislators, Wright notes, seek power within the legislative body because they want to be able to propose and pass legislation.

Legislators are forced to pursue these goals in a very uncertain and ever-changing environment. They are in a bind; although they have explicit and straightforward goals, they do not know precisely how to achieve them. According to Wright, this is where lobbyists come in. The job of a lobbyist is to provide government officials with information—information that will (it is hoped) affect the way these government officials behave. The information that lobbyists provide to government officials is designed to reduce uncertainty and help legislators learn how best to achieve their goals.

Information: What Kinds Lobbyists Use. Although Wright applies his theory only to legislative lobbying, his basic theory can be applied to virtually all state government officials as well as to the public. When state lobbyists lobby, they provide three types of information to the people they lobby: (1) political information about the status and prospect of a proposed or potential government decision; (2) career-relevant information about the implications of a particular course of action for a government official's political career; and (3) policy-analytic information about "the likely economic, social, or environmental consequences" of a particular course of action (Wright 1996, 88).

Using This Information. In 2010 the California legislature considered a bill that would have, among other things, banned single-use plastic bags in grocery stores and some pharmacies and retail stores across the state. Ultimately, the state assembly passed the bill, but the state senate rejected it. The arguments used by both sides nicely illustrate the role of information in lobbying.

According to Wright's theory, each member of the California state legislature asked himself or herself the following types of questions when considering how to vote on the bill: How do my constituents feel about this bill? If I vote for the bill, how will it affect my chances of reelection? Will the bill negatively affect the state's economy or unemployment rate? "Ban the bag" lobbyists representing environmental groups tried to convince legislators to support the ban by giving them the information they would need to answer the myriad questions they faced (Joyce 2010; Wood 2010). The bill, they argued, would improve the quality of the environment, at both the state level and the global level, because plastic bag pollution would be reduced. Their arguments also touched on electoral considerations. Lobbyists argued that supporting the ban was smart politically because there was a lot of evidence that Californians supported strong environmental regulations.

Lobbyists against the ban, some of whom represented plastic bag manufacturing companies, focused primarily on the economic effects of the bill. A ban, they said, would cost the state (and other states) jobs in the plastics industry. This was not only bad for the state, they argued, it was also hazardous to the electoral health of legislators who would face angry voters during a time of economic distress.

The battle over California's plastic bag bill provides some support for Wright's communications theory of lobbying. In short, lobbyists on both sides of the battle used information, among other things, to try to get their way. In most cases, lobbying is at least in part about providing information. Although many people tend to think of lobbying as bestowals of money, gifts, food, or booze, it usually takes the form of providing government officials with information. Even when lobbyists lobby the public through indirect lobbying, they rely heavily on information.

INTEREST GROUP POWER IN THE STATES

Early pluralist scholars, including Arthur Bentley (1908) and David Truman (1951), argued that a multitude of interests would exist in a democracy. To these scholars, it was natural for people to join groups representing their interests, and policy was therefore the product of competition among many groups. Robert Dahl (1956, 150) argued that "any active and legitimate group will make itself heard," though he also acknowledged that not all groups were equally powerful. However, even though pluralists argued that groups of all kinds could influence government decisions, critics argued that some groups were very powerful, while others were virtually powerless. For example, E. E. Schattschneider (1960) famously argued that some interests occupied a privileged political position, and policies often reflected a bias toward elites, business, and the wealthy. A few scholars in this mold even suggested that policies could be bought and sold like commodities (Mueller 1983). More recently, a more balanced view of **interest group power** has emerged. Neopluralist scholars, building on the work of Charles Lindblom (1977) and Terry Moe (1980), have noted that under some conditions groups are quite powerful, and under others they are not. Neopluralists agree with pluralists that a wide range of groups exist and could exert influence, but they also agree with their critics, acknowledging that some groups occupy an advantaged position (McFarland 2004). To summarize, neopluralists tend to acknowledge that although business interests are certainly advantaged, they do not always prevail, particularly if their wishes conflict with public opinion on salient issues. Influence, they argue, is contingent on political and environmental factors.

So just how powerful are interest groups? And under what conditions are they likely to get what they want from government? These questions are very difficult to answer, and assessing interest group strength and power is very difficult (primarily because each government decision has multiple causes). Difficulty also arises from the fact that group power can be viewed in several ways. For example, group power could be viewed as a specific group's ability to achieve its goals (individual group power). Group power could also be viewed in terms of the most powerful interest groups in a society (overall interest group power). The differences between these views are obvious when one considers that a specific group may be very successful in getting what it wants, but may be viewed as relatively powerless in the state overall. Similarly, a specific group may be widely perceived as very influential, but it may often lose political battles. A final way to view group power is to consider **group system power**—that is, the overall influence of interest groups relative to political parties and other political institutions and actors.

Individual Group Power

Appraising the power of an individual group is challenging, if not impossible, primarily because individual group power is the ability of a specific organization to achieve its goals as *it* defines them. The only way to truly assess individual group power is through an internal evaluation by the group itself. Unfortunately, this means that outside observers (such as political scientists) can never really know how powerful any single interest group is. One thing is certain, however: many interest groups in the states consider themselves powerful even though neither the broader public nor government officials view them this way.

There are several explanations for this disparity. First, some groups are only fleetingly active and thus may not be on the radar screens of many public officials over the long term. For example, an association of truck owners may work to defeat increased restrictions on truck weight limits. Such a group would probably do its work in relative obscurity, but nevertheless would consider its efforts successful. Second, although some groups are perennial players in state politics, others come and go as issues rise and fall on the government's agenda. For example, in 2001 and 2002 a group called the Committee on State Taxation registered to lobby in North Carolina because of a tax-related bill introduced in the legislature (Newmark 2008a). In 2003, however, the group did not register because the bill was not considered by the state legislature. Similarly, it is not unusual for coalitions of groups to form to address a specific issue, only to dissolve once the issue has been resolved. Such was the case in the fight over Proposition 8 (the California Marriage Protection Act) in California, which defined marriage in the state as between one man and one woman. Many of the coalitions that formed to lobby the public on the issue were no longer needed once the vote had been held on the initiative. Groups that are active only intermittently may appear to outsiders as ineffectual, whereas in reality they are inactive because either they have already received what they wanted from state government, or state government is simply not considering any issues of importance to them. Third, a group may focus on an issue that is far from public view and of minor public concern. For example, a professional association of beauticians may work with an executive agency to write regulations concerning the occupational licensing process. Rarely are beauticians seen as powerful interests in the states, but a professional association representing beauticians may be very successful in achieving its limited goals. Some groups involved in the regulatory process are very successful because they have captured their area of concern through the dependence of bureaucrats on their expertise.

Who's Running the State? Overall Interest Group Power

In our quest to understand overall interest group power, we owe a great deal to community power scholars such as Floyd Hunter (1953) and Robert Dahl (1961), who decades ago asked questions about who governed and sought a greater understanding of what interests were influential in communities. More recently, state interest group experts Clive Thomas and Ronald Hrebenar (1990, 1996, 1999, 2004) have made the most comprehensive attempt at assessing overall interest group power in the fifty states. Their rankings offer the best indication of overall interest group power in the states and likely provide a reliable indication of the most active interests.

According to the most recent rankings (Nownes, Thomas, and Hrebenar 2007), general business interests are the most powerful types of groups in the states, followed by teachers' organizations, utilities, manufacturers, hospitals, insurance-related interests, physicians, contractors, local governments, and lawyers. Although there has been some fluctuation in power since the 1980s, the power rankings have been fairly stable. Some interests, such as gaming, contractors and developers, tourism, and hospitals, have made gains over the years, whereas others, such as state employees, banks and financial institutions, and the oil and gas industry, have seen declines in their relative rankings.

What do these rankings mean collectively? On the one hand, they seem to confirm the views of pluralists, who hold that numerous interests are powerful. The rankings reflect the fact that many interests are represented by groups before state government. On the other hand, the rankings clearly show that there is a notable bias in the pressure system. In addition to business interests in the top spot, other business-related interests, including utilities, manufacturers, insurers, and contractors and developers, are in the top ten, seemingly confirming the suspicions of pluralism's critics, who argue that there is an elite, upper-class, business-oriented bias in the interest group universe. Typically, many of the most powerful interest groups in the states lobby for low levels of regulation, relatively low wages, and policies that lead to large profits. But before one accepts the most extreme version of the "business dominates everything" argument, one must keep in mind that not all business interests want the same thing. For example, the lobbying goals of a solar energy company are probably very different from those of an oil company. The solar energy company may want stricter regulations and higher taxes on fossil fuels (which may cause people to turn to solar), whereas the latter would be adamantly opposed to both. Moreover, business interests do not always get what they want (Page, Shapiro, and Dempsey 1987; Smith 2000), and it is likely that business group influence is mitigated by public opinion (Gray et al. 2004; Witko and Newmark 2005) and countermobilization by opposing interests such as labor unions. Finally, it is important to keep in mind that the power rankings are based on the assessments of public officials, scholars, and journalists, and so they may not reflect actual effectiveness in promoting legislation or furthering their causes.

Group System Power

Another way to conceptualize interest group power in the states is to consider the overall impact of interest groups and their general strength in a state. Thomas and Hrebenar classified states' interest group systems as dominant, dominant/complementary, complementary, complementary/subordinate, or subordinate relative to other actors and factors (Nownes, Thomas, and Hrebenar 2007). These other actors and factors include the strength of political parties, the strength of the executive branch, political culture, competition with other interests, and statutory or constitutional opportunities or constraints.

In dominant states such as Alabama, Florida, Hawaii, and Nevada, interest groups have a great deal of influence, more than other political actors. In the several rankings compiled by Thomas and Hrebenar (1990, 1996, 1999, 2004; Nownes, Thomas, and Hrebenar 2007), no state's interest group system has ever been categorized as subordinate or totally lacking in power. In the latest rankings, just over half the states (twenty-six) are categorized as having dominant/complementary interest group systems; interest group systems in fifteen states are placed in the complementary category. In states with complementary group systems, groups must work in conjunction with other actors to get things done; they find their abilities to influence government constrained by other political actors. Most often, groups are constrained by or must work with political parties, but they may also be constrained by or must work with a strong chief executive, active citizens, or other powerful groups. The reason that a state is characterized in a certain way is often a reflection of state politics, immigration and migration, demographic characteristics, and economic factors.

A Concluding Word on Group Power in the States

Although there are some common influences across the states, the impact of groups in a particular state is a product of the unique ways in which these influences interact and change. For example, since Democrat Brian Schweitzer became governor of Montana in 2005, interest groups appear to have become less powerful in the state because the governor has taken the lead on many issues and vetoed legislation popular with some business interests in his state. In some states, the power of certain individual groups and the perception of the power of individual interests may hold firm or even increase at a time when the same groups and interests are declining in other states. Thus, although some common denominators do exist across the states, changes in single group power, overall interest group power, and group system power often depend on the individual circumstances in a state.

CONCERNS AND PROBLEMS: REGULATION OF INTEREST GROUPS IN THE STATES

In 2005 lobbying at the state level became a billion-dollar business for the first time. Over 40,000 registered lobbyists representing 50,000 organizations sought to influence the 40,000 laws passed and $1.4 trillion in appropriations made by the various state legislatures in 2005 (Laskow 2006). Even though interest groups and lobbyists are indispensable to vibrant liberal democracies, including those in the American states, they can and often do have negative effects on a political system (Thomas 2004a).

Critics cite four specific concerns about interest groups in the American states. First, as vehicles of representation, interest groups are far from ideal in that they do not represent all segments of society equally. Their bias is toward the better-educated, higher-income majority culture (whites in most states), and toward the males in that population. Second, resources—mainly money—do matter, and those groups that have the most resources, particularly business firms, trade associations, and professional associations, tend to be the most successful in gaining access to state government officials. Third, extensive resources—including money, good lobbyists, and favored status with government officials—mean that some groups exert power out of proportion to their numbers of members. In some instances, a powerful interest group can even thwart the will of a much larger number of people. Finally, because the stakes are so high, some interest groups and lobbyists resort to illegal means to achieve their policy goals; unfortunately, some government officials will oblige them.

Regulations

Over the years, concerns about undue influence and corruption, as well as a desire to reach an improved state of democracy, have led to greater regulation of interest groups (Thomas 2004a). Some states have made substantial efforts to regulate the behavior of lobbyists and lawmakers, while others' efforts are little more than window dressing. For example, Wisconsin, Washington, and Connecticut have had relatively strict regulations on lobbying behavior in place for some time (Newmark 2005). Other states have increased regulation following ethics violations or illegal activities by lobbyists and lawmakers. Following scandals in South Carolina (1990) and Kentucky (1992), for example, these states adopted among the most restrictive lobbying laws in the country. Prior to their respective scandals, these states had among the weakest lobbying laws in the nation (Newmark 2005, 2008a). Other states have not been as aggressive in regulating lobbying activity, even after political scandals. As part of a series of bills dealing with ethics, Alabama limited lobbying spending, but the state still allows unlimited spending by lobbyists on food, lodging, and transportation for "educational functions" for legislators (Reilly 2010). Overall, Alabama's lobbying regulation is somewhat weak compared with that of other states. One of the barriers to states regulating legislative, lobbying, or ethical behaviors is that lawmakers often receive some benefit—monetarily, electorally, or otherwise—from lobbyists, and restricting these benefits is not in a legislator's interest. Accordingly, the legislature has little reason to act collectively because most lawmakers will benefit individually. Because many state lawmakers are not well compensated, particularly those in states with less professional legislatures, free dinners or paid-for social events are considered just the small perks of the job.

Still, the states have sought to regulate lobbying and interest group activity in a number of ways. For example, in all fifty states both lobbyists and interest groups must register with the secretary of state's office or some other government unit. To register, interest groups and lobbyists submit basic information about their organization and pay a fee to the state, which can vary from no specified fee listed in statute (which is the case in eleven states, including Arkansas, Delaware, and Hawaii) to $1,000 annually in Illinois (National Conference of State Legislatures 2010b). In Kansas, the amount ranges from $35 to $360, depending on the amount of money spent in a lobbying capacity. The norm, however, is about $100. Early research suggested that registration requirements would serve as a barrier to entry for new interests (Brinig, Holcombe, and Schwartzstein 1993). However, subsequent scholarship found evidence to the contrary (Lowery and Gray 1997). A modest fee of $100–200 and a small amount of paperwork do not stop an organization from registering as an interest group in a given state.

The states vary in how they define an interest group and whom they consider a lobbyist. These definitions determine whether lobbyists or interest groups must register with a state. For example, North Carolina includes *legislative lobbying* and *public employees as lobbyists* in its definition of a lobbyist, while states such as South Carolina and Washington include these criteria as well as *elected officials as lobbyists* and *administrative agency lobbying* as part of their definitions (Newmark 2008a).

All states require registration and basic reporting of lobbying activities, but they vary in the frequency with which they require the reporting or disclosure of lobbying activity and in the detail that must be provided. In the interest of openness, some states require both lobbyists and lawmakers to disclose to whom they give money and from whom they accept money or gifts. The logic behind disclosure laws is that lawmakers will think twice before accepting contributions from interests with questionable reputations. Liberal "good government" advocates, campaign finance reformers, and those concerned with public corruption argue that the public has the right to know where money comes from. In Oklahoma, for example, disclosure is required of any aggregate gifts valued in excess of $50 during a six-month period given to state officials or members of their families (National Conference of State Legislatures 2010b).

Other ways to regulate lobbying include prohibiting certain activities such as gift giving by lobbyists, or prohibiting lawmakers or other governmental officials from receiving certain things. Thus regulations often restrict the behavior of lobbyists, lawmakers, or both. Regulations of activity also vary across states, with some states such as South Carolina and Wisconsin restricting even giving a cup of coffee to a legislator. Nebraska restricts lobbyists from giving, and lawmakers from receiving, more than $50 in aggregate gifts in one month. Campaign contributions, however, are exempted. Contingency fees—fees charged only if the lobbyist is successful in achieving some desired goal such as the passage of a piece of legislation—are prohibited in forty-three states and limited by another three states (National Conference of State Legislatures 2010a).

Donors give to politicians either when they run for office or once they are in office. Campaign finance legislation also serves as a means of regulating lobbying activity; in this case, the regulation occurs when candidates run for office. And the states can differentiate campaign contributions from gifts given during a legislative session. Again, states may place restrictions on PACs that distribute funds to candidates.

Regardless of the definition of lobbying, disclosure requirements, prohibited activities, and campaign finance restrictions, it is necessary to consider the penalties for violating laws aimed at regulating lobbyists and lawmakers. This is perhaps the most difficult part of lobbying regulation to assess. Each state regulates lobbying and legislative activity by means of a number of constitutional and statutory provisions. Some states have harsh penalties; others give little more than a slap on the wrist for violations. Some states have minimum penalties; others have maximum penalties. Vermont, for example, has a $10,000 limit on civil penalties for each violation (National Conference of State Legislatures 2011). Whether or not this is a severe penalty is debatable.

Another factor that limits our ability to assess the states' efforts in regulating lobbying is that states can restrict the behavior of lobbyists and lawmakers either by specifically targeting lobbyists and lawmakers or by adopting general ethics laws. All states have ethics commissions or boards, but not all of them are centralized, and not all of them have the same jurisdiction and abilities. States must have the resources, legal authority, and gumption to pursue ethics concerns, corruption, or violations of lobbying laws. States with centralized ethics commissions typically are able to pursue investigations, whereas those without them may not have the personnel or funding to conduct complex investigations (Vaughan and Newmark 2008). At times, it boils down to an attorney general or district attorney who decides to invest limited resources in going after public officials or those who might influence them. And despite the fact that these law enforcement officials are supposed to be independent of those they investigate, there is the possibility that they have to decide to probe for information on the behavior of people with whom they interact regularly. Furthermore, the states vary in how well their officials behave and in the procedures for filing ethics complaints. Therefore, some attorneys general, ethics commissions, or district attorneys have a greater number of cases than others.

After serving in the state legislature for some time, lawmakers develop relationships with their colleagues. These relationships may give an unfair advantage to former lawmakers who leave public service to lobby for their own businesses or clients. Thus the majority of states restrict former lawmakers from lobbying for up to two years after they leave office (Kerns 2001/2009). These "revolving door" laws are designed to limit former lawmakers in using their connections in the legislature to influence policy. According to the National Conference of State Legislatures (2010c), eight states have a two-year waiting period, twenty-one states have a one-year wait, and four others have partial restrictions on when former lawmakers can lobby. Seventeen states, including Arkansas, Maine, Texas, and Vermont, have no revolving door laws.

Does It Matter?

Because of variations among the states in the extent and the stringency of enforcement of lobby laws, the question arises: Do these laws and regulations make a difference? We believe they do for two reasons. First, lobbying laws and other lobbying regulations unquestionably have made it easier for people to find out who is lobbying whom, how they are doing it, and for what. Disclosure increases the potential for public and press scrutiny of lobbying. The availability of more information for public disclosure has probably been the element of lobbying regulation that has had the most significant effect on state politics and government. Most of the regulatory issues just addressed come to light only when a public official engages in questionable behavior and the media report it. The majority of the public is unaware of the state laws regulating lobbyist and interest group behavior, and the media are the means by which citizens become aware of political misbehavior. When prominent officials are involved or the alleged transgressions involve serious criminal activity, the media certainly take note. The Tennessee Waltz scandal in 2005, for example, involved several Tennessee state lawmakers, at least one lobbyist, and bribery charges. In essence, the Federal Bureau of Investigation conducted a "sting" operation in which its agents pretended to be lobbyists for a company that needed legislative favors. The agents offered legislators money in exchange for their support of legislation, and several lawmakers agreed to take the money. This, of course, is against the law. Because of the officials involved and the severity of the accusations, the scandal generated a lot of attention in the state.

Second, lobbying laws and regulations have apparently affected the behavior of entrenched interest groups and their lobbyists in the states. Restraint in dealings with public officials, greater concern for their group's public image, and a higher degree of professionalism among lobbyists appear to be the three major effects. Lobbyists, especially those representing powerful interest groups, are today much less likely to use blatant strong-arm tactics than they were in the past because their activities are now closely scrutinized. Even dominant interests, such as Microsoft in Washington State, prefer to use low-key approaches buttressed by public relations campaigns. The challenge ahead for the states is to balance regulating access to decision makers with ensuring a democratic ability to have that access.

CONCLUSION

Politics in the states changes quickly. But there is one constant: interest groups. Interest groups are and always have been crucially important actors in all fifty states. In this chapter we have attempted to give you a broad overview of interest group politics in the states.

In closing, we wish to make a few observations. First, although interest groups have always been active in the states, it appears that there are now more groups in more states than ever before. Second, interest group communities in the states are more diverse than ever before. Today, in all fifty states (to different extents, of course), citizens' groups, charities, think tanks, government entities, and other types of interest groups lobby alongside the traditional business and professional association powerhouses. Third, lobbying in the states is more professional than ever before. State lobbyists are no longer good ol' boys or sleazy glad-handers (if they ever were). Many state lobbyists today are sophisticated professionals who rely on often sophisticated information gathering and lobbying techniques to try to get their way. Finally, all of this takes place within a complex political system populated by a multitude of entities and actors, all operating under certain constraints (or opportunities) provided by a state's statutory and constitutional law.

KEY TERMS

associations, 106

communications theory of lobbying, 118

direct techniques, 112

energy-stability-area (ESA) model, 109

group system power, 120

indirect techniques, 112

institutional interests, 106

interest group, 106

interest group power, 119

lobbying, 106

lobbyist, 106

state interest group system, 107

traditional membership group, 106

REFERENCES

Bentley, Arthur F. 1908. *The Process of Government: A Study of Social Pressures.* Chicago: University of Chicago Press.

Boehmke, Frederick J. 2002. "The Effect of Direct Democracy on the Size and Diversity of State Interest Group Populations." *Journal of Politics* 64: 827–844.

Bowling, Cynthia J., and Margaret R. Ferguson. 2001. "Divided Government, Interest Representation, and Policy Differences: Competing Explanations of Gridlock in the Fifty States." *Journal of Politics* 63: 182–206.

Bowman, Ann O'M., and Neal D. Woods. 2010. "Expanding the Scope of Conflict: Interest Groups and Interstate Compacts." *Social Science Quarterly* 91: 669–688.

Brinig, Margaret F., Randall G. Holcombe, and Linda Schwartzstein. 1993. "The Regulation of Lobbyists." *Public Choice* 77: 377–384.

Brisbin, Richard A., Jr., Robert Jay Dilger, Allan S. Hammock, and L. Christopher Plein. 2008. *West Virginia Politics and Government,* 2d ed. Lincoln: University of Nebraska Press.

Dahl, Robert A. 1956. *A Preface to Democratic Theory.* Chicago: University of Chicago Press.

———. 1961. *Who Governs? Democracy and Power in an American City.* New Haven, Conn.: Yale University Press.

Elazar, Daniel J. 1984. *American Federalism: A View from the States,* 3d ed. New York: Harper and Row.

Esterling, Kevin M. 2004. *The Political Economy of Expertise: Information and Efficiency in American National Politics.* Ann Arbor: University of Michigan Press.

Gray, Virginia, and David Lowery. 1995. "Interest Representation and Democratic Gridlock." *Legislative Studies Quarterly* 20: 531–552.

———. 1996. *The Population Ecology of Interest Representation: Lobbying Communities in the American States.* Ann Arbor: University of Michigan Press.

———. 2001a. "The Expression of Density Dependence in State Communities of Organized Interests." *American Politics Research* 29: 374–391.

———. 2001b. "The Institutionalization of State Communities of Organized Interests." *Political Research Quarterly* 54: 265–284.

Gray, Virginia, David Lowery, Matthew Fellowes, and Andrea McAtee. 2004. "Public Opinion, Public Policy, and Organized Interests in the American States." *Political Research Quarterly* 57: 411–420.

Hrebenar, Ronald J., and Clive S. Thomas, eds. 1987. *Interest Group Politics in the American West.* Salt Lake City: University of Utah Press.

———. 1992. *Interest Group Politics in the Southern States.* Tuscaloosa: University of Alabama Press.

———. 1993a. *Interest Group Politics in the Midwestern States.* Ames: Iowa State University Press.

———. 1993b. *Interest Group Politics in the Northeastern States.* University Park: Pennsylvania State University Press.

Hunter, Floyd. 1953. *Community Power Structure: A Study of Decision Makers.* Chapel Hill: University of North Carolina Press.

Joyce, Ed. 2010. "Calif. Enviro Groups Urge Passage of Plastic Bag Bill." KPBS.com, June 1, 2010. www.kpbs.org/news/2010/jun/01/calif-enviro-groups-urge-passage-plastic-bag-bill/.

Kerns, Peggy. 2001/2009. "Revolving Door Laws." National Conference of State Legislatures, Denver, January 2009. www.ncsl.org/default.aspx?tabid=15312.

Laskow, Sarah. 2006. "State Lobbying Becomes Billion-Dollar Business." Center for Public Integrity, Washington, D.C., December 20. www.publicintegrity.org/hiredguns/report.aspx?aid=835.

Lindblom, Charles E. 1977. *Politics and Markets: The World's Political-Economic Systems.* New York: Basic Books.

Lowery, David, and Virginia Gray. 1993. "The Density of State Interest Group Systems." *Journal of Politics* 55: 191–206.

———. 1997. "How Some Rules Just Don't Matter: The Regulation of Lobbyists." *Public Choice* 91: 139–147.

McFarland, Andrew S. 2004. *Neopluralism: The Evolution of Political Process Theory.* Lawrence: University Press of Kansas.

Moe, Terry M. 1980. *The Organization of Interests: Incentives and the Internal Dynamics of Political Interest Groups.* Chicago: University of Chicago Press.

MSNBC. 2004. "California Gives Go-ahead to Stem-Cell Research: Proposition 71 Provides $3 Billion in State Funding Over Next Decade." MSNBC.com, November 3. www.msnbc.msn .com/id/6384390/ns/health-cloning_and_stem_cell.

Mueller, Dennis C., ed. 1983. *The Political Economy of Growth.* New Haven, Conn.: Yale University Press.

National Conference of State Legislatures. 2010a. "Ethics: Contingency Fees for Lobbyists." National Conference of State Legislatures, Denver, June. www.ncsl.org/default.aspx?tabid =15351.

———. 2010b. "Lobbyist Activity Report Requirements." National Conference of State Legislatures, Denver, July. www.ncsl.org/default.aspx?tabid=15356#ok.

———. 2010c. "'Revolving Door' Prohibitions against Legislators Lobbying State Government after They Leave Office." National Conference of State Legislatures, Denver, November. www .ncsl.org/default.aspx?tabid=15334.

———. 2011. "Criminal Penalties for Public Corruption/Violations of State Ethics Laws." National Conference of State Legislatures, Denver, January. www.ncsl.org/default .aspx?tabid=15319#VT.

National Institute on Money in State Politics. 2011a. "Colorado 2010." www.followthemoney.org/ database/state_overview.phtml?y=2010&s=CO.

———. 2011b. "Lobbyist Map, Total Lobbyists for 2009." www.followthemoney.org/database/ graphs/lobbyistlink/lobbymap.phtml?p=0&y=2009&l=0.

———. 2011c. "National Overview Map." www.followthemoney.org/database/nationalview.phtml.

———. 2011d. "Nevada 2010." www.followthemoney.org/database/state_overview.phtml?y=2010 &s=NV.

———. 2011e. "South Dakota 2010." www.followthemoney.org/database/state_overview.phtml? y=2010&s=SD.

Newmark, Adam J. 2005. "Measuring State Legislative Lobbying Regulation, 1990–2003." *State Politics and Policy Quarterly* 5: 182–191.

———. 2008a. "Interest Groups and Lobbying in North Carolina: Density, Diversity, and Regulation." In *The New Politics of North Carolina,* ed. Christopher A. Cooper, and H. Gibbs Knotts, 85–105. Chapel Hill: University of North Carolina Press.

———. 2008b. "Strategic Lobbying: The Nature of Legislator/Lobbyist Relations." *Journal of Political Science* 36: 1–32.

Nownes, Anthony J. 2006. *Total Lobbying: What Lobbyists Want (and How They Try to Get It).* New York: Cambridge University Press.

Nownes, Anthony J., and Krissy Walker DeAlejandro. 2009. "Lobbying in the New Millennium: Evidence of Continuity and Change in Three States." *State Politics and Policy Quarterly* 9: 429–455.

Nownes, Anthony J., and Patricia K. Freeman. 1998a. "Female Lobbyists: Women in the World of 'Good Ol' Boys.'" *Journal of Politics* 60: 1181–1201.

———. 1998b. "Interest Group Activity in the States." *Journal of Politics* 60: 86–112.

Nownes, Anthony, Clive S. Thomas, and Ronald J. Hrebenar. 2007. "Interest Groups in the States." In *Politics in the American States: A Comparative Analysis*, 9th ed., ed. Virginia Gray and Russell L. Hanson, 98–126. Washington, D.C.: CQ Press.

Page, Benjamin I., Robert Y. Shapiro, and Glenn R. Dempsey. 1987. "What Moves Public Opinion?" *American Political Science Review* 81: 23–44.

Reilly, Ryan J. 2010. "Amid Bingo Bribery Scandal, Alabama Institutes Lobbying Reform." Talkingpointsmemo.com, December 28. http://tpmmuckraker.talkingpointsmemo.com/2010/12/amid_bingo_bribery_scandal_al_institutes_lobbying.php.

Rosenthal, Alan. 2001. *The Third House: Lobbyists and Lobbying in the State*s, 2d ed. Washington, D.C.: CQ Press.

Schattschneider, E. E. 1960. *The Semisovereign People: A Realist's View of Democracy in America*. New York: Holt, Rinehart and Winston.

Smith, Daniel A., and Caroline J. Tolbert. 2004. *Educated by Initiative: The Effects of Direct Democracy on Citizens and Political Organizations in the American States*. Ann Arbor: University of Michigan Press.

Smith, Mark A. 2000. *American Business and Political Power: Public Opinion, Elections, and Democracy*. Chicago: University of Chicago Press.

Thomas, Clive S. 2004a. "The Concerns and the Major Approach for Addressing Them: An Overview." In *Research Guide to U.S. and International Interest Groups*, ed. Clive S. Thomas, 357–359. Westport, Conn.: Praeger Publishers.

———. 2004b. "Lobbyists: Definitions, Types, and Varying Designations." In *Research Guide to U.S. and International Interest Groups*, ed. Clive S. Thomas, 151–154. Westport, Conn.: Praeger.

Thomas, Clive S., and Ronald J. Hrebenar. 1990. "Interest Groups in the States." In *Politics in the American States: A Comparative Analysis*, 5th ed., ed. Virginia Gray, Herbert Jacob, and Robert B. Albritton, 123–158. Glenview, Ill.: Scott, Foresman.

———. 1991. "Nationalization of Interest Groups and Lobbying in the States." In *Interest Group Politics*, 3d ed., ed. Allan J. Cigler and Burdett A. Loomis, 63–80. Washington, D.C.: CQ Press.

———. 1996. "Interest Groups in the States." In *Politics in the American States: A Comparative Analysis*, 6th ed., ed. Virginia Gray and Herbert Jacob, 122–158. Washington, D.C.: CQ Press.

———. 1999. "Interest Groups in the States." In *Politics in the American States: A Comparative Analysis*, 7th ed., ed. Virginia Gray, Russell L. Hanson, and Herbert Jacob, 113–143. Washington, D.C.: CQ Press.

———. 2004. "Interest Groups in the States." In *Politics in the American States: A Comparative Analysis*, 8th ed., ed. Virginia Gray and Russell L. Hanson, 100–128. Washington, D.C.: CQ Press.

Truman, David B. 1951. *The Governmental Process: Political Interests and Public Opinion*. New York: Knopf.

Vaughan, Shannon K., and Adam J. Newmark. 2008. "The Irony of Ethics Research: When the Sun Don't Shine on Enforcement." *Public Voices* 10: 87–95.

Witko, Christopher, and Adam J. Newmark. 2005. "Business Mobilization and Public Policy in the U.S. States." *Social Science Quarterly* 86: 356–367.

Wolak, Jennifer, Adam J. Newmark, Todd McNoldy, David Lowery, and Virginia Gray. 2002. "Much of Politics Is Still Local: Multi-State Lobbying in State Interest Communities." *Legislative Studies Quarterly* 27: 527–555.

Wood, Daniel B. 2010. "California Set to Ban Plastic Bags." *Christian Science Monitor*, August 30. www.csmonitor.com/Environment/2010/0830/California-set-to-ban-plastic-bags.

Wright, John R. 1996. *Interest Groups and Congress: Lobbying, Contributions, and Influence.* Needham Heights, Mass.: Allyn and Bacon.

Yackee, Susan Webb. 2009. "Private Conflict and Policy Passage: Interest-Group Conflict and State Medical Malpractice Reform." *Policy Studies Journal* 37: 213–231.

SUGGESTED READINGS

Print

Allen, Mahalley D. "Laying Down the Law? Interest Group Influence on State Adoption of Animal Cruelty Felony Laws." *Policy Studies Journal* 33 (2005): 443–457. A study of the effects of citizens' group lobbying on state animal cruelty policies.

Bergan, Daniel E. 2009. "Does Grassroots Lobbying Work? A Field Experiment Measuring the Effects of an E-mail Lobbying Campaign on Legislative Behavior." *American Politics Research* 37 (2009): 327–352. Reports the results of a field experiment designed to determine the effectiveness of a grassroots lobbying campaign in New Hampshire.

Cigler, Allan J., and Burdett A. Loomis, eds. *Interest Group Politics*, 7th ed. Washington, D.C.: CQ Press, 2007. An edited collection of essays about interest groups in the United States. Most of the articles concern interest groups in Washington, but one (the essay by Virginia Gray and David Lowery) is about interest group politics in the states, and several are general articles that contain information relevant to interest groups in the states.

Nownes, Anthony J., and Krissy Walker DeAlejandro. "Lobbying in the New Millennium: Evidence of Continuity and Change in Three States." *State Politics and Policy Quarterly* 9 (2009): 429–455. Presents results from a survey of lobbyists in three states, examining the tactics and techniques of state lobbyists.

Internet

American League of Lobbyists. www.alldc.org/. From this professional association for lobbyists, information for both the practitioner and the student of lobbying.

California Secretary of State. www.cal-access.ss.ca.gov/Lobbying/. Provides directories of interest groups, lobbyists, and lobbying firms registered to lobby in America's most populous state, as well as links to California's lobbying laws and regulations.

Center for Public Integrity's Iwatch News Service. http://www.iwatchnews.org/local/states-disclosure. Contains stories on ethics laws and the violation thereof in the states.

National Conference of State Legislatures. www.ncsl.org. A source of copious information on the structure and activities of American state legislatures.

National Institute on Money in State Politics. www.followthemoney.org. Presents information on campaign contributions and lobbying activity in all fifty states.

CHAPTER 5

 The Initiative Process

SHAUN BOWLER AND TODD DONOVAN

About half the states, most of them in the West, have some type of **direct democracy** process that gives voters a direct say in shaping public policy. These states allow voters to use the initiative process to draft laws and, if a sufficient number of signatures are collected from registered voters, place them on the state's ballot. As we shall see, each state using initiatives has a unique set of rules regulating the process, and so how the process affects state politics varies. In principle, however, the process should weigh heavily in state politics. It offers a fundamentally different vision of how government *should* work that significantly alters that way it in fact *does* work. In states with the initiative process, voters and politicians will adopt roles that are quite different than those adopted in states without the initiative. Where direct democracy processes are in places, voters are likely to be more active and politicians more constrained than in states that lack these processes.

About half—twenty-four—of the fifty states have the initiative process. In recent decades, voters in states that use the initiative process have decided on many critical matters of policy—with battles over several of these setting the stage for major policy debates at the national level. Antitax initiatives from the late 1970s, for example, foreshadowed the Reagan-era federal tax cuts of the early 1980s. More recently, initiatives in California, Florida, and Washington targeting affirmative action set the tone for national debate on the policy in the late 1990s. From 2004 to 2008, voters in several states considered the fate of controversial ballot measures that would ban same-sex marriage. Indeed, initiative efforts in the states are sometimes part of larger campaigns designed to shape the national agenda as much as set policy in a particular state. Initiative activists with an eye to the national stage seek to place their proposals on the ballot in multiple states to promote their causes. Same-sex marriage, term limits, and other issues have been part of this feature of initiative politics, with the result that they often spread beyond the borders of a single state (Magleby 1998).

That said, most of the proposals that reach a state's ballot are likely to be home-grown. This does not mean that all or even most initiatives are the product of the average citizen who rallies at the grassroots to challenge an established order. The initiative process is also used by political parties, incumbent politicians, candidates for office, wealthy individuals, and powerful interest groups (Smith and Tolbert 2001; Ellis 2002). In addition, several initiative states have spawned individual policy entrepreneurs who, though never holding office, use multiple initiatives to reshape their states' policy agendas (Donovan, Bowler, and McCuan 2001). In this context, over the last decade citizens in initiative states have voted on issues such as gun control, access to abortion, gay rights, services for immigrants, bilingual education, criminal sentencing, taxation, gambling, insurance reform, environmental protection, campaign finance reform, and term limits.

ORIGINS OF INITIATIVES IN THE UNITED STATES

The initiative process was first introduced in 1898 in South Dakota and first used in 1904 in Oregon.[1] A series of other states followed South Dakota and adopted the initiative—eighteen between 1898 and 1918—as disaffected social movements such as labor groups, farmers (the Grange movement, the Farmers' Alliance), single-taxers, Prohibitionists, evangelists, and good government "goo goos" pressed for a more direct say in their government (Lawrence, Donovan, and Bowler 2009). State governments that often seemed to these **Populists** and **Progressives** as too corrupt and too beholden to special interests were targeted for reform with the initiative and referendum devices. These direct-democracy tools were part of a larger set of reforms, including direct election of U.S. senators, direct primary elections, and restrictions on political parties that were designed to weaken the control that powerful economic actors had over government (Lawrence, Donovan, and Bowler 2009).

It is important to put these reforms in context. At the turn of the twentieth century, campaign contributions were unregulated, and bribery and graft were not uncommon in state legislatures (Schuman 1994; Sutro 1994). Powerful business interests were able to finance a political party or a coalition of legislators in exchange for favorable treatment. As one observer noted in the 1880s, the Oregon legislature consisted of "briefless lawyers, farmless farmers, business failures, bar-room loafers,

---

1. Nebraska had allowed use of the initiative in cities the year before, in 1897.

Fourth-of-July orators [and] political thugs" (quoted in Schuman 1994, 949). To Populist and Progressive reformers of that era, legislators could not be trusted to serve the public interest (Sutro 1994).

Cain and Miller (2001) distinguish between the Progressive and Populist roots of the initiative process both in terms of the different social bases of these movements and in terms of what each wanted from reforms. The Populists maintained that common people were trustworthy and competent but that elected legislators were neither (Cain and Miller 2001, 35). The explicit intent of the Populists was to take power away from incumbent politicians, vested interests, and party machines and give it to voters. Progressives were more sympathetic to the legislative process but wanted to "liberate representative government from [the] corrupt forces so that it might become an effective instrument for social reform" (Cain and Miller 2001, 36). In their study of the origins of the initiative process, Bridges and Kousser (2011) highlight the importance of the public itself in conditioning how careful politicians were in granting the reform. After all, the initiative process required legislators to give up power to the voters. Bridges and Kousser note that the initiative was more likely to be introduced when reforming politicians were confident that the voters using the initiative agreed with progressive policies.

A WIDE VARIETY OF INITIATIVE SYSTEMS

Each of the twenty-four states that currently allow initiatives has its own unique version of the process.

Most western states that adopted the initiative early on now allow citizens to draft **constitutional initiatives** as well as **statutory initiatives**.[2] Many of these states also require relatively few signatures to qualify measures. After 1918, the window of opportunity for the spread of wide open direct democracy in the United States closed. Only a few states adopted the initiative after this early period. Only Alaska included the initiative in its constitution when it was admitted to the Union (1959), and Wyoming (1968), Illinois (1970), Florida (1970), and Mississippi (1992) have adopted it since.

Being removed from the immediate context of the Populist zeal for direct democracy, each of these late-adopting states has a breed of initiative that is much more restrained than what is found in California, Oregon, and much of the rest of the American West. Three late-adopting states allow constitutional initiatives only, with severe restrictions on their subject matter or restrictive provisions for qualification (Florida, Illinois, and Mississippi). As such, initiatives are rarely used in these states.[3] In 2006 Florida voters passed an amendment requiring a 60 percent

2. Statutory initiatives change the law, not the constitution; constitutional initiatives change the constitution. Amending state constitutions is typically much harder to accomplish than making statutory changes. One reason is that initiatives that seek to amend constitutions have higher qualification requirements.

3. See Initiative and Referendum Institute (2010b) for evidence on use.

supermajority to approve future initiatives—a rule that may further increase the difficulty of passing initiative amendments there. Arizona's Proposition 112 (2010) was just one of a series of efforts aimed at limiting the initiative process. It tried to make the signature-gathering process a little harder, and other legislative proposals sought to force initiatives that changed spending to identify revenue sources. Although the public remains quite supportive of the initiative process in most states where it is used, state legislators are less enthusiastic (Bowler et al. 2001). There is evidence that public opinion in California—a high-initiative-use state—is becoming tolerant of reform proposals that might moderate initiative use (Baldassare and Dyck 2006). Proposals for expanding initiative use to additional states (such as New Jersey—see Holman 2002) have failed to advance.

Many of the early-adopting, Populist-inspired states have relatively liberal rules on qualification combined with provisions for constitutional and statutory initiatives. More than three hundred initiatives have appeared on California ballots since the state adopted direct democracy, and even more in Oregon. The number of ballot measures that have qualified across all states have steadily increased since the 1960s. After a decline in the 1940s and 1950s, the use of initiatives reached a new peak in the 1990s, when there were nearly four hundred initiatives on state ballots—far more than any other decade (Ellis 2002). The frequency of use across states varies considerably, with frequent users such as Oregon, California, Colorado, North Dakota, and Arizona offset by states such as Illinois, Wyoming, and Mississippi, which barely use the process. McGrath (2011) reports that from 1976 to 2004 an average of 2.6 initiative proposals were on the ballot during a two-year electoral cycle. But this average masks great variation because the number on the ballots ranged from zero to eighteen, depending on the state (McGrath 2011, table 1). The five states with the most frequent use of the initiative historically—in order, Oregon, California, Colorado, North Dakota, and Arizona—have averaged more than three initiatives per election since the Progressive era (Tolbert, Lowenstein, and Donovan 1998). Many, in fact most, of these initiatives failed. In 2010, for example, of the forty-two initiatives on the ballot, only 43 percent were approved, putting that year's success rate "slightly above the long run historical approval rate of 41%" (Initiative and Referendum Institute 2010a). And yet even though so many initiatives fail, they can have a powerful effect on the design of state political institutions and on the political agenda.

INITIATIVES AS A FORM OF DIRECT DEMOCRACY

While we refer to the "initiative process" throughout this chapter, several distinct types of direct democracy have been adopted in the United States. Although frequently lumped together, it is important to note the differences among them. The four main types of direct citizen voting on policy questions are the direct initiative, the indirect initiative, the popular referendum, and the legislative referendum. Under the **legislative referendum**, citizens vote on statutes or constitutional amendments, or both, that have previously been enacted by the state legislature or proposed by the legislature. This process allows for public feedback on major actions—most often constitutional changes or long-term bond borrowing plans—supported by elected officials. Use of legislative referendums is quite widespread, with nearly every advanced democratic nation other than the United States (Butler and Ranney 1994) and nearly every American state having some provisions for them—particularly for state constitutional matters.

Initiatives and popular referendums are another matter, and may be thought of as forms of direct democracy because control over whether a public vote is held rests outside of the legislature. Through the **popular referendum** process (also known as the popular veto), if enough voter signatures are collected, a bill previously approved by the legislature is put before voters for a binding yes or no vote. With the exceptions of Florida and Mississippi, every state that adopted initiatives also adopted popular referendums at the same time (Magleby 1984).

With **direct initiatives,** it is the initiative's proponents, rather than the legislature, who write the legislation that the public will vote on: qualified measures simply go straight to the ballot in the next election. A few states use **indirect initiatives**, which allow the state legislature to adopt a proposal once it qualifies but also gives lawmakers the option of coming up with an alternative measure to place on the ballot alongside the original initiative. Most states with initiatives have direct initiatives only. However, a few (Maine, Massachusetts, Wyoming) have indirect initiatives only. Five others—Michigan, Nevada, Ohio, Utah, and Washington—have both. The distinction between direct and indirect initiatives is not always precise. Depending on the state, the "indirect" initiative question may go on the ballot if the legislature rejects it, submits a different proposal, or takes no action. Alaska's and Wyoming's initiative processes are usually considered indirect. However, instead of requiring that an initiative be submitted to the legislature for action, they require only that an initiative not be placed on the ballot until after a legislative session has convened and adjourned.

INITIATIVES AND AGENDA SETTING

For our purposes, we treat direct and indirect initiatives as one category in which citizens or groups outside the legislature initiate policy proposals. We focus on initiatives rather than popular referendums because they have the greatest policy impact and generate the most heated discussions among observers of state politics.

Under the initiative process, citizens, interest groups, and others who are outside of the government decide whether to place a question on the ballot, when to ask it, and what the details of the law will be. The initiative grants the power to make policy directly to the citizens and is a direct expression of both majority rule and popular sovereignty in a way quite distinct from a purely representative form of government. Although the process may be distinct from representative institutions, it does interact with them. As we note later, Elizabeth Garrett calls states that have both direct and representative democracy "hybrid" democracies (Garrett 2005a, 2005b, 2005c).

SUBJECT MATTER

What, then, can voters decide on in initiative states? Most states follow legislative practice in limiting a proposal to a single subject. Some states add further restrictions.[4] Oklahoma, for example, has restrictions on how often a proposal can be made, and Mississippi imposes a string of restrictions on the kinds of policy areas that may be proposed. In general, though, most anything can be raised via the initiative.[5]

Although some states may review the proposal prior to circulating petitions to check for proper form, very few states allow amendment or revision of propositions without the proponent's consent. Of the twenty-four states that use the initiative process, only six have much of a pre-election review at all, and four more (Colorado, Idaho, Montana, and Washington) have a largely advisory process. In terms of other forms of legal review only, Florida's court has been known to regularly nullify initiatives on single-subject grounds, declaring that single-subject evaluations should be applied more rigorously to initiatives than legislative bills (Lowenstein 1995, 282). Since 2000, however, state courts in California, Colorado, Nevada, and Oregon have become more rigid in the application of their state's single-subject requirements (Miller 2009). At times, this has meant that a single initiative must be split into several questions that are put before voters (Ellis 2002, 144–146; also see the discussion in the *Columbia Law Review* on the difficulty of defining the "subject" of an initiative with any precision (Cooter and Gilbert, 2010; Hasen and Matsusaka 2010).

In summary, there are few limits on the kinds of issues that can reach the ballot—from taxation through issues such as the death penalty, regulation of euthanasia, abortion, drug use, rights for gays and lesbians, and prohibitions on the hunting of specific animals (such as wolves and mountain lions). A wide assortment of animal welfare measures have appeared on ballots recently, including measures in California banning the consumption of horsemeat and regulating the treatment of calves, egg-laying hens, and pregnant pigs; an Oklahoma initiative banning cockfighting; and a constitutional initiative in Florida to protect pregnant pigs (all four of these were approved). Other issues reaching the ballot are clearly designed to limit what legislators can do: issues such as term limits, spending limits, and campaign finance reforms. Many of these are such polarizing matters that incumbent legislators may not wish to have floor votes on them, whereas others are often matters that many self-interested incumbents might resist.

---

4. For a list of restrictions, see National Conference of State Legislatures (2006).
5. A few states prohibit measures dealing with the judiciary, bills of rights, or tax questions.

Throughout the twentieth century, a surprising degree of stability existed in the subject matter on which voters were asked to decide (Magleby 1994; see also Tolbert, Grummel, and Smith 2001). The most common types of initiatives since 1980 have been governmental reform measures such as term limits and campaign finance regulation (23 percent) and taxation questions (22 percent). Social and moral issues (17 percent) and environmental measures (11 percent) are the next most common types of questions (Magleby 1994; Tolbert, Grummel, and Smith 2001). Apart from an upsurge in the proportion of measures dealing with the environment and a slight decline in the proportion dealing with governmental reform, the general subject matter on ballots at the end of the 1990s was relatively similar to that appearing in the early decades of the twentieth century.

GETTING ON THE BALLOT

The actual impact of an initiative on state politics may depend on how easy the initiative process is to use and on the nature of the demands of interest groups in a state. There is considerable variation in how easy it is for citizens to use the process across the twenty-four states that have some version of direct democracy. Independent of ease, there is also considerable variation in the level of demand for initiatives in each state. Putting aside for a moment the state-specific details of qualification procedures,[6] most states share four basic steps in the initiative process:

1. A proposal is drafted by proponents.
2. The proposal is forwarded to a state office for review (usually for form, not legal content). An official title and summary of the measure are issued (a few states allow proponents to write the title).
3. Proponents circulate petitions that include the title, a summary, and text of the law for registered voters to sign.
4. A state office verifies that the correct number of signatures has been gathered. If so, the proposal goes to the ballot.

These steps may sound relatively straightforward, but their actual practice can raise some quite difficult issues.

Take, for example, the first two steps: drafting and filing a proposal. It is important to underscore that, at least in certain states, anyone with a few spare dollars can submit a proposal on just about any topic—indeed, in the state of Washington anyone with just $5 and a bee in the bonnet can start the initiative process. Far more proposals are thus submitted for title and summary than ever qualify for the ballot. Although many commentators have expressed doubts about the advisability of a process in which anyone with a few dollars can make a policy proposal, it is true

---

6. For a more detailed discussion of California's initiative process, see "Initiatives," California Secretary of State, www.ss.ca.gov/elections/elections.htm.

that the costs and logistics of collecting signatures weed out all but the best funded and best organized proponents.

Important differences can be found across states in the qualification stage, when petitions are circulated for signatures. Most states require a minimum number of signatures, expressed in terms of a percentage of the votes cast for governor in the previous election. This percentage ranges from 3 percent in Massachusetts to 15 percent in Arizona. Some states also have requirements about the origins of the signatures: they cannot come simply from one area or city but from a broad area, usually defined in terms of counties. Nebraska requires that 5 percent of signatures come from at least two-fifths of the counties, and Wyoming requires signatures from two-thirds of all counties. States vary, too, in how much time is allowed to gather signatures. Although some states allow more than a year (Missouri, Utah), Oregon has a fairly stringent ninety-day time limit for collecting signatures.

In general, the percentage thresholds for collecting signatures were put into place when the initiative process was first adopted, but as the populations of states have grown over the last century, so too have the raw numbers of signatures required. But time limits for circulation have not changed. Thus, whereas in 1900 it might have taken fewer than 170 signatures a day to qualify in a state with 250,000 voters, today it would require more than 1,000 signatures a day if that same state has 1.6 million voters.[7] In some states, the pace of signature collection now makes it difficult for any proposal to reach the ballot unless proponents pay professional petition firms to collect signatures for them. This situation has led some observers to argue that an "initiative industrial complex" has subverted the Populists' vision of the initiative process. But in fact the use of paid signature collectors (Beard and Schultz 1914) and professional initiative campaign staffs (McCuan et al. 1998) has been part of the process in some states since early in the twentieth century. It should come as no surprise that businesses expert in gathering signatures originated in California and that they export their services to initiative proponents in other states. These companies, along with other, non-California firms, hire subcontractors who employ temporary workers to gather the signatures. Some of these petition management firms advertise that they will guarantee qualification—for a set price. A typical qualification effort might cost $1–2 per signature. In fact, it could cost over $1 million to put a proposal on the California ballot. Even in a smaller state such as Washington or Oregon, the cost may approach $300,000.

Several states, including Washington and Colorado, passed laws banning the use of paid signature gathering. In 1988 the U.S. Supreme Court overturned these laws in *Meyer v. Grant*, 486 U.S. 414, arguing that the First Amendment protected paid petitioning as a form of political speech. It is little wonder, then, that most proposals fail to make it to the ballot, and that those that do qualify require financial

7. This example reflects the situation in Oregon, assuming a 6 percent signature requirement and a ninety-day time frame.

backing by wealthy groups (unions, professional associations, or trade groups) or wealthy individuals who act as patrons for a group promoting some policy. Indeed, many observers argue that as qualification costs increase only special interests and the wealthy will be able to get their measures on the ballot in many states (see Schrag 1998; Broder 2000; Haskell 2001; Ellis 2002). Examples of the wealthy groups include Microsoft cofounder Paul Allen, who paid for a school choice measure in Washington, and billionaire financier George Soros, who has spent hundreds of thousands of dollars supporting medical marijuana initiatives in several states such as Arizona, California, Colorado, and Nevada.

As for the signature-gathering process itself, the states vary in their requirements. In California, for example, those who wish to get a constitutional initiative amendment on the ballot have to gather signatures equivalent to 8 percent of the number of votes for governor (5 percent for a statutory initiative). As of 2008, this meant they had to gather approximately 694,000 valid signatures (434,000 for statutory initiatives) within 150 days. Organizing such an effort is a huge task in and of itself. It is made harder by the fact that many signatures turn out to be invalid. People may sign joke names, or they may not be registered voters. Initiative proponents must therefore "over-gather" signatures, and in California they typically must turn in 1.1 million total signatures in order to secure the 694,000 valid signatures needed to qualify for the ballot. It is not surprising, then, that the vast majority of initiative proposals fail to qualify and therefore fail to make it onto the California ballot—that is, even after drafting a proposal, giving it to the secretary of state's office, paying California's $200 fee, and starting a petition drive, the overwhelming majority of proposals never receive enough signatures to reach the ballot. During Oregon's 2000 election cycle, for example, petitioners filed 166 proposals—one-quarter of which were filed by Oregon Taxpayers United. Yet only twenty-six measures appeared on the ballot (meaning that 84 percent of proposals did not even qualify for the ballot).

Some states are much more frequent users of the initiative than others, which in part reflects the limits placed on the use of initiatives. States that impose geographical restrictions on where signatures come from or that limit the scope of the initiative's subject matter—Illinois is especially restrictive—reduce the number of initiatives appearing on their ballots. Banducci (1998, 117) demonstrates that signature-gathering regulations do matter. Even when several other factors are accounted for, significantly fewer initiatives emerge in states that require proponents to collect more signatures per day.

Table 5-1 is a simple descriptive index of how difficult it is to qualify for the ballot in each state. The index accounts for whether only statutes or only constitutional measures are allowed, whether the length of the qualifying period is limited, whether requirements are imposed for a geographic distribution of signatures, whether the proportion of voters' signatures required for qualification is relatively high, and whether the substance of what can be decided by initiative is limited.

Table 5-1   Index of Qualification Difficulty and Initiative Use

State	Year initiative process adopted	Qualification difficulty[a]	Number of initiatives from adoption to 2010	Number from 1976 to 1996	Number from 1996 to 2010
Oregon	1902	0	355	86	78
California	1911	1	340	98	102
Colorado	1912	1	215	46	57
North Dakota	1914	1	179	34	15
Arkansas	1909	2	120	16	10
Idaho	1912	2	28	13	8
Michigan	1908	2	72	18	13
Ohio	1912	2	77	18	14
South Dakota	1898	2	64	24	21
Arizona	1912	3	172	29	36
Massachusetts	1918	3	72	25	20
Missouri	1906	3	81	18	20
Montana	1904	3	77	27	22
Oklahoma	1907	3	85	11	5
Utah	1900	3	20	9	4
Washington	1912	3	163	39	51
Florida	1972	4	32	14	21
Illinois	1970	4	1	1	0
Maine	1908	4	52	23	21
Nebraska	1912	4	46	13	15
Nevada	1904	4	54	13	24
Alaska	1959	5	47	18	25
Mississippi	1992	5	2	1	1
Wyoming	1968	6	6	4	1

SOURCES: Assembled by the authors from data in David B. Magleby, *Direct Legislation: Voting on Ballot Propositions in the United States* (Baltimore: Johns Hopkins University Press, 1984); National Conference of State Legislatures, "Initiative States Ranked in Order of Use, 1898–1999," and "Initiative States Ranked in Order of Use, 1990–2004" (Denver: National Conference of State Legislatures, 2000, 2005), www.ncsl.org/programs/legman/elect/inrank.htm; and Initiative and Referendum Institute, www.iandrinstitute.org/data.htm.

a. Higher scores equal more difficulty. Points are added to the index if (1) only statutes or only constitutional measures are allowed; (2) the length of the qualifying period is limited; (3) a geographical distribution of signatures is required; (4) the proportion of voter signatures required for qualification is between 7 and 10 percent; (5) the proportion of voter signatures required for qualification exceeds 10 percent; and (6) there are substantive limits on the subject matter of initiatives.

Oregon, which has none of these limitations, tops the list with the most initiatives, and Mississippi, one of the most restrictive states, ranks near the bottom in initiative use. The correlation between this index and the number of initiatives qualifying in these states in the 1990s is moderately strong (Pearson's $r = -0.74$).[8] The imperfect correlation reflects in part that items in the index are weighted equally despite the fact that some—such as geographical requirements for signatures—may be much more of an impediment to qualification than others.

Liberal qualification rules are not the sole determinant of how many initiatives make it to the ballot. States with more people per state representative, with stronger

8. Pearson's r reflects the degree of linear relationship between two variables. It ranges from -1 to $+1$, where $+1$ reflects a perfect positive relationship, and -1 reflects a perfect negative one.

interest group systems, and with more professionalized legislatures are also likely to have more initiatives (Banducci 1998).

It is clear from Table 5-1 that initiative politics plays a much bigger role in western states, particularly the Pacific Coast states, where liberal qualification laws combine with relatively dense interest group communities. Eastern and midwestern states with initiatives tend to have more restrictive qualification rules, but they also may have political party organizations that play a larger role in structuring political competition, thereby reducing demands for the use of initiatives (Dwyre et al. 1994). Many more initiatives reach state ballots west of the Mississippi than elsewhere.

INITIATIVE CAMPAIGNS AND ELECTIONS

Getting onto the ballot is just the first major hurdle. Once qualified, a person or group sponsoring an initiative still has a campaign to wage. The campaign stage of the initiative process has attracted considerable attention from scholars. Since publication of the seminal works of David Magleby (1984) and Thomas Cronin (1989), initiative campaigns have probably been the most studied aspect of American direct democracy. A common argument is that well-financed groups are advantaged in the campaign process. Some take this critique further and argue that well-financed campaigns may manipulate voters into passing policies that they actually do not prefer. Criticism of the process at this stage thus falls into two broad categories: a critique of the role of special interests and a critique of the process for making too many demands on voters. We address each of these in turn in this section.

The argument that special interests dominate the initiative process is a plausible one. After all, if up to $1 million may be needed to qualify a proposal, let alone campaign for one, initiative politics obviously requires significant resources—resources that only groups may possess.

Elections in California give some insight into how much spending can be involved.[9] In the 2010 general election, a total of $147 million was spent by proposition supporters and opponents on their campaigns for and against nine initiatives on the California ballot that year, although the record remains the over $477 million spent in 2008 on ballot measures, including over $140 million spent to qualify and support (or oppose) initiatives that affected gambling on Native American reservations in California. Money does not, however, guarantee victory. Retailers outspent wholesalers in 2006 during a $12 million campaign over a Massachusetts initiative that would have allowed wine sales in supermarkets, but voters soundly rejected the retailers' initiative.

9. Much of political scientists' understanding of initiative politics comes from the Pacific Coast and Colorado. We know much less about the initiative experience in, for example, the midwestern states of Missouri and Michigan. In part this situation reflects the importance of the Pacific Coast. In part, too, it reflects the generally more data-friendly governments in those states.

These enormous sums are possible because the U.S. Supreme Court views initiative campaigns differently than it views candidate contests. In *Buckley v. Valeo*, 424 U.S. 1 (1976), the Court recognized that large contributions to candidates may create the appearance that a candidate for office is corrupt. This ruling allows Congress and the states a limited ability to override First Amendment concerns and regulate the size of contributions to candidates. By contrast, contributions to initiative campaigns are viewed as attempts at direct communication with voters rather than attempts to influence elected officials. The Court reasoned in *First National Bank of Boston v. Bellotti*, 435 U.S. 765 (1978), that voters cannot do any favors for the donor, so they found no state interest in limits on contributions to initiative campaigns. The *Bellotti* decision was the Court's first to explicitly extend free speech rights to corporations (Tolbert, Lowenstein, and Donovan 1998). Put simply, there are no limits on what can be spent on initiative campaigns.

Most initiative campaign spending is devoted to television advertising. How do voters respond? Because anyone with the money can bring an issue to the ballot, some initiatives may focus on the narrow concerns of a particular group or economic sector. But voters may be unfamiliar with the issues of interest to such groups—issues such as the regulation of health maintenance organizations, tort reform, securities litigation, regulation of car insurance, or the status of tribal casinos. In such circumstances, they may find it difficult to decide. After all, voters are simply asked to vote yes or no on ballot initiatives; there are no party labels on the ballot and few other cues to guide them when they vote. To complicate matters, in each election they may also be asked their opinion on several ballot initiatives.

This scenario would seem to be fertile ground for the impact of manipulative TV ad campaigns. Well-heeled special interests, the argument goes, can afford to get any issues they want onto the ballot. Once on the ballot, these same interests can afford to buy spin doctors, campaign managers, and the TV ads needed to get voters to vote for things they do not really want or that even harm the public interest (Schrag 1998; Broder 2000). It is, we should say, a plausible argument and has to be taken seriously by initiative supporters and opponents alike. We address this argument by breaking it into its two component parts: first, that economic interests—not citizen interests—dominate the process, and second, that voters are readily swayed by TV ad campaigns. We will examine each of these arguments in turn.

Do Economic Interest Groups or Citizen Groups Dominate the Process?

One way to assess the argument about the abilities of special interests to get issues on the ballot is to ask whether narrowly focused economic interests (such as banks, industry groups, corporations, and professional associations) outspend other, broader-based citizen groups. Another is to ask whether these economic groups tend to win the initiative contests they finance.

One of the most careful studies of the role of interest groups in the initiative process is Elisabeth Gerber's 1999 study *The Populist Paradox*. It is difficult, of course, to cleanly divide up the proponents and opponents of initiatives into "economic" interests and other, broader-based interests. Gerber defines *economic groups* as those whose members and donors are almost exclusively firms and organizations rather than individual citizens. Examples are the Missouri Forest Products Association, California Beer and Wine Wholesalers, and Washington Software Association (Gerber 1999, 69–71), and specific business firms such as casino operators and tobacco giant Phillip Morris. Gerber's study of contributions from eight states found that more than $227 million was contributed to ballot measure campaigns between 1988 and 1992, of which 68 percent came from narrowly based economic groups. One interesting finding was that a *negative* relationship existed between the amounts contributed by economic, professional, and business groups in support of an initiative and the probability that that initiative would pass (Gerber 1999, 110).

In another study, Gerber (1998) found that, although economic interests did outspend citizen groups, most of the economic group spending was defensive—that is, nearly 80 percent of economic group contributions were aimed at trying to defeat measures, while nearly 90 percent of citizen spending was in support of measures. Economic group spending in opposition is often well spent. Donovan et al. (1998, 90) also show that narrow economic groups regularly defeat initiatives supported by a broad, diffuse constituency, but Gerber (1998, 18–19) found that measures supported by citizens' groups and opposed by economic groups pass at rates higher than average.

When economic interest groups spend in favor of their own initiatives, they rarely win. Gerber (1999, 137) concluded that economic groups are at a disadvantage in initiative contests because they "lack the resources required to persuade a statewide electoral majority" to vote yes on many things. Another study looking at fifty-three California initiative contests from 1986 to 1996 found that the pass rate of propositions benefiting narrow interests was only 14 percent—a much lower figure than for propositions affecting broad-based groups (Donovan et al. 1998, 96). In short, although a high level of spending in support of an initiative does not appear to have a strong association with passage, a high level of spending against does. Banducci (1998) estimates that a dollar spent by the campaign advocating defeat of an initiative has almost twice as much impact on the eventual vote share than a dollar spent by the side advocating passage. So-called special interests do not often seem to write public policy via the initiative, but they are successful at blocking many proposals that might affect them (Lupia and Matsusaka 2004). However, interest group campaign spending is not irrelevant. A detailed study of spending in California in 2000–2004 found that a $155,000 increase in TV advertising (one hundred ads) was associated with 1.1 percent more support for the "yes" side in a campaign, while a corresponding change in opposition spending lowered support by 0.6 percent (Stratmann 2006; de Figueiredo, Ji, and Kousser 2011).

Groups do not just affect the initiative process; they also are affected by it. A wider range of interest groups mobilize in initiative states. The ability to propose legislation directly to the people also changes the opportunities that interest groups have to represent people, benefiting the interests of citizens who typically have less access to the legislative process than business groups (Boehmke 2005)—that is, the initiative may not just be for insider groups or special interests, but may well benefit grassroots groups as well.

Are Voters Swayed by Ad Campaigns? How Voters Decide on Initiatives

It is more than plausible to suppose that voters are vulnerable to misleading advertising by initiative campaigns. Research suggests, however, that voters may be able to make reasonable choices on initiatives. On some issues such as abortion or gay rights, voters are perfectly capable of making up their own minds. On more complex issues, they may rely on information cues to help (Lupia 1994; Bowler and Donovan 1998; Lupia and McCubbins 1998). One way they do this is by noticing elite endorsements (Lupia 1994; Bowler and Donovan 1998; Karp 1998). If, for example, voters see a prominent Democrat supporting a proposition, then Democratic voters are likely to support the proposition and Republicans oppose it. Of course, voting on the basis of simple cues does not establish that citizens understand the details of the proposals they decide on. It may explain, however, why so few examples of successful initiatives are later found to be unpopular with the voters who approved them.

But how do voters receive the cues? In ten states the secretaries of state mail voters a ballot pamphlet that lists each ballot proposal and includes arguments for and against the proposition (Dubois and Feeney 1992, 126). In those states, key information cues are given to voters in the pamphlet. For many, finding out who signed the arguments pro and con is the single most important source of information they use when making their decisions (Bowler and Donovan 1998, 2002b). A second way that voters may find cues about an initiative is through TV ads paid for by the campaigns advocating or opposing it. Surveys show that typical voters believe that initiative campaigns are attempts to mislead (Bowler et al. 2001, 370), and that voters discount the usefulness of political ads (Bowler and Donovan 2002b). However, these ads often do provide useful cues to voters. One study of initiative campaign TV ads from several states found that these ads often provide cues such as the names of sponsors or opponents as well as the names of prominent groups, newspapers, and politicians who have taken positions on the measure. Voters in Washington and California report using multiple sources of information when deciding on initiatives, and less than 2 percent of those who used TV ads relied on that information source exclusively (Bowler and Donovan 2002b).

Spending on initiative TV ads and other campaign material probably increases public awareness of the initiatives that are the subject of the ads (Bowler and Donovan 1998; Nicholson 2003; Stratmann 2006). Once an ad or series of ads is broadcast, then general awareness of the initiative question is raised, and at that point citizens might pay a little more attention to the news or the ballot pamphlet. This may explain in part why one study found higher levels of general knowledge about politics in states with prominent initiative campaigns (Smith 2002).

One of the changes over the last decade in elections generally has been the greater use of the Internet and social networking media. Campaigns of all varieties are increasingly targeting voters through Web sites and social networking sites such as Facebook and YouTube. Use of the Web may also offset the spending advantages one side enjoys in the campaigns for and against ballot initiatives.

Both of these aspects of Web-based campaigns depend in part on the way voters use the information they find on the Web. Figure 5-1 shows the results for California in 2010 comparing Google Insight search data in that state for the two governors (averaged together) and nine propositions (averaged together) to show the proportion of searches. Although the figure does not show the number of searches, it does give some indication of when searches take place. The similar patterns seen in other states suggest two points. First, voters do indeed search for information

Figure 5-1   Proportion of Google Searches for Gubernatorial Candidates and Propositions by Date, California, 2010

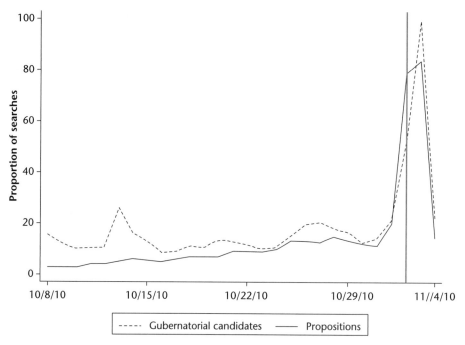

SOURCE: Google Insight, www.google.com/insights/search/#.

NOTE: Graph shows proportion of searches for gubernatorial candidates (average of searches for Democrat Jerry Brown and Republican Meg Whitman) as well as proportion of searches for nine propositions (Proposition 19 through Proposition 27) just past election day 2010. It does not show the number of searches.

about ballot propositions on the Web and so do indeed develop sources of information other than TV ads. Second, the pattern of the search is similar to that for candidates in that voters' searches for information seem to intensify closer to the election, but for propositions the searches seem to begin later than for candidate elections.

Initiatives and the Context of State Electoral Politics

Initiative campaigns can alter a state's political context or electoral mood by helping to define the major issues at stake, and candidates can take advantage of that fact. Classic examples are California Republican Pete Wilson's come-from-behind reelection in 1994 benefiting from an anti–illegal immigration initiative (Proposition 187). More recent examples are measures addressing same-sex marriage from 2004 to 2008. Work by Nicholson (2005) represents the best treatment yet of the relationship between the issues raised in initiative contests and the ways in which candidates try to use the issues for their own purposes (also see Donovan, Tolbert, and Smith 2008, 2009). Nicholson (2005) addresses as well the reverse effect: when the popular views of candidates are shaped by ballot initiatives. There is also systematic evidence that initiatives affect who participates in state elections. Recent studies have shown that initiative use increases turnout (Tolbert, Grummel, and Smith 2001; Tolbert, Bowen, and Donovan 2009). An analysis by Mark Smith (2001) suggests that highly salient initiatives have the greatest effect, particularly in off-year (nonpresidential year) state elections.

Journalists such as James Dao (2004) of the *New York Times* have credited George W. Bush's narrow reelection in 2004 (by a 118,000-vote margin in Ohio) to conservative voters mobilized by the state's same-sex marriage ban initiative. Most academic studies (Abramowitz 2004; Hillygus and Shields 2005; Donovan, Tolbert, and Smith 2008) stress that other issues were more important than same-sex marriage in the 2004 presidential race, and none finds that the Ohio initiative was decisive in Bush's victory. However, surveys found that concern about same-sex marriage was a stronger predictor of voting for Bush in states where same-sex marriage was on the 2004 ballot, and Ohio voters who said they came to the polls because of the marriage initiative were overwhelmingly supportive of Bush (Donovan, Tolbert, and Smith 2008). Some candidates use state initiatives to make the differences between themselves and an opponent explicit. In 2006 Democrat Claire McCaskill defeated Missouri's incumbent U.S. senator, Jim Talent, in part by embracing a stem cell research initiative that Talent opposed.

Daniel Smith has described how parties use initiatives to promote wedge issues they hope will split their opponents' base of support (Smith and Tolbert 2001). Major examples from the last decade are the issues of affirmative action and immigration initiatives. Republicans adopted and promoted a California initiative to restrict affirmative action (Proposition 209 in 1996) and another measure to restrict services to illegal immigrants (Proposition 187 in 1994). David Magleby

(1998) has highlighted the ways in which initiatives spread across state boundaries and, in some instances, even to national prominence as an example of the ways in which initiative politics at the state level can have implications beyond the state itself. Whether because they are planned by political parties or because state interest groups pay attention to and communicate with each other, similar measures often emerge in different states. In 2006, for example, eminent domain measures were on the ballot in twelve states, and tobacco and smoking issues were the focus of ten measures.

This discussion has focused on initiative campaigns and elections and the direct effects initiatives have on a state's political context. Initiatives also shape state politics in other ways, by changing how people see themselves as citizens.

EFFECTS OF INITIATIVES ON CITIZENS AND STATE POLITICS

A body of democratic theory proposes that people learn how to be citizens by making decisions in groups and by participating in politics (see Pateman 1970). Greater democratic participation may therefore have an educative role for citizens. Some scholars maintain that ballot initiatives, by forcing people to deliberate about public issues, are a form of participatory democracy that leads to a more engaged, informed, and interested citizenry. Direct voting on policy matters, this logic suggests, may increase discussion about public policy and, at least at a minimal level, force voters to think more about the policy issues on the ballot.

Recent studies find that there might be some merit to these ideas. As noted earlier, initiatives are associated with higher voter turnout. In fact, some voters will turn out and vote on an initiative contest when the candidate races on the ballot might otherwise have led them to stay home. In 2004 four of the five propositions in the state of Washington saw more votes cast than were cast in the race for lieutenant governor, and all five saw more votes cast than were cast for secretary of state and treasurer.

The presence of highly visible initiatives on a state ballot may also be associated with higher levels of general knowledge about politics. Smith (2002) found that voters have higher levels of factual knowledge about politics where initiatives are used more frequently. Bowler and Donovan (2002a) found that citizens in states with frequent initiative use feel more competent when participating in politics, are more likely to think that they "have a say," and are more likely to think that public officials care about what they think.

INITIATIVES AND MINORITIES

Many people worry that the initiative process could be used to harm minorities, particularly groups such as gays and lesbians and racial, ethnic, linguistic, and religious minorities (Gamble 1997; Hajnal, Gerber, and Louch 2002). Those who worry about repressive majorities point to a series of antiminority measures that have appeared on ballots. Initiatives have emerged proposing the repeal of affirmative action in California, Florida, Michigan, and Washington. And initiatives concerning immigration, bilingual education, and the declaration of English as the official language of the United States have appeared in several states (Citrin, Reingold, and Walters 1990). Initiatives and referendums to ban same-sex marriage appeared on thirteen state ballots in 2004 and eight more in 2006. One key question, then, is whether the initiative process as a whole is repressive of minorities.

Hajnal, Gerber, and Louch (2002) ask how often racial and ethnic minority voters are on the losing side when they vote on initiatives. If the initiative process is repressive, then ethnic minorities should be consistently in the voting minority. They find, however, that minority voters are no more likely to be supporting the losing side in an initiative contest than white and non-Hispanic voters. The reason for this is quite straightforward: members of ethnic minorities are concerned about the same series of issues as everyone else and not just a single issue. On some of these issues they are in the opinion majority; on others they are not.

Gay rights have been one of the more contentious areas of initiative politics and minority rights because politically conservative Christian activists have repeatedly sought to use the initiative process to attack gay rights (Gamble 1997). Early examples of these attempts are a 1988 California proposal to quarantine those with AIDS. From the 1970s through 2000, proposals of this severity mostly failed at the state level (Donovan and Bowler 1998). By moderating their proposals, however, proponents have had much more success with measures such as those calling for the defense of marriage. By the end of 2006, twenty-three states had approved constitutional amendments defining marriage as between a man and a woman. Only two states—Arizona and Colorado—rejected variants of these measures.

Regardless of whether antiminority measures pass or fail, they may have effects on the public's regard for minorities. By simply targeting a minority group, initiatives can change the public's attitudes about the group (or about policies that benefit the group), and mass opinion can become less tolerant of the targeted minority group (Wenzel, Donovan, and Bowler 1998). Cain and Miller (2001, 52) argue that the "limited evidence does suggest that the initiative process . . . is sometimes prone to produce laws that disadvantage relatively powerless minorities—and probably is more likely than legislatures to do so." Indeed, Haider-Markel, Querze, and Lindaman (2007) find that pro–gay rights laws are more likely to be approved by legislatures than by voters, whereas antigay outcomes are more likely under direct democracy than in a legislature.

INITIATIVES AND STATE POLICY

Some scholars posit that the initiative process benefits public policy because it then better reflects the preferences of voters. The effect need not stem from passage of an initiative, or its even reaching the ballot. Rather, the mere existence of the initiative process can change how legislators behave. If legislators know that there is a credible threat of passage of a popular measure by initiative, they might have greater incentives to pass some version of it themselves in order to maintain some ability to shape the eventual policy. Initiatives can also send legislators signals about the public's wishes on key policy matters (Romer and Rosenthal 1979; Gerber 1996).

In states without the initiative process, legislators face different pressures and may have fewer clear signals about what the public wants. Some studies find that certain public policies in initiative states—spending on certain state programs, abortion regulations, death penalty laws, and some civil rights policies—more closely match public opinion in those states than in non-initiative states (Matsusaka 1995; Gerber 1996, 1999; Arceneaux 2002). Others find no such effect (Lascher, Hagen, and Rochlin 1996; Camobreco 1998). Many of these studies examine different policy areas, however, and use different methods. Gerber (1996, 1999) finds that when the initiative process is present in a state, state death penalty and parental abortion notification laws better reflect that state's public opinion. Lascher, Hagen, and Rochlin (1996) have investigated a menu of different policies. Matsusaka (2001, 2007) argues that if the proper statistical models are used, there is evidence that states with initiatives have policies that more closely match voter preferences (but see Lax and Phillips 2011).

Initiative Effects on State Governance Policies

One policy area in which the initiative has a clear, direct impact is in what Tolbert, Lowenstein, and Donovan (1998) call **governance policies**. Voters in initiative states frequently pass measures that amend the political system itself. By giving groups outside the legislature a tool to craft policies, initiatives can advance policies that run counter to the self-interests of elected officials. States with the initiative process are much more likely to have adopted policies that constrain how legislators govern: term limits, supermajority requirements for new taxes, tax and expenditure limitations (Tolbert, Lowenstein, and Donovan 1998), and campaign finance reforms (Pippen, Bowler, and Donovan 2002).

The general effect of these reforms has been to give state politics a different character in initiative states. Supporters of the initiative process say this is just as it should be. One of the original purposes of the initiative as an institution was to make policy more responsive to voter demands. If, for example, legislatures kept increasing taxes beyond the willingness of voters to pay, then the initiative would allow someone to put in place mechanisms to restrain future tax increases—such as California's Proposition 13 (1978), Oregon's Measure 5 (1990), Colorado's Taxpayer Bill of Rights (TABOR) amendment (1991), or Washington's I-695 (2000). When voters grow weary of the initiative-induced fiscal constraints they place on their legislators, they may eventually vote to suspend the constraints—as Colorado voters did with the "TABOR Timeout" proposition in 2005.

Similarly, if legislators do not allocate enough money to a particular program, then groups outside the legislature can demand that money be allocated directly to that program via the initiative. Education unions have been skilled at promoting such initiatives. The California Teachers' Association, for example, passed Proposition 98 in 1988 to mandate that a fixed percentage of state general fund revenues go to K–12 education, and in 2000 the Washington Education Association sponsored the successful initiative I-732, which mandated pay raises for Washington State's teachers. It is important to remember that these mandates for increased spending and limits on revenue can constrain legislatures both in the present and potentially in the future. The extent of constraint depends on how (or if) a state constitution allows legislators to amend or repeal initiatives that voters approved. Term limits are another example of initiative-induced constraints on legislators. Initiative states tend to have term-limited legislatures; non-initiative states—with the exception of Louisiana—do not (Cain and Miller 2001, 49).

Initiative Effects on State Fiscal Policy

By opening lawmaking and constitutional amendment processes to those outside of the legislature, a state's political system can be reengineered by the visionary—and the vindictive. Direct democracy has given outsiders, particularly antitax advocates, the opportunity to institutionalize rules that constrain taxing and spending without having to specify where the government cuts will come. It also gives groups seeking their slice of the budget pie an additional point of access. This means voters may be asked to cut property taxes, increase tobacco taxes, guarantee a certain share of general funds for education, or authorize teacher pay raises and smaller class sizes. A single ballot could therefore contain choices for cutting some taxes, raising others, issuing public debt for specific projects, and increasing spending on specific programs. In most states, choices about increasing spending need not be linked to specific proposals about where the revenue will come from. Likewise, choices about cutting taxes typically need not be linked to specific programs that will lose funding. As time goes on, the disconnect between spending and revenue may worsen.

Little is known about how voters reason about such choices over time. The electorates in several states have voted on fiscal matters in ways that may seem on the surface somewhat contradictory. Washington voted to limit revenues in 1992 and to cut taxes in 1999; voters then approved dramatic increases for spending on education in 2000. While continuing to support property tax limits, the California electorate later mandated funds for K–12 education and approved a sales tax increase to fund police and fire protection. Likewise, voters in other states have said no to one kind of tax (usually property) while approving others (usually targeted sales taxes or lotteries). One reason for this may be that people tend to be more aware of, and hostile to, property taxes than sales taxes (Bowler and Donovan 1995).

The consequences of these **fiscal initiatives** on, for example, state budgets and bond ratings may be more enduring than the effects of other initiatives that pass

(Donovan and Bowler 1998; New 2010). All of this raises several important questions about voters, initiatives, and state fiscal policies: When given such a free hand in budgeting, do voters consider the fiscal trade-offs implicit in such choices? Are they as capable of budgeting as a legislature?

A fiscal crisis may result if they are not. Some see Oregon as an object lesson. Measure 5 in 1990 was followed by anti–property tax Measure 47 in 1996, which was intended to fix the problems in Measure 5. Two subsequent measures originating in the legislature sought to increase taxes to avoid budget cuts. But both of these measures (28 in 2003 and 30 in 2004) were defeated. Observers see Oregon's state and local finances as overly reliant on user fees and locked into rounds of fiscal crisis and poor or interrupted public services in part because a core of organized, motivated antitax policy entrepreneurs have held sway in initiative politics (Thompson and Green 2004). Others, however, see Oregon as an example of a state in which citizens simply prefer the combination of lower taxes and fewer services to higher taxes and more services.

The fiscal position of initiative states is thus likely to be different from that in non-initiative states, with initiative states imposing more constraints on politicians than non-initiative states. One problem with this is that legislators may have greater difficulty writing coherent budgets in initiative states. Peter Schrag (1998), one of the fiercest and also one of the most thoughtful critics of the initiative process, is especially scathing on this point. It may be that various initiative mandates and restrictions leave politicians with relatively little budgetary wiggle room, which may be especially problematic during economic downturns.

THE LEGISLATURE'S ROLE: IMPLEMENTATION AND AMENDABILITY

The initiative process undoubtedly constrains elected officials. But some state legislatures are more insulated from the effects of initiatives than others. If a state does not allow constitutional amendments, for example, or does not allow some types of fiscal measures to be passed through the initiative, then that state's initiative measures are likely to place fewer constraints on its legislature. Statutory initiatives are more readily amended or repealed by the legislature in some states (such as Colorado, Maine, Idaho, and Missouri), whereas other states require waiting periods, supermajorities, or both before an initiative can be amended. California is the only state in which the legislature can neither amend nor repeal an initiative statute. By contrast, where legislatures are more insulated from the initiative process, voters may pass a proposal, only to have it changed by a legislature later on.

Table 5-2 ranks states in terms of how much their legislatures may be insulated from the effects of the initiative process. This ranking is based on our nine-item index of the factors that insulate a state legislature from that process.

California—with constitutional amendments, no legislative ability to amend statutes, no restrictions on fiscal initiatives, and no indirect initiatives—stands out as the least insulated. Wyoming, Maine, and Massachusetts rank as the most insulated from the effects of an initiative. In states at the opposite end of the continuum from California, legislatures have the discretion of ignoring, rejecting, or modifying voter-approved initiatives.

The potential effects of initiatives on the legislature—and on policy—are better illustrated when Table 5-1 and Table 5-2 are considered together. For example, although the Arkansas legislature may have less formal control over initiatives that pass than the Oregon legislature (Table 5-2), it is easier to qualify initiatives in Oregon (Table 5-1). Meanwhile, with relatively easy qualification processes, high initiative use, and limited legislative insulation from the effects of initiatives, California and Oregon's version of direct democracy gives voters the most power. Not surprisingly, then, a considerable body of work considers the workings of the initiative in these two states.

Even without the power of formal amendment, legislators may still find ways around fully implementing initiatives they find too burdensome. This is the theme of *Stealing the Initiative*, by Elisabeth R. Gerber et al. (2001, 109). The authors take as a starting point the idea that "initiatives do not implement or enforce themselves." Some initiatives try to build in enforcement provisions that make it harder for politicians to "cheat" the popular will, but most measures have to leave some discretion to politicians either wittingly or, in the

Table 5-2 State Legislature Insulation from the Initiative Process

State	Legislative insulation index[a]
California	1
Arkansas	2
Arizona	3
Michigan	3
North Dakota	3
Oregon	3
Colorado	4
Idaho	4
Oklahoma	4
South Dakota	4
Utah	4
Washington	4
Illinois	5
Nevada	5
Florida	5
Alaska	6
Missouri	6
Montana	6
Nebraska	6
Ohio	6
Mississippi	7
Maine	8
Massachusetts	8
Wyoming	9

SOURCES: Assembled by the authors from data in National Conference of State Legislatures, *Final Report and Recommendations of the NCSL I&R Task Force* (Denver: National Conference of State Legislatures, 2002); and Elisabeth R. Gerber, "Legislative Response to the Threat of the Popular Initiative," *American Journal of Political Science* 40 (1996): 99–128.

a. Higher scores reflect the fact that the legislature has greater ability to affect initiatives and is more insulated from their effects. Points are added to the index (1) if the state has a single-subject rule; (2) if there are limits on the substance of initiatives; (3) if there are limits on fiscal initiatives; (4) if the legislature can amend or repeal initiative statutes; (5) if the legislature can repeal initiative statutes without a waiting period; (6) if the legislature can repeal initiative statutes without a supermajority; (7) if the state has no constitutional initiatives; (8) if the state has direct and indirect initiatives; and (9) if the state has indirect initiatives only.

case of badly drafted initiatives, unwittingly. Take, for example, John Matsusaka's finding that spending in initiative states is lower at the state level but higher at the local level (Matsusaka 1995). One explanation for this is that state governments can avoid citizen-initiated tax and expenditure limitations (TELs) by establishing new local jurisdictions—special service districts—that are not affected by earlier antitax initiatives (Bowler and Donovan 2001). In the 1990s, initiative states saw a flowering of special governments such as sewer districts, water districts, fire districts, and the like, in part in response to TELs imposed at the state level. Thus one way around TELs at the state level is to push taxing and spending down to counties and special governments. The result is that "the policy impact of most initiatives reflects a compromise between what electoral majorities and government actors want" (Gerber et al. 2001, 110).

Governing is different in initiative states, but this does not mean that the initiative process has supplanted the role of the legislature. Some journalists go so far as to suggest that initiatives have rendered some state legislatures meaningless. Yet the evidence suggests that the legislature is able to manage within the constraints imposed by the initiative process. Depending on whether one is a supporter or opponent of the initiative process, state legislatures can be seen as capable of either defending themselves or subverting popular wishes. After all, if most initiatives are defeated at the ballot box, or may be amended after they have passed, or not be fully implemented by state government, it is pretty clear that the critics of the process are greatly overstating the threat that initiatives pose to republican government.

Elizabeth Garrett (2005a, 2005b, 2005c) has coined the term *hybrid democracy* to refer to politics in the states that have the initiative process. Garrett is careful to note that this hybrid form of democracy may have some downsides, but there are upsides, too, in terms of how representative and direct democracy affect each other and are not isolated from each other (Garrett 2005c). As noted in this chapter, candidates can use ballot initiatives to help mobilize voters to turn out to vote, and ballot initiatives can help raise issues that color how voters see candidates. There is, then, an interrelationship between the institutions of representative and direct democracy and, indeed, between direct democracy and the courts.

THE COURT'S ROLE: LEGAL CHALLENGES

Legislators, political parties, and interest groups are not the only actors who influence the fate of initiatives. Initiatives are embedded in the system of checks and balances through the judicial process. Initiatives, like any other law, must be consistent with both the U.S. Constitution and the relevant state constitution, and must abide by the state's regulations on the initiative process as well.

As noted earlier, in almost all states the state courts play no role in evaluating measures before they are voted on. But they do play a substantial role once measures are approved by the voters. Courts tend to reason that no one has legal standing to challenge an initiative—in terms of constitutionality, conformity with single-subject rules, and other matters—until it has passed and actually has begun to affect policy. If state and federal courts did provide a preelection review of a measure's constitutionality, they would, they fear, be overstepping their role and affecting voter decisions. Because of this resistance by the state and federal courts to ruling on initiatives before elections, voters quite often approve measures that are later invalidated by the courts. In 2010, for example, California's Proposition 8 (2008) that sought to ban same-sex marriage was overruled in federal court (see Miller 2009).

Observers of initiatives disagree somewhat on what the courts' proper role should be. Advocates of the "juris-populists" approach argue that because initiatives are the direct, undiluted expression of popular will, the courts should give greater deference to initiatives than they might give to bills approved by legislatures (Cain and Miller 2001). In practice, however, state and federal courts treat initiative laws just like laws passed by legislatures. Ellis (2002) notes that some legal scholars argue that initiatives should be given even greater scrutiny than legislative bills because initiatives are not subject to the same checks and balances as other laws (that is, there is no possibility of a veto threat by the governor) and because initiatives have not been vetted through the rigors of the legislative drafting process. Others argue for greater court activity prior to elections to prevent campaigns on unconstitutional initiatives (see Haskell 2001; Ellis 2002).

Still other observers worry that some state courts, particularly those selected or reappointed via popular election, might be reluctant to overturn voter-approved initiatives out of fear that voters will punish them when they stand for reelection (Eule 1990). Some observers believe that, in practice, the courts have become too willing to strike down initiatives. Miller (1999) found that most state initiatives in the set of states he examined were challenged in court, with 40 percent overturned in whole or in part. This high level of litigation might reflect the willingness of those who lose at the ballot box to try and find a way to win through the courts and so give judges an opportunity to exercise power. Holman and Stern (1998) found that plaintiffs challenging successful initiatives in court are able to **venue shop**—that is, they can file cases in different districts of either state or federal courts in order to find those judges most likely to grant them a favorable ruling.

According to Mads Qvortrup (2001, 197), the "courts increasingly are encroaching upon decisions made by the citizens themselves." He notes that more than half of the recent initiatives in three states have been challenged by the courts, and over half of those challenges resulted in invalidation of the initiative. An increasing number of these sorts of challenges seem to come in federal rather than state courts, providing another instance of ways in which the initiative process within one state will have implications for, and interact with, institutions beyond that state (Magleby 1998).

Although it may be tempting, and even easiest, to see direct democracy in the states as a process not just distinct from but to some extent isolated from other kinds of processes and institutions, the works of scholars such as Garrett, Gerber, and Magleby remind us that the process both affects and is affected by the representative institutions of the state and by the broader federal system.

LONG-TERM EFFECTS OF INITIATIVES

All of this creates the potential for initiative-fueled cycles of change. Initiatives may alter state policy directly by providing an additional point of access for groups seeking to change the substance of what government does. Thus advocates of the decriminalization of drugs, physician-assisted suicide, increases in the minimum wage, or nearly any other policy could in effect do an end run around the legislature and take their appeals straight to the voters.

More important, initiatives have effects on state policies that are less direct but potentially more enduring. As discussed earlier, the existence of the initiative device may affect how legislators behave by increasing the likelihood that they will take note of the public's substantive policy preferences—that is, it gives groups an additional tool to use in pressuring legislators into passing something that might be popular with voters. In the long run, then, in some policy arenas legislatures in initiative states may come to adopt policies more in line with public preferences.

But direct democracy provides more than just another access point to the legislative process. It allows those outside of the legislature and the traditional centers of power to permanently change the institutions of government that structure how policy is made. Initiatives have been used to rewrite state rules about how judges sentence criminals, about how much a state can collect through existing taxes, and about how much the legislature can spend in a given year. Initiatives have been used to change rules about how legislatures approve new taxes, and initiatives have placed limits on how often legislators can run for reelection. These rule changes have consequences in the long run; they limit the range of policy options available to future legislatures.

This situation is particularly evident in the states that allow constitutional initiatives. To illustrate how radically different politics in initiative states are from, say, U.S. politics generally, consider who drives the process of amending the U.S. Constitution or other constitutions in non-initiative states. At the federal level, supermajorities of both houses of Congress are required to propose amendments that must then be approved by at least three-quarters of the states—usually by the state legislatures. At both stages, incumbent representatives control the process. In non-initiative states, a state constitutional amendment may be referred to the voters for approval, but again, the amendment is written by the legislature. Under these conditions, changes in rules about how politics are conducted are largely shaped by actors who have to live with the consequences but who also have a vested interest in those consequences.

CONCLUSION

Critics of the initiative process have advanced sustained critiques against the process as a kind of faux populism. Instead of making politics more democratic or more responsive to the will of the voters, they argue, the initiative process may simply give well-established interests yet another point of access to the system or tie up the policymaking system of the state. Consequently, there are consistent calls for reform. Most reforms to the process, however, are generated from within the state's political institutions and are often couched in terms of a desire to protect the "integrity" of the process and prevent corruption or the appearance of corruption (see, for example, Drage 2001). But many reforms seem intent on maintaining the integrity of the process by making it harder to use. The reforms that seek to limit the role of paid activists (as Colorado sought to do; see Drage 2001, 230) or give greater say to the politicians prior to a vote (as the California suggestions seek to do) also mean limits on propositions. Although attempts at reform seem—and quite possibly are—driven by the purest of intentions, some of the consequences of the proposed reforms might be to raise the hurdles higher for those who would use the process.

Attempts to limit the initiative process have met legal obstacles (Drage 2001). A bigger obstacle is a political one. Direct democracy continues to have a large appeal to voters. The process is hugely popular wherever it is employed. Perhaps, then, after the "third rail" of Social Security comes the "fourth rail" of direct democracy. Even as voters recognize that the process could be improved, there is little agreement on what should be altered: Signature gathering? The majorities required? A limitation on what can be passed? It is all too easy to limit the process until it is—as in Illinois and Mississippi—a case of direct democracy in name only. It is easy enough to neuter the process; it is harder to keep its good qualities. When voters are surveyed—whether in initiative or non-initiative states—they usually express overwhelming support for the process. To be sure, voters have some concerns, but the popular appeal of the process remains deeply rooted. Indeed, how could it not? One of the main assumptions of the U.S. Constitution is that of popular sovereignty, and one has to try very hard not to see the initiative process as a logical consequence of that assumption. As Americans continue to work out the implications of their Constitution, it seems reasonable to expect a widening, not a narrowing, of the use of direct democracy. American government is the people's government, and it is presumably for the people to decide how their government functions. Still, the question remains: Can direct democracy be too much of a good thing?

KEY TERMS

REFERENCES

Abramowitz, Alan. 2004. "Terrorism, Gay Marriage, and Incumbency: Explaining the Republican Victory in the 2004 Presidential Election." *The Forum* 2: Article 3.

Arceneaux, Kevin. 2002. "Direct Democracy and the Link between Public Opinion and State Abortion Policy." *State Politics and Policy Quarterly* 2: 372–387.

Baldassare, Mark, and Joshua Dyck. 2006. "The Nature and Limits of Support for Direct Democracy." Paper presented at the American Political Science Association, Philadelphia, August 31–September 3.

Banducci, Susan. 1998. "Direct Legislation: When Is It Used and When Does It Pass?" In *Citizens as Legislators: Direct Democracy in the United States*, ed. S. Bowler, T. Donovan, and C. Tolbert. Columbus: Ohio State University Press.

Beard, Charles, and Bril E. Schultz. 1914. *Documents on the State-wide Initiative, Referendum, and Recall.* New York: Macmillan.

Boehmke, Fredrick. 2005. *The Indirect Effect of Direct Democracy: How Institutions Shape Interest Group Systems.* Columbus: Ohio State University Press.

Bowler, Shaun, and Todd Donovan. 1995. "Popular Responsiveness to Taxation." *Political Research Quarterly* 48: 77–99.

———. 1998. *Demanding Choices: Opinion and Voting in Direct Democracy.* Ann Arbor: University of Michigan Press.

———. 2001. "Fiscal Illusion and State Tax and Expenditure Limitations." Paper presented at the State of the States Conference, Texas A&M University, College Station, March 2–3.

———. 2002a. "Democracy, Institutions and Attitudes about Citizen Influence on Government." *British Journal of Political Science* 32: 371–390.

———. 2002b. "Do Voters Have a Cue? TV Ads as a Source of Information in Referendum Voting." *European Journal of Political Research* 41: 777–793.

Bowler, Shaun, Todd Donovan, Max Neiman, and Johnny Peel. 2001. "Institutional Threat and Partisan Outcomes: Legislative Candidates' Attitudes toward Direct Democracy." *State Politics and Policy Quarterly* 1: 364–379.

Bridges, Amy, and Thad Kousser. 2011. "Where Politicians Gave Power to the People: Adoption of the Citizen Initiative in the U.S. States." *State Politics and Policy Quarterly* 11: 167–197.

Broder, David S. 2000. *Democracy Derailed: Initiative Campaigns and the Power of Money.* New York: Harcourt.

Butler, David, and Austin Ranney, eds. 1994. *Referendums around the World: The Growing Use of Direct Democracy.* Washington, D.C.: AEI Press.

Cain, Bruce E., and Kenneth P. Miller. 2001. "The Populist Legacy: Initiatives and the Undermining of Representative Government." In *Dangerous Democracy? The Battle over Ballot Initiatives in America*, ed. Larry J. Sabato, Howard Ernst, and Bruce A. Larson. Lanham, Md.: Rowman and Littlefield.

Camobreco, John F. 1998. "Preferences, Fiscal Policies, and the Initiative Process." *Journal of Politics* 60: 891–929.

Campbell, Anne. 1997. "The Citizen's Initiative and Entrepreneurial Politics: Direct Democracy in Colorado, 1966–1994." Paper presented at the Western Political Science Association meeting, Tucson.

Citrin, Jack, Beth Reingold, and Evelyn Walters. 1990. "The Official English Movement and the Symbolic Politics of Language in the United States." *Western Political Quarterly* 43: 553–560.

Cooter, Robert D., and Michael D. Gilbert. 2010. "Sidebar: Reply to Hasen and Matsusaka." *Columbia Law Review* 110: 59–62. www.columbialawreview.org/assets/sidebar/volume/110/59_Cooter.pdf.

Cronin, Thomas. 1989. *Direct Democracy: The Politics of Initiative, Referendum, and Recall.* Cambridge, Mass.: Harvard University Press.

Dao, James. 2004. "Same-Sex Marriage Issue Key to Some GOP Races." *New York Times,* November 4.

de Figueiredo, John M., Chang Ho Ji, and Thad Kousser. 2011. "Financing Direct Democracy: Revisiting the Research on Campaign Spending and Citizen Initiatives." *Journal of Law, Economics, and Organization.* http://jleo.oxfordjournals.org/content/early/2011/06/23/jleo.ewr007.abstract.

Donovan, Todd, and Shaun Bowler. 1998. "Responsive or Responsible Government?" In *Citizens as Legislators: Direct Democracy in the United States,* ed. S. Bowler, T. Donovan, and C. Tolbert. Columbus: Ohio State University Press.

Donovan, Todd, Shaun Bowler, and David S. McCuan. 2001. "Political Consultants and the Initiative Industrial Complex." In *Dangerous Democracy? The Battle over Ballot Initiatives in America,* ed. Larry J. Sabato, Howard Ernst, and Bruce A. Larson. Lanham, Md.: Rowman and Littlefield.

Donovan, Todd, Shaun Bowler, David McCuan, and Kenneth Fernandez. 1998. "Contending Players and Strategies: Opposition Advantages in Initiative Elections." In *Citizens as Legislators: Direct Democracy in the United States,* ed. S. Bowler, T. Donovan, and C. Tolbert. Columbus: Ohio State University Press.

Donovan, Todd, Caroline Tolbert, and D. Smith. 2008. "Priming Presidential Votes by Direct Democracy." *Journal of Politics* 4: 1217–1231.

———. 2009. "Political Engagement, Mobilization, and Direct Democracy." *Public Opinion Quarterly* 73: 98–118.

Drage, Jeannie. 2001. "State Efforts to Regulate the Initiative Process." In *The Battle Over Citizen Law Making,* ed. M. Dane Waters. Durham, N.C.: Carolina Academic Press.

Dubois, Philip L., and Floyd F. Feeney. 1992. *Improving the California Initiative Process: Options for Change.* Berkeley: California Policy Seminar, University of California.

Dwyre, Diana, M. O'Gorman, J. Stonecash, and R. Young. 1994. "Disorganized Politics and the Have-Nots: Politics and Taxes in New York and California." *Polity* 27: 25–47.

Ellis, Richard. 2002. *Democratic Delusions: The Initiative Process in America.* Lawrence: University Press of Kansas.

Eule, Julian. 1990. "Judicial Review of Direct Democracy." *Yale Law Journal* 99: 1504.

Gamble, Barbara S. 1997. "Putting Civil Rights to a Popular Vote." *American Journal of Political Science* 91: 245–269.

Garrett, Elizabeth. 2005a. "Crypto-Initiatives in Hybrid Democracy." *Southern California Law Review* 78: 985.

———. 2005b. "Hybrid Democracy." *George Washington University Law Review* 73: 1096.

———. 2005c. "The Promise and Perils of Hybrid Democracy." The Henry Lecture, University of Oklahoma Law School, October 13. http://clhc.usc.edu/centers/cslp/assets/docs/cslp-wp-048.pdf.

Gerber, Elisabeth R. 1996. "Legislative Response to the Threat of the Popular Initiative." *American Journal of Political Science* 40: 99–128.

———. 1998. "Interest Group Influence in the California Initiative Process." Background paper no. 115. San Francisco: Public Policy Institute of California.

———. 1999. *The Populist Paradox: Interest Group Influence and the Promise of Direct Legislation.* Princeton, N.J.: Princeton University Press.

Gerber, Elisabeth R., Arthur Lupia, Mathew D. McCubbins, and D. Roderick Kiewiet. 2001. *Stealing the Initiative: How State Government Responds to Direct Democracy.* Upper Saddle River, N.J.: Prentice Hall.

Haider-Markel, Donald P., Alana Querze, and Kara Lindaman. 2007. "Lose, Win, or Draw? A Re-examination of Direct Democracy and Minority Rights." *Political Research Quarterly* 60: 304–314.

Hajnal, Zoltan, Elisabeth R. Gerber, and Hugh Louch. 2002. "Minorities and Direct Legislation: Evidence from California Ballot Proposition Elections." *Journal of Politics* 64: 154–177.

Hasen, Richard L., and John G. Matsusaka. 2010. "Sidebar: Some Skepticism about the 'Separable Preferences' Approach to the Single Subject Rule: A Comment on Cooter & Gilbert." *Columbia Law Review* 110. www.columbialawreview.org/sidebar/volume/110/35_Hasen.pdf.

Haskell, John. 2001. *Direct Democracy or Representative Government? Dispelling the Populist Myth.* Boulder, Colo.: Westview Press.

Hillygus, D. Sunshine, and Todd G. Shields. 2005. "Moral Issues and Voter Decision Making in the 2004 Presidential Election." *PS: Political Science and Politics* 38: 201–209.

Holman, Craig. 2002. *An Assessment of New Jersey's Proposed Limited Initiative Process.* New York: Brennan Center for Justice at NYU School of Law.

Holman, Craig, and Robert Stern. 1998. "Judicial Review of Ballot Initiatives: The Changing Role of State and Federal Courts." *Loyola of Los Angeles Law Review* 31: 1239–1266.

Initiative and Referendum Institute. 2010a. "Election Results 2010: Tea Party Spillover." *Ballotwatch* (newsletter), November. http://iandrinstitute.org/BW%202010-2%20Election%20Results%20%2811-6%29.pdf.

———. 2010b. "Initiative Use." September. http://iandrinstitute.org/IRI%20Initiative%20Use%20%282010-1%29.pdf.

Johnson, Claudius. 1944. "The Adoption of the Initiative and Referendum in Washington." *Pacific Northwest Quarterly* 35: 291–304.

Karp, Jeffrey A. 1998. "The Influence of Elite Endorsements in Initiative Campaigns." In *Citizens as Legislators: Direct Democracy in the United States*, ed. S. Bowler, T. Donovan, and C. Tolbert. Columbus: Ohio State University Press.

Lascher, Edward L., Michael G. Hagen, and Steven A. Rochlin. 1996. "Gun behind the Door? Ballot Initiatives, State Policies, and Public Opinion." *Journal of Politics* 58: 760–775.

Lawrence, Eric, Todd Donovan, and Shaun Bowler. 2009. "Adopting Direct Democracy: Testing Competing Explanations of Institutional Change." *American Politics Research* 37: 1024–1047.

Lax, Jeffrey, and Justin Phillips. 2011. "The Democratic Deficit in the States." *American Journal of Political Science.* http://onlinelibrary.wiley.com/doi/10.1111/j.1540-5907.2011.00537.x/abstract.

Lowenstein, Daniel H. 1995. *Election Law: Cases and Materials.* Durham, N.C.: Carolina Academic Press.

Lupia, Arthur. 1994. "Shortcuts versus Encyclopedias: Information and Voting Behavior in California Insurance Reform Elections." *American Political Science Review* 88: 63–76.

Lupia, Arthur, and John Matsusaka. 2004. "Direct Democracy: New Approaches to Old Questions." *Annual Review of Political Science* 7: 463–482.

Lupia, Arthur, and Mathew D. McCubbins. 1998. *The Democratic Dilemma: Can Citizens Learn What They Need to Know?* New York: Cambridge University Press.

Magleby, David B. 1984. *Direct Legislation: Voting on Ballot Propositions in the United States.* Baltimore: Johns Hopkins University Press.

———. 1994. "Direct Legislation in the American States." In *Referendums around the World*, ed. David Butler and Austin Ranney. Washington, D.C.: AEI Press.

———. 1998. "Ballot Initiatives and Intergovernmental Relations in the United States." *Publius: The Journal of Federalism* 28: 147–163.

Matsusaka, John. 1995. "Fiscal Effects of the Voter Initiative: Evidence from the Last 30 Years." *Journal of Political Economy* 103: 587–623.

———. 2001. "Problems with a Methodology Used to Evaluate the Effect of Ballot Initiatives on Policy Responsiveness." *Journal of Politics* 63: 1250–1256.

———. 2007. "Disentangling the Direct and Indirect Effects of the Initiative Process." Working paper available at http://www-bcf.usc.edu/~matsusak/Papers/Matsusaka_Direct_vs_Indirect_2007.pdf.

McCuan, David, Shaun Bowler, Todd Donovan, and Ken Fernandez. 1998. "California's Political Warriors: Campaign Professionals and the Initiative Process." In *Citizens as Legislators: Direct Democracy in the United States*, ed. S. Bowler, T. Donovan, and C. Tolbert. Columbus: Ohio State University Press.

McGrath, Robert. 2011. "Electoral Competition and the Frequency of Initiative Use in the U.S. States." *American Politics Research.* http://apr.sagepub.com/content/39/3/611.short.

Miller, Kenneth P. 1999. "The Role of Courts in the Initiative Process." Paper presented at the annual meeting of the American Political Science Association, Atlanta, August.

———. 2009. *Direct Democracy and the Courts.* Cambridge, U.K.: Cambridge University Press.

National Conference of State Legislatures. 2006. "Initiative Subject Restrictions," August 3. www.ncsl.org/programs/legismgt/elect/SubRestrict.htm.

New, Michael. 2010. "U.S. State Tax and Expenditure Limitations: A Comparative Political Analysis." *State Politics and Policy Quarterly* 10: 25–50.

Nicholson, Stephen P. 2003. "The Political Environment and Ballot Proposition Awareness." *American Journal of Political Science* 47: 403–410.

———. 2005. *Voting the Agenda.* Princeton, N.J.: Princeton University Press.

Pateman, Carole. 1970. *Participation and Democratic Theory.* Cambridge, U.K.: Cambridge University Press.

Pippen, John, Shaun Bowler, and Todd Donovan. 2002. "Election Reform and Direct Democracy: The Case of Campaign Finance Regulations in the American States." *American Politics Research* 30: 559–582.

Qvortrup, Mads. 2001. "The Courts v. the People: An Essay on Judicial Review of Initiatives." In *The Battle over Citizen Law Making*, ed. M. Dane Waters. Durham, N.C.: Carolina Academic Press.

Romer, Thomas, and Howard Rosenthal. 1979. "The Elusive Median Voter." *Journal of Public Economics* 12: 143–170.

Schrag, Peter. 1998. *Paradise Lost: California's Experience, America's Future.* New York: New Press.

Schuman, David. 1994. "The Origin of State Constitutional Direct Democracy: William Simon U'Ren and 'The Oregon System.' " *Temple University Law Review* 67: 947–963.

Smith, Daniel A. 1998. *Tax Crusaders and the Politics of Direct Democracy.* New York: Routledge.

Smith, Daniel A., and Caroline Tolbert. 2001. "The Initiative to Party: Partisanship and Ballot Initiatives in California." *Party Politics* 7: 781–799.

Smith, Mark A. 2001. "The Contingent Effects of Ballot Initiatives and Candidate Races on Turnout." *American Journal of Political Science* 45: 700–706.

———. 2002. "Ballot Initiatives and the Democratic Citizen." *Journal of Politics* 64: 892–903.

Stratmann, Thomas. 2006. "Is Spending More Potent For or Against a Proposition? Evidence from Ballot Measures." *American Journal of Political Science* 50: 788–801.

Sutro, Stephen. 1994. "Interpretations of Initiatives." *Santa Clara Law Review* 34: 945–976.

Thompson, Fred, and Mark T. Green. 2004. "Vox Populi? Oregon Tax and Expenditure Limitation Initiatives." *Public Budgeting and Finance* 24: 73–87.

Tolbert, Caroline J., Daniel C. Bowen, and Todd Donovan. 2009. "Initiative Campaigns: Direct Democracy and Voter Mobilization." *American Politics Research* 37: 155–192.

Tolbert, Caroline, John Grummel, and Daniel Smith. 2001. "The Effects of Ballot Initiatives on Voter Turnout in the American States." *American Politics Review* 29: 625–648.

Tolbert, Caroline, Daniel H. Lowenstein, and Todd Donovan. 1998. "Election Law and Rules for Using Initiatives." In *Citizens as Legislators: Direct Democracy in the United States*, ed. S. Bowler, T. Donovan, and C. Tolbert. Columbus: Ohio State University Press.

Wenzel, James, Todd Donovan, and Shaun Bowler. 1998. "Direct Democracy and Minorities: Changing Attitudes about Minorities Targeted by Initiatives." In *Citizens as Legislators: Direct Democracy in the United States*, ed. S. Bowler, T. Donovan, and C. Tolbert. Columbus: Ohio State University Press.

SUGGESTED READINGS

Print

Boehmke, Fredrick. *The Indirect Effect of Direct Democracy: How Institutions Shape Interest Group Systems*. Columbus: Ohio State University Press, 2005. A rich study of how the existence of the initiative process affects interest group representation.

Gerber, Elisabeth R. *The Populist Paradox: Interest Group Influence and the Promise of Direct Legislation*. Princeton, N.J.: Princeton University Press, 1999. Examines the role of groups in initiative campaigns and concludes that it is difficult for economic groups to sell most of their initiatives to voters.

Nicholson, Stephen. *Voting the Agenda: Candidates, Elections, and Ballot Propositions*. Princeton, N.J.: Princeton University Press, 2005. Shows that initiatives affect the issues that voters use when evaluating candidates.

Smith, Daniel, and Caroline J. Tolbert. *Educated by Initiative: The Effects of Direct Democracy on Citizens and Political Organizations in the American States*. Ann Arbor: University of Michigan Press, 2004. Demonstrates how initiatives facilitate greater citizen engagement and participation.

Internet

Centre for Research on Direct Democracy. www.c2d.ch/index.php. A Web site that offers information about the initiative and referendum experience outside the United States.

Initiative and Referendum Institute. http://iandrinstitute.org/. Located at the University of Southern California, perhaps the best Web site on the subject of initiatives and referendums, containing not only a series of reports and information on them, but also a book section.

National Conference of State Legislatures (NCSL). www.ncsl.org/. Web site containing material related to state elections, including initiatives and referendums, as well as a wealth of other material on policy and politics at the state level.

National Institute for Democracy. http://ni4d.us/. The Web site of a lobby group that seeks to introduce the initiative nationwide and so provides a very positive view of the process.

Offices of the secretary of state. Ballot propositions in California seem to be the best documented, but the offices of the secretary of state in many states will also provide information that give a sense of what it takes to get a proposal on the ballot. For examples of current proposals, see these secretary of state sites: Arizona, www.azsos.gov/election/IRR/; California, www.sos.ca.gov/elections/; Colorado, www.sos.state.co.us/pubs/elections/Initiatives/InitiativesHome.html; and Washington, www.sos.wa.gov/elections/.

Public Policy Institute of California (PPIC). www.ppic.org/main/home.asp. Reports and studies related to the initiative process as well as a wealth of other material on policy and politics at the state level.

CHAPTER 6

 Legislative Politics in the States

KEITH E. HAMM AND GARY F. MONCRIEF

State legislatures fascinate students of institutions as well as students of individual behavior. As institutions, state legislatures present an array of organizational and structural arrangements. Indeed, there is probably more variation among state legislatures than any other institution of state government. For example, some legislatures are very large (the New Hampshire House has four hundred members), and others are quite small (the upper chamber in Alaska is composed of twenty senators, and the Nevada and Delaware Senates have twenty-one). The districts represented by individual legislators range widely in size as well. Representatives in Maine, Vermont, and Wyoming—and many representatives in New Hampshire—are from districts with fewer than 10,000 members, whereas each member of the Arizona, California, Florida, Illinois, New Jersey, New York, Ohio, Texas, and Washington lower chambers represents more than 100,000 people.[1] In fact, state senators in Texas (815,000) and California (930,000) represent more people than any member of the U.S. House of Representatives.

Political scientists often categorize state legislatures by their degree of professionalization based on session length, size of legislative operations, and salary. **Professionalization** refers to the capacity of the legislature to act as an effective and independent institution. But it also affects individual legislators and whether they view their legislative job as a part-time endeavor or a full-time career. State legislatures differ substantially on these and other dimensions (see Table 6-1 for some

1. See Squire and Moncrief (2010, 22–28) for more about differences in constituency and district magnitudes.

Table 6-1 Measures of Legislative Professionalization

State	Base compensation[a]	Estimated unvouchered allowance[a]	Estimated maximum compensation[a]	Session (months)[b]	Permanent staff[c]	Kurtz category[d]/ Squire's index
California	$95,000	$33,000	$128,000	9	2,067	Prof I/2
New York	80,000		80,000	12	2,676	Prof I/1
Michigan	80,000	12,000	92,000	12	973	Prof I/4
Pennsylvania	78,000		78,000	12	2,918	Prof I/3
Wisconsin	50,000	10,000	60,000	12	640	Prof II/10
Massachusetts	58,000		58,000	12	903	Prof II/7
Ohio	61,000		61,000	12	465	Prof II/5
Illinois	68,000	21,000	89,000	12	980	Prof II/6
New Jersey	49,000		49,000	12	940	Prof II/11
Florida	30,000		30,000	2	1,457	Prof II/15
Alaska	50,000	17,000	67,000	3	325	Hybrid/12
Arizona	24,000	4,000	28,000	3.5	598	Hybrid/8
Hawaii	49,000	9,000	58,000	3	355	Hybrid/9
Colorado	30,000		30,000	4	230	Hybrid/16
Texas	7,000	12,000	19,000	5/0	2,090	Hybrid/14
North Carolina	14,000	9,000	23,000	4	321	Hybrid/21
Washington	42,000	5,000	47,000	3	597	Hybrid/13
Maryland	44,000		44,000	3	562	Hybrid/19
Connecticut	28,000		28,000	4	490	Hybrid/17
Oklahoma	38,000	13,000	51,000	4	293	Hybrid/20
Missouri	36,000	12,000	48,000	4.5	474	Hybrid/18
Iowa	25,000	14,000	39,000	3.5	191	Hybrid/24
Minnesota	31,000	6,000	37,000	3.5	590	Hybrid/27
Nebraska	12,000		12,000	4	228	Hybrid/25
Oregon	22,000	10,000	32,000	5/1	298	Hybrid/23
Delaware	42,000	7,000	49,000	5.5	74	Hybrid/30
Kentucky	19,000	9,000	28,000	3.5	406	Hybrid/33
Virginia	18,000	6,000	24,000	2	391	Hybrid/32
Louisiana	17,000	17,000	34,000	2.5	666	Hybrid/26
South Carolina	10,000	12,000	22,000	5	270	Hybrid/28
Tennessee	19,000	17,000	36,000	4.5	277	Hybrid/37
Arkansas	15,000		15,000	2/1	405	Hybrid/42
Alabama	1,000	50,000	51,000	3.5	467	Hybrid/45
Vermont	10,000	21,000	31,000	4.5	60	Citizen I/41
Idaho	16,000	10,000	26,000	3	81	Citizen I/36
Nevada	9,000	8,000	17,000	4/0	293	Citizen I/29
Rhode Island	13,000		13,000	5.5	284	Citizen I/34
Kansas	12,000	14,000	26,000	4.5	150	Citizen I/31
West Virginia	20,000	9,000	29,000	2	219	Citizen I/35
Georgia	17,000	17,000	34,000	3.5	605	Citizen I/38
New Mexico	0	7,000	7,000	1.5	172	Citizen I/40
Mississippi	10,000	12,000	22,000	3.5	164	Citizen I/39
Indiana	23,000	12,000	35,000	3	239	Citizen I/22
Maine	12,000	7,000	19,000	4	169	Citizen I/43
Montana	4,000	5,000	9,000	3.5/0	127	Citizen II/44

Table 6-1 *(Continued)*

State	Base compensation[a]	Estimated unvouchered allowance[a]	Estimated maximum compensation[a]	Session (months)[b]	Permanent staff[c]	Kurtz category[d]/ Squire's index
Utah	7,000	10,000	17,000	1.5	114	Citizen II/46
South Dakota	6,000	6,000	12,000	2	55	Citizen II/47
Wyoming	4,000		4,000	2	39	Citizen II/48
North Dakota	7,000		7,000	3.5/0	32	Citizen II/49
New Hampshire	100		100	5	147	Citizen II/50

a. The figures in the third and fourth columns are estimates only and should be treated as such. They represent the estimated *maximum* amount if a legislator was eligible for and claimed every expense allowance and per diem possible. They were computed by Moncrief as 2010 base salary plus unvouchered expense allowances for those legislators outside the capital city area, as reported by the National Conference of State Legislatures (NCSL) and the Utah Legislative Compensation Commission (Supplemental Report, December 2010). For states with legislatures that meet every two years (biennial), or those with a mandated short session and long session every other year, the compensation figures are averaged. Figures are rounded to the nearest thousand, except for New Hampshire. Note that many New York legislators receive additional compensation for service in designated "leadership positions."

b. Accurate calculation of session length is always difficult for the following reasons. First, some states report as calendar days, others as actual days in session (legislative days). Second, depending on political context and issues, the number of days in session varies widely year to year in many states. And, third, the use of special sessions varies by year. For these reasons, reporting of specific numbers of days is somewhat misleading, and therefore we have opted instead to provide the average number of months in a session. For states that meet only biennially, we report figures for both years separately. For all other states, we average the two sessions, using data from 2009 and 2010 as reported by the NCSL.

c. Data are taken from National Conference of State Legislatures, "Size of State Legislative Staff: 1979, 1988, 1996, 2003, and 2009," www.ncsl.org/default.aspx?tabid=14843. The 2009 permanent staff are used here as the benchmark because they are likely to be the professional, full-time staff. Over 80 percent of all legislative staff members are in the category of permanent staff. However, in some states the session-only staff is a significant part of the workforce. States in which session-only staff makes up at least half of the total staff are Kansas, Nevada, New Mexico, North Carolina, North Dakota, and Wyoming.

d. Data are taken from National Conference of State Legislatures, "Full and Part-Time Legislatures," wwww.ncsl.org/default.aspx?tabid=16701. Karl Kurtz creates five categories of legislatures in descending order of legislative professionalization ("red," "red-light," "white," "blue-light," and "blue"). For our purposes, we designate these as Prof I (red), Prof II (red-light), Hybrid (white), Citizen I (blue-light), and Citizen II (blue). Numbers represent Squire's 2009 professionalism index rankings as found in Peverill Squire, *The Evolution of American Legislatures* (Ann Arbor: University of Michigan Press, 2012).

comparisons). For example, some state legislatures (Pennsylvania and New York) meet virtually full time, much like the U.S. Congress. Others (North Dakota and Montana) meet only a few months every other year.

Obviously, compensation for legislators is likely to be tied to the time commitment required of those legislators. California state legislators receive an annual base salary of $95,000, plus a per diem expense that can bring the total compensation package to at least $128,000. By contrast, state legislators in New Hampshire receive $100 per year for their work, and those in New Mexico receive no annual compensation at all, but are reimbursed for daily expenses.

The magnitude of legislative operations also differs considerably. One commonly used measure is the number of legislative staff personnel. Although the California, New York, Pennsylvania, and Texas state legislatures each employ over 2,000 people as staff, there are fewer than fifty full-time legislative staff members in North Dakota and Wyoming.

All of these differences matter in terms of the effectiveness and independence of state legislatures in policymaking. And they matter in terms of the types of people who are attracted to service in the state legislature. Put another way, the incentives and costs of legislative service are different in different states (Squire 2007). Because legislative professionalization varies by state, and because it has implications for both the institution and the individuals serving in the institutions, it is the focus of considerable research (see Squire and Hamm 2005; Kousser 2005; Malhotra 2006, 2010; Woods and Baranowski 2006; and Squire 2007 for recent examples).

Although there is marked variation in the professionalization of state legislatures, most are more professional today than they were a generation ago (Rosenthal 2009, 183–188). For example, many state legislatures met only every other year until the 1960s. Legislatures were viewed at that time as unrepresentative of the general public, controlled by so-called good ol' boys—older white males from rural areas. They met for only brief periods and were poorly staffed, ill-equipped, and generally appeared to be dominated by the governor or a handful of powerful interest groups. Today, all but four or five legislatures hold annual sessions, pay better salaries, and have bigger staffs than they did a generation ago. If one thinks of legislative professionalization as a continuum, almost all state legislatures have moved (some only slightly, some a great deal) in the direction of greater professionalization in the last thirty years.[2] Moreover, even the more part-time legislatures demand a greater time commitment than in the past. Not surprisingly, there is a strong relationship between the level of professionalization of the legislature and the time required of its members to fulfill their legislative duties (Kurtz et al. 2006).

Although it is true that virtually all legislatures have progressed along the "professionalization" continuum over the last fifty years, it is equally true that this trend has slowed—perhaps even reversed—in some states recently. California legislators' pay was cut by 18 percent, effective December 2010. The total number of full-time staff in state legislatures has declined.[3] Twenty states reported fewer full-time staff in 2009 compared with 2003—mostly a result of cutbacks because of the budget shortfalls experienced by states in recent years.

Just as there are important institutional differences today among legislatures, other significant differences have a bearing on the individual legislators from state to state. For example, the incentive structure for the individual legislator is different in a part-time, low-pay, low-staff legislature than in the more professional ones (Maddox 2004). There are also differences in what is known as the "opportunity structure" (Squire 1988).

The prospects for state legislators to advance to higher office vary significantly across the states. For example, the eighty members of the California Assembly have

---

2. King (2000, table 1) identifies four states that actually *regressed* on the professionalism scores between 1964 and 1994. They are Georgia, Massachusetts, New Hampshire, and New Mexico.

3. The National Conference of State Legislatures (NCSL) conducts periodic surveys of state legislative staff, and the most recent enumeration was in 2009. According to the NCSL, the fifty state legislatures have a total of 27,567 full-time staff. In 2003 the total was 28,067, and in 1996 the figure was 27,822. See National Conference of State Legislatures (2009b).

an abundance of other electoral positions for which they may run, including forty state senate seats, fifty-three seats in the U.S. House, eight state constitutional offices, and the mayor's office in several large California cities. Advancement prospects are much bleaker for the four hundred members of the New Hampshire House of Representatives, because the state has only twenty-four state senate seats, two seats in the U.S. House, and only one position elected statewide—the governor's.

Although the individual costs and benefits of legislative service vary from state to state, it is also true that today almost all state legislators behave more like professional politicians than they did a generation ago. And yet the extent of change is not uniform across all legislatures. As one might expect, the behavioral changes seem to be greatest in the more professional, careerist legislatures. Although many of the changes and improvements made to the state legislative institutions in the past generation are positive, it is clear that state legislatures are not held in particularly high regard by the general public. There are many reasons for this situation, including a lack of public understanding about how legislatures operate (Rosenthal 2009, 8–26; Squire and Moncrief 2010, 240). They are, indeed, complex institutions, charged with solving very difficult societal problems.

Another reason for this lack of regard is that candidates who run for legislative office often find it easy to campaign against the legislature itself. Candidates for governor rarely attack the office of governor but instead focus on the other candidates who are running for governor. Candidates for judicial positions (in many states judges are elected) do not rail against the judicial system but instead promote their own qualifications for the office. And yet candidates for the legislature often campaign against the "do-nothing" legislature, characterizing it as "controlled by special interests" and urging the voters to "throw the bums out." Over time, such rants cannot help but drag down the public image of the state legislature.

Finally, Americans have never been fond of the idea of politics as a career. But it is clear that it has become more of a career in many state legislatures over the last twenty or thirty years. By the late 1980s, legislators in some states were staying in office for longer periods of time than ever before (although probably not for as long as the general public seems to think). The electoral system appeared to be so heavily biased in favor of incumbents that challengers seemed to have little chance of winning a seat. The public reaction in many states was to support the movement to limit the number of terms a legislator could serve. Term limits, which are now the law in fifteen states, are discussed later in this chapter.

THE ELECTORAL ARENA

The nature of the electoral system affects legislative politics. Two important characteristics of the electoral system are the electoral formula and **district magnitude.** At the general election, virtually all states use a plurality (also known as first-past-the-post) electoral formula for choosing legislators. It is the simplest of all electoral formulas: whoever gets the most votes wins. District magnitude (the number of legislators chosen from each district) varies a bit from state to state. Most states employ single-member districts (SMDs) exclusively. However, some states use multimember districts (MMDs) in the lower chamber. The most common multimember arrangement is the two-member district, although a few states have districts with three or more members.[4]

Most of the MMDs are free-for-all districts, in which all candidates in the district run against one another. The two (in a two-member district) candidates receiving the highest vote counts are declared the winners. Some states employ **post-designate** (also known as position-designate or seat-designate) MMDs, in which the candidates must declare for which seat in the district they are running (for example, seat A or B). In effect, such systems operate as a series of single-member elections within the same district.

These characteristics of the electoral system make some difference (Snyder and Ueda 2007). There is some evidence that legislators representing SMDs are more likely to vote in accordance with the constituency median than are MMD representatives (Cooper and Richardson 2006; Bertelli and Richardson 2008). Furthermore, the role of political parties is probably greater in campaigns and elections in multi-member districting systems because members of the same party tend to run as a team. Historically, minorities (racial, ethnic, or the minority political party) were less likely to be elected in MMDs. Because of the potential to discriminate against minorities, many states (especially southern states, under court mandate) eliminated most of their free-for-all MMDs during the 1960s and 1970s. Today, roughly 87 percent of all state legislators are elected in single-member (or seat-designate multimember) districts, with a plurality rule.

Redistricting

The terms **reapportionment** and **redistricting** are often used interchangeably in the United States, although technically they are not synonymous. Apportionment refers to the allocation of seats within the polity; reapportionment suggests a change in the number of seats allocated to subunits within the polity. Redistricting is simply the redrawing of the electoral boundaries without a change in the actual number of seats or districts. At the congressional level, reapportionment occurs after each decennial census. The 435 seats of the U.S. House of Representatives are reallocated so that some states gain House seats and some lose seats, based on population shifts within the country. Because representatives in state legislatures are no longer allocated to political subdivisions, the task is not one of reapportionment but rather one of redistricting.

The question of apportionment of legislative bodies is ultimately a question of how Americans view the concept of representation. In what way do they intend to represent the various interests and components of society?

---

4. See Squire and Moncrief (2010, table 1-6, 28).

With the exception of the U.S. Senate, the decision in the United States has been resolved in favor of population equality as the basis of representation. The idea is that each person's vote should be of equal value, and in the context of the American system that idea has translated into equal populations per legislative district. Thus each district must contain roughly the same number of people.[5]

One of the most dramatic changes in the electoral system occurred in what has come to be known as the "reapportionment revolution" of the 1960s. Prior to 1962, the U.S. Supreme Court took a hands-off approach to the issues of state legislative reapportionment and redistricting. The constitutions of most states mandated that their lower chambers be apportioned according to equal population standards, but this requirement was simply ignored in many of these states and absent in other states. Moreover, many state constitutions provided for equal representation of counties in the state senates (usually one senator per county, regardless of population). The result of the county rule in the senates and the disregard for the population rule in many lower chambers was that many state legislatures were severely malapportioned according to population standards. For example, in 1962 in Connecticut, Florida, and Vermont more than 50 percent of the seats in the lower chambers were controlled by a mere 12–13 percent of the state population (Ansolabehere and Snyder 2008, 50–51). In Alabama, 26 percent of the total population could elect a majority of house members (Scher, Mills, and Hotaling 1997).

The situation changed dramatically when the U.S. Supreme Court decided a series of cases in the 1960s and early 1970s.[6] First, the Court reversed its previous position and decided that reapportionment issues were justiciable and that the courts could (and would) intervene in reapportionment matters. This had the effect of forcing states to honor their own constitutional requirements that lower chambers be apportioned by population. Second, the Court determined that state senates also must be apportioned according to population standards, effectively eliminating the standard of county representation in state upper chambers. The effect of these decisions was dramatic: it greatly increased the number of state legislators from urban and suburban areas and sharply reduced the number of legislators from rural areas. Ansolabehere and Snyder (2008) found that a significant policy shift occurred in some state legislatures after this reshuffling. Moreover, along with other changes in society (such as implementation of the Voting Rights Act of 1965 and the increasing political participation of women in the late

5. The U.S. Supreme Court does permit some latitude at the state legislative level. Generally, an overall population deviation of up to 10 percent between the most populous and least populous districts is permissible. But see *Larios v. Cox*, 300 F. Supp. 2d 1320 (N.D. Ga. 2004), and Bullock (2010, 185) for potential change in this policy.

6. Many court cases have had an important bearing on state legislative reapportionment-redistricting issues, but the early ones of significance include *Baker v. Carr*, 369 U.S. 186 (1962); *Reynolds v. Sims*, 377 U.S. 533 (1964); *Lucas v. Forty-Fourth General Assembly of Colorado*, 377 U.S. 713 (1964); *Whitcomb v. Chavis*, 403 U.S. 124 (1971); and *White v. Regester*, 412 U.S. 755 (1973).

1960s), these reapportionment decisions helped pave the way for significant increases in the number of women and minorities serving in state legislatures today.

Although redistricting has always been a highly politicized matter, recent events may increase the partisan nature of the process. For example, in 2003, after gaining majority status in the Texas legislature, Republicans moved to redraw the congressional district lines (states are responsible for drawing their own congressional districts). The U.S. Supreme Court upheld this practice as a matter of state policy authority.

The dramatic Republican gains in state legislative seats in the 2010 state legislative elections likely will have an effect as well. Twenty of the ninety-nine state legislative chambers changed from Democratic to Republican control. Thus because redistricting is the responsibility of the legislature in most states, the Republican Party gained an important advantage in many of them. This advantage is not unlimited, however.

Redistricting procedures differ among the states on two important dimensions. First, there are differences in the mapmaking institutions from one state to another (McDonald 2004). Currently, the mapmaking institution in thirty-five states is the legislature itself. In the remaining fifteen states, the institution is an independent redistricting commission. Commissions are especially prevalent in the western states; with California recently adopting the commission format, eight western states now use this procedure.

The actual degree of independence (from the legislature) and the manner in which the commission is constituted differ from one state to another. Moreover, the specific rules or principles for drawing districts, usually found in the state code or constitution, differ. Depending on the specificity of these rules or principles, they serve as constraints on the mapmaking institutions (Winburn 2008; Forgette, Garner, and Winkle 2009; Bullock 2010).

Furthermore, because of advances in technology and greater access to census data and redistricting software programs, the ability of the public to be involved in the redistricting process is much greater in the 2011–2012 redistricting cycle than ever before (Altman and McDonald 2012). Indeed, it is possible that redistricting—always a litigious exercise—may become even more prone to court challenges as individuals and organizations who feel aggrieved by newly adopted plans contest such plans with their own.

The Issue of Minority Representation

Although population equality among districts has been the principal concern of the courts, they have paid considerable attention to protecting racial and ethnic minority groups. During the 1960s and 1970s, the U.S. Supreme Court directed its efforts toward ensuring that minority voting strength was not diluted. In particular, the Court struck down some state districting plans that had included MMDs. In some states, African American populations were sufficiently large and geographically compact so that the creation of SMDs would likely lead to the election of African Americans to the state legislature. However, by creating MMDs states were able to undermine the voting strength of blacks, subsuming the minority population into larger multimember districts. This practice was particularly common in the southern states. Although never claiming that MMDs were by nature unconstitutional, the Court rejected their use in cases in which MMDs would have the effect of reducing the potential influence of racial and ethnic minorities.[7]

During the 1980s and 1990s, however, the states' approaches to redistricting changed. Based in part on case law,[8] but largely on directives from the U.S. Department of Justice, they began to maximize the number of districts in which racial minorities constituted a majority, a process known as **affirmative gerrymandering.** However, in a series of cases in the mid- to late 1990s the U.S. Supreme Court indicated an unwillingness to support the move toward affirmative gerrymandering.[9]

Legislative Consequences of the Electoral System

Electoral systems are often judged by their translation of electoral votes into legislative seats. The issue is the extent to which a particular percentage of votes (say, 40 percent) yields a commensurate percentage of seats in the legislative chamber. A system in which the votes-to-seats ratio is 1 (for example, 40 percent of the votes and 40 percent of the seats, or 40:40 = 1.00) is said to be proportional. The dominant system in the United States—SMDs with plurality—tends to be disproportional (Bullock 2010, 20–21). Specifically, the party that receives the most votes statewide will almost always receive an even higher percentage of seats in the legislature. This phenomenon may be heightened by gerrymandering. Thus the party that receives, say, 55 percent of the popular vote statewide will usually command 60–65 percent of the legislative seats.

Moreover, the relative weakness of party loyalty among American voters means that individual candidates have a strong incentive to cultivate a "personal vote" among the electorate. The upshot is that American elections, at both the national and state levels, are basically candidate-centered (rather than party-centered) contests. Running for the legislature puts a premium on personal ambition and drive, devotion to the local district and its needs, and attention to the political issues that can help mobilize voter support in the district.

By contrast, the role of the legislature in governing the state requires a much different set of skills. First of all, it requires collective action, which in turn requires

---

7. See, for example, *Whitcomb v. Chavis* and *White v. Regester.*

8. See, in particular, *Thornburg v. Gingles,* 478 U.S. 30 (1986).

9. See, for example, *Abrams v. Johnson,* No. 95-1425 (1997); *Shaw v. Hunt,* 116 S. Ct. 1894 (1996); and *Johnson v. DeGrandy,* 512 U.S. 997 (1994).

bargaining, negotiation, and compromise. This dilemma of legislative representation—serving the constituency and making policy for the state—provides the strain and conflict that make legislative life both interesting and frustrating. This tension between the electoral needs of individual legislators and the policymaking needs of the legislative institution appears to be particularly great today. The annual struggle by the California legislature to set a state budget is an example (Rosenthal 1998).

RUNNING FOR THE LEGISLATURE

Beginning in the late 1960s, state legislatures underwent a modernization movement designed to increase their capacities to perform the tasks of policymaking, oversight, and constituent service. These efforts led to "what is perhaps the most dramatic metamorphosis of any set of U.S. political institutions in living memory" (Mooney 1995, 47). Many assumed that as the institution of the state legislature changed, so would the individuals serving as legislators. Whether this is true is unclear. What is certain is that the cost-benefit structure for serving in the state legislature has changed in many states, and this probably has contributed to changes in the nature of recruitment.

Candidate recruitment is a product of many factors, including the nature of the state political system; the specific rules of candidacy and nomination; the political conditions in the specific legislative district, including the role of local party organizations; and the individual attributes and decision-making calculus of the potential candidates themselves. These factors—what might be called "the electoral context"—affect who runs for state legislative office (Moncrief, Squire, and Jewell 2001; Gaddie 2004; Sanbonmatsu 2006; Hamm and Hogan 2008; Masket 2009). The electoral context is highly variable in different states (Squire and Moncrief 2010).

To what extent do Democrats and Republicans contest elections, compete effectively, and win office? In the following section, we describe patterns in legislative elections and consider explanations for them.

Electoral Contestation, Competition, and Winning

The first step in the electoral process involves selection of candidates by the major parties. In most states, this decision is made in a party primary. Key issues involve who may vote in the primary and what percentage of the vote determines the winner. The primary winner is determined in most states by a simple plurality. For example, if candidates X, Y, and Z contest the Republican primary for a specific state legislative seat, and they receive 25 percent, 36 percent, and 39 percent of the vote, respectively, then candidate Z would receive the Republican nomination. However, some states (Alabama, for example) require the primary winner to receive a majority of the vote. In this example, a runoff primary would then be held between the two top vote-getters (Y and Z) to determine who would receive the party's nomination for the general election contest.

The typical general election is a contest between Democrats and Republicans, although a smattering of third-party candidates (for example, from the Libertarian Party) and independents is sometimes on the ballot. How frequently does a contest between Democrats and Republicans occur? Table 6-2 helps to answer this question for two time periods (1996–2006 and 2009–2010) for forty-eight state legislative houses. The most striking aspect of the data in the second column for the elections between 1996 and 2006 is the wide range in contestation within each level of professionalization. Overall, though, the Democrats and Republicans challenged each other in at least 75 percent of the general election races in roughly one-fourth of the states. This level of contestation was more likely to occur in the most professional legislatures, probably because they tend to have larger, more heterogeneous, and therefore more competitive districts.

Has contestation for state legislative office increased or decreased over time? We chronicled the development of political parties contesting for office from 1968 to 1995 in a previous edition of this volume (Hamm and Moncrief 2007). A comparison of results from the 1996–2006 period with those from the earlier period shows that the percentage of contested state legislative offices declined in more states than it increased. Some states experienced very significant declines, exceeding 20 percent, with the most spectacular decline of 32 percent occurring in Rhode Island. Although increases in contesting for office happened less frequently during the most recent decade, significant increases did occur in states that were traditionally dominated by one party, including increases of 20 percent or more in Alabama, Arkansas, Hawaii, and Oklahoma.

Given the heightened level of political activity surrounding the 2010 election, did contestation for state legislative office increase? As shown in column (2) of Table 6-2, no single pattern emerges. However, the level of contestation was at least 10 percent higher in the 2009–2010 elections in ten state legislative house chambers, exceeding 20 percent in Virginia and Rhode Island.

It is one thing for a party to contest a legislative seat; it is quite another to be truly competitive—that is, to have a reasonable chance of winning the seat. Some legislative districts are so dominated by one party that the opposition party has little chance of winning even when it contests the election. Such a situation makes it more difficult to recruit quality candidates for the losing party. How competitive are the two parties in the states? If we define *competitive* as an election in which the loser received at least 40 percent of the vote, then state legislative elections are not very competitive. Only in North Dakota were 50 percent or more of the races competitive in 1996–2006; in ten states less than 20 percent of the races were competitive. In contrast with our earlier findings on contestation, then, competition seems to be lowest in professional legislatures for reasons we address in a later discussion of incumbency.

In a majority of states, the percentage of competitive races declined from 1968–1995 to 1996–2006. Although some of the decrease was relatively minor, in

Table 6-2   Level of Two-Party Contestation and Two-Party Competition in State Legislative Houses, 1996–2010

State	Two-party contestation[a]		Two-party competition[b]	
	1996–2006 (1)	2009–2010 (2)	1996–2006 (3)	2009–2010 (4)
Professional legislatures				
Michigan	98	98	25	30
New Jersey	94	94	34	23
California	90	93	23	20
Ohio	85	84	27	31
New York	74	74	12	23
Wisconsin	62	69	32	39
Pennsylvania	60	54	14	20
Illinois	51	64	15	16
Massachusetts	32	44	9	27
Hybrid legislatures				
Minnesota	94	97	43	46
Hawaii	85	90	32	25
Washington	78	65	41	47
Oregon	77	90	38	37
Colorado	74	83	37	42
Connecticut	65	74	22	41
Iowa	64	68	37	46
Alaska	66	60	32	23
Maryland	62	68	29	25
Missouri	62	57	27	20
Oklahoma	59	47	26	18
Kansas	54	57	22	24
North Carolina	52	63	29	30
Delaware	52	68	21	29
Arizona	52	52	32	25
Alabama	48	40	17	18
Virginia	45	69	21	24
Tennessee	45	56	19	24
Kentucky	45	51	25	25
Florida	43	52	23	18
Texas	38	37	17	21
Mississippi	38	n/a[c]	15	n/a[c]
South Carolina	30	30	13	10
Citizen legislatures				
Maine	84	93	47	49
Nevada	82	95	43	36
North Dakota	80	75	56	42
South Dakota	73	60	40	36
Montana	72	71	37	41
Utah	70	79	29	20
New Hampshire	71	84	44	44
West Virginia	69	62	31	38
Vermont	61	55	39	37
Indiana	56	71	24	33
Idaho	53	54	26	23
New Mexico	48	47	23	20
Wyoming	46	50	27	18
Rhode Island	38	63	12	29
Arkansas	37	33	25	21
Georgia	37	35	16	8

SOURCES: 1996 and 1998 election data: Keith E. Hamm and Robert E. Hogan, "Testing the Effects of Campaign Finance Laws in State Legislative Elections" (project funded by the National Science Foundation, SES-0215450, 2002); 2000–2006 data: collected by the authors from statistics Web sites; 2010 data: http://ballotpedia.org/wiki/index.php/State_legislative_elections_results,_2010. Percentage entries calculated by the authors.

a. Entries are percentages indicating frequency of Democratic versus Republican challenge.

b. Defined as the losing candidate receiving at least 40 percent of the two-party vote.

c. n/a = not applicable; no election was held in this two-year period.

sixteen states it exceeded 10 percent, being greater than 20 percent in Connecticut and Indiana. Increases in competition were less common, and in only four states did the change exceed 10 percent. In Arkansas, the change was greater than 20 percent. An examination of the data for the 2009–2010 elections reveals no consistent pattern—see column (4) of Table 6-2. There were significantly more competitive seats (at least a 5 percent increase) in sixteen chambers, whereas competition dropped off by 5 percent in another thirteen chambers. Somewhat surprisingly, significant increases in competition occurred in professional state legislatures.

Contestation and competition are important, but winning is ultimately what counts. An examination of the share of state legislative seats won by the two parties since 1960 underscores several trends. First, the greatest change has occurred in the southern states. In 1960 the Democrats won 94 percent of all races in the South, but by 2010 this figure had fallen to 46 percent (National Conference of State Legislatures 2010). After the 2010 election, Republicans claimed majority control in eighteen of the twenty-two southern chambers, whereas they had controlled no chamber forty years earlier. Second, in nonsouthern states the percentage of seats won by the two parties has fluctuated. Republicans won 62 percent of the seats in 1968, but claimed just 41 percent in 1974, probably as a result of the Watergate scandal. Third, since 1962 the president's party always lost seats in midterm elections except for two elections. In 1998 the Democrats with Bill Clinton in the White House actually gained about three dozen seats, and in 2002 the Republicans with George W. Bush as president gained about 180 seats. The typical pattern reemerged in 2006 with the Republicans losing about 320 state legislative seats (National Conference of State Legislatures 1996; Hansen 2000; Storey 2006). The tumultuous events surrounding the 2010 midterm elections illustrate the potential volatility of the electorate. In that election, the Republicans captured not only the U.S. House of Representatives, but gained roughly seven hundred state legislative seats, the most significant increase in more than forty years. In light of the election results, Republicans held more seats at the state legislative level than at any time since 1928 (National Conference of State Legislatures 2010). More important, many of these seat changes translated into changes in chamber control.

What Affects Legislative Election Outcomes?

State legislative elections may be viewed in two ways. From one perspective, state legislative elections are battles between Democrats and Republicans. Thus the focus is on trying to explain the percentage of the vote received by each party. From another perspective, the battle is one between incumbents and challengers. This view is more candidate-centered and focuses on what influences the percentage of the vote received by each type of candidate, regardless of party. From either perspective, election outcomes are conceptualized as a function of some combination of incumbency, campaign expenditures, past party strength, and, to a lesser extent, characteristics of the challenger (such as the campaign skills and name recognition of the challenger) and officeholder (such as voting record).

Party Strength. In states in which political parties are competitive, election outcomes are often affected by the partisan makeup of the district. The impact of party strength, however, varies across the states. In addition, the electoral impact of district party strength is greater in some years than in others.

The tumultuous 1994 election illustrates the potential volatility of the electorate and seems to call into question the impact of party strength. In 1994 the Republicans captured not only the U.S. House of Representatives but also seventeen state chambers. Outside the South, the Democratic share of seats won was the lowest since the 1968 election. Nevertheless, an analysis of the pattern of control of lower-house seats during 1992–1996 in eight states shows that 82 percent were won by the same party in all three elections (Frendreis and Gitelson 1997). Part of the reason for this outcome is that only one in three seats was contested in all three elections. And yet, at the same time, one should not underplay the extent of change in some states.

Incumbency. State legislators, if they seek reelection, have a high probability of winning. This is true in both single-member districts (Carsey et al. 2008) and multimember districts (Hirano and Snyder 2009). The reelection rate has grown in recent years, approaching 95 percent under normal circumstances (Carsey et al. 2008).

The probability of reelection varies across states. What factors account for this variation? Two studies—Berry, Berkman, and Schneiderman (2000) and Carey, Niemi, and Powell (2000)—that looked at elections over the periods 1970–1989 and 1992–1994, respectively, found that the probability of reelection is higher when (1) the length of term is two years (as opposed to four years); (2) the legislator is a member of a more professional legislature; (3) redistricting is under the control of the incumbent's own party (rather than divided control or control by the opposite party); and (4) the incumbent was unopposed in the previous election (rather than being contested).[10]

Why is the level of legislative professionalism such a strong influence on incumbency and thus on electoral outcomes? The argument is that by providing members with more institutional resources (such as staff, free mailings to constituents, and district offices), professional legislatures reduce the impact of other variables (such as presidential coattails or a poor economy) on election outcomes. "Because members of a highly professional legislature should be able to take advantage of available resources to focus attention on themselves through both their legislative and campaign activities, they are more likely than members of less professionalized

---

10. The last two variables were included only in the Berry, Berkman, and Schneiderman (2000) study.

bodies to be able to shield themselves from external forces" (Berry, Berkman, and Schneiderman 2000, 863).

Effects of Campaign Spending. Clearly, money matters in U.S. elections, including state legislative elections. Research shows convincingly that the candidate who spends the most money usually wins, but this finding does not mean that money alone was the reason for victory. Incumbents, who usually have a high chance of reelection, generally have a substantial advantage over challengers in their abilities to attract campaign contributions, and therefore enjoy a similar advantage in their abilities to outspend challengers. This spending disparity between incumbents and challengers is particularly great in the states with the more professional legislatures. The reason for this disparity is clear: it does not cost much to run for the state legislature in the rural states with citizen legislatures, and a challenger is more likely to be able to raise the $5,000 or so that it takes to be competitive. By contrast, it may cost $100,000 or more to run a competitive campaign in Illinois or California, and most challengers simply cannot raise that amount of money.

Does the amount of money spent on the campaign directly affect the share of votes that a candidate receives? Generally, the answer is yes. And it seems to be especially true in primary elections, where candidates are able to increase their vote shares by spending larger amounts of money. In general elections, the impact of expenditures on the percentage of the vote won appears to vary from state to state and from year to year.

State Legislative Campaigns. During the last few decades, electioneering practices in the United States have undergone dramatic changes. Political campaigns have become more candidate-centered as grassroots campaigning and party organizational support have given way to mass media contacts and professional consultants. Modern electioneering practices are certainly embraced by some state legislative candidates; they enlist the assistance of political consultants, conduct polls to gauge the preferences of voters, target tailored messages to specific segments of the population, and contact voters via radio and television. Meanwhile, the Internet has increasingly gained favor as a campaign tool, especially among candidates in the more professional state legislatures (Herrnson, Stokes-Brown, and Hindman 2007). Overall, then, a growing number of state legislative candidates are now employing such techniques, but the use of these techniques is conditioned by the level of available funds, the competitive situation of the candidate, the congruence of the legislative district with television media markets, and a host of other constituency characteristics (Hogan 1998; Faucheux and Herrnson 1999; Moncrief, Squire, and Jewell 2001; Squire and Moncrief 2010).

THE STATE LEGISLATORS

Obviously, institutions do not run themselves. They are social inventions, implying that they are created by and for people. In this section, we take a look at the people who serve in legislatures.

Who Are They?

The composition of most state legislatures is more diverse today than it was a generation ago. Here we explore changes in the gender, race, and ethnicity of state legislators that have resulted in more diverse legislatures (Table 6-3).

Gender. Although women make up a majority of the voting population, they have never been a majority in any U.S. state legislature.[11] In 1894 the first three women to serve in a state legislature were elected to the Colorado House of Representatives (Cox 1996). In 1925, 141 women were serving in state legislatures (Cox 1996). By 1973 there were 424 women state legislators, and that number increased in every electoral cycle for the next twenty years. But by the mid-1990s the percentage of legislative seats held by women had leveled off at about 22 percent and did not increase appreciably until the 2006 and 2008 elections, when the percentage of women rose by almost 2 percentage points, to 24.5 percent. By 2009 women held at least 30 percent of the legislative seats in about a dozen states, half of them western states. Although the number of women state legislators declined somewhat after the 2010 election, women held over one-third of the legislative seats in Arizona, Hawaii, and Vermont and 41 percent of the seats in Colorado. For the most part, southern states continued to have lower female representation (under 14 percent in Alabama and Oklahoma, and less than 10 percent in South Carolina in 2011).

Although it is important from the point of view of symbolic representation that more women now serve in legislatures, ultimately does their presence make a difference behaviorally and in terms of public policy? Recent research suggests that it does, but only after the number of women who are elected reaches a critical mass. In those state legislatures with the highest proportion of female legislators, women are more likely to exhibit policy priorities related to issues of women, children, and family. In states with the lowest levels of female representation, these gender differences in legislative priorities are absent (Thomas 1994).

Meanwhile, there is a growing disparity between the proportion of female legislators in the two political parties (Sanbonmatsu 2006). This disparity has obvious implications for the nature of policymaking, depending on which party is in control of the legislative chamber. Recent figures indicate that more than 31 percent of all Democratic state legislators are women, while only 16 percent of Republican state legislators are women (Center for the American Woman and Politics 2011). Moreover, this gender gap between the parties is growing; the GOP has become more male and the Democratic Party more female since 1994. The gender gap in legislative office is particularly dramatic in a few states: in Colorado almost 60 percent of the Democratic state legislators are women, while less than 19 percent of the Republican state legislators are female. In Idaho, the figures are

---

11. However, in 2009–2010 women constituted a majority of a single chamber of a state legislature for the first time ever. The New Hampshire Senate contained thirteen women and eleven men (Center for the American Woman and Politics 2009).

Table 6-3   Measures of Diversity in State Legislatures

State	Total seats (house + senate)	Percentage female (2011)	Percentage black (2009)	Percentage Latino (2009)
Alabama	140	14%	25%	0%
Alaska	60	23	2	0
Arizona	90	34	2	14
Arkansas	135	22	10	0
California	120	27	11	23
Colorado	100	40	2	3
Connecticut	187	29	8	4
Delaware	62	26	8	2
Florida	160	24	16	9
Georgia	236	23	22	1
Hawaii	76	33	0	0
Idaho	105	27	0	1
Illinois	177	29	18	7
Indiana	150	21	8	1
Iowa	150	21	0	0
Kansas	165	27	4	2
Kentucky	138	18	5	0
Louisiana	144	16	18	0
Maine	186	28	0	0
Maryland	188	31	23	2
Massachusetts	200	24	5	3
Michigan	148	21	15	2
Minnesota	201	32	1	1
Mississippi	174	14	29	0
Missouri	197	23	10	1
Montana	150	23	0	1
Nebraska	49	22	4	0
Nevada	63	29	11	8
New Hampshire	424	24	0	0
New Jersey	120	28	13	7
New Mexico	112	28	2	44
New York	212	23	16	8
North Carolina	170	22	19	1
North Dakota	141	15	0	0
Ohio	132	21	14	0
Oklahoma	149	13	4	1
Oregon	90	28	2	1
Pennsylvania	253	17	8	0
Rhode Island	113	26	3	3
South Carolina	170	9	22	0
South Dakota	105	20	0	0
Tennessee	132	18	14	1
Texas	181	21	9	20
Utah	104	18	0	4
Vermont	180	38	1	0
Virginia	140	19	10	1
Washington	147	31	1	2
West Virginia	134	16	2	0
Wisconsin	132	24	0	1
Wyoming	90	16	1	2
Total	7,382	23.3%	8.5%	3.3%

SOURCES: Center for the American Woman and Politics, "Fact Sheet: Women in State Legislatures Office 2011," www.cawp .rutgers.edu/Facts.html#leg; National Conference of State Legislatures, "Numbers of African American Legislators 2009," www.ncsl .org/default.aspx?tabid=14767; National Conference of State Legislatures, "Number of Latino Legislators 2009," at www.ncsl.org/ default.aspx?tabid=14776.

55 and 21 percent, respectively.[12] These partisan differences explain why female representation in state legislatures declined when Republicans made electoral gains in 2010.

Legislators have their greatest impacts through the organizational positions they hold—the committee and leadership posts. In the 1970s, women were usually assigned to and chaired committees dealing with those issues traditionally thought of as women's concerns (health and welfare), and they were underrepresented on rules, fiscal, and business affairs committees. By the late 1980s, women were still frequently assigned to and chaired health and welfare committees, but they had significantly increased their representation on budget committees, although they were still underrepresented on business committees in most states (Thomas 1994, 66–67). In terms of chairing committees, by 1993–1994 women were overrepresented as chairs on education, health, and social and human services committees and underrepresented on banking and financial institutions, energy, insurance, and rules committees (Darcy 1996). Nevertheless, one study concluded that "women are not discriminated against when committee chairs are selected" (Darcy 1996, 892). Increasingly, women are also assuming the most powerful positions in state legislatures. As of 2009, women were serving as senate presidents or presidents pro tempore in twelve states and as house Speaker in five states, and over 25 percent of all committee chairs were women (Center for the American Woman and Politics 2009).

Race and Ethnicity. Another area of diversification is racial-ethnic characteristics. Fifty years ago, almost no African Americans or Hispanics served in state legislatures. By 2009 African American legislators constituted 8.5 percent ($N = \sim600$) of all state legislators. Hispanic legislators were a much smaller but growing proportion, roughly 3.3 percent ($N = 243$). Clearly, the percentage of minority legislators is correlated with the size of the minority population in the state (Casellas 2009). An interesting recent line of inquiry is the legislative behavior of African Americans (Gay 2007) and Latinos (Preuhs and Juenke 2011) elected from majority-minority districts.

The largest proportions of African American state legislators are in southern states (over 20 percent of the legislators in Alabama, Georgia, Maryland, Mississippi, and South Carolina are black). The largest proportions of Latino legislators are found in New Mexico (44 percent), California (23 percent), Texas (20 percent), and Arizona (14 percent). Asian American and Pacific Islander legislators are prevalent in Hawaii (more than 50 percent) and California (about 5 percent), and Native Americans make up more than 12 percent of the Oklahoma and 7 percent of the Montana legislatures (Verhovek 2007).

12. Calculated by the authors from information on the Web sites of the Center for the American Woman and Politics (CAWP) and the NCSL, March 2011.

The recruitment patterns for black and white legislators appear to be somewhat different. For example, black legislators receive their start in politics outside of government (the civil rights movement, churches, or unions), whereas white legislators are more likely to start in state or local government (Button and Hedge 1996). African American legislators usually represent majority-black urban districts, whereas white legislators tend to represent white rural or suburban districts.

Scholars disagree about whether African American state legislators face discrimination within their legislatures. One study found that black legislators were more likely to perceive discrimination within the legislature than white legislators (Button and Hedge 1996). Black lawmakers report the greatest amount of discrimination in the Deep South legislatures, and the least amount of discrimination in the Rim South, probably because of the fact that blacks in this area represent a sizable number of white constituencies. In a study of the perceived effectiveness of North Carolina legislators, race was a significant variable. African American legislators received lower effectiveness scores even after controlling for political party affiliation, seniority, and leadership status (Haynie 2001).

Legislative Turnover and Legislative Careers

Table 6-4 shows the average turnover for elections over the last eight decades. Several observations arise from these data. First, turnover in state senates is generally slightly lower than turnover in state houses. In part, this difference stems from the fact that state senators usually serve four-year terms, and the terms are staggered so that only half of the senate is elected at a time.

The second observation is that the mean turnover dropped rather steadily in every decade until the 1990s. However, in the 1990s and the first decade of the twenty-first century the average turnover actually increased slightly. This trend is largely due to the advent of **term limits** in over a third of the states, beginning in the 1990s. Turnover is also slightly higher in recent decades because of an increase in the so-called wave elections in 1994, 2006, and 2010, in which national electoral waves favoring one party brought many new members into every state legislature.

Some members leave office involuntarily. Most frequently and obviously, this occurs when a legislator is forced out of office as a result of electoral defeat. As noted earlier, most incumbents win reelection, but at least a few incumbents lose in each election. Death accounts for about one-fourth of those instances in which a legislator vacates the office before completing the term. The third

Table 6-4 Average Turnover per Election in State Legislatures, by Decade, 1931–2009 (percent)

	House	Senate
1931–1940	59%	51%
1941–1950	51	43
1951–1960	45	40
1961–1970	41	37
1971–1980	32	29
1981–1990	24	22
1991–2000	25	23
2001–2009	25	22

SOURCE: Gary F. Moncrief, Richard Niemi, and Lynda Powell, "Time, Turnover, and Term Limits: Trends in Membership Stability in State Legislatures," *Legislative Studies Quarterly* 29 (2004): 357–381; 2001–2009 updates calculated by the authors.

most common reason for involuntary departure is that a legislator has been arrested, indicted, convicted of a crime, or otherwise forced from the legislature for some unethical behavior. This reason does not account for the bulk of the departures, but in some states the effect is quite noticeable. In the early 1990s, two extreme cases surfaced: in South Carolina sixteen legislators went to jail in a Federal Bureau of Investigation sting operation (Rosenthal 1998), and in Kentucky fifteen legislators were convicted on corruption charges.

State legislatures, through their state constitutions, statutes, or chamber rules, can choose from a wide variety of options to discipline members, including expulsion, censure, sanctions, and reprimands. The power to expel a member is rarely used. Only seventeen of ninety-one state legislative chambers that responded to a questionnaire indicated that they have taken this most serious action (American Society of Legislative Clerks and Secretaries 1998). This does not mean that state legislatures are unwilling to investigate serious charges; in the most serious cases members simply resign rather than wait to be expelled. The upsurge in ethics laws and codes has not only clarified what actions are impermissible but also has increased the frequency with which legislative chambers must investigate their members for violations.

Another reason for involuntary departure is found now in fifteen states: term limits. Until the early 1990s, legislators in the fifty states could serve until they were defeated. But that situation began to change in the early 1990s when voters, using the initiative process, approved limitations on legislators' tenure in nineteen states.[13] In addition, legislators in Utah voted to place limits on themselves, and in Louisiana the legislature placed the term limits issue on the ballot and the voters approved it. Subsequent court actions have overturned term limits in Massachusetts, Oregon, Washington, and Wyoming. The Idaho state legislature repealed the term limits law in 2002, and the Utah state legislature did the same in 2003, leaving fifteen states with term limits. As expected, turnover has increased in most states with term limits, averaging 12–18 percent higher than in states without term limits, depending on the year (Moncrief, Niemi, and Powell 2008). The 2010 election produced extraordinary turnovers in states in which term limits and partisan waves converged; in Michigan the turnover was 54 percent in the House and 76 percent in the Senate. In Missouri, the turnover in 2010 reached 46 percent in the House. Although a variety of states have term limits, the limits differ in two important respects: (1) the particular limit on the number of years of continuous service allowed, and (2) whether there is a lifetime ban on subsequent service, or simply a limit on the number of years of consecutive service (Sarbaugh-Thompson 2010). On the basis of these criteria, term limits are most severe in the California Assembly, Arkansas House, and Michigan House, where a lifetime ban exists after serving

13. Only in Mississippi and North Dakota did a majority of the citizens vote against term limits propositions.

six years. In Louisiana, by contrast, a member may serve twelve years consecutively in each chamber.

The adoption of term limits has led to numerous predictions and propositions about their potential impact on legislators and the legislative process. Within the last few years, empirical studies testing these propositions have emerged (see Mooney 2009 for a detailed review). The most comprehensive study to date (Kurtz, Cain, and Niemi 2007; also see Kousser 2005 and Carey et al. 2006) yields the following findings: (1) turnover increases in term-limited states, but the extent of that increase depends on the nature of the term limit and level of professionalization in a given legislature; (2) with the exception of California, there is virtually no evidence that term limits have increased the diversity in state legislatures; (3) term limits weaken the connection between legislators and their districts—term-limited legislators spend less time on casework and constituency communication; (4) although term limits may have reduced the power of some particular lobbyists, they have not reduced the overall influence of interest groups as a whole; (5) the diminished institutional knowledge in term-limited states has increased the influence of staff, especially partisan staff; and (6) term limits facilitate a shift of power away from the legislature and toward the executive branch of government. Furthermore, there is evidence that power within the legislature is shifting toward the upper chamber (Apollonio and La Raja 2006). Several reasons account for this finding, but the most important is that in term-limited states most senators have served in the house, whereas few senators who are termed out are likely to then run for the lower chamber. Because political conditions, constitutional structures, and term limit laws vary from state to state, recent research has focused on teasing out the more nuanced, "contextual" effects of term limits (Kousser 2006; Sarbaugh-Thompson 2010; Sarbaugh-Thompson et al. 2010; Miller, Nicholson-Crotty, and Nicholson-Crotty 2011).

Representing Constituents

In a representative democracy, legislators presumably represent their constituents. This simple statement, however, hides a complex political phenomenon. What do the terms *constituency* and *representation* mean? Legislators use the term *constituency* in several different ways. From this perspective, one views the constituency not as a single entity but as a "nest of concentric circles" (Fenno 1978, 1). The largest circle represents the geographic constituency—that is, the entire population living within the legal boundaries of the district. Occupying a smaller circle are the legislator's supporters, the reelection constituency. A subset of the reelection constituency is composed of the legislator's strongest supporters or loyalists—the primary constituency. The smallest circle is confined to political confidants and advisers—those thought to be good friends—otherwise known as the personal constituency (Fenno 1978). At any one time, a legislator may be focusing on one or more of these constituencies.

The concept of representation is also difficult to grasp. One useful way of conceptualizing representation is in terms of the legislator being "responsive" to the constituents in terms of policy, service, and allocation of public goods.

Policy responsiveness involves the correspondence between the constituents' preferences and the behavior of the elected official. Alan Rosenthal (1998, 19) notes that "it is much more difficult, however, for representatives to act as agents of their constituency on policy matters." Why? First, some legislators, sometimes called trustees, use their own judgment because they lack confidence in the views of organized groups in their district or they believe that voters want their legislator to lead on critical issues. Second, as noted, the relevant constituency is not always obvious. Should the member be concerned with the total population, those who voted, or those who cast their vote for him or her? Third, for those delegates or legislators who want to follow the wishes of their constituents, the problem is that most people do not have an opinion, save on the major issues (Rosenthal 2004, 40–42). Moreover, broader contextual factors may be at work, especially in chambers dominated by one party (Gamm and Kousser 2010). Service responsiveness refers to the advantages and benefits the representative is able to secure for particular constituents. Legislators are, in effect, asked to help acquire a divisible resource for particular individuals. Requests can span a wide range—for example, a legislator may be asked to help a citizen receive government assistance in the form of a job or unemployment compensation, or to help a business that has a disagreement with a state agency over licensing, taxes, or paperwork. Constituents most commonly contact their state legislators for information or for help with bureaucratic red tape and, to a lesser extent, with requests for jobs. Constituents less frequently contact their legislators about easing government regulations, intervening in local disputes, or helping with nongovernmental organizations (Freeman and Richardson 1996). The common term for this type of activity is **casework.**

What role does casework play in the job of the average legislator? Veteran legislators find that constituents' demands for services have increased significantly, and so they are spending more time on casework. And freshmen feel casework is an area in which they can make an immediate impact (Reeher 2006, 62). Meanwhile, "legislators in all types of legislative institutions find tremendous increases in the pressures of the job, as well as in the demand for and time spent on constituent service" (Moncrief, Thompson, and Kurtz 1996). What determines the amount of time that a legislator and the legislator's staff devote to casework? The most recent research finds that several factors appear to have an impact. At the individual level, legislators who place a high value on casework, who favor greater government spending, and who perceive that they will benefit electorally are more likely to devote more time, including staff time, to casework (Freeman and Richardson 1996). Conversely, legislators who place a low value on casework, who believe in a more limited role for government, and who do not see any electoral benefit from casework are less inclined to devote much time to such activities. The type of legislature in which one serves also has an impact. Legislators who serve in bodies that have a tradition of supporting constituency service, offer career incentives for members, and provide personal staff or district offices are more likely to devote more time to casework (Freeman and Richardson 1994). In their recent study, Kurtz et al. (2006) find a strong correlation between commitment to casework and constituent contact and the total time spent on the legislative job.

Legislators often seek government goods and services for their districts. "They are general rather than individual benefits, but they frequently benefit one part of the district or one group more than others" (Jewell 1982, 135). This type of "allocation responsiveness" is often associated with pork barrel projects, which benefit a specific district but are paid for by everyone. Proponents of term limits argue that such limits will reduce allocational responsiveness, because legislators will not have the incentive to pursue pork barrel projects as a reelection tool. The results from an empirical study of term limits suggest that this may indeed be the case. Legislators in term-limited states report spending less time than legislators in other states in securing government money and projects for their districts (Carey et al. 2006).

THE LEGISLATURES

Basic patterns of organization and leadership are common to most legislatures, but subtle differences make each legislature unique. This section explores the commonalities and differences in the structure of state legislatures.

Organizational Features

A comparative analysis of state legislatures reveals numerous differences in these organizations. Six important factors are the number of chambers, size, chamber leadership patterns, party caucuses, committees, and staff.

Number of Chambers and Size. In forty-nine of the fifty states, the legislature (also called the general assembly or general court in some states) is composed of two chambers. The upper chamber is called the senate in all states; the lower chamber is usually called the house of representatives (although in some states it is referred to as the assembly, the house of delegates, or general assembly). The Nebraska legislature is a unicameral body with just one chamber, a senate. State senates range in size from a low of twenty members in the Alaska Senate to a high of sixty-seven in the Minnesota Senate. The lower houses exhibit greater variability; the smallest is the Alaska House of Representatives with only forty legislators and the largest the New Hampshire House of Representatives with four hundred members. The size of the legislative body affects both the structural and procedural aspects of life in the legislature—for example, the greater the number of members in the chamber, the greater the degree of hierarchical organizational structure, the more limited the floor debate, and the greater the specialization among members.

Chamber Leadership. In the forty-nine lower houses, the chamber leader, referred to as the Speaker, is elected by the members of the house. Greater variation is found among the state senates. The membership elects a president in twenty-three state senates and a Speaker in one. The lieutenant governor presides in twenty-six, but as a member of the executive branch the lieutenant governor has limited power in most of these legislatures.[14] The real power resides with the president pro tempore, who is chosen by the senate members themselves.

Although some legislative leaders have served in that capacity for a number of terms, a recent study found that 86 percent of senate presidents, house Speakers, and majority and minority leaders changed between 1990 and 1997 (Hansen 1997). Until at least the early 1990s, the career path to the top leadership position was becoming more institutionalized as the legislatures themselves institutionalized (Freeman 1995; Squire and Moncrief 2010, 133–134). Although the path to the top post varied, an apprenticeship in another leadership position (such as majority leader or chair of an important committee) was common. This trend will probably continue to be the norm in those state legislatures not faced with term limits. If an apprenticeship norm is to be followed in the legislatures with term limits, future chamber leaders will have to be given major leadership positions (for example, committee chair or majority leader) early in their legislative careers—usually in their second or third terms at the latest. A key factor in these states is the ability to raise campaign funds. "In almost every state the ability and commitment of the prospective speaker to raise campaign funds, recruit candidates, and help candidates and incumbent legislators get elected has been a critical factor in the selection process" (Bowser et al. 2003, 125).

The job of the legislative leader is more complex today than it was in the past. Internal responsibilities include acting as the chief administrative officer, building legislative coalitions, and providing services and information to individual members, to name only a few. Leaders also have external responsibilities, including being party spokesperson, interacting with the executive, serving as the interchamber representative, holding press conferences, and preparing for campaigns (Wright 2005).

Analyzing legislative leadership patterns in twenty-two states, Malcolm Jewell and Marcia Whicker (1994) provide a framework for research. They contend that legislative leadership is to a certain extent dependent on context. A key factor is the structure of the institution, including the power of the legislature relative to that of other key state political actors, its level of professionalization and representativeness,

---

14. In six southern state senates—Alabama, Georgia, Mississippi, South Carolina, Tennessee, and Texas—the lieutenant governor has the power to appoint members to committees (Council of State Governments 2010).

the nature of its legislative rules, and the degree of party **polarization**. The legislative setting also affects the leader's power. For example, the fewer the restrictions on leadership tenure, the greater is the leader's ability to affect policy. The larger the size of the party majority and the greater the degree of party cohesion and loyalty, the greater is the impact of the power of the leader. Leaders also have access to a range of tools and techniques. For example, leaders find their power to influence public policy increases as their power to appoint committee members increases, as the size of the professional leadership staff increases, and as the techniques for controlling the party caucuses also increase. Finally, personal leadership style and goals are thought to affect the leader's power.

In terms of the formal institutional powers of house Speakers, a recent study indicates that Speakers have potentially significant powers in four areas: appointing party leaders and committee chairs, controlling the committee system, controlling house procedures, and not being limited in the number of years that a Speaker may serve (see Table 6-5). Speakers are more likely to have greater formal powers in states with higher levels of party competition and more likely to have weaker powers in state legislatures that serve as springboards for higher office.

Party Caucuses. In most state legislatures, members of the same political party belong to a party caucus. Although these groups dominated the state legislative process in the years after the Civil War and into the twentieth century, their role today is somewhat diminished. Caucuses may perform a multiplicity of functions: choosing the party leadership, keeping members informed, discussing policy to help leaders assess membership opinion, building cohesion, and mobilizing votes (Jewell and Whicker 1994, 100).

The importance of party caucuses varies among the state legislatures. In general, party caucuses are most important in the legislative process in small chambers with evenly matched parties. They are least important in large chambers with one dominant party (Francis 1989, 45). An analysis of party caucuses in formerly one-party legislatures, mostly in the South, found that when the minority party (at the time of the study, it was usually the Republican Party) is more competitive in the electoral realm, the party caucuses become more complex in terms of meeting more frequently, having formal leadership and formal rules, providing information, and acting in formulating policies (Anderson 1997).

Committees. State legislatures face a daunting problem: there is not enough time in a legislative session for the entire legislative membership to adequately discuss and debate each proposed bill. To solve this workload problem, legislatures create smaller working groups called committees to initially review, analyze, and rewrite bills that have been introduced. Because it is inefficient to assign a group of legislators to review only one bill or one specific issue and then break up, these small working groups usually exist for the life of a particular legislative session. To further enhance the division of labor, each committee generally has jurisdiction over a given policy area (for example, education or health). Jurisdiction is more likely set

Table 6-5 Speakers' 2001 Institutional Power Index, by Level of Professionalism

State	Appointment powers	Committee powers	Procedure powers	Tenure powers	Total index
Professional legislatures					
New York	5.0	4.0	4.0	5.0	18
New Jersey	3.0	4.0	5.0	5.0	17
Wisconsin	3.0	4.0	4.5	5.0	16.5
Illinois	5.0	2.5	2.5	5.0	15
Michigan	3.0	4.0	4.5	3.0	14.5
Massachusetts	5.0	2.5	2.5	4.0	14
California	5.0	3.5	2.5	3.0	14
Ohio	3.0	4.0	2.5	4.0	13.5
Pennsylvania	3.0	1.0	4.0	5.0	13
Hybrid legislatures					
Delaware	3.0	4.0	5.0	5.0	17
Maryland	4.0	4.0	4.0	5.0	17
Mississippi	3.0	4.0	4.5	5.0	16.5
Tennessee	3.0	4.0	4.5	5.0	16.5
Alabama	3.0	4.0	4.0	5.0	16
North Carolina	3.0	4.0	4.0	5.0	16
Oregon	3.0	4.0	4.0	5.0	16
Arizona	3.0	4.0	4.5	4.0	15.5
Louisiana	3.0	4.0	4.0	4.5	15.5
Iowa	1.0	5.0	4.0	5.0	15
Virginia	3.0	4.0	3.0	5.0	15
Colorado	3.0	2.5	4.5	4.0	14
Florida	5.0	4.0	4.0	1.0	14
Missouri	3.0	2.5	4.5	4.0	14
South Carolina	1.0	4.0	4.0	5.0	14
Texas	4.0	1.0	4.0	5.0	14
Kansas	1.0	4.0	3.5	5.0	13.5
Connecticut	4.0	2.5	4.0	2.0	12.5
Oklahoma	1.0	4.0	4.5	3.0	12.5
Minnesota	1.0	2.5	3.5	5.0	12
Alaska	1.0	1.0	4.0	5.0	11
Hawaii	1.0	0.0	4.5	5.0	10.5
Kentucky	2.0	1.0	2.5	5.0	10.5
Washington	3.0	0.0	2.5	5.0	10.5
Citizen legislatures					
West Virginia	5.0	4.0	4.5	5.0	18.5
Indiana	4.0	4.0	5.0	5.0	18
New Hampshire	5.0	4.0	4.0	5.0	18
Idaho	3.0	4.0	4.5	5.0	16.5
Utah	3.0	4.0	4.5	5.0	16.5
New Mexico	3.0	4.0	4.0	5.0	16
Vermont	3.0	4.0	4.0	5.0	16
Georgia	3.0	4.0	3.5	5.0	15.5
Montana	3.0	2.5	5.0	4.0	14.5
Nevada	3.0	4.0	2.5	4.5	14
Rhode Island	1.0	4.0	4.0	5.0	14
Maine	3.0	4.0	2.5	3.0	12.5
South Dakota	3.0	4.0	4.5	1.0	12.5
Arkansas	3.0	0.0	4.5	3.0	10.5
North Dakota	1.0	1.0	4.0	1.0	7
Wyoming	1.0	1.0	2.5	1.0	5.5

S O U R C E : Modified from Nancy Martorano, "Distributing Power: Exploring the Relative Powers of Presiding Officers and Committees in the State Legislative Process," paper presented at the 2004 annual meeting of the American Political Science Association, Chicago, September 2–5.

by the chamber leadership or a management committee rather than by rule (American Society of Legislative Clerks and Secretaries 1998). Membership on committees is usually restricted to just those legislators serving in one chamber or the other. In at least twenty-nine state legislatures, however, and especially in Maine, Massachusetts, and Connecticut, some joint committees composed of members from both chambers exist (Hamm and Hedlund 1994).

Committee systems at the state level have changed extensively over time. A recent study chronicles the development of committee systems in thirty-eight chambers during the twentieth century (Hamm and Hedlund 2006). At the beginning of the century, the typical standing committee system in a state legislature consisted of a relatively large number of committees; the size of each committee was relatively small; and each legislator had a significant number of committee assignments. Committee names were stable from session to session and jurisdiction was generally quite narrow, sometimes limited to a single institution or problem. Starting in the 1940s, the total number of committees, committee positions, and mean number of assignments per member declined to a nadir in the 1970s and then increased slightly. Indications are that the number of committees or the average size of committees is a function of the size of the legislature, whereas the degree of committee specialization at the individual level is a function of the stability of the legislative membership (Francis 1989).

The roles that standing committees play today in the legislative process vary among the ninety-nine state legislative chambers. In one set of legislative chambers, the key decision-making power is lodged mainly in the committees. In a second set of legislatures, the critical decisions are made by either the majority party leadership or the majority party caucus. And in a third set, power is shared between the standing committees and the leadership or the caucus. According to a study conducted in the early 1980s, in nearly two-thirds of the chambers the shared committee–leadership/caucus model prevails (Francis 1989). Committees are generally most important in chambers in which one party dominates (Francis 1989). An unexplored research question is whether committees remain important in chambers that moved in recent years from being one-party dominant to a more balanced two-party system (such as the Georgia Senate).

The ability of committees to play a meaningful role in the legislative process can also be affected by the rules governing the operation of the legislature. These rules are found in state constitutions, state statutes, and the formal rules and regulations of legislative chambers. For example, committees in the Oregon House have significant influence over policy content because the rules permit them to introduce bills with the committee listed as the author, offer substitute bills in place of the original, have committee amendments automatically incorporated into the bill rather than have each amendment accepted or rejected by the floor, and make it very difficult to amend legislation on the floor by requiring unanimous consent to accept the amendment. The committees also are important in the lawmaking process because all bills must be referred to committee and bills reported from committee go directly to the calendar. In other words, the rules carve out a central role for committees in the legislative process. Committees do not have such favorable rules in most state legislatures. At the other end of the spectrum, committees in Maine must report every bill to the floor even if a majority of the committee members oppose the bill's passage.

Staff. A major change in state legislatures during the last thirty years has been the growth of legislative staff: "State legislatures have moved away from dependence on external sources for information in favor of in-house staff resources" (Neal 1996, 24).

Legislative staff are not equally distributed among the state legislatures. During the 2009 legislative session, 2,751 staff were employed by the New York legislature (2,676 full time and 75 part time), whereas the Vermont legislature had only eighty-six (sixty full-time) staff positions (National Conference of State Legislatures 2009b). Because staff are a component of professionalism, it is not surprising that professional legislatures have substantially more staff than either the hybrid legislatures or the citizen legislatures. Professional legislatures have on average nine full-time staff members for each legislator; this figure drops to fewer than three in hybrid legislatures and to one in citizen legislatures.

Legislative staff vary in type (Neal 1996; National Conference of State Legislatures 2009b). In all state legislatures, the chief parliamentary officers and staff are involved in the lawmaking and administrative processes. They deal with tasks such as introducing bills, preparing calendars, tracking amendments offered during debate, and posting hearing schedules. Leadership staff members work directly for legislative leaders or for party caucuses, and the typical leadership staff engage in policy research, constituent services, and administrative duties.

Staff provide a variety of services, but the most important function is communication: staff members are the eyes and ears of the leadership. They keep the leadership informed about the concerns and needs of the members. Staff members supplement the work of assistant leaders or party whips by keeping members informed about what is going on in the chamber and in committees. Before an important roll call vote, they help to poll the party membership. They keep the membership informed about the wishes of the leadership, the scheduling of legislation, and the status of members' bills. Finally, staff members frequently represent the leadership in behind-the-scenes negotiations on bills, either at the committee stage or when bills are pending on the floor (Jewell and Whicker 1994).

Research staff compile background information on bills, respond to members' requests for information, and sometimes provide staff support for committees. Legal services staff, armed with their legal experience, draft bills, conduct legal research, and may be involved in administration and enforcement of ethics codes. Legislative program evaluation staff engage in program evaluation and performance auditing. Legislative fiscal staff undertake fiscal analysis, budget review, and revenue review for state legislatures. These staff members usually examine budget requests made by state agencies and make suggestions to the state legislators about these requests. Personal staffers—that is, those who work for individual legislators—are usually found in legislatures that meet almost full time.

Choosing Leaders and Subgroups

Once legislators have been chosen in district elections, the legislative chamber must be organized to conduct business. In effect, three processes, sometimes intersecting, are occurring: choosing chamber leaders, choosing legislative party leaders, and choosing committee chairs and members.

Chamber Leaders. In most state legislatures, the majority party caucuses determine which of their members will serve as presiding officers. In these state legislatures, significant politicking takes place before the caucus meets as candidates try to line up votes. In some instances, it becomes apparent that one candidate has captured a majority of the vote, and the losing candidate withdraws before the caucus meets. In others, a short meeting is held at which only one ballot is necessary to elect the party's nominee. And in still others, a protracted battle takes place in which no one is initially able to assemble a winning coalition.

There is no guarantee that the members of the majority party caucus will abide by the caucus decision. In such cases, at least six scenarios are likely, ranging from little or no impact to a complete restructuring of the legislature. The first scenario is that a few members may vote for the minority party candidate, but their defection is not significant enough to change the outcome. A second possibility is that several party dissidents may simply withhold their support, making it impossible for the majority party candidate to win the position and ultimately forcing the candidate to withdraw. In a third scenario, a dissident faction of the majority party teams up with the minority party to elect one of the dissidents as Speaker, but there is no long-term impact.

A fourth scenario has more lasting consequences, but in it a member of the majority party does serve as Speaker. This situation occurred in the Texas House at the outset of the 2009 session when Republicans held a 76–74 advantage in the chamber. Several Republicans had chaffed under Speaker Tom Craddick's rigid control of the legislative process. After the 2008 elections, a dissident group of eleven Republicans settled on one of their own, Joe Straus, to lead the charge against Craddick. Because the Speaker in Texas is chosen by all the members in a House floor vote, the goal is to lock up at least seventy-six votes. After Straus released a list of eighty-five supporters (seventy Democrats and fifteen Republicans), Craddick and those loyal to him dropped their opposition to Straus (*Texas Weekly* 2009). Thus, although a member of the majority party was elected Speaker, the bulk of the initial support came from members of the minority party. As a result, the Democrats played more of a role in the 2009 legislative session than in the previous three sessions.

The fifth scenario is more unusual in that the leadership is acquired by the minority party with the help of a few votes by disgruntled members of the majority party. Ralph G. Wright, the Democratic Speaker of Vermont from 1985 to 1991, came to power this way (Wright 2005).

The final scenario is really unusual in that almost all members of the majority party, including the majority party leader, throw their support behind a minority party legislator.[15]

What happens if the two parties have an identical number of seats? This is a possibility in the sixty-one chambers with an even number of seats, and it has actually occurred forty times since 1966, including in the Alaska Senate (four sessions) and the Montana House (three sessions) (National Conference of State Legislatures 2009a). In 2011, for example, Democrats and Republicans had an equal number of seats in the Alaska Senate and the Oregon House. To resolve the situation, several solutions have been adopted. The most common is to have co-leaders, alternating either daily or monthly in running the floor session, and co–committee chairs. For example, the evenly split Oregon House in the 2011 legislative session decided to have the co-leaders trade off being presiding Speaker every other day (Lehman 2011). In a variant of this approach, the chamber leadership changes partisan control at the end of the first year of a two-year session. Another way is to elect the leader from one party but to give the bulk of the committee chairs to members of the other party. Sometimes, the issue is settled by state law. A final possibility is that the majority coalition will be bipartisan, which has been the case for the last few sessions in the Alaska Senate (Forgey 2010).[16]

We have discussed the organization of the legislature as if it involves only the decisions of the members of that chamber. Although that is generally true today, in past years the governor, particularly in some southern states, was the kingmaker. In a most unusual occurrence, in 2002 the newly elected Democratic governor of New Jersey, James McGreevey, convinced the newly elected Democratic majority in the assembly to accept his choice as Speaker. The Democratic caucus acquiesced after members of the governor's team issued sufficient threats to future political careers. As a result, a backbencher with only two years of legislative experience became what was considered to be the third most powerful politician in New Jersey government, bypassing those who had held key legislative positions in previous sessions (Diamond 2002).

Party Leaders. Legislatures also must choose their political party leaders. The formal legislative party organization varies among the state legislative chambers.

15. This happened in the Pennsylvania House in 2007. Even though the Democrats held a 102–101 advantage, a few renegade Democrats were willing to vote for the incumbent Republican Speaker. Almost all of the Democrats then settled on a plan to elect a Republican Speaker, but with the understanding that the Democrats would be able to control House committees and the agenda on the House floor (Thompson 2007).

16. Even though there were ten Democrats and ten Republicans in the 2011 legislative session, a sixteen-member Bipartisan Working Group that included ten Democrats and six Republicans became the senate's majority caucus (Forgey 2010).

Legislative party organizations can be placed on a continuum from simple to relatively complex. At one extreme—Mississippi—there is no formal party organization. The simplest organization is one in which each party has a floor leader (majority or minority party) responsible for leading debate on the floor and working with the Speaker in setting the agenda (Alaska Senate). More complex organizations (New York Assembly) have a more detailed leadership structure, including positions such as assistant majority leader, whip, and majority caucus chair.

The actual selection of the key party leaders usually takes place in the party caucus in which the legislators from that party vote for their officers. In essence, then, the leaders are chosen by their peers. In some chambers, however, the elected chamber leader, who is also the party leader, appoints the majority leader and other party officials (such as in the Connecticut Senate). In a few legislative bodies (such as the Illinois Senate and New York Senate), the elected chamber leader also carries the title of majority leader, thereby fusing power in one person. Another option is to forgo a majority leader designation and designate the elected chamber leader to serve as the party chair. In the Ohio Senate, for example, there is no majority leader, and the senate president, the elected chamber leader, presides over the majority party caucus.

Committee Chairs and Members. After the selection of the chamber and party leadership, the standing work groups for the legislature are designated. The committee assignment process is a key organizational decision in which members are allocated for the duration of the legislative session to concentrate on certain policy areas. The leadership's ability to control appointments is crucial to governing the chamber. As Jewell and Whicker (1994, 95) note, "The ability of the majority-party leadership to appoint, and if necessary to remove, committee chairs is one of its greatest sources of power." The elected chamber leader (Speaker, president, or president pro tempore) selects committee chairs in about 70 percent of the state legislative chambers. In other states, committee chairs may be selected by the majority leader, by a chamber committee, by substantive committee members, by the entire chamber, by chamber seniority, or by committee seniority.

Across all state legislatures, the most frequent considerations in appointing committee chairs are political party, the competency or talent of the member, and the preference of the member, followed by the member's seniority in the chamber, tenure on the committee, and support in the leadership election. Less important are occupation, geographic location of the member's district in the state, gender, and ethnic representation (American Society of Legislative Clerks and Secretaries 1998).

Legislators are appointed to committees in a variety of ways. In about half of the legislative chambers, legislators of the majority political party are appointed by the top leader (Speaker, president), and in about one in four chambers this responsibility falls to the president pro tempore, Speaker pro tempore, or majority leader. In roughly one in ten chambers, a committee on committees or a rules committee performs this task. Seniority is the rule in only a few chambers, such as the Arkansas Senate and Utah Senate (American Society of Legislative Clerks and Secretaries 1998). Even greater control is possible if the majority party leaders are able to dictate which minority party members will be appointed to specific committees. In several states, the minority leader has some influence over which members of the minority party will be assigned to the various committees (American Society of Legislative Clerks and Secretaries 1998).

THE LEGISLATURE AT WORK

As governmental institutions, state legislatures perform several important functions. For one thing, they make policy. Legislatures are not the only policymaking institutions in the states, but they are at the center of the process. Thus when most people are asked "What do legislatures do?" their first response is usually "They pass bills" or "They make laws for the state."

But legislatures perform other tasks as well. One of the most important is **appropriations.** Legislatures must approve the budget for the state, and the recent extended, severe economic recession has made this a particularly important and yet difficult task. Technically, appropriations can be considered part of the lawmaking function because budgets are constructed by means of the appropriations bills passed by the legislature. But budget setting is such an important issue and dominates many state legislative sessions to such a degree that we treat it as a function separate from the regular, substantive lawmaking process. State budgets today are multibillion-dollar propositions. Not only does the state budget allocate funds for the various state agencies, but local governments (especially cities and school districts) receive substantial appropriations from the state budget.

Governors have a powerful influence over the state budgetary process because in most states it is the governor's office, acting on the basis of projected revenue, that first makes revenue estimates and then submits a proposed budget to the legislature. Moreover, the governor can claim to represent the fiscal interests of the entire state, whereas legislators have a natural tendency to first look out for the budgetary interests of their individual districts. Nevertheless, few legislatures today are willing to abdicate the appropriations function entirely to the executive branch. Most legislatures have added their own revenue estimation and budget review staff to provide themselves with an independent analysis of the budget needs of the various state agencies (Rosenthal 1998, 315), and in about a dozen states the legislature exerts a powerful independent force over the budget process (Squire and Moncrief 2010).

A third function of state legislatures is **administrative oversight.** Because they have primary responsibility for passing legislation but not for administering these laws, the legislature seeks a check on the ways in which the various state agencies are operating. This is a difficult task for state legislatures, many of which meet only part time and have limited staff assistance. Moreover, for most legislators the personal incentive to invest vast amounts of time in oversight is generally not very great. Nevertheless, legislatures, to varying degrees, make an effort to perform oversight. One way legislators seek oversight of state agencies is through budget hearings. Most state legislatures also exercise some control by reviewing administrative rules and regulations. This review, which is now an institutionalized routine in many states, is a way to ensure that the administrative agencies are following legislative intent in the way the laws are executed.

Finally, legislatures perform **constituency service.** In truth, this function is more closely associated with the individual legislator than with the legislative institution, but legislators use institutional resources (such as staff personnel) to perform this service. One form of constituent service is casework. Such service is often in the form of interceding in a constituent's behalf with a state agency, handling requests from constituents for information, or even helping them find jobs (Freeman and Richardson 1996). In contrast with the oversight function, legislators have a strong incentive to perform casework and believe it helps them win reelection.

Another form of constituent service is securing a "particularistic" benefit for a district such as a new road or airport. Sometimes referred to as pork or pork barrel projects, these benefits are particularistic because they benefit a specific segment of the population (the legislator's district), but the costs are borne universally (the entire state foots the bill through the state budget). Obviously, this particular type of action is closely tied to the appropriations process.

The Legislative Process

The basic process of passing a bill into law is generally similar in all state legislatures (see Box 6-1 for a summary of the legislative process), but there are differences in the details from one state to another.[17] Moreover, the formal process is only part of the story. Personalities, outside events, and timing are all factors that affect the likelihood that any particular proposal will wend its way through the process to become law.

Most bills do not become law. The average for the fifty states is about 20 percent, but the success rate varies greatly from one state to another. Many factors account for this variation, but one study finds that more professional legislatures and those chambers that do not impose a limit on the number of bills a legislator can introduce tend to pass lower proportions (Squire 1998). Another study found that both

---

17. Most official state legislative Web sites nowadays include a description of "how a bill becomes law" in that specific state; see, for example, www.cga.ct.gov/html/bill.pdf (Connecticut), www.legislature.idaho.gov/about/howabillbecomeslaw.htm (Idaho), www.ncga.state.nc.us/NCGAInfo/Bill-Law/bill-law.html (North Carolina), and www.house.state.oh.us/jsps/Bill.jsp (Ohio).

Box 6-1   The Legislative Process

Bill is drafted

The ideas for bills come from a variety of sources, including interest groups, administrative agencies, the governor's office, constituents, or the legislator herself. A bill may be drafted by an individual legislator, but more likely she will use the drafting service provided by the legislative staff. After the legislator approves the draft, she may seek cosponsors for the proposal.

Introduction and first reading

The draft becomes a bill when the sponsoring legislator "drops" the bill—that is, gives it to the clerk of the chamber, who assigns the bill a number. The bill is given its first reading at this point.

In an effort to keep the institutional workload manageable, a few state legislatures limit the number of bills an individual legislator can introduce each year. In most states with such rules, exceptions are permitted for certain types of bills (for example, local bills that affect only a legislator's district rather than the state as a whole).

Another method of containing the workload is to impose bill introduction deadlines, which many state legislatures now employ. Under such rules, individual legislators cannot introduce bills after a specified day (for example, the twenty-fifth day of the session).

Committee referral

The bill is assigned to one of the substantive standing committees of the chamber. Because different committees are composed of different legislators, the decision about which committee should get the bill can sometimes be an important determinant of the bill's ultimate fate. In most states, the power of referral rests with the presiding officer.

Subcommittee

Some state legislatures make extensive use of subcommittees as a way to divide the workload within the committee. Some states use subcommittees infrequently, usually to consider a particular issue such as reapportionment.

Committee hearings

Generally, the most extensive discussion and review of a bill occurs in hearings before the committee (or subcommittee). It is here that most public input will occur. This input, in the form of public testimony, is often dominated by lobbyists for interest groups, who testify in favor of or opposition to the bill, or who argue for specific changes in the bill. Control over the hearing process (including, in most states, the decision on whether to schedule hearings) is usually in the hands of the committee chair. However, the rules of some state legislatures require all bills to receive a public hearing.

Committee action

After the bill has been reviewed and considered, the committee may report the bill out with one of several recommendations. The committee action at this stage is critical to the potential success of the bill. The possible recommendations include "Do Pass," "Do Not Pass," "No Recommendation," "Refer to Another Committee," "Withdraw from Consideration," "Amend," "Substitute," or "Table."

Perhaps 90 percent of the bills that receive a favorable ("Do Pass") recommendation from the committee will ultimately pass when the bill comes up for a floor vote. An unfavorable recommendation ("Do Not Pass") is rare in most states; if the committee does not favor the bill it will simply not hold hearings, or it will vote to put the bill aside ("Table"). However, a few states require all legislation to be reported from committee to floor. In these states, a "Do Not Pass" recommendation is common, because the committee does not have the option of killing the bill through inaction.

Committees often recommend amendments to a bill. If substantial changes are needed, the committee may offer a substitute bill for the original one. When committee amendments or substitute bills arise, the full membership of the chamber will have an opportunity to accept or reject the proposed changes in a separate vote prior to voting on passage of the bill itself.

Box 6-1 *(Continued)*

Once the bill is reported from committee, it is placed on the second reading calendar. If committee amendments were reported, the legislature, operating as the Committee of the Whole, considers whether to adopt the proposed amendments. Amendments offered by other members (floor amendments) are usually in order at this stage as well. If amendments to the bill are adopted, the bill must be rewritten to reflect the changes. This is known as engrossment.

Third reading and floor vote

In most state legislative chambers, the floor debate and floor vote occur at this stage. In order for a bill to pass, a simple majority of those present and voting is required in most states. Thus, if there are one hundred members, and on a given bill the vote is forty-five "yeas," forty "nays," and fifteen "not present" or "abstaining," the bill would pass. However, a few states require a true majority of the chamber to vote in favor of a bill in order for it to pass. If a true majority is required, the vote just described (45–40–15) would mean the bill fails, because a "true majority" in a chamber with one hundred members is fifty-one. Under these circumstances, "taking a walk" on a bill has the same effect on the vote outcome as voting "nay."

Reconsideration

In keeping with the deliberative nature of legislatures, there is usually a provision that a vote on a bill can be reconsidered within twenty-four to forty-eight hours of the vote. Occasionally, a bill will pass one day, be reconsidered, and fail the next day. Or it may fail and subsequently be reconsidered and passed.

Action in the second chamber

The steps in the second chamber are generally identical to those listed above, from introduction through third reading and floor debate. Most states require sequential action, meaning that the bill is not referred to the second chamber until it has worked its way through the chamber in which it was originally introduced. However, some states (like Congress) permit concurrent introduction, meaning that versions of the bill are introduced in both chambers at the same time.

Conference committees

To become law, a bill must pass both chambers in precisely the same form. If a bill passes each chamber, but in different forms (for example, amendments were added in one chamber), a resolution of these differences is necessary. If neither chamber is willing to accede to the changes made by the other chamber, then a conference committee is created in an effort to work out an acceptable compromise. In most cases, the presiding officers appoint three or four members of each chamber to serve as the conferees. If a majority of the conference committee can negotiate an agreement, this new version of the bill is submitted for approval via floor vote in each chamber. If the conference report is accepted by the floor in both chambers, the bill passes. If either chamber rejects the conference report, or if the conferees cannot agree on a compromise version of the bill, the bill dies.

Conference committees are more prevalent in some state legislatures than in others. In some states, they have become a very significant part of the legislative process.

Governor's action

Once a bill is passed in identical form in both chambers, the bill is sent to the governor. The governor may sign it into law or veto it. Vetoes are most common under conditions of divided government (the governor is from one party and the legislative majority is from the other party), but they occur in almost all legislative sessions. The provisions for overriding a gubernatorial veto vary a bit from state to state; the most common rule is that a legislature must muster a two-thirds majority in each chamber to override the governor's veto. Only about 5 percent of gubernatorial vetoes are overridden.

N O T E : For detailed tables of legislative rules and procedures in all fifty states, see American Society of Legislative Clerks and Secretaries in cooperation with the National Conference of State Legislatures, *Inside the Legislative Process* (Denver: National Conference of State Legislatures, 2000).

the number of bills and the proportion of bills enacted is inversely related to the number of interest groups in the state. In other words, the more interest groups, the more difficult it is to get legislation passed (Gray and Lowery 1995). This observation thus leads to another one: a good deal of the power of interest groups and lobbyists rests in the power to block.

One reason so many bills fail to become law is that the legislative process is loaded with obstacles, all of which must be overcome. The forces opposing a bill need to be successful only at any one stage to block the proposed legislation, whereas the bill's proponents must win at each step. A bill can be effectively killed (and many are) in committee. Or it may be gutted through floor amendments. Or it might be defeated in the floor vote. It might even be passed on the floor and defeated on a reconsideration motion. The bill can lose at any of these stages, in either chamber. Or it may die because a conference committee cannot produce an acceptable compromise. Or the governor may veto it. Some bills die simply because time runs out. It is not uncommon for a few bills to pass one chamber, be reported favorably out of committee in the second chamber, and yet be left to languish on the second or third reading calendar because the legislature adjourns the session.

Nor is it unusual for a specific piece of legislation to be introduced several years before it ultimately passes. Some proposals are so different from the status quo that it takes several years for the legislators to become educated about the issue, or for public opinion to become sufficiently solidified on a proposed solution. Interest groups, in particular, often take a long-term view, knowing a bill will not pass this year or perhaps even next year, but eventually "its time will come" (a common phrase in the legislative halls).

Influences on Legislative Policymaking

Many factors are involved in the policymaking process. Some of these factors have to do with the nature of the legislative institution. For one thing, compromise is valued; after all, majority coalitions are needed for both the committee vote and the floor vote. Moreover, because of the bicameral structure of state legislatures (except Nebraska's), negotiation between the chambers is often necessary.

Another consideration is time, and in several ways. First, most state legislatures meet in session only part time (two to four months a year). As the end of the session approaches, time becomes a critical consideration. Because there is not enough time to process all the proposals, the leadership often takes control of the legislative agenda in the last few weeks of the session and decides which bills will come to the floor for a vote and which will die on the second or third reading calendar.

Second, because it takes time for legislation to be drafted, introduced, and heard in committee, the workflow of legislatures is different in the beginning of the session than at the end. In the first month or so, legislators spend most of their time in committees and less time debating and voting on the floor. The pace appears to be slow and deliberative, even ponderous. As the session progresses, action on the floor picks up as more and more bills flow out of the committees. In the last few weeks, most of the committee work is complete and floor activity often becomes frenetic, with perhaps dozens of roll call votes occurring in a single day.

Third, legislators (and legislation) are affected by electoral cycles. Some types of policies (for example, tax increases and perhaps highly emotional issues such as abortion) are less likely to be considered during an election year because legislators fear the consequences for their own careers.

Most legislation that comes to a floor vote is relatively noncontroversial and comprises bills that make only minor changes in existing law. The decision-making process on such legislation is routine, and the roll call votes are often unanimous or nearly unanimous. During the course of the entire session, only a hundred or so bills may generate considerable controversy at the floor stage. Of course, these are the bills that are most salient to the general public and the media and that may cause considerable angst for the legislators as they cast their votes.

The focus on how legislators vote on final passage of bills can mask the importance of their behavior at earlier stages. Committee votes, for example, are less visible to the general public. There is evidence that roll call votes on the floor (which are recorded) are not necessarily accurate reflections of the positions taken by the legislators on the same bills in committee, where votes are often not recorded. Procedural votes (for example, a vote to recommit a bill to committee or to hold a bill on the second reading calendar) sometimes allow legislators to kill a bill without a formal roll call. And yet advances in technology help to open the system to more public scrutiny. Today, virtually all state legislatures maintain Web sites, and many of these report floor votes and even committee hearings and votes.

State legislators rely on cues from many sources during the policymaking process. Some of these sources, such as legislative staff, may be more influential at the bill formulation or the committee stages than at the floor vote stage. The committee report itself is often an important cue.

The extent of party voting varies by state legislature and circumstance (Wright and Schaffner 2002; Jenkins 2006). When a party holds a slim majority of seats in the chamber, legislators are more likely to feel pressure to toe the party line than when the party commands a large majority (more than 60 percent of the seats). In states in which the party plays an important role in nominating candidates, members are also more likely to vote with the party on important votes. In recent years, ideology has appeared to be playing a larger role in voting decisions (Jenkins 2006, 2008; Yamane and Oldmixon 2006).

Indeed, an important issue in American politics is whether political parties and their supporters are becoming more polarized. Most scholars who study this phenomenon agree that parties in the U.S. Congress have grown more polarized over time (see, for example, Layman, Carsey, and Horowitz 2006 and McCarty, Poole, and Rosenthal 2006). Does this trend hold in the U.S. states? Only a handful of studies have examined this question. We suggest four tentative conclusions from the research conducted to date. First, the degree to which parties are polarized on legislative roll calls varies substantially across the states. In one study of eleven legislatures, the authors found the highest level of polarization in California and the lowest in Louisiana. Second, when viewed across time (that is, the 1994–2004 legislative sessions), the level of polarization has remained stable in some legislatures, such as the New Jersey Assembly, and increased in others, such as the Ohio House (Shor, Berry, and McCarty 2010). Third, an intriguing finding from the California Assembly suggests that the more outsiders (such as party bosses, party activists, and interest groups) control the nomination process, the more likely party polarization develops (Masket 2009). And fourth, although the impact of term limits has been substantial on some aspects of the legislative process, they do not seem to have affected the level of party polarization (Wright 2007).

Interest groups exert substantial influence over the legislative process in many states. In part, this influence arises from lobbyists' roles as important sources of information for legislators, particularly in states with limited staff and time. In states with a dominant economic interest (such as agriculture in Kansas), legislators are often predisposed toward protecting that group. Recognizing the importance of the state legislature in policymaking, many interest groups are increasingly active in state legislative elections. This interest often takes the form of campaign contributions to selected candidates who are supportive of a group's agenda.

Another avenue for interest groups and others is the initiative process, as described in Chapter 5 of this text. Only about half of the states permit the direct initiative as a method of policymaking, and its use varies widely among those states. But as Bowler and Donovan point out in Chapter 5, the mere existence of the initiative process in a state may alter legislative behavior. For one thing, legislators are more likely to be attentive to those publics that have the means to organize an initiative drive. In some cases, legislators may act on an issue because of the threat that an initiative will otherwise be filed. Thus on some issues this form of direct democracy probably makes the legislature more sensitive to public opinion. But initiatives can also be used to limit the legislature's options, especially on fiscal matters. Tax and expenditure limitations (TELs) are often the product of the initiative process. By either limiting tax increases or mandating spending (or both), TELs further politicize the appropriations process. And, of course, some initiatives are aimed directly at the legislative institution itself—the issue of term limits is an obvious example.

Governors are also important players in the legislative process. Through the State of the State address and the budget message, both delivered at the beginning of the legislative session, the chief executive is able to help shape the policy agenda (Kousser and Phillips 2009). The ultimate weapon in the gubernatorial arsenal is the veto.

Ultimately, the most important cue source for most legislators is their own perception of constituent opinion. When public opinion in the district is clearly on one side of a specific issue, the legislator will rarely vote against it, but very few issues elicit a clear and unified voice from one's constituency. On the vast majority of bills, legislators are relatively unconstrained by constituent opinion, although they may feel constrained by the opinions or wishes of specific segments of their constituencies. Legislators are particularly attentive to those individuals or groups within their districts who have the ability to mobilize enough voters to potentially affect the outcome of the legislator's next election.

CONCLUSION

Legislatures are complex organizations. In part, this complexity stems from the fact that to be productive legislatures must reach some consensus among a majority of members. But the members are elected from different electoral districts, representing constituencies that are often very different. This fact of legislative life is not fully appreciated by the general public.

State legislatures are similar in many respects. For example, all state legislatures are expected to carry out the same functions: policymaking, budget appropriations, administrative oversight, and constituent service. But legislatures differ from one state to another in many ways, too. Many of these differences are captured in the concept of professionalization, which reflects the differences in time commitment, monetary incentives, and staff support that one finds across the state legislatures. Other differences are the size of the legislative districts represented, the costs of campaigning for legislative office, and the degree of diversity among the legislators themselves. Further differences emerge from the ways in which the legislatures are organized and the specific rules under which they operate. It is these differences, and their consequences, that make state legislatures so interesting.

As a group, state legislatures face immense challenges in the years to come. Some of these challenges stem from the ongoing changes in federalism; states (and therefore state legislatures) are again emerging as important partners in the federal relationship. Other challenges stem from economic and social changes within a particular state—changes that bring both opportunities and problems that must be addressed by the legislatures. Still other changes, such as term limits, are aimed directly at the legislative institution itself. State legislatures under term limits are forced to adapt in many ways (Kousser 2005).

This issue of adaptation and change in state legislatures will be a particularly interesting one to follow in the coming years. In the past generation, state legislatures have undergone many reforms aimed at modernizing the legislative institution. These reforms included upgraded physical facilities, larger staffs, longer sessions, and higher salaries for legislators. Although these changes were important in extending the capacity of the legislative institution to do its job, they had the additional consequence of altering the incentive structure for those who serve in state legislatures. Because many legislatures now meet for longer periods, it becomes increasingly difficult for the individual legislator to juggle both a private career and public service. Moreover, the larger staffs and improved physical facilities have made the legislature a more attractive place to be. The legislature has also become a more diverse place; many more women and people of color are serving in state legislatures today than just twenty-five years ago.

Years ago, many legislators served only one or two terms and then left public service because the benefits (both psychological and economic) simply did not outweigh the costs (in terms of time away from family and business). This is no longer true in many states. Thus the changes wrought to improve state legislatures also had an effect on those who serve in the legislatures. Dissatisfaction with what the public increasingly perceives as "career" legislators has created a backlash against legislators, which in turn affects the institution itself. This is one of the important dilemmas that legislators and the public must face in the years to come: Can they build effective legislative institutions and at the same time discourage legislators from long-term service?

KEY TERMS

administrative oversight, 194
affirmative gerrymandering, 171
appropriations, 194
casework, 184
constituency service, 195
district magnitude, 167

polarization, 187
post-designate, 168
professionalization, 163
reapportionment, 168
redistricting, 168
term limits, 181

REFERENCES

Altman, Micah, and Michael P. McDonald. 2012. "Technology for Public Participation in Redistricting." In *Reapportionment and Redistricting in the West*, ed. Gary Moncrief. Lanham, Md.: Lexington Books.

American Society of Legislative Clerks and Secretaries. 1998. *Inside the Legislative Process*. Denver: National Conference of State Legislatures.

Anderson, R. Bruce. 1997. "Electoral Competition and the Structure of State Legislatures: Organizational Complexity and Party Building." PhD diss., Rice University.

Ansolabehere, Stephen, and James M. Snyder Jr. 2008. *The End of Inequality: One Person, One Vote and the Transformation of American Politics*. New York: Norton.

Apollonio, D. E., and Raymond La Raja. 2006. "Term Limits, Campaign Contributions, and the Distribution of Power in State Legislatures." *Legislative Studies Quarterly* 31: 259–281.

Berry, William D., Michael B. Berkman, and Stuart Schneiderman. 2000. "Explaining Incumbency Reelection." *American Political Science Review* 94: 859–874.

Bertelli, Anthony, and Lilliard E. Richardson Jr. 2008. "Ideological Extremism and Electoral Structure: Multimember versus Single-Member Districts." *Public Choice* 137.

Bowser, Jennifer Drage, Rich Jones, Karl T. Kurtz, Nancy Rhyme, and Brian Weberg. 2003. "The Impact of Term Limits on Legislative Leadership." In *The Test of Time: Coping with Legislative Term Limits,* ed. Rick Farmer, John David Rausch Jr., and John C. Green, 119–132. Lanham, Md.: Lexington Books.

Bullock, Charles S., III. 2010. *Redistricting: The Most Political Activity in America.* Lanham, Md.: Rowman and Littlefield.

Button, James, and David Hedge. 1996. "Legislative Life in the 1990s: A Comparison of Black and White State Legislators." *Legislative Studies Quarterly* 21: 199–218.

Carey, John M., Richard G. Niemi, and Lynda W. Powell. 2000. *Term Limits in the State Legislatures.* Ann Arbor: University of Michigan Press.

Carey, John M., Richard G. Niemi, Lynda W. Powell, and G. Moncrief. 2006. "The Effects of Term Limits on State Legislatures: A New Survey of the 50 States." *Legislative Studies Quarterly* 31: 105–134.

Carsey, Thomas, Richard Niemi, William Berry, Lynda Powell, and James Snyder Jr. 2008. "State Legislative Elections, 1967–2003." *State Politics and Policy Quarterly* 8: 430–443.

Casellas, Jason. 2009. "The Institutional and Demographic Determinants of Latino Representation." *Legislative Studies Quarterly* 34: 399–426.

Center for the American Woman and Politics. 2009. "Factsheet: Women in State Legislatures 2009." www.cawp.rutgers.edu/Facts.html#leg.

———. 2011. "Factsheet: Women in State Legislative Office 2011." www.cawp.rutgers.edu/Facts .html#leg.

Cooper, Christopher, and Lilliard Richardson Jr. 2006. "Institutions and Representational Roles in U.S. State Legislatures." *State Politics and Policy Quarterly* 6: 174–194.

Council of State Governments. 2010. *The Book of the States 2010.* Table 4.14, Lieutenant Governors: Powers and Duties. http://knowledgecenter.csg.org/drupal/system/files/ Table_4.14_0.pdf.

Cox, Elizabeth. 1996. *Women State and Territorial Legislators, 1895–1995: A State-by-State Analysis, with Rosters of 6,000 Women.* Jefferson, N.C.: McFarland Press.

Darcy, Robert. 1996. "Women in the State Legislative Power Structure: Committee Chairs." *Social Science Quarterly* 77: 889–898.

Diamond, Randy. 2002. "The Consensus Candidate." *State Legislatures* 28: 20–24.

Faucheux, Ron, and Paul Herrnson. 1999. "See How They Run: State Legislative Candidates." *Campaigns and Elections* (August).

Fenno, Richard. 1978. *Homestyle.* Boston: Little, Brown.

Forgette, Richard, Andrew Garner, and John Winkle. 2009. "Do Redistricting Principles and Practices Affect U.S. State Legislative Electoral Competition?" *State Politics and Policy Quarterly* 9: 151–175.

Forgey, Pat. 2010. "Bipartisan Coalition to Again Control Senate, Keeps Stevens in Charge." *Juneau Empire,* November 4. www.juneauempire.com/stories/110410/sta_730859930.shtml.

Francis, Wayne. 1989. *The Legislative Committee Game: A Comparative Analysis of Fifty States.* Columbus: Ohio State University Press.

Freeman, Patricia. 1995. "A Comparative Analysis of Speaker Career Patterns in U.S. State Legislatures." *Legislative Studies Quarterly* 20: 365–375.

Freeman, Patricia, and Lilliard E. Richardson Jr. 1994. "Casework in State Legislatures." *State and Local Government Review* 26: 21–26.

———. 1996. "Explaining Variation in Casework among State Legislators." *Legislative Studies Quarterly* 21: 41–57.

Frendreis, John, and Alan Gitelson. 1997. "Shifting Partisan Fortunes in Electoral Politics." Paper presented at the annual meeting of the Southern Political Science Association, Norfolk, Va., November 5–8.

Gaddie, Ronald Keith. 2004. *Born to Run: Origins of the Political Career.* Lanham, Md.: Rowman and Littlefield.

Gamm, Gerald, and Thad Kousser. 2010. "Broad Bills or Particularistic Policy? Historical Patterns in American State Legislatures." *American Political Science Review* 104: 151–170.

Gay, Caludine. 2007. "Legislating without Constraints: The Effect of Minority Districting on Legislators' Responsiveness to Constituency Preferences." *Journal of Politics* 69: 442–456.

Gray, Virginia, and David Lowery. 1995. "Interest Representation and Democratic Gridlock." *Legislative Studies Quarterly* 20: 531–552.

Hamm, Keith E., and Ronald D. Hedlund. 1994. "Committees in State Legislatures." In *The Encyclopedia of the American Legislative System,* ed. Joel J. Silbey. New York: Charles Scribner's Sons.

———. 2006. "Legislative Professionalization and Committee Systems: Institutional versus Individual-Level Impact." Research paper prepared for the twentieth International Political Science Association World Congress, Fukuoka, Japan.

Hamm, Keith E., and Robert Hogan. 2008. "Campaign Finance Laws and Candidacy Decisions in State Legislative Elections." *Political Research Quarterly* 61: 458–467.

Hamm, Keith E., and Gary F. Moncrief. 2007. "Legislative Politics in the States." In *Politics in the American States: A Comparative Analysis,* 9th ed., ed. Virginia Gray and Russell L. Hanson. Washington, D.C.: CQ Press.

Hansen, Karen. 1997. "Living within Term Limits." *State Legislatures* (June): 13–19.

———. 2000. "The New Political Parity." *State Legislatures* (December): 12–15.

Haynie, Kerry L. 2001. *African American Legislators in the American States.* New York: Columbia University Press.

Herrnson, Paul, Atiya Kai Stokes-Brown, and Matthew Hindman. 2007. "Campaign Politics and the Digital Divide." *Political Research Quarterly* 60: 31–42.

Hirano, Shigeo, and James Snyder Jr. 2009. "Using Multimember District Elections to Estimate the Sources of the Incumbency Advantage." *American Journal of Political Science* 53: 292–306.

Hogan, Robert E. 1998. "The Role of Political Campaigns in State Elections." PhD diss., Rice University.

Jenkins, Shannon. 2006. "The Impact of Party and Ideology on Roll-Call Voting in State Legislatures." *Legislative Studies Quarterly* 31: 235–257.

———. 2008. "Party Influence on Roll Call Voting: A View from the U.S. States." *State Politics and Policy Quarterly* 8: 239–262.

Jewell, Malcolm E. 1982. *Representation in State Legislatures.* Lexington: University of Kentucky Press.

Jewell, Malcolm E., and Marcia Whicker. 1994. *Legislative Leadership in the American States.* Ann Arbor: University of Michigan Press.

King, James. 2000. "Changes in Professionalism in U.S. State Legislatures." *Legislative Studies Quarterly* 25: 327–343.

Kousser, Thad. 2005. *Term Limits and the Dismantling of State Legislative Professionalism.* New York: Cambridge University Press.

———. 2006. "The Limited Impact of Term Limits: Contingent Patterns in the Complexity and Breadth of Laws." *State Politics and Policy Quarterly* 4: 410–429.

Kousser, Thad, and Justin H. Phillips. 2009. "Who Blinks First: Legislative Patience and Bargaining with Governors." *Legislative Studies Quarterly* 34: 55–86.

Kurtz, Karl, Bruce Cain, and Richard Niemi, eds. 2007. *Institutional Change in American Politics: The Case of Term Limits*. Ann Arbor: University of Michigan Press.

Kurtz, Karl, Gary Moncrief, Richard Niemi, and Lynda Powell. 2006. "Full-Time, Part-Time, and Real Time: Explaining State Legislators' Perceptions of Time on the Job." *State Politics and Policy Quarterly* 6: 322–338.

Layman, Geoffrey C., Thomas M. Carsey, and Juliana Menasce Horowitz. 2006. "Party Polarization in American Politics: Characteristics, Causes, and Consequences." *Annual Review of Political Science* 9: 83–100.

Lehman, Chris. 2011. "Evenly Divided Oregon House Elects Co-Speakers." National Public Radio. www.npr.org/2011/01/25/133201775/Evenly-Divided-Oregon-House-Elects-Co-Speakers.

Maddox, Jerome. 2004. "Opportunity Costs and Outside Careers in U.S. State Legislatures." *Legislative Studies Quarterly* 29: 517–544.

Malhotra, Neil. 2006. "Government Growth and Professionalism in U.S. State Legislatures." *Legislative Studies Quarterly* 31: 563–584.

———. 2010. "Disentangling the Relationship between Legislative Professionalism and Government Spending." *Legislative Studies Quarterly* 33: 387–414.

Masket, Seth. 2009. *No Middle Ground: How Informal Party Organizations Control Nominations and Polarize Legislatures*. Ann Arbor: University of Michigan Press.

McCarty, Nolan, Keith E. Poole, and Howard Rosenthal. 2006. *Polarized America: The Dance of Ideology and Unusual Riches*. Cambridge, Mass.: MIT Press.

McDonald, Michael. 2004. "A Comparative Analysis of Redistricting Institutions in the United States, 2001–2002." *State Politics and Policy Quarterly* 4.

Miller, Susan M., Jill Nicholson-Crotty, and Sean Nicholson-Crotty. 2011. "Re-Examining the Institutional Effects of Term Limits in U.S. State Legislatures." *Legislative Studies Quarterly* 36: 71–97.

Moncrief, Gary F., Richard Niemi, and Lynda Powell. 2008. "Turnover in State Legislatures: An Update." Paper presented to the annual meeting of the Western Political Science Association, San Diego, March.

Moncrief, Gary F., Peverill Squire, and Malcolm Jewell. 2001. *Who Runs for the Legislature?* Upper Saddle River, N.J.: Prentice Hall.

Moncrief, Gary F., Joel A. Thompson, and Karl T. Kurtz. 1996. "The Old Statehouse, It Ain't What It Used to Be." *Legislative Studies Quarterly* 21: 57–72.

Mooney, Christopher. 1995. "Citizens, Structures, and Sister States: Influences on State Legislative Professionalism." *Legislative Studies Quarterly* 20: 47–67.

———. 2009. "Term Limits as a Boon to Legislative Scholarship: A Review." *State Politics and Policy Quarterly* 9: 204–228.

National Conference of State Legislatures. 1996. "Fate of President's Party in State Legislative Elections, 1960–1996." www.ncsl.org/programs/legismgt/elect/presprty.htm.

———. 2009a. "In Case of a Tie." www.ncsl.org/default.aspx?tabid=17278.

———. 2009b. "Size of State Legislative Staff." www.ncsl.org/default.aspx?tabid=14843.

———. 2010. "Republicans Exceed Expectations in 2010 State Legislative Elections." www/ncsl.org/?tabid=21634.

Neal, Tommy. 1996. *Lawmaking and the Legislative Process: Committees, Connections, and Compromises*. Denver: National Conference of State Legislatures.

Preuhs, Robert, and Erik Gonzalez Juenke. 2011. "Latino U.S. State Legislators in the 1990s: Majority-Minority Districts, Minority Incorporations and Institutional Position." *State Politics and Policy Quarterly* 11: 48–75.

Reeher, Grant. 2006. *First Person Political: Legislative Life and the Meaning of Public Service.* New York: NYU Press.

Rosenthal, Alan. 1998. *The Decline of Representative Democracy: Process, Participation, and Power in State Legislatures.* Washington, D.C.: CQ Press.

———. 2004. *Heavy Lifting: The Job of the American Legislature.* Washington, D.C.: CQ Press.

———. 2009. *Engines of Democracy: Politics and Policymaking in State Legislatures.* Washington, D.C.: CQ Press.

Sanbonmatsu, Kira. 2006. *Where Women Run: Gender and Party in the American States.* Ann Arbor: University of Michigan Press.

Sarbaugh-Thompson, Marjorie. 2010. "Measuring 'Term Limitedness' in U.S. Multi-State Research." *State Politics and Policy Quarterly* 10: 199–217.

Sarbaugh-Thompson, Marjorie, John Strate, Kelly Leroux, Richard Elling, Lyke Thompson, and Charles Elder. 2010. "Legislators and Administrators: Complex Relationships Complicated by Term Limits." *Legislative Studies Quarterly* 35: 57–89.

Scher, Richard K., Jon L. Mills, and John J. Hotaling. 1997. *Voting Rights and Democracy.* Chicago: Nelson-Hall.

Shor, Boris, Christopher Berry, and Nolan McCarty. 2010. "A Bridge to Somewhere: Mapping State and Congressional Ideology on a Cross-Institutional Common Space." *Legislative Studies Quarterly* 35: 417–448.

Snyder, James, Jr., and Michiko Ueda. 2007. "Do Multimember Districts Lead to Free-Riding?" *Legislative Studies Quarterly* 32: 649–679.

Squire, Peverill. 1998. "Membership Turnover and the Efficient Processing of Legislation." *Legislative Studies Quarterly* 23: 23–32.

———. 2007. "Measuring State Legislative Professionalism: The Squire Index Revisited." *State Politics and Policy Quarterly* 7: 211–227.

Squire, Peverill, and Keith Hamm. 2005. *101 Chambers: Congress, State Legislatures, and the Future of Legislative Studies.* Ann Arbor: University of Michigan Press.

Squire, Peverill, and Gary Moncrief. 2010. *State Legislatures Today: Politics under the Domes.* Upper Saddle River, N.J.: Longman.

Storey, Tim. 2006. "Chalk One Up for the GOP." The Thicket at State Legislatures: Elections, November 28. http://ncsl.typepad.com/the_thicket/elections/index.html.

Texas Weekly. 2009. "Play It Backwards." January 9. http://texasweekly.com/node/3538.

Thomas, Sue. 1994. *How Women Legislate.* New York: Oxford University Press.

Thompson, Charles. 2007. "Democrats Get House, GOP Gets Speaker." *Harrisburg Patriot News,* January.

Verhovek, Sam Howe. 2007. "Indians Stake Claim in Politics." *Boston Globe,* April 29. www.boston.com/news/nation/articles/2007/04/29/indians_stake_claim_in_politics/.

Winburn, Jonathan. 2008. *The Realities of Redistricting: Following the Rules and Limiting Gerrymandering in State Legislative Redistricting.* Lanham, Md.: Lexington Books.

Woods, Neal, and Michael Baranowski. 2006. "Legislative Professionalism and Influence on State Agencies." *Legislative Studies Quarterly* 31: 585–609.

Wright, Gerald. 2007. "Do Term Limits Affect Legislative Roll Call Voting? Representation, Polarization, and Participation." *State Politics and Policy Quarterly* 7: 256–280.

Wright, Gerald, and Brian Schaffner. 2002. "The Influence of Party: Evidence from the State Legislatures." *American Political Science Review* 96: 367–380.

Wright, Ralph G. 2005. *Inside the Statehouse: Lessons from the Speaker.* Washington, D.C.: CQ Press.

Yamane, David, and Elizabeth A. Oldmixon. 2006. "Religion in the Legislative Arena: Affiliation, Salience, Advocacy, and Public Policymaking." *Legislative Studies Quarterly* 31: 433–460.

SUGGESTED READINGS

Print

Reeher, Grant. *First Person Political: Legislative Life and the Meaning of Public Service.* New York: NYU Press, 2006. A look inside the legislative job, based on interviews with state legislators in Connecticut, New York, and Vermont.

Rosenthal, Alan. *Engines of Democracy: Politics and Policymaking in State Legislatures.* Washington, D.C.: CQ Press, 2009. The latest in Rosenthal's long line of highly readable and thematic observations about state legislatures.

Squire, Peverill. *The Evolution of American Legislatures: Colonies, Territories, and States, 1619–2009.* Ann Arbor: University of Michigan Press, 2012. An analysis of the origins of legislatures in the United States.

Squire, Peverill, and Keith E. Hamm. *101 Chambers: Congress, State Legislatures, and the Future of Legislative Studies.* Columbus: Ohio State University Press, 2005. Compares and contrasts Congress and the state legislatures on histories, fundamental structures, institutional and organizational characteristics, and members.

Squire, Peverill, and Gary Moncrief. *State Legislatures Today: Politics under the Domes.* Upper Saddle River, N.J.: Longman, 2010. An introduction to the institutional variety found in state legislatures and the work of state legislators around the country.

Internet

National Conference of State Legislatures. www.ncsl.org. A vast array of information on state legislatures and issues.

State Legislatures Ballotpedia. http://ballotpedia.org/wiki/index.php/Portal:State_legislatures. A compendium of information and links to state legislative institutions.

The Thicket at State Legislatures. http://ncsl.typepad.com/the_thicket/. A "bipartisan blog by and for legislative junkies" on the Web site of the National Conference of State Legislatures and open to all manner of legislative subjects for discussion.

CHAPTER 7

Governors and the Executive Branch

MARGARET FERGUSON

A governor is the most visible political actor in a state and is viewed by many citizens as the personification of the state itself. This elected officeholder sits atop the state's political and governmental hierarchy. The state legislature, bureaucracy, press, politics, and policies all bear the imprint of the governor.

Governors are expected to fill a long roster of roles. A handbook written to assist new governors lists the following: head of the executive branch, legislative leader, head of party, national figure, family member, and ceremonial chief (National Governors Association 1978). Other roles are equally broad in responsibility, such as intergovernmental actor and policy leader, and some are narrower in scope, such as chief crisis manager (National Governors Association 1978; Morehouse 1987). Some roles are constant, while others fluctuate over time. For example, since the terrorist attacks on the United States of September 11, 2001, the governor's role as crisis manager has been growing in importance.

Governors have not always been at the top of the pecking order in their states, nor have they always been at the center of state activities. The negligible powers and responsibilities given to the earliest state governors reflected the antipathy that citizens of the colonial period felt toward executive power—a dislike carried over from their experiences with imposed colonial governors. During the next two centuries, governors gradually gained more power, and many of the early restrictions placed on them were reduced or removed. This transformation happened in a series of incremental steps and in varying degrees across the states. In many states, new restrictions and new challenges faced governors as state governments evolved.

Beginning with the democratization movement in the early nineteenth century, the selection of governors moved from the legislature to direct election by the people. This shift empowered governors with newfound popular legitimacy. However, this "pursuit of representativeness" also imposed new restrictions on the governor as other state administrative officials came to be selected by direct popular election (Kaufman 1963, 36). States placed some important administrative functions outside the control of the governor and into the hands of others directly responsible to the people. This shift created multiple centers of power in the executive branch, sometimes setting the governor up with competition from other elected officials.

As patronage and corruption increased in the era following the Civil War, many reformers charged that legislative bodies could not effectively run the states or administer public programs, and they pressed for more changes in the form of state governments. Restrictions were placed on both gubernatorial and legislative powers, and a drive began to raise the competence of state government—in fact, governments at all levels—through the use of **merit systems** and civil service personnel procedures. For the first time, "what you know" became more important than "who you know" in state government. Furthermore, as new responsibilities were undertaken, new agencies, boards, and commissions were established to handle them—again, often outside the direct control of any executive official. These "Progressive" efforts to obtain "neutral competence" in running government were an attempt to separate politics from administration. Governors and legislators were obviously on the political side, and these reforms were meant to maintain that separation. Perhaps ironically, state government reform actually weakened governors in important ways.

In the last fifty years, constitutional revision and executive branch reorganization have clarified the lines of state government authority. Governors now have longer terms of office, the opportunity to serve successive terms, and more staff support. In addition, they have considerable budget authority to help control the executive branch and stronger veto power to use in their legislative negotiations. At the same time, however, the strength and reach of the civil service and merit systems have increased, providing state employees with a degree of protection and even insulation from the governor.

This chapter examines the current status of the American governorship and answers the following questions. First, who are governors and how do they reach office? What is the nature of gubernatorial politics? Second, what powers do states give governors so they can fulfill their roles? To what extent do these powers vary across the fifty states? Third, what are the major roles that all governors must perform? How do these roles provide governors with greater informal powers to achieve their goals, and how do they work with the legislatures and bureaucracies? Fourth, what options are available to governors after their tenures in office? In a sense, this chapter follows the trajectory of the men and women who seek to be governor, win the election, serve as governors, and move on from the governorship. Each step influences what happens during the next, and as this chapter explains, these are not discrete steps.

Throughout the chapter, I highlight differences across the states, the governorships, and the governors to point out the diversity inherent in the Union. This should not overshadow the larger point of understanding, however, which is how similar these actors, their offices, and their responsibilities are.

BECOMING GOVERNOR

In theory, anyone who meets the constitutional qualifications for office can become governor. In practice, some people are much more likely than others to occupy the governor's chair. In this section, I consider why this is so.

Where You Have Been Makes a Difference

A basic clue to what a particular public office is all about, and its position within any political power hierarchy, is who seeks and fills that office. Of interest are some of the career steps governors pursue prior to the governorship. The first step of interest is their entry level onto the gubernatorial ambition ladder. Table 7-1 indicates that more than half the governors serving between 1900 and 2011 began their political careers either as state legislators or in law enforcement.[1] This was especially true between 1950 and 1980, when nearly three out of five governors used these offices as their entry points. The importance of the state legislature as the first step is increasing—two of every five governors entering office since 1950 began their elective careers there.

Also climbing in importance as first steps are local elective positions[2] and service in the U.S. Congress.[3] The prominence of the path that begins by serving in administrative positions en route to the governorship has declined sharply since 1980.[4]

The second step of interest is these governors' last or penultimate position prior to becoming the chief executive. Table 7-2 indicates that just under three-fifths of the governors' penultimate positions between 1900 and 2006 were other statewide elective offices, the state legislature, or law enforcement. Since 1981, there has been a considerable shift in governors' launching pads. Other statewide elective offices

1. Law enforcement includes county and city attorneys, district attorneys, U.S. attorneys, judges at all levels, personnel from the Central Intelligence Agency (CIA) and Federal Bureau of Investigation (FBI), and state attorneys general (even if elected by statewide vote).

2. This category comprises all elective offices at the local level except county and city attorneys and district attorneys.

3. This category refers to seats in the U.S. House of Representatives or U.S. Senate.

4. Administrative positions refer to all public offices at the local, statewide, and federal levels that are not elective. Some offices are appointive, and others are career positions. No law enforcement offices are included in this category. At the state level, elective offices in some states (such as state auditor) are administrative in others.

Table 7-1 Entry Level or First Elected Office of a Governor's Career, 1900–2011 (in percentages)

	1900–1949	1950–1980	1981–2011	1900–2011
Number of governors	**501**	**324**	**234**	**1,059**
Legislative	29%	35%	39%	33%
Law enforcement	19	23	13	19
Administrative	15	15	6	13
Local elective	10	11	17	11
No prior office	8	10	11	11
Other	13	1	2	7
Statewide elective	5	4	8	5
Congress	0.4	2	3	1

SOURCES: For 1900–1980, see Larry Sabato, *Goodbye to Good-Time Charlie: The American Governorship Transformed,* 2d ed. (Washington, D.C.: CQ Press, 1983), 36–39; 1981–2006 data assembled by Thad Beyle; 2007–2011 data assembled by the author.

NOTE: Columns may not add to 100 because of rounding.

Table 7-2 Penultimate or Stepping-Stone Office of a Governor's Career, 1900–2011 (in percentages)

	1900–1949	1950–1980	1981–2011	1900–2011
Number of governors	**501**	**324**	**234**	**1,059**
Statewide elective	19%	22%	30%	23%
Legislative	18	24	13	18
Law enforcement	19	19	12	17
Administrative	14	10	4	11
Congress	10	9	18	11
No prior office	8	10	13	10
Local elective	7	5	9	7
Other	6	0	1	3

SOURCES: For 1900–1980, see Larry Sabato, *Goodbye to Good-Time Charlie: The American Governorship Transformed,* 2d ed. (Washington, D.C.: CQ Press, 1983), 36–39; 1981–2011 data assembled by the author.

NOTE: Columns may not add to 100 because of rounding.

now account for three out of ten of the governors, and law enforcement positions have declined considerably, to only 12 percent. Also rising in importance are U.S. congressional and senatorial seats.

Elective statewide positions—whether lieutenant governor, secretary of state, state treasurer, state attorney general, or state auditor—obviously can be a strong jumping-off position for candidates for the governorship. Also included in this category are former governors who run and win the office again.

The number of individuals moving from the U.S. Congress to the governorship has increased, from about 10 percent between 1900 and 1980 (Sabato 1978, 40) up to 18 percent between 1981 and 2011. Part of the political calculus in making this type of move is the ability to do so without jeopardizing one's current congressional or U.S. Senate seat. Some states have off-year gubernatorial elections, which allow some members of Congress to campaign for governor while retaining their federal seats. In other states, the timing of the party nominations permits a member of Congress to hold the congressional seat until the nomination is won and then resign in time for the election campaign (Sabato 1983, 41).

By and large, the evidence suggests that previous electoral experience (with the attendant visibility) at the congressional, statewide, or state legislative levels is one of the most important steps to the governorship. Most governors have had such electoral experience.

Today, the governorships nationwide are characterized by somewhat greater diversity. No longer is the governor's chair a spot for only white males. In 2011 six women were serving as governor, and over half the states have had at least one female governor. There are currently two Latino governors: Susana Martinez of New Mexico (that state's first female governor) and Brian Sandoval of Nevada. Two African American men have served as governor since Douglas Wilder was elected in Virginia in 1990. African American David Paterson of New York (who is also the only legally blind governor to date) succeeded to the office upon the resignation of Eliot Spitzer in 2008. Deval Patrick of Massachusetts is the only African American governor as of 2011. Bobby Jindal of Louisiana and Nikki Haley of South Carolina are the first two Indian American governors.

The Election Campaign: High Costs for the States' Highest Office

During the last few decades, the costs of running for and winning the governor's seat have escalated rapidly. In 1956 the average cost of a gubernatorial campaign was estimated to be $100,000 (up to $300,000 in the more populated states). Those 1956 dollars would be equal to just over $800,000 and just under $2.5 million, respectively, in 2011 dollars.

Looking at all governors running in the 1977 and 1980 elections, the combined total cost was $650 million; for the 2003 through 2006 elections, the total cost was double that, at nearly $1.3 billion.[5] The four-year bank of elections between 2007 and 2010 was even more expensive, with total costs topping $1.6 billion. The largest jumps in the level of expenditures came in the years in which thirty-six states held their gubernatorial elections: 1982, 1986, 1990, 1998, 2002, 2006, and 2010. In the 1980s, these jumps were tied to the adoption of new (at the time) and expensive campaign techniques and technologies—including direct mail, computerized field operations, and an increase in television advertisements—by gubernatorial campaigns across the fifty states. Since the late 1980s, the cost of these elections leveled off in the high $600 million range, but that changed with the 2002 elections, when spending topped $1 billion in the thirty-six gubernatorial races. This increase was driven in part by a rise in the level of electoral competitiveness; twenty-four new governors were elected in 2002, when only sixteen incumbent governors ran and four of them lost. In the 2006 elections, the expenditures dropped back to $815

5. All dollar figures and amounts in this section are in 2011 equivalent U.S. dollars based on the Consumer Price Index (CPI-U). The CPI-U is based on 1982–1984 = 100. The 1956 CPI-U was equal to 27.2 of that index base, and the 2011 CPI-U was equal to 226.0 of that index base.

million because twenty-five of the twenty-seven incumbent governors won their races and only eleven new governors were elected. Campaigns in 2010 spent $1.1 billion (as much as all four previous years combined).[6]

Although large states might be expected to have expensive gubernatorial races, some of the most expensive races have been in southern states, where one-party Democratic dominance is being replaced by costly two-party, candidate-oriented campaigns. The average cost of governor's races has escalated steeply over the last five elections in Texas ($59 million), Virginia ($32.7 million), Florida ($28.7 million), North Carolina ($23.2 million), and Louisiana ($22.9 million).

The reasons for such costs and their continuing escalation are many. Changes in the style of campaigning are the most significant among them. With the transformation of state political parties and the decline of party identification among voters, candidates cannot afford to depend on the party regulars to deliver the needed votes. Going from county to county and meeting with the local politicos may solidify some votes and bring together part of a winning coalition, but doing so takes time, reaches too few people, and does not deliver enough votes.

The old "ground war" approach has been replaced by the newer "air war" campaigns. The most direct path to potential voters is through the costly mass media. Opinion polls, political consultants, media consultants, direct-mail persuasion and fund-raising, telephone banks, "micro-targeting" of voters (the use of commercial databases to craft individual messages), and rapid travel throughout the state are all expensive, but needed. Governor's races are generally more expensive when political parties are weak, an open seat is up, the race is highly contested from nomination to general election, or there is a partisan shift as a result of the election or an incumbent is unseated (Beyle 1996, 10–14). Which of these factors is the most significant probably varies not only by state but also by candidate and by circumstances. The recent trend toward self-financed candidates such as Meg Whitman in California (who spent $144 million of her own money in the 2010 governor's race, but lost) has also inflated costs.

Campaign spending is important in that in most races the candidate who spends the most wins the election. It is also true, however, that this is a bit of a circular argument in that the candidate most likely to win (a popular incumbent, for example) is better able to raise (and therefore spend) money than is a challenger. Research indicates that both incumbent party candidates and out-party candidates benefit electorally from greater spending. However, spending is most effective for in-party candidates, indicating that raising more money does not necessarily level the playing field for the out-party challenger (Partin 2002). However, Bardwell (2005) cautions that the relationship between spending and votes for incumbents is exaggerated and largely disappears once incumbent popularity is accounted for.

---

6. Thirty-seven states held elections in 2010; Utah candidates spent some $5 million in a special election.

As noted earlier, popular incumbents are better able to raise money, and so their popularity, rather than the spending of campaign dollars, predicts their ultimate success.

In 2010 incumbents typically spent more than challengers, though there are exceptions. In Massachusetts, Deval Patrick spent considerably less than his closest opponent, Charlie Baker, and slightly less than independent candidate Tim Cahill. Patrick still won with 48 percent of the vote. By contrast, in Ohio incumbent Ted Strickland was outspent and defeated by challenger John Kasich.

Although political observers assume that campaigns "matter," scholars of election outcomes have often found otherwise. However, it is known that higher-intensity gubernatorial campaigns result in higher levels of information among the electorate and therefore presumably a more educated vote choice (Partin 2001).

Research on gubernatorial elections often compares gubernatorial campaigns to other statewide races such as those for U.S. Senate seats because they share electoral constituencies. This work has revealed that, for example, compared with senators, gubernatorial incumbents are somewhat more vulnerable because they tend to attract higher-quality challengers (Squire and Fastnow 1994). A major question among those studying gubernatorial elections is whether governors (like presidents) are held accountable for the state of the economy. Most voting studies say yes, though findings vary on how much the state of the economy affects assessments of gubernatorial performance relative to other influences (see, for example, Chubb 1988; Stein 1990; Atkeson and Partin 1995; Niemi, Stanley, and Vogel 1995; Svoboda 1995; and King 2001). Some research finds a linkage between presidential popularity and gubernatorial elections (Carsey and Wright 1998). Retrospective voting, or holding governors accountable at the ballot box for their prior performance, is particularly strong when the governor and legislature share party attachments (Leyden and Borelli 1995). In summary, as noted earlier, races for governor are expensive and high profile. The outcomes are influenced by the performance of the incumbents, some assessment of the state of the economy, and, perhaps surprisingly, the performance of the president (particularly when the governor and president share a party attachment).

Gubernatorial Popularity

Gubernatorial popularity is another topic of interest to researchers and observers of governors. Studying this topic has become much easier since Thad Beyle and his colleagues made these data readily available (www.unc.edu/~beyle/). Popularity is thought to be important for a variety of reasons. Some scholars argue that more popular governors are more likely to achieve their policy goals (Rosenthal 1990; Ferguson 2003). More directly, popularity is related to the electoral fortunes of governors because positive assessments of gubernatorial performance often predict success at the ballot box. However, these are not the same thing. Because electoral results represent only a single point in time, votes might not be representative of public attitudes about gubernatorial performance more generally. In fact, it turns out that only in election years do voters hold governors accountable for unpopular actions such as tax increases. In other years, even something as noteworthy as a tax increase does not have a direct negative effect on the popularity of the governor (MacDonald and Sigelman 1999).

Much like the study of elections, research on gubernatorial popularity often revolves around economic effects. Does the popularity of governors erode under poor economic conditions in the same way that presidential popularity suffers? Although research has very clearly shown that the public holds presidents accountable for the performance of the national economy, scholars have found competing evidence on whether governors are similarly held accountable. Some evidence suggests that governors and presidents share a similar fate. Gubernatorial popularity suffers under high state unemployment. Sadly for governors, however, they do not experience a commensurate boost in popularity from low unemployment (Hansen 1999). Other research finds no effect and points out that other factors such as partisanship are more important (Crew and Weiher 1996; MacDonald and Sigelman 1999). Some observers believe that Americans view the performance of governors through the lens of presidential politics. According to this "presidency-centered" model, because of the president's high level of visibility, people hold all members of the president's party responsible for economic conditions. Other observers assert that the popularity of governors derives from things the governor does or does not do, not some assessment connecting the governor to the president (Orth 2001). This finding indicates that, when assessing responsibility and giving credit or laying blame, people (quite sensibly) distinguish among the responsibilities of different government actors.

Researchers clearly have some work yet to do to sort out these differing findings. It could be that unemployment rates affect the popularity of some governors but not others (Adams and Squire 2001; Crew et al. 2002). If so, gubernatorial popularity is idiosyncratic and the unique features of individual incumbents and constituent expectations are at least as important as the economic variables that are so often discussed. Finally, perhaps citizens are actually rather sophisticated in their assessments of gubernatorial performance. They recognize that governors have limited influence over the state economy and essentially no influence over the national economy (Howell and Vanderleew 1990). Because of this understanding, people judge their governors on the unemployment situation in their state relative to levels in the country at large. Therefore, whatever the level of unemployment in a state, governors are rewarded when state unemployment is less than the national average and punished when it is higher (Cohen and King 2004). Voters assign different responsibilities to different governmental actors and hold them accountable accordingly.

Those who assert that gubernatorial approval is idiosyncratic often point to the importance of the individual people who hold the office, in addition to the economic effects often thought to be important. However, unlike the state of the economy, the important characteristics of an individual governor are difficult to study systematically. Researchers who have tried to measure how much governors' personality features affect their popularity have found that governors' personalities do affect their popularity in predictable ways. As political observers instinctively know, some governors are popular simply because they have appealing personalities (Barth and Ferguson 2002).

THE POWERS OF GOVERNORS: A COMPARISON

Another important consideration is how much and what kind of power resides in the governor's office. Power, however, is not an easy thing to define. As Schlesinger (1965, 1971) has shown, some governors are strong, some are weak, and some fall in between. Political actors can draw power from a variety of sources. Some power comes from the office, some from the political context, and some from the personality or skill of the actors themselves. Reasons for strength can derive variously from personality, personal wealth, electoral mandate, party or interest group structure, state statute, or the **formal powers** of the office itself. The type of power can also vary within a particular state; for example, a governor may have considerable power over the executive branch but little in working with the legislature. Alternatively, a governor may have little power with either of these but have a close relationship with the president, which confers some significant power in the intergovernmental arena and even in the state. And some governors holding institutionally weak governorships still manage to exert quite a lot of power within their states.

The governors of the most populous states—California, New York, and Texas—are particularly important. They have greater influence in national political conventions with their large state delegations and in Congress with their larger congressional delegations. Meanwhile, they are often elevated to a potential presidential candidacy simply because they are the governors of these states. The national press covers them closely, giving their state activities a national tinge. In short, these governors have national power because of the states they head. In the 1980s, a former governor of California, Ronald Reagan, won the presidency twice, and in 1996 the sitting governor of California, Pete Wilson, tried but failed. And then there is Texas governor George W. Bush, who won the 2000 and 2004 presidential races.

This section focuses on the powers governors have within their own states: those powers they bring to the office themselves and those powers provided them by the state constitution, state statutes, and the voters. At the end of the section, I consider some alternative means of capturing the power of the governorship.

The Personal Power of Governors

Each person who serves as governor possesses a set of personal attributes that can be turned into either a strength or a weakness, depending on the situation.

Based on the influential categorization scheme devised and regularly updated by Thad Beyle, I look at four separate indicators of the personal strength of the governors serving as of the spring of 2011.

Electoral Mandate (EM). The margin of victory by which governors win their seats is an indicator of the size of the electoral mandate. The premise is that the larger the margin of victory, the stronger the governor will be. Governors who win by a wide margin can use that margin politically by declaring that the people cast their votes overwhelmingly so that a particular goal could be achieved. Governors who win by a narrow margin and those who succeed to office cannot effectively use this argument.

Position on the State's Political Ambition Ladder (AL). The political ambition indicator places governors on the state's political ambition ladder in relation to their previous positions. The premise is that a governor progressing steadily up from sub-state to statewide elective office to the governorship will be stronger than governors who start at the top with the governorship as their first office. Officials elected to a variety of offices have worked their way through each level and have learned en route what to expect and what is expected of them. They also have developed friends and allies who will support them (as well as enemies and ingrates who will not). The governor for whom it is the first elective office must build such an understanding and relationships on the job.

The Personal Future of Governors as Governors (PF). Governors who are near the beginning of their terms and who have the ability to run again have more power than do governors who are nearing the end of their terms in office, are retiring, or are term-limited. Governors up for reelection are able to go out to the voters again and seek the electoral mandate voters can provide, and at the same time possibly help supporters and hurt detractors. Governors who cannot run again become lame ducks with little political potential remaining.

Being a lame duck can be frustrating for governors. They have the trappings and formal powers of office but lack the political power and wallop they once had. They not only lose the potential clout needed to attract the support of those who are not necessarily their friends and allies, they also lose the support of their friends and allies.

Gubernatorial Performance Ratings (GP). Performance as governor is another aspect of the **personal power** of governors. There are many ways in which scholars might measure the performance of the governors of the fifty states. Two of them rely on asking people—involved observers and the public—just how well they think the governor of their state is performing. The premise in using perception data is that those governors who are seen as performing in a relatively positive way add to their own personal power and will be more effective than will those who are not performing well. But what constitutes a good performance by a governor? On what basis do observers make their judgments?

One factor in some evaluations is that the governor has achieved some level of success in economic development efforts. This can be especially important when a state has experienced a weak economic period during or just before the governor's term in office, and thus successes in seeking and obtaining new businesses and new jobs would be important. Or it could be that the governor is just serving during good economic times and is receiving good marks for that. A second factor is how well the current governor compares with recent predecessors. Clearly, if a governor is under a dark cloud for doing (or not doing) something or for an action or inaction by someone else in the administration, the comparison will be negative. Another factor is the governor's ability to keep state functions stable and working in accordance with what voters want.

The second way to measure gubernatorial performance is by the proliferating state-level public opinion polls. They provide some fairly consistent results on how well citizens, registered voters, or likely voters feel that their governor is performing. These results are usually made public by the news media that pay for the polls or by a university center that conducts the polls.

In such polls, the reasons for the respondents' assessments are obscure, but how they rate their governor's performance becomes part of the politics surrounding the governor. The categories of responses used vary from "approve, disapprove" to "excellent, good, average, fair, poor." What everyone looks for is the percentage of positive responses in the ratings of the governor, although most political consultants believe that the negative assessments are more meaningful in political terms.

The reasons for these ratings are not always clear, but their impact is potentially great. For those on the low side of the scale, their administrations are jarred, and their political future is unclear, if not damaged beyond repair. For those on the high side of the scale, these public opinion poll ratings become part of their political and personal arsenal in their attempts to achieve results.

The Personal Power of Governors: Summary. To assess and compare how the fifty state governors in 2011 fared in their personal power, the scores of each of the indicators just described can be combined into a single index, which weights them all equally. Each state's scores on the four separate indicators (with each indicator measured on a five-point scale) are averaged to create an overall five-point scale. In the nine states in which no public approval polls were available, the scores of the three remaining factors are averaged to create the overall rating.

As indicated in the governor's personal power column in Table 7-3, thirty-two of the governors fell in the 4.0–5.0 category, and all the governors' scores averaged to 3.8. In summary, most governors do bring their own brand of personal power to the governorship. Some fall toward the weaker side, but they are outweighed by the considerably larger number on the stronger side.

The Institutional Powers of Governors

The **institutional powers** of the governorship are those powers given to the governor by the state constitution, state statutes, and the voters when they vote on

Table 7-3   Personal Powers of the Governors, by State, 2011

State	Electoral mandate (EM)[a]	Ambition ladder (AL)[b]	Personal future (PF)[c]	Gubernatorial performance (GP)[d]	Governor's personal power index score (GPP)[e]
Alabama	5	5	5	n/a	4.00
Alaska	5	5	2	5	4.25
Arizona	5	5	3	3	4.00
Arkansas	5	1	3	5	3.5
California	5	5	5	3	4.5
Colorado	5	2	5	4	4.00
Connecticut	2	2	2	5	2.75
Delaware	5	5	5	n/a	5.00
Florida	2	1	5	2	2.50
Georgia	4	5	5	2	4.00
Hawaii	5	5	5	n/a	5.00
Idaho	4	5	5	3	4.25
Illinois	2	5	5	3	3.75
Indiana	5	5	3	4	4.25
Iowa	4	5	5	3	4.25
Kansas	5	5	5	4	4.75
Kentucky	5	5	4	4	4.50
Louisiana	5	5	4	4	4.50
Maine	2	5	5	3	3.75
Maryland	5	5	3	4	4.25
Massachusetts	2	1	5	3	2.75
Michigan	5	1	5	2	3.25
Minnesota	2	5	5	n/a	4.00
Mississippi	5	1	1	3	2.50
Missouri	5	5	5	3	4.50
Montana	5	1	1	n/a	1.75
Nebraska	5	5	3	5	4.50
Nevada	5	5	5	3	4.50
New Hampshire	4	1	5	5	3.75
New Jersey	3	5	5	3	4.00
New Mexico	4	5	5	4	4.50
New York	5	5	5	4	4.75
North Carolina	3	5	4	2	3.50
North Dakota	5	5	2	n/a	3.00
Ohio	2	5	5	2	3.50
Oklahoma	5	5	5	n/a	5.00
Oregon	2	5	5	3	3.75
Pennsylvania	4	5	5	2	4.00
Rhode Island	2	5	5	2	3.50
South Carolina	3	5	5	2	3.75
South Dakota	5	5	5	n/a	5.00
Tennessee	5	5	5	3	4.5
Texas	5	5	5	5	5.00
Utah	5	5	5	5	5.00
Vermont	2	5	5	n/a	4.00
Virginia	5	5	3	3	4.00

(Continued)

Table 7-3   Personal Powers of the Governors, by State, 2011 *(Continued)*

State	Electoral mandate (EM)[a]	Ambition ladder (AL)[b]	Personal future (PF)[c]	Gubernatorial performance (GP)[d]	Governor's personal power index score (GPP)[e]
Washington	3	5	5	1	3.50
West Virginia	5	5	5	3	4.50
Wisconsin	3	5	5	3	4.00
Wyoming	5	1	5	4	3.75
Fifty-state average	4.1	4.2	4.1	3.3	3.80

S O U R C E S : Electoral mandate: www.unc.edu./~beyle and author's data; ambition ladder: individual governors' Web sites and author's data; personal future: *The Book of the States, 2007* (Lexington, Ky.: Council of State Governments, 2007), and author's data; gubernatorial performance: author's data; governor's personal power: see note.

a. EM—electoral mandate: 5 = landslide win, won by eleven or more points; 4 = comfortable majority of six to ten points; 3 = narrow majority of three to five points; 2 = tight win of two or less points or a plurality win of under fifty points; 1 = succeeded to office (source: www.unc.edu/~beyle).

b. AL—governor's position on the state's political ambition ladder: 5 = steady progression; 4 = former governors; 3 = legislative leader or member of U.S. Congress; 2 = sub-state position to governor; 1 = governorship is first elective office (source: individual governors' Web sites and www.unc.edu/~beyle).

c. PF—personal future of the governor: 5 = early in term, can run again; 4 = late in term, can run again; 3 = early in term, term-limited; 2 = succeeded to office, can run for office; 1 = late in final term (source: *Book of the States, 2010* and *2011* [Lexington, Ky.: Council of State Governments, 2010, 2011], and www.unc.edu/~beyle).

d. GP—gubernatorial job performance rating in public opinion polls: 5 = over 60 percent positive job approval rating; 4 = 50–59 percent positive job approval rating; 3 = 40–49 percent positive job approval rating; 2 = 30–39 percent positive approval rating; 1 = less than 30 percent job approval rating; n/a = no polling data available (source: www.unc.edu/~beyle).

e. GPP—governor's personal powers index score, which is the sum of the scores of EM, AL, PF, and GP divided by four and rounded to the nearest tenth of a point, except for those states without a GP score where the sum is divided by three and rounded to the nearest tenth of a point.

constitutions and referenda. In a sense, these powers are the structure into which the governor moves after being elected to office.

Separately Elected State-Level Officials (SEP). The concept of a plural executive is alive and well in many of the states. Instead of following the presidential model, with a president and vice president as the only elected executive branch officials, most of the states have opted to allow voters to select a range of state officials.[7] Although reducing the number of separately elected executive branch officials is a common goal of reformers, states have generally rejected such reforms. Between 1955 and 1994, the number of separately elected officials at the state level dropped from 514 (in the forty-eight states) to 511 (in the fifty states). However, the average only dropped from 10.7 per state to 10.2 per state (Beyle 1995). In 2006, 308 separately elected officials served twelve major offices in the states (Hovey and Hovey 2007)—up from 306 such officials in 1972.

Each of these separate offices has its own political support network that is often resistant to changes in how leadership is selected. Some of these offices serve as

7. However, some people still argue for the plural executive model in the states. See Robinson (1998) for an argument based on a study of several of these separately elected officials in Wyoming.

launching pads for individuals seeking higher elective offices and are part of the state's political ambition ladder. It is often just not worth the struggle to change how they are selected; too much political effort and capital would be expended for too little real political gain.

For the governor, this means working with other officials who have similar claims to a statewide political constituency. Although elected officials in charge of carrying out administrative processes—such as secretaries of state or controllers—may seem innocuous by definition, they can cause a governor considerable problems. Tensions between governors and lieutenant governors have led to bizarre political situations in which governors have been wary of leaving their states lest the lieutenant governor sabotage the governor's programs while serving as acting governor. The Republican governor of North Carolina once found himself being sued by the separately elected Democratic attorney general in one case while simultaneously being represented by the same attorney general in another (Council of State Governments 1992, 29).

Tenure Potential (TP). How long governors can serve and whether they can succeed themselves for more than one term are important factors in determining just how much power they have. One argument is that those having the possibility of a longer stay in the office are better able to carry out their programs. But this can cut both ways: if limits were put on gubernatorial terms, governors might move faster and more decisively to achieve their goals and not be afraid of the voters' retribution at the ballot box when a necessary yet unpopular decision has to be made.

During the country's earliest years, ten of the governors of the thirteen original states had one-year terms, another a two-year term, and two had three-year terms. Now, forty-eight of the fifty state governors have four-year terms, and only two—in New Hampshire and Vermont—have two-year terms.

Another significant shift has taken place since 1960: the states have borrowed presidential term limits. The Twenty-second Amendment to the U.S. Constitution, adopted in 1951, states: "No person shall be elected to the office of President more than twice." This amendment was a direct reaction to the four terms to which President Franklin D. Roosevelt was elected. In 1960 only six states restricted their governors to two four-year terms (Schlesinger 1965, 220). But with the rise of the term limits movement, many states began to impose such a restriction, and by 2007 a total of thirty-six had done so.

The Power of Appointment (AP). One of the first decisions facing governors-elect is whom to appoint to key positions in the state administration. This power of appointment is fundamental to a governor's administration, especially in relation to the state bureaucracy. But the appointive power is also part of the governor's legislative role because gubernatorial promises of appointments to high-level executive positions or to the state judiciary can be the coin spent for support for particular legislation.

The history of state governors' appointment powers is one of growth from weak beginnings. The rise in the number of separately elected officials during the nineteenth century and the ad hoc proliferation of state agencies, often headed by boards and commissions, added to the problem of gubernatorial control. This diluted gubernatorial power was the backdrop for twentieth-century reforms to increase the governor's appointive power. The assumption underlying these reforms was that governors who can appoint officials without the involvement of any other authority can be held accountable for these officials' actions. Such governors are more powerful than those who must have one or both houses of the legislature confirm an appointment. Governors who only approve appointments rather than initiate them have even less appointive power. Weakest are those governors who neither appoint nor approve but have a separate body to do so and those who have no opportunity to appoint because the officials who head agencies are elected separately.

One caveat about this appointive power index is in order: a politically shrewd governor with an efficient political operation in the governor's office can probably orchestrate many of the selection decisions made by boards, commissions, and department or agency heads. Thus the governor might not be as powerless as the constitutional or statutory language might suggest.

Control over the Budget (BP). The **executive budget**, centralized under gubernatorial control, is a twentieth-century response to the chaotic fiscal situations found in state government at the turn of that century. Contained in one document, an executive budget seeks to place under the chief executive's control all the agency and department requests for legislatively appropriated funds; it also reflects the governor's own policy priorities. This document is then transmitted to the legislature for its consideration and ultimate passage. Putting the governor at the top of the centralized budget process in the executive branch and making the governor the chief lobbyist for the budget in the legislature places much power in the governor's hands.

What the governor can do is develop and present the state budget as the fiscal road map for the next fiscal year or biennium. The legislature can often undo much of this effort, however, as the budget bill works its way through the legislative process. In some states, the governor's proposed budget is described as dead on arrival because the legislature intends to build the state's next budget on its own. Moreover, when conflicts about the budget arise within executive branch agencies and between the agencies and the governor, the legislature is where agency grievances can be heard. The greater the power to make changes in the governor's proposed budget and the more the legislature is willing to do so, the less potential budget power is left for the governor. Of course, not all gubernatorial-legislative relationships are adversarial in nature, and what the governor proposes usually does set the agenda for debate and decision.

State legislatures have sought even more involvement in the budgetary process to regain some of the budgetary powers lost to governors. They have developed legislative oversight procedures, tried to require legislative appropriation or approval of federal grant funds flowing into the state, and sought to involve legislative committees in administrative budgetary shifts taking place during the fiscal year.

The budgetary powers of both executive and legislative branch actors are actually somewhat limited. For example, most states earmark their gasoline taxes for highway or mass transportation uses, and some earmark taxes on alcohol for various purposes or allot a fraction of their sales taxes to local governments. Tolls and fees for bridges, highways, and other state-established public authorities are retained by the agencies collecting them to finance their own activities and projects. In recent decades, states have faced more federal mandates for spending on Medicaid, certain environmental problems, prisons, and disabled persons. A governor's budgetary power is thus reduced when appropriated funds are earmarked or otherwise diverted by legislative prescription, when public authorities raise or expend independent income, or when federal mandates direct state expenditures. Most states provide their governors with full budget power and their legislatures with unlimited power to change a governor's proposed budget.

The Veto Power (VP). Governors possess the formal power to veto bills and, in most states, parts of bills passed by the legislature. This is the most direct power the governor can exercise in relation to the legislature. There are many differences in the veto power extended to governors: total bill veto, item veto of selected words, and item veto to change the meaning of words (National Association of State Budget Officers 1997, 19–31).

The **veto**, although a direct power over the legislature, also provides governors with some administrative powers because it gives them the ability to stop agencies from gaining support in a legislative end run around their governor's or their budget office's adverse decision. This is especially true in those forty-four states in which the governor can veto particular items in an agency's budget without rejecting the entire bill (Benjamin 1982; Moe 1988). Several states have gone further by allowing the governor to place conditions on approval of a full bill with amendments to the bill or rewording of the lines (Moe 1988).

The veto and its use involve two major actors: the governor and the legislature. It is an act of the legislature that a governor must sign or veto; however, the legislature can vote to override the veto and thus make a law without the governor's signature. In fact, more than a few states even allow their legislatures to recall bills from the governor before the governor has acted on the bill, thereby creating a negotiating situation—an informal alternative to the veto (Benjamin 1982). This tactic can allow the governor to become part of the legislative process with de facto amendatory power as the governor and the legislature negotiate the bill's contents (Benjamin 1982; Moe 1988).

The requirements for legislative override range from only a majority of members present and voting to a special majority, such as a vote of three-fifths of the legislature. Although the threat of a legislative override has not been great in the past, the number of gubernatorial vetoes overridden by legislatures has grown somewhat. Some would argue that the use of the veto is a sign of gubernatorial weakness rather than strength because strong governors win the battle through negotiation rather than confrontation with the legislature. Moreover, a governor using a veto risks embarrassment at the hands of the legislature. It is a power to be used sparingly (National Governors Association 1978).

Party Control (PC). Partisanship is a key variable in a governor's relationship with the legislature. If the governor's party also controls the legislature, partisan conflicts can be minimized and the governor's agenda is more likely to succeed. Cooperation should be the style of their relationship. If the governor and the legislative leadership are not of the same party, partisan conflicts all too often characterize the relationship and the governor's ability to achieve goals is lessened. Because each state except Nebraska has two houses in its legislature, it is quite possible that at least one house will be controlled by the opposition party.

Recent decades have seen a growing trend toward a "power split" in state governments (Sherman 1984), a situation of divided government in which one party holds the governor's office and the other party controls one or more of the legislative houses. In 2011 there were seventeen power splits. V. O. Key Jr. called this power split a "perversion" of separation of powers, allowing partisan differences to present an almost intractable situation (Key 1956, 52), but not all view this situation with alarm. In 1984 Gov. Lamar Alexander of Tennessee indicated that "it makes it harder, sometimes much harder; but the results can be better, sometimes much better" (Sherman 1984, 9). The outcome depends on how individual leaders handle a power split (van Assendelft 1997) and the type of legislation being considered (Bowling and Ferguson 2001).

When the governor's party is in the minority but controls a sizable number of seats, it is more difficult for the opposition majority to change the governor's budget or override the governor's veto. However, open and easygoing personalities can often overcome partisan differences or, as Governor Alexander said, "If you have good, well-meaning leaders, it's likely to be much better than any other process" (quoted in Sherman 1984, 12).

Because seventeen states had a power split in 2011, it is not surprising to see in the party control column in Table 7-4 that only five governors had a legislature in which their party had a substantial majority (holding more than 75 percent of legislative seats). Nebraska's governor had to deal with a unicameral (one-house) legislature elected on a nonpartisan basis. Only Rhode Island's governor faced a legislature controlled by a substantial majority of the opposition party in 2011.

Table 7-4 Governors' Institutional Powers, by State, 2010

State	Separately elected executive branch officials (SEP)[a]	Tenure potential (TP)[b]	Appointment power (AP)[c]	Budget power (BP)[d]	Veto power (VP)[e]	Party control (PC)[f]	Total	GIPI[g]
Alabama	1.5	4	2.5	4	4	4	20	3.3
Alaska	2.5	4	3.5	5	2.5	3.5	21	3.5
Arizona	2	4[h]	2.5	4	2.5	4	20	3.3
Arkansas	2	4[i]	2	2	2	4	16	2.7
California	1	4	2	4	2.5	4	17.5	2.9
Colorado	4	4	3	2	2.5	3	18.5	3.1
Connecticut	4	5	3	2	2.5	4	20.5	3.4
Delaware	2	4[j]	3	4	5	4	22	3.3
Florida	3	4	3	2	2.5	4	18.5	3.1
Georgia	1	4	1.5	5	2.5	4	18	3
Hawaii	5	4	2.5	2	5	5	23.5	3.9
Idaho	1	5	2	1	2.5	5	16.5	2.75
Illinois	4	5	3.5	2	5	4	23.5	3.9
Indiana	3	4[k]	3.5	5	0	4	19.5	3.25
Iowa	3	5	3.5	2	2.5	3	19	3.2
Kansas	3	4	2.5	5	2.5	4	21	3.5
Kentucky	2.5	4	3	4	2.5	3	19	3.2
Louisiana	2	4[l]	4	2	2	3	17	2.8
Maine	5	4	3	2	2	3.5	20	3.25
Maryland	4	4[m]	3	5	5	4	25	4.2
Massachusetts	4	5	3	5	4	5	26	4.3
Michigan	4	4	3	4	4	4	23	3.8
Minnesota	4	5	3.5	2	2	4	20.5	3.4
Mississippi	3	4	2	5	5	3	22	3.7
Missouri	2	4	2.5	4	2.5	2	17	2.8
Montana	3	4[n]	3	5	2.5	2	19.5	3.25
Nebraska	4	4[o]	3	2	2.5	3	18.5	3.1
Nevada	2.5	4	2.5	5	0	4	18	3
New Hampshire	5	2	2.5	4	0	3	16.5	2.75
New Jersey	5	4	4	4	5	2	24	4
New Mexico	4	4	3.5	5	2.5	2	21	3.5
New York	4	5	3	2	5	3	22	3.7
North Carolina	3	4	2.5	2	1.5	2	15	2.5
North Dakota	3	5	3.5	5	2.5	4	23	3.8
Ohio	4	4[p]	3	5	2.5	4	22.5	3.75
Oklahoma	1	4[q]	1.5	2	2	4	14.5	2.4
Oregon	1.5	4[r]	2	2	2.5	3	15	2.5
Pennsylvania	4	4	3	5	2.5	2	20.5	3.4
Rhode Island	4	4	3	2	0	1	14	2.3
South Carolina	1	4[s]	2.5	2	2.5	4	16	2.7
South Dakota	3	4	3	5	3	4.5	22.5	3.75
Tennessee	2	4[t]	4.5	2	2	4	16.5	2.75
Texas	2	5	1.5	2	2.5	4	17	2.8
Utah	4	5	3	2	2.5	5	21.5	3.6
Vermont	2	2	2.5	5	0	4	15.5	2.6
Virginia	2.5	3	3.5	5	3	3	20	3.3
Washington	1	5	4	5	5	4	24	4
West Virginia	2	4	3	5	2.5	4	20.5	3.4

(Continued)

Table 7-4 Governors' Institutional Powers, by State, 2010 *(Continued)*

State	Separately elected executive branch officials (SEP)[a]	Tenure potential (TP)[b]	Appointment power (AP)[c]	Budget power (BP)[d]	Veto power (VP)[e]	Party control (PC)[f]	Total	GIPI[g]
Wisconsin	3	5	1.5	4	2.5	4	20	3.3
Wyoming	2	4[u]	3	2	5	5	21	3.5
Fifty-state average	2.9	4.1	2.85	3.5	2.65	3.7	19.7	3.3

SOURCE: All data are from *The Book of the States, 2010*, vol. 42 (Lexington, Ky.: Council of State Governments, 2010), and updated as needed for 2010 election results and other information.

a. SEP—separately elected executive branch officials: 5 = only governor or governor/lieutenant governor team elected; 4.5 = governor or governor/lieutenant governor team, with one other elected official; 4 = governor/lieutenant governor team with some process officials (attorney general, secretary of state, treasurer, auditor) elected; 3 = governor/lieutenant governor team with process officials, and some major and minor policy officials elected; 2.5 = governor (no team) with six or fewer officials elected, but none are major policy officials; 2 = governor (no team) with six or fewer officials elected, but two are major policy officials; 1.5 = governor (no team) with six or fewer officials elected, but two are major officials; 1 = governor (no team) with seven or more process and several major policy officials elected.

b. TP—tenure potential of governors: 5 = four-year term, no restraint on reelection; 4.5 = four-year term, only three terms allowed; 4 = four-year term, only two terms permitted; 3 = four-year term, no consecutive election permitted; 2 = two-year term, no restraint on reelection; 1 = two-year term, only two terms permitted.

c. AP—governor's appointment power in six major functional areas: corrections, K–12 education, health, highway/transportation, public utilities regulation, and welfare. The six individual offices scores are totaled and then averaged and rounded to the nearest 0.5 for the score. 5 = governor appoints, no other approval needed; 4 = governor appoints and a board, council, or legislature approves; 3 = someone else appoints and the governor approves or shares appointment; 2 = someone else appoints and the governor and others approve; 1 = someone else appoints and no approval or confirmation needed; 0 = separately elected statewide official.

d. BP—governor's budget power: 5 = governor has full responsibility, legislature may not increase executive budget; 4 = governor has full responsibility, legislature can increase by special majority vote or subject to item veto; 3 = governor has full responsibility, legislature has unlimited power to change executive budget; 2 = governor shares responsibility, legislature has unlimited power to change executive budget; 1 = governor shares responsibility with another elected official, legislature has unlimited power to change executive budget.

e. VP—governor's veto power: 5 = governor has item veto, and a special majority vote of the legislature is needed to override a veto (three-fifths of legislators elected or two-thirds of legislators present); 4 = governor has item veto, with a majority of legislators elected needed to override; 3 = governor has item veto, with only a majority of the legislators present needed to override; 2.5 = governor has item veto power on appropriations only, with a special majority vote needed to override; 2 = governor has item veto power on appropriations only, with a majority of legislators elected needed to override; 1.5 = governor has no item veto, with a special legislative majority needed to override; 1 = governor has no item veto, with only a simple legislative majority needed to override; 0 = governor has no veto power.

f. PC—gubernatorial party control: 5 = governor's party has a substantial majority (75 percent or more) in both houses of the legislature; 4.5 = governor's party has a substantial majority in one house and nearly a substantial majority in the other; 4 = governor's party has a simple majority in both houses (under 75 percent) or a substantial majority in one house and a simple majority in the other; 3.5 = governor's party has a simple majority in one house, and split control in the other; 3 = split control in the legislature or a nonpartisan legislature; 2 = governor's party has a simple minority (25 percent or more) in both houses or a simple minority in one house and a substantial minority (under 25 percent) in the other; 1 = governor's party has a substantial minority in both houses.

g. GIPI—governor's institutional powers index. To assess and compare how the fifty governors fared in their institutional powers, the scores of each indicator were combined into a single additive index. The six indicator scores for each state's governorship are averaged to remain within the framework of the five-point scale, and the average across all fifty states is 3.3.

h. Arizona—absolute two-term limitation, but not necessarily consecutive.

i. Arkansas—same as in Arizona.

j. Delaware—eligible for eight of any period of twelve years.

k. Indiana—after two consecutive terms, must wait for four years or one full term before being eligible again.

l. Louisiana—same as in Indiana.

m. Maryland—same as in Indiana.

n. Wyoming—eligible for eight of sixteen years because of a Wyoming Supreme Court ruling that held term limits to be unconstitutional.

o. Nebraska—same as in Indiana.

p. Ohio—same as in Indiana.

q. Oklahoma—same as in Indiana.

r. Oregon—eligible for eight out of any period of twelve years.

s. South Carolina—same as in Indiana.

t. Tennessee—same as in Indiana.

u. Wyoming—same as in Montana.

The Institutional Powers of Governors: Summary. These six elements can be combined to comprise the governor's institutional powers index (GIPI). Each state's scores on each element are averaged to create an overall five-point scale. Actual values range from a low of 2.3 in Rhode Island to a high of 4.3 in Massachusetts. The fifty-state average is 3.3. See Table 7-4 for explanations of how values are assigned and for values by state for each element.

Overall Gubernatorial Powers in the Fifty States. The two sets of gubernatorial powers can be combined into one overall ten-point index of **gubernatorial powers**. The results, presented in Table 7-5, show an average score of 7.3. At the high side of this combined index with scores of 8.0 or greater are ten states—Delaware, Maryland, New Jersey, and New York in the Northeast; Alabama in the South; Kansas in the Midwest; and Hawaii, New Mexico, South Dakota, and Utah in the West. At the low end of the scale with scores under 6.5 are nine states—Connecticut and Rhode Island in New England; Arkansas, Florida, Mississippi, North Carolina, and South Carolina in the South; and Montana and Oregon in the West. Of course, these ratings change as incumbents are replaced with a new group of men and women bringing with them their own personal styles and strengths or weaknesses. This combined index attempts to account for a variety of elements thought to contribute to the power of governors.

Gubernatorial Power: Other Approaches

This chapter has presented a long-standing framework for understanding gubernatorial power. Scholars of the governorship have made use of this index in slightly varying forms for many years, particularly as a mechanism for comparing the powers of governors across the states using a common metric. A substantial body of literature has employed the institutional

Table 7-5 Summary of Personal and Institutional Powers of Governors, by State, 2011

State	Score
Hawaii	8.90
South Dakota	8.75
Utah	8.60
Maryland	8.45
New York	8.45
Alabama	8.30
Delaware	8.30
Kansas	8.25
New Jersey	8.00
New Mexico	8.00
West Virginia	7.90
Texas	7.80
Alaska	7.75
Kentucky	7.70
Illinois	7.65
Nebraska	7.60
Indiana	7.50
Nevada	7.50
Washington	7.50
Iowa	7.45
California	7.40
Minnesota	7.40
Oklahoma	7.40
Pennsylvania	7.40
Arizona	7.30
Louisiana	7.30
Missouri	7.30
Virginia	7.30
Wisconsin	7.30
Ohio	7.25
Tennessee	7.25
Wyoming	7.25
Colorado	7.10
Massachusetts	7.05
Michigan	7.05
Georgia	7.00
Idaho	7.00
Maine	7.00
North Dakota	6.80
Vermont	6.60
New Hampshire	6.50
South Carolina	6.45
Oregon	6.25
Arkansas	6.20
Mississippi	6.20
Connecticut	6.15
North Carolina	6.00
Rhode Island	5.80
Florida	5.60
Montana	5.00
Fifty-state Average	7.40

SOURCE: Calculated from Tables 7-3 and 7-4.

NOTE: Each state's score is the sum of its overall scores in Tables 7-3 and 7-4.

powers index as a proxy for the power that derives from the office. Those who employ the index do so generally in the context of examining the relative importance of social, economic, and political variables on state policy outputs (Dometrius 1979). These studies have looked at a variety of issues of significance to policymaking in the states. They range from investigations of gubernatorial support of agency budget requests (Sharkansky 1968) to the effect of formal powers on administrative oversight (Hebert, Brudney, and Wright 1983; Brudney and Hebert 1987) to studies of gubernatorial effectiveness in the legislative arena (Dilger, Krause, and Moffett 1995) and the success of gubernatorial proposals (Ferguson 2003). Other scholars assert that individual elements of the index should be broken out and, most important, used to predict success in the appropriate context (Dometrius 1979; Gross 1991; Barrilleaux and Berkman 2003; Ferguson 2003). Although several scholars have expressed some concerns about the limitations of the index, no one has offered a comparable substitute. Other scholars warn about use of the index over time. Krupnikov and Shipan (2011) point out changes that have accompanied the presentation of the index over the years that make its use potentially problematic.

Other scholars remind their peers that formal powers are merely potential power. They must be skillfully mobilized by a governor if they are to be of any use (Sigelman and Dometrius 1988). Finally, many scholars have asserted that formal powers are necessary but not sufficient tools for governors attempting to lead—in whatever arena (Bernick 1979; Sigelman and Dometrius 1988; Durning 1991; Dilger, Krause, and Moffett 1995; Ferguson 2003). The indices of power presented here are therefore only a small piece of understanding gubernatorial power. And there are certainly other means of capturing this fundamental notion.

Krupnikov and Shipan (2011) argue for a more nuanced understanding of gubernatorial budget power. They turn to indicators developed by the National Association of State Budget Officers of the role of the governor in various steps in the budget process. These indicators are (1) the governor's ability to spend federal funds without legislative approval; (2) the governor's line item veto power; (3) the governor's power to reorganize departments related to the budget without legislative approval; (4) the governor's ability to reduce the budget without legislative approval in addition to a traditional indicator from *The Book of the States*; and (5) whether the governor has sole authority for preparing the budget.

Other scholars have recently looked for other means of understanding gubernatorial power. Drawing on the presidency literature, some have begun to examine the unilateral power wielded by governors. Executive orders (at both the national and state levels) have traditionally received little scholarly attention because they were formerly believed to have only narrow significance relevant only to the execution of the law. Recent scholarship, however, questions this assumption. For example, Ferguson and Bowling (2008) find that governors in all fifty states employ executive orders and that they are used for a variety of purposes. Although many of these executive orders are symbolic in nature, many others are more substantive. Ferguson and Foy (2011) have taken a closer look at other means of unilateral power in the governorship. Examining Indiana's governor (a weak governor according to the institutional powers index), they find that governors can accomplish many of their policy goals by unilateral action, meaning they need not concern themselves with working with the state legislature, nor must they always employ executive orders when not pursuing legislation. Instead, governors can pursue many types of what they call "executive action," including giving orders to state agency heads, issuing policy memos, or simply entering into contracts with outside service providers to create a change in state policy. In 2007, for example, Indiana governor Mitch Daniels changed the state's welfare intake system by directing the relevant agency to enter into a contract for services with IBM. The legislature was not consulted and, upon reconvening, it held hearings and raised objections. But the decision had already been made, and changes had already been put in place.

BEING GOVERNOR

The true measure of governors and their administrations is how well they actually perform the various roles assigned to them. Are they able to translate their potential powers into effective action? What additional informal powers must they use to achieve the goals of their administrations?

As governor of Tennessee, Lamar Alexander argued that a governor's role was to "see the state's few most urgent needs, develop strategies to address them, and persuade at least half the people that he or she is right" (Alexander 1986, 112). For Alexander, the governor's main role is policymaking. A former governor of Vermont, Madeleine Kunin (1985–1991), agreed and asserted that "the power of a governor to set the tone and define the values of a state administration is enormous." She also felt that "as governor, I had the incredible luxury to dream on a grand scale" (Kunin 1994, 11–12).

The Governor as Policymaker

The goals of a gubernatorial administration are those policy directions a governor wishes to emphasize while in office. The types of policy priorities vary greatly across the activities of state government and depend on several factors, including the governor's own personal interests and outside events.

From a series of interviews with former governors, several themes emerged on how they believed they exerted policy leadership. Most saw their role as that of an issue catalyst, picking the issue up from the public, focusing it, and seeking to take action on it. Some others saw their role as that of a spectator viewing policy issues arising out of conflicts between actors on the state scene, whether they were special interest groups, the bureaucracy, or the mayor of the state's largest city. Finally, a few saw the governor as a reactor to accidents of history and other unanticipated events. In the eyes of these governors, leadership was more a process of problem solving and conflict resolution than agenda setting (National Governors Association 1981, 1).

Various basic changes have aided governors in exerting policy leadership. The first level of change has taken place in the governor's office itself. In recent years, the office has increased greatly in size, ability, functions, and structure. What used to amount to a few close associates working together with the governor has now been transformed into a much larger and more sophisticated bureaucratic organization in many of the states.

There have also been changes in the governor's extended office—the budget and planning agencies—which are increasingly being moved closer to the governor. In the most recent changes, governors have developed more aggressive offices of policy management, often following the federal model by creating a state-level office of management and budget. One of the most critical roles of these agencies is "to provide the governor an independent source of advice on a broad range of state policy issues" (Flentje 1980, 26). They can also assist by reaching into the departments and agencies to help them implement policy directions and decisions.

These changes, and others, highlight the basic fact that governors have had to improve their policy capacity substantially to govern, especially in administering their state's executive branch. But governors can vary on how they use this capacity, how much they believe it really helps them, and how well they perform in this role.

Governors in the Legislative Arena

One of the most important roles of governors in the modern period is that of legislative leader. Armed with the status and stature of the governorship, governors take the lead in lawmaking. Although governors are not members of the legislative branch, the tools of the office of governor and the political environment in the states encourage governors to take an active role. These formal powers include the veto, the power to present a State of the State address, the power to call special sessions of the legislature, and the power to prepare and administer the budget. Informal and enabling resources are also important for the role of legislative leader. Informal resources such as personality, the popularity of the governor, a popular mandate, and skill and charisma assist the governor in legislative leadership, as do enabling resources such as a strong professional staff (Dilger, Krause, and Moffett 1995; Ferguson 2003).

Public policymaking is a long, complicated process. Thus the legislative leadership role of the governor encompasses at least two of the "phases" of the policy process. Governors can use their resources to bring problems to the attention of the legislature (agenda setting) and then to attempt to influence the types of solutions adopted (policy formulation). During the agenda-setting phase, public officials identify problems requiring governmental action. Though any number of issues might be of concern to governors, unresolved conflicts that have a bearing on the lives of large numbers of people tend to be the issues that make it to the public agenda (Gleiber and Shull 1992). During this phase, the governor can make a large contribution (Rosenthal 1990; Bernick and Wiggins 1991; Gross 1991; Herzik 1991). The governor's role as agenda setter arises from several sources, most notably the responsibility to prepare the budget, to present State of the State addresses, and to call special sessions (Jewell 1969; Francis and Weber 1980; Ransone 1985; Bernick and Wiggins 1991). The visibility of the office also offers governors access to the media and the public and the opportunity to claim credit, which encourages gubernatorial agenda setting (Beyle and Muchmore 1983; Rosenthal 1990; Bernick and Wiggins 1991).

After a policy question is placed on the agenda, the work of understanding state problems, gathering information, and researching and drafting potential solutions begins. Although this phase is primarily the domain of legislators, governors have a role to play here as well. Legislative committees typically do much of the work on possible laws. Legislative leaders exert a lot of influence over which bills make it out of committee, which ones make it to the floor of the chamber for consideration, and which ones finally pass. Governors have legislative liaisons to work the legislature on their behalf, and they also rely on others such as party leaders and legislative allies to act on their behalf. Meanwhile, department heads may be mobilized to present information to the legislature and lobby in behalf of the governor's initiatives.

Anyone hoping to win adoption of a piece of preferred legislation must forge a coalition of supporters through bargaining (Neustadt 1980). Bargaining requires having something of value to offer to someone else. Although governors, like everyone else who hopes to pass legislation, must engage in this time-consuming bargaining process, they, with their many tools, are especially well placed to win. For example, the governor can offer support on a member's "pet legislation" in exchange for that member's support for the governor's initiatives. Governors also benefit from the symbolic importance of the governorship as they engage in bargaining with legislators. They can invoke the symbolism of the office to convince some legislators to change their minds. In short, if the governor calls a member into the executive office and looks across a desk marked by the great seal of the state and asks a member for support, that member may find it difficult to say no.

Governors can also perform special services for members by helping their constituents with problems. A legislator who has sought and received help from the governor's office for a constituent may be more willing to cast a vote in favor of the governor's legislative goals later on. Governors can create goodwill with a legislator as well by granting a constituent of that legislator a key appointment in exchange for the member's support on proposed legislation. Finally, governors may offer legislators their political support by raising money and making campaign appearances (Rosenthal 1990).

Research on the governor's role in the legislative agenda has most often centered on the use of the veto (and its impact) and the governor's role in budget making. Scholarship on budgeting has given the governor center stage. In most states, historically the budget has been a primary domain of the governor (Sharkansky 1968; Gross 1980; Moncrief and Thompson 1980; Abney and Lauth 1985; Gosling 1985, 1986). However, state legislators are key actors here as well. Although this varies across the states, some scholarship has found a trend toward greater legislative branch budget activity and the end of executive dominance of the budgetary process (Gosling 1985; Thompson 1987; Rosenthal 1990; Clynch and Lauth 1991). Others characterize the budgetary process in the twenty-first century as more balanced, dominated by neither the legislature nor the executive, with each playing a key role (Barrilleaux and Berkman 2003; Goodman 2007; Dometrius and Wright 2009). What predicts the balance of power? It appears that institutionally strong governors can dominate budgetary agendas and also block legislative alternatives, though both of these actions cause governors to accrue a variety of costs (Breunig and Koski 2009). However, highly professionalized legislatures are better able to bargain with the governor and hold out for and achieve their desired outcomes (Kousser and Phillips 2009).

The veto has also been the subject of much scholarship. Governors rarely use the veto. Indeed, as noted earlier, the use of the veto might be interpreted as evidence of weakness rather than strength; it could indicate failure to achieve the governor's goals at some previous stage (Beyle 1990; Rosenthal 1990). What prompts governors to ultimately employ the veto? Does it stem from personal characteristics or from institutional arrangements? Governors in similar institutional situations behave in predictably similar ways. For example, governors with greater formal powers issue more vetoes. Governors also respond to the rules. Governors in states with more stringent override rules use more vetoes. Governors also respond to the context. Governors issue more vetoes under divided government and when they are lame ducks. Perhaps because governors are so strategic about the use of vetoes, they are rarely overridden (Wiggins 1980; Wilkins and Young 2002).

The amendatory and item vetoes to which most governors have access presumably offer them more flexibility in influencing legislation once it reaches their desks. The item veto grants the governor the opportunity to strike out certain elements of a bill, particularly unwanted spending (Dearden and Husted 1993). Although not much research has been conducted on the use of these vetoes, there is some evidence that these are useful tools for governors attempting to influence the actions of the legislature (Bernick and Wiggins 1991).

A better understanding of the larger role of the governor in the legislative domain requires research that links specific gubernatorial proposals to specific legislative enactments. Although this is not an easy task, some scholars have done research along these lines (Bernick and Wiggins 1991; Gross 1991; Ferguson 2003). This scholarship sheds some light on gubernatorial success at legislative leadership. Most important for the governor is political party. The strength of the governor's party in the legislature is critical for gubernatorial success (Morehouse 1996; Hall 2002). However, even support from the governor's own party is not guaranteed. Gubernatorial partisans are more supportive and opposing party members are less supportive in election years (Hall 2002). Prior experience serving in the legislature helps the governor, while involvement in a major scandal hurts (Ferguson 2003).

Factors related to the political, economic, and institutional environments also help to explain success of gubernatorial proposals (Ferguson 2003).

In summary, it is not impossible for governors to convince the required numbers of legislators to support their policy preferences, but it is not a simple task. It is significantly more difficult than simply convincing the legislature to take up a particular agenda item for consideration. No matter the difficulty, the governor's role in both agenda setting and policy formulation makes legislative leadership among the most important jobs of modern governors. At the same time, this role is a reminder of the limitations of power in the American political system. Even officials as prominent and powerful as governors are not typically able to make law single-handedly. They must work with others through an established and complicated process to achieve their policy goals.

Overseeing the Bureaucracy

In addition to serving as legislative leaders, governors today are in name and in practice the chief executives of their states. Control of the bureaucracy is a constant struggle as governors compete with legislators for control in this arena, in addition to bureaucrats themselves (Abney and Lauth 1986; Rosenthal 1990; Abney and Lauth 1998; Elling 2004). Because legislatures write the laws and delegate a significant amount of discretion to the executive branch officials who must implement them, legislators retain the right to oversee how that discretion is exercised. In addition to governors and legislators, executive branch officials themselves sometimes seek to make their own choices. Based on their knowledge and expertise, these officials form preferences about how the laws implemented by their agencies should be managed. Even if such administrators are appointed by the governor, they may not always agree with the governor's policy positions. Agency heads with significant experience and a broad set of political supporters outside the governor's mansion may actually be able to pursue their policy interests to the exclusion of the governor's goals.

The struggle to control state bureaucracy is one of the long-standing conflicts of state politics. Multiple actors have a legitimate claim on influencing what the bureaucracy does. All three sets of actors (governors, legislators, and agency heads) are today more professional and have more resources to influence the bureaucracy. Thus all three sets of actors could exert control over the bureaucracy. However, the extent to which each has actually exerted control has varied over time. Interested legislators can hold hearings about agency operations. They can also pass legislation to add to, alter, or even abolish programs. Perhaps most important, legislators remain the key actors in the budgetary process, and they are responsible for approving administrative spending requests.

Nevertheless, if there is a battle between the governor and the legislature for executive control, being a single actor gives the governor an edge. Legislatures rarely act in pursuit of a unified goal because they are made up of many members. Moreover, legislators are likely to place less emphasis on exerting influence in this arena. The work is very time-consuming; holding hearings, reviewing agency rules and regulations, and examining spending decisions require a very large time commitment on the part of a concerned legislator, and such oversight rarely results in any substantive policy change. As legislatures have become more professionalized, legislators increasingly concern themselves with lawmaking, campaigning, and constituency work, all of which typically take precedence over oversight of the bureaucracy (Wright 1967; Bowling and Wright 1998a). More professionalized legislatures have more resources, however, and with their longer terms, lower membership turnover, and more legislative staff, legislatures are more capable of providing direction to the bureaucracy (Potoski and Woods 2001). Although only a few legislatures can be called truly professional, to the extent that more are becoming professionalized, legislatures may be more influential in executive oversight.

As it stands today, though, the tools that governors possess give them an advantage. Most states now have a central personnel agency, headed by a gubernatorial appointee, rather than a semiautonomous civil service commission. Governors also appoint a significant number of other high-level administrative officials. Surveys of state administrators seem to indicate that gubernatorial influence is on the rise. In the 1960s, state agency heads believed the legislature exerted more influence over them than the governor (Wright 1967). However, by the 1990s at least half of agency heads reported that governors exerted greater control, and less than a third said the legislature was more influential (Bowling and Wright 1998b). This change has taken place despite the fact that governors spend less time on this role than their other responsibilities. Executive branch leadership is a challenging job and the benefits are not always clear (Elling 1992).

Much like research on gubernatorial leadership in the legislative arena, studies of gubernatorial influence over the bureaucracy tend to examine the effect of institutional powers (Dometrius 2002; Elling 2004; Woods 2004). Though not all scholarship finds a significant relationship between institutional powers collectively and executive influence over the bureaucracy (Potoski and Woods 2001), scholarship almost universally points to the importance of the appointment power (Abney and Lauth 1983; Hebert, Brudney, and Wright 1983; Brudney and Hebert 1987; Bowling and Wright 1998a). Governors appoint a great number of executive branch officials. Although many top-level actors remain outside gubernatorial appointment, states have taken steps to "shorten the ballot" and thereby give governors greater control (Elling 2004).

The creation of an infrastructure in the governor's office has undeniably empowered the governor. This growth in the gubernatorial office has accompanied the growth of state government generally and the related growing workload for governors. The creation of a modern gubernatorial office presumably empowers governors seeking to oversee the bureaucracy (Bowman, Woods, and Stark 2010).

Some scholars point to the importance of newer resources such as economic analysis (cost-benefit analysis, economic impact analysis, or regulatory analysis), program evaluation, and administrative rule review as possible sources of gubernatorial influence over the bureaucracy (Woods and Baranowski 2007). Administrative rule review is the ability to modify or strike down administrative rules crafted by state agencies. The degree to which governors have this power varies greatly across the states. In some states, the governor may review existing rules, but in other states the governor has review authority only over newly proposed rules. This situation limits the efficacy of this power. Some states give the governor power of approval before proposed rules can take effect (Grady and Simon 2002; Woods 2004).

Reinventing Government

Governors are responsible for overseeing the large and often unwieldy state bureaucracies. The appointment power offers some help, but this power has proven inadequate for governors who hope to truly direct state administration. To that end, most states have given their governors the authority to reorganize the executive branch. A typical **reorganization** involves consolidating the responsibilities of many separate agencies into a smaller number on the basis of broad functional categories. Reorganization is purported to reduce wasteful duplication and coordinate the delivery of services. Reorganization also usually brings the heads of the consolidated agencies under the managerial authority of the governor, giving the governor greater authority over the implementation of law. The ability to reorganize the state bureaucracy has long been considered an important tool for controlling the bureaucracy (Rosenthal 1990; Beyle 1995; Elling 2004; Gormley 2006).

Although reorganization is the most common form of bureaucratic reform, some observers dismiss such reorganization as too limited to have much real effect. In *Reinventing Government: How the Entrepreneurial Spirit Is Transforming the Public Sector,* Osborne and Gaebler (1993) call for a more aggressive approach. A major element of their call for reinvention is the idea of catalytic government, meaning governments should determine which services to provide and how they are to be funded, but the actual implementation of these services need not be done by government employees. A closely related idea is called competitive government. This concept advocates bringing competition into the arena of service delivery—using economic principles to ensure that services are delivered efficiently and effectively.

States have, to varying degrees, adopted the ideas of reinvention into their administration of services. Privatization is a common approach whereby states contract with private for-profit or nonprofit organizations for the provision of certain services. States have employed private contractors for services such as highway construction for many years. Building maintenance, food delivery, clerical services, and security services are other examples of areas in which states often hire private contractors. In recent decades, the use of privatization has moved into other arenas such as managing daycare, adoption, and foster services; managing Medicaid claims; and overseeing employee training and placement. A few states have even experimented with privately run correctional facilities, but with some rather dire results in some instances when riots broke out because of the poor training of guards and high prisoner to guard ratios.

The most common reason states offer for contracting out is that private providers can deliver services of equal or better quality at a lower cost than a government agency. Privatization also makes sense when the need for a particular service is short-lived, because hiring someone else to provide it rather than building a state apparatus would be quicker and cheaper. Privatization has not been uniformly successful, however. In some cases, costs have indeed declined, but sometimes that decline has been accompanied by a decline in either the quantity or quality of services. The fact that outside contractors usually need to make a profit to stay in business may encourage them to cut corners, resulting in a poor-quality product. Another criticism of contracting out is that it lowers accountability to the public. Citizens who wish to complain about the provision of a service may have difficulty discovering who is actually responsible because people at so many levels are involved.

Although none of the current reforms has been fully successful in achieving all they set out to accomplish, states continue to experiment with these and other means of improving the work of government. The work of state bureaucracies continues to be scrutinized and is often viewed with disfavor. This disfavor will always create an impetus to try to alter "business as usual" so that public officials, especially governors, can claim to be addressing the concerns of the public.

In the Middle of Intergovernmental Relations

The world that a governor must address is not constrained by the boundaries of the state. In an earlier time, out-of-state efforts made by governors were limited to occasional trips to attract industry, to attend the socially oriented governors' conferences, and to participate in the presidential nominating conventions every four years. In recent decades, however, the states and the governors have found that they need to focus on the issues, problems, and government activities that are part of the larger intergovernmental system in which individual states are lodged. Some of these issues may concern several states concurrently, such as a pollution problem with a common river. Others are regional in scope, such as higher education in the South following World War II and the establishment of the Education Commission of the States in the mid-1960s. Still others, such as health and welfare reform, are national in scope, and thus all states and governors have a stake in the actions of Congress and the national executive branch. In the 2000s, some governors have emerged as leaders in attempts to battle greenhouse gas emissions and global climate change. Governors and their Canadian counterparts have also entered into compacts to set targets for reductions in greenhouse gases and identify best practices (Burke and Ferguson 2010).

Gubernatorial relations with a state's congressional delegation are complex and subject to different types of difficulties. At the purely political level, a governor may be seen as a potential challenger for a U.S. senator's seat or even a congressional seat. Meanwhile, more and more members of Congress are eyeing gubernatorial chairs. On policy matters, a governor may give attention to particular issues because of the state's interest or for the benefit of states in general. Congressional delegation members also have their own interests that may or may not coincide with the governor's expressed interests. Therefore, the degree of cooperation between these two sets of political actors can vary greatly; some governors find their delegations remote, inaccessible, and suspicious of any joint venture, and others find camaraderie.

In 2010 twenty-eight states maintained offices in Washington. The creation of these offices and the sheer number of states that have established them indicate that governors do not believe they can rely on their congressional delegations to speak up for the needs of their state governments in policy negotiations. Interestingly, this is not a recent development. The "cooperative federalism" of the 1930s provided new opportunities for the states to seek assistance from the federal government, and governors took steps to position themselves to pursue those benefits. Among those opportunities was vying for federal war contracts. New York and Connecticut, with their industrial bases and entrepreneurial governors, were the first states to establish Washington offices to work to secure these benefits, and New York's office has remained in continual operation since that time (Jensen and Emery 2011).

In recent years, a new factor—length of tenure—has entered the politics of intergovernmental relations. Longer tenure is important in the governor's intergovernmental role. Relations need time to mature, and the activities undertaken are complex and take time to perform effectively. Furthermore, leadership in intergovernmental organizations gives governors a platform for airing their views and for actually affecting policy. But term limitations restrict governors in their abilities to fulfill this intergovernmental role, especially in holding leadership positions. Thus states may be shortchanging themselves by limiting the tenure they allow their governors (Grady 1987). As the movement to limit terms of public officials grows and succeeds, this particular role of governors may also be curtailed. Those advocating term limits have been more concerned about internal political dynamics than this intergovernmental role. However, those concerns appear to have been misplaced. Governors serving multiple terms do not appear to lose their efficacy as state leaders during lengthy tenures (Lammers and Klingman 1986). Because of the negative ramifications of term limits for gubernatorial leadership, perhaps these tenure limitations should be reconsidered.

Working with the Media

Probably the most significant source of informal power available to governors is their relationship with the public through the media and through other modes of contact. Most governors have used media contact with the people to gain election to office, and so they are well aware of the potency of this informal power. Once in office, however, the governor's relationship with the press undergoes a subtle yet important change. The governor is no longer the head of the army of attack but is the head of the army of occupation, the new administration in the state capital.

Although the media's attention to state government and its activities has waned in recent years, the media still watch the governor with a keen eye, often evaluating gubernatorial performance not only against the promises but against previous administrations and the needs of the state. Furthermore, the media can become suddenly very interested in the activities and conduct of someone the governor has brought into the administration. Stories of official misconduct sell newspapers and make the evening news more exciting—or so many in the media believe.

Governors have the opportunity to dominate the news from the state capital by carefully planning when press conferences are held during the day and when press releases are distributed. If they time it right, their story is on the evening television news and in the morning papers, where the audiences are large. A governor's communications or press relations office can determine a portion of the news that airs about a gubernatorial administration.

Governors do vary, however, in their approach to and openness with the media. Some hold press conferences routinely and others hold them only on specific occasions. Individual interview sessions with members of the press are regular fare for some governors, whereas others are more protective of their time and interactions with the media.

The advice that incumbents offer new governors indicates just how sensitive governors are to this relationship: "The media expects you to do well. Thus, doing well isn't news." "When you hold a press conference and are going to face the lions, have some red meat to throw them or they'll chew on you." "Never make policy at a news conference." "Never argue with a person who buys ink by the barrel" (Beyle and Huefner 1983, 268).

How well do governors actually do in this relationship? Do the new governors heed the advice of their more experienced peers? Are they able to make that switch from campaigner to governor effectively? Obviously, the answer is that it varies by individual governor. But governors seeking reelection do not need poor media relations, which are hard to overcome. After all, the media are the primary vehicles by which voters get a reading on how their governor is performing.

Another part of a governor's public role is primarily reactive. The governor's office receives many letters, visits, and telephone calls. Most of these must be answered. Each response probably affects two to five people among the extended family and friends of the recipient. Thus the number of contacts between the governor or the governor's staff and the public, either directly or indirectly, is very high. How well the governor's office handles these interactions can become an important part of the public's perception of the governor's performance.

Some governors take an activist stance toward the public and generate citizen contacts through a variety of approaches. Some capitalize on their ceremonial role by appearing at county fairs, cutting ribbons at shopping centers, attending dedication ceremonies, and crowning beauty queens. These activities often can require a considerable investment of time.

Not the least of a governor's relations with the media and their statewide constituency is responding to an emergency situation. This response can include calling out the National Guard to help maintain control in the aftermath of a disaster such as an earthquake, hurricane, or tornado. A governor must then make a personal visit to the site of a disaster to see the damage and to talk with the people who have suffered in the calamity—and possibly reap the political rewards. In fact, it is probably a liability for any governor to fail to appear under such circumstances.

The governor, through this public role, has the potential to set the state's public agenda and focus attention on it. A governor's priorities can become the state's priorities unless unforeseen crises or problems arise or the media themselves are inadequate to the task.

LEAVING THE GOVERNORSHIP

According to former Vermont governor Madeleine Kunin (1994), "There are two climaxes in political life: rising to power and falling from it." At the end of a gubernatorial term, a governor usually has several options. Many can and do seek reelection to the governor's chair. Indeed, in recent decades some governors have virtually turned a gubernatorial chair into their own private property as they served for several terms. Although seeking reelection as an incumbent usually provides a major campaign advantage, winning reelection (and sometimes renomination) is not always an easy task.

The Unplanned Departure

Why do incumbent governors lose? In a few situations, a single issue can pinpoint the cause of a governor's defeat, and that issue may be something that the governor has little control over, such as a souring economy. In other cases, a defeat is the result of an accumulation of several issues and concerns about the governor's administration. Scandals and incompetence—administrative, political, or personal—are also significant factors in the defeat of incumbent governors.

In some situations, incumbents just overstayed their welcomes and were blocking others from the office, or the voters in the party primary or general election wanted someone new in the office. The Republican resurgence across the nation and in the South, specifically, demonstrates that changing politics and voter preferences can be the cause.

Between 1970 and 2006, there were 519 separate gubernatorial elections, and 313 incumbent governors sought reelection to another term. Although most—75 percent—of these incumbents won, seventy-seven governors did lose, twenty in their own party primary process and fifty-seven in the general election. Furthermore, as of 2011 twenty-three governors had been removed from office by a criminal court decision or impeachment, or they chose to resign in the face of such scandals.

Recall is one mechanism (available in nineteen states) for removing public officials before their term in office is complete. In 2002 California governor Gray Davis, a Democrat, won his second term with a 47.3 percent plurality. Shortly after that election, a group opposed to Davis began circulating a petition to hold a recall election. They were able to gather enough signatures, and in 2003 a recall and replacement election was held. Davis was recalled from office by a vote greater than 55 percent; Arnold Schwarzenegger, a Republican, was then chosen by the voters to serve out the remainder of Davis's term. In the volatile politics of 2011, there are movements afoot in a handful of states to force recall elections for public officials, including governors. It is too early to tell whether any of these drives will ultimately be successful.

Some states seem to experience more than their share of corruption in the governor's office. For example, of the nine men who have served as governor of Illinois since 1953, five (William Stratton, Otto Kerner, Daniel Walker, George Ryan, and Rod Blagojevich) were indicted for crimes committed either during their time in office or for illegal activity after leaving office. Four of these governors were ultimately convicted of their crimes, which ranged from racketeering and mail fraud to bribery and bank fraud. Governor Stratton was acquitted on charges that he employed campaign funds for private purposes. Most recently, in late June 2011 Governor Blagojevich was convicted on nearly all of the twenty federal charges levied against him, most famously trying to sell the U.S. Senate seat left vacant by Barack Obama's election to the presidency. In December 2011, the governor was sentenced to 14 years in prison. Governor Blagojevich was the first Illinois governor ever to be impeached. Before his impeachment and removal from office, Arizona governor Evan Meacham's 1988 conviction on impeachment charges was the first in seventy-five years. Interestingly, another Arizona governor, Fife Symington, was convicted of bank fraud and resigned from office in 1997. Symington was ultimately pardoned by President Bill Clinton (whose life he had saved from a riptide off Cape Cod).

In summary, governors seeking to stay in office or to regain office are vulnerable to the ambitions of others within their party and the state, to a desire on the part of voters for a change, to issues directly affecting the electorate's wallets or lives (jobs, the economy, taxation, the environment), and to allegations of misconduct or poor performance.

Onward and Upward

Staying in office is only one of several options that an incumbent governor may weigh. For some governors, the position is one step on a ladder that they hope leads to a higher office, such as the U.S. Senate or even the presidency. After all, four of the five most recent presidents had been governors—Jimmy Carter, Ronald Reagan, Bill Clinton, and George W. Bush. Governors are ubiquitous potential presidential nominees in both parties. The governorship, with the executive experience it engenders, serves as an excellent training ground for the presidency. Furthermore, some observers argue that the executive experience governors brought to the presidency actually helped to create the modern presidency (Ambar 2012).

Some governors move on to appointed national-level positions, such as the several governors who were appointed to cabinet-level offices during the George W. Bush administration: Secretary of Health and Human Services Tommy Thompson of Wisconsin (1987–2001); Administrator of the Environmental Protection Agency Christine Todd Whitman of New Jersey (1994–2001); Secretary of Homeland Security Tom Ridge of Pennsylvania (1995–2001); Secretary of Agriculture Mike Johanns of Nebraska (1999–2005); and Mike Leavitt of Utah (1993–2003), who served as both the secretary of health and human services and the administrator of the Environmental Protection Agency. Two New Hampshire governors became chief of staff to the president: Sherman Adams (1949–1953) for Dwight D. Eisenhower, and John Sununu (1983–1989) for George H. W. Bush.

Why did New Hampshire governors do so well in these presidential administrations? The early New Hampshire presidential primary is crucial to the presidential nomination process, and winning candidates remember the help given them by the governor. Now that the presidential primary process has changed so that many states vote early, other governors could reap the benefits of supporting the candidate who eventually wins the presidential race.

Some other governors move into leadership positions in the corporate world or in higher education: former governor of North Carolina Terry Sanford (1961–1965) became president of Duke University; former governor of Tennessee Lamar Alexander became president of the University of Tennessee; and former governor of New Jersey Tom Kean (1982–1990) became president of Drew University. However, one has to be impressed most with the large number of governors for whom the governorship was their ultimate elected public office. They sought the office, served, and returned to their private lives—often to lucrative law practices that might have included representing clients before the state legislature, state agencies, or state courts. Unfortunately, some governors were prosecuted for their misconduct while in office or prior to becoming governor, and some later served terms in prison.

Succession

The governor's office can be vacated before the official end of a term because of death, incapacity, impeachment, resignation, or recall. In such cases, a state must have a line of succession in place to ensure that the office is not left unattended. All states specify at least one person in their line of succession, although states vary in the procedures they employ. A variety of questions might arise as to whether states have sufficient policies in place and whether those policies are appropriate. The National Lieutenant Governors Association argues that states should consider questions such as the following: When should succession be triggered? Who is in the line of succession, and in what order? How deep is the line of succession? If incapacity is deemed to be temporary, how is incapacity determined? Once succession is triggered, does the new official become the "acting" governor, or does that person assume the title and all powers of the office (Hurst 2009)? If individuals from other branches of government are in line to succession, do they retain their other positions? If so, this raises some significant questions about violations of the separation of powers (Gulley 2011). In forty-three states, the lieutenant governor is first in line for succession to the governorship. The remaining states—Arizona, Oregon, and Wyoming—designate the secretary of state as first in line, while Maine, New Hampshire, Tennessee, and West Virginia name the senate president to this role.

Who will take over in the absence of the governor is not an inconsequential consideration. For example, in 2003 Gov. Frank O'Bannon of Indiana suffered a stroke and lingered in a coma for days before his death. Indiana law details how gubernatorial incapacitation is determined. The House Speaker and Senate president must file a letter with the state supreme court indicating that the governor is incapacitated. The supreme court must then meet within forty-eight hours to rule on the question. On September 10, 2003, the Speaker and Senate president filed such a letter regarding Governor O'Bannon, and the court declared the governor incapacitated, making the lieutenant governor acting governor. The governor died three days later, on September 13, and Joe Kernan, O'Bannon's lieutenant, became governor. Two governors resigned the governorship in New Jersey within four years in the early 2000s, and the acting governors continued to serve as Senate president, presiding over action in the Senate while heading the executive branch. New Jersey did not, at the time, have a lieutenant governor, but the state recently elected its first one.

Finally, if one needed additional evidence of its importance, the events of September 11, 2001, brought into clear focus the need to have clear and deep lines of succession to account for unexpected events, so that states facing enormous challenges need not do so without a governor at the helm (Hurst 2009).

Leaving

Most governors find a good life after being governor. But as former Michigan governor William Milliken (1969–1983) observed, they must plan their departure and "take advantage of the lessons learned by those who have already gone down the path." This means preparing for the new administration while winding down the old and preparing for their own new life. The National Governors Association developed a worst-case scenario to alert outgoing governors to what can happen without such planning and to suggest some strategies to follow to avert such problems (National Governors Association 1990).

All this sounds quite rational, but in the white heat of politics, especially when the governor is defeated at the polls, these steps are not easy to take, nor does there seem to be enough time to plan them. Although states generally make provisions for their incoming governors, they tend to ignore their outgoing ones. The exiting governors suddenly lose all the perquisites of being governor: staff, cars, drivers, schedulers, office equipment, telephones, and so forth. Hence the lament of former governor Calvin L. Rampton of Utah: "I never realized how much of a man's life he spends looking for a parking place" (quoted in Weeks 1984, 73).

CONCLUSION

The governorship is the highest elective office in a state and is, in some cases, the stepping-stone to an even higher office. The governor symbolizes the state to many, and when state government falters or errs, the public often holds the governor accountable. In recent years, the states have refurbished their governments, bidding "Goodbye to Goodtime Charlie" and in doing so have generally attracted a new breed of very capable people to serve as governor (Sabato 1978). But there are still signs that, although a few "Goodtime Charlies" remain, there is also a good chance that a handful of governors will lose their moral or ethical compasses in either seeking or holding the office.

This chapter has provided a view of the governorship through the eyes of the governors themselves and of those who watch and study what governors do. It has described the politics of becoming governor; the tools—both personal and institutional—available to the governor; the major roles now being performed by governors; and how, in performing these roles, governors have informal powers of considerable magnitude. Not only do governors sit atop the state governments and the state political system, but, through their informal powers, they can also set and dominate the state's policy agenda and have an impact on regional and national agendas.

KEY TERMS

executive budget, 222	merit system, 209
formal power, 216	personal power, 217
gubernatorial power, 227	reorganization, 235
institutional power, 218	veto, 223

REFERENCES

Abney, Glenn, and Thomas P. Lauth. 1983. "The Governor as Chief Administrator." *Public Administration Review* 43: 40–49.

———. 1985. "The Line Item Veto in the States." *Public Administration Review* 45: 372–377.

———. 1986. *The Politics of State and City Administration.* Albany: State University of New York Press.

———. 1998. "The End of Executive Dominance in State Appropriations." *Public Administration Review* 58: 388–395.

Adams, Greg D., and Peverill Squire. 2001. "A Note on the Dynamics and Idiosyncrasies of Gubernatorial Popularity." *State Politics and Policy Quarterly* 1: 380–393.

Alexander, Lamar. 1986. *Steps along the Way: A Governor's Scrapbook.* Nashville, Tenn.: Thomas Nelson.

Ambar, Saladin. 2012. *The Hidden Prince: How Governors Helped Build the Modern Presidency, 1976–1932.* Philadelphia: University of Pennsylvania Press.

Atkeson, Lonna Rae, and Randall W. Partin. 1995. "Economic and Referendum Voting: A Comparison of Gubernatorial and Senatorial Elections." *American Political Science Review* 89: 99–107.

Bardwell, Kedron. 2005. "Reevaluating Spending in Gubernatorial Races: Job Approval as a Baseline for Spending Effects." *Political Research Quarterly* 58: 97–105.

Barrilleaux, Charles, and Michael Berkman. 2003. "Do Governors Matter? Budgeting Rules and the Politics of State Policymaking." *Political Research Quarterly* 56: 409–417.

Barth, Jay, and Margaret R. Ferguson. 2002. "American Governors and Their Constituents: The Relationship between Gubernatorial Personality and Public Approval." *State Politics and Policy Quarterly* 2: 268–282.

Benjamin, Gerald. 1982. "The Diffusion of the Governor's Veto Power." *State Government* 55: 99–105.

Bernick, E. Lee. 1979. "Gubernatorial Tools: Formal vs. Informal." *Journal of Politics* 41: 656–664.

Bernick, E. Lee, and Charles W. Wiggins. 1991. "Executive-Legislative Relations: The Governor's Role as Chief Legislator." In *Gubernatorial Leadership and State Policy,* ed. Eric Herzik and Brent Brown. New York: Greenwood Press.

Beyle, Thad. 1990. "Governors." In *Politics in the American States: A Comparative Analysis,* 5th ed., ed. Virginia Gray, Herbert Jacob, and Robert Albritton, 568–573. Boston: Little Brown.

———. 1995. "Enhancing Executive Leadership in the States." *State and Local Government Review* 27: 18–35.

———. 1996. "Governors: The Middlemen and Women in Our Political System." In *Politics in the American States: A Comparative Analysis,* 6th ed., ed. Virginia Gray and Herbert Jacob. Washington, D.C.: CQ Press.

Beyle, Thad L., and Robert Huefner. 1983. "Quips and Quotes from Old Governors to New." *Public Administration Review* 43: 268–270.

Beyle, Thad L., and Lynn Muchmore. 1983. *Being Governor: The View from the Office.* Durham, N.C.: Duke University Press.

Bowling, Cynthia J., and Margaret R. Ferguson. 2001. "Divided Government, Interest Representation, and Policy Differences: Competing Explanations of Gridlock in the Fifty States." *Journal of Politics* 63: 182–206.

Bowling, Cynthia J., and Deil S. Wright. 1998a. "Change and Continuity in State Administration: Administrative Leadership across Four Decades." *Public Administration Review* 58: 429–445.

———. 1998b. "Public Administration in the United States: A Half-Century Administrative Revolution." *State and Local Government Review* 30: 52–64.

Bowman, Ann O'M, Neal D. Woods, and Milton R. Stark II. 2010. "Governors Turn Pro: Separation of Powers and the Institutionalization of the American Governorship." *Political Research Quarterly* 63: 304–315.

Breunig, Christian, and Chris Koski. 2009. "Punctuated Budgets and Governors' Institutional Powers." *American Politics Research* 37: 1116–1138.

Brudney, Jeffrey L., and F. Ted Hebert. 1987. "State Agencies and Their Environments: Examining the Influence of Important External Actors." *Journal of Politics* 49: 186–206.

Burke, Brendan, and Margaret Ferguson. 2010. "Going Alone or Moving Together: Canadian and American Middle Tier Strategies on Climate Change." *Publius* 40: 436–459.

Carsey, Thomas M., and Gerald C. Wright. 1998. "State and National Factors in Gubernatorial and Senatorial Elections." *American Journal of Political Science* 42: 994–1002.

Chubb, John E. 1988. "Institutions, the Economy, and the Dynamics of State Elections." *American Political Science Review* 82: 133–154.

Clynch, Edward J., and Thomas P. Lauth. 1991. "Conclusion: Budgeting in the American States—Conflict and Diversity." In *Governors, Legislatures, and Budgets,* ed. Edward J. Clynch and Thomas P. Lauth. New York: Greenwood Press.

Cohen, Jeffrey E., and James D. King. 2004. "Relative Unemployment and Gubernatorial Popularity." *Journal of Politics* 66: 1267–1282.

Council of State Governments. 1992. *The Book of the States, 1992–1993.* Lexington, Ky.: Council of State Governments.

———. 1996. *The Book of the States, 1996–1997.* Lexington, Ky.: Council of State Governments.

Crew, Robert E., Jr., David Branham, Gregory R.Weiher, and Ethan Bernick. 2002. "Political Events in a Model of Gubernatorial Approval." *State Politics and Policy Quarterly* 2: 283–297.

Crew, Robert E., Jr., and Gregory R. Weiher. 1996. "Gubernatorial Popularity in Three States: A Preliminary Model." *Social Science Journal* 33: 39–55.

Dearden, James A., and Thomas A. Husted. 1993. "Do Governors Get What They Want? An Alternative Examination of the Line-Item Veto." *Public Choice* 77: 707–723.

Dilger, Robert J., George A. Krause, and Randolph R. Moffett. 1995. "State Legislative Professionalism and Gubernatorial Effectiveness, 1978–1991." *Legislative Studies Quarterly* 20: 553–571.

Dometrius, Nelson C. 1979. "Measuring Gubernatorial Power." *Journal of Politics* 41: 589–610.

———. 2002. "Gubernatorial Approval and Administrative Influence." *State Politics and Policy Quarterly* 2: 251–267.

Dometrius, Nelson C., and Deil S. Wright. 2009. "Governors, Legislatures, and State Budgets across Time." *Political Research Quarterly* 63: 783–795.

Durning, Dan. 1991. "Education Reform in Arkansas: The Governor's Role in Policymaking." In *Gubernatorial Leadership and State Policy,* ed. Eric Herzik and Brent Brown. New York: Greenwood Press.

Elling, Richard C. 1992. *Public Management in the States: A Comparative Study of Administrative Performance and Politics.* Westport, Conn.: Praeger.

———. 2004. "Administering State Programs: Performance and Politics." In *Politics in the American States: A Comparative Analysis,* 8th ed., ed. Virginia Gray and Russell L. Hanson, 261–289. Washington, D.C.: CQ Press.

Ferguson, Margaret R. 2003. "Chief Executive Success in the Legislative Arena." *State Politics and Policy Quarterly* 3: 158–182.

Ferguson, Margaret R., and Cynthia J. Bowling. 2008. "Executive Orders and Administrative Control." *Public Administration Review* 68: S20–S28.

Ferguson, Margaret R., and Joseph J. Foy. 2011. "Unilateral Power: Beyond Executive Orders." *Proceedings of the Annual Meeting of the Midwest Political Science Association.* Chicago: Midwest Political Science Association.

Flentje, H. Edward. 1980. *Knowledge and Gubernatorial Policy Making*. Wichita: Wichita State University, Center for Urban Studies.

Francis, Wayne L., and Ronald E. Weber. 1980. "Legislative Issues in the 50 States." *Legislative Studies Quarterly* 5: 407–421.

Gleiber, Dennis W., and Steven A. Shull. 1992. "Presidential Influence in the Policymaking Process." *Western Political Quarterly* 45: 441–467.

Goodman, Doug. 2007. "Determinants of Perceived Gubernatorial Budgetary Influence among State Executive Budget Analysts and Legislative Fiscal Analysts." *Political Research Quarterly* 60: 43–54.

Gormley, William T. 2006. "Accountability Battles in State Administration." In *State of the States*: 4th ed, ed. Carl E. Van Horn, 101–119. Washington, D.C.: CQ Press.

Gosling, James J. 1985. "Patterns of Influence and Choice in the Wisconsin Budgetary Process." *Legislative Studies Quarterly* 10: 457–482.

———. 1986. "Wisconsin Item-Veto Lessons." *Public Administration Review* 46: 292–300.

Grady, Dennis O. 1987. "Gubernatorial Behavior in State-Federal Relations." *Western Political Quarterly* 40: 305–318.

Grady, Dennis O., and Kathleen M. Simon. 2002. "Political Restraints and Bureaucratic Discretion: The Case of State Government Rule Making." *Politics and Policy* 30: 646–677.

Gross, Donald A. 1980. "House-Senate Conference Committees: A Comparative State Perspective." *American Journal of Political Science* 24: 769–778.

———. 1991. "The Policy Role of Governors." In *Gubernatorial Leadership and State Policy*, ed. Eric Herzik and Brent Brown. New York: Greenwood Press.

Gulley, Dwight. 2011. "In Absentia: An Examination of Policy on State Gubernatorial Succession." *Proceedings of the 2011 Annual Meeting of the Midwest Political Science Association*. Chicago: Midwest Political Science Association.

Hall, Thad E. 2002. "Changes in Legislative Support for the Governor's Program Over Time." *Legislative Studies Quaterly* 27: 107–122.

Hansen, Susan B. 1999. " 'Life Is Not Fair': Governors' Job Performance Ratings and State Economies." *Political Research Quarterly* 52: 167–188.

Hebert, F. Ted, Jeffrey L. Brudney, and Deil S. Wright. 1983. "Gubernatorial Influence and State Bureaucracy." *American Politics Research* 11: 243–263.

Herzik, Eric. 1991. "Policy Agendas and Gubernatorial Leadership." In *Gubernatorial Leadership and State Policy*, ed. Eric Herzik and Brent Brown. New York: Greenwood Press.

Hovey, Kendra, and Harold Hovey. 2007. "D-12—Number of Statewide Elected Officials, 2006." In *CQ's State Fact Finder, 2007*. Washington, D.C.: CQ Press.

Howell, Susan E., and James M. Vanderleeuw. 1990. "Economic Effects on State Governors." *American Politics Research* 18: 158–168.

Hurst, Julia Nienaber. 2009. *Executive Branch Successors and the Line of Succession*. Florence, Ky.: National Lieutenant Governors Association.

Jensen, Jennifer M., and Jenna Kelkres Emery. 2011. "The First State Lobbyists: State Offices in Washington during WWII." *Journal of Policy History* 23: 117–149.

Jewell, Malcolm. 1969. *The State Legislature: Politics and Practices*, 2d ed. New York: Random House.

Kaufman, Herbert. 1963. *Politics and Policies in State and Local Governments*. Englewood Cliffs, N.J.: Prentice Hall.

Key, V. O., Jr. 1956. *American State Politics*. New York: Knopf.

King, James D. 2001. "Incumbent Popularity and Vote Choice in Gubernatorial Elections." *Journal of Politics* 63: 585–597.

Kousser, Thad, and Justin H. Phillips. 2009. "Who Blinks First? Legislative Patience and Bargaining with Governors." *Legislative Studies Quarterly* 34: 55–86.

Krupnikov, Yanna, and Charles R. Shipan. 2011. "Measuring Gubernatorial Power: A New Approach." *Proceedings of the Annual Meeting of the Midwest Political Science Association.* Chicago: Midwest Political Science Association.

Kunin, Madeleine. 1994. *Living a Political Life.* New York: Knopf.

Lammers, William W., and David Klingman. 1986. "Durable Governors as Political Leaders: Should We Limit Tenure?" *Publius: The Journal of Federalism* 16: 53–72.

Leyden, Kevin M., and Stephen A. Borelli. 1995. "The Effect of State Economic Conditions on Gubernatorial Elections: Does Unified Government Make a Difference?" *Political Research Quarterly* 48: 275–290.

MacDonald, Jason A., and Lee Sigelman. 1999. "Public Assessments of Gubernatorial Performance: A Comparative State Analysis." *American Politics Research* 27: 201–215.

Moe, Ronald C. 1988. *Prospects for the Line Item Veto at the Federal Level: Lessons from the States.* Washington, D.C.: National Academy of Public Administration.

Moncrief, Gary F., and Joel A. Thompson. 1980. "Partisanship and Purse Strings: A Research Note on Sharkansky." *Western Political Quarterly* 33: 336–340.

Morehouse, Sarah M. 1987. "Money Versus Party Effort: Nominating the Governor." Paper presented at the annual meeting of the American Political Science Association, Chicago, September 4–7.

———. 1996. "Legislative Party Voting for the Governor's Program." *Legislative Studies Quarterly* 21: 359–381.

National Association of State Budget Officers. 1997. *Budget Procedures in the States.* Washington, D.C.: National Association of State Budget Officers.

National Governors Association. 1978. *Governing the American States.* Washington, D.C.: National Governors Association.

———. 1981. *Reflections on Being Governor.* Washington, D.C.: National Governors Association.

———. 1990. *The Governor's Final Year: Challenges and Strategies.* Washington, D.C.: National Governors Association.

Neustadt, Richard. 1980. *Presidential Power: The Politics of Leadership from FDR to Carter.* New York: Wiley.

Niemi, Richard G., Harold W. Stanley, and Ronald J. Vogel. 1995. "State Economies and State Taxes: Do Voters Hold Governors Accountable?" *American Journal of Political Science* 39: 936–957.

Orth, Deborah A. 2001. "Accountability in a Federal System: The Governor, the President, and Economic Expectations." *State Politics and Policy Quarterly* 1: 412–432.

Osborne, David, and Ted Gaebler. 1993. *Reinventing Government: How the Entrepreneurial Spirit Is Transforming the Public Sector.* New York: Penguin.

Partin, Randall W. 2001. "Campaign Intensity and Voter Information: A Look at Gubernatorial Contests." *American Politics Research* 29: 115–140.

———. 2002. "Assessing the Impact of Campaign Spending in Governors' Races." *Political Research Quarterly* 55: 213–233.

Potoski, Matthew, and Neal D. Woods. 2001. "Designing State Clean Air Agencies: Administrative Procedures and Bureaucracy Autonomy." *Journal of Public Administration Research and Theory* 11: 203–222.

Ransone, Coleman. 1985. *The American Governorship.* Westport: Conn.: Greenwood Press.

Robinson, Julia E. 1998. "The Role of the Independent Political Executive in State Governance: Stability in the Face of Change." *Public Administration Review* 58: 119–128.

Rosenthal, Alan. 1990. *Governors and Legislatures: Contending Powers*. Washington, D.C.: CQ Press.

Sabato, Larry. 1978. *Goodbye to Good-Time Charlie: The American Governorship Transformed*. Lexington, Mass.: Lexington Books.

———. 1983. *Goodbye to Good-Time Charlie: The American Governorship Transformed*. 2d ed. Washington, D.C.: CQ Press.

Schlesinger, Joseph A. 1965. "The Politics of the Executive." In *Politics in the American States*, ed. Herbert Jacob and Kenneth N. Vines. Boston: Little, Brown.

———. 1971. "The Politics of the Executive." In *Politcs in the American States*, 2d ed., ed. Herbert Jacob and Kenneth N. Vines. Boston: Little, Brown.

Sharkansky, Ira. 1968. "Agency Requests, Gubernatorial Support, and Budget Success in State Legislatures." *American Political Science Review* 62: 1220–1231.

Sherman, Sharon. 1984. "Powersplit: When Legislatures and Governors Are of Opposing Parties." *State Legislatures* 10: 9–12.

Sigelman, Lee, and Nelson C. Dometrius. 1988. "Governors as Chief Administrators: The Linkage between Formal Powers and Informal Influence." *American Politics Research* 16: 157–170.

Squire, Peverill, and Christina Fastnow. 1994. "Comparing Gubernatorial and Senatorial Elections." *Political Research Quarterly* 47: 705–720.

Stein, Robert M. 1990. "Economic Voting for Governor and U.S. Senator: The Electoral Consequences of Federalism." *Journal of Politics* 52: 29–53.

Svoboda, Craig J. 1995. "Restrospective Voting in Gubernatorial Elections: 1982 and 1986." *Political Research Quarterly* 48: 135–150.

Thompson, Joel A. 1987. "Agency Requests, Gubernatorial Support, and Budget Success in State Legislatures Revisited." *Journal of Politics* 49: 756–779.

van Assendelft, Laura A. 1997. *Governors, Agenda Setting, and Divided Government*. Lanham, Md.: University Press of America.

Weeks, George. 1984. "Gubernatorial Transitions: Leaving There." *State Government* 57: 73–78.

Wiggins, Charles W. 1980. "Executive Vetoes and Legislative Overrides in the American States." *Journal of Politics* 42: 1110–1117.

Wilkins, Vicky M., and Garry Young. 2002. "The Influence of Governors on Veto Override Attempts: A Test of Pivotal Politics." *Legislative Studies Quarterly* 27: 557–575.

Woods, Neal D. 2004. "Political Influence on Agency Rule Making: Examining the Effects of Legislative and Gubernatorial Rule Review Powers." *State and Local Government Review* 36: 174–185.

Woods, Neal D., and Michael Baranowski. 2007. "Governors and the Bureaucracy: Executive Resources as Sources of Administrative Influence." *International Journal of Public Administration* 30: 1219–1230.

Wright, Deil S. 1967. "Executive Leadership in State Administration: Interplay of Gubernatorial, Legislative, and Administrative Power." *Midwest Journal of Political Science* 11: 1–16.

SUGGESTED READINGS

Print

Beyle, Thad L., ed. *Governors in Hard Times*. Washington, D.C.: CQ Press, 1992. A multiauthored, ten-state set of case studies on how the governors of those states coped with the economic downturn of the late 1980s and early 1990s, with some lessons learned that could be useful in the current economy.

Clynch, Edward J., and Thomas P. Lauth. *Governors, Legislatures, and Budgets*. New York: Greenwood, 1991. In addition to an overview of the process of budgeting in the states, includes chapters on the budget process in thirteen states and offers important insights into the varied and complex realm of budgeting in state governments.

Ferguson, Margaret R. *The Executive Branch of State Government: People, Process, and Politics.* Santa Barbara, Calif.: ABC CLIO, 2006. Examines the history, structure, and politics of the governorship and the executive branch. Topics include formal and informal powers; seeking, winning, and leaving the office; and the many roles and responsibilities of the modern American governorship. Also contains entries on specific features of the executive branch in each of the fifty states.

Leal, David L. *Electing America's Governors: The Politics of Executive Elections.* Basingstoke, U.K.: Palgrave Macmillan. 2006. Compares gubernatorial elections with those for Senate and the presidency. Leal finds that gubernatorial elections are more similar to presidential than senatorial elections and therefore are best understood as "executive" elections.

Shribnick, Ethan G. *A Legacy of Innovation: Governors and Public Policy.* Philadelphia: University of Pennsylvania Press. 2008. Tracks the evolution of gubernatorial leadership as it has dealt with issues such as conservation, transportation, civil rights, education, globalization, and health care.

van Assendelft, Laura A. *Governors, Agenda Setting, and Divided Government.* Lanham, Md.: University Press of America, 1997. A four-state case study of the problems governors have in setting and achieving their policy agendas when there is divided partisan control of government.

Internet

American State Administrators Project. www.auburn.edu/outreach/cgs/ASAP/. A project consisting of a forty-year set of surveys of state agency heads and top executives in all fifty states. The surveys have been conducted the fourth and eighth year of every decade since the project's inception in 1964. It now surveys administrators heading some one hundred types of state agencies across the country.

Center on the American Governor, Eagleton Institute of Politics, Rutgers University. http://governors.rutgers.edu/index.php. Program that seeks to promote research and discussion on the role of the governor in the United States. It is building a virtual archive and plans to sponsor a range of academic activities and public forums on topics and issues relating to the office of governor across the country as well as the administrations of selected holders of the office in New Jersey and other states.

Government Performance Project. www.governing.com/gpp/2005/intro.htm. A joint effort by *Governing* magazine and the Maxwell School of Citizenship and Public Affairs at Syracuse University to create report cards for the fifty states and the thirty-five largest cities (based on revenues) in the United States. The grades are based on an assessment of government performance in five areas: management of finances, personnel, infrastructure, information technology, and the use of performance measures.

National Association of State Budget Officers. http://nasbo.org/. The professional membership organization for state finance officers for more than sixty years. NASBO is the instrument through which the states collectively advance state budget practices. The organization regularly collects data about state budget practices and expenditures, among other fiscal matters.

National Governors Association. www.nga.org. A bipartisan organization of the nation's governors that provides a venue for governors and their staffs to share ideas and policy solutions as well as lobby Congress on issues of importance to the states. The Web site includes the biographies of the current governors as well as a searchable database of former governors for each of the states.

National Lieutenant Governors Association. www.nlga.us/. The professional association for the elected officials who are first in line of succession to the governors in the states. Members meet, foster interstate cooperation, and share best practices. The Web site reports on the current leadership activities of the lieutenant governors as well as the policy resolutions passed by the association since 1990.

Thad Beyle's Web site. www.unc.edu/~beyle/. A site containing data on gubernatorial power, job approval ratings derived from state public opinion polls, and campaign spending since the 1970s.

CHAPTER 8

State Courts

Politics and the Judicial Process

MELINDA GANN HALL

State courts are perhaps the most enigmatic of political institutions. Frequently the focus of controversy, these courts decide some of the most salient and publicly visible issues on the American political agenda, generating heated debates and provoking accusations of "judicial activism" and "legislating from the bench." In the process, state courts can place themselves squarely in conflict with the other institutions of government and on the opposite side of the political fence from their respective citizenries. In response, state legislatures can retaliate by refusing to raise judges' salaries, altering court jurisdictions, and using legislation and state constitutional amendments to attack the courts publicly and undo their rulings. Similarly, citizens in all but twelve states can sanction sitting judges by refusing to return them to office at election time.

An excellent illustration is the highly publicized dispute over the Iowa Supreme Court's ruling in *Varnum v. Brian,* 763 N.W.2d 862 (2009). In this case, a unanimous seven-member court used the state constitution to invalidate a 1998 statute defining marriage exclusively as the union between one man and one woman, requiring instead that the state extend the right to marry to same-sex couples. The court's decision, which was consistent with the previous rulings of the high courts of Massachusetts, California, and Connecticut but incompatible with the laws of virtually all of the states and the underlying principles of the federal Defense of Marriage Act, immediately set into motion a successful campaign to retaliate against the court for purportedly overstepping the bounds of judicial authority. In

2010, the three supreme court justices who were up for reelection were resoundingly defeated at the polls. Grumblings in the Republican-controlled House continue, with some members seeking to convince the Iowa General Assembly to impeach the four remaining justices of the *Varnum* majority. For now, however, the right of same-sex couples to marry is constitutionally protected in Iowa.

The controversy over same-sex marriage in Iowa follows in the wake of a similar controversy in California. In May 2008, the California Supreme Court ruled in *In re Marriage Cases,* 183 P.3d 384 (2008), that the state constitution guaranteed same-sex couples the right to marry. From May through November, some eighteen thousand same-sex marriages were performed in California. However, voters immediately responded to the court's decision with Proposition 8, a ballot initiative approved in the November 2008 election that invalidated the court's decision by defining marriage as between opposite-sex partners only. In turn, the successful adoption of Proposition 8 sparked litigation over whether state constitutional amendments could be used to restrict civil rights and whether the same-sex marriages already performed were valid. The California Supreme Court decided these issues in 2009, ruling that both Proposition 8 and the marriages were consistent with California law. Efforts continue by numerous groups to undo Proposition 8 and reinstate same-sex marriage in California, and the battle continues across the American states on this deeply divisive issue in which courts play a central role.

Despite these overtly political interactions on the issue of same-sex marriage and the decisive impact generally of state court decisions on public policy and political discourse, state courts fundamentally are legal institutions explicitly charged with resolving disputes using established principles of law. In fact, the American legal culture creates strong normative expectations about the proper basis on which cases should be decided and the means through which the judiciary should, or should not, participate in politics. These expectations uniformly insist that courts remain outside the political realm. Perhaps most extreme is the widely accepted theory of **mechanical jurisprudence,** which describes the process of judging as the objective, straightforward application of existing laws to the established facts of the cases. Of course, mechanical jurisprudence largely represents a normative ideal, but the fact remains that from judges one expects strict adherence to the rule of law, independence from external pressures, and impartiality in choosing winners and losers.

Reconciling these countervailing realities of courts as political and legal institutions goes to the very heart of understanding the politics of judging and the role of state judiciaries in American democracy. Although the process of evaluating courts is complicated by the fact that the judicial role varies from state to state, there are some basic propositions, firmly grounded in the scientific literature, that accurately describe state judicial politics (Hall 1999, 2007a).

First and foremost, state courts play a decisive role in allocating wealth and power in the United States. Many of the most divisive issues in society are presented to courts in the form of lawsuits, and the sheer volume of litigation processed annually in state courts affects the lives of millions of Americans, even in the most mundane types of cases. Second, judges have discretion in interpreting law, particularly in the states' highest courts. On many issues, the law simply is not a vice that rigidly binds decisions, especially when new issues or new technologies emerge or where constitutions are involved. Third, like other political actors, judges have well-defined political preferences and act to promote those preferences when deciding cases. Generally speaking, judges are politically knowledgeable and have their own agendas. Moreover, it is inevitable that judges will draw on their own personal values when existing law is not an adequate guide for their decisions. Finally, the exercise of preferences is constrained by the formal rules structuring the institution (including state and federal law) and by the overall context within which each court operates. In short, some judges are much freer than others to pursue their own goals and shape political outcomes.

This chapter builds on these fundamental tenets by exploring various aspects of the judicial function, including the ways in which state courts serve their citizenries and participate in politics. Specifically, the work of state courts is examined, starting with the organization and size of these institutions and their caseloads. Similarly, outcomes are explored, including the degree to which state courts engage in redistributive politics through **tort cases.** Thereafter, the representative function of state courts is considered, including the controversy over electing judges. Finally, state courts are examined within the system of checks and balances, especially the extent to which courts act as a countermajoritarian force. The overall point is straightforward yet compelling: state courts are vitally important institutions that play a critical role in state politics, even under the most restrictive conditions.

THE ORGANIZATION OF STATE COURTS

This exploration of state courts begins with a prototypical organizational scheme for state judiciaries:

Court(s) of last resort

⇑

Intermediate appellate courts

⇑

General jurisdiction trial courts

⇑

Limited jurisdiction trial courts

At the bottom of the judicial hierarchy are the **limited jurisdiction trial courts,** which hear misdemeanors (usually traffic violations), small claims (usually involving less than $10,000), and other relatively minor disputes. Overall, these courts process huge caseloads using abbreviated procedures and rarely permit appeal.

Above these courts are the **general jurisdiction trial courts**, which decide cases not delegated to the limited jurisdiction trial courts. These courts hear the most important matters at the trial level, including felony prosecutions and civil disputes involving sizable sums of money.

At the appellate level, forty-one states have **intermediate appellate courts**, which hear appeals from the general jurisdiction trial courts. Generally speaking, because each major case is entitled to one appeal, these courts have nondiscretionary dockets mandating review of the cases properly filed. However, eleven states (Delaware, Maine, Montana, Nevada, New Hampshire, North Dakota, Rhode Island, South Dakota, Vermont, West Virginia, and Wyoming) do not have intermediate appellate courts, largely because their caseloads do not require them. Instead, all appeals in these eleven states go directly to the **court of last resort** (usually called the supreme court), which has a mandatory docket. Otherwise, state supreme courts have discretionary dockets, allowing the justices to decide whether to grant or deny review in each case.

Intermediate appellate courts fundamentally alter the function of state supreme courts by removing the burden of frivolous or routine appeals. Although these cases still can be appealed to the states' highest courts after being reviewed in the lower appellate courts, they are heard again only if the supreme court agrees to do so. However, when intermediate appellate courts are present, high courts tend to select the most important and politically relevant cases, including those with far-reaching policy consequences. Overall, in the states that have intermediate appellate courts, state judiciaries can process more appeals, and state supreme courts can largely confine themselves to the most pressing issues of state politics.

The organizational scheme just presented necessarily understates how complex state court systems really can be. For example, some states have complicated concurrent jurisdictional arrangements between the limited and general jurisdiction trial courts, and all state courts of last resort have mandatory jurisdiction in some types of cases (such as death penalty cases and cases in which trial courts have invalidated statutes). Similarly, in a small subset of cases (such as those dealing with certain tax questions and regulating the practice of law), state supreme courts have original jurisdiction, hearing cases on the facts for the first time as in a trial court.

Although cases from state courts of last resort can be appealed to the U.S. Supreme Court if there are issues of federal law, there is little chance that state supreme court decisions will be reviewed by the nation's highest court. In its 2005 term, the U.S. Supreme Court decided the "fewest number of cases in modern history" (Barnes 2007, A04), disposing of a mere eighty-two cases with written opinions. In the 2009 term, the Court decided only seventy-seven cases with full opinions (Administrative Office of the U.S. Courts 2010, 82). Most of these cases are taken from the lower federal courts, and matters governed entirely by state law are outside the federal courts' jurisdiction. Practically speaking, state supreme courts really are courts of last resort.

The reach of state courts is not restricted to state law or state politics. In fact, state courts play a vital role in interpreting federal law and in deciding important issues on the national political agenda. In criminal prosecutions, for example, fundamental principles of the Bill of Rights and Fourteenth Amendment are regularly interpreted and implemented by state courts, subject to mandates set by the U.S. Supreme Court.

Judgeships in the States

One important dimension of state judicial power is the size of the state court bench, described in Table 8-1 as the number of authorized judgeships. To place these figures in context, consider that in the federal court system there are 352 judgeships in the Bankruptcy Courts (a division of the District Courts), 678 in the District Courts (the general jurisdiction trial courts), 179 in the Courts of Appeals (the intermediate appellate courts), and 9 in the Supreme Court (the court of last resort), for a total of 1,218 (Administrative Office of the U.S. Courts 2010). When viewed in relation to the states, where the total number of authorized judgeships is 30,811, federal judges represent a mere 4 percent of the overall bench in the United States. In fact, four states (California, Georgia, New York, and Texas) each have court systems that outsize the entire federal judiciary, and North Carolina falls just fourteen judges short.

Across the states, judiciaries differ considerably (see Table 8-1). South Dakota, with only fifty-seven judges in the entire system, operates the smallest judiciary (National Center for State Courts 2010a). Coming in second is Vermont, with sixty-five judges. In fact, fourteen states each have fewer than two hundred judges. At the other extreme, New York has the largest bench—3,593 judges—followed by Texas with 3,271. Overall, eight states each authorize more than a thousand judgeships for their various courts. Clearly, then, some states are managing complicated court systems, while others have a less challenging task.

Of course, one would expect larger judiciaries in the most populated states, which presumably have bigger caseloads. However, Table 8-1, which also standardizes the total number of judgeships by population, reveals some interesting deviations from this expectation. Some of the most populated states operate some of the smallest court systems. At the lowest end on this measure are highly populated states such as California and Florida, which have fewer than six judges per 100,000 people. At the other end are smaller states such as North Dakota, Wyoming, and Louisiana, which authorize, respectively, 22.0, 22.1, and 22.9 judgeships per 100,000 people. In short, state court systems vary widely in size and can be ranked on this dimension, but these ranks change when size relative to the citizenry is considered.

Table 8-1   Authorized Judgeships in State Courts, 2008

State	Total state bench	Court of last resort	Intermediate appellate courts	General jurisdiction trial courts	Limited jurisdiction trial courts	Judges per 100,000
Alabama	610	9	10	144	447	13.0
Alaska	138	5	3	48	82	20.1
Arizona	428	5	22	164	237	6.6
Arkansas	345	7	12	118	208	12.0
California	2,134	7	105	2,022	n/a	5.8
Colorado	541	7	16	150	368	11.0
Connecticut	330	7	10	180	133	9.4
Delaware	125	5	n/a	24	96	14.3
Florida	989	7	61	599	322	5.4
Georgia	1,506	7	12	199	1,288	15.5
Hawaii	79	5	6	45	23	6.1
Idaho	133	5	3	40	85	8.7
Illinois	920	7	45	868	n/a	7.2
Indiana	416	5	16	308	87	6.5
Iowa	360	7	9	344	n/a	12.0
Kansas	521	7	13	243	258	18.6
Kentucky	282	7	14	145	117	6.6
Louisiana	1,020	7	53	247	713	22.9
Maine	76	7	n/a	53	16	5.8
Maryland	350	7	13	153	177	6.2
Massachusetts	411	7	25	82	297	6.3
Michigan	621	7	28	221	365	6.2
Minnesota	304	7	16	281	n/a	5.8
Mississippi	530	9	10	51	460	18.0
Missouri	806	7	32	368	399	13.5
Montana	159	7	n/a	49	103	16.4
Nebraska	144	7	6	55	76	8.1
Nevada	154	7	n/a	64	83	5.9
New Hampshire	102	5	n/a	24	73	7.7
New Jersey	802	7	32	411	352	9.3
New Mexico	306	5	10	88	203	15.4
New York	3,593	7	71	455	3,060	18.5
North Carolina	1,205	7	15	209	974	13.0
North Dakota	141	5	n/a	42	94	22.0
Ohio	1,056	7	68	391	590	9.2
Oklahoma	656	14[a]	12	241	389	18.0
Oregon	457	7	10	178	262	12.1
Pennsylvania	1,045	7	24	434	580	8.3
Rhode Island	148	5	n/a	27	116	14.0
South Carolina	790	5	9	68	708	17.5
South Dakota	57	5	n/a	39	13	7.1
Tennessee	602	5	24	154	419	9.7
Texas	3,271	18[b]	80	444	2,729	13.5
Utah	235	5	7	79	144	8.6
Vermont	65	5	n/a	37	23	10.5
Virginia	419	7	11	157	244	5.4
Washington	416	9	22	229	156	6.3
West Virginia	385	5	n/a	65	315	21.2
Wisconsin	510	7	16	241	246	9.1
Wyoming	118	5	n/a	22	91	22.1
Total	30,811	340	951	11,300	18,220	10.1

SOURCES: Compiled from data reported by the National Center for State Courts, *State Court Caseload Statistics: An Analysis of 2008 State Court Caseloads* (Williamsburg, Va.: National Center for State Courts, 2010); and U.S. Census Bureau, "Annual Estimates of the Population for the United States, Regions, States, and for Puerto Rico: April 1, 2000 to July 1, 2009," NST-EST2009-01, www .census.gov/popest/states/NST-ann-est.html.

NOTE: n/a = not applicable.

a. Oklahoma has two courts of last resort, one for criminal cases (Court of Criminal Appeals) and the other for civil cases (Supreme Court). Each court has seven judges.

b. Texas has two courts of last resort, one for criminal cases (Court of Criminal Appeals) and the other for civil cases (Supreme Court). Each court has nine judges.

A reasonable speculation might be that states with lower judge-to-population ratios are slower and less efficient, but there have been no systematic tests of this hypothesis.

Salaries in State Judiciaries

A different way of thinking about state judiciaries is to consider salaries for state court judges. Salaries are significant because they may affect the qualifications of attorneys who are drawn to public service, the extent to which there might be competition for judgeships, and the willingness of judges to remain on the bench. As a comparative base, the annual salaries for federal judges are $213,900 in the Supreme Court, $184,500 in the Courts of Appeals, and $174,000 in the District Courts (United States Courts 2010).

As Table 8-2 indicates, the salaries for state court judges are generally lower than those for their federal counterparts, averaging $135,273 in the trial courts, $138,288 in the intermediate appellate courts, and $150,801 in the courts of last resort (National Center for State Courts 2010b, 1–3). As with authorized judgeships, however, there is considerable variation across the states. Topping the salary scale is California (where salaries exceed those in the federal courts): supreme court, $218,237; intermediate appellate courts, $204,599; and trial courts, $178,789. Just behind California is Illinois, where supreme court salaries are $207,066; intermediate appellate court salaries, $194,888; and trial court salaries, $178,835. At the opposite end are South Dakota, Montana, and Mississippi. In Mississippi, which ranks last, supreme court salaries are $112,530 and trial court salaries are $104,170.

As for each specific type of court, the salaries range across the states from $104,170 to $178,835 in the general jurisdiction trial courts (a $74,665 difference), from $105,050 to $204,599 in intermediate appellate courts (a $99,549 difference), and from $112,530 to $218,237 in the courts of last resort (a $105,707 difference).

Though interesting, these figures do not reflect differences across the states in cost of living. When salaries for general jurisdiction trial court judges are adjusted to take into account actual spending power, perceptions about the best- and worst-paying judgeships change. In some of the most dramatic shifts in trial court salaries, California declines from second to twentieth, Alaska drops from third to twenty-fourth, New York goes from twentieth to forty-sixth, and Hawaii goes from twenty-third to last. In fact, at the bottom are Vermont, Maine, and Hawaii. Alternatively, Mississippi rises in rank from fiftieth to fortieth, and West Virginia goes from forty-third to thirty-fourth. All things considered, Illinois, Tennessee, and Delaware offer the best trial court salaries when cost of living is considered. Overall, the difference between the best- and worst-paying judgeships with cost of living considered is $107,052.

Table 8-2 Salaries in State Courts, 2010

State	Supreme court	Intermediate appellate court	General trial court	Adjusted general trial court
Alabama	$180,005	$178,878	$134,943	$144,712
Alaska	188,604	178,188	174,396	130,956
Arizona	155,000	150,000	145,000	139,158
Arkansas	145,204	140,732	136,257	150,752
California	218,237	204,599	178,789	134,707
Colorado	139,660	134,128	128,598	125,462
Connecticut	162,520	152,637	146,780	116,956
Delaware	185,050	n/a	168,850	162,110
Florida	157,976	150,077	142,178	144,114
Georgia	167,210	166,186	144,752	155,668
Hawaii	151,118	139,924	136,127	81,116
Idaho	119,506	118,506	112,043	118,698
Illinois	207,066	194,888	178,835	188,168
Indiana	151,328	147,103	125,647	134,446
Iowa	163,200	147,900	137,700	145,702
Kansas	135,905	131,518	120,037	130,269
Kentucky	135,504	130,044	124,620	138,536
Louisiana	149,572	142,477	136,544	141,980
Maine	119,476	n/a	111,969	97,710
Maryland	162,352	149,552	140,352	113,591
Massachusetts	145,984	135,087	129,694	110,190
Michigan	164,610	151,441	139,919	150,437
Minnesota	145,981	137,552	129,124	124,877
Mississippi	112,530	105,050	104,170	113,540
Missouri	137,034	128,207	120,484	131,010
Montana	113,964	n/a	106,870	107,484
Nebraska	142,760	135,622	132,053	145,459
Nevada	170,000	n/a	160,000	158,200
New Hampshire	146,917	n/a	137,804	116,479
New Jersey	185,482	175,534	165,000	127,146
New Mexico	123,691	117,506	111,631	112,867
New York	151,200	144,000	136,700	107,349
North Carolina	137,249	131,531	124,382	128,341
North Dakota	130,228	n/a	119,330	121,043
Ohio	141,600	132,000	121,350	128,701
Oklahoma	137,655	130,410	124,373	137,720
Oregon	125,688	122,820	114,468	102,667
Pennsylvania	186,450	175,923	161,850	161,224
Rhode Island	156,213	n/a	140,642	113,514
South Carolina	137,171	133,741	130,312	131,791
South Dakota	118,173	n/a	110,377	109,017
Tennessee	165,336	159,840	154,320	171,603
Texas	150,000	137,500	132,500	146,067
Utah	145,350	138,750	132,150	139,530
Vermont	129,245	n/a	122,867	100,930
Virginia	183,839	168,322	158,134	161,790
Washington	164,221	156,328	148,832	141,643
West Virginia	121,000	n/a	116,000	122,142
Wisconsin	144,495	136,316	128,600	130,680
Wyoming	131,500	n/a	125,300	125,694
Average	150,801	138,288	135,273	131,479

SOURCE: National Center for State Courts, *Survey of Judicial Salaries* (Williamsburg, Va.: National Center for State Courts, 2010).

NOTE: n/a = not applicable.

THE WORK OF STATE COURTS

State courts process staggering caseloads that collectively represent the vast majority (about 98 percent) of the nation's litigation. In 2008, the most recent year for which data are available, state trial courts processed 106,000,000 filings (National Center for State Courts 2010c, 20). Of these, 54.2 percent involved traffic violations, 20.1 percent were criminal cases, 18.3 percent were civil cases, 5.4 percent were domestic relations, and 2.0 percent involved juveniles. By contrast, filings in the federal trial courts for roughly the same period (October 2008 through September 2009) totaled 1,985,345, of which 1,402,816 (or 70.7 percent) were bankruptcy filings (Administrative Office of the U.S. Courts 2010, 14). Even excluding traffic cases, which are a huge part of the annual workload, state courts are handling an incredible volume of cases, both overall and in relation to the federal courts.

State litigation and the subsequent decisions of judges in these matters have profound effects on the daily lives of Americans. Excellent examples are divorce and other matters of family law (including adoption and child custody), probate, and serious crime. In fact, the federal courts are restricted to cases involving federal law or the United States as a party and to a diversity of citizenship cases involving high-dollar disputes between citizens of different states under state law. The average citizen is not likely to be party to these types of disputes except bankruptcy.

State Court Caseloads

Table 8-3 provides a detailed look at filings in state trial courts. As the table illustrates, there is an extraordinary range across the states in judicial workload, not only for filings but also when rates are calculated by dividing filings by state population.

A look at civil litigation in 2008 is revealing. The total number of filings in state courts ranged from 25,545 in Vermont to 1,852,112 in New York. As for rates, the highest are found in Maryland, which has an astonishing rate of 18,005 filings per 100,000 people, and in Virginia at 13,098. Least litigious by rate are Hawaii (2,493), Mississippi (2,363), and Tennessee (1,130).

A different picture emerges when looking at criminal filings, both overall and for the general jurisdiction trial courts only, which handle the most serious crimes. As Table 8-2 documents, Texas had 2,565,242 criminal filings in 2008, compared with 17,862 in Vermont. Regarding rates, Arkansas and Delaware handle the most criminal cases overall, and Massachusetts and New Mexico process the least. For the general jurisdiction trial courts specifically, California and North Dakota are at the top, and Wyoming and Massachusetts are at the bottom.

Finally, at the appellate level California is the most litigious state, and Wyoming is the least. In fact, the difference between California and Wyoming is 35,436 appellate filings annually. As for rates, Louisiana is first and Rhode Island is last. As with the trial courts, notable differences across the states in appellate caseloads suggest

Table 8-3 Caseloads in State Courts, 2008

State	Total cases	Total civil cases	Civil rate per 100,000	Total criminal cases	Criminal rate per 100,000 adults	General jurisdiction criminal rate per 100,000 adults	Total appellate cases	Appellate rate per 100,000
Alabama	504,805	224,447	4,812	275,075	7,897	2,350	5,283	113
Alaska	65,678	25,616	3,733	39,414	8,251	1,319	648	94
Arizona	1,111,707	343,888	5,290	763,038	15,993	1,285	4,781	74
Arkansas	723,483	140,867	4,933	580,700	27,261	3,867	1,916	67
California	2,923,919	1,163,889	3,166	1,724,310	6,453	6,453	35,720	97
Colorado	516,507	324,301	6,566	187,796	5,110	1,102	4,410	89
Connecticut	429,100	260,218	7,432	167,483	6,353	6,353	1,399	40
Delaware	348,212	65,265	7,475	282,277	42,993	1,541	670	77
Florida	2,951,629	1,419,204	7,743	1,503,985	10,629	2,773	28,440	155
Georgia	990,653	335,641	3,465	649,760	9,127	2,138	5,252	54
Hawaii	145,072	32,116	2,493	112,209	11,522	774	747	58
Idaho	216,972	82,253	5,398	133,695	12,271	994	1,024	67
Illinois	1,165,719	642,701	4,982	512,133	5,372	5,372	10,885	84
Indiana	824,257	512,956	8,044	307,275	6,503	5,431	4,026	63
Iowa	279,495	184,370	6,140	91,962	4,089	4,089	3,163	105
Kansas	255,629	195,021	6,960	57,866	2,810	2,187	2,742	98
Kentucky	539,630	284,899	6,673	251,252	7,805	993	3,479	81
Louisiana	663,707	288,155	6,532	364,760	11,375	5,047	10,792	245
Maine	115,566	43,593	3,311	71,218	7,081	1,473	755	57
Maryland	1,328,281	1,014,391	18,005	310,788	7,415	1,995	3,102	55
Massachusetts	480,300	424,672	6,535	51,940	1,047	130	3,688	57
Michigan	1,846,369	824,665	8,244	1,012,366	13,694	960	9,338	93
Minnesota	416,267	236,782	4,536	176,570	4,583	4,583	2,915	56
Mississippi	NA	69,439	2,363	NA	NA	NA	1,217	41
Missouri	511,607	318,115	5,381	189,227	4,297	4,297	4,265	72
Montana	117,725	64,779	6,696	52,247	7,249	1,008	699	72
Nebraska	263,179	119,386	6,694	141,814	10,789	773	1,979	111
Nevada	346,248	187,511	7,211	156,489	8,089	757	2,248	86
New Hampshire	133,257	54,519	4,143	77,774	7,881	1,285	964	73
New Jersey	1,683,540	918,527	10,579	757,009	11,594	1,822	8,004	92
New Mexico	125,145	93,370	4,706	30,079	2,105	1,847	1,696	85
New York	2,617,570	1,852,112	9,501	749,317	5,108	554	16,141	83
North Carolina	2,447,701	591,007	6,408	1,853,505	26,584	2,150	3,189	35
North Dakota	74,031	33,727	5,258	39,962	8,306	8,306	342	53
Ohio	1,830,895	915,127	7,967	901,902	10,526	1,194	13,866	121
Oklahoma	323,173	209,142	5,742	110,209	4,083	4,083	3,822	105
Oregon	300,176	202,283	5,336	93,433	3,274	3,274	4,460	118
Pennsylvania	1,031,533	463,311	3,722	553,290	5,833	1,952	14,932	120
Rhode Island	110,124	67,518	6,424	42,283	5,267	715	323	31
South Carolina	1,172,962	346,478	7,734	823,309	24,570	3,739	3,175	71
South Dakota	87,187	58,416	7,264	28,410	4,826	4,826	361	45
Tennessee	246,995	70,240	1,130	173,196	3,696	3,696	3,559	57
Texas	3,499,513	913,184	3,754	2,565,242	14,686	1,607	21,087	87
Utah	257,015	133,650	4,884	121,922	6,572	2,116	1,443	53
Vermont	43,910	25,545	4,112	17,862	3,793	3,793	503	81
Virginia	2,186,555	1,017,606	13,098	1,163,226	19,857	3,180	5,723	74
Washington	672,104	307,898	4,701	358,463	7,367	924	5,743	88
West Virginia	228,073	81,166	4,473	144,496	10,245	664	2,411	133
Wisconsin	448,603	300,005	5,331	144,510	3,446	3,446	4,088	73
Wyoming	67,658	36,782	6,905	30,592	7,765	514	284	53

SOURCE: Compiled from data reported by the National Center for State Courts, *State Court Caseload Statistics: An Analysis of 2008 State Court Caseloads* (Williamsburg, Va.: National Center for State Courts, 2010), 54–60, 69–75, 84–89.

NOTE: NA = not available.

that the role and impact of state judiciaries differ considerably from one state to another.

State Trial Court and Supreme Court Dockets

A different perspective on the work of state courts emerges from a closer look at the relative mix of criminal and civil cases. By comparing civil and criminal dockets, one can ascertain the extent to which state courts specialize in criminal or civil litigation and concomitantly the specific role state courts might be playing within their respective political systems. Although some state courts focus heavily on criminal cases and basically function as agents of social control, others largely mediate private interests and engage in distributive and redistributive politics.

As Table 8-3 illustrates, state courts at the trial level can be specialists in civil or criminal law. About half of the states receive more civil than criminal filings. The specialization in criminal cases is pronounced in Arkansas, Delaware, Hawaii, and North Carolina, where criminal caseloads are at least triple the civil caseloads. Alternatively, twenty-five states process more civil filings than criminal filings, even when the limited jurisdiction trial courts and their high volumes of traffic cases are taken into account. Kansas, Maryland, Massachusetts, and New Mexico receive at least three times as many civil filings as criminal filings.

Figure 8-1 describes the dockets of state supreme courts. Unlike many of their trial court counterparts, state supreme courts tend to specialize in civil litigation. At one extreme, the Alaska Supreme Court almost exclusively is a forum for private interests. Less than 4 percent of the high court's docket in Alaska involves criminal cases, in part because crime rates are quite low. Other states show a similar though less extreme focus, even those that tend to see higher crime rates. For example, Alabama, New Jersey, Ohio, Oregon, and Virginia devote about 80 percent of their dockets to civil appeals. Alternatively, four state supreme courts (Arizona, Florida, Indiana, and North Carolina) specialize in criminal matters, although not to the extent of the state supreme courts preoccupied with civil litigation. The North Carolina Supreme Court, the court of last resort most focused on criminal cases as a proportion of the overall docket, still reserves about 34 percent of its docket for civil matters.

In short, state judiciaries differ not only in litigation volume but also in the types of cases typically resolved. Just as the job description for judges varies from one state to the next, so do the demands placed on courts and the interests being served.

Although there are few systematic explanations for why caseloads vary across the states, litigation rates appear to reflect the "social complexity, politics, policies, and legal structures" of the states, particularly when the courts are the most viable forum for addressing particular types of claims (Yates, Davis, and Glick 2001, 137). For example, social complexity in the form of urbanization reduces

Figure 8-1   Composition of State Supreme Court Dockets, 1995–1998

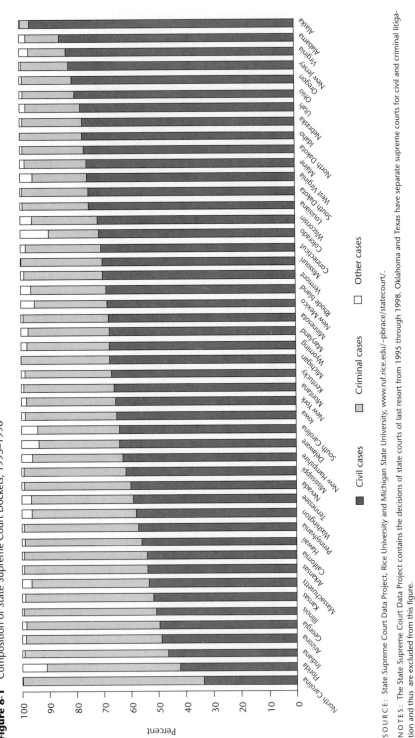

SOURCE: State Supreme Court Data Project, Rice University and Michigan State University, www.ruf.rice.edu/~pbrace/statecourt/.

NOTES: The State Supreme Court Data Project contains the decisions of state courts of last resort from 1995 through 1998. Oklahoma and Texas have separate supreme courts for civil and criminal litigation and thus are excluded from this figure.

opportunities for the informal redress of grievances and thus increases litigiousness. Similarly, vigorous interpartisan competition is linked to responsive government, thereby reducing the need for an alternative forum like the judiciary to seek particular political outcomes. State policies such as welfare benefits influence litigation by creating incentives or disincentives to use courts as arenas to pursue redistributive results. And tort reform reduces the ability to litigate while providing some compensation to victims in the form of no-fault insurance benefits.

Similarly, studies of state supreme courts suggest that the types of cases heard and their ultimate dispositions are the product of institutional and other contextual forces operating on courts, as well as strategic calculations by justices and litigants. For example, studies of abortion have established that the propensity to accept these cases on appeal and then to overturn state statutes is related to variables such as whether judges are elected; divided versus unified government; the presence or absence of state privacy provisions; predictions by litigants of the likelihood of winning; and the relative ideological preferences of the court, the legislature, and the public (Brace, Hall, and Langer 1999, 2001). In other words, the work of state courts is not the product of random events but instead reflects the systematic impact of factors structuring politics in general and state politics in particular.

QUALITY OF JUSTICE ISSUES: WHO WINS

One of the most pressing issues for state trial courts is the proliferation of tort cases and the steep monetary awards that these cases sometimes produce. Tort cases are civil cases involving injury, negligence, or misconduct, such as automobile accidents, premises liability, product liability, professional malpractice, and slander or libel. In tort cases, trial courts and juries have been criticized for what are often described as ridiculously high awards, especially in product liability and medical malpractice cases. In fact, the issue of medical malpractice is driving many states and the federal government to consider placing statutory caps on monetary awards, which are alleged to be responsible for unfavorable trends such as the rising costs of health care.

One interesting way to think about torts is in the context of the demands they place on the judicial system. Not only are tort cases an important source of business for state judiciaries, but they also are likely to consume considerable resources through the process of trials. In 2005 torts accounted for about 61 percent of all civil trials in the United States, compared with contract disputes at 33 percent and real property cases at 6 percent (Bureau of Justice Statistics 2008, 2). Among torts, the most common claims were automobile liability (35 percent) and medical malpractice (9 percent). Coming in third, at about 7 percent, were premises liability claims, or cases alleging harm from inadequately maintained or dangerous property.

More intriguing than caseloads, however, are outcomes, or who wins. In fact, it is interesting to compare the outcomes in tort trials with the outcomes in contract disputes, the other major area of civil litigation. In 2005, win rates in tort and contract disputes were, respectively, 52 percent and 66 percent (Bureau of Justice Statistics 2008, 4). Thus it appears that when tort claimants choose to take cases all the way to trial, they are more likely to win than lose, but not at the same rate as plaintiffs in contract cases. Also as one might expect, within the broad subject area of torts, win rates differ considerably. Plaintiffs are most successful (win rates that exceed 60 percent) in animal attack and automobile accident cases, and are least successful in medical malpractice (23 percent), product liability not involving asbestos (20 percent), and false arrest or imprisonment (15.5 percent).

It is important to note that win rates reflect successes at trial and do not include cases that were dismissed by the court or that were filed and then settled out of court between the parties. Also, the figures just reported are aggregated across the states. The extent to which these patterns vary by state is not known, although substantial diversity should be anticipated. Finally, there is an inherent bias in access to civil courts. Because of the costs associated with litigation, many economically disadvantaged people and groups are precluded from ever going to court in the first place.

Monetary awards in civil trials provide another perspective on tort litigation. Despite the conventional wisdom that torts routinely produce sizable if not exorbitant monetary awards, the median award in tort trials in 2005 was $24,000 compared with $35,000 in contract cases (Bureau of Justice Statistics 2008, 5). However, 5 percent of all tort awards were at least $1 million compared with 3.5 percent of contract cases. Overall, these cases involving huge sums are likely to generate controversy even when the courts determine that such amounts are merited.

Finally regarding civil litigation, it is essential from the standpoint of justice to ask whether particular categories of litigants have an inherent advantage or disadvantage in the judicial process. The classic concern is whether litigants with greater resources and experience in the courts (the haves) are more likely to prevail over those who are less economically advantaged and less likely to use the courts on a repeat-player basis (the have-nots). Haves generally are defined as businesses, groups, and governments; have-nots are individuals.

Although the reports currently available on state trial courts do not isolate win rates in cases pitting these interests against each other, win rates in power asymmetric tort cases in state supreme courts are displayed in Figure 8-2. As would be predicted for the trial courts, the states vary considerably in the extent to which have-not litigants are successful against the haves. Across the states, win rates vary from 20 percent to almost 60 percent. Overall, these patterns suggest much the same as for workloads: state courts differ markedly in the types of interests being represented. In this regard, a broader lesson about state politics merits observation: caution should be exercised when attempting to generalize based on data limited to

Figure 8-2 Wins by Have-Nots in Asymmetric Civil Litigation in State Supreme Courts, 1995–1998

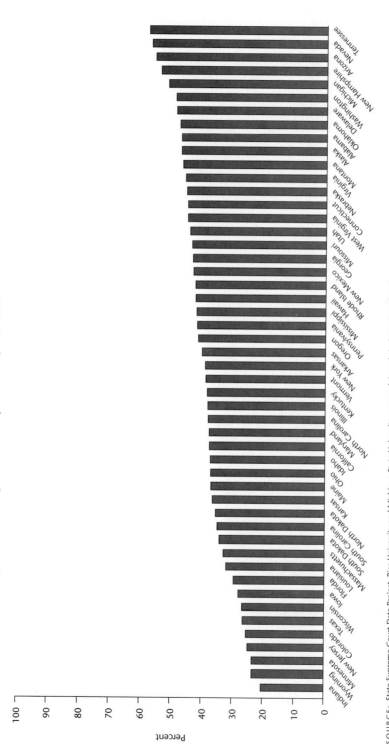

S O U R C E :   State Supreme Court Data Project, Rice University and Michigan State University, www.ruf.rice.edu/~pbrace/statecourt/.

N O T E :   The State Supreme Court Data Project contains data on the decisions of state courts of last resort from 1995 through 1998.

single states or select subsets of states. When it comes to descriptions of state judicial politics, one size does not fit all. The same principle applies to deriving conclusions about individual states from state aggregations.

There are systematic explanations for why tort cases appear on state supreme court dockets and, once docketed, who wins. Brace and Hall (2001) found that features of state court systems (particularly professionalization), the supply of legal services, and public preferences are critical in determining access to the courts and the subsequent outcomes in civil cases involving asymmetric power relationships. Professionalization, which reflects a variety of factors related to staff size, salaries, and budgets, reduces the flow of cases to state supreme courts by producing more satisfactory outcomes in the lower courts. Alternatively, larger numbers of attorneys, elected judges, and liberal citizenries all promote these cases and encourage liberal outcomes. In other words, understanding courts as agents of the economically privileged or the economically underprivileged is predicated on understanding the larger political context.

SELECTION AND REPRESENTATION

Although the fundamental purpose of state courts is to resolve legal disputes, these institutions perform other important functions, including democratic representation. Perhaps most basic is symbolic representation through which judges represent the citizenry by sharing important immutable characteristics. Studies suggest that symbolic representation in state courts may enhance institutional legitimacy and promote decisions better reflective of the interests of traditionally underrepresented groups, who now collectively make up the majority of the population (Hurwitz and Lanier 2003, 2008).

Diversity in State Courts

Improving the diversity of state courts has been an important goal for the last several decades, not only to increase the representation of historically disadvantaged groups but also to enhance the quality of the bench by expanding the interests and experiences of judges. Overall, evidence suggests that these efforts have been somewhat successful. Hurwitz and Lanier (2008, 53) document that 36 percent of the judges in state courts of last resort and 34 percent in state intermediate appellate courts are women and racial minorities. These figures are consistent with those for the U.S. Courts of Appeals, where about 34 percent are women or racial minorities (Hurwitz and Lanier 2008, 62), but fall short of the 44 percent on the U.S. Supreme Court resulting from President Barack Obama's recent appointments.

Despite conventional wisdom, there do not appear to be any systematic differences in diversity on the state court bench across methods of judicial selection. Hurwitz and Lanier (2008) essentially confirm that politically underrepresented groups do not seem to have an inherent advantage or disadvantage in any selection method currently used to staff the state court bench, a finding that comports with those of earlier studies (Glick and Emmert 1987; Hurwitz and Lanier 2003).

State Courts and the Electoral Connection

Among the many enduring controversies in state politics is the debate revolving around how best to select judges. Although all courts provide symbolic representation by reflecting traits fundamental to political and personal identity, most state judiciaries are linked directly to their citizenries through the process of elections. It is on this linkage that much of the current controversy over judicial selection centers, particularly because of the changing character of judicial elections and their possible impact on judicial legitimacy.

Generally speaking, debates about judicial selection largely reflect preferences about the seemingly incompatible goals of judicial independence and electoral accountability. Proponents of a strongly independent judiciary prefer that judges be appointed, whereas advocates for accountability favor judicial elections. However, both positions reflect underlying beliefs about the best ways to promote justice and to place state courts in state politics. As Tarr (2006, 3) effectively summarizes:

> Underlying the endemic conflict over judicial independence and judicial accountability are differing assessments of what are the most serious threats to the rule of law. Proponents of judicial independence emphasize the danger that pressures on judges may induce them to abandon their commitment to the rule of law in favor of what is popular or politically acceptable. But advocates of accountability see the danger primarily in the absence of checks on judges, which frees them to pursue their political or ideological or professional agendas at the expense of fidelity to law.

Preferences about judicial selection similarly reflect values about which groups should control access to political power and monitor judicial performance. Some selection processes allow political elites (the governor, state legislature, state bar association, and attorneys) to exert more influence than the citizenry, while others place power in the hands of the citizenry. Table 8-4 categorizes states by the method used to select the court of last resort and also lists terms of office.

As Table 8-4 indicates, the large majority of states prefer to have a formal electoral connection between their citizens and highest courts. Overall, thirty-eight states select or retain judges in partisan, nonpartisan, or retention elections. The terms of office range from six to twelve years in elected courts and from six years to lifetime tenure in appointed courts. Indeed, the reliance on elections or appointment systems with fixed terms is one of the principal differences between state courts and the federal judiciary, where judges are appointed with lifetime tenure.

The most popular method for selecting state supreme court justices is the **Missouri Plan** or "merit" plan, which is a hybrid system combining initial appointment with subsequent retention elections. As Table 8-4 documents, the Missouri Plan is used in sixteen states. In this particular method, a nominating commission

Table 8-4   Selection Systems and Terms of Office for State Supreme Courts

Partisan election	Term	Nonpartisan election	Term	Retention election (Missouri Plan)	Term	Appointment	Term
Alabama	6	Arkansas	8	Alaska	10	Connecticut	8
Illinois[a]	10	Georgia	6	Arizona	6	Delaware	12
Louisiana	10	Idaho	6	California	12	Hawaii	10
New Mexico	8	Kentucky	8	Colorado	10	Maine	7
Pennsylvania[a]	10	Michigan[b]	8	Florida	6	Massachusetts	Life
Texas	6	Minnesota	6	Indiana	10	New Hampshire	Life
West Virginia	12	Mississippi	8	Iowa	8	New Jersey	7
		Montana	8	Kansas	6	New York	14
		Nevada	6	Maryland	10	Rhode Island	Life
		North Carolina	8	Missouri	12	South Carolina	10
		North Dakota	10	Nebraska	6	Vermont	6
		Ohio[b]	6	Oklahoma	6	Virginia	12
		Oregon	6	South Dakota	8		
		Washington	6	Tennessee	8		
		Wisconsin	10	Utah	10		
				Wyoming	8		

S O U R C E : Data reported by the American Judicature Society, *Judicial Selection in the States*, www.judicialselection.us; data are revised to reflect the coding rules in notes a and b.

a. Initially select judges in partisan elections but use retention elections for subsequent terms.

b. Do not list partisan affiliations in the general elections but use partisan caucus or partisan primary to nominate candidates.

appointed by the governor screens candidates for each judgeship and ultimately recommends a short list; the governor then makes the official appointment from the commission's list. Thereafter, the nominee immediately assumes office, but within a short time—usually the next general election—he or she faces a retention vote from the state electorate. Challengers are not allowed to enter these elections. Instead, voters are asked to retain, or not retain, the incumbent. If successful, the judge begins a regular term of office and will come up for reelection again as each term expires. If voters decide not to retain, the judge is removed and the selection process begins anew. In the states using retention elections, terms range from six to twelve years.

Almost as popular as the Missouri Plan are nonpartisan elections, which are used in fifteen states. The defining characteristic of these elections is the absence of partisan labels in general elections. In Michigan and Ohio, however, partisan processes are used to nominate candidates, so that the partisan affiliations of the candidates are readily identifiable by the politically observant for the general elections, even though this information is not reported on the ballot. Overall, the terms of office in states using nonpartisan elections range from six to ten years.

As Table 8-4 also indicates, in twelve states supreme court justices are appointed. These appointments are made by the state legislature (South Carolina and Virginia) or by the governor (with or without a nominating commission) subject to confirmation by the state legislature (one or both houses) or judicial selection commission (Hawaii). Appointive systems are perhaps the most varied of the selection methods, but they all preclude any direct connection between voters and the bench. At the same time, appointments in nine of the twelve states are limited to specific terms. Justices in these states serve terms ranging from six to fourteen years and must be reappointed by a commission or state legislature. Only Massachusetts, New Hampshire, and Rhode Island grant lifetime tenure (subject to any mandatory retirement-age provisions).

Finally, seven states use partisan elections, in which candidates' partisan affiliations are listed on the ballot. However, the picture is somewhat complicated. Illinois and Pennsylvania use partisan elections for each justice's first term and retention elections for all subsequent terms. Consistent with other selection schemes, terms of office in partisan elections range from six to twelve years.

Interestingly, eight states use different methods for staffing the lower courts than their supreme court. For trial courts, Indiana, New York, and Tennessee use partisan elections, and California, Florida, Maryland, Oklahoma, and South Dakota use nonpartisan elections. Overall, ten states use partisan elections, twenty states use nonpartisan elections, nine states use the Missouri Plan, and eleven states use appointment methods. At the trial court level, the Missouri Plan is the least preferred method of judicial selection.

Historically, the mission of the judicial reform movement, which was part of the Progressive movement in state politics early in the twentieth century, was to eliminate the partisan election of judges. In large part, this goal has been achieved. In the early 1960s, twenty states used partisan elections to staff the high court bench, fourteen states used nonpartisan elections, eleven states used gubernatorial or legislative appointment, and only five states used the Missouri Plan (Hall 1999, 132–133). Today, partisan elections have become the least popular way to choose supreme court justices.

In recent years, the aim of the reform movement has shifted toward ending judicial elections altogether, although there is considerable debate about the wisdom of this choice and the accuracy of some of the claims against judicial elections (see, for example, Bonneau and Hall 2009). The American Bar Association is now advocating a gubernatorial appointment plan without legislative confirmation (American Bar Association 2003). Primarily, the concern is that the legitimacy of courts may be threatened by recent trends in judicial elections, including dramatic increases in the costs of seeking office and the fact that judges must solicit funding from attorneys and parties who may later appear in court.

Underlying these concerns is a rapidly evolving body of law governing the conduct of judicial elections brought about by recent decisions of the U.S. Supreme Court. Particularly important is *Republican Party of Minnesota v. White*, 536 U.S. 765 (2002), in which the U.S. Supreme Court effectively eliminated "announce" restrictions preventing judicial candidates from expressing their views on political issues likely to come before their courts. More recently, the ruling in *Citizens United v. Federal Election Commission*, 175 L. Ed. 2d 753 (2010), invalidated federal campaign finance reform legislation that prevented corporations and labor unions from advertising independently of the candidates within thirty days of an election. Although the Court viewed these restrictions as unconstitutionally impinging on the First Amendment rights of these groups, critics predict a storm of unrestrained special-interest influence in the electoral process for all political offices. In fact, this decision was openly condemned by President Obama in his 2010 State of the Union address, which inspired a whispered (yet visible to the cameras) defense from Justice Samuel A. Alito Jr. that the president's criticisms were "not true." Finally, in *Caperton v. Massey Coal Company*, 173 L. Ed. 2d 700 (2009), the Supreme Court held that elected judges who benefit from significant campaign contributions or independent expenditures have a constitutional obligation to recuse themselves from any case involving those parties. *Caperton* illustrates the rising profile of state supreme court elections and the desire of powerful interests to seek to control who serves in these vitally important institutions, and yet the desire at the same time that courts remain impartial arbiters of society's conflicts.

In fact, there is some evidence that judicial elections have become more competitive. For example, the contestation rates in supreme court elections from 1986 through 2008 (see Table 8-5) reveal that prior to 1992 only about one-third of all incumbents seeking reelection in nonpartisan elections faced any risk of electoral challenge. Since then, the clear majority have had to defend their seats against challengers. In fact, in 2004 the contestation rate in nonpartisan elections reached 73.1 percent. A similar pattern is evident in partisan elections, except that partisan elections always have been competitive by this measure. Indeed, it seems quite likely now that a high proportion of incumbents in partisan elections will face challengers, although the 2008 elections produced the lowest contestation rate since 1992.

However, defeat rates, also displayed in Table 8-5, tell a different story. The odds of an incumbent losing a retention election are slight. Only about 2 percent (or 7) of the 361 incumbents seeking reelection from 1986 through 2008 were ousted from office. Moreover, there do not appear to be any discernable temporal trends in these elections. Importantly, this extraordinary incumbency advantage cannot be explained by judicial competence. Studies (for example, Hurwitz and Lanier 2008) clearly show that there are no observable differences in the quality of judges across selection systems.

Defeat rates in nonpartisan elections also do not exhibit any obvious temporal trends but are significantly higher than those for retention elections. Overall, the defeat rate in nonpartisan elections from 1986 through 2008 was 6.7 percent, with a range of 0–17.9 percent in any given election cycle. The most competitive year for nonpartisan elections was 2008, during which the defeat rate more than doubled from the previous election cycle.

Most dramatic are defeat rates in partisan elections, which averaged 25.8 percent over the period 1986–2008 and ranged from 15.8 percent to 45.5 percent across election cycles. Surprisingly, defeat rates in partisan elections have declined notably.

Table 8-5 Contestation and Defeats in State Supreme Court Elections, 1986–2008

	Retention elections		Nonpartisan elections			Partisan elections			All elections		
	Number running	Defeat rate	Number running	Contest rate	Defeat rate	Number running	Contest rate	Defeat rate	Number running	Contest rate	Defeat rate
1986	33	9.1	24	16.7	4.2	18	61.1	22.2	75	35.7	10.7
1988	28	0.0	15	33.3	6.7	19	73.7	15.8	62	55.9	6.5
1990	34	0.0	24	37.5	4.2	18	72.2	33.3	76	52.4	9.2
1992	23	4.3	22	54.5	9.1	20	65.0	25.0	65	59.5	12.3
1994	27	0.0	17	52.9	5.9	11	81.8	36.4	55	64.3	9.1
1996	23	8.7	23	65.2	4.3	11	100.0	36.4	57	76.5	12.3
1998	41	0.0	18	66.7	0.0	12	91.7	33.3	71	76.7	5.6
2000	30	0.0	27	63.0	7.4	11	90.9	45.5	68	71.1	10.3
2002	29	0.0	18	61.1	5.6	11	90.9	18.2	58	72.4	5.2
2004	27	3.7	26	73.1	3.8	10	90.0	30.0	63	77.8	7.9
2006	39	0.0	27	55.6	7.4	12	100.0	8.3	78	69.2	1.3
2008	27	0.0	28	57.1	17.9	10	80.0	10.0	65	63.2	9.2
Total	361	1.9	269	53.5	6.7	163	80.4	25.8	793	63.7	8.4

SOURCE: Author's data, collected from various official state reports. Odd-year elections are combined with the previous year for reporting purposes.

The defeat rate in 2006 was the lowest of the series, a pattern that continued in 2008.

Although the results of the 2010 elections are just now being assembled and analyzed, the preliminary results are intriguing. In 2010 the defeat rates in retention, nonpartisan, and partisan elections were, respectively, 8.8 percent, 10.0 percent, and 0.0 percent. The defeat rate in retention elections, caused by the three defeats in Iowa mentioned at the outset of this chapter, was the highest since 1996 but did not really exceed previous loss rates in 1986 and 1996. In nonpartisan elections, the defeat rate declined by 44 percent over the previous election cycle, and in partisan elections there was a precipitous drop in defeats to none at all in 2010.

Overall, the *White* decision and other recent changes in the campaign context do not appear to have had much of an effect on contestation or defeat rates in state supreme court elections, with the exception of the defeat rates in the 2008 nonpartisan elections and the 2010 retention elections. However, these trends are offset by sharp declines in defeat rates in partisan elections since 2004 and nonpartisan elections in 2010, as well as declines in contestation rates in nonpartisan elections since 2006. In fact, Bonneau, Hall, and Streb (2011) confirmed this conclusion more systematically for both state supreme courts and state intermediate appellate courts. Although it is too soon to draw definitive conclusions, early evidence suggests that the *White* decision and other changes in the electoral context may not have had the impact expected, at least with respect to the incumbency advantage. Whether *White* and other recent decisions have had other effects, such as changing the content of campaigns or the role of independent spending, remains to be seen.

Drawing substantive conclusions from contestation and defeat rates is an excellent illustration of the essentially normative nature of the judicial selection debate. Whether the rates of contestation and defeat are good news or bad news depends largely on the reader's preferences. Those who favor electoral accountability as a means of best ensuring judicial integrity will hail the seemingly strong connections between citizens and the bench brought about by nonpartisan and partisan elections. Overall, it is clear that voters do not blindly favor incumbents in these elections.

These conclusions are consistent with other empirical evidence that judicial elections, particularly partisan elections, make a great deal of sense, democratically speaking. Among other things, challengers are strategic in deciding whether to take on incumbents (Bonneau and Hall 2003, 2006). Particularly vulnerable are newly appointed incumbents and incumbents who won their previous elections by narrow margins. In other words, the most electorally insecure are those who were never chosen by voters in the first place or are relatively unpopular. Similarly, the electorate when voting has the capacity to distinguish between quality and nonquality challengers (Hall and Bonneau 2006) and to make issue-based choices even when partisan labels are not on the ballot (Baum 1987; Hojnacki and Baum 1992; Hall 2001a). Finally, rather than being alienated by aggressive, costly campaigns, citizens are mobilized to vote by these races (Hall 2007b; Hall and Bonneau 2008). Thus to accountability advocates, partisan elections, and to a lesser extent nonpartisan elections, appear to be working well, even if there are concerns about the influence of special interests and the campaign negativity that currently plague elections generally.

For advocates of judicial independence, the recent trends in electoral competition in nonpartisan and partisan elections are disturbing. In particular, heated campaigns place pressures on state court judges to acquiesce to the popular preferences in order to avoid electoral defeat. In fact, a significant literature confirms that state supreme court justices chosen under competitive conditions and who are approaching the end of their terms are likely to engage in strategic voting to retain their seats (Hall 1987, 1992, 1995; Brace and Hall 1997)[1] and may be deterred from seeking reelection in the first place (Hall 2001b). From a different perspective, competitive elections require extensive fund-raising, thereby promoting the appearance of impropriety when sitting judges accept campaign contributions from donors later appearing before their courts. Because of these trends, appointive systems or the Missouri Plan are viewed as a better way to choose judges.

Regardless of one's preferences about how state court judges should be selected and to a large extent despite the empirical evidence, the controversy over electing

---

1. Even this empirical finding can be interpreted to support or oppose judicial elections. Justices taking public preferences into account when deciding cases may be a legitimate pressure on judges to follow the law rather than decide cases as they wish.

judges will continue. There simply is no perfect system for selecting judges, nor is there any way to remove partisan politics or other political judgments from the process. Elective systems may be too closely connected to representative politics, and appointive systems can be characterized by elitism, cronyism, and intense partisanship.

JUDICIAL REVIEW IN CHECKS AND BALANCES

State courts participate fully in the system of checks and balances through the exercise of judicial review, which empowers courts to invalidate the actions of the other branches of government that are inconsistent with the state or federal constitution. It is primarily in this way that courts find themselves pitted directly against the other primary actors in state politics on some of the most controversial issues on the American political agenda. Generally speaking, when courts invalidate statutes or other official acts, they are acting as a **countermajoritarian** force by undermining legislative or other popular majorities.

Because such cases often are politically explosive, a single case can place a court on the political hot seat even when the court upholds the action in question. However, it becomes difficult to fly under the political radar when courts actually overturn statutes, ordinances, executive orders, or ballot initiatives. Figure 8-3 shows the rates at which state supreme courts invalidate actions as a proportion of all constitutional challenges. In some states, the tendency to exercise judicial review is significant. Overall, eleven supreme courts are active players in the game of checks and balances by invalidating in at least one of every three opportunities. Particularly interesting are the Minnesota, Oregon, and Oklahoma Courts of Criminal Appeals, which reverse popular majorities about as often as not. These courts are more likely to experience unhappy relations with state government than those in other states with less confrontational decisional propensities.

Alternatively, as Figure 8-3 shows, the courts of last resort in some states are not likely to engage in constitutional conflicts. Particularly notable are Connecticut, Indiana, Maine, and Michigan, which did not invalidate any actions on constitutional grounds during the period covered by the figure. Generally, the extent to which state supreme courts accept these cases and then invalidate on constitutional grounds reflects a series of strategies and contextual contingencies in state political environments (Brace, Hall, and Langer 1999, 2001; Langer 2002).

In the game of checks and balances, certain types of constitutional conflicts are especially controversial because they involve issues that are the most politically salient to the other branches of government. Two excellent examples are restrictive abortion regulations, which are important to executives and legislatures for solidifying popular support in conservative states, and campaign and election laws, which influence the electoral fortunes of public officials. On these types of issues, courts are less likely to invalidate statutes when the fear of retaliation is greatest, such as when the executive and legislature are controlled by the same political party

Figure 8-3 Success Rate of Constitutional Challenges in State Supreme Courts, 1995–1998

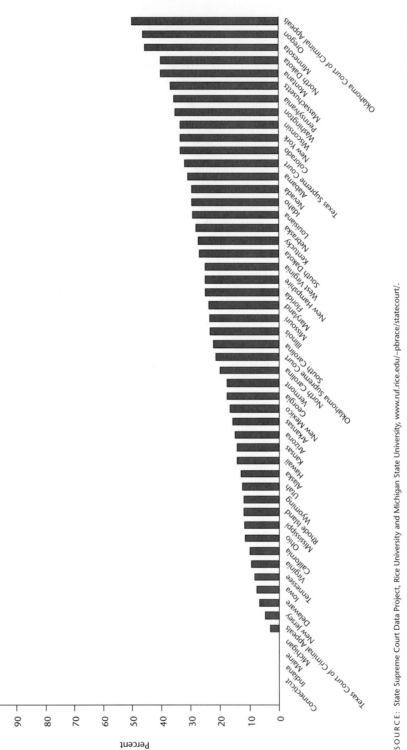

SOURCE: State Supreme Court Data Project, Rice University and Michigan State University, www.ruf.rice.edu/~pbrace/statecourt/.

NOTES: The State Supreme Court Data Project contains data on the decisions of state courts of last resort from 1995 through 1998. Oklahoma and Texas have separate supreme courts for civil and criminal litigation.

and thus can more readily retaliate by passing legislation or proposing constitutional amendments to undermine court rulings (Brace, Hall, and Langer 1999, 2001; Langer 2002).

On questions less salient to the other branches and more relevant to citizens, judges must weigh their concerns about legislative or gubernatorial reprisals against constituency pressures, their own ideological preferences, and rulings of the U.S. Supreme Court. Politically volatile is the death penalty—an issue on which the state courts have been particularly active. For example, in rulings in *State (of Kansas) v. Marsh*, 102 P.3d 445 (2004), and *People (of the State of New York) v. LaValle*, 817 N.E.2d 341 (2004), the Kansas and New York high courts invalidated death penalty statutes. Another excellent example is *Nebraska v. Mata*, 745 N.W.2d 229 (2008), in which the Nebraska Supreme Court declared that executions by electrocution, the only method authorized at the time in Nebraska, violated the state constitution.

Of course, courts can place themselves squarely at odds with the other branches of government and with the voters without exercising judicial review. In death penalty cases, courts do not have to invalidate a statute in order to overturn a death sentence. Instead, reviewing death sentences for procedural irregularities or proportionality is an inherent component of the due process function of appellate courts. By carefully scrutinizing these cases and holding trials to the strictest of standards, state supreme courts restrict the application of the death penalty and greatly lessen its reach. In fact, state supreme courts overturned convictions or death sentences in sixty-eight capital cases in 2009 (Bureau of Justice Statistics 2010, 13).

CONCLUSION

State courts are often considered legal institutions that are largely disconnected from politics. However, normative perceptions of the proper role of courts and the primacy of the rule of law often obscure reality. In fact, state judiciaries, individually and collectively, have a resounding impact on state politics. In addition to processing almost staggering caseloads involving issues most directly relevant to the American public, state courts engage in distributive and redistributive politics, represent the citizenry both directly and symbolically, and can actively serve as countermajoritarian agents. These roles differ considerably across the states, and it will only be through more research and systematic analysis that scholars will achieve accurate, comprehensive depictions and explanations of the various manifestations of these vital institutions. Even so, it is evident that in many ways state courts can serve to connect citizens to the institutions of state government, give preference to particular interests, and undermine legislative or other popular majorities. Without understanding courts and their effects, Americans are left with unsatisfactory explanations of many important dimensions of state politics and policy.

KEY TERMS

countermajoritarian, 273

courts of last resort, 254

general jurisdiction trial courts, 254

intermediate appellate courts, 254

limited jurisdiction trial courts, 253

mechanical jurisprudence, 252

Missouri Plan, 267

tort case, 253

REFERENCES

Administrative Office of the U.S. Courts. 2010. "Judicial Business of the United States Courts." www.uscourts.gov/uscourts/Statistics/JudicialBusiness/2010/JudicialBusinespdfversion.pdf.

American Bar Association Commission on the 21st Century Judiciary. 2003. *Justice in Jeopardy.* Chicago: American Bar Association.

Barnes, Robert. 2007. "Justices Continue Trend of Hearing Fewer Cases." *Washington Post,* January 7, sec. A.

Baum, Lawrence. 1987. "Explaining the Vote in Judicial Elections: The 1984 Ohio Supreme Court Elections." *Western Political Quarterly* 40: 361–371.

Bonneau, Chris W., and Melinda Gann Hall. 2003. "Predicting Challengers in State Supreme Court Elections: Context and the Politics of Institutional Design." *Political Research Quarterly* 56: 337–349.

———. 2009. *In Defense of Judicial Elections.* New York: Routledge.

Bonneau, Chris W., Melinda Gann Hall, and Matthew J. Streb. 2011. "*White* Noise: The Unrealized Effects of *Republican Party of Minnesota v. White* on Judicial Elections." *Justice System Journal* 32: 247–268.

Brace, Paul, and Melinda Gann Hall. 1997. "The Interplay of Preferences, Case Facts, Context, and Rules in the Politics of Judicial Choice." *Journal of Politics* 59: 1206–1231.

———. 2001. " 'Haves' versus 'Have Nots' in State Supreme Courts: Allocating Docket Space and Wins in Power Asymmetric Cases." *Law and Society Review* 35: 393–418.

Brace, Paul, Melinda Gann Hall, and Laura Langer. 1999. "Judicial Choice and the Politics of Abortion: Institutions, Context, and the Autonomy of Courts." *Albany Law Review* 62: 1265–1303.

———. 2001. "Placing State Supreme Courts in State Politics." *State Politics and Policy Quarterly* 1: 81–108.

Bureau of Justice Statistics. 2008. "Civil Bench and Jury Trials in State Courts, 2005." Washington, D.C.: U.S. Department of Justice.

———. 2010. "Capital Punishment, 2009—Statistical Tables." Washington, D.C.: U.S. Department of Justice.

Glick, Henry R., and Craig Emmert. 1987. "Selection Systems and Judicial Characteristics: The Recruitment of State Supreme Court Judges." *Judicature* 70: 228–235.

Hall, Melinda Gann. 1987. "Constituency Influence in State Supreme Courts: Conceptual Notes and a Case Study." *Journal of Politics* 49: 1117–1124.

———. 1992. "Electoral Politics and Strategic Voting in State Supreme Courts." *Journal of Politics* 55: 427–446.

———. 1995. "Justices as Representatives: Elections and Judicial Politics in the American States." *American Politics Quarterly* 23: 485–503.

———. 1999. "State Judicial Politics: Rules, Structures, and the Political Game." In *American State and Local Politics: Directions for the 21st Century,* ed. Ronald E. Weber and Paul Brace. New York: Chatham House.

———. 2001a. "State Supreme Courts in American Democracy: Probing the Myths of Judicial Reform." *American Political Science Review* 92: 315–330.

———. 2001b. "Voluntary Retirements from State Supreme Courts: Assessing Democratic Pressures to Relinquish the Bench." *Journal of Politics* 63: 1112–1140.

———. 2007a. "Competition as Accountability in State Supreme Court Elections." In *Running for Judge: The Rising Political, Financial, and Legal Stakes of Judicial Elections,* ed. Matthew J. Streb. New York: New York University Press.

———. 2007b. "Mobilizing Voters in State Supreme Court Elections: Competition and Other Contextual Forces as Democratic Incentives." *Journal of Politics* 69: 1162–1174.

Hall, Melinda Gann, and Chris W. Bonneau. 2006. "Does Quality Matter? Challengers in State Supreme Court Elections." *American Journal of Political Science* 50: 20–33.

———. 2008. "Mobilizing Interest: The Effects of Money on Ballot Roll-Off in State Supreme Court Elections." *American Journal of Political Science* 52: 457–470.

Hojnacki, Marie, and Lawrence Baum. 1992. " 'New Style' Judicial Campaigns and Voters: Economic Issues and Union Members in Ohio." *Western Political Quarterly* 45: 921–948.

Hurwitz, Mark S., and Drew Noble Lanier. 2003. "Explaining Judicial Diversity: The Differential Ability of Women and Minorities to Attain Seats on State Supreme Court and Appellate Courts." *State Politics and Policy Quarterly* 3: 329–352.

———. 2008. "Diversity in State and Federal Appellate Courts: Change and Continuity across 20 Years." *Justice System Journal* 29: 47–70.

Langer, Laura. 2002. *Judicial Review in State Supreme Courts: A Comparative Study.* Albany: State University of New York Press.

National Center for State Courts. 2010a. *State Court Caseload Statistics: An Analysis of 2008 State Court Caseloads.* Williamsburg, Va.: National Center for State Courts.

———. 2010b. *Survey of Judicial Salaries.* Williamsburg, Va.: National Center for State Courts.

———. 2010c. *Examining the Work of State Courts, 2008.* Williamsburg, Va.: National Center for State Courts.

Tarr, G. Alan. 2006. "Creating and Debating Judicial Independence and Accountability." Paper presented at the annual meeting of the American Political Science Association, Philadelphia, August 31–September 3.

United States Courts. 2010. "Judicial Salaries Since 1968." www.uscourts.gov/Viewer.aspx?doc=/uscourts/JudgesJudgeships/docs/JudicialSalarieschart.pdf.

Yates, Jeff, Belinda Creel Davis, and Henry R. Glick. 2001. "The Politics of Torts: Explaining Litigation Rates in the American States." *State Politics and Policy Quarterly* 12: 127–143.

SUGGESTED READINGS

Print

American Bar Association Commission on the 21st Century Judiciary. *Justice in Jeopardy.* Chicago: American Bar Association, 2003. An excellent summary of the issues involved in the controversy over electing judges, including arguments from the ABA about why electing judges should be abandoned.

Hall, Melinda Gann. "On the Catalysm of Judicial Elections and Other Popular Antidemocratic Myths." In *What's Law Got to Do with It? What Judges Do, Why They Do It, and What's at Stake,* ed. Charles Gardner Geyh. Palo Alto, Calif.: Stanford University Press, 2011. A comprehensive essay on the disjuncture between empirical political science and the advocacy community on the judicial elections controversy.

Kritzer, Herbert M., Paul Brace, Melinda Gann Hall, and Brent T. Boyea. "The Business of State Supreme Courts, Revisited." *Journal of Empirical Legal Studies* 4 (2007): 427–439. A look at the dockets of state supreme courts over time, including how the workloads of these courts have changed.

Streb, Matthew J. *Running for Judge: The Rising Political, Financial, and Legal Stakes of Judicial Elections.* New York: NYU Press, 2007. The latest edited volume on judicial elections, with essays from some of the most respected scholars, who offer a variety of perspectives.

Internet

American Judicature Society. www.ajs.org/selection/sel_stateselect.asp. Details processes for selecting judges in the states as well as the various reforms under way.

National Center for State Courts. www.ncsconline.org. A wealth of information on the state courts, including topical reports and data.

State Law (WashLaw: Washburn University School of Law). www.washlaw.edu/uslaw/states/allstates/. Links to state law search, legal libraries, municipal codes, local county courthouse addresses, draft and uniform model acts, state and local tax agencies, Uniform Commercial Code locator, and other state agencies.

State Supreme Court Data Project. www.ruf.rice.edu/~pbrace/statecourt/. Source for the State Supreme Court Data Project, a multiuser database containing information about the cases decided in all state supreme courts from 1995 to 1998, as well as related information.

CHAPTER 9

State Corrections Policy

JOHN WOOLDREDGE

Throughout the 1980s, news portrayals of the police and courts as being "soft" on criminals contributed to public dissatisfaction with crime control strategies across the United States (Roberts 1992). Responding to this dissatisfaction, state officials enacted tougher laws and imposed stiffer penalties on individuals convicted of crimes. The last two decades of the twentieth century saw nationwide an increase of 50 percent in the rate of incarceration in state prisons. As a result, the population of state prisons skyrocketed, from 300,000 inmates in 1980 to 1.5 million in 2000 (Blumstein and Beck 1999).

Although the population has since fallen to 1.4 million, prison officials in many states report that inmate crowding has become one of the most important problems they face—now, and in the foreseeable future (Mauer 2006). To address this problem, states have built new prisons, some of them with "supermax" compounds for securing the most dangerous criminals. The construction of new prisons or the expansion of existing facilities continues to be a priority in some states today, and state legislatures have had to struggle with whether to fund new prisons by raising taxes or cutting spending in other programs.

This chain of events, in which a solution to one problem generates new issues or concerns, is typical of public policy. It is especially visible in **corrections policy**, the complex set of procedures for managing persons found guilty in a court of law of misdemeanor or felony crimes. Correctional policies are implemented by the state or federal government, depending on which laws are broken. Offenders whose crimes fall under the jurisdiction of state courts are handled via state corrections policy. This policy varies widely across states because of their diverse political, social, and economic environments. This chapter describes some of the most important differences in state sentencing policies and prison management procedures and explains them in terms of differences in ideology, legal practices, and state resources.

SENTENCING IN THEORY AND IN PRACTICE

Many factors affect the types of corrections policies implemented by a particular state, including the dominant sentencing philosophies adopted by public officials and the resources available for implementing those philosophies. Because of differences in ideology and resources, no two states have identical policies for dealing with offenders. States can be grouped on the basis of policy similarities, however, and more generally in terms of their sentencing philosophies.

Philosophies and Justifications for Incarceration

Four primary **sentencing philosophies** guide correctional practices in the United States: retribution, deterrence (both general and specific), incapacitation, and rehabilitation. *Retribution* involves punishing offenders in proportion to the harm they inflict on society. The state represents the voice of the people in condemning the offender. Removing punishment from the hands of those who are emotionally involved contributes to greater equity in the treatment of offenders.

Retribution is compatible with general *deterrence*, which makes use of punishment to discourage others from committing similar crimes. A retributive approach to punishment promotes consistency in punishment, which, if publicized, educates citizens about what can happen to them if they choose to commit the same crime. Also compatible with retribution is specific or individual deterrence, or punishment for the purpose of deterring the offender who committed the crime. By contrast, *incapacitation* aims to prevent future crimes by the offender by removing them from society via incarceration or execution. This philosophy generates different practices in comparison with retribution because the punishment might actually be harsher relative to the crimes committed.

Rehabilitation emphasizes the treatment and reform of offenders. Underlying this philosophy is the assumption that the sources of an individual's deviant behavior can be identified and treated. It is generally believed that the most effective means of rehabilitation are in the community rather than in prison (or a **correctional facility**), and so a state's emphasis on rehabilitation usually coincides with a preference for community sanctions.

Most states have adopted elements of all four philosophies, depending on the crimes committed, unique circumstances surrounding the offenses, and the attributes of offenders and their life situations. Some of the differences in state policies reflect varying emphases on the four philosophies for different crimes and offenders.

Sentencing Models as Reflections of Different Philosophies

Many states have created sentencing commissions charged with developing sentencing schemes that express the underlying philosophies of punishment for criminals. A greater emphasis on rehabilitation is sometimes reflected in indeterminate sentencing schemes with relatively broad ranges for prison terms, based on the idea that the length of time needed to reform an offender cannot be determined in advance. States with a greater focus on retribution or incapacitation, by contrast, generally follow some type of determinate sentencing scheme with narrower sentence ranges than those under indeterminate schemes. Even across states with determinate sentencing, however, there remains considerable variation in sentence lengths for the same crimes.

Recent sentencing reforms reflect interest in curbing judicial discretion in order to promote greater uniformity in sentencing, and there has been a nationwide trend away from indeterminate sentencing and toward determinate sentencing. This evolution is part of the **get-tough movement** noted earlier, with more states adopting a less tolerant stance toward convicted offenders. Some of the more common practices associated with determinate sentencing include sentencing guidelines (judges are "guided" toward particular terms of imprisonment or alternatives to incarceration based on a series of factors and presumptions), truth-in-sentencing (imprisoned offenders must serve a minimum percentage of the sentence imposed in court), mandatory sentences (automatic prison sentences of a particular length for certain types of crimes and offenders), and parole guidelines (parole boards are limited in their discretion to grant and terminate parole). Thirty-one states are now operating under sentencing guidelines or other forms of determinate sentencing (Stemen and Rengifo 2011).

The information displayed in Table 9-1 describes different types of **sentencing schemes,** based on whether states have truth-in-sentencing, parole, or mandatory or voluntary sentencing guidelines. States are ordered by rank according to their policy liberalism (defined in Chapter 1) to help readers discern patterns in these schemes. Each state has also been assigned a rank on sentencing policy "toughness," which is a composite index reflecting the adoption of mandatory sentencing guidelines, truth-in-sentencing, the abolition of parole, three-strikes laws, minimum prison terms for up to six offender groups, and incarceration rates in state prisons.

To maintain consistency with the index of policy liberalism, the higher ranks in the sentencing policy "toughness" index reflect more conservative (tougher)

Table 9-1 State Sentencing Policies and Dates Enacted (Repealed)/Reenacted, Ranked by Policy Liberalism

Jurisdiction	Policy liberalism	Sentencing policy "toughness"	Truth-in-sentencing	Abolished parole	Mandatory guidelines	Voluntary guidelines
California	1	46	1994	1976		
New York	2	35	1995			
New Jersey	3	7	1997			
Vermont	4	12				
Connecticut	5	29	1995			
Hawaii	6	11				
Maryland	7	24				1983
Rhode Island	8	16				
Oregon	9	20	1995	1989	1989	
Maine	10	19	1995	1975		
Massachusetts	11	2				
Minnesota	12	6	1993	1980	1980	
Wisconsin	13	14	1999	1999		1985 (1994)/2000
Montana	14	10				
Washington	15	26	1990	1984	1984	
New Mexico	16	1	1999			
West Virginia	17	2				
Illinois	18	42	1996	1978		
New Hampshire	19	31				
Alaska	20	8			1980	
Delaware	21	21	1990	1990		1987
Michigan	22	9	1995		1999	1984 (1998)
Colorado	23	13				
Pennsylvania	24	38	1996		1982	
Iowa	25	29	1996			
Kentucky	26	3				
Missouri	27	34	1994			1997
Ohio	28	22	1996	1996	1996 (2006)	2006
Kansas	29	4	1995	1993	1993	
North Carolina	30	33	1994	1994	1994	
Nevada	31	17				
Georgia	32	18	1995			
Nebraska	33	5				
South Carolina	34	42	1996			
Indiana	35	43		1977		
Virginia	36	40	1995			1991
Utah	37	28	1985			1985
Arizona	38	36	1994	1994		
Tennessee	39	23	1995		1989	
North Dakota	40	41	1995			
Alabama	41	39				
Idaho	42	45				
Oklahoma	43	22	1998			
South Dakota	44	15				
Wyoming	45	27				
Florida	46	44	1995	1983	1994 (1998)	1983 (1993)
Mississippi	47	37	1995	1995		
Texas	48	30				
Louisiana	49	32	1997			1992
Arkansas	50	25				

SOURCES: For ranks for policy liberalism, see Chapter 1 in this volume; for the remainder of the data in this table, see Benjamin Steiner and John Wooldredge, "Comparing State versus Facility Level Effects on Crowding in U.S. Correctional Facilities," *Crime and Delinquency* 54 (2008): 259–290; Don Stemen and Andres Rengifo, "Policies and Imprisonment: The Impact of Structured Sentencing and Determinate Sentencing on State Incarceration Rates, 1978–2004," *Justice Quarterly* 28 (2011): 174–201.

NOTE: Ranks on policy liberalism: 1 = most liberal, 50 = most conservative; ranks on sentencing policy toughness: 1 = most liberal, 46 = toughest policy (with some states tied on rank).

corrections practices.[1] The correlation between state policy liberalism and sentencing toughness is roughly 0.38 (Pearson's *r*, *p* < .01), indicating a fair amount of correspondence between the two ranks where more policy-liberal states tend to have more lenient sentencing practices and lower incarceration rates. There are exceptions to this correspondence, however, such as California, which is one of the most policy-liberal states and yet has a prison population that is nearly twice the size of what its state facilities were designed to house.

Table 9-1 lists the different combinations of various sentencing policies and when they were introduced in each state. The year in which sentencing guidelines were implemented is important because the typical guideline schemes introduced in the 1980s are more rigid than those implemented in the 1990s. For example, the guidelines enacted in Ohio in 1996 were based on the Ohio Sentencing Commission's decision to avoid the matrix-style grid of earlier schemes (such as Minnesota's) because of a perception that such a scheme removed too much judicial discretion and resulted in overly harsh sentences for particular offenders.[2]

States such as Washington and California have also enacted three-strikes laws that force criminals to serve lengthy prison terms upon their third felony conviction. These laws have placed enormous demands on prison resources because of the costs involved. In California, for example, a twenty-five-year minimum prison sentence for a third strike costs more than $600,000. Sentencing commissions are now forced to deal with prison crowding when they recommend legislation because of the fivefold increase in prison populations since 1980. This situation has led to decriminalization in some states, particularly for drug laws; offenses that once mandated prison sentences have been redefined as lower-level felonies with recommended sentences of community supervision.

Perhaps the biggest obstacle to formulating effective corrections policy is the difficulty in anticipating all possible consequences of policy change, such as the

1. The index is based on the most recent information for six policies and practices affecting the severity of sentences for criminals. The first policy is whether a state has mandatory sentencing guidelines. States are ranked higher if they operate under guidelines, and higher still if they follow guidelines implemented in the 1980s (earlier schemes were more rigid than subsequent schemes). The second policy is whether states follow truth-in-sentencing, with higher ranks assigned to states requiring completion of higher percentages of the prison terms stated in courts. The next two policies are binary variables indicating whether states abolished parole and whether they adopted three-strikes legislation. The number of sentences for which a minimum length of time in prison is required for particular offenders and crimes is counted for each state, with higher ranks for states with more of these minimum sentences (including minimums for habitual offenders, narcotics offenses, repeat violent offenders, sex offenders, crimes involving guns, and drunk driving). Finally, states are ranked on their incarceration rates per 100,000 residents. To maintain consistency with the index of policy liberalism, higher ranks reflect more conservative (tougher) corrections practices. Each of these scales was standardized, and all of the standardized scales were summed to create a unique score for each state.

2. The matrix-style grid used to determine sentences in some states consists of two dimensions that rate both the severity of an offense and an offender's prior criminal record. Numerical scores appear along each axis of the grid, and the intersection of a particular row and column designates a prison term. Judges are permitted to override designated terms in special circumstances, for documented reasons.

impact of sentencing reforms on prison inmate crowding. Interstate differences in corrections policy may be easier to appreciate because they are based on state differences in philosophies and economies that shape sentencing schemes and, in turn, all of the limits placed on available resources for punishment and correction.

Disjuncture between Sentencing Philosophies and the Law

Laws and legal processes shaped by sentencing philosophies are imperfect reflections of those philosophies. This is another source of interstate differences in sentencing based on subjective interpretations of philosophies such as retribution and rehabilitation. For example, retributive punishments in the U.S. legal system are defined in terms of varying lengths of incarceration in jail or prison, execution (in capital cases only), and financial restitution (in less serious cases involving stolen or damaged property). However, no term of imprisonment is a true reflection of the exact harm inflicted on society by an offender because there is no objective measure of harm. Some crimes can inflict physical, emotional, and economic pain on an individual, not to mention the pain inflicted on the victim's family, and it is impossible to gauge these harms in order to derive punishments of equal weight.

The sheer number of criminal laws further complicates the situation by multiplying such calculations literally hundreds of times. For these reasons, the idea of retribution has evolved into a practice whereby punishments are graded according to the seriousness of offenses, which has led to disparities across states in the absolute length of incarceration ascribed for particular crimes. For example, many (not all) states separate the length of imprisonment for armed robbery and burglary by five years, but the minimum prison sentence for burglary ranges from one to five years across states, while the minimum sentence for armed robbery typically ranges from three to ten years.

There are also differences across states in the factors that the law says should be considered in determining proportionate punishments. Offense severity is always the primary consideration when determining proportionate punishments, but there is disagreement over the relevance of an offender's culpability and criminal history. Mitigating factors (information or evidence favoring less severe sanctions for a particular crime) and aggravating factors (information/evidence favoring more severe sanctions) also vary across states. For example, when considering whether to execute a defendant convicted of first-degree murder, mitigating factors in some states include whether the offender was under substantial duress at the time of the crime and whether the offender had no prior criminal record. Aggravating factors in such cases might include whether the offender created a grave risk of death for others aside from the victim and whether the offender agreed to commit the act in exchange for payment or other pecuniary gain.

Sentencing disparities across states are also influenced by the role of victims in the sentencing process. Growing public concern over victim harm and the absence of victims' rights during the last half of the twentieth century led to an ideology of restorative justice, in which the offender and victim participate in sentencing decisions geared toward helping the offenders understand their harm to others and motivating them to "repair" their injuries. The growing popularity of this ideology has coincided with thirty-two states modifying their own constitutions to protect victims' rights—for example, including victims in public proceedings related to the crime, giving timely notice of the release of suspects, enforcing the victim's right to speak at sentencing, and protecting victims (National Center for Victims of Crime 2009).

Perhaps the greatest disparity in sentencing across states stems from differences in the resources for rehabilitation. Drug treatment programs vary in quality and quantity across states, a fact that generates interstate differences in whether a drug offender is treated in the community or is sent to prison. Diversion programs for drug offenders also vary widely, which can lead to differences in the official criminal records for similarly situated offenders across states.

Policy versus Practice: Limitations of Sentencing Models

Just as sentencing philosophies do not always translate into laws that perfectly reflect those philosophies, the implementation of laws is not always uniform. Interstate differences in political ideologies and the organization of trial courts of general jurisdiction contribute to differences in levels of disjuncture between policy and practice, as noted in Chapter 8. Also, a state government's adoption of sentencing guidelines that reduce judicial discretion does not imply that all court actors across all trial courts necessarily favor the reform. On the contrary, judges often bemoan efforts to change their methods of decision making (Griffin and Wooldredge 2001). Some judges are merely uncomfortable with change itself, but other judges perceive these reforms as challenges to their authority.

The orientation of judges has implications for the implementation of sentencing reforms. Guidelines necessarily conflict with a philosophy of individualized justice and as such could be undermined by judges through their greater willingness to approve particular charge or sentence reductions (or both) in plea agreements (Wooldredge 2009). Thus depending on their attitudes toward sentencing guidelines, some judges may be more passionate than others about maneuvering around the restrictions placed on their discretion. To the extent that judicial actors in one state are more opposed to sentencing guidelines, the outcomes may differ from those in a state where judges support the same guidelines.

These considerations suggest the importance of political influences on incarceration rates and the impact of political ideologies on statewide differences in practice. Yates and Fording (2005) show how more conservative political environments contributed to the rising incarceration rates during the latter part of the twentieth century, when crime rates either remained level or increased at a much slower pace. The greater popularity of the more punitive ideologies that characterized the get-tough movement emerged against a backdrop of growing political conservatism.

Therefore, differences in political environments and degrees of conservatism may account for statewide differences in imprisonment rates and corrections policy.

Another motivation underlying the implementation of more structured sentencing schemes has been more effective control of incarceration rates (Reitz 1999; Frase 2000). This effort is consistent with those to curb judicial discretion, because a state's judiciary ultimately determines the proportions of convicted offenders sent to prison, and failure to reduce judicial discretion can lead to decision making without consideration of the resources available for confinement. In short, more structured sentencing schemes should provide greater control over prison "inputs" and, in light of the dramatic increases in state incarceration rates since 1980, should ultimately help to *reduce* prison populations. Despite interest in reducing prison populations, however, recent evidence indicates a relatively weak correspondence between more structured sentencing schemes and state prison incarceration rates (Stemen and Rengifo 2011). On the other hand, there is evidence to suggest that fluctuations in incarceration rates follow state political ideologies very closely (Percival 2010), possibly reflecting differences between conservatives and liberals in levels of tolerance toward offenders and the different priorities of these groups regarding incapacitation versus crime prevention (Beckett and Western 2001).

This observation can be tied to the earlier discussion of how state-level sentencing reforms may not be very effective in achieving their aims. The scale of state policy liberalism described in Chapter 1 might be a more accurate proxy of judicial interest in and willingness to keep prison populations at manageable levels, assuming that judges in more liberal states are likely to be more liberal themselves as a consequence of being elected by more liberal constituencies.

Juvenile Court Philosophies and Practices

Separate courts for young offenders were originally created because the goals of juvenile justice once differed from those of adult criminal justice. The belief back then was that juveniles should not be punished like adults because the young are less responsible for their crimes (that is, they are less likely to act on their own free will owing to their immaturity, and they are more easily influenced by their environments). Focusing instead on the goal of personal reform, legislators distinguished juvenile courts from adult courts in terms of law, procedure, and possible sanctions. The emphasis on reform instead of punishment meant that costly due process procedures could be minimized. Guilt was presumed upon entry into the juvenile justice system, and under the doctrine of *parens patriae* the court assumed a guardian role in order to determine the course of action that would reflect the best interest of each child.

States differ in terms of when juvenile courts were first established, the legal age cutoffs for jurisdiction over juveniles (fourteen, fifteen, sixteen, or seventeen), how much emphasis is placed on treatment, levels of due process, and possible sanctions. No two states maintain the same system of juvenile justice. Some of the differences that have evolved over the last forty years are whether juveniles should receive *Miranda* warnings by officers, can be housed in adult jails, can be waived to adult court (for their processing and punishment), and can be eligible for the death sentence. Also at issue is the role of prosecutors vis-à-vis juveniles and the rates of institutionalization of juveniles. In short, juveniles may be treated more or less as adults, depending on the state in which they are processed.

Generally speaking, there is movement toward harsher sanctions for juveniles, although states vary in their juvenile law and court procedures. Most states now have waiver laws that permit the prosecution of juveniles in adult criminal courts. Consistent with the get-tough movement, these laws expose juveniles to the same punishments (including death) available for adults, although juveniles waived to adult court also then have the same due process protections accorded adults. Some states do not practice juvenile waiver, however, and others have adopted cumbersome processes that make waivers rare. A dozen states are now in the process of revising their transfer statutes in order to expedite juvenile waivers. There are also interstate differences in the applicable ages and crimes for which juveniles may be transferred. In Arkansas, juveniles sixteen years and older can be waived to adult court for any felony. The age cutoff in Michigan is lower (fourteen years and older), but it is applicable to fewer crimes: murder, attempted murder, arson, aggravated assault, armed robbery, kidnapping, first-degree criminal sexual conduct, carjacking, bank robbery, and escape (Steiner and Wright 2007).

States no longer house juveniles in adult jails and municipal lockups, but the process of getting states to comply with this federal directive (one of many under the Juvenile Justice and Delinquency Prevention Act of 1980) took nearly twenty years. Similarly, most states now involve district attorneys in juvenile court processes, in contrast to the time when prosecutors in some states merely reviewed intake officers' recommendations to charge juveniles. As for juveniles incarcerated in detention centers, facility populations range from virtually zero in some states (such as Wyoming) to tens of thousands (Florida) to hundreds of thousands (California). Finally, the U.S. Supreme Court's decision in *Stanford v. Kentucky,* 492 U.S. 361 (1989), permits the execution of persons aged sixteen or seventeen at the time of their offense, but states vary in their willingness to actually sentence juveniles to death.

Varying Impacts of the Get-Tough Movement

The movement toward determinate sentencing schemes grew out of an interest in more consistent punishments for particular crimes. This interest is grounded primarily in a due process perspective, but it also reflects the idea that general deterrence is more effective when individuals understand exactly what would happen to them if caught for engaging in crime. The ambiguous sentences under indeterminate schemes are believed to be ineffective deterrents when the same types of offenses result in very different sentences (for example, one offender might serve only one year in prison while another, similarly situated offender serves ten years). The get-tough movement, however, has been uneven. Although the United States experienced nearly a fivefold increase in imprisonment rates after 1980, this rate of increase was not uniform across states. Substantive interstate differences were found in the number of facilities, incarceration rates, and size of inmate populations, as depicted in Table 9-2. Some of these differences might reflect differences in state populations and resources for crime control, but they might also indicate interstate differences in the emphases placed on incarceration and the average length of prison sentences. As for a link between state policy liberalism and an emphasis on incarceration, the correlation between policy liberalism and state incarceration rates for 2009 is 0.62 (Pearson's r, $p < .001$). This relationship is stronger than the already noted correlation between policy liberalism and sentencing policy "toughness" ($r = 0.40$) and suggests that a more general level of policy liberalism might be more indicative of a judicial body's interest in punishment severity as opposed to whether a state has adopted more specific elements of "tougher" sentencing.

There appears to have been a slight reversal in prison incarceration rates beginning in 2008 and continuing through 2009, when the national rate of admissions in state prisons dropped from a mean rate of 452 per 100,000 population in 2005 for all fifty states to a mean rate of 410 in 2009 (Harrison and Beck 2006; West and Sabol 2010). The most recent published estimate of the population of offenders held in state prisons is roughly 1.4 million (as of December 31, 2009), which indicates a decline in the population for the first time in over twenty-five years. There were exceptions to the general trend of decreasing incarceration rates, but incarceration rates have either declined or remained relatively stable across thirty-eight states. It is too soon to determine whether this is the beginning of a new trend across states in the size of their prison populations.

If they continue, the recent decline in rates of incarceration could lead to a significant decline in prison populations across the country. The decline in incarceration rates is already having ripple effects on other aspects of state corrections, such as in Kentucky, where it is no longer necessary to house convicted felons in jail until prison bed space becomes available. None of Kentucky's prisons operate over their design capacity, and there is no longer a waiting list for prison space. This trend comes with one disadvantage, however: local jails no longer receive state monies for housing convicted felons.

Fiscal Crises and Prison Population Size versus Composition

Because all state governments deal with the budget constraints caused by the recent economic recession, a common focus of budget cuts is on corrections and, in particular, prison facilities and operations. Perhaps ironically, the same conservatives who wanted tougher criminal sentences just a few years ago are now adamant about reducing spending. Attention has turned to closing existing facilities

Table 9-2 Incarceration Rates, Inmate Populations, and Facilities, 2009

State	Incarceration rate per 100,000 residents	Prisoners held in state prisons on December 31, 2009	Number of state facilities
Maine	150	2,206	5
Minnesota	189	9,986	13
New Hampshire	206	2,731	5
Rhode Island	211	3,674	7
Massachusetts	213	11,316	13
North Dakota	228	1,486	4
Utah	232	6,533	2
Nebraska	243	4,474	7
Washington	271	18,233	14
Vermont	277	2,220	8
New Jersey	291	25,382	23
Iowa	292	8,813	9
New York	298	58,687	63
Kansas	305	8,641	10
New Mexico	316	6,519	8
Hawaii	317	5,891	8
West Virginia	346	6,367	10
Illinois	349	45,161	34
Alaska	357	5,285	15
Montana	368	3,605	6
Wisconsin	369	23,153	28
North Carolina	369	39,860	73
Oregon	373	14,403	9
Wyoming	377	2,075	3
Connecticut	382	19,716	21
Maryland	382	22,255	22
Pennsylvania	406	51,429	28
South Dakota	420	3,434	3
Tennessee	426	26,965	15
Ohio	446	51,606	34
Delaware	447	6,794	8
Indiana	447	28,808	18
Colorado	450	22,795	31
Michigan	457	45,478	52
California	458	171,275	87
Nevada	470	12,482	16
Idaho	476	7,400	9
Kentucky	478	21,638	15
Virginia	480	38,092	47
Missouri	509	30,563	22
South Carolina	512	24,288	22
Arkansas	522	15,208	21
Georgia	526	53,371	60
Florida	559	103,915	69
Arizona	580	40,627	15
Texas	648	171,249	111
Alabama	650	31,874	18
Oklahoma	657	26,397	26
Mississippi	702	21,482	29
Louisiana	881	39,780	14

SOURCES: Populations adapted from Heather West and William Sabol, *Prisoners in 2009* (Washington, D.C.: U.S. Department of Justice, Bureau of Justice Statistics, 2010); facility figures provided by James Stephan, *Census of State and Federal Correctional Facilities, 2005* (Washington, D.C.: U.S. Department of Justice, Bureau of Justice Statistics, 2008).

(as in Colorado and Kansas) and using more alternatives to incarceration (as in New Jersey and Ohio) (Steinhauer 2009). States such as Kentucky and Indiana are even revisiting their criminal sentencing statutes (Associated Press 2011). It is possible, therefore, that the recent drop in incarceration rates is an indication that government conservatives are easing up on their "get-tough" ideology in order to deal with their budget woes.

Regardless of the lower incarceration rates since 2008, African American men continue to make up larger portions of inmate populations. Scholars disagree over whether this is a consequence of sentencing discrimination or the disproportionately greater involvement of African American men in felony crime. No one disputes the fact that roughly half of the nation's prison population consists of African Americans, a group that constitutes less than 20 percent of the general population. Marc Mauer (2006) contends that a move from indeterminate to determinate sentencing may only make matters worse for minorities if a new scheme simply redefines particular offenses more common among African Americans as more "serious." For example, a sentencing scheme that dictates more severe sanctions for selling crack cocaine might affect African Americans more than whites if African Americans are arrested more often for the offense. A study of police arrest practices in New York City described how the police there are more apt to frisk African Americans compared with whites, resulting in higher rates of drug arrests among African Americans and thus higher rates of imprisonment for this group (Ridgeway 2007). The implication is that sentencing reforms driven by the get-tough movement may be affecting the demographics of state prison populations, and this impact may vary across states depending on differences in reforms.

Overall, one in three African American males is under supervision, either in prison or under community sanctions (Seiter 2008). According to David Karp and Todd Clear (2000), some prosecutors and judges are making conscious efforts to clean up particular neighborhoods by being harder on offenders from those communities. Unfortunately, because of the higher concentrations of minorities in economically disadvantaged neighborhoods, this process may further tighten legal controls over African Americans.

STATE'S RESPONSIBILITIES TO PRISON INMATES

State sentencing policies differ, and so do the prisons in which those sentences are served. Facilities in eastern states tend to be older than those in the west, for example. Older prisons provide harsher living conditions because they were built in an era when incarceration was meant to be punitive and when much less was known about the link between architectural design and safety. Since then, prisoners have gained some relief from court decisions that affect prison conditions, and rising prison populations have compelled states to develop more efficient and effective forms of incarceration. In the process, some of the differences among states are fading, although the range of variation remains wide.

Inmates' Rights and Sentencing Philosophies

The **inmates' rights movement** was sparked by the politicization of inmates during the civil rights movement and the disproportionate incarceration of African Americans in the 1960s. A flood of litigation by prisoners followed, which brought these matters to the attention of the courts. The lawsuits changed the course of corrections policy in the United States by establishing the substantive rights of prison inmates.

Prisoners in all fifty states now have rights guaranteed in the U.S. Constitution and potentially safeguarded by the U.S. Supreme Court. These rights include freedom of speech, freedom of association with outsiders as well as other inmates, freedom of religion, access to courts, procedural due process when accused of violating facility rules, protections against self-incrimination during custodial interrogations, access to facility programs, racial desegregation, searches and seizures, privacy, medical treatment (and the right to refuse it), and physical safety.

Depriving inmates of personal freedoms was once a key element of their punishment. During the inmates' rights movement, prisoners gained access to some limited forms of personal property, conjugal visitation and furloughs, freedoms regarding clothing and appearance, and freedom from corporal punishment by staff. Physical confinement was the only remaining deprivation, and public complaints about "coddling" prisoners were common during the 1970s and 1980s. During the last three decades, some state policymakers reacted to these perceptions by introducing harsher prison environments—reintroducing the chain gang in Alabama, for example—or adding super maximum security prisons that isolate inmates from each other (Allen et al. 2010).

States differ on the scope of inmates' rights depending on the emphasis each state places on the four sentencing philosophies described earlier. Litigation filed by inmates held in state prisons is most often handled by state courts because states operate under different bodies of correctional law. Prisoners' rights protected under state constitutions vary, too. These differences are substantial, but the general trend is toward more stringent conditions of confinement, perhaps a reflection of a more conservative U.S. Supreme Court (Collins 2004).

Conditions of Confinement as Cruel and Unusual Punishment

The Eighth Amendment prohibits the imposition of cruel and unusual punishment, and is applicable to state prisons through the due process clause of the Fourteenth Amendment. Beginning in the 1970s, both state and federal courts were assigned the task of evaluating prisons with this in mind. The U.S. Supreme Court has held that correctional practices are "cruel and unusual" when they are disproportionately severe for the offense, they are of such character as to "shock the conscience," they go beyond that which is necessary to achieve their aim, and the method of imposition is arbitrary (Barak 2007).

Because courts did not interfere with prison policies for nearly two hundred years, it is no surprise that the court evaluations of prison facilities beginning in the 1970s revealed some barbaric practices and confinement conditions. In the early 1980s, eight entire state prison systems were deemed unconstitutional. Another twenty-one states included at least one facility found in violation of the Eighth Amendment. A new era of prison growth took place during the 1990s based on these court assessments, and more than six hundred new prisons were built across the country (Branham 2005).

The areas of contention falling under the general category of cruel and unusual punishments for prison inmates include deficiencies in medical care, excessive use of force by correctional officers, and the physical conditions of confinement. Regarding medical care, prison staff must act with "deliberate indifference" to an inmate's "serious medical needs" (including mental problems) before the action can be considered cruel and unusual. An officer's use of excessive force is often a complicated issue for the courts. On the one hand, correctional officers can resort to force in order to stop a fight between two inmates, quell a prison riot, and deal with noncompliant inmates during cell searches and head counts. On the other hand, the decision to use force is left to an officer's discretion, and discretion is applied differently by different officers.

Some inmate grievances about the physical conditions of confinement have focused on crowding, improper diet, poor heating, rodent infestations, lack of fire safety, poor plumbing, and inmate violence. Inmate crowding is a common complaint because most states have facilities with populations larger than they were built to hold. It is common for prison administrators to deal with this issue by placing two inmates in a cell designed for one. According to the courts, double-bunking is not unconstitutional so long as inmates are not confined to their cells for extended periods of time each day.

As for an inmate's right to a safe environment, an important problem that has received considerable attention over the last several years is the sexual victimization of inmates by other inmates and staff. The Prison Rape Elimination Act (PREA) of 2003 was intended to deal with this problem, and the Bureau of Justice Statistics (BJS) is required as part of the act to compile information on the incidents and effects of sexual victimization in prisons each year. A review of the BJS reports on the subject (available at www.bjs.usdoj.gov) reveals no substantive changes over the last several years in the prevalence of sexual victimization in state prisons despite implementation of PREA in 2003. The latest figures indicate that 4.4 percent of prison inmates were sexually victimized by other inmates or staff in 2008–2009, and that roughly 88,500 prison and jail inmates were subjected to these abuses during the same period (Beck and Harrison 2010). Some of the highest victimization rates among men were found in Texas (8.6 percent) and Louisiana (7.5 percent), whereas the highest rates for women were found in Wisconsin (11.9 percent) and Virginia (11.4 percent) (Beck and Harrison 2010). Because Texas and Louisiana have among the highest incarceration rates in the country, it is possible that higher victimization rates among male inmates are a by-product of higher incarceration rates.

Issues Related to Crowded Prison Environments

The unprecedented growth in prison populations has forced prison administrators and government officials to consider the consequences of institutional crowding for the safety of both staff and inmates; adequate resources for medical care and psychological counseling; the ability to maintain proper surveillance of all inmates; and the availability of recreation, work assignments, vocational training, and education programs (Camp et al. 2003).

The most common response to crowding has been to build more prisons, but the recent budget crises faced by state governments have essentially eliminated this as a viable option, at least in the near future. Also, critics of this strategy argue that building more prisons merely allows more people to be sent to prison (Blumstein and Beck 1999), and that new prison construction might have contributed to the growth of the nation's prison population in recent decades. Prison construction has also been uneven across states, resulting in much larger increases in inmate populations for some states than others.

The threats to staff and inmate safety posed by crowding are the biggest concerns for prison administrators because of the costs associated with prison riots, litigation dealing with the state's failure to protect inmates, and staff turnover. More crowded facilities bring motivated offenders physically closer to one another and also inhibit effective supervision by officers, thereby creating more opportunities for violence. From a different perspective, inmates in more crowded environments are more likely to feel greater anxiety, stress, and depression (Wooldredge 1997).

Prison Programs and Inmate Classification

Despite the get-tough movement during the last few decades, all states retain various programs that were once associated with the goal of rehabilitation. More than 90 percent of all state prisons offer educational programs for inmates, and over half of inmates participate in these programs (Harlow 2003). Mental health programs are offered in every prison because roughly 16 percent of prison inmates are diagnosed with mental health problems (Ditton 1999). Substance abuse programs are also common in prisons; nearly 70 percent of all state prison inmates are considered regular drug users (National Center on Addiction and Substance Abuse 2002). Recreation is available in all prisons as well, although the public sometimes objects to inmates being allowed to "enjoy" weight lifting, aerobics, basketball, billiards, Ping-Pong, and board games. Incarceration is inherently a form of deprivation, and it can produce harmful effects. For example, physical isolation combined with lengthy prison sentences at California's Pelican Bay Prison led many inmates to seek treatment for psychological disorders, only to be placed back in physical isolation after their treatment. To address such problems, **correctional classification** instruments have been developed to place inmates in facilities appropriate to their individual needs (within the limits posed by the severity of an inmate's crime and the risk that the inmate might escape or engage in violent behavior). In addition to being more humane, the practice makes it easier to manage large and diverse prison populations.

Risk classification is also used to reduce the odds of attempted escapes and violence by placing inmates in the most appropriate environments. Assessment of the risk that an inmate will engage in misconduct can result in the inmate being placed in a facility with the least restrictive controls necessary to minimize the risk and facilitate adaptation to confinement. Inmates are classified in terms of the necessary security level of a facility and the type of housing within a facility (cells versus dormitories and single versus double occupancy in a cell).

All states have relatively well-developed prisoner classification systems, although they differ in the degree to which they continually review and update their systems. For example, in response to the rising female inmate population, states need to better evaluate the unique mental health needs of female inmates, but very few states have effectively addressed this issue. Virginia, Oklahoma, and Rhode Island are, however, some of the exceptions to this deficiency (Austin and Hardyman 2004).

PRISON ORGANIZATION AND MANAGEMENT

Roughly 1,300 state prisons are operating today. In response to court intervention in prison affairs, growing inmate populations, and greater public awareness of prison operations, the vast majority of states have created a **department of corrections** (or a similar agency) to oversee state prison operations and guide prison administration. Forty-three states have departments of corrections that report to either the governor's office (thirty-two states) or to state boards or commissions (eleven states), and another six states have agencies operating under state departments of public safety or social services (Seiter 2008). Most of these agencies are also responsible for overseeing community corrections.

Each state's department of corrections or similar agency has a director who works with the governor and the legislature in developing and refining correctional policies, and who ultimately is responsible for effective management and operations. These directors are appointed by either the governor (in twenty-four states) or state boards or commissions; the latter are composed of gubernatorial appointees. Many departments of corrections have developed their own offices of legislative affairs that inform and update state legislatures about corrections policy, new proposals, and media coverage of critical issues as they emerge. Many departments of corrections also include legal offices that deal with inmate litigation and the possible legal ramifications of new correctional policies. Separate from the legal office is an internal affairs office that deals with the illegal and unethical actions of prison staff.

The primary administrative functions of the central office for each department of corrections include accounting (developing budgets and keeping track of spending) and prison construction. The corrections budget is a part of each state's budget that must be approved by the state legislature. Overseeing prison construction involves selecting architects and approving designs, supervising all construction, and starting up operations in new prisons. The central office typically handles issues related to labor relations such as affirmative action, contract negotiations, and training. Some departments of corrections also provide funding to county jails in order to improve operations, and jail inspections are often carried out by the central office to ensure that these facilities are in compliance with jail standards.

Table 9-3 lists the number of full-time-equivalent employees in each state's department of corrections, and each department's annual budget. Most of the budget is spent on employees' wages, salaries, and benefits. As the number of inmates have increased, so too have the number of employees needed to administer and staff prisons, especially in states that emphasize rehabilitation and a correspondingly wide range of prison programs. This is evident in the column on the far right of Table 9-3, which ranks states according to the amount spent on corrections per prisoner. In many states, the average annual cost of incarceration exceeds the price of attending a private college or university.

In some states, prison employees are a potent political force by virtue of their large number—there are 54,344 full-time prison staff in California and 44,745 full-time staff in Texas. Correctional officers are also unionized in many states, which not only increases their political force but also places greater demands on state budgets because of contract negotiations. During the recent economic recession, states such as Ohio threatened to lay off as much as 20 percent of the correctional officer workforce. But the officers' union intervened and salvaged all positions.

Why are prisons so expensive, and why do they cost more in some states than others? Answers to these questions require an examination of the inner workings of prisons. Every prison has a warden or a superintendent, with two or three assistant wardens. Prisons also include uniformed staff (in charge of security) and professional staff (in charge of treatment programs). A third group of staff deals with personnel issues, facility maintenance, internal accounting, and inmate services such as food, laundry, health, and job assignments.

Large offender populations pose a number of security problems, including prison riots, attempted escapes, inmate-on-inmate violence, dangers to staff, and staff abuses of inmates' rights. Many newer prisons are designed to decentralize authority and increase supervision over inmates. Dividing a prison into separate autonomous living areas (called pods or dormitories) allows tighter control over smaller numbers of inmates, analogous to creating several prisons within a prison (Fairweather and McConville 2000). A podular facility, for example, which is designed to hold 450 inmates, might be divided into three wings holding 150 inmates each. Each wing maintains a separate management staff, including a unit

Table 9-3 Corrections Employees and Expenditures, 2007

State	Employees (FTE) Total[a]	Per prisoner[b]	Annual spending Total[c]	Per prisoner[b]
Massachusetts	5,947	0.53	$878,056,000	$77,594
Wyoming	1,018	0.49	126,169,000	60,804
Maine	1,267	0.57	126,673,000	57,422
Washington	8,581	0.47	952,978,000	52,267
Maryland	11,892	0.53	1,157,766,000	52,023
New Jersey	10,164	0.40	1,319,948,000	52,003
Rhode Island	1,736	0.47	172,162,000	46,860
Utah	3,166	0.48	301,100,000	46,089
Vermont	1,197	0.54	101,302,000	45,632
New Mexico	3,962	0.61	291,164,000	44,664
Nebraska	2,824	0.63	198,847,000	44,445
New York	34,095	0.58	2,591,379,000	44,156
New Hampshire	1,320	0.48	112,857,000	41,324
Montana	1,161	0.32	143,466,000	39,796
Alaska	1,767	0.33	210,204,000	39,774
Minnesota	3,990	0.40	379,616,000	38,014
California	54,344	0.32	6,466,958,000	37,758
Oregon	4,999	0.35	542,474,000	37,664
North Dakota	660	0.44	55,565,000	37,392
Michigan	16,828	0.37	1,685,004,000	37,051
Wisconsin	9,232	0.40	851,641,000	36,783
Delaware	2,816	0.41	244,736,000	36,022
West Virginia	3,298	0.52	213,974,000	33,607
Connecticut	7,486	0.38	617,988,000	31,344
Kansas	3,588	0.42	268,636,000	31,089
South Dakota	875	0.25	106,073,000	30,889
Hawaii	2,357	0.40	179,322,000	30,440
Colorado	6,766	0.30	689,346,000	30,241
Pennsylvania	17,161	0.33	1,514,846,000	29,455
North Carolina	21,070	0.53	1,147,569,000	28,790
Virginia	14,224	0.37	1,079,101,000	28,329
Ohio	16,679	0.32	1,450,522,000	28,108
Iowa	3,085	0.35	237,279,000	26,924
Arkansas	5,111	0.34	394,550,000	25,944
Idaho	1,862	0.25	190,791,000	25,783
Illinois	12,060	0.27	1,139,669,000	25,236
Georgia	19,491	0.37	1,332,364,000	24,964
Florida	28,945	0.28	2,440,853,000	23,489
Indiana	7,337	0.25	599,867,000	20,823
Nevada	3,765	0.30	261,167,000	20,923
Oklahoma	5,663	0.21	541,284,000	20,506
Arizona	8,915	0.22	826,193,000	20,336
Kentucky	4,114	0.19	438,238,000	20,253
Missouri	12,303	0.40	601,655,000	19,686
Tennessee	7,133	0.26	509,065,000	18,879
South Carolina	7,808	0.32	436,117,000	17,956
Texas	44,745	0.26	3,043,667,000	17,773
Alabama	4,971	0.16	444,035,000	13,931
Mississippi	3,535	0.16	283,252,000	13,186
Louisiana	7,089	0.18	499,385,000	12,533

SOURCE: Expenditure and employment figures were retrieved from U.S. Department of Justice, Bureau of Justice Statistics, "Corrections," http://bjs.ojp.usdoj.gov/index.cfm?ty=pbdetail&iid=2315.

a. Total employees is the number of full-time-equivalent (FTE) employees on March 31, 2007.

b. Per prisoner results are based on state prison populations as of December 31, 2009.

c. Total expenditures include direct and capital outlays for institutions and other state corrections.

manager and a handful of case managers and counselors. Case managers develop each inmate's programming plan, and counselors deal with the more routine inmate functions such as arranging visits, phone calls, and work assignments.

Prisons are labor-intensive operations, and correctional officers are the core workforce. The minimum qualifications to become an officer vary widely across states, although in most states the only educational requirement is a high school degree or GED, accompanied by a relatively brief training stint at an "academy," ranging anywhere from a few weeks to six months. Correctional officers supervise and control inmates primarily through strict enforcement of rules and procedures, operation of security technology (surveillance cameras, electronic doors, and non-lethal and lethal weapons), and communication with inmates.

Line officers are assigned to specific areas within a facility, including inmate housing areas, work areas, classrooms, recreation yard, administration and reception areas, and along the perimeter of the prison grounds. Officers are generally rotated in these jobs to reduce boredom, prevent burnout, and ease the stress associated with particular area assignments (especially in housing areas and on the recreation yard). The organization of officers follows a military hierarchy: line officers, sergeants (in charge of the line officers and filling in behind them when short-handed), lieutenants (in charge of investigating misconduct by inmates or officers and for initiating the disciplinary process), and captains (basically in charge of paperwork).

One of the few commonalities in corrections policy across states is a vertical chain of command. Each level in the chain receives directives from the level immediately above, with ultimate authority resting with the prison warden. Goal achievement relies on the warden, but the safety of the prison environment relies on every staff member completing work tasks successfully.

Prison security means preventing inmate escapes, inmate movement into restricted areas, gatherings of "large" groups of inmates that might precipitate violence, and victimization of other inmates and staff. Security is maintained in state prisons by means of inmate classification systems, the physical security of a facility (defined by the amount of control over population movement and level of difficulty when attempting escape), strict enforcement of rules (including staff rules), total surveillance of inmate movement, preventing inmates from accessing contraband (items posing potential threats to the safety of the environment), an inmate disciplinary system, use of administrative or punitive segregation (isolating inmates in separate housing units because they pose a danger to others), and riot preparedness. Resources are also needed to control drug trafficking inside prisons because of the large number of these offenders who manage to have drugs smuggled into their facilities. The number of drug offenders in prison increased by nearly 70 percent during the 1990s (Seiter 2008).

Inmates are restricted in terms of their movement within a facility, and there are several head counts of inmates each day. Most inmates also spend a portion of each day in structured routines such as work assignments, education, and counseling (these activities help to keep inmates under surveillance and out of trouble). Restrictions on movement are greater in more secure facilities. Thus facility environments differ dramatically because of the differences in security level.

Consistent with the rising inmate population and the heavier reliance over time on a vertical chain of command for effective prison management is the growth and complexity of prison bureaucracies. As a result, the expenditures for state departments of corrections have increased tremendously. To some extent, state differences in corrections expenditures reflect differences in prison populations, differences in economies, and differences in sentencing philosophies.

MANAGING DEATH ROW INMATES AND OTHER SPECIAL POPULATIONS

Capital punishment is the execution of an offender (by the state) after conviction for a capital crime. The definition of a capital crime varies slightly across states, but in most states it is limited to first-degree murder with at least one aggravating factor (for example, killing a police officer, committing murder during a rape or robbery, killing multiple victims, or committing another murder after being previously convicted of a murder). Many states also define treason against the state as a capital offense. For example, in the 1990s members of the "Republic of Texas" movement claimed that the annexation of Texas by the United States was illegal. Richard McLaren, the leader of a faction of this group, was arrested for kidnapping and treason against the state of Texas in 1997, both capital offenses. Only a handful of states have defined other crimes (for example, train wrecking, capital drug trafficking, aircraft piracy) as capital offenses. After the terrorist attacks on the United States on September 11, 2001, many states created new laws related to terrorist acts, and twelve states specifically treat the violation of terrorist laws as capital offenses punishable by death (Lyons 2002). Several other states treat terrorist acts as aggravating factors in capital offenses such as first-degree murder. By contrast, twelve states do not define capital crimes and therefore do not administer the death penalty (Snell 2010).

Since the U.S. Supreme Court's ruling in *Furman v. Georgia,* 408 U.S. 238 (1972), that the death penalty cannot be applied unequally for similarly situated offenders, states have instituted bifurcated trials in capital cases. These jury trials operate in two stages: guilt is determined at the first stage, which is followed by the second or sentencing stage for persons who are found guilty. At the second stage, the jury is presented with mitigating and aggravating circumstances that focus on the crime itself (such as whether the murder was committed during another offense such as rape or robbery), the victim (such as the degree of involvement or provocation), the defendant (such as whether previously convicted of murder), or some combination of these circumstances. If sentenced to death, the convicted defendant has an automatic appeal and review of the sentence. The appeal is in place to ensure that the sentence was not imposed because of the prejudices or emotions of the jury, that the sentence is consistent with the evidence, and that similarly situated defendants have been sentenced to death in the past.

Capital punishment has existed in most states since their inception, although there were no executions in the country between 1968 and 1976, when widespread opposition to the death penalty coincided with the rehabilitation era, the U.S. Supreme Court's ruling in *Furman v. Georgia,* and the cumbersome appeals process. Executions resumed in 1977, after the U.S. Supreme Court in *Gregg v. Georgia,* 428 U.S. 153 (1976), defined the elements that must be met for a constitutional application of the death penalty. The case of *Ring v. Arizona,* 536 U.S. 584 (2002), also addressed the issue of fairness in the application of the death penalty; the Supreme Court ruled that juries must decide the sentences of persons convicted of crimes for which the penalty is death.

State executions increased dramatically in the 1990s, although the annual number has yet to match the peak numbers of the 1930s, which ranged from 150 to 199 a year across the states. The highest number of executions since 1976 was the ninety-eight executions in 1999, and these occurred in only one-third of the states with the death penalty. The annual number of executions is small, however, relative to the number of inmates on death row.

Roughly 3,173 inmates are currently on death row awaiting execution in thirty-six states. This bottleneck is attributable to the lengthy appeals process (and, to a lesser extent, the occasional election of governors who formally or informally ban executions during their administrations). The demographics of death row inmates reveal a disproportionate representation of African Americans (42 percent of all death row inmates) and men (98 percent). Racial disparities in actual executions were not quite as dramatic in 2009, although African Americans were still overrepresented (roughly 27 percent of all executions), raising concerns about possible racial bias (Snell 2010).

States with capital punishment use one or two of five methods of execution. The types of execution for each state are displayed in Table 9-4, along with the number of inmates on death row in each state as of December 31, 2009, and each state's rank on the cumulative number of executions since 1977. (These ranks reveal wide differences across the states in execution trends. A comparison of Tables 9-2 and 9-4 also reveals that ten of the top twelve states ranked on executions also have some of the highest incarceration rates in the country.) Lethal injection typically involves a three-part "cocktail" beginning with an injection of sodium thiopental (rendering unconsciousness) followed by pancuronium (a muscle relaxant causing paralysis), and finally potassium chloride (to stop the heart). Lethal injection has come under the greatest attack for being "cruel and unusual" because a person might not be unconscious before the heart has been stopped.

Table 9-4 Death Penalty Statistics for States with Capital Punishment

State	State rank on executions since 1977	Death row inmates on December 31, 2009	Lethal injection	Electrocution	Gas	Hanging	Firing squad
Texas	1	331	✓				
Virginia	2	13	✓	✓			
Oklahoma	3	79	✓	✓			✓
Florida	4	389	✓	✓			
Missouri	5	51	✓		✓		
Georgia	6	101	✓				
Alabama	7	200	✓	✓			
North Carolina	8	159	✓				
South Carolina	9	55	✓	✓			
Ohio	10	165	✓				
Arkansas	11	40	✓	✓			
Louisiana	11	83	✓				
Arizona	12	131	✓		✓		
Indiana	13	14	✓				
Delaware	14	17	✓			✓	
California	15	684	✓		✓		
Illinois	16	16	✓	✓			
Nevada	16	80	✓				
Mississippi	17	60	✓				
Utah	18	10	✓				✓
Tennessee	19	89	✓	✓			
Maryland	20	5	✓				
Washington	21	8	✓			✓	
Kentucky	22	35	✓	✓			
Montana	22	2	✓				
Nebraska	22	11	✓				
Pennsylvania	22	218	✓				
Oregon	23	31	✓				
Connecticut	24	10	✓				
Colorado	24	2	✓				
Idaho	24	14	✓				
New Mexico	24	2	✓				
South Dakota	24	2	✓				
Wyoming	24	1	✓		✓		
Kansas	25	9	✓				
New Hampshire	25	1	✓			✓	
New Jersey	25	0	✓				
New York	25	0	✓				

SOURCE: Adapted from Tracy Snell, *Capital Punishment, 2009—Statistical Tables* (Washington, D.C.: U.S. Department of Justice, Bureau of Justice Statistics), 6, 11, 17, 18.

Differences in the degree to which state legislatures pursued more punitive sentencing philosophies during the "get-tough" era have contributed to interstate differences in the use of capital punishment, and the careful reader will also note the correspondence between each state's rank on sentencing policy "toughness" from Table 9-1 and that state's corresponding rank on executions from Table 9-4.

Despite these interstate differences, nationwide capital punishment was more widespread during the 1980s and 1990s, indicating a general disillusionment with rehabilitation and a desire to see more severe punishments. As of 2010, roughly

65 percent of Americans supported the death penalty, although this percentage represented the lowest level of support for the death penalty in the last twenty-five years (Newport 2010). Despite this "majority" support, Americans continue to worry about the possibility of executing innocent persons. DNA tests have been used to exonerate death row inmates in Arizona, Florida, Idaho, Illinois, Louisiana, Maryland, Oklahoma, Pennsylvania, and Virginia. In 2003 this concern prompted Illinois governor George Ryan to commute the sentences of all death row inmates, and Illinois became a non–death penalty state in 2011.

The number of annual executions has dropped since 1999, from ninety-eight in 1999 to forty-seven in 2010 (Snell 2010). The decline is consistent with the trend toward lower incarceration rates described earlier and possibly reflects a reversal of the policy of "getting tougher" with offenders. Another reason for the drop in executions during 2010 was the inability of some states to obtain enough sodium thiopental from the sole manufacturer, Hospira Inc. The manufacturer initially declared that it would resume production of the drug in Italy, but Italian authorities stepped in and declared that the drug would not be exported overseas if it was to be used for executions. So far, California and Oklahoma have delayed executions because of the shortage of the drug, and several other states claim to have only enough for one more execution. Great Britain has also refused to export the drug to the United States, and now the European Union is considering a formal policy to permanently ban exports of the drug.

Inmate populations have become more heterogeneous over the last few decades as a consequence of the dramatic increase in the prison population. This situation has placed new demands on prison administrators and staff in order to manage special offenders such as juveniles housed in adult facilities, drug offenders, mentally ill persons, the elderly, extremely violent offenders, sex offenders, and individuals with infectious diseases such as HIV. Each of these groups requires additional resources or programs for its unique needs during incarceration.

The percentage of the prison population consisting of drug offenders has increased dramatically since state and federal governments began their crackdowns on drug offenders in the 1980s, but the incarceration rates of drug offenders still vary widely across states (Human Rights Watch 2000). Nevertheless, a regional pattern exists; the highest rates of incarceration for drug offenders are predominantly in the eastern half of the country, especially along the East Coast.

More than 10 percent of inmates have reported spending time in a mental hospital or undergoing treatment for mental illness prior to their incarceration. Throughout the 1970s and 1980s, courts grew less tolerant of defendants being found "not guilty by reason of insanity," and so the insanity defense became less successful in keeping offenders out of prison. The advent of the "guilty but insane" verdict allowed states to send mentally ill offenders to prison instead of hospitals. This development forced prison administrators to create an infrastructure for meeting the needs of the mentally ill (programs, health care professionals, antipsychotic drugs) while also addressing related security issues (separate living units and more supervision to prevent the mentally ill from harming others or themselves). Mental health screening is now a large part of the prison intake process, which is conducted by correctional psychologists.

Two factors have contributed to an increase in the mean age of prison inmates over the last twenty years: mandatory sentences (and related policies under guide-line schemes) that prevent judges from deliberately keeping older offenders out of prison, and the aging of the general population in the United States. Larger propor-tions of inmates over forty-five years of age—elderly inmates—have placed heavy demands on health care resources in prison, which in turn drives up the average annual cost of incarceration for these individuals. Aside from medical resources, there are additional demands for age-appropriate recreation, transportation for individuals who have difficulty walking, less physically demanding work assign-ments, and efforts to prevent victimization by younger inmates.

Despite increases in the average age of prison inmates across all fifty states, there are differences in the age composition of inmate populations that place heavier demands on some states than others. The average age of prisoners in New York State is thirty-six years, and the higher proportion of inmates over age sixty has forced the state to consider how to deal with larger numbers of inmates facing dementia (Associated Press 2007). By contrast, the average age of inmates in South Dakota is thirty years and falls well below the national average of thirty-six (South Dakota Department of Corrections 2007).

The numbers of extremely violent offenders being sent to prison are also growing across states, which is why many states have built **supermax prisons** to manage the most dangerous offenders. The sole purpose of these prisons is control (via separate cells, twenty-three-hour lockdown, limited access to staff, and no access to other inmates), and there is no treatment programming. The structural and staff resources needed to build and manage these prisons are more expensive than for any other type of facility, and they place enormous demands on the annual budgets of a state's depart-ment of corrections. This is one reason why many states operate supermax units within existing prisons instead of operating completely separate supermax facilities. There are now forty-four states with either separate supermax facilities or units desig-nated as such in existing prisons, and no state has more than one supermax prison.

The number of prison beds designated for supermax inmates ranges broadly across states. The southern and western regions of the country have roughly 14,000 beds for these offenders, with the rest of the states totaling fewer than 6,000 beds (Mears 2006). New York accounts for more than one-third of the 6,000. This makes sense in view of the population of New York, although some of the much smaller states in the South and West (such as Arizona and Mississippi) have more than 1,700 beds for these offenders.

The rising incarceration rates of sex offenders have also placed heavy demands on prison resources. The numbers of incarcerated sex offenders increased sevenfold between 1980 and 2004, owing in part to tougher legislation regarding rape, child molestation, and other forms of sexual assault (Harrison and Beck 2006). DNA testing also led to a dramatic increase in conviction rates for these offenders during this period. They need special treatment programs and are often confined for indefinite periods of time based on their need for treatment, thereby making it more difficult to plan for an offender's release and impeding effective management of prison resources (such as bed space).

CRITICAL ISSUES IN CORRECTIONS

State governments face many critical issues regarding the incarceration and management of offenders, and the salience of these issues varies across states with their different political, social, and economic environments. The issues include the reintegration of large numbers of offenders back into the community after release from prison (post-prison policies), the use of privatization to meet incarceration demands, and community alternatives to incarceration.

Post-Prison Policies

The growth in prison populations since 1980 has made it more difficult for parole agencies to effectively monitor the growing numbers of individuals released from prison. The transition from the prison cell to the community is not easy for former offenders, especially after lengthy prison terms during which they have been isolated from their social environments. Despite the abolition of parole boards in some states, the numbers of ex-inmates placed on parole across the country have increased by 18 percent since 2000 (Glaze, Bonczar, and Zhang 2010). Enormous caseloads severely hinder parole officers' abilities to enforce their clients' conditions of supervision—that is, the rules on the post-release behaviors of parolees such as not leaving the jurisdiction without permission; not associating with known criminals; not accessing firearms; and complying with financial obligations to family, or victims, or both. Problems related to monitoring are state-specific, however, and some states have abolished parole altogether. The parole population of Maine on December 31, 2009, was only thirty-one, but California had more than 106,000 parolees (Glaze, Bonczar, and Zhang 2010).

There are also differences across states in the degree to which released prisoners are subjected to **state disenfranchisement laws** that prohibit parolees or felony probationers from voting. Thirty-five states do not allow one or both of these groups to vote (Porter 2010). Delaware and Wyoming also deny voting rights for a five-year period after an offender's sentence has been served. The procedures for restoring voting rights are often plagued by red tape, and many ex-offenders do not bother to attempt to register to vote. More than 4 million adults are currently or permanently disenfranchised. The impact of these laws has been especially severe for African American men (Manza and Uggen 2006).

Post-prison policies related to certain groups of sex offenders are also relevant to restriction of the post-prison rights of offenders. Concerns about the high recidivism rates of sexual predators and pedophiles have led sixteen states to enact civil commitment statutes allowing states to file petitions to indefinitely commit to mental institutions or correctional facilities, for purposes of confinement and psychiatric treatment, sex offenders who are being released from prison. If committed, an offender cannot be released until a mental health professional declares that the person no longer poses a danger to society. Problems with these statutes include the lack of consensus on what constitutes effective treatment for sex offenders, the natural conflict between the goals of confinement and treatment in correctional facilities, and the fact that release care is problematic because of the public's growing concerns about sexual predators residing in their communities—see, for example, *Kansas v. Hendricks*, 521 U.S. 346 (1997).

Privatization

Since 1980, all states have been forced to confront issues such as inmate crowding and the needs of special offender groups (which in turn affect sentence lengths, available programs, and the safety of prisons). State governments have relied more heavily in recent years on nongovernment or private enterprises to handle various aspects of prison construction and management. States vary in their reliance on **privatization,** depending on the seriousness of inmate crowding and costs of incarceration. As of 2009, for example, Maine did not rely on private prisons, whereas Texas housed more than 19,000 inmates in private facilities (West and Sabol 2010).

In order to deal with budget deficits, states such as Ohio are in the process of privatizing some state prisons by contracting with the private sector. Critics of this form of privatization have identified potential problems related to delegating the use of deadly force to nongovernment agencies, declining program quality because of the desire to increase profits, rising labor costs when unions are involved in contract negotiations, shutting down facilities because of bankruptcy, and finding the state liable for mistakes that led to an inmate's death or other violations of their civil rights (Kinkade and Leone 1993).

Alternatives to Incarceration

Community corrections have become more popular than privatization for dealing with rising prison populations and budgets. The most popular programs include intensive supervised probation (ISP), boot camp, house arrest supplemented with electronic monitoring, and community residential centers.

ISP requires offenders to report to a probation officer five times a week, to provide a complete weekly schedule of all activities to officers, and to be accessible at any time when officers decide to check up on the offender's scheduled activities. Boot camps are designed for younger, first-time offenders and are run as military boot camps (including dress codes, physical exercise, hard labor, and an emphasis on discipline). Most camps also add educational and substance abuse programs. House arrest, or community control, forces an offender to remain inside the home except for travel to and from work and for other approved activities, including food shopping and family responsibilities. It is commonly accompanied by electronic monitoring that requires an ankle bracelet equipped with a tracking device so that officers know where an offender is at all times. Finally, community residential centers, or halfway houses, allow offenders to work in the community during the day while they spend their nights in a residential structure housing from thirty to two hundred persons. Offenders placed on house arrest or in a halfway house often have to pay a portion of the costs for these sanctions. As long as proper risk assessments are conducted (to prevent high-risk offenders from being placed in the community), all of these options generally coincide with the same recidivism rates as for prisoners and are cheaper than incarceration.

The degree to which states rely on community alternatives to incarceration depends primarily on levels of crowding in state facilities, and more recently on their budget deficits in conjunction with the costs of incarceration, but the dominant sentencing philosophies in a state also play important roles. The largest numbers of offenders placed in community programs are found in states with the highest levels of inmate crowding—California, Florida, Georgia, Ohio, and Texas (Glaze, Bonczar, and Zhang 2010). The use of alternatives in several other states, however, seems to be driven more by sentencing philosophies than by limited prison resources. Massachusetts and New Jersey, for example, place large numbers of offenders in the community, and both states are relatively low on the scale of the get-tough policies described in Table 9-1.

A qualification to the above is that the recent economic recession has forced even the "toughest" states to reconsider their sentencing policies. Until recently, the available resources for incarceration were based heavily on the degree to which state legislatures pursued tougher policies for criminals. But, as noted earlier, the "tougher" states are now backtracking on higher corrections spending because of recent budget crises. The fact that no two states maintain identical policies and practices underscores that it is the level of each state's commitment to the "get-tough" movement balanced against each state's level of budget deficits that now matters most for shaping state corrections policies.

KEY TERMS

correctional classification, 294
correctional facility, 280
corrections policy, 279
department of corrections, 294
get-tough movement, 281
inmates' rights movement, 291

privatization, 304
sentencing philosophies, 280
sentencing schemes, 281
state disenfranchisement law, 303
supermax prison, 302

REFERENCES

Allen, Harry, Edward Latessa, Bruce Ponder, and Clifford Simonsen. 2010. *Corrections in America: An Introduction*, 11th ed. Upper Saddle River, N.J.: Prentice Hall.

Associated Press. 2007. "New York Prison Creates Dementia Unit as Inmate Population Ages." *International Herald Tribune: Americas,* May 28.

———. 2011. "Indiana Commission Starts Anew with Sentencing Changes." *HeraldTimesOnline,* June 25. www.heraldtimesonline.com/.

Austin, James, and Patricia Hardyman. 2004. *Objective Prison Classification: A Guide for Correctional Agencies.* Washington, D.C.: National Institute of Corrections.

Barak, Greg. 2007. *Battleground Criminal Justice.* Westport, Conn.: Greenwood Publishing.

Beck, Allen, and Paige Harrison. 2010. *Sexual Victimization in Prisons and Jails Reported by Inmates.* Washington, D.C.: U.S. Department of Justice, Bureau of Justice Statistics.

Beckett, Katherine, and Bruce Western. 2001. "Governing Social Marginality: Welfare, Incarceration, and the Transformation of State Policy." *Punishment and Society* 3: 43–59.

Blumstein, Alfred, and Allen Beck. 1999. "Population Growth in U.S. Prisons, 1980–1996." *Crime and Justice: A Review of Research* 26: 17–61.

Branham, Lynn. 2005. *The Law and Policy of Sentencing and Corrections.* St. Paul, Minn.: Thomson/West.

Camp, Scott, Gerald Gaes, Neal Langan, and William Saylor. 2003. "The Influence of Prisons on Inmate Misconduct: A Multilevel Investigation." *Justice Quarterly* 20: 501–533.

Collins, William. 2004. "Bumps in the Road to the Courthouse: The Supreme Court and the Prison Litigation Reform Act." *Pace Law Review* 24: 651–674.

Ditton, Paula. 1999. *Mental Health and Treatment of Inmates and Probationers.* Washington, D.C.: U.S. Department of Justice, Bureau of Justice Statistics.

Fairweather, Leslie, and Sean McConville. 2000. *Prison Architecture.* San Francisco: Elsevier.

Frase, Richard. 2000. "Is Guided Discretion Sufficient? Overview of State Sentencing Guidelines." *St. Louis University Law Journal* 44: 425–450.

Glaze, Lauren, Thomas Bonczar, and Fan Zhang. 2010. *Probation and Parole in the United States, 2009.* Washington, D.C.: U.S. Department of Justice, Bureau of Justice Statistics.

Griffin, Timothy, and John Wooldredge. 2001. "Judicial Reactions to Sentencing Reform in Ohio." *Crime and Delinquency* 47: 491–512.

Harlow, Caroline Wolf. 2003. *Education and Correctional Populations.* Washington, D.C.: U.S. Department of Justice, Bureau of Justice Statistics.

Harrison, Paige, and Allen Beck. 2006. *Prisoners in 2005.* Washington, D.C.: U.S. Department of Justice, Bureau of Justice Statistics.

Human Rights Watch. 2000. "Punishment and Prejudice: Racial Disparities in the War on Drugs." www.hrw.org/reports/2000/usa.

Karp, David R., and Todd R. Clear. 2000. "Community Justice: A Conceptual Framework." In *Boundary Changes in Criminal Justice Organizations.* Vol. 2, *Criminal Justice 2000.* Washington, D.C.: U.S. Department of Justice, Office of Justice Programs.

Kinkade, Patrick, and Matthew Leone. 1993. "Issues and Answers: Prison Administrators' Responses to Controversies Surrounding Privatization." *Prison Journal* 72: 57–76.

Lyons, Donna. 2002. "States Enact New Terrorism Crimes and Penalties." *NCLS State Legislative Report* 27 (November).

Manza, Jeff, and Christopher Uggen. 2006. *Locked Out: Felony Disenfranchisement and American Democracy.* New York: Oxford University Press.

Mauer, Marc. 2006. *Race to Incarcerate,* 2d ed. New York: New Press.

Mears, Daniel. 2006. *Evaluating the Effectiveness of Supermax Prisons.* Washington, D.C.: Urban Institute.

National Center for Victims of Crime. 2009. "About Victims' Rights." Washington, D.C.: National Center for Victims of Crime. www.victimlaw.info/victimlaw/pages/victimsRight.jsp.

National Center on Addiction and Substance Abuse at Columbia University. 2002. *Trends in Substance Abuse and Treatment Needs among Inmates.* Washington, D.C.: U.S. Department of Justice, National Institute of Justice.

Newport, Frank. 2010. "In U.S., 64% Support Death Penalty in Cases of Murder." Gallup Press Release, November 8, 2010.

Percival, Garrick. 2010. "Ideology, Diversity, and Imprisonment: Considering the Influence of Local Politics on Racial and Ethnic Minority Incarceration Rates." *Social Science Quarterly* 91: 1063–1082.

Porter, Nicole. 2010. "Expanding the Vote: State Felony Disenfranchisement Reform, 1997–2010." The Sentencing Project, Washington, D.C. www.sentencingproject.org.

Reitz, Kevin. 1999. "The Status of Sentencing Guidelines Reforms in the U.S." *Overcrowded Times* 10: 1–14.

Ridgeway, Greg. 2007. "Analysis of Racial Disparities in the New York Police Department's Stop, Question, and Frisk Practices." RAND Corporation (TR-534), Santa Monica, Calif.

Roberts, Julian. 1992. "Public Opinion, Crime, and Criminal Justice." *Crime and Justice: A Review of Research* 16: 99–180.

Seiter, Richard. 2008. *Corrections: An Introduction.* Upper Saddle River, N.J.: Pearson Prentice Hall.

Snell, Tracy. 2010. *Capital Punishment, 2009—Statistical Tables.* Washington, D.C.: U.S. Department of Justice, Bureau of Justice Statistics.

South Dakota Department of Corrections. 2007. "Miscellaneous Adult Statistics." South Dakota Department of Corrections. www.state.sd.us/corrections/miscellaneous_stats.htm.

Steiner, Benjamin, and Emily Wright. 2007. "Assessing the Relative Effects of State Direct File Waiver Laws on Violent Juvenile Crime: Deterrence or Irrelevance?" *Journal of Criminal Law and Criminology* 96: 1451–1477.

Steinhauer, Jennifer. 2009. "To Cut Costs, States Relax Prison Policies." *New York Times*, March 24.

Stemen, Don, and Andres Rengifo. 2011. "Policies and Imprisonment: The Impact of Structured Sentencing and Determinate Sentencing on State Incarceration Rates, 1978–2004." *Justice Quarterly* 28: 174–201.

West, Heather, and William Sabol. 2010. *Prisoners in 2009.* Washington, D.C.: U.S. Department of Justice, Bureau of Justice Statistics.

Wooldredge, John. 1997. "Explaining Variation in Perceptions of Inmate Crowding." *Prison Journal* 77: 27–40.

———. 2009. "Short- versus Long-term Effects of Ohio's Switch to More Structured Sentencing on Extra-legal Disparities in Prison Sentences in an Urban Court." *Criminology and Public Policy* 8: 285–312.

Yates, Jeff, and Richard Fording. 2005. "Politics and State Punitiveness in Black and White." *Journal of Politics* 67: 1099–1121.

SUGGESTED READINGS

Print

Crime and Justice: A Review of Research. Edited by Michael Tonry and published by the University of Chicago Press, a refereed series of volumes of commissioned essays on crime-related research subjects.

DiIulio, John. Governing Prisons: A Comparative Study of Correctional Management. New York: Free Press, 1987. An interesting comparison and evaluation of prison organization and leadership in three very different states: California, Michigan, and Texas.

Irwin, John, and James Austin. *It's About Time: America's Imprisonment Binge,* 3d ed. Belmont, Calif.: Wadsworth, 2001. A description of the trends in the U.S. prison populations of both men and women, and policy-related explanations for the ongoing prison population explosion that began in the 1980s.

Latessa, Edward, and Harry Allen. *Corrections in the Community,* 4th ed. Cincinnati: Anderson, 2009. Thorough descriptions of all aspects of community alternatives to incarceration, with historical overviews of current trends and practices.

Internet

Bureau of Justice Statistics Publications. www.ojp.usdoj.gov/bjs/pubalp2.htm. Along with the Sourcebook of Criminal Justice Statistics, the most current national- and state-level statistics on sentencing practices, incarceration rates, prison populations, and probation and parole caseloads.

National Criminal Justice Reference Service. www.ncjrs.gov/whatsncjrs.html. Provides information to support research, policy, and program development on the many aspects of corrections policy, including crime, law enforcement, and the criminal justice system.

Sentencing Project. www.sentencingproject.org/. A nonprofit organization that advocates penal reform and publishes news and recommendations, but be aware of its point of view.

Sourcebook of Criminal Justice Statistics. www.albany.edu/sourcebook/. Along with Bureau of Justice Statistics Publications, provides the most current national- and state-level statistics on sentencing practices, incarceration rates, prison populations, and probation and parole caseloads.

CHAPTER 10

Fiscal Policy in the American States

ROBERT C. LOWRY

Fiscal policy arises from decisions about government revenues, spending, and borrowing. Elected officials must periodically decide how to raise the money needed to pay for public programs and what programs merit the use of those resources. To do so, they must make trade-offs between different revenue sources, between spending on different public programs, and between higher spending and lower taxes or less borrowing. Even if the "best" choice seems obvious to a disinterested observer, achieving it may be difficult because of the incentives faced by voters and elected officials. Voters naturally prefer low taxes but high spending on programs that benefit them. Elected officials want to fund programs that help their constituents and their own chances for reelection, while avoiding blame for any painful decisions.

State governments face many more statutory and constitutional restrictions on fiscal policymaking than does the national government. Some of these constraints were adopted when state constitutions were first written, but many others were imposed by voters through the use of ballot initiatives (see Chapter 5). These constraints generally seek to restrict the fiscal scale of state government relative to the population or the economy and to discourage the accumulation of large amounts of public debt. Satisfying these constraints is especially difficult when tax revenues are down, demand for programs that provide a social safety net is up, and states have made commitments to benefits for retired state employees that extend far into the future.

Fiscal policymaking also offers scholars of state government and politics opportunities to study the effects of many other political and economic variables. Every state adopts a budget at least every other year, and all states have similar options when deciding how to raise and spend public monies. Revenues, expenditures, and debt are measured in continuous dollar amounts that can be compared across states and (after adjusting for inflation) time. This unit of measurement also facilitates the use of statistical models to test hypotheses. A great deal of research on state fiscal policy analyzes the effects of variables such as partisan control of elected offices, the relative powers of the governor and state legislature, the ideology of elected officials and voters, organized interest groups, and constitutional or statutory constraints.

In this chapter, I first examine the differences in the scope and scale of state governments and major explanations for differences in fiscal scale. Next, I summarize the primary constitutional and statutory constraints that shape state fiscal policy. I then discuss state government revenues, comparing the extent to which different states rely on different kinds of taxes and fees; discuss state government debt and future obligations such as employees' pensions; describe the budget process and the use of rainy day funds to guard against future contingencies; and touch briefly on the composition of state government expenditures. Finally, I discuss the politics of scarcity in the context of the severe economic conditions that states currently face.

THE SCOPE AND SCALE OF STATE GOVERNMENT

Before comparing the fiscal scale—that is, the levels of revenue and spending by state government—in different states, I will first adjust for differences in scope by making a distinction between total revenue or spending and **general revenue or spending**. The difference is due to state-owned liquor stores, public utilities, and insurance trusts (U.S. Census Bureau 1992). Liquor stores and utility companies are examples of state-owned enterprises that generate their own revenues to cover their own expenses. In 2009 seventeen states generated revenue from liquor stores, and twenty-one states did so from public utility companies (U.S. Census Bureau 2009). All states also administer one or more insurance trusts for public employee retirement and social insurance systems. These are financed by contributions tied to public employees' compensation, plus net earnings on their investment assets (U.S. Census Bureau 1992). Virtually all academic research on state fiscal policy concentrates on general revenues and expenditures.

Turning to scale, Figure 10-1 shows own-source general revenue per capita for each state in **fiscal year** 2009. This revenue includes that collected by state government through taxes or other charges imposed on state residents and economic activity occurring within the state's borders. It therefore captures the fiscal scale of state government as felt by voters in their pocketbooks. Own-source general revenue per capita tends to be high in New England (except for New Hampshire), New

York, and New Jersey; it is lowest in the Southeast, and also low in the Midwest. General spending is financed by own-source general revenue, net intergovernmental revenue (IGR) transfers, and in some cases borrowing. A map showing general spending per capita does not look terribly different from Figure 10-1. The specific values obviously change, but few states shift from one quintile to another in the rankings.

There is a great deal of variation across the states in fiscal scale. Alaska is a special case because of its reliance on taxes and fees applied to the extraction of nonrenewable natural resources (see Chapter 1). Even after excluding Alaska, own-source general revenue and general spending per capita are more than twice as high for the state ranked second (Wyoming in both cases) as for the states ranked fiftieth (Georgia and Florida, respectively). The interquintile ranges are $2,864–4,220 per capita for own-source general revenue and $4,525–6,105 per capita for general spending. Thus the fiscal scale of the state ranked eleventh is about 47 percent larger than that of the state ranked fortieth when measured by own-source general revenue, and 35 percent larger when measured by general spending.

What might explain differences in fiscal scale across states? Two obvious factors are ability to pay and preferences for public services. States with larger **tax bases** generate more own-source revenue and have greater expenditures (Alt and Lowry

Figure 10-1 Own-Source General Revenue per Capita, 2009

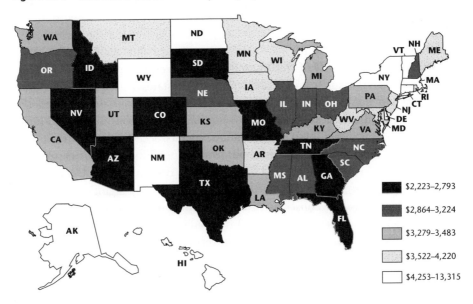

SOURCE: U.S. Census Bureau, *2009 Annual Survey of State Government Finances*, www.census.gov/govs/state/.

1994; Besley and Case 2003; Matsusaka 2004; Primo 2007). The connection is sufficiently strong that some studies measure fiscal scale as a percentage of personal income or gross domestic product, similar to Figure 2-1.

With respect to preferences about the appropriate levels of revenue and spending, most people would probably expect states controlled by Democrats to have higher taxes and spending than states controlled by Republicans. Determining the effect of partisan control on fiscal scale is surprisingly tricky, however. First, not all Republicans or all Democrats have the same preferences. During most of the twentieth century, for example, Democrats in the southern states were much more conservative than those in the rest of the country (Erikson, Wright, and McIver 1993). Second, partisan control of government is often divided and can change abruptly, whereas fiscal scale tends to change gradually. It is relatively rare for the same party to be in control long enough to achieve its desired target (Alt and Lowry 2000). Still, if one party consistently wins a majority of races for governor and state legislature over a number of election cycles, this factor should be reflected in measures of fiscal scale. Alt and Lowry (1994) estimate separate models of general revenues and spending in southern and nonsouthern states during 1968–1987, and calculate implied fiscal scale targets from the results. They estimate that nonsouthern Democrats target a substantially larger fiscal scale relative to income than Republicans, with southern Democrats falling in between. Alt and Lowry (2000) find that Democrats tend to increase fiscal scale in the first two years after they achieve unified control of state government, whereas Republicans tend to decrease fiscal scale. Reed (2006) also finds that tax burdens increase more if Democrats control the legislature, but Primo (2007) obtains mostly insignificant results for combined state and local spending.

It might also be expected that liberal states have larger fiscal scale than conservative states. Systematic tests of this hypothesis have been hampered by the lack of reliable and valid measures of ideology across all fifty states. Besley and Case (2003) found that partisanship and ideology had independent effects on spending and taxes in forty-nine states[1] during 1960–1993; states with more liberal citizens as measured by Berry et al. (1998) or where Democrats occupy a larger fraction of seats in the lower house of the legislature tax and spend more. Matsusaka (2004) finds no statistically significant effect of ideology on combined *state and local* government expenditures during 1970–2000, but a marginally significant effect on *state* spending, with more conservative states spending less.

Differences in fiscal scale as measured by spending also depend on the relative success of different states in attracting intergovernmental revenue transfers (Alt and Lowry 1994; Matsusaka 2004; Primo 2007). As Figure 2-2 in Chapter 2 shows, there is only a loose connection between the taxes a state's residents pay to the federal

---

1. Nebraska is omitted because it has a nonpartisan legislature. Besley and Case (2003) label their dependent variables "total spending" and "total taxes." However, it appears from their summary statistics that the former is actually general expenditures, while the latter is clearly not total revenues.

government and intergovernmental grants to state and local governments. Although much of the variation in IGR transfers can be explained by measures of need, political factors matter as well. Federal transfers per capita are greater to smaller states that have disproportionate representation in the U.S. Senate (Lee and Oppenheimer 1997). Research has also found that the distribution of federal funds for at least some programs is affected by partisanship (Levitt and Snyder 1995) and organized groups representing state interests (Lowry and Potoski 2004).

Fiscal scale also depends on institutions, which may be defined as "the rules of the game in a society or, more formally, . . . the humanly devised constraints that shape human interaction" (North 1990, 3). Different kinds of constraints are discussed in greater detail in the next section, but states that allow voter initiatives tend to have smaller state fiscal scale (Matsusaka 2004; Primo 2007), although some scholars do not find statistically significant results (Besley and Case 2003). Another recent line of research suggests fiscal scale is greater in states with more transparent budgeting rules that make it easier for voters, the media, and interest groups to understand the budget and hold elected officials accountable (Alt and Lowry 2010). The basic intuition is that voters are willing to trust politicians with greater tax revenues if they are confident they can observe how and why spending decisions are made.

Finally, fiscal scale varies in the short run because of the business cycle and the need to maintain fiscal balance. Revenue from taxes and fees falls during a recession. The usual government response is a cut in spending despite increased demands for public assistance. There is also evidence that both Democrats and Republicans adjust general revenues in response to the previous year's deficit or surplus in order to maintain fiscal balance (Alt and Lowry 1994; Poterba 1994).

State governments raise and spend money for pretty much the same purposes across all fifty states, but the amounts they raise and spend vary significantly. Reasons for long-term differences in fiscal scale include differences in the abilities of state residents to pay for public services, preferences for government programs, transfers of revenue from the federal government, and institutions that govern how decisions are made. In addition, cyclical differences in scale occur within each state because of the business cycle and adjustments needed to maintain fiscal balance. The adjustments required during the recent "great recession" have been large and painful in many states.

INSTITUTIONS AFFECTING STATE FISCAL POLICY

State fiscal policy in the United States is constrained by institutions to a far greater degree than is national fiscal policy. Virtually all of these constraints are self-imposed, not from above (Rodden and Eskeland 2003). Some constraints affect overall fiscal scale, others affect the composition of revenues or expenditures, and still others affect the way that fiscal policy responds to unexpected events. Although a great deal of research in recent years has focused on specific institutions, their full effect in any particular state may depend on the combination of institutions in place.

To begin, all states share certain fundamental features that affect all kinds of policymaking. Separation of powers is an important institutional feature because it allows for the possibility that the executive and legislative branches will be controlled by different parties. Divided governments tend to have implied targets for fiscal scale in between those implied for unified Democrats or Republicans, and are also slower to react to unexpected events (Poterba 1994; Alt and Lowry 1994, 2000). Other important differences across states discussed in earlier chapters are the existence of ballot initiatives (Chapter 5), the degree of legislative professionalism (Chapter 6), and the formal powers of the governor (Chapter 7). Both the governor and legislators are elected, but only the governor has the entire state for a

Table 10-1 State Fiscal Policy Institutions

State	Budget cycle (1)	Transparency (2)	Supermajority vote — Budget (3)	Taxes (4)	No deficit carryover (5)	Tax and expenditure limits (6)	Debt restriction (7)
Alabama	Annual	0.44			X		X
Alaska	Annual	0.44			X	X	
Arizona	Biennial	0.33		X	c	X	X
Arkansas	Biennial	0.33	X	X	X		
California	Annual	0.55	a	X	d	X[e]	
Colorado	Annual	0.67			X	X[e]	X
Connecticut	Biennial	0.77			c	X	X
Delaware	Annual	0.77		X	X	X	X
Florida	Annual	0.44		X	X	X	X
Georgia	Annual	0.88			X		
Hawaii	Biennial	0.44			X	X	X
Idaho	Annual	0.56			X	X	X
Illinois	Annual	0.56	b		c		X
Indiana	Biennial	0.11			d	X	X
Iowa	Annual	0.67			X	X	X
Kansas	Biennial	0.56			X		X
Kentucky	Biennial	0.56			X		X
Louisiana	Annual	0.56		X	d	X	X
Maine	Biennial	0.33			X	X	X
Maryland	Annual	0.67			c		X
Massachusetts	Annual	0.57			c	X[e]	X
Michigan	Annual	0.67			c,d	X[e]	X
Minnesota	Biennial	0.33			X		
Mississippi	Annual	0.67	X	X	X	X	X
Missouri	Biennial	0.56			X	X[e]	X
Montana	Biennial	0.63			X		
Nebraska	Biennial	0.33			X		X
Nevada	Biennial	0.78		X	X	X	X
New Hampshire	Biennial	0.22			X		X
New Jersey	Annual	0.78			c	X	X

constituency. Thus the governor might favor programs that generate benefits spread widely across the state, whereas legislators are mostly concerned with the benefits to their own districts (Barrilleaux and Berkman 2003). Several studies have concluded that more professionalized legislatures are associated with higher spending, but Malhotra (2006, 2008) argues that causation is reversed, because states that prefer larger state government also have more professional legislatures. The ballot initiative tends to have a negative effect on fiscal scale (Matsusaka 2004; Primo 2007), and this effect is due to the existence of the initiative power, without regard to how it is used.

Table 10-1 lists several additional institutions that affect fiscal policy. Column (1) shows whether each state has an annual or biennial budget cycle. Column (2) shows the state's score as of 2000 on an index measuring transparent budget

Table 10-1   *(Continued)*

State	Budget cycle (1)	Transparency (2)	Supermajority vote — Budget (3)	Taxes (4)	No deficit carryover (5)	Tax and expenditure limits (6)	Debt restriction (7)
New Mexico	Annual	0.56			X		X
New York	Annual	0.44			c		X
North Carolina	Biennial	0.78			X		X
North Dakota	Biennial	0.33			X		X
Ohio	Biennial	0.33			X	X	X
Oklahoma	Annual	0.56		X	X	X	
Oregon	Biennial	0.11		X	X	X	X
Pennsylvania	Annual	0.67			c		X
Rhode Island	Annual	0.89	X		X	X	X
South Carolina	Annual	0.56			X	X	X
South Dakota	Annual	0.56		X	X		X
Tennessee	Annual	0.44			X	X	X
Texas	Biennial	0.33			c	X	X
Utah	Annual	1			X	X	X
Vermont	Annual	0.25			c, d		
Virginia	Biennial	0.44			X		X
Washington	Biennial	0.67			d	Xe	
West Virginia	Annual	0.67			c		
Wisconsin	Biennial	0.33			c, d		X
Wyoming	Biennial	0.78			X		X

SOURCES: Columns (1), (3)–(5), and (7): National Association of State Budget Officers, *Budget Processes in the States* (Washington, D.C.: National Association of State Budget Officers, 2008); column (2): James E. Alt, David Dreyer Lassen, and Shanna S. Rose, "The Causes of Transparency: Evidence from U.S. States," *IMF Staff Papers* 53 (2006): 30–57; column (5): National Conference of State Legislatures, "NCSL Fiscal Brief: State Balanced Budget Provisions," Denver, 2010; column (6): Michael J. New, "U.S. State Tax and Expenditure Limitations: A Comparative Political Analysis," *State Politics and Policy Quarterly* 10 (2010): 25–50.

a. California voters eliminated a two-thirds vote requirement in November 2010.

b. Three-fifths supermajority required after June 1.

c. The National Conference of State Legislatures reports deficit may be carried forward.

d. The National Association of State Budget Officers reports deficit may be carried forward.

e. Spending or revenue limit adopted by initiative.

processes, with higher scores indicating more transparency (Alt, Lassen, and Rose 2006). Columns (3) and (4) indicate whether the state requires a supermajority vote in the legislature to pass a budget or tax increase, respectively. Although only a handful of states require more than a majority to adopt a budget, eleven states require more than a majority to raise taxes.

Column (5) indicates whether each state prohibits a budget deficit from being carried forward into the next fiscal year. Every state but Vermont has some sort of **balanced-budget law,** but some of these laws require only that the governor propose a balanced budget or that the legislature pass a balanced budget (National Association of State Budget Officers 2008). Laws that have more bite require a state to offset a deficit in one fiscal year with a projected surplus in the next year, or to finish the year with revenue and spending in balance. These laws tend to result in greater reaction to the previous fiscal year's deficit or surplus and sometimes require midyear adjustments (Alt and Lowry 1994; Poterba 1994). States that lack these laws are more likely to exhibit a "political business cycle," in which government spending increases in the years before an election and decreases in the years after an election (Rose 2006). However, different sources disagree on exactly which states have these laws.[2] The National Conference of State Legislatures (2010b) explains that some states do not explicitly prohibit carrying forward a deficit but have other provisions that create the same effect. Column (5) indicates that three states currently allow deficits to be carried forward, thirty-three states have explicit or unambiguous prohibitions, and fourteen states have other provisions that some but not all experts believe have the same effect.

Column (6) shows whether a state has a specific limit on state government revenue or spending. **Tax and expenditure limits (TELs)** can take a variety of forms, but generally limit the growth in revenue or spending per capita to the rate of inflation, or a fixed percentage of personal income (Poterba and Reuben 1999). New (2010) finds that TELs are most effective when imposed on the legislature by a ballot initiative.

Finally, Column (7) shows whether there are restrictions on a state's ability to accumulate **general obligation debt**—that is, debt that can be repaid out of general fund revenues as opposed to dedicated fees. Some states do not allow general obligation debt at all, others limit it to a maximum dollar amount or a percentage of the tax base, and others require voter approval (National Association of State Budget Officers 2008).

Measuring the effect of fiscal institutions can be tricky for several reasons. First, as the discussion here has indicated, it is not always clear how to measure differences in laws across states (Bowler and Donovan 2004). Second, it is not always clear whether the institution has a causal effect on outcomes. For example, does a

---

2. The studies cited in this paragraph all rely on coding by the Advisory Commission on Intergovernmental Relations (1992).

provision for voter initiatives independently restrain state government taxes and spending, or do more conservative states have voter initiatives and also lower levels of taxes and spending? The case for a causal effect is strongest when institutions have been in place for a long time and are difficult to change. Most constitutional provisions for voter initiatives were adopted during the Progressive Era early in the twentieth century (Matsusaka 2004, but also see Marschall and Ruhil 2005). By contrast, states are constantly changing their budgeting rules, and the average level of transparency has increased over the last twenty years, although Alt and Lowry (2010) allow for possible endogeneity in their analysis.

Finally, the full effect of one type of institution may depend on the presence of other institutions. For example, Matsusaka (2004) suggests that voter initiatives have a direct effect on revenue, but their effect on spending is conditional on the presence of a balanced budget requirement. Similarly, Primo (2007) and Inman (2003) argue that strong balanced budget laws are effective only in states that have politically independent courts to ensure enforcement.

Institutions—the rules of the game—can affect fiscal policy by ruling out certain choices and altering the ability of selected actors to influence decisions. Research has established correlations between a number of institutions and fiscal policy outputs, but causation is harder to demonstrate for institutions such as transparency rules that are evolving. Meanwhile, there is great interest in this subject outside of academia because would-be reformers are constantly looking for ways to improve the rules that govern public decision making.

STATE GOVERNMENT GENERAL REVENUE

State government general revenue may be divided into intergovernmental transfers and own-source revenue. I will deal with the intergovernmental transfers only briefly here because Chapter 2 addresses intergovernmental relations. As for own-source revenue, there is great variation in the extent to which different states rely on different kinds of taxes and fees, and several interesting controversies are currently receiving attention.

Intergovernmental Transfers

In 2009 about one-third of state government general revenue was generated from net intergovernmental transfers. About 95 percent of these transfers came from the federal government. Although many governors actively seek to increase federal transfers to their state, these revenues come with strings attached. First, they can only be used for designated purposes. The largest share by far is for Medicaid; other areas receiving substantial federal assistance are food and nutrition subsidies, public housing, highways and public transportation, and education and welfare programs (U.S. Census Bureau 2009, 2011). Second, many of these transfers take the form of matching funds, meaning that the state must come up with a specified contribution from own-source revenues for each dollar of federal funds. By lowering the effective price to state government of a dollar's worth of designated services, matching federal funds affect how state governments spend own-source revenues as well as the overall composition of state government expenditures (Nicholson-Crotty, Theobald, and Wood 2006). Federal transfers may also come with other strings attached, as discussed in Chapter 2.

Own-Source Revenue

State governments in the United States rely on own-source revenue more than subnational governments in any other federal country except Canada (Rodden and Eskeland 2003). Moreover, states have almost complete autonomy to adopt whatever taxes or fees they choose, provided they do not unduly burden interstate commerce or violate due process or make eligibility to vote conditional on paying a poll tax (see Article 1, section 8, of the U.S. Constitution, together with the Fourteenth and Twenty-fourth Amendments).

As shown in Figure 10-2, the aggregate composition of own-source revenue for all fifty states changed substantially from 1945 to 2009. In 1945 the largest share of

Figure 10-2 Composition of Aggregate Own-Source General Revenue, 1945–2009

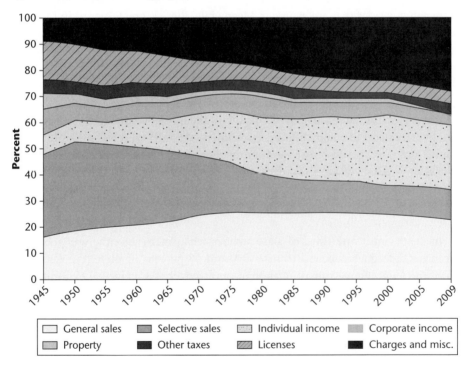

SOURCES: U.S. Census Bureau, *Statistical Abstract of the United States*, various years, www.census.gov/compendia/statab/; U.S. Census Bureau, *2009 Annual Survey of State Government Finance*, www.census.gov/govs/state/.

NOTE: Property taxes are combined with other taxes in 2009.

own-source revenue was generated by selective sales taxes, followed by general sales taxes and license taxes. Among them, these three sources accounted for almost 63 percent of own-source general revenue. By 2005 the reliance on selective sales taxes and license taxes had decreased substantially, whereas the reliance on individual income taxes, charges and miscellaneous fees, and even general sales taxes had increased. These three sources each accounted for about 25 percent of the total, with selective sales taxes accounting for another 11 percent and the rest spread among corporate income taxes, property taxes, license taxes, and all other taxes. The shares of revenue from general sales and individual income taxes were down slightly in 2009 compared with 2005 because of the 2007–2009 recession.

Table 10-2 shows the percentage of own-source general revenue that each state generated from different types of taxes and fees in 2009. Categories differ slightly from Figure 10-2 because of the detail that is available for recent years. I have combined property taxes with "other" taxes, and show separate figures for current charges and miscellaneous revenues. *Current charges* are defined as "charges imposed for providing current services or for the sale of products in connection with general government activities" (U.S. Census Bureau 1992).

The aggregate figures at the bottom of Table 10-2 mask major differences across states. Five states (Alaska, Delaware, Montana, New Hampshire, and Oregon) have no general sales tax. Seven states (Alaska, Florida, Nevada, South Dakota, Texas, Washington, and Wyoming) have no individual income tax, and two other states (New Hampshire and Tennessee) tax unearned income only. At the other extreme, Florida, Tennessee, and Washington generate more than 40 percent of own-source general revenues from general sales taxes, and New York and Oregon generate more than 40 percent from individual income taxes.

Several states are able to take advantage of special circumstances to limit their reliance on general sales and income taxes. Alaska is the only state that has no general sales tax and no individual income tax. Instead, Alaska generates more than 80 percent of its own-source general revenue from other taxes and miscellaneous. These consist largely of severance taxes and other fees derived from mineral leases for oil. Revenue from these sources fluctuates greatly from year to year (Barrett et al. 2003), but often generates large budget surpluses. In 1976 Alaska adopted a constitutional amendment requiring that at least 25 percent of this revenue be placed in an investment fund that pays dividends to Alaska residents. Since 1990, dividends have averaged over $1,200 per resident per year.[3] Ten other states rich in natural resources generate significant revenue from severance taxes and royalties (Brunori 2005).[4] In addition, Delaware has created a niche as the favorite home of private business corporations, and it generates

---

3. Alaska Permanent Fund Corporation, 2011, www.apfc.org.

4. They are Kentucky, Louisiana, Montana, New Mexico, North Dakota, Oklahoma, Texas, Washington, West Virginia, and Wyoming.

Table 10-2 Percentage Composition of Own-Source General Revenues, 2009

State	General sales tax	Selective sales tax	Individual income tax	Corporate income tax	License taxes	Other taxes	Current charges	Miscellaneous other
Alabama	15.5	16	19.9	3.7	3.6	3.5	27.5	10.4
Alaska	n/a	2.7	n/a	6.9	1.5	43.1	6	39.8
Arizona	35.8	10.8	16.2	3.7	2.5	5.7	12	13.3
Arkansas	27	9.6	21.8	3.4	3.2	7.8	19.7	7.5
California	23	5.9	35.3	7.6	6.7	1.9	11.3	8.4
Colorado	15.5	8.6	32.1	2.4	2.7	2.1	21.7	15
Connecticut	20.1	13.1	39.1	2.7	2.2	1.9	12.3	8.6
Delaware	n/a	9.3	17.8	4.1	22.5	1.1	20.6	24.6
Florida	44.6	17.7	n/a	4.3	4.2	3.3	14.4	11.6
Georgia	24.6	7.9	36.2	3.2	2.2	0.5	15	10.3
Hawaii	35.5	9.6	19.3	1.1	2.1	0.3	20	12.1
Idaho	28.3	8.7	27.6	3.3	6.3	0.3	14.2	11.3
Illinois	19.6	18.4	24.1	7.2	6.4	1.1	12.1	11.2
Indiana	30.2	12.9	21	4.1	3.4	0.9	16.8	10.7
Iowa	20.8	10.1	25.6	2.5	6.2	0.8	22.9	11.1
Kansas	22.8	8.4	28	3.8	3.1	2.5	22.4	9
Kentucky	20.4	12.9	23.7	2.8	3.4	6.5	21.1	9.2
Louisiana	20.4	14.1	20.3	4.2	3.2	6.8	14.2	16.8
Maine	20.1	12.5	27.2	2.8	4.8	1.8	13.3	17.4
Maryland	18.6	11	31.2	3.6	3.3	5.2	15.5	11.6
Massachusetts	13.3	7.7	36.5	6.2	2.6	1.5	13.9	18.4
Michigan	27.2	10.6	17.7	2.1	4.1	7.1	20.1	11.2
Minnesota	23.2	15.9	36.9	4.1	5.4	5.6	1.9	7
Mississippi	35.2	12.9	17.3	3.8	4.7	1.4	17.7	7.2
Missouri	20.4	10.5	32.1	1.9	4.3	0.4	17.1	13.3
Montana	n/a	14.6	22.9	4.5	8.2	16.3	13.9	19.4
Nebraska	26.7	9.1	28.4	3.5	3	0.3	17.3	11.7
Nevada	39.1	34.1	n/a	n/a	7.6	10.1	10.6	8.5
New Hampshire	n/a	22	2.6	13.1	6	12.7	21.8	21.8
New Jersey	22.6	9.2	28.6	6.9	3.9	2.7	15	11.1
New Mexico	22.4	7.2	11	2.4	2.5	12	15.7	26.8
New York	12.9	10.6	42.8	5.1	1.8	2.3	9.7	14.8
North Carolina	18.2	12.7	35	3.3	5.3	0.6	14.8	10.1
North Dakota	17	9.4	10.4	3.6	4	23.3	20.6	11.7
Ohio	20.8	13.7	23.7	1.5	8.2	0.2	20.8	11.1
Oklahoma	17.9	8.2	21	2.8	8.2	9.3	18.3	14.4
Oregon	n/a	6.1	44.6	2.1	7	1.1	20.9	18.2
Pennsylvania	20	15.6	22.5	4.1	5.9	2.8	17.7	11.4
Rhode Island	19.8	13.9	23.4	2.6	2.4	0.9	15.6	21.4
South Carolina	22.5	9	18.2	1.7	3.5	0.3	32	12.8
South Dakota	34.3	14.8	n/a	2.2	8.7	0.4	15.4	24
Tennessee	41.9	10.8	1.5	5.4	7.5	1.8	15.5	15.6
Texas	35.2	17.6	n/a	n/a	11.6	3.9	18	13.6
Utah	19.4	7.3	25.8	2.7	4	1.1	28.1	11.5
Vermont	9.4	14.7	15.7	2.5	2.9	28.4	16.5	9.9
Virginia	12.6	8.5	33.4	2.4	2.5	1.8	25.5	13.3
Washington	44.2	13.6	n/a	n/a	4.1	10.4	17.7	10
West Virginia	15.1	15.2	21.2	5.7	2.6	5.3	18.3	16.4
Wisconsin	19.8	12.4	28.9	3.2	4.4	1	18.1	12.1
Wyoming	26.7	3.5	n/a	n/a	4.1	40.2	5.1	20.4
Median	20.4	10.8	22.7	3.3	4.1	2.2	16.9	11.7
U.S. Total	22.9	11.5	24.7	4.1	5	3.7	15.7	12.4

SOURCE: U.S. Census Bureau, State Government Finance Data, Summary Table Spreadsheet, 2009.

NOTE: n/a = not applicable.

substantial revenue from incorporation fees. Florida and Nevada rely heavily on taxes applied to tourism and gambling, respectively.

Aside from these special cases, what affects the decision to rely on different kinds of taxes and fees? First, to be classified as a "tax" by the Census Bureau, revenue must be visible to the taxpayer and not disguised or included as part of some other charge (U.S. Census Bureau 1992). Thus some of the shift over time from taxes to current charges and miscellaneous may reflect attempts to hide the true cost of government (Bowler and Donovan 1995), as well as polls indicating broad support for raising revenue through user fees and other specific charges rather than general-purpose taxes (Matsusaka 2004).

Four considerations used when comparing different types of taxes are (1) potential for raising revenue, (2) consequences for equity, (3) effects on behavior, and (4) ease of administration and compliance (Rosen 1992; Brunori 2005). A comparison of individual income taxes, general sales taxes, and selective sales taxes will illustrate these considerations.

The overall trend from 1945 to 1985 was clearly in the direction of greater reliance on individual income taxes, but the percentage of own-source general revenues from this source has crept up only slightly since 1985. Individual income taxes have the potential to raise a great deal of revenue. However, income fluctuates with the business cycle, and so income tax revenues are low in the same years that expenditures on public assistance programs are high. The equity consequences of taxes are frequently measured by whether they are regressive, neutral, or progressive. A **regressive tax** is one in which people with lower incomes pay a higher percentage of their income in taxes; a **progressive tax** is one in which people who are better off bear a disproportionately large share of the cost of public services. Individual income taxes could, in principle, be structured either way, but in practice they are progressive.[5] These taxes are also relatively easy to administer because many states use the same definitions, exemptions, and deductions as the federal income tax code (Brunori 2005).

Individual income taxes are often criticized because they reduce the private returns from economically productive activity. Thus, high marginal income tax rates dampen economic growth. This effect may be offset in part by exemptions and deductions for certain activities, but these same features tend to detract from the perceived fairness of the tax as well as make it more difficult to administer (Brunori 2005). Finally, individual income taxes can be a political hard sell because the people they hit hardest—those with high incomes—vote more often and make more campaign contributions than other people (Schlozman, Verba, and Brady 1999).

---

5. The degree of progressivity varies, depending on the income brackets used, the difference between the highest and lowest marginal rates, and the specific exemptions or deductions allowed (Council of State Governments 2009). Even a flat-rate income tax is mildly progressive if all taxpayers are allowed a fixed personal exemption (Brunori 2005).

The aggregate reliance on the general sales taxes also increased from 1945 to 1975, and has remained relatively constant since then. General sales taxes are usually calculated as a percentage of the retail price for tangible goods. They could be applied to services as well, but many kinds of services have traditionally been exempt (Barrett et al. 2003; Brunori 2005). Thus a student at a private college pays sales tax on textbooks purchased at the bookstore, but probably not on tuition. A survey conducted in 2007 asked state tax officials which of 168 services they taxed. Only seven states taxed even half the services listed, only seven taxed any professional services at all, and only four (Delaware, Hawaii, New Mexico, and Washington) taxed all of the professional services listed (Federation of Tax Administrators 2008).

General sales taxes nevertheless have the potential to generate a great deal of revenue, and may be more stable than income taxes because people have to buy food, clothing, and so on even in a recession. However, these taxes are usually regressive, because the amount people spend on consumer purchases does not rise as fast as income. Many states address this aspect of these taxes by making "necessities" exempt from general sales taxes,[6] but such exemptions cut into the revenue base, and people with low incomes still tend to spend a greater percentage of their incomes on non-essential consumer items than do people with high incomes. These exemptions also increase the administrative costs to vendors who must collect sales tax revenues and then turn them over to the state (Brunori 2005), and they can result in some apparently arbitrary distinctions. In Ohio, for example, iced tea is considered a food and therefore exempt from sales tax, but fruit juice is not (Barrett et al. 2003). A few states have tried extending the sales tax to include more services, which would broaden the tax base and potentially make it less regressive, especially if professional services such as legal advice and accounting are included. However, these proposals have been met with strong political opposition (Barrett et al. 2003). Maryland and Michigan adopted laws extending sales taxes to more services in 2007 and 2008, respectively, but both laws were rescinded before they could even be implemented (Federation of Tax Administrators 2008).

Selective sales taxes are taxes on specific items that typically are calculated per unit rather than as a percentage of the sale. Thus gasoline taxes are so many cents per gallon. In addition to gasoline and other motor fuels, selective sales taxes are often applied to tobacco products and alcoholic beverages. The aggregate revenue from selective sales taxes, adjusted for both population and inflation, actually grew from 1945 to 2009, but did not keep up with the growth in the state fiscal scale as a whole. The tax base for these revenues is by definition limited, and attempts to raise more revenue by increasing the tax rate will be at least partially offset by a decrease in the quantity sold. Selective sales taxes may also be regressive. They may

---

6. Necessities typically include food and medicine and sometimes clothing. Some states have a sales tax holiday in August before the start of the school year (Brunori 2005).

be politically popular, however, if they apply only to products that the majority consider undesirable or that create social costs.

Corporate income taxes have never been a major source of revenue for most states, and they declined as a percentage of aggregate own-source general revenue from 7.9 percent in 1980 to 4.1 percent in 2009. Brunori (2005) argues that one reason for this decline is the comparative advantage that corporations enjoy in organizing political opposition to taxes, as well as their ability to employ experts who can minimize their tax obligations. In addition, states frequently grant tax breaks to specific firms in an attempt to attract or retain investment and jobs. This sort of interstate competition may be characterized as a prisoner's dilemma, where all states would be better off if none of them offered tax breaks, but no state wants to be left at a competitive disadvantage.

Property taxes accounted for nearly half of state government revenue prior to the 1930s (Brunori 2005), but by 1945 they were relatively unimportant. Property taxes remain the major source of revenue for local governments. They are based on assessments that are often viewed as unfair, are regressive, and are highly visible because they are paid in large lump sums. As a result, they tend to be very unpopular (Bowler and Donovan 1995; Barrett et al. 2003). Some states have adopted state-wide legal limits on local property taxes (Matsusaka 2004). Property taxes may also be applied to tangible personal property such as automobiles, boats, and airplanes, but these are, if anything, even less popular than taxes on real property (Brunori 2005). Voter opposition to the "car tax" was a major factor in recent gubernatorial elections in Virginia and California (Hill 2003; Lewis 2007).

Finally, license taxes are similar to selective sales taxes except that they are based on the type of activity being licensed (such as hunting, fishing, driving, incorporating a business, and selling alcoholic beverages) and the length of time the license is valid. They have essentially the same strengths and weaknesses as selective sales taxes, and have also become less important relative to other types of taxes.

Current Controversies

As states constantly seek to raise revenue by means that are at least politically palatable, if not popular, controversies inevitably arise. Three issues currently receiving attention include **sin taxes**, lotteries, and remote sales.

So-called sin taxes are taxes applied to activities that are often associated with undesirable behavior and that may impose costs on the rest of the population. The most common examples are selective sales taxes on tobacco and alcohol and direct gaming taxes. (Motor fuel taxes apply to activities that generate negative externalities but are not viewed as undesirable, per se. Moreover, nearly everyone drives, whereas not everyone drinks, smokes, or gambles.) These taxes are often politically popular, but they suffer from a problem of inconsistent justifications. Some supporters see them as a good way to generate revenue from a subset of the population that is engaging in undesirable activities. Others see them as a tool to discourage the behavior being taxed. The problem, of course, is that the two objectives of raising revenue and discouraging behavior are incompatible.

Another variation on the sin taxes controversy exists in Nevada, which is the only state with legalized prostitution. Brothels there are subject to various local taxes, but Nevada has no state individual or corporate income tax. The lobbyist for the Nevada Brothel Association has promoted the idea of a state "entertainment tax" applied to prostitution, which he admits is a hedge against the probability that some future legislature will make prostitution illegal throughout the state. So far, most members of the legislature are opposed to the tax (Friess 2009).

Still further variations are gaming taxes and state-operated lotteries. Gaming taxes and lotteries are often controversial because many people believe that the state should not be encouraging gambling, and because these taxes and lotteries are perceived to be a regressive source of revenue used to provide benefits for middle- and upper-class residents (Brunori 2005). Before 1989, only Nevada (beginning in 1931) and New Jersey (1976) had legalized casino gambling. Now, twenty-one states have commercial or racetrack casinos (American Gaming Association 2011),[7] and every state but Hawaii and Utah has at least some form of legalized gambling (Brunori 2005). Nevada raises nearly one-quarter of its revenue from gambling taxes and fees, and other states are increasingly turning to casinos as a source of revenue (Brunori 2005). Forty-four states since 1964 have created legal lotteries that generate revenue for state and local governments (North American Association of State and Provincial Lotteries 2011). Although in 2009 the net proceeds amounted to only about 1.8 percent of aggregate own-source general revenue, Delaware, Rhode Island, South Dakota, and West Virginia each rely on their lottery for at least 5 percent of own-source general revenue (U.S. Census Bureau 2011).

Just as states are constantly looking for new forms of revenue, they also are seeking to eliminate opportunities for taxable activities to evade their jurisdiction. Because of the growing popularity of shopping by mail order and over the Internet, sales from vendors located out of state have become a significant drain on general sales tax revenues. The problem is that sales taxes normally are first collected by the vendor and then passed on to the state. The U.S. Supreme Court ruled in 1992 that states cannot compel a vendor who does not have a "physical presence" in a state to collect sales and use taxes[8] (*Quill v. North Dakota*, 504 U.S. 298). Rather than collecting these taxes, out-of-state vendors seek to obtain a competitive advantage by advertising that their sales are not subject to tax. (In fact, buyers are supposed to remit the tax themselves, but few individuals do and enforcement is prohibitively difficult.) Because of the growth in Internet sales, this is a serious concern for state governments. The Supreme Court explicitly stated in *Quill v. North Dakota* that

---

7. As discussed in Chapter 2, many Native American tribes operate casinos and other gambling establishments, and the adjacent state typically gets a share of the proceeds.

8. Use taxes are sales taxes paid by residents in one state on purchases made in another state (Rosen 1992, 491).

Congress has the power to decide "whether, when and to what extent the states may burden interstate mail-order concerns with a duty to collect use taxes," but Congress has not done so. Several states have responded by passing "Amazon tax" laws that say an online business such as Amazon.com has the necessary presence if it pays affiliates within a state to market its goods. However, these laws are being challenged in the courts (Grovum 2010).

STATE GOVERNMENT DEBT AND FUTURE OBLIGATIONS

In addition to intergovernmental transfers and own-source revenue, state governments fund their programs by borrowing money through the bond market. States do not borrow extensively to finance operations, but they do borrow to finance capital projects such as new buildings and highways. States may issue general obligation bonds that are backed by their "full faith and credit," meaning that they can be repaid from any tax or fee revenues, or they may use "revenue bonds" that are backed by a specific revenue stream such as user fees (Kiewiet and Szakaly 1996). As noted earlier, state government borrowing backed by full faith and credit is heavily constrained by various statutory or constitutional limitations (Kiewiet and Szakalay 1996; National Association of State Budget Officers 2008).

Figure 10-3 shows the total debt outstanding per capita in 2009, by state. The map looks quite similar to that in Figure 10-1, showing own-source general revenue per capita. Although this similarity is not too surprising, ability to repay debt is generally measured by the size of the tax base rather than tax revenues, because the tax base represents the pool of resources that could be tapped if necessary. Some states tax their base at a higher rate than others. California, for example, ranks nineteenth out of fifty states in debt relative to own-source general revenue, but only twenty-eighth in debt as a percentage of gross state product because its own-source general revenues are relatively low compared with the size of its economy.

When states borrow money, they pay interest rates based on the perceived risk to lenders. Although no state has defaulted on its debt since the nineteenth century,[9] there is always some risk that lenders will not be paid on time or that the terms of the loan may need to be renegotiated. Perceived risk to lenders is summarized by bond ratings. In 2008 nine states received Standard and Poor's highest bond ratings of AAA, and California had the lowest ratings of any state at A– (U.S. Census Bureau 2011). Bonds rated BBB or better are considered to be investment grade.

Some studies have concluded that the bond ratings states receive and the interest they pay are affected by political and institutional as well as economic variables. Various studies have found that states with strong balanced budget laws receive higher ratings or pay lower interest rates, but Lowry and Alt (2001) argue that the effect of these laws is conditional on actual fiscal balance. They also find that

---

9. Eight states and the Territory of Florida defaulted on bond payments in the 1840s, and there were waives of defaults by municipal governments in the 1870s and 1930s (Inman 2003).

Figure 10-3   Total Debt Outstanding per Capita, 2009

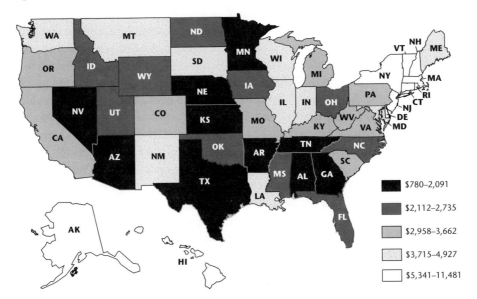

SOURCE: U.S. Census Bureau, *2009 Annual Survey of State Government Finances,* www.census.gov/govs/state/.

Democratic administrations are penalized more than Republican administrations by bond markets for running deficits. Poterba and Reuben (1999) find that more liberal states (as measured by interest group scores of U.S. senators) pay higher interest rates, and interest rates also depend on balanced budget rules and spending and revenue limits. Krueger and Walker (2008) find that states with divided government or frequent changes in partisan control are perceived as riskier by bond markets—a situation attributable, they argue, to the fact that markets are less certain about whether current policies will be maintained in the future.

Bonded debt is not the only form of future financial obligation that states have. Like many large private employers, state governments provide their employees with benefits, including retirement and health care. Many state government retirement plans are "defined benefit" plans, in which the state commits to paying its employees a certain amount every year after they retire for as long as they live. Some states that have these plans have not been making sufficient contributions to the retirement fund to meet their projected financial obligations (Pew Center on the States 2010). Moody's Investors Service recently announced that it will include unfunded pension liabilities as a form of debt when deciding how to rate state government bonds (Walsh 2011).[10] Despite the recent increase in attention, some analysts

10. Many states also have underfunded future health benefits, but Moody's will not take notice of this on the theory that health benefits can be renegotiated (Walsh 2011).

believe that concerns about state government debt and future obligations are over-stated (Lav and McNichol 2011).

FITTING ENDS TO MEANS

Fiscal policy consists of many decisions about specific taxes and fees and funding for specific programs that must be made by elected state officials. Revenue depends on tax legislation that can be adopted in the same way as other bills (see Chapter 6); spending is determined by budgets that must be adopted periodically according to a preset schedule. The budget process presents many opportunities for negotiation and gamesmanship. Players sometimes miscalculate in the final stages, leading to at least a partial suspension of government services until a new agreement can be reached.

Timing Issues

A state government budget is a document that specifies the funds appropriated for specified purposes for a future time period measured in fiscal years, given projected revenues over that same time period. A fiscal year is twelve months in length, but it does not coincide with a calendar year. All but four states use fiscal years beginning July 1, with the number of the fiscal year corresponding to the calendar year in which it ends (Council of State Governments 2009). Thus the data shown in Figure 10-1 for these states reflect revenues received between July 1, 2008, and June 30, 2009. The four exceptions are Alabama (October 1), Michigan (October 1), New York (April 1), and Texas (September 1). Having a fiscal year that begins in the middle of the calendar year gives new officeholders whose terms start in January a chance to debate the contents of the budget without having to wait an entire year before making decisions. Moreover, the largest single category of state government expenditures is education, so it makes sense to start the fiscal year in the middle of the summer, when schools are not in session.

Another difference across states is the frequency with which the budget must be adopted. As shown in Table 10-1, twenty-seven states adopt a budget annually; twenty-three do so biennially. Adopting a budget biennially saves considerable time and creates a longer planning horizon, but it also limits a state's ability to respond quickly to changes in demand for public services or economic conditions, and it weakens transparency and accountability for the results (Alt, Lassen, and Rose 2006).

State governments often fund projects such as the construction of roads and buildings that take more than a year or two to complete. These are treated in a separate document known as a **capital budget**. The planning horizon for a capital budget ranges from one to ten years, with five or six years being most frequent. It typically includes land purchases, construction or renovation of buildings, and equipment purchases over a minimum dollar amount. Differences across states occur in the minimum expenditure required to qualify and the treatment of maintenance and repair costs. In most states, a centralized agency oversees capital projects and helps to coordinate the capital budget with the operating budget. In some states, the two budgets are merged into a single document (National Association of State Budget Officers 2008).

Although capital outlays amounted to just 6.4 percent of aggregate general spending in fiscal year 2009 (U.S. Census Bureau 2009), elected officeholders may take a particular interest in capital projects because they are visible and long-lasting and provide location-specific benefits to voters. For example, a state legislator likely stands to gain more politically from a new classroom building for the community college in her district than from her support for appropriations to pay the operating expenses at all of the public colleges and universities throughout the state (see Weingast, Shepsle, and Johnsen 1981).

The Budget Process

Budgetary legislation differs from other legislation in that it must be completed in time for the start of the fiscal year. To accomplish this, states have developed a specific series of steps and assigned responsibility for each step to different actors (National Association of State Budget Officers 2008). These steps do not always occur in the same sequence and the process is often iterative, with initial estimates of revenues and spending being challenged and updated throughout. Nevertheless, the entire process is choreographed and subject to deadlines.

An important early step is the preparation of revenue estimates. These estimates project how much revenue the state government will generate over the coming fiscal year(s), assuming that the current tax and fee schedules remain in place. If changes to the existing tax or fee schedules are being considered, separate revenue estimates will be needed for them. These estimates depend on assumptions about the state of the economy, and thus are subject to manipulation in ways that may be hard to detect. Small changes in assumptions about growth rates, inflation rates, or the timing of events can affect the revenue estimate in ways that make a budget look prudent or reckless. A governor who campaigns on the promise of ambitious new programs might want to use an optimistic set of assumptions about the economy so that it looks like plenty of revenue will be available. If these estimates turn out to be inaccurate, the governor can blame the resulting shortfall on bad luck rather than mismanagement. An important question, therefore, is who prepares the revenue estimates? The most common answer is an agency within the executive branch, but some states use a joint executive-legislative commission to reach a consensus, and a few even use private consultants (National Association of State Budget Officers 2008).

Simultaneous with the preparation of revenue estimates, administrative agencies are asked to prepare requests for appropriations subject to guidelines from the governor's office. In most states, the governor's budget is submitted to the legislature shortly after the start of the new legislative session, but a few states call for it to be submitted before the session convenes. The legislature then holds hearings on appropriations bills and ultimately adopts a budget subject to revenue estimates and any requirements for fiscal balance. As with other legislation, the governor may sign or veto the budget. In forty-three states, the governor has a third option, which is to use a line-item veto to accept some, but not all, of the legislature's budget. The governor's specific powers in each state vary by the smallest unit that can be vetoed and the number of votes in the legislature required to override a veto (see Chapter 7).

As the start of the new fiscal year approaches and the time for bargaining grows short, all sorts of interesting maneuvers may occur. A last-minute rush to get something passed can create opportunities for legislators or the governor to demand funding for pet projects or other concessions as the price of their support. Especially if the two chambers of the legislature are controlled by different parties, a game of "chicken" may develop where both sides refuse to make concessions in the hope that the other side will blink first (Alt and Lowry 1994).

Although the same sort of dynamic occurs at the national level, the pressure to reach an agreement is greater in state budgeting for two reasons. First, as shown in Table 10-1 most states face institutional constraints that limit their abilities to avoid hard choices by running a deficit. Second, twenty-two states do not allow the fiscal year deadline to be effectively extended with a continuing resolution that says funding for programs will continue at the current level for some period of time. In these states, if a budget is not adopted by the start of the fiscal year, the state government must shut down. An additional eleven states do not have a specific provision and it is not known what would happen, but these states have always passed their budgets on time (National Conference of State Legislatures 2008).

Occasionally, negotiations fail to produce an agreement and the government ceases to function for a time. Since 2002, nineteen states have started one or more fiscal years without a budget, and five of these experienced at least a partial government shutdown (National Conference of State Legislatures 2010a). For example, in 2006 New Jersey had to shut down all but essential services for the first time in its history. Roughly 45,000 state employees were placed on involuntary furloughs until the impasse was resolved a week into the fiscal year. Perhaps worse from a public relations standpoint, the state lottery stopped selling tickets, and twelve Atlantic City casinos ceased operations because of the absence of state inspectors. According to the initial estimates, the shutdown cost the state $3.2 million a day in lottery sales and gambling taxes (Jones and Chen 2006).

Rainy Day Funds

An additional tool that state governments use to maintain fiscal balance is the **rainy day fund**, sometimes known as a "budget stabilization fund." This is a designated account into which the state deposits funds in good years, and from which it can withdraw funds to avoid running a deficit in bad years. Some states mandate deposits using a formula based on personal income or general revenues, or deposit some of the proceeds from designated revenue sources. By 2008 all states except Kansas and Montana had some sort of rainy day fund (National Association of State Budget Officers 2008).

Rainy day funds have been used commonly only for about two decades, and states continue to experiment with the rules governing their use. Some states place a cap on the maximum amount in the fund, some have supermajority requirements for votes to withdraw funds, some have rules requiring rapid replenishment of funds once withdrawn, and so on (National Association of State Budget Officers 2008). Having too many rules can defeat the purpose of a fund meant to be used for unforeseen contingencies. And yet allowing elected officials complete discretion to dip into the fund may lead to failure to maintain adequate reserves for true emergencies.

Although having a rainy day fund helps to smooth state government spending over good times and bad, money that is kept in reserve is money not being used to provide public services. Most states therefore maintain a relatively modest reserve. In 2009 actual rainy day fund balances were just 4.3 percent of aggregate general spending. Five states had balances greater than 10 percent of spending, but twenty-two states had balances less than 2 percent of spending (National Association of State Budget Officers 2010).

STATE GOVERNMENT GENERAL EXPENDITURES

This chapter focuses more on the fiscal scale of state government, revenue sources, and budget processes than state government spending on specific programs. This section briefly addresses intergovernmental revenue transfers to local governments and the composition of state government spending. Several other chapters in this book address specific policy areas.

Intergovernmental Revenue Transfers to Local Governments

In fiscal year 2009, just as intergovernmental revenue transfers from the federal government accounted for about one-third of aggregate state government general revenues, intergovernmental transfers to local governments accounted for about one-third of aggregate general expenditures. In some cases, these are the same dollars, because federal aid to local governments routed through the state is classified as intergovernmental transfers twice (U.S. Census Bureau 1992). However, the fact that the two transfer streams are currently balanced is largely coincidental. Whereas federal transfers to states have increased significantly as a share of general revenue since 1945, the percentage of state general spending going to local governments has actually dropped slightly during the same time period.

Figure 10-4 Composition of Aggregate General Expenditures, 1945–2009

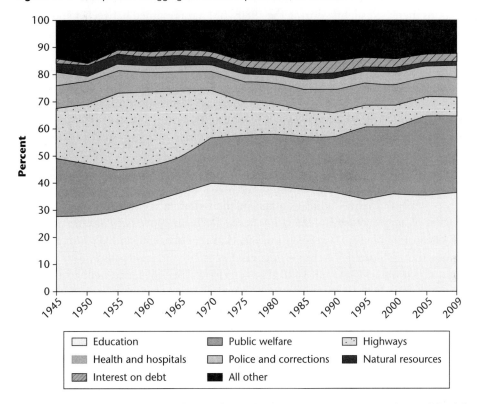

SOURCES: U.S. Census Bureau, *Statistical Abstract of the United States,* various years, www.census.gov/compendia/statab/; U.S. Census Bureau, *2009 Annual Survey of State Government Finance,* www.census.gov/govs/state/.

Composition of General Spending

Figure 10-4 shows the composition of aggregate state general spending, including transfers to local governments, by function since 1945. Education was already the largest category in 1945, but grew steadily relative to other functions until 1970 and has remained a fairly constant share of spending since. The percentage of general spending devoted to highways grew until the late 1950s, when it was nearly as large as education, and then it dropped sharply. Highways accounted for only about 7 percent of general spending in 2009 compared with 28 percent in 1955. Public welfare passed highways as the second largest category in the early 1970s and has continued to grow relative to other functions. This growth stems primarily from the rapid increase in Medicaid spending (National Association of State Budget Officers 2010), which is classified as public welfare rather than health care in state government finance reports. The percentages of aggregate spending on other functions have remained relatively constant. Health care and hospitals consistently account for 7–9 percent of general spending. The share devoted to police and corrections increased slightly during the 1980s, but has remained between 4 and 5 percent since 1990. State governments spend relatively little on natural resources and a variety of other functions in the "all other" category, which also includes government administration. The share of aggregate general spending devoted to interest payments on the debt grew slightly from 1970 to 1990 but remained below 5 percent and has decreased in more recent years. By contrast, net interest payments have consumed at least 5 percent of federal outlays every year since 1946 and at least 10 percent every year from 1981 through 2001 (*Economic Report of the President* 2010).

An examination of state-by-state data reveals that the composition of general spending is much more consistent across states than is the composition of own-source general revenue. Education and public welfare accounted for 36.3 and 28.2 percent of aggregate general spending, respectively, in 2009. They are the two largest categories in every state except Alaska, Hawaii, Louisiana, and Wyoming, where "other and unallocable" is first or second. Highways and health and hospitals each account for about 7 percent of aggregate general spending, and neither accounts for more than 13.5 percent in any state. No state devotes more than 5.8 percent of general spending to police and corrections, and only Montana and Wyoming devote more than 3.4 percent to natural resources. Finally, interest on the general debt accounts for just 2.9 percent of aggregate general spending, and no more than 8.9 percent in any state.

Although many studies have focused on state spending in specific areas such as welfare programs, higher education, or primary and secondary schools, few studies have tried to model the trade-offs between different functions. Nicholson-Crotty, Theobald, and Wood (2006) look at the trade-offs between changes in spending funded by own-source general revenue on education, public welfare, highways, and health and hospitals for all fifty states during 1972–1996. After controlling for different measures of need, they find that liberal states spend more than conservative states on public welfare relative to each of the other three categories, and more on health care and highways relative to education. Relative changes in state spending on different functions also reflect relative changes in federal intergovernmental transfers. This finding implies that the federal government is able to influence state-level budgetary tradeoffs through its intergovernmental transfers.

THE POLITICS OF SCARCITY IN DIFFICULT TIMES

Fiscal policy is one area in which the rhetoric of campaigning and the reality of governing are likely to clash head-on. Candidates for office would much rather make promises about what they are going to do for voters once elected than give warnings about what they cannot do. The fundamental fact, however, is that resources are limited but wants are not.

An extreme example of what can occur after a candidate takes office is provided by Alabama governor Bob Riley. Riley, a Republican, was elected governor in 2002 after serving three terms in Congress. As a candidate, he bragged that he never voted for a tax increase in Congress and promised not to raise taxes as governor. Less than one year later, however, he pushed the largest tax increase in Alabama history through the state legislature. The changes required an amendment to the state constitution, which Riley supported on the grounds that it would eliminate the deficit inherited from his predecessor, allow for needed investments in education, and make the state tax code less regressive. His own state party denounced him, while Democrats were divided (or maybe just confused!). Meanwhile, the amendment was defeated, 67–33 percent (Russakoff 2003). Although Riley managed to win reelection in 2006, Alabama continues to rank near the bottom among states in per capita own-source general revenue and spending.

More recently, some candidates for governor have had no choice but to acknowledge the need for tough decisions. The severe recession that began in late 2007 led to a significant drop in revenues from sales and income taxes, while increasing the demand for programs such as Medicaid and unemployment insurance. The American Recovery and Reinvestment Act of 2009 (the federal stimulus) provided a surge in intergovernmental revenue that helped many states weather fiscal years 2010 and 2011, albeit not without making midyear cuts in spending for numerous programs (National Association of State Budget Officers 2010). Now the federal stimulus funds have dried up, and own-source tax revenues are not expected to recover for several more years. Meanwhile, Medicaid costs are projected to continue growing, and bond markets are becoming increasingly concerned about the failure of many states to fully fund their employee pensions and other benefits. As a result, the politics of scarcity have become the "politics of austerity" for many states. The newly elected Democratic governor of New York, Andrew Cuomo, for one, proclaimed his state to be "functionally bankrupt" (Fletcher 2011).

Solving the political calculus of scarcity (let alone austerity) is going to be difficult. First, there is the argument that raising taxes when unemployment is high and incomes are stagnant is bad economic and social policy. Second, various statistical analyses have shown that voters tend to punish incumbent governors at the ballot box for tax increases (Kone and Winter 1993; Niemi, Stanley, and Vogel 1995), particularly if taxes rose more than in neighboring states (Besley and Case 1995). Although voter reactions may depend on whether the incumbent governor is a Democrat or Republican, whether the incumbent's party also controls the legislature, and whether the process by which decisions are made is transparent (Lowry, Alt, and Ferree 1998; Alt and Lowry 2010), opposition to broad-based tax increases is widespread (Matsusaka 2004).

About the only way to justify a broad-based increase in taxes may be to show that it is needed to avoid cuts in spending that would be even more painful. Under normal circumstances, cutting spending can be extremely difficult. For one thing, candidates typically find upon assuming office that the ever-popular targets of waste, fraud, and abuse do not account for more than a minor share of government spending. For another, elected officeholders face the temptation to use public resources to fund projects that benefit their own voting constituents. Under the current circumstances, however, the combination of reduced revenues and institutional constraints mandating balanced budgets may leave governors and legislators with literally no options other than raising taxes or cutting spending on programs that enjoy broad support (National Association of State Budget Officers 2010; Fletcher 2011).

Theoretically, yet another option is to borrow, but whereas the federal government routinely borrows to finance operating deficits, state governments are strongly discouraged from doing so. Moreover, balanced budget laws and other institutions at the state but not the national level may generate reinforcing expectations about what constitutes "responsible" fiscal management (Briffault 1996; Lowry and Alt 2001). The difference between federal and state governments is due, at least in part, to the fact that the former must finance national defense and is also viewed as the responder of last resort in the case of large-scale crises (Alesina and Perotti 1996).

Elected state officials who feel caught between competing demands and constraints may be tempted to use creative accounting and other gimmicks. Such tactics cannot be sustained forever, however, and research on the effects of transparent budget procedures suggests that obfuscation can lead to a lower probability of reelection for the governor (Alt and Lowry 2010). Another way to avoid constraints might be to shift spending from the state to local governments (Matsusaka 2004). In recent years, voter initiatives have been used widely in many states to place even more restrictions on revenues, spending, and borrowing. This tide may have crested, however, and there are some signs it is waning. The provision in Colorado's Taxpayer Bill of Rights limiting the growth in tax revenue per capita to the rate of inflation was suspended by voters in November 2005 (Johnson 2005). In 2010 California voters approved an initiative that removed the requirement of a two-thirds supermajority to pass a budget and made it a simple majority. At the same time, however, they added a two-thirds requirement for votes to raise certain fees (Hoeffel 2010).

Overall, state politicians making fiscal policy decisions are faced with a greater need to acknowledge trade-offs than their national counterparts because of the institutional constraints they face. During normal times, they have been able to make such decisions while responding to the preferences of their constituents for different kinds of taxes and spending priorities. Now and in the immediate future, their task has become more difficult. The next few years will tell which states enact tax increases despite the political risk involved, which make painful spending cuts, and whether any states prove incapable of solving the politics of scarcity in difficult times.

KEY TERMS

balanced-budget law, 316
capital budget, 327
fiscal year, 310
general obligation debt, 316
general revenue (or general
   spending), 310
progressive tax, 321

rainy day funds, 329
regressive tax, 321
sin tax, 323
tax and expenditure limits
   (TELs), 316
tax base, 311

REFERENCES

Advisory Commission on Intergovernmental Relations. 1992. *Significant Features of Fiscal Feder-alism,* Vol. 1. Washington, D.C.: Advisory Commission on Intergovernmental Relations.

Alesina, Alberto, and Roberto Perotti. 1996. "Fiscal Discipline and the Budget Process." *American Economic Review* 86 (May): 401–407.

Alt, James E., David Dreyer Lassen, and Shanna S. Rose. 2006. "The Causes of Transparency: Evidence from U.S. States." *IMF Staff Papers* 53: 30–57.

Alt, James E., and Robert C. Lowry. 1994. "Divided Government, Fiscal Institutions, and Budget Deficits: Evidence from the States." *American Political Science Review* 88: 811–828.

———. 2000. "A Dynamic Model of State Budget Outcomes under Divided Partisan Government." *Journal of Politics* 62: 1035–1069.

———. 2010. "Transparency and Accountability: Empirical Results for U.S. States." *Journal of Theoretical Politics* 22: 379–406.

American Gaming Association. 2011. "Industry Information: State Information: Statistics." www .americangaming.org.

Barrett, Katherine, Richard Greene, Michele Marianai, and Anya Sostek. 2003. "The Way We Tax: A 50-State Report." *Governing,* February, 20–97.

Barrilleaux, Charles, and Michael Berkman. 2003. "Do Governors Matter? Budgeting Rules and the Politics of State Policymaking." *Political Research Quarterly* 56: 409–417.

Berry, William D., Evan J. Ringquist, Richard C. Fording, and Russell L. Hanson. 1998. "Measuring Citizen and Government Ideology in the American States, 1960–93." *American Journal of Political Science* 42: 327–348.

Besley, Timothy, and Anne Case. 1995. "Incumbent Behavior: Vote-Seeking, Tax Setting, and Yardstick Competition." *American Economic Review* 85: 25–45.

———. 2003. "Political Institutions and Policy Choices: Evidence from the United States." *Journal of Economic Literature* 41: 7–73.

Bowler, Shaun, and Todd Donovan. 1995. "Popular Responsiveness to Taxation." *Political Research Quarterly* 48: 79–99.

———. 2004. "Measuring the Effect of Direct Democracy on State Policy: Not All Initiatives Are Created Equal." *State Politics and Policy Quarterly* 4: 345–363.

Briffault, Richard. 1996. *Balancing Acts: The Reality behind State Balanced Budget Requirements.* New York: Twentieth Century Fund Press.

Brunori, David. 2005. *State Tax Policy: A Political Perspective,* 2d ed. Washington, D.C.: Urban Institute Press.

Council of State Governments. 2009. *The Book of the States.* Lexington, Ky.: Council of State Governments.

Economic Report of the President. 2010. Washington, D.C.: Government Printing Office.

Erikson, Robert S., Gerald C. Wright, and John McIver. 1993. *Statehouse Democracy: Public Opinion and Policy in the American States.* New York: Cambridge University Press.

Federation of Tax Administrators. 2008. "FTA Survey of Services Taxation—Update." July. www .taxadmin.org/fta/pub/services/btn/0708.html.

Fletcher, Michael A. 2011. "Governors from Both Parties Plan Painful Cuts amid Budget Crises across the U.S." *Washington Post*, February 7.

Friess, Steve. 2009. "Nevada Brothels Want to Pay Tax, but State Says No." *New York Times*, January 26.

Grovum, Jake. 2010. "The 'Amazon Tax' War Escalates." *Stateline*, April 26. www.stateline.org/live/ details/story?contentId=479651.

Hill, John. 2003. "License Fee Rollback Rife with Uncertainties." *Sacramento Bee*, November 10, A1.

Hoeffel, John. 2010. "Election 2010: Assessing the Results." *Los Angeles Times*, November 4, AA7.

Inman, Robert P. 2003. "Transfers and Bailouts: Enforcing Local Fiscal Discipline with Lessons from U.S. Federalism." In *Fiscal Decentralization and the Challenge of Hard Budget Constraints*, ed. Jonathan Rodden, Gunnar S. Eskeland, and Jennie Litvack, 35–84. Cambridge, Mass.: MIT Press.

Johnson, Kirk. 2005. "Colorado Cap on Spending Is Suspended." *New York Times*, November 3, A16.

Jones, Richard G., and David W. Chen. 2006. "Corzine Ends New Jersey Shutdown and Approves Budget." *New York Times*, July 8, 22.

Kiewiet, D. Roderick, and Kristen Szakaly. 1996. "Constitutional Limitations on Borrowing: An Analysis of State Bonded Indebtedness." *Journal of Law, Economics, and Organization* 12: 62–97.

Kone, Susan L., and Richard Winters. 1993. "Taxes and Voting: Electoral Retribution in the American States." *Journal of Politics* 55: 22–40.

Krueger, Skip, and Robert W. Walker. 2008. "Divided Government, Political Turnover, and State Bond Ratings." *Public Finance Review* 36: 259–286.

Lav, Iris J., and Elizabeth McNichol. 2011. "Misunderstandings Regarding State Debt, Pensions, and Retiree Health Costs Create Unnecessary Alarm." Center on Budget and Policy Priorities, January 20. www.cbpp.org/cms/index.cfm?fa=view&id=3372.

Lee, Frances E., and Bruce I. Oppenheimer. 1999. *Sizing Up the Senate: The Unequal Consequences of Equal Representation.* Chicago: University of Chicago Press.

Levitt, D. Stephen, and James M. Snyder. 1995. "Political Parties and the Distribution of Federal Outlays." *American Journal of Political Science* 39: 958–980.

Lewis, Bob. 2007. "Ex-Gov. Gilmore Eyes GOP White House Bid." *Washington Post*, January 9. www.washingtonpost.com.

Lowry, Robert C., and James E. Alt. 2001. "A Visible Hand? Bond Markets, Political Parties, Balanced Budget Laws, and State Government Debt." *Economics and Politics* 13: 49–72.

Lowry, Robert C., James E. Alt, and Karen E. Ferree. 1998. "Fiscal Policy Outcomes and Electoral Accountability in American States." *American Political Science Review* 92: 759–774.

Lowry, Robert C., and Matthew Potoski. 2004. "Organized Interests and the Politics of Federal Discretionary Grants." *Journal of Politics* 66: 513–533.

Malhotra, Neil. 2006. "Government Growth and Professionalism in U.S. State Legislatures." *Legislative Studies Quarterly* 31: 563–584.

———. 2008. "Disentangling the Relationship between Legislative Professionalism and Government Spending." *Legislative Studies Quarterly* 33: 387–414.

Marschall, Melissa J., and Anirudh V.S. Ruhil. 2005. "Fiscal Effects of the Voter Initiative Reconsidered: Addressing Endogeneity." *State Politics and Policy Quarterly* 5: 327–355.

Matsusaka, John G. 2004. *For the Many or the Few: The Initiative, Public Policy, and American Democracy.* Chicago: University of Chicago Press.

National Association of State Budget Officers. 2008. *Budget Processes in the States.* Washington, D.C.: National Association of State Budget Officers.

———. 2010. *Fiscal Survey of the States.* Washington, D.C.: National Association of State Budget Officers.

National Conference of State Legislatures. 2008. "Procedures When the Appropriations Act Is Not Passed by the Beginning of the Fiscal Year." www.ncsl.org/default.aspx?tabid=12616.

———. 2010a. "Late State Budgets." www.ncsl.org/default.aspx?tabid=17823.

———. 2010b. "NCSL Fiscal Brief: State Balanced Budget Provisions." www.ncsl.org/documents/fiscal/StateBalancedBudgetProvisions2010.pdf.

New, Michael J. 2010. "U.S. State Tax and Expenditure Limitations: A Comparative Political Analysis." *State Politics and Policy Quarterly* 10: 25–50.

Nicholson-Crotty, Sean, Nick A. Theobald, and B. Dan Wood. 2006. "Fiscal Federalism and Budgetary Tradeoffs in the American States." *Political Research Quarterly* 59: 313–321.

Niemi, Richard G., Harold W. Stanley, and Ronald J. Vogel. 1995. "State Economies and State Taxes: Do Voters Hold Governors Accountable?" *American Journal of Political Science* 39: 936–957.

North, Douglass C. 1990. *Institutions, Institutional Change, and Economic Performance.* New York: Cambridge University Press.

North American Association of State and Provincial Lotteries. 2011. "Member Lotteries." www.naspl.org.

Pew Center on the States. 2010. "The Trillion Dollar Gap: Underfunded State Retirement Systems and the Roads to Reform." Pew Charitable Trusts, Philadelphia.

Poterba, James M. 1994. "State Responses to Fiscal Crisis: The Effects of Budgetary Institutions and Politics." *Journal of Political Economy* 102: 799–821.

Poterba, James M., and Kim S. Rueben. 1999. "State Fiscal Institutions and the U.S. Municipal Bond Market." In *Fiscal Institutions and Fiscal Performance*, ed. James M. Poterba and Jürgen von Hagen, 181–208. Chicago: University of Chicago Press.

Primo, David M. 2007. *Rules and Restraint: Government Spending and the Design of Institutions.* Chicago: University of Chicago Press.

Reed, W. Robert. 2006. "Democrats, Republicans, and Taxes: Evidence that Political Parties Matter." *Journal of Public Economics* 90: 725–750.

Rodden, Jonathan, and Gunnar S. Eskeland. 2003. "Lessons and Conclusions." In *Fiscal Decentralization and the Challenge of Hard Budget Constraints*, ed. Jonathan Rodden, Gunnar S. Eskeland, and Jennie Litvack, 431–466. Cambridge, Mass.: MIT Press.

Rose, Shanna. 2006. "Do Fiscal Rules Dampen the Political Business Cycle?" *Public Choice* 128: 407–431.

Rosen, Harvey S. 1992. *Public Finance*, 3d ed. Homewood, Ill.: Irwin.

Russakoff, Dale. 2003. "Ala. Voters Reject Tax Increase; Referendum Results Seen as Warning to Officials Nationwide." *Washington Post*, September 10, A02.

Schlozman, Kay Lehman, Sidney Verba, and Henry E. Brady. 1999. "Civic Participation and the Equality Problem." In *Civic Engagement in American Democracy*, ed. Theda Skocpol and Morris P. Fiorina, 427–460. Washington, D.C.: Brookings.

U.S. Census Bureau. 1992. *Government Finance and Employment Classification Manual.* www.census.gov/govs/www/class.html.

———. 2009. *2009 Annual Survey of State Government Finances.* www.census.gov/govs/state/.

———. 2011. *Statistical Abstract of the United States.* www.census.gov/compendia/statab/.

Walsh, Mary Williams. 2011. "Moody's to Factor Pension Gaps in States' Ratings." *New York Times*, January 27.

Weingast, Barry R., Kenneth A. Shepsle, and Christopher Johnsen. 1981. "The Political Economy of Benefits and Costs: A Neoclassical Approach to Distributive Politics." *Journal of Political Economy* 89: 642–664.

SUGGESTED READINGS

Print

Besley, Timothy, and Anne Case. "Political Institutions and Policy Choices: Evidence from the United States." *Journal of Economic Literature* 41 (2003): 7–73. Summarizes a large literature and presents findings on the effects of a variety of political institutions on fiscal outcomes for American states.

Brunori, David. *State Tax Policy: A Political Perspective*, 2d ed. Washington, D.C.: Urban Institute Press, 2005. A thorough and accessible discussion of different kinds of taxes and fees used by state governments and the political arguments for and against their use.

Matsusaka, John G. *For the Many or the Few: The Initiative, Public Policy, and American Democracy*. Chicago: University of Chicago Press, 2004. Analyzes the effects of voter initiatives on state fiscal scale throughout the twentieth century and presents data on preferences for taxes and spending drawn from opinion polls.

Primo, David M. *Rules and Restraint: Government Spending and the Design of Institutions*. Chicago: University of Chicago Press. 2007. Analyzes the effects of fiscal institutions on spending at both the state and federal levels. It emphasizes the need for enforcement mechanisms that are compatible with politicians' rational incentives.

Rodden, Johnathan, Gunnar S. Eskeland, and Jennie Litvack. *Fiscal Decentralization and the Challenge of Hard Budget Constraints*. Cambridge, Mass.: MIT Press, 2003. Contains chapters on the fiscal practices of subnational governments in the United States, Canada, Norway, Germany, Argentina, Brazil, India, China, South Africa, the Ukraine, and Hungary. It allows readers to place American state governments in a cross-national perspective.

Internet

Center on Budget and Policy Priorities. www.cbpp.org. Nonpartisan research organization with a particular focus on how policy decisions affect low- and moderate-income families and individuals. Areas of research include state budget and tax issues.

Federation of Tax Administrators. www.taxadmin.org. Comparisons of state tax systems and information on policy issues of common concern presented by an organization that provides services to tax collection agencies in the fifty states, Washington, D.C., New York City, and Puerto Rico.

National Association of State Budget Officers. www.nasbo.org. Access to annual surveys and state expenditure reports as well as news about issues concerning state fiscal policy provided by the professional organization for all state budget officers of the fifty states and U.S. territories.

Pew Center on the States. www.pewcenteronthestates.org. The Pew Center's "States' Fiscal Health Project" focuses on the problems faced by state governments in light of current economic conditions. Includes reports on future financial obligations stemming from underfunded employee benefits.

Tax Foundation. www.taxfoundation.org. Various measures of tax burdens and rankings for all fifty states provided by this nonpartisan tax research group that seeks to educate taxpayers about sound tax policy and the size of the tax burden.

CHAPTER 11

 State Health and Welfare Programs

MARK CARL ROM

The American states were mugged by the Great Recession of 2007–2009. Before the assault, states were flush, and perhaps even a little tipsy. During it, they needed additional care precisely when they could least afford it. Now, they remain seriously ill. They are slowly recovering, but their prognosis is uncertain. Meanwhile, there is a major new "doctor" in the house: President Barack Obama's Patient Protection and Affordable Care Act (ACA).

The ACA, if implemented, will dramatically alter the nation's health care landscape. Two elements of the ACA in particular will affect state policies (Center for Healthcare Research and Transformation 2011). The first substantially expands the Medicaid program by broadening eligibility to all poor individuals. The second directs the states to establish "health insurance exchanges" for individuals and small businesses. If the states choose not to do this, the federal government will do it for them.

It is a challenging time for state health and welfare programs and policies. This chapter focuses on the most important programs that deliver medical services and economic support to the needy, as well as state policies for health and welfare more generally. I attempt to answer several questions: What are the major health and welfare programs in the nation, and what roles do the states play in designing,

The author wishes to thanks to Mia Martinez and Rose Tutera-Baldauf for their able research assistance and Sabra Bissette Ledent for her skillful editing.

funding, and implementing them? What are the main patterns of the state programs over time and across the states regarding recipients, benefits, and expenditures? What are the states now doing to reform their health and welfare programs? What are the politics of these programs? What are the states doing to promote personal health and economic independence so that these medical and income support programs will be less necessary in the future? And how will the ACA affect them if it is upheld by the Supreme Court, which will ultimately rule on the law's constitutionality because of the numerous legal challenges to the law?

THE PROGRAMS

Social welfare programs transfer income or provide services to individuals to improve the quality of their lives. The vast majority of social welfare spending is not aimed specifically at those living in poverty. Social Security and Medicare are national programs that serve the elderly. State involvement is confined to public assistance (or **means-tested) programs.** State governments administer a broad variety of welfare programs, involving, for example, medical care, cash assistance, food, energy, housing, job training, and education. Much, but not all, welfare assistance is considered an entitlement: any person eligible for benefits can obtain them, and the government is obligated to provide the benefits necessary to fill all claims. In 2008 state and federal governments spent about $610 billion on public assistance programs (U.S. Census Bureau 2011, 350).

Medicaid

Medicaid provides medical care to low-income persons who are aged, blind, or disabled; to poor families with children; and to certain other pregnant women and children (for a summary of Medicaid eligibility, services, and financing, see Klees, Wolfe, and Curtis 2010). The federal and state governments share responsibility for Medicaid. The federal government establishes program guidelines on eligibility, services, and financing, and state governments design and administer the program. The federal and state governments split the cost of the program based on the federally established matching rate that requires the more affluent states to pay a higher share of the cost.

The federal government requires states to provide a broad list of Medicaid-covered medical services, including inpatient and outpatient hospital services as well as physicians' services, to the **categorically needy.** States are permitted to offer additional services, such as medications, eyeglasses, or psychiatric care, and to place limits on recipients' use of the services.

Until 2014, when the Affordable Care Act is scheduled to expand program eligibility, Medicaid will not provide medical assistance to all those in poverty. Beginning in 2014, all individuals under age sixty-five living in families with incomes below 138 percent of the "family poverty line" become eligible for Medicaid if the ACA is fully implemented. Until then, all states must provide Medicaid to individuals in "categorically needy" groups—for example, those eligible for Supplemental Security Income (SSI)—although the states have broad discretion to determine who is eligible to receive Medicaid services. States can also provide coverage to those **"medically needy"** individuals who have extensive health needs but who do not quite fall within the administrative definition of "poor." As of 2008, thirty-four states (and the District of Columbia) offered at least some services to the medically needy (Klees, Wolfe, and Curtis 2010, 24). States are required to provide more extensive services to the categorically needy than to the medically needy.

Medicaid does not have its own team of doctors. Instead, states reimburse private health care providers who deliver services to Medicaid recipients. States decide, within federal guidelines, the reimbursement rates. The states are required to set reimbursement rates high enough so that Medicaid services will actually be available to recipients, at least to the extent that health care services are available to other residents in the state. Health care providers cannot charge Medicaid patients additional fees above these amounts.

Medicaid is the King Kong of state welfare programs: it alone accounts for about 60 percent of public assistance spending. In 2010 Medicaid served over 60 million individuals at a cost to the states of some $150 billion (National Association of State Budget Officers 2011, 43), which was about a third of the program's total cost. Medicaid consumed about 22 percent of all state spending in that year, and for many states it was the largest single budget item (National Association of State Budget Officers 2011, 43).

Temporary Assistance for Needy Families

The Temporary Assistance for Needy Families (TANF) program aspires to improve the economic conditions of poor families and reduce their dependence on government by promoting work, encouraging marriage, and reducing out-of-wedlock pregnancies.[1] Created in 1996, TANF replaced the Aid to Families with Dependent Children (AFDC) program, fulfilling President Bill Clinton's promise to "end welfare as we know it." Although established by the federal government, TANF gives the states substantial authority to determine who is eligible, what obligations they face, and what benefits they receive, as well as how the program will be designed, implemented, and evaluated.

Unlike Medicaid, TANF is not an entitlement program; states can deny benefits to any family or category of poor family—and some have done so with gusto. Each year the federal government gives each state a block of funds to pay for the program, based on a federal formula. The states are required to spend at least 80 percent as

---

1. For a summary, see Office of Family Assistance, "Temporary Assistance for Needy Families: Eighth Annual Report to Congress," U.S. Department of Health and Human Services, Administration for Children and Families, www.acf.hhs.gov/programs/ofa/data-reports/annualreport8/chapter00/chap00.htm.

much as they did for AFDC in 1994. If they impose effective work requirements, they need spend only 75 percent as much. The states can—and do—use a substantial portion of their TANF funds for purposes other than providing cash benefits.

When TANF was reauthorized by the federal government in 2006, the federal government agreed to provide the states with $16.6 billion a year between 2006 and 2010, implying that the "real" federal support for this program would decline at the pace of inflation. The American Recovery and Reinvestment Act of 2009 (better known as the "Stimulus Bill") provided an additional $5 billion for 2009–2010. Perhaps because assistance provided through TANF was already low, few states (California, Florida, and Hawaii) cut benefits further during the recession (National Association of State Budget Officers 2010, 11).

Supplemental Security Income

The SSI program provides cash payments to elderly, blind, and disabled persons who are also poor (for a summary, see Social Security Administration 2010b). Maximum SSI benefits are available to those persons who are without other resources. Benefits are reduced as a recipient's earned income rises, or if the recipient is living with another person.

SSI is the second-largest state-supported cash assistance program, but it is mainly a federal program. The federal government establishes eligibility requirements, sets national benefit levels, and administers the program; states have the option of supplementing the **federal benefit standard.** All but six states—Arkansas, Arizona, Mississippi, North Dakota, Tennessee, and West Virginia—provide some form of supplemental benefits, although typical benefits are quite small (Social Security Administration 2011). The federal government pays for federal benefits and administration; the state governments fund the supplemental benefits and their administrative costs. Federal SSI benefits are indexed to inflation, so recipients receive the same cost-of-living adjustments as do Social Security beneficiaries; as with TANF, state benefits are not indexed.

THE POLITICS

In 2009 the Medicaid, TANF, and SSI programs together spent approximately $450 billion to assist some 50 million recipients (Social Security Administration 2010a, 16).[2] These programs are a complex mix of federal and state designs, funds, and administration. What factors influence the programmatic mix? Economic and demographic attributes are certainly important, but political factors ultimately dominate. The reasons for this are clear. Economic and demographic conditions provide policymakers with opportunities and constraints, but these conditions do

2. Also see Kaiser Family Foundation, "Total Medicaid Spending," www.statehealthfacts.org/comparetable.jsp?ind=177&cat=4&sub=47&yr=90&typ=4&sort=a; Center for Budget and Policy Priorities, "TANF Spending Factsheet," http://npc.umich.edu/news/events/safetynet/tanf-spending-factsheet.pdf.

not by themselves make policies; politicians do. Politicians make program decisions based on their electoral concerns, their ideological beliefs, and their pragmatic judgments about what is best for their constituents, state, and country.

Federalism

The United States is a federalist country. Authority over health and welfare policy is shared—not always agreeably—among the state and national governments. This sharing has three main implications for state policies. First, states do not have sole jurisdiction over health and welfare policy because they are constrained by national laws. Second, the state and federal governments often attempt to gain control over health and welfare programs and shift burdens to the other party. Efforts toward control take the form of federal mandates, which require the states to perform certain functions and obtain waivers whenever they want to establish their own standards. For their part, states are often tempted to play these programs in order to obtain the maximum federal financial support at minimum cost to themselves.

Third, state governments compete, and at times cooperate, with each other. Some of the competition is political, as ambitious politicians strive to build their national reputations by developing innovative programs to address social problems. The competition can also be economic, as politicians seek to make their states more attractive for businesses and workers and less attractive to the poor who consume welfare dollars. Political and economic competition can lead in different directions; politicians have reasons for making their states distinctive but not so distinctive that they scare away economic resources. Politicians do not want their states to become "welfare magnets."

Internal Politics

State policy choices are also influenced by political, economic, and demographic factors that vary across states and over time. The political cultures, ideologies, institutions, and public opinions of states all affect their health and welfare policies (Rom 2012b). The economic conditions of the states, their wealth, and the sources of it can influence state politicians as they choose among policies. The states also differ in the age of their populations, the composition of their families, and the ethnicity of their citizens, each with potential significance for their policies.

Political culture affects policy choices, as Chapter 1 explained. In moralist political cultures, "both the general public and the politicians conceive of politics as a public activity centered on some notion of the public good and properly devoted to the advancement of the public interest" (Elazar 1970, 174). By contrast, traditionalist political cultures view politics as a way of preserving the status quo, and individualist political cultures view it as a way of gaining personal enrichment. Moralist political cultures tend to be more activist and generous in their health and welfare programs than traditionalist or individualist ones. A state's political culture changes only slowly, and so it is the most stable of the political variables.

Political ideology involves the durable views of politicians about what the government should do and how it should do it. Americans tend to have conservative or liberal ideologies about health and welfare programs; liberals are generally in favor of expanded benefits and more inclusive eligibility standards, and conservatives typically prefer more restrictive benefits and eligibility. Political culture is related to, but by no means identical to, political ideology (Erikson, Wright, and McIver 1993, 150–176). Moralist states are not necessarily liberal, nor are individualist states invariably conservative, although traditionalist states almost always are conservative. Political conservatives in moralist states might believe that governments best help the poor by making welfare difficult to obtain; liberals in individualist states might seek to increase welfare spending merely to enhance their own political fortunes.

The political institutions of American governments—their legislatures, bureaucracies, political parties, interest groups, electoral systems—can also influence health and welfare policies. In general, governments with professional legislatures and competent bureaucracies are more active in developing programs and openhanded in supporting them. Interest groups are more involved, and more influential, in some states than in others and in some issues than others (Gray et al. 2004). States with more highly mobilized publics and more competitive elections may also be more likely to support social welfare programs (Rom 2012b).

Policymakers pay attention to public opinion, and these opinions vary across the states, over time, and among health and welfare issues (Berry et al. 1998). The citizens of Minnesota and Mississippi, for example, have different opinions about the appropriate role of their governments in social policy, and those state policies in part reflect these opinions. Still, the sentiments of the nation as a whole also change over the years, with the public looking more favorably on welfare recipients in the 1960s than more recently. The American public also appears to be more sympathetic to programs that provide goods and services (such as food and health care) to the poor instead of cash. Certain types of recipients are more politically popular. The "deserving poor" (the disabled, children, and the elderly, for example) are viewed sympathetically and provided greater governmental support, whereas the "undeserving poor" (such as young men and women bearing children out of wedlock) are scorned by the public (Katz 1986). Public approval of programs that promote work is much stronger than of programs that do not help the poor help themselves.

Interest groups are also active in welfare and especially health politics (Gray et al. 2009). Medical providers have an interest in how health programs are designed, administered, and financed. Certain types of patients—particularly the elderly and disabled—have organizations that routinely promote their claims (but welfare mothers usually do not). Interest groups are less involved in income assistance programs, where the main actors are typically welfare officials, charities, and religious organizations.

Economic and Demographic Factors

Social welfare policies intend to address economic conditions, but the policies are also influenced by the conditions they hope to alter. The principal economic factors influencing health and welfare policies are both cyclical (like the seasons) and structural (like the climate). As for the cyclical, when the economy goes into recession, more people become poor, the number of people eligible for welfare programs increases, and program costs rise. When the economy is growing, fewer people are eligible for benefits and so program costs fall. Structural shifts, such as the transition from an economy based on labor to one driven by technology, are usually slower to occur and longer lasting. The economic and demographic structure of the population establishes the durable conditions in which social welfare programs operate.

Figure 11-1 compares state poverty rates in 1999 and 2009. Poverty rates vary substantially across states, with the rate in New Mexico twice that of Utah, for example. Only five lucky states had lower poverty rates in 2009 than in 1999. In the least fortunate states—such as Arizona, Indiana, and South Dakota—poverty rates soared. Even though poverty rates grew among the states and across racial groups, family types, and ages (except the elderly), the median family income was actually higher in the United States in 2009 than in 1999. Therefore, the higher poverty rates do not reflect a poorer country, but one with more families living in poverty.

The economic and demographic characteristics of the states provide the context for politicians. Richer states have more resources to devote to health and welfare programs, if they wish to do so. States with more favorable demographics have fewer welfare needs. Those in the greatest need of help—the young, minorities, female-headed families—are also likely to have the least political power. Ultimately, neither resources nor needs determine what policies will be chosen; policymakers do.

Interstate Competition

The states are politically independent of each other, and yet they are all part of a nationwide economic and political system. State politicians seeking to develop a national reputation therefore have incentives to conduct bold policy experiments. When running for president, Bill Clinton of Arkansas and George W. Bush of Texas pointed to the educational reforms they had pioneered as the governors of their states. If innovations prove successful or otherwise attractive politically, other states often imitate them. This pattern of state innovation and diffusion is well recognized in American politics (Walker 1969).

States also engage in economic competition with each other in the finance, commerce, and labor arenas. Politicians find it far easier to run for reelection if they can boast that under their direction their state has a booming economy and low taxes. This interstate economic competition has convinced some scholars that states are ill-suited to direct welfare programs (Peterson 1995). The logic behind

Figure 11-1   Poverty Rates in the American States, 1999 and 2009 (in percentages)

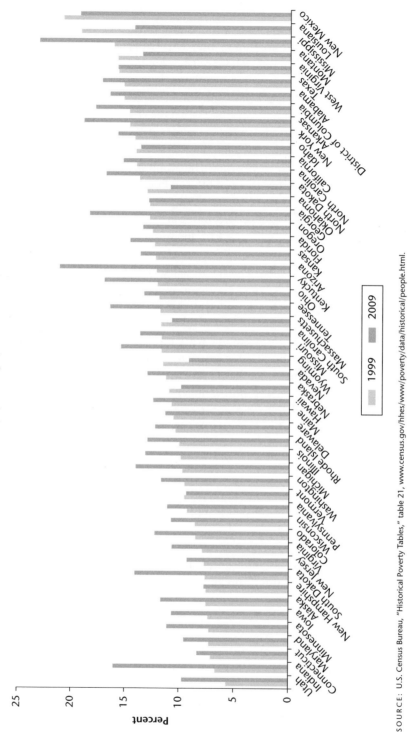

SOURCE: U.S. Census Bureau, "Historical Poverty Tables," table 21, www.census.gov/hhes/www/poverty/data/historical/people.html.

this claim is simple. Individuals, whether citizens or politicians, are assumed to act in their own self-interest. If a state offers generous health and welfare benefits, it will become a **welfare magnet,** attracting the poor who need benefits and repelling the affluent who pay the taxes to support them. Politicians thus have incentives to prevent their states from becoming welfare magnets; in fact, states have incentives to provide welfare programs that are less generous than the programs of their neighbors. If each state acts the same way, welfare benefits would become increasingly stingy and welfare eligibility increasingly stringent as states "race to the bottom." There is solid evidence that interstate competition has restricted state welfare generosity (Rom 2012b).

It is worth remembering that state policy choices are far more complicated than a simple tallying of economic, demographic, and political forces would suggest. Policies vary among the states for unique historical reasons. An unusually forceful leader, a public scandal, a temporary surge in public opinion can all have lasting effects on policy choice, not only for the individual states but also for the nation. Massachusetts governor Mitt Romney approved the universal health care insurance program that would become the model for President Obama's Patient Protection and Affordable Care Act. Vermont governor Peter Shumlin campaigned on a promise to create a "single-payer" health care system for the state—and he succeeded. As Shumlin put it, "We want to figure this one out and get it right. Then we hope that perhaps that others will follow" (NPR 2011).

THE PATTERNS

Turning to the patterns—and the anomalies—in health and welfare policies, this section examines the broad trends since 1980 in recipients and expenditures for Medicaid, TANF, and SSI.

Trends in Number of Recipients

The welfare caseloads between 1980 and 2010 are shown in Figure 11-2. Each program has a different trajectory. Medicaid has grown, and grown, and grown still further, increasing by over 40 million people in thirty years. Increases during the 2000s reflect the rising number of Americans without private insurance, the growing poverty rates, and the expansion of Medicaid eligibility. If the ACA is fully implemented, Medicaid enrollments are expected to grow by another 20 million by 2019 (Foster 2011). AFDC, by contrast, was stable during the 1980s before undergoing what seemed to be alarming growth in the early 1990s, which helped trigger the 1996 reforms that ended the program. After TANF was created in 1996, the number of recipients fell by more than two-thirds before edging up during the recession. SSI caseloads, by contrast, have grown slowly over the entire period.

These trends—strong growth in Medicaid rolls, decline in TANF, and stability in SSI—are important for state politics and policy. These trends are not linked solely to economic or demographic changes. They do reflect the clear preference of state

Figure 11-2 Welfare Recipients, by Program, 1980–2010

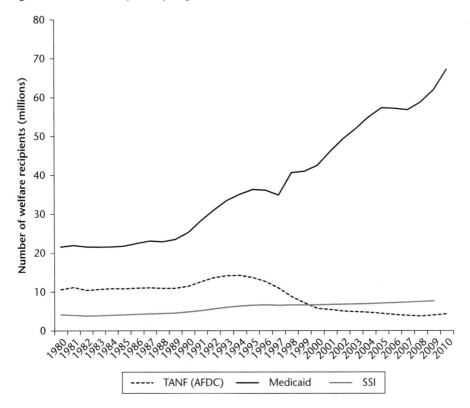

SOURCES: AFDC/TANF: Administration for Children and Families, "Data & Reports," www.acf.hhs.gov/programs/ofa/data-reports/index.htm. Medicaid: Center for Medicare and Medicaid Services, "Medicare and Medicaid Statistical Supplement," table 13.4, www.cms.gov/MedicareMedicaidStatSupp/LT/itemdetail.asp?filterType=dual,%20keyword&filterValue=2010&filterByDID=0&sortByDID=1&sortOrder=ascending&itemID=CMS1248022&intNumPerPage=10; 2009–2011 estimates from Vernon K. Smith, Kathleen Gifford, Eileen Ellis, Robin Rudowitz, and Laura Snyder, "Hoping for Economic Recovery, Preparing for Health Reform: A Look at Medicaid Spending, Coverage, and Policy Trends," Kaiser Commission on Medicaid and the Uninsured, 2010, 31, www.kff.org/medicaid/upload/8105.pdf. SSI: 1980–1989: U.S. House of Representatives, Committee on Ways and Means, *The Green Book 2000*, table 3.19; 1990–2000: U.S. Social Security Administration, "Annual Statistical Supplement 2001, SSI," www.ssa.gov/policy/docs/statcomps/supplement/2001/7a.pdf; 2000–2009: U.S. Social Security Administration, Office of Retirement and Disability Policy, "Annual Statistical Supplement 2010," table 7A.3, www.ssa.gov/policy/docs/statcomps/supplement/2010/7a.html#table7.a3.

and national politicians for providing medical care to the elderly, disabled, and children who are poor, while withholding income support from impoverished, able-bodied adults, who presumably should not have to rely on the government for support.

Trends in Expenditures

Program spending trends have closely paralleled those for recipients: Medicaid has soared, TANF has shrunk, and SSI has grown modestly. In 2010 total spending for Medicaid was about $366 billion, with the states paying about one-third of the total; by contrast, total TANF spending was a mere $31 billion, with the states paying almost exactly half. SSI was larger than TANF at about $50 billion, but only a modest slice (less than $5 billion) of this comes from state coffers (Social Security Administration 2011). In real dollars, the states spend substantially less on TANF and SSI today than they did during the 1970s, and vastly more on Medicaid. Increasingly, welfare spending *is* health care spending.

As TANF spending has declined, its purposes have changed. Under AFDC, most spending was for cash assistance, with the remainder covering administration and other services. But only about 35 percent of the $31 billion that state and federal governments spent on TANF programs in 2009 went toward cash benefits, with the other 65 percent going toward a wide variety of other purposes, including work-related activities, child care, and transportation (Administration for Children and Families 2010).

The ACA, if implemented, will have an enormous impact on Medicaid. It is predicted that between 2014 and 2019 the ACA will add a total of $455 billion in additional Medicaid spending *above* what would otherwise be expected. Of that amount, 91 percent would be picked up by the federal government because of the higher federal matching rate for newly eligible enrollees (Centers for Medicare and Medicaid Services 2010, iv). Overall, Medicaid spending is expected to more than double, reaching $840 billion in 2019.

State Welfare Benefits and Recipients

The national trends, then, are diverging recipient populations and program expenditures, with Medicaid growing rapidly, SSI growing slowly, and TANF generally shrinking. These trends have not affected all states equally, nor have all states responded in the same way to the changing times.

Benefits. It is difficult to report state welfare benefits succinctly because welfare recipients have different needs and states offer different services. Thus each state has a different mix of recipients joining and leaving the rolls at various times. For example, the elderly and disabled account for only 25 percent of the Medicaid caseload nationally (Smith et al. 2010, 12), but they account for over two-thirds of Medicaid spending. States with higher proportions of persons in these categories will therefore have higher costs than other states, all else being equal. In addition, states vary in how—and how well—they administer their welfare programs, and such variation influences administrative costs per recipient.

Figure 11-3 shows the average annual payments in 2008 to all Medicaid recipients by state, ranked in declining order, as well as the average payments to disabled recipients, who are, as noted earlier, the most expensive category of recipients individually as well as overall. The average annual state Medicaid benefits per recipient in 2008 were $5,051. New York, the state with the highest spending per recipient ($9,000), spent three times as much as the lowest state, Wisconsin ($3,000). State Medicaid spending on the disabled is even more variable, with per

Figure 11-3 Annual Medicaid Benefits per Person, by State, for All Recipients and Disabled Recipients, 2008

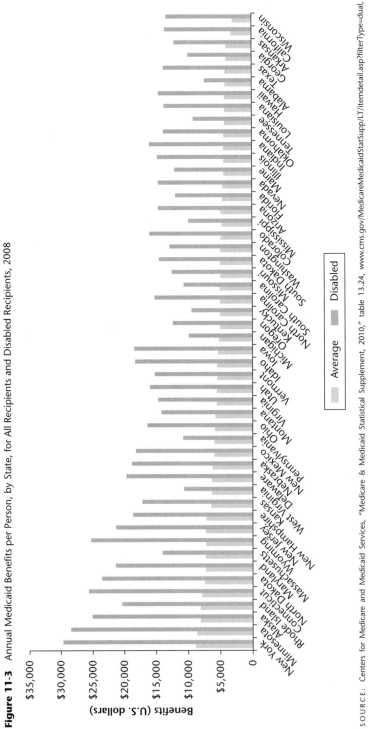

SOURCE: Centers for Medicare and Medicaid Services, "Medicare & Medicaid Statistical Supplement, 2010," table 13.24, www.cms.gov/MedicareMedicaidStatSupp/LT/itemdetail.asp?filterType=dual,%20keyword&filterValue=2010&filterByDID=0&sortOrder=ascending&itemID=CMS1248022&intNumPerPage=10.

recipient spending more than four times higher in New York ($30,000 a year) than in Alabama ($7,400). These differences are much greater than the variation in the cost of living across the states, and they indicate real distinctions in how the states treat their low-income residents. Higher spending on medical care does not invariably translate into better care, of course, but it is reasonable to suspect that when spending levels are too low, care also suffers.

For TANF, forty-three states spend more on noncash assistance than on cash benefits, especially in the most generous states: the top ten spend an average of less than 20 percent of TANF funds on cash benefits. The most generous state—Illinois—spent nearly $20,000 per recipient in 2008, of which only $1,200 was in the form of cash assistance. The least generous state—Tennessee—spent about $2,200 per recipient, evenly divided between cash and noncash assistance. A TANF recipient in Arkansas would on average receive a check for about $75 a month. That amount would not go far, even in Arkansas.

Historically, there has been a modestly strong relationship between state generosity in Medicaid and TANF: if a state had relatively high expenditures in one program, it was likely to be more generous in the other as well. As Medicaid and TANF have become increasingly separated programmatically, however, they have also become more disassociated in terms of their generosity. By 2009 state TANF expenditures and Medicaid benefits were almost entirely unrelated (the correlation coefficient was 0.07). For example, Wisconsin has the lowest per recipient Medicaid spending and the sixth highest TANF expenditures per recipient, whereas Rhode Island has the fourth highest Medicaid spending and only the thirty-third highest TANF expenditures.

More affluent states generally support more generous social welfare programs than their poorer peers (the correlation coefficient between per capita income and Medicaid benefits is 0.57 and between income and TANF spending is 0.39). The relationship between prosperity and generosity does not hold in every state, however. Virginia is fairly affluent (seventh highest income) and nevertheless stingy in its TANF expenditures (fortieth); West Virginia is poor (next to last in per capita income), but is willing to spend on health care (thirteenth highest Medicaid expenditures). Perhaps surprisingly, welfare generosity is more closely tied to economic affluence than to political ideology. The correlations between "state government ideology" (as defined by Berry et al. 2010) and Medicaid and TANF benefits are 0.24 and 0.19, respectively.

Virtually every state enacted measures to control Medicaid spending during the recession. A record number of states—twenty in 2010 alone—trimmed Medicaid benefits. For example, Arizona, California, Hawaii, and Massachusetts ceased offering some or all adult dental services (Smith et al. 2010, 7). Even more states cut providers' (such as physicians) reimbursement rates. Even though cutting the amount that Medicaid pays to providers does allow states to save money in the short run, it also threatens the ability of states to ensure that enough providers will offer Medicaid services. If the rates fall too low, providers may refuse new patients or cease to participate entirely.

Recipients. A few broad patterns can be identified in Medicaid and TANF case-loads across states and over time. First, between 2003 and 2009 Medicaid popula-tions were vastly bigger than TANF caseloads in *every state:* the narrowest gap was in Nevada, where less than 1 percent of residents were enrolled in TANF and almost 10 percent were on the Medicaid rolls in 2009. Second, despite large differences in the rates of change across states and among programs, most states had growing Medicaid caseloads and falling TANF caseloads. On average, 18.5 percent of state residents received Medicaid during 2009 compared with 17.9 percent in 2003. In 2009 the state with the proportionately (and absolutely) largest Medicaid popula-tion was California, where almost 30 percent of the residents received Medicaid services at some point during that year. The state with the smallest caseload was Nevada, with just under 10 percent of Nevadans receiving Medicaid benefits. The increase in Medicaid caseloads was not spread evenly across the states, however; eighteen states saw declining caseloads between 2003 and 2009, although the declines were generally modest. A few states (Iowa, Massachusetts, Michigan, and Pennsylvania) had increases of over 20 percent in their Medicaid populations. TANF caseloads fell 25 percent, from an average of 1.6 percent to 1.2 percent, on top of the one-third caseload decline experienced from 1998 to 2003.

The relationship between program generosity and caseload might seem obvious: states with higher benefits would have relatively larger caseloads both because more people would be eligible for benefits and because benefits would be more desirable to obtain. But this is definitely not the case, at least for TANF. There is a fairly strong negative correlation (–0.41) between TANF expenditures per recipient and the relative size of the caseload. With a fixed budget, the response to larger case-loads must by definition be lower average expenditures, and vice versa. In the old days, caseloads drove spending. Today, policy drives caseloads, and spending runs on autopilot.

Medicaid caseloads and expenditures are mildly and negatively correlated (–0.20): states that have relatively large Medicaid populations have somewhat lower per recipient expenditures than states with smaller caseloads. The most extreme example is California, which has the largest Medicaid population and the lowest per recipient expenditures. As usual, there are exceptions to the pattern; New York has the most expensive Medicaid program per recipient, and it also has the second largest caseload overall.

HEALTH CARE REFORM

During the 1960s and 1970s, the federal government was the leading innovator in welfare policy; more recently states have been in the vanguard. State health care reform proposals are usually built around three goals: (1) controlling costs, both for the state's citizens and for the state itself; (2) providing access so that the health care needs of citizens are met; and (3) providing high-quality care, but this goal, while important, is more controversial and difficult to define.

To accomplish these goals, state policymakers have focused on three types of reforms: (1) expanding insurance coverage for children and other vulnerable populations; (2) making insurance more affordable and available to individuals and the small-business community; and (3) controlling short-term and long-term health care costs. This section examines the bold health insurance reforms in Massachusetts and Vermont, Medicaid managed care, and insurance for children. It concludes with a discussion of state efforts to develop the health insurance exchanges mandated by the ACA.

Universal Health Care Coverage in Massachusetts

Massachusetts led the way in health insurance innovation when in 2006 it enacted legislation to provide nearly universal insurance. The law requires all individuals to purchase health insurance or face stiff tax penalties. Businesses with ten or more employees must offer health insurance or pay a "fair share" contribution to help workers buy insurance on their own. To help low-income individuals obtain insurance, Massachusetts expanded Medicaid eligibility and established the Commonwealth Care Health Insurance Program, which provides sliding-scale subsidies to individuals earning less than 300 percent of the poverty line, with poor individuals paying no premiums at all.

By 2010 over 98 percent of Massachusetts residents were covered by health insurance, by far the highest coverage rate in the country. Access to health care had improved and so had affordability, although one-fifth of survey respondents reported problems finding a doctor who would see them or paying their medical bills.

Still, health care in Massachusetts remains too costly. In response, Gov. Deval Patrick has proposed a new plan to control costs and transform the medical payment system by creating "accountable care organizations" that would reward doctors for how healthy they keep their patients, not how much service they provide (Salsberg 2011). Despite concerns over cost, the Massachusetts program retains broad support, with about two-thirds of the public supporting the reforms, most employers believing the reforms were good for the state, and the vast majority of doctors concurring that the program had improved (or did not harm) the quality of care (Blue Cross Blue Shield of Massachusetts Foundation 2011, 3).

"Single-Payer" Health Care Reform in Vermont

In 2011 Vermont took a big step toward becoming the first state to adopt a "single-payer" health care system when Gov. Peter Shumlin signed a health reform law with overwhelming support in the state legislature. The law calls for establishing Green Mountain Care (GMC), the government-run insurer that will cover all residents. The program will provide all Vermonters—the state hopes—with comprehensive, affordable, high-quality, publicly financed health care coverage. Green Mountain will pay providers a fixed sum to care for a specific population, giving them incentives to favor preventive care and control costs. The Green Mountain Care board, composed of five governor-appointed and Senate-confirmed members, will oversee GMC's payment and delivery system in order to provide quality care and to control its costs (Teague 2011).

The law will not be phased in until at least 2014, and two barriers must be surmounted for the program to become operational. First, Vermont must obtain waivers from the federal government to create Green Mountain Care and the single-payer system. And second, the state must develop a plan to finance the system, which would involve a combination of public and private money.

Progress toward implementation depends on Vermont's political environment. Most private insurers will oppose implementation; after all, the plan could put them out of business in that state. Fortunately for Vermont, its largest health insurer, Blue Cross/Blue Shield, supports the plan because it is poised to administer the payments system (Klein 2011). Because businesses that already provide health insurance would have to pay into the system, they might find the taxes too high and drop coverage or consider moving elsewhere. Pharmaceutical companies, which are not favored by the plan, are sure to dispatch their lobbyists to stall, change, or eliminate it.

Medicaid Managed Care

Initially, Medicaid was a **fee-for-service program**: medical providers were simply reimbursed for their services. States established reimbursement rates, and medical providers were required to accept the reimbursements as payment in full for their services. But this system did not please providers, who believed the rates were too low; nor did it guarantee access to care for Medicaid recipients, who often found it hard to obtain services. Under the system, total costs grew rapidly as providers sought higher payments and recipients sought more care.

Such fee-for-service problems, also experienced by private insurers, led insurance firms to experiment with **managed care programs.** One important element in many programs is that they are **capitated**—that is, the program receives a fixed amount of money per enrolled person to provide a set of services. If the program spends less than this amount per patient, it runs a surplus; if it spends more, it incurs a loss. This situation creates incentives for programs to reduce costs by delivering care efficiently; by minimizing unnecessary care; and, many fear, by withholding appropriate care.

Managed care programs now dominate both the private and public health insurance markets, with over 90 percent of those with private insurance and 70 percent of those with Medicaid in managed care (Kaiser Family Foundation 2010a, 1). Only the two most rural states, Alaska and Wyoming, lack managed care programs.

Two trends in Medicaid managed care are worth noting. First, private managed care organizations are playing a diminishing role as recipients increasingly enroll in Medicaid-only or Medicaid-dominated organizations. Second, many states now offer (or mandate) Medicaid managed care programs for more complex populations than "regular" families and children, such as those with "disabilities and chronic illnesses, persons with HIV/AIDS, and 'dual eligibles'—low income seniors and severely disabled individuals who are covered by both Medicare and Medicaid" (Kaiser Family Foundation 2010a, 3–4). To serve these more complex populations, states are now seeking innovative ways in which to coordinate and manage care (see Kaiser Family Foundation 2010a, 4–5).

State Children's Health Insurance Program

Based in part on state experiments, the federal government created the Children's Health Insurance Program (CHIP) in 1997 to help states create or expand programs providing medical care to children in moderately poor families. At that time, about one-quarter of the nation's poor children lacked health insurance. With CHIP, the vast majority now have it, and those who do not are often eligible but not yet enrolled. Initially, the federal government provided funding to the states based on each state's proportion of the nation's poor and uninsured children. The states provided matching funds, at a lower rate than for Medicaid, and administered CHIP. The states can use federal funds to expand Medicaid to include CHIP, to create a separate CHIP program, or both. Today, the states pick up about 30 percent of the tab for CHIP, with the federal government providing the rest.

Unlike Medicaid, CHIP is not an entitlement program. Instead, the federal government provides each state with a block grant that it can spend at its discretion, within federal guidelines. For example, the states can require cost-sharing for CHIP services—that is, families participating in CHIP may have to pay for services, although seventeen states have chosen not to use this option—and limit benefits in ways that are not allowable in Medicaid. If CHIP spending is higher than states have budgeted, they can establish waiting lists for the program or otherwise limit enrollment.

Congress encouraged the states to expand CHIP eligibility and simplify enrollment when it reauthorized CHIP in 2009 (Kaiser Family Foundation 2009a). Federal funding for the program was substantially increased, relying on the federal cigarette tax as the main source of the necessary revenue. Meanwhile, the states' block grants were altered to reflect how much they actually were spending or were expected to spend in the future. The reauthorized CHIP was expected to provide an additional 6.5 million children with health insurance coverage (Kaiser Family Foundation 2009a).

States are using their discretion to design an assortment of CHIPs. Eleven states have incorporated CHIP into their existing Medicaid programs, while the other thirty-nine states have created separate programs. It appears, however, that the states with combined programs have had somewhat better outcomes.[3] States also have broad flexibility on setting eligibility standards. Forty-seven states cover children from families with incomes at 200 percent of the federal poverty level or higher; twenty-five states children in families with incomes up to 250 percent of the poverty level or higher; and sixteen states children in families with incomes up to 300 percent of the poverty level or higher. States can, at their discretion, cover "lawfully-residing immigrant children"—that is, children who were born in the United States to undocumented workers—without imposing a five-year waiting period. By 2011 twenty-one states had opted to provide coverage to such children, and seventeen states were providing coverage to lawfully residing pregnant immigrants.[4]

State Health Insurance Exchanges

The ACA requires each state to have in place by 2014 a "health insurance exchange" that would serve as an "Expedia" for residents shopping for health insurance. The states can design their own exchanges either individually or in groups. If they choose not to develop exchanges, the federal government will do it for them.

The exchanges have several purposes (Kaiser Family Foundation 2009b). First, they present consumers with a choice of private health insurance plans from an approved list so that the plans can be compared by price and benefits. To promote this function, exchanges would be structured so that services and costs are standardized, thereby making the comparisons easier and limiting the ability of insurance companies to vary benefits in order to attract healthier (and lower-cost) enrollees. Consumers would also receive information on performance measures of the various insurance plans. Second, the exchanges would facilitate enrollment by providing information and assistance on eligibility and subsidies. Third, the exchanges would help make insurance more portable, enabling consumers to maintain their insurance as they move from job to job or between Medicaid and subsidized private insurance for those with low and variable incomes. And fourth, the exchanges would help the states reform their insurance markets by, for example, determining how much insurance premiums and coverage can vary.

Most states are moving toward creating exchanges. By June 2011, thirty-two states had introduced legislation to establish exchanges, and at least six other states appeared headed in that direction. Ten states had already enacted legislation establishing exchanges, with California leading the way when it approved the idea in the fall of 2010. Only one state (Louisiana) had officially rejected the notion of creating an exchange, whereas Massachusetts has already established one (Center for Budget and Policy Priorities 2011, 1–3).

---

3. Georgetown University Health Policy Institute, "Coordinating Medicaid and CHIP," http://ccf .georgetown.edu/index/background-coordinating.

4. Georgetown University Health Policy Institute, "Medicaid and CHIP Programs," http://ccf .georgetown.edu/index/medicaid-and-schip-programs.

As they take steps toward establishing exchanges, states will consider the political and policy opportunities and challenges. Exchanges give states an opportunity to maintain regulatory authority over the health insurance market; coordinate eligibility rules and benefits across Medicaid, CHIP, and the exchanges; mitigate risk selection among the insurance policies offered within and outside the exchange; and promote the state's reform priorities. The challenges are to create a new program at a time of great fiscal stress, ensure that the exchange is "self-sustaining" by 2015 as required by the ACA, and hold administrative costs down while satisfying voter demands for good service (Carey 2010, 2).

States will continue to confront two core problems: caring for the ill and controlling costs. Even during the recession, many states expanded Medicaid eligibility or simplified enrollment procedures. Despite enormous budget pressures, forty-one states expanded Medicaid in 2010. Although most expansions were quite modest, some states (such as Colorado and Wisconsin) adopted broader reforms, and Connecticut decided to enroll childless adults ahead of the ACA requirement that they do so by 2014 (Smith et al. 2010, 7). Still, the states are likely to remain under heavy stress from Medicaid in the coming years. As the expanded federal support for Medicaid ends in 2011, it is expected that state Medicaid spending will grow as much as 25 percent in 2012, even though state revenues are still at pre-recession levels (Smith et al. 2010, 9). If the states have to expand their Medicaid programs further, as required by the ACA, the budgetary pressures will intensify.

PREVENTION

Health and welfare programs provide care to the sick and assistance to the poor. But they do relatively little to prevent individuals from becoming sick or needing public assistance. U.S. health and welfare programs emphasize treatment rather than prevention.

From a policy perspective, this approach makes little sense, but from a political perspective there are good reasons to emphasize treatment over prevention. Policymakers usually face a situation in which people need immediate assistance and there is not enough money to help them with their needs and at the same time prevent others from requiring the same assistance later. As demands for treatment are almost always louder than requests for prevention, the former is politically favored over the latter. Yet the maxim is true: a dime of prevention is worth a dollar of cure. It is cheaper to stay well than to become healed, to stay out of poverty than to get out of it.

State health and welfare policies have, to their credit, tilted somewhat more to prevention in recent years. Medicaid managed care has a better chance to emphasize wellness programs such as prenatal care, well baby care, and routine screenings, among others, than did the traditional Medicaid. The ACA requires insurance companies to provide recommended preventive care free and, to the extent that state exchanges actually enroll individuals in insurance, more people will have access to this care. As a matter of policy, however, the federal and state governments typically spend far more on treatment than prevention, at least on matters of public health: spending on prevention has never reached 10 percent of overall health expenditures (Miller et al. 2008).

Even when both political parties are committed to prevention they may have strong differences about what real prevention is. Liberals generally view prevention as a set of positive incentives offered by the government—that is, programs must provide education or services so that citizens can become physically strong and economically self-sufficient. Conservatives usually reject this view, placing responsibility for physical and economic health more squarely on the individual citizens. Government, from the conservative perspective, mainly creates incentives for persons to become dependent and diseased by providing welfare and health benefits in the first place. Accordingly, government practices prevention best by ensuring that individuals bear the consequences of their own actions.

All this said, it is worth considering: Why do people become ill and in need of medical care? Although the answers no doubt involve social and even metaphysical elements, I will focus on behavioral answers: people need medical treatment in part because of the way they behave. Behavior is in turn affected by social forces, genetic endowments, personal choices, and public policies. State efforts at prevention therefore need to address behaviors.

Behavioral factors are largely responsible for about half of all premature deaths each year. Almost two decades ago, researchers demonstrated that three big factors—tobacco use, obesity and lack of exercise, and abuse of alcohol—caused about 40 percent of all deaths and 75 percent of premature deaths in the United States. The other major factors—preventable microbial or toxic agents, firearms, sexual behavior, motor vehicles, and illicit drugs—accounted for most of the other 25 percent of premature deaths (McGinnis and Foege 1993). The big three remain devastating today: tobacco use is responsible for nearly 500,000 deaths each year, obesity and lack of exercise for about 400,000 deaths, and alcohol abuse for some 60,000 fatalities (Danaei et al. 2009).

Behavioral risks that damage public health have distinctive politics. All involve personal activities—smoking cigarettes, eating too much and exercising too little, drinking alcohol, shooting firearms, and having unsafe sex—that raise strong emotions in the political arena (Meier 1994). Because these activities involve the highly personal behaviors of millions of people, they are difficult for governments to control or change. However, there is some good news on the behavioral front: the rate of fatalities linked to driving while intoxicated has fallen by almost 30 percent in the past decade, although drunk driving is still responsible for about one-third of traffic fatalities.[5] Smoking rates dropped steadily for almost forty years, although

---

5. National Highway Traffic Safety Administration, "Traffic Safety Fact 2009: Alcohol Impaired Driving," www-nrd.nhtsa.dot.gov/Pubs/811385.PDF.

they now appear to have stabilized at about 20 percent of the adult population (Centers for Disease Control and Prevention 2009). Other behaviors are less susceptible to change. The public's willingness to adopt healthier sexual behaviors has not been firmly established, and America has not proved capable of greatly reducing its gun violence. Other trends are worrisome: in 2011 the "slimmest" state was "fatter" than the "fattest" state twenty years ago (Trust for America's Health 2011).

Tobacco

Tobacco use, especially cigarette smoking, is by far the largest behavioral threat to public health. The magnitude of the problem can be difficult to grasp: each year tobacco kills the equivalent of the 9/11 terrorist attacks—every third day.

In the mid-1990s, various state governments concluded that smoking-related health problems imposed large costs on the public through the Medicaid and Medicare programs and began to challenge the tobacco companies to reduce smoking rates. Four states (Florida, Minnesota, Mississippi, and Texas) successfully pressed their claims against the tobacco industry before the industry reached a global settlement with all fifty states in November 1998. Under the terms of the settlement, tobacco companies will pay an expected $246 billion to the states over twenty-five years (Action on Smoking and Health 1998).

A large portion of the revenues from this settlement was supposed to be used to reduce smoking rates. However, pledges notwithstanding, most states have failed to use this windfall primarily to reduce tobacco use. State spending on tobacco control declined substantially in the early 2000s, and during the recession the states increasingly diverted the tobacco settlement revenues to other purposes. In 2011 the states were expected to devote a mere 2 percent of those funds (or about $500 million of the $25 billion) to programs to prevent smoking or to help smokers to quit, representing nearly a 30 percent decline over the previous three years. Only two states—Alaska and North Dakota—were spending as much as the Centers for Disease Control and Prevention (CDC) had recommended, and only five other states were spending even half of the CDC-recommended amount. Nevada, New Hampshire, and Ohio had allocated no funds whatsoever to smoking prevention programs (Wilson 2010).

States are using various other means to reduce tobacco-related risks, although the intensity of the effort has varied across the states and over time. By the end of 2010, twenty-seven states had passed "comprehensive" bans on smoking in all public places and workplaces, including restaurants and bars (American Lung Association 2010, 3). Eleven states enacted comprehensive laws in 2006–2007, but the pace has been slowing: only six more states approved comprehensive bans during the next three years. Every state requires smoke-free indoor air in some places to some extent, but seven states (Indiana, Kentucky, Mississippi, South Carolina, Texas, West Virginia, and Wyoming) continue to allow smoking in workplaces, restaurants, and bars (Centers for Disease Control and Prevention 2011b).

All states also have cigarette excise taxes, with an average charge of $1.46 per pack (and the federal government imposing an additional $1.01 per pack). New York has the highest tax, at $4.35 per pack; Missouri has the lowest, at $0.17 (American Lung Association 2011b, 3). Still, the CDC has concluded that state cigarette taxes are not nearly high enough to cover the economic costs of smoking; it estimated the average economic productivity lost per pack at $5.16, the average medical expenses lost per pack at $5.31, and the cost to Medicaid per pack at $1.63 (Centers for Disease Control and Prevention 2006). It is clear that higher cigarette taxes reduce demand for cigarettes. For example, Rhode Island raised its cigarette tax from $0.71 in 2001 to $3.46 in 2009, and during that period the rate of smoking among high school students fell from almost 25 percent to about 13 percent (American Lung Association 2011b, 3).

States also make it more difficult for youth to smoke. All states prohibit the sale and distribution of tobacco products to minors, and forty-three states have laws that bar minors from buying, possessing, or using tobacco products.[6] No state allows vending machine sales of cigarettes to minors, and most states have other policies to prevent or restrict teen smoking.

States are taking additional steps to prevent or reduce smoking. Hawaii, for example, now requires its Medicaid managed care plans to cover all smoking cessation medications and to provide at least one type of anti-smoking counseling. Kentucky, a major tobacco-producing state, substantially improved access to cessation treatment for its Medicaid population. By the end of 2010, six state Medicaid programs were providing comprehensive coverage for all Food and Drug Administration–approved cessation medications and counseling services. Several states also provide such services for state employees and their families (American Lung Association 2011c, 10–11).

Laws do not necessarily mean results, however, because state enforcement of tobacco laws is notoriously lax, particularly for sales to minors.[7] Although the smoking rates among youth are much lower than they were two decades ago, cigarettes remain the most commonly abused substance among those in high school. About 20 percent of seniors are currently smokers (Johnston et al. 2011, 30).

Diet and Activity

Diet and activity contribute to about 400,000 premature deaths each year (Danaei et al. 2009). The problem is that Americans in general eat too much and exercise too little. Over 60 percent of Americans were overweight in 2009, and 27 percent of adults were obese (Mendes 2010). And yet state and federal policymakers have done

6. American Lung Association, "Search SLATI Database," www.lungusa2.org/slati/search.php.

7. Campaign for Tobacco-Free Kids, "Enforcing Laws Prohibiting Cigarette Sales to Kids Reduces Youth Smoking," www.tobaccofreekids.org/research/factsheets/pdf/0049.pdf.

much less to reduce the threats to public health from obesity than from tobacco or alcohol.

Because of the political dynamics of obesity, it is difficult for policymakers to take effective action to reduce or prevent the obesity epidemic (Engelhard, Garson, and Dorn 2009). Obesity has no clear villains, nor are there silver bullet policies. However, as the weight of the evidence about the harms of obesity has grown along with the weight of the American public, state legislatures, if not the public, have become increasingly concerned.

The major policy focus has been on childhood obesity. There has been a flurry of legislative activity to reduce youth obesity and to promote exercise (National Conference of State Legislatures 2010a). This activity includes some form of **body mass index (BMI)** or fitness screening programs for schoolchildren, diabetes screening and management, and insurance coverage for obesity prevention. In 2009 forty laws or resolutions addressing youth obesity were enacted, with the most popular laws involving school nutrition. A similar number of laws were approved in 2008 (National Conference of State Legislatures 2009, 2010a).[8]

Policy initiatives have not just targeted children, although addressing adult obesity has proven to be a much greater challenge for the states. Forty states impose taxes on sugared beverages and snacks (some states impose taxes on all groceries), but these taxes are too low to reduce the demand for junk food (Brownell and Frieden 2009). States that have tried to impose larger and broader junk food taxes have not fared well. For example, in 2008 New York governor David Patterson proposed an 18 percent tax on soft drinks, but this proposal faced overwhelming opposition in the legislature and among the public and was not even seriously considered. Public opinion on junk food taxes varies widely, depending on the survey, but it is most supportive when the tax revenues are dedicated to obesity prevention and reduction efforts (Brownell and Frieden 2009). And yet the public appears skeptical that junk food taxes would actually do anything to reduce obesity (Montopoli 2010). Although states are starved for revenue and a well-crafted junk food tax could fatten public coffers while slimming down the public's waistlines, the states remain reluctant to take the next step in that direction.

The ACA includes provisions that give states opportunities, incentives, or mandates to promote wellness (which includes weight management, among other behaviors). In response to the ACA, as well as to their own political concerns, the states have been busy. In 2010 over eighty wellness measures were introduced in state legislatures. Among other things, they allowed "insurance discounts, rebates and incentives to people who buy individual coverage for participating in a wellness program," permitted those who participated in a wellness program to enjoy

---

8. For a summary list of laws, see Kaiser Family Foundation, "State Laws Addressing Childhood Obesity, 2010," www.statehealthfacts.org/comparetable.jsp?ind=52&cat=2&sub=14.

discounts in group rates of insurance, raised "awareness about wellness and the benefits of healthy lifestyles," created wellness commissions or studies, established wellness and prevention programs for public employees, and created wellness-related tax credits (National Conference of State Legislatures 2010b).

Because of the complexities of reducing obesity, it is unclear whether the states can make an impact on this problem. So far, they have not; the rate of obesity continues to grow. And the medical costs will probably grow apace. In 2008 it was estimated that health problems associated with obesity were costing the nation some $150 billion in medical expenses, with Medicaid and Medicare bearing much of the burden (Finkelstein et al. 2009).

Alcohol

Every year, some 60,000 Americans die at least in part from abusing alcohol. These deaths can occur through alcohol's effect on the body (for example, cirrhosis of the liver or fetal alcohol syndrome) and, more important, on behavior. Between a quarter and a half of all homicides, assaults, car and boat fatalities, drowning and fire fatalities, and the like can be attributed in part to alcohol consumption (Emergency Nurses Association, Injury Prevention Institute 2006).

There are old and new politics of alcohol. The call for prohibition by a mainly religious element within the country defined the old politics. The public health consequences or the costs and benefits of alcohol use did not enter into the debate; it was just about whether drinking was a sin. This politics still prevails in many parts of the country. Although no states maintain prohibition, numerous dry counties dot the map, especially through the parts of the country known as the Bible Belt. It is no small irony that the Jack Daniels distillery, which produces Tennessee bourbon, is located in a dry county.

The new politics of alcohol is divided sharply between personal use and public misuse. Millions of Americans drink moderately, and there is little opposition to responsible alcohol use. Alcohol use is not inherently harmful, and medical research suggests that moderate consumption might, in some circumstances, be healthful. The alcohol companies themselves urge their buyers to drink in moderation, albeit at the end of commercials relentlessly promoting their products.

Virtually no one defends excessive drinking. Public misuse—especially drunk driving—is vigorously attacked around the country. Groups such as Mothers against Drunk Driving (MADD) and its offshoots such as Students against Drunk Driving (SADD) have mobilized much political and social support for their goal. The states have led the way in these attacks, although not always willingly. The major impetus to state action was the 1984 federal law that required states to enact a minimum drinking age of twenty-one by 1986 or lose a portion of their federal highway funds (O'Malley and Wagenaar 1991). Prior to this law, only fourteen states prohibited the purchase of alcohol by those under the age of twenty-one, but by 1988 all fifty states prohibited it. All fifty states have also made it a crime for a driver to have a blood alcohol content (BAC) of 0.08 or above—up from fifteen states in the mid-1990s when the typical BAC was 0.10 (Insurance Institute for Highway Safety 2007).

States continue to tighten the tap on drinking and driving. In 2009, 229 bills were introduced in forty-six states to reduce drunk driving further, and twenty-five states adopted new laws. Forty-three states have laws imposing stiffer penalties, such as additional fines or ignition interlock devices, on drivers with high BAC levels. Nine states require ignition interlocks—devices that prevent a car from starting if the driver has alcohol on the breath—for all those convicted of drunk driving (Savage, Tiegen, and Farber 2010, 1, 6–8). The federal Transportation Equity Act requires the states to impose specific sanctions on repeat offenders, and by the end of 2009 thirty-nine states had enacted legislation bringing them into compliance.

The combination of tougher drunk driving laws, heavier penalties for violators, and expanded enforcement, together with changing social mores, has contributed to the substantial reduction in the rate of deaths, injuries, and accidents attributed to alcohol-influenced driving. The alcohol-related traffic fatality rate has declined almost continually over the last twenty-five years, and in 2009 it was at the lowest level since these statistics have been collected (Century Council 2010, 8).

Firearms

Horrific violent crime is a staple of American life. In 2011 the lead story was the attempted assassination of Rep. Gabrielle Giffords in a shooting spree in Tucson, Arizona, that left six dead and nineteen wounded. Just over a year earlier, twelve persons were murdered and another thirty-one wounded by a lone gunman at the Fort Hood army base in the largest, but hardly the only, mass shooting that occurred in 2009 (Associated Press 2009). And no one will forget the slaughter at Virginia Tech in Blacksburg, Virginia, in 2007, in which thirty-two students and faculty were slaughtered in the classrooms and halls.

As shocking as these crimes were, they do not reveal a trend toward a more dangerous society. Violent crime rates in 2009 were at their lowest levels since data-gathering began in 1973. The rates of murder, rape, robbery, and assault were all less than a third of their peaks in the 1970s (Bureau of Justice Statistics 2011). Surely, that is news worth celebrating.

Just as surely, the United States remains unique among wealthy nations in the toll taken by firearms. Each year, firearms are associated with more than 30,000 fatalities by homicide, suicide, and accident (Xu et al. 2010, 89). Unlike the violent crime rate, the fatality rate for firearms has not budged from about 10 deaths per 100,000 persons over the last decade. Not all groups are at equal risk, however: men are six times more likely than women to be killed by a firearm, and black men are twice as likely as white men to die from a bullet (Xu et al. 2010, 91). The extent of firearm violence varies widely from state to state and over time. In general, the southern and western states have much higher levels of violence than states in the Northeast or Midwest. Louisiana, for example, had over eleven firearm-related homicides per 100,000 residents in 2007, whereas New Hampshire had one-twentieth that amount. The fifty-state average was about 4 per 100,000 residents.[9]

Unique as well is the constitutional right of individuals to own guns. The Second Amendment states, "A well regulated Militia, being necessary to the security of a free state, the right of the people to keep and bear Arms, shall not be infringed," but not until recently did the Supreme Court consider whether this right extended to individuals. In *District of Columbia v. Heller*, 554 U.S. 570 (2008), and *McDonald v. City of Chicago*, 561 U.S. 3025 (2010), the Court narrowly decided (in two 5–4 votes) that federal, state, and local governments cannot violate fundamental individual rights to gun ownership. Under these rulings, then, state and local governments cannot *ban* firearms entirely; the extent to which firearms can be regulated remains an open question.

States themselves have a wide variety of policies to regulate and control the purchase, carrying, or ownership of firearms, and over the years many attempted to strengthen these laws.[10] The advocates of more permissive gun laws have perhaps had more numerous victories. In 2011 Wisconsin enacted one of the nation's strongest "right to carry" laws, leaving Illinois as the only state that does not provide citizens an option for carrying concealed weapons (National Rifle Association [NRA] 2011c). The NRA has also been extraordinarily successful in pressing for state "Castle Doctrine" laws, which allow citizens to use force—including deadly force— "against an attacker in their home and any place where they have the legal right to be," while also protecting individuals from civil lawsuits from the attacker when force is used (National Rifle Association 2001b). First adopted by Florida in 2005, similar laws have since been approved in twenty-six other states, most recently by Pennsylvania in 2011.

One gun policy issue aligns the interests of gun control supporters and Second Amendment advocates: the belief that the mentally ill should not have access to firearms. This issue rose on the policy agenda after the Virginia Tech shootings, and again after the attempt on Representative Giffords's life. In 1968, spurred by Sirhan Sirhan's assassination of Sen. Robert F. Kennedy, who was running for the presidential nomination, the federal government approved legislation barring anyone with a history of severe mental illness from buying firearms, but that ban was never vigorously enforced. Although more than 2.5 million mentally ill persons were prohibited from purchasing weapons under this law, at the time of the Virginia Tech massacre the FBI database contained only some 235,000 names because federal law did not require the states to report this information, nor did it give

9. Bureau of Justice Statistics, *Sourcebook of Criminal Justice Statistics,* www.albany.edu/source book/pdf/t300012007.pdf.

10. For a state-by-state summary of laws and regulations on firearms, see National Rifle Association (2011a).

them any funding to do so. The federal government subsequently required the states to share the names of the mentally ill and supplied funding to do so, but only a fraction of the pledged funds were actually distributed and no penalties have yet been enforced. The results are hardly encouraging: by the time the deadline for reporting had passed, nine states had not supplied any names and seventeen other states had given twenty-five names or fewer, indicating that the background checklists are still woefully incomplete (Associated Press 2011). Political agreement does not necessarily mean policy compliance.

Sexual Behavior

Alas, one of life's greatest pleasures is one of its greatest problems. Unprotected sexual intercourse can kill, injure, and deprive—and not just by transmitting the virus that causes AIDS. The good news is that AIDS is no longer the death sentence it once was; improved treatment regimes reduced the number of persons dying from AIDS from 33,000 in 1996 to just over 17,000 in 2008. The sad news is that 1–1.2 million Americans are living with HIV, about 20 percent of them "undiagnosed and unaware of their condition" (Centers for Disease Control and Prevention 2011a). Unprotected sexual intercourse also contributes to approximately 30,000 deaths annually from "excess infant deaths" (from unintended pregnancies), cervical cancer (linked to certain sexually transmitted diseases), and hepatitis B infection. In addition, some 15 million persons become infected with a sexually transmitted disease (STD) each year, and about half of all pregnancies are unplanned (American Pregnancy Association 2011).

Although prescription drugs are now available to render HIV a chronic condition rather than an invariably fatal disease, they pose substantial financial challenges for some states' public health systems. Every state is home to persons with HIV/AIDS (PWAs), but AIDS is not spread uniformly across the country: California, Florida, and New York alone accounted for about 40 percent of total AIDS cases up through 2008.[11] A large proportion—about 40 percent of those with HIV receiving medical care—are enrolled in Medicaid, most often because they are both poor and disabled (see Kaiser Family Foundation 2009c for a discussion). The result is that much of the health care cost of HIV/AIDS is borne by the public sector; in 2008 the federal and state governments spent about $7.5 billion on AIDS through Medicaid (Kaiser Family Foundation 2009c). The federal government picked up the entire tab for the "dual eligibles" who also received benefits through Medicare. States with large numbers of PWAs, in particular, have thus been under tremendous pressure to contain the costs the PWAs have imposed on the public. A principal way in which these states have tried to cope is to seek **Medicaid waivers** so that PWAs can receive home or community-based, long-term care rather than

---

11. Kaiser Family Foundation, "Estimated Numbers of Persons Living with an AIDS Diagnosis, All Ages, 2008," www.statehealthfacts.org/comparemaptable.jsp?ind=516&cat=11.

more expensive hospitalization, and at least fifteen states have experimented with this approach.

The politics of sex has been characterized by the struggle between those who view sexual behavior as a moral issue and those who consider it a policy issue only to the extent that sexual behavior threatens public health (Rom 2012a). The attitudes and policy preferences of those holding these views are fundamentally different. The "moral issue" group believes that government policy should encourage or enforce only "moral" sex—that is, monogamous relations within a heterosexual marriage—by advocating "abstinence only" education. The "policy issue" group argues that sexual relations between consenting individuals are acceptable to the extent that they do not cause unintended pregnancies or spread disease. Therefore, this group favors "comprehensive education" focusing on risk reduction as the appropriate policy. States' policies toward sexual behavior have to a large extent mirrored these divisions within their populations—more conservative states and localities have emphasized abstinence only; more liberal states and localities, comprehensive education.

The politics of sex have been especially unhelpful in welfare policy. Unprotected sexual intercourse is literally the beginning of the nonmarital births to teenagers that put families at risk of needing public assistance. But prevention policies that tell teenagers either to "just say no" or "just be safe" apparently have little impact on teenage pregnancy rates. It is intriguing—a hopeful sign—that policies emphasizing both moral restraint and safer sex are more successful at reducing unwanted pregnancies and sexually transmitted diseases than either approach alone (Manlove et al. 2002). However, during the administration of President George W. Bush, the federal government provided states with financial inducements to offer abstinence-only education, and the states generally accepted those inducements (Bleakley, Hennessy, and Fishbein 2006; Guttmacher Institute 2006). Although some states have moved away from an exclusive focus on abstinence, those policies still dominate sex education (Kaiser Family Foundation 2010b).

Meanwhile, it is apparent that youth who become pregnant, or who impregnate, often have academic, economic, and emotional difficulties before conception occurs. Dropping out of school, living in poverty, and having little hope for the future help create conditions that lead teenagers to become parents (Lawson and Rhode 1993). Research suggests that it is important to address teenagers' social conditions as a way of preventing teen pregnancies. Rather than focusing on pregnancy prevention by itself, public policy needs to improve the educational, economic, and emotional circumstances of the adolescents most at risk (Sawhill 2001). Perhaps the best form of birth control is the realistic hope for a better future if childbearing is delayed. Providing such realistic hope for teenagers is not always an easy task, even for parents. The states face even greater challenges in providing this hope: the United States has the highest rates of teen pregnancy in the industrialized Western world.

But there are glimmers of hope. Although high by international standards, the U.S. teen pregnancy rate was at an historical low in 2009, having fallen by 37 percent over the last twenty years (Reinberg 2011). The decline was attributed both to decreasing sexual activity among teens and to higher contraceptive use. Predictably, the teen birthrate varies dramatically from state to state. The states with the highest birthrates tended to be southern states with high poverty rates (such as Mississippi, New Mexico, and Texas, with over sixty births per 1,000 teens). Those with the lowest tended to be more affluent northern states (Massachusetts, New Hampshire, and Vermont, with about twenty births per 1,000 teens).[12]

HEALTH OUTCOMES: STATE COMPARISONS

States have adopted various policies to improve the health of their residents. The states' progress can be assessed by what they are doing ("outputs") or what they have accomplished ("outcomes"). The first approach focuses on state policies by, for example, using "report cards" that have been developed by various organizations. In 2007, when the previous edition of this book was published, the states were not performing well in their policy choices: the overall "grade point average" (GPA) was 1.94 (or just below a C). The "good students" appeared to be the usual suspects: New York and California were both in the top three. Other states were more surprising: Arkansas ranked fourth, for example. Some states scored quite high on some measures and much lower on others. For example, Pennsylvania rated an A– for obesity prevention and a D+ for tobacco control, while South Carolina earned an F for tobacco and an A– for obesity. Perhaps the generally poor scores indicated that the rating organizations were tough graders. More likely, these grades reflected the fact that the states had not been particularly engaged in health promotion.

The second approach focuses on health outcomes. Outcomes allow the states to be compared against each other rather than against some standard as in the report cards. Outcomes are influenced by policies, but policies do not determine them; other powerful social, economic, and demographic determinants are at work.

Outcomes can be measured in different ways, but here the states are rated based on a single salient indicator of the main behavioral risks: tobacco use, obesity and inactivity, alcohol abuse, firearms, and sexually transmitted diseases. "Tobacco" is defined as the percentage of the adult population that currently smokes cigarettes, which ranges from a low of 9 percent in Utah to a high of nearly 27 percent in West Virginia. "Overweight" averages the percentage of adults who are overweight and those who do not exercise regularly. Again, Utah is the healthiest state on this dimension, although the overweight average is still a shocking 50 percent. And again, West Virginia is the laggard with fully two-thirds of its adults overweight or

12. Kaiser Family Foundation, "Teen Birth Rate per 1,000 Population Ages 15–19, 2008," www .statehealthfacts.org/comparemaptable.jsp?ind=37&cat=2.

Table 11-1   State Behavioral Health Rankings

State	Overall rank	Tobacco	Weight	Alcohol	Firearms	STDs
Utah	1	1	1	2	24	5
Vermont	2	13	2	33	14	3
Connecticut	3	3	10	46	4	20
California	4	2	19	28	18	28
Hawaii	5	7	6	34	1	39
Colorado	6	19	3	30	23	30
Oregon	7	10	7	23	21	10
Massachusetts	8	5	12	39	3	9
Idaho	9	16	9	13	33	6
Washington	10	11	15	25	15	16
Minnesota	11	9	20	49	10	7
New Jersey	12	6	27	18	7	8
Arizona	13	4	29	21	44	29
New Hampshire	14	21	17	27	8	1
Montana	15	33	4	37	38	13
District of Columbia	16	8	5	48	51	51
New York	17	15	21	31	5	41
Maine	18	29	13	24	11	2
Rhode Island	19	17	30	43	2	18
New Mexico	20	31	14	11	42	43
Illinois	21	22	23	40	12	40
Maryland	22	12	37	9	30	34
Virginia	23	32	18	16	25	26
Wyoming	24	36	11	26	43	21
Iowa	25	20	34	45	6	15
Nebraska	26	25	26	42	13	12
North Dakota	27	27	24	50	16	11
Kansas	28	23	33	20	22	24
Texas	29	18	38	22	29	35
Delaware	30	26	25	44	19	45
Florida	31	24	36	15	31	27
South Dakota	32	14	44	47	9	23
Wisconsin	33	35	22	51	17	22
Pennsylvania	34	30	31	32	27	19
Alaska	35	39	8	41	48	49
Georgia	36	28	42	5	35	31
Nevada	37	43	16	38	46	25
Michigan	38	34	28	35	28	38
North Carolina	39	37	40	12	32	37
Missouri	40	41	32	36	34	36
Indiana	41	42	39	17	26	17
Ohio	42	46	35	29	20	33
South Carolina	43	40	46	10	37	47
Arkansas	44	47	41	7	45	44
Oklahoma	45	49	43	14	36	32
Tennessee	46	38	50	1	41	42
Louisiana	47	45	47	19	50	48
Kentucky	48	50	45	8	40	14
Alabama	49	44	48	6	47	46
Mississippi	50	48	49	4	49	50
West Virginia	51	51	51	3	39	4

SOURCES: All data from Kaiser Family Foundation, www.statehealthfacts.org, except alcohol use, from Centers for Disease Control and Prevention, www.cdc.gov/alcohol/data-table.htm#binge-states.

inactive. "Alcohol" is the percentage of adults who engage in binge drinking, defined as consuming five or more drinks in a single day. Tennessee is the most abstemious (7 percent), perhaps because in much of the state alcohol cannot be legally bought, whereas about a quarter of Wisconsin's adults are binge drinkers. "Firearms" is firearm deaths per 100,000 persons. Here, Louisiana is the deadliest state (twenty deaths), and Hawaii is the most peaceful (2.6 deaths). "STD" is the number of cases of chlamydia—the most common sexually transmitted disease—per 10,000 persons. In New Hampshire, the rate is sixteen; in Mississippi, it is more than four times higher.

To create the overall ranking, the individual risk factors were weighted roughly by the importance of that factor in causing premature deaths—for every 1 million premature deaths, the overall index assumes that 500,000 were caused by smoking, 400,000 by diet and lack of activity, 60,000 by alcohol abuse, 20,000 by firearms, and 20,000 by sexual behavior (so, for example, the smoking rate was multiplied by 0.5, the obesity/inactivity rate by 0.4, and so forth).

Table 11-1 shows the overall rankings as well as the ranking for each factor. Those states at the very top and very bottom are probably not surprising: West Virginia, Mississippi, and Alabama are better known for college football than for healthy lifestyles, whereas Utah and Vermont may elicit wholesome images of hiking and skiing. More interesting are how the personalities of the states come through in the differing kinds of risks they apparently accept or avoid. Hawaii is among the healthy leaders for tobacco, weight, and firearms, but it is a comparative laggard in alcohol and STDs. West Virginia, highest in most risks, is comparatively safe in terms of alcohol and STDs, although one wonders if this also reflects data-reporting priorities.

CONCLUSION

How well and how quickly the states will recover from the recession are not yet known. Whether the ACA will be implemented is uncertain. But of this one can be confident: the states will continue to grapple with poverty and the health care needs of their citizens. How they do so will reflect the economic, social, and demographic features of the states because those features affect the choices that state politicians make. One hopes that future editions of this volume will reveal states that are more prosperous and healthier. Time will tell.

KEY TERMS

body mass index (BMI), 361
capitated, 354
categorically needy, 340
federal benefit standard, 342
fee-for-service program, 354

managed care program, 354
means-tested program, 340
Medicaid waiver, 365
medically needy, 341
welfare magnet, 347

REFERENCES

Action on Smoking and Health. 1998. http://ash.org.

Administration for Children and Families. 2010. "TANF Financial Data." www.acf.hhs.gov/programs/ofs/data/.

American Lung Association. 2010. "State Legislated Actions on Tobacco Issues 2010." www.lungusa2.org/slati/reports/SLATI_2010_Final_Web.pdf.

———. 2011a. "Laws that Prevent Stronger Local Tobacco Control Laws." www.lungusa2.org/slati/appendixe.php.

———. 2011b. "State Cigarette Taxes." www.lungusa2.org/slati/reports/cigarette-tax-fact sheet072011.pdf.

———. 2011c. "State of Tobacco Control 2010." www.stateoftobaccocontrol.org/ala-sotc2010.pdf.

American Pregnancy Association. 2011. "Statistics." www.americanpregnancy.org/main/statistics.html.

Associated Press. 2009. "Raw Data: Past Deadly U.S. Mass Shootings," April 3. www.foxnews.com/story/0,2933,512480,00.html.

———. 2011. "Few States Follow Mental Health Laws," February 18. www.foxnews.com/us/2011/02/17/ap-finds-states-follow-mental-health-gun-law/.

Berry, William D., Richard C. Fording, Evan J. Ringquist, Russell L. Hanson, and Carl Klarner. 2010. "Measuring Citizen and Government Ideology in the American States: A Re-appraisal." *State Politics and Policy Quarterly* 10: 117–135.

Berry, William D., Evan J. Ringquist, Richard C. Fording, and Russell L. Hanson. 1998. "Measuring Citizen and Government Ideology in the American States." *American Journal of Political Science* 42: 327–348.

Bleakley, Amy, Michael Hennessy, and Martin Fishbein. 2006. "Public Opinion on Sex Education in U.S. Schools." *Archives of Pediatric Adolescent Medicine* 160: 11.

Blue Cross Blue Shield of Massachusetts Foundation. 2011. "Health Reform in Massachusetts: Expanding Access to Health Insurance Coverage—Assessing the Results." http://bluecrossfoundation.org/Health-Reform/~/media/D0DDA3D667BE49D58539821F74C723C7.pdf.

Brownell, Kelly D., and Thomas R. Freiden. 2009. "Ounces of Prevention: The Public Policy Case for Taxes on Sugared Beverages." *New England Journal of Medicine* 360: 1805–1808.

Bureau of Justice Statistics. 2011. "National Crime Victimization Survey Violent Crime Trends, 1973–2008." Office of Justice Programs, U.S. Department of Justice. http://bjs.ojp.usdoj.gov/content/glance/tables/viortrdtab.cfm.

Bureau of Labor Statistics. 2011. "Labor Force Statistics." U.S. Department of Labor. http://data.bls.gov/pdq/SurveyOutputServlet.

Carey, Robert. 2010. "Health Insurance Exchanges: Key Issues in State Implementation." State Coverage Initiatives, Robert Woods Johnson Foundation. www.rwjf.org/files/research/70388.pdf.

Center for Budget and Policy Priorities. 2011. "Analysis of State Health Insurance Exchange Legislation: Establishment Status and Governance Issues." www.cbpp.org/files/CBPP-Analysis-of-Exchange-Legislation-Establishment-and-Governance.pdf.

Center for Family Policy and Research. 2011. "The State of Children and Families: 2011." http://mucenter.missouri.edu/MOchildfam11.pdf.

Center for Healthcare Research and Transformation. 2011. "Guide to State Requirements and Policy Choices in the Affordable Care Act." www.chrt.org/public-policy/policy-briefs/guide-to-state-requirements-and-policy-choices-in-the-affordable-care-act/.

Centers for Disease Control and Prevention. 2006. "State Data Highlights." www.cdc.gov/tobacco/data_statistics/state_data/data_highlights/2006/00_pdfs/DataHighlights06table4.pdf.

———. 2009. "Vital Signs: Current Cigarette Smoking Among Adults Aged ≥ 18 Years—United States, 2009." *Morbidity and Mortality Weekly Report* 59: 1135–1140. www.cdc.gov/mmwr/preview/mmwrhtml/mm5935a3.htm.

———. 2011a. "HIV/AIDS: Basic Statistics." www.cdc.gov/hiv/topics/surveillance/basic.htm #dpdhi.

———. 2011b. "State Smoke-Free Laws for Worksites, Restaurants, and Bars—United States, 2000–2010." *Morbidity and Mortality Weekly Report* 60: 472–475. www.cdc.gov/mmwr/ preview/mmwrhtml/mm6015a2.htm?s_cid=mm6015a2_w.

Centers for Medicare and Medicaid Services. 2010. "Medicare and Medicaid Statistical Supplement: 2010 Data." www.cms.gov/MedicareMedicaidStatSupp/09_2010.asp#TopOfPage.

Century Council. 2010. "State of Drunk Driving Fatalities in America, 2009." www.centurycouncil .org/files/material/files/SODDFIA.pdf.

Danaei, Goodarz, Eric L. Ding, Dariush Mozaffarian, Ben Taylor, Jurgen Rehm, Christopher J. L. Murray, and Majid Ezzati. 2009. "The Preventable Causes of Death in the United States: Comparative Risk Assessment of Dietary, Lifestyle, and Metabolic Risk Factors." *PLoS Medicine* 6: 1–24. www.plosmedicine.org/article/info%3Adoi%2F10.1371%2Fjournal.pmed.1000058.

Elazar, Daniel J. 1970. "The States and the Political Setting." In *Policy Analysis in Political Science,* ed. Ira Sharkansky. Chicago: Markham.

Emergency Nurses Association, Injury Prevention Institute. 2006. "Alcohol and Injury Facts." www.ena.org/ipinstitute/fact/ENAIPFactSheet-Alcohol.pdf.

Engelhard, Carolyn L., Arthur Garson Jr., and Stan Dorn. 2009. "Reducing Obesity: Policy Strategies from the Tobacco Wars." Urban Institute, Washington, D.C. www.urban.org/uploaded pdf/411926_reducing_obesity.pdf.

Erikson, Robert S., Gerald C. Wright, and John R. McIver. 1993. *Statehouse Democracy: Public Opinion and Policy in the American States.* Cambridge, U.K.: Cambridge University Press.

Finkelstein, Eric A., Justin G. Trogdon, Joel W. Cohen, and William Dietz. 2009. "Annual Medical Spending Attributable to Obesity: Payer- and Service-Specific Estimates." *Health Affairs* 28: 822–831.

Foster, Richard D. 2011. "Statement on the Estimated Effect of the Affordable Care Act on Medicare and Medicaid Outlays and Total National Health Care Expenditures." Subcommittee on Health, Committee on Energy and Commerce, U.S. House of Representatives, May 16. www .dhhs.gov/asl/testify/2011/03/t20110330e.html.

Gray, Virginia, David Lowery, Matthew Fellowes, and Andrea McAtee. 2004. "Public Opinion, Public Policy, and Organized Interests in the American States." *Political Research Quarterly* 57: 411–420.

Gray, Virginia, David Lowery, James Monogan, and Erik K. Godwin. 2009. "Incrementing toward Nowhere: Universal Health Care Coverage in the States." *Publius: The Journal of Federalism* 40: 82–113.

Guttmacher Institute. 2006. "In Brief: Facts on Sex Education in the United States." www.gutt macher.org/pubs/fb_sexEd2006.html.

Insurance Institute for Highway Safety. 2007. "DUI/DWI Laws." www.iihs.org/laws/state_laws/ dui.html.

Johnston, L. D., P. M. O'Malley, J. G. Bachman, and J. E. Schulenberg. 2011. "Monitoring the Future National Survey Results on Drug Use 1975–2010. Institute for Social Research, University of Michigan. www.monitoringthefuture.org/pubs/monographs/mtf-vol1_2010 .pdf.

Kaiser Family Foundation. 2009a. "Children's Health Insurance Program Reauthorization Act of 2009 (CHIPRA)." Kaiser Commission on Medicaid and the Uninsured. www.kff.org/medicaid/ upload/7863.pdf.

———. 2009b. "Explaining Health Care Reform: What Are Insurance Exchanges?" www.kff.org/ healthreform/upload/7908.pdf.

———. 2009c. "Fact Sheet: Medicaid and HIV/AIDS." www.kff.org/hivaids/upload/7172_04 .pdf.

———. 2010a. "Medicaid and Managed Care: Key Data, Trends, and Issues." Kaiser Commission on Medicaid and the Uninsured. www.kff.org/medicaid/upload/8046.pdf.

———. 2010b. "State Sex and STD/HIV Education Policy, as of August 1, 2010." www.state healthfacts.org/comparetable.jsp?ind=567&cat=11.

Katz, Michael B. 1986. *In the Shadow of the Poorhouse: A Social History of Welfare in America.* New York: Basic Books.

Klees, Barbara S., Christian J. Wolfe, and Catherine A. Curtis. 2010. "Brief Summaries of Medicare and Medicaid." Centers for Medicare and Medicaid Services, U.S. Department of Health and Human Services. www.cms.gov/MedicareProgramRatesStats/Downloads/MedicareMedicaidSummaries2010.pdf.

Klein, Ezra. 2011. "Vermont Closing in on Single Payer." *Washington Post,* May 9. www.washington post.com/blogs/ezra-klein/post/vermont-closing-in-on-single-payer/2011/05/09/AFvtBm ZG_blog.html.

Lawson, Annette, and Deborah L. Rhode, eds. 1993. *The Politics of Pregnancy: Adolescent Sexuality and Public Policy.* New Haven, Conn.: Yale University Press.

Manlove, Jennifer, Elizabeth Terry-Humen, Angela Romano Papillo, Kerry Franzetta, Stephanie Williams, and Suzanne Ryan. 2002. *Preventing Teenage Pregnancy, Childbearing, and Sexually Transmitted Diseases: What the Research Shows.* Washington, D.C.: Child Trends. www .childtrends.org/PDF/K1Brief.pdf.

McGinnis, J. Michael, and William H. Foege. 1993. "Actual Causes of Death in the United States." *JAMA,* November 10, 2207–2212.

Meier, Kenneth J. 1994. *The Politics of Sin: Drugs, Alcohol, and Public Policy.* New York: M. E. Sharpe.

Mendes, Elizabeth. 2010. "Six in 10 Overweight or Obese in U.S., More in '09 than in '08." www .gallup.com/poll/125741/six-overweight-obese.aspx.

Miller, George, Charles Roehrig, Paul Hughes-Cromwick, and Craig Lake. 2008. "Quantifying National Spending on Wellness and Prevention." *Advances in Health Economics and Health Services Research* 19: 1–24. www.altarum.org/publications-resources-health-systems-research/quantifying-national-spending.

Montopoli, Brian. 2010. "Poll: Most Oppose Tax on Junk Food." CBS News, January 7. www .cbsnews.com/8301–503544_162–6068825–503544.html.

National Association of State Budget Officers. 2010. *The Fiscal Survey of the States.* http://nasbo .org/Publications/FiscalSurvey/tabid/65/Default.aspx.

———. 2011. *The Fiscal Survey of the States.* www.nasbo.org/LinkClick.aspx?fileticket=yNV8Jv3 X7Is%3d&tabid=38.

National Conference of State Legislatures. 2009. "Childhood Obesity—2008 Update of Legislative Policy Options." www.ncsl.org/default.aspx?tabid=13883.

———. 2010a. "Childhood Obesity—2009 Update of Legislative Policy Options." www.ncsl.org/default.aspx?tabid=19776.

———. 2010b. "2010 Wellness Legislation." www.ncsl.org/default.aspx?tabid=20434.

National Rifle Association. 2011a. "Federal and State Firearms Laws." www.nraila.org/gunlaws/#?st=IA.

———. 2011b. "Pennsylvania Governor Signs NRA-Backed Castle Doctrine into Law." www .nraila.org/News/Read/NewsReleases.aspx?ID=15275.

———. 2011c. "Wisconsin State Legislature Passes Landmark Right-to-Carry Legislation." www .nraila.org/News/Read/NewsReleases.aspx?ID=15254.

NPR (National Public Radio). 2011. "Vermont Steps Closer to Single-Payer Health Plan." http://m.npr.org/news/Health/136502764?page=2.

O'Malley, Patrick M., and Alexander Wagenaar. 1991. "Effects of Minimum Drinking Age Laws on Alcohol Use, Related Behaviors, and Traffic Crash Involvement by American Youth: 1976–1987." *Journal of Studies on Alcohol* 52: 478–491.

Peterson, Paul E. 1995. *The Price of Federalism.* Washington, D.C.: Brookings.

Reinberg, Stephen. 2011. "U.S. Teen Birth Rate Hits Record Low." MedicineNet.Com. www.medicinenet.com/script/main/art.asp?articlekey=142728.

Rom, Mark Carl. 2012a. "Below the (Bible) Belt: The Politics of Sexuality Education." In *Curriculum and the Culture Wars: When and Where Is Religion Appropriate in the Public Schools?* ed. Melissa Deckman and Joseph Prud'homme. New York: Peter Lang.

———. 2012b. "Social Welfare Policy." In *Oxford Handbook of State and Local Politics,* ed. Donald Haider-Markel. New York: Oxford University Press.

Salsberg, Bob. 2011. "Governor Patrick Unveils Plan to Curb Massachusetts Health Care Costs." *Herald News.* www.heraldnews.com/business/x372398102/Gov-Patrick-unveils-plan-to-curb-Mass-health-care-costs.

Savage, Melissa A., Anne Teigen, and Nicholas Farber. 2010. "Traffic Safety and Public Health: State Legislative Action 2009." National Conference of State Legislatures, Transportation Series #4. www.ncsl.org/documents/transportation/09trafficsafety.pdf.

Sawhill, Isabel. 2001. *What Can Be Done to Reduce Teen Pregnancy and Out-of-Wedlock Births?* Washington, D.C.: Brookings.

Smith, Vernon K., Kathleen Gifford, Eileen Ellis, Robin Rudowitz, and Laura Snyder. 2010. "Hoping for Economic Recovery, Preparing for Health Reform: A Look at Medicaid Spending, Coverage, and Policy Trends." Kaiser Commission on Medicaid and the Uninsured. www.kff.org/medicaid/upload/8105.pdf.

Social Security Administration. 2010a. "SSI Annual Statistical Report 2009." www.ssa.gov/oact/ssir/SSI10/toc.html.

———. 2010b. "2010 SSI Annual Report." Washington, D.C.

———. 2011. "Understanding Supplemental Security Income SSI Benefits." www.ssa.gov/ssi/text-benefits-ussi.htm.

Teague, Patrick M. 2011. "Vermont Takes Steps Down the Single-Payer Path." Health Policy Hub. http://blog.communitycatalyst.org/index.php/2011/05/26/vermont-takes-steps-down-the-single-payer-path/.

Trust for America's Health. 2011. "F as in Fat: How Obesity Threatens America's Future." http://healthyamericans.org/report/88/.

U.S. Census Bureau. 2011. *Statistical Abstract of the United States, 2011.* Washington, D.C.: Government Printing Office.

Walker, Jack L., Jr. 1969. "The Diffusion of Innovation in the American States." *American Political Science Review* 63: 830–899.

Wilson, Beth. 2010. "States Spending Just 2% of Tobacco Settlement Funds on Smoking Prevention." *American Medical News.* www.ama-assn.org/amednews/2010/12/13/prsa1213.htm.

Xu, Jiaquan, Kenneth D. Kochanek, Sherry L. Murphy, and Betzaida Tejada-Vera. 2010. "Deaths: Final Data for 2007." *National Vital Statistics Reports* 58: 1–136. www.cdc.gov/NCHS/data/nvsr/nvsr58/nvsr58_19.pdf.

SUGGESTED READINGS

Print

2011 State Expenditure Report. Washington, D.C.: National Association of State Budget Officers, 2011. www.nasbo.org/Publications/StateExpenditureReport/tabid/79/Default.aspx. Annual reports that summarize the main trends in state spending on health and welfare and other policies, as well as the major policy changes states make in response to fiscal challenges.

Rom, Mark Carl. "Social Welfare Policy." In *Oxford Handbook of State and Local Politics,* ed. Donald Haider-Markel. New York: Oxford University Press, 2012. A synthesis and summary of political science research on state health and welfare programs.

Rowe, Gretchen, Mary Murphy, and Ei Yin Mon. *Welfare Rules Databook: State Policies as of July 2009.* Washington, D.C.: Urban Institute, 2010. www.acf.hhs.gov/programs/opre/welfare_employ/state_tanf/databook09/databook09.pdf. State-by-state summaries of eligibility, benefits, and requirements between 1996 and 2009.

Internet

Centers for Medicare and Medicaid Services (U.S. Department of Health and Human Services). www.cms.hhs.gov/. Links to information and data on the Medicaid and SCHIP programs.

Office of Family Assistance, Administration for Children and Families (U.S. Department of Health and Human Services). www.acf.hhs.gov/programs/ofa/. Links to information on recent program developments provided by the office that oversees the TANF program.

State Health Facts (Kaiser Family Foundation). www.statehealthfacts.org. A wide array of data on health status and health programs and summaries of data across states and state-by-state profiles.

State Health Policy (Commonwealth Fund). www.commonwealthfund.org/. The State Health Policy section of the Web site evaluates state health care systems, explores possible reforms, and tracks public opinion on health policy.

CHAPTER 12

The Politics of Education

MICHAEL B. BERKMAN AND ERIC PLUTZER

The iconic one-room schoolhouse represents the simplest form of government in which residents pool resources to erect a basic structure and hire a teacher. And it embodies the ideal, still widely held today, that schools should be controlled locally and governed democratically.

At the outset of the twentieth century, there were over 200,000 one-room schoolhouses operating in the United States, with large multi-school systems in the nation's big cities. At this time, education was also becoming the responsibility of the states. Soon, the right to a free education would be enshrined in most state constitutions. Connecticut's constitution, for example, requires that "there shall always be free public elementary and secondary schools in the state."

It would not take long for the federal government to become interested in public education as well. Beginning with emergency assistance to pay teachers and school construction projects during the Great Depression, the federal role has grown. Today, education policy is a complex mix involving national, state, and local governments, with parents, citizens, unions, and advocacy organizations seeking to influence policy at all three levels.

POLICY AND THE POLITICS OF EDUCATION

Education policy is frequently contentious, with lively debates on how much to spend, how to raise funds to support educational spending, and what goes on inside the schools themselves. This chapter focuses on the debates over money and over what students should learn.

Debates over money raise thorny questions about how much to spend on instruction, about whether generous expenditures actually result in a better education, and about the best and most equitable ways to raise revenues. Debates over curriculum link schools to the wider political and policy discussions in the broader society: Should sex education include instruction on the proper use of condoms? Should social studies emphasize the multicultural heritage of racial and ethnic groups that make up the United States? Should language arts instruction emphasize phonics or "whole language" approaches? The intensity of political clashes rooted in culture and values intensifies when the arena is public schools because all sides in these debates see the stakes as especially high when it comes to the education of their children.

Federalism and Intergovernmental Relations

Debates over money and curriculum are complicated by the tangled web of policymaking that includes the local, state, and federal governments. Should state governments play a role in equalizing spending across communities? Or should spending depend only on local preferences and what each community can afford? Should the learning goals in math or science be the same in every classroom in a school district or even in every classroom in a state? Should they be the same in every state in the nation? To what extent should teachers and school districts be held accountable for how well they teach? The ideals of local control that Americans associate with the one-room schoolhouse are constantly put to the test in contemporary educational policymaking.

Who Decides?

Most fundamentally, all of these questions raise a profound issue: Who decides? To answer this question, one needs to consider three key elements:

1. The nation's democratic heritage, which provides guidance on *who should decide.*
2. The legal framework of various levels of government and the federal courts, which establish who has the *authority to decide* policy and to resolve differences of opinion and values.
3. The actual power held by key actors in the education policy process, especially governors, teachers' unions, and parents. Understanding the power of key actors explains *who actually decides.*

DEMOCRACY IN AMERICA: WHO *SHOULD* DECIDE?

The strong tradition of local control of public education in the United States goes hand in hand with the idea of **political responsiveness**—the idea that governing bodies should adhere closely to majority preferences. School districts are often small and encourage the direct involvement of local citizens; school district financial decisions are frequently subject to citizen approval by referenda; and many New England schools are to this day still governed by town hall meetings. Perhaps more than any other domain of the nation's life, Americans project onto their schools an ideal of direct citizen participation in governance.

And yet the American political tradition also has, since its inception, been wary of majoritarianism. Small, socially homogeneous communities, James Madison argues in *Federalist* 10, may pursue goals so zealously that they trample the rights of others (Madison 1961). As a result, federal courts have been heavily involved in public education to ensure that the civil rights and civil liberties of students are always protected against policies passed by the majority. Likewise, the Progressive movement from the 1890s to the 1920s promoted electoral and managerial reforms that would insulate policymaking from the excesses of partisan politics. More recently, many conservatives have championed market mechanisms to shift power from elected governmental bodies to the parents of school-age children.

As education has become increasingly important in the overall competitiveness of individual states and the country as a whole, the role of educational experts has increased. Although Americans embrace the idea of policymaking by citizen politicians, they are increasingly relying on experts in pedagogy, test design, special needs education, analysis of low-performing schools, and so on. These experts typically work in state departments of education and exert influence on governors, legislatures, and individual school districts. Recently, experts in the federal government have begun to play a larger role in determining what school districts must do to obtain federal funds.

Teachers have influence as well. There is a long-standing willingness to give teachers considerable autonomy in deciding how to teach in their own classrooms, allowing them to adapt to the needs of their students and the sensibilities in their communities. And yet this willingness is now being contested as teachers are increasingly being held accountable for the results of their efforts in the classroom. Indeed, greater **accountability**, "the idea of holding schools, districts, educators, and students responsible for results," has been at the heart of many recent battles and policies about public education (*Education Week* 2004).

Finally, parents are expected to have primary responsibility for raising their children. Parents represent a subset of local citizens, who can, of course, vote in school board elections and participate in school governance. But parents often seek additional power to influence the curriculum, to decide how funds are spent (and raised), and to customize their children's educational experience (such as by deciding which school their child attends, by removing their children from lessons they believe conflict with their values, or by removing their child from the public school system altogether).

In summary, questions about who should decide have complex answers. Strong traditions in the American experience variously point to local citizens, the federal courts, educational experts, teachers, and parents. Each of these groups vies for influence in a system of governance that begins with state government, but extends to local school boards, on the one hand, and fiscal imperatives driven by the national government, on the other.

AUTHORITY AND GOVERNANCE AT THE STATE LEVEL

All states have a state board of education—a political body responsible to the public that makes policies. A board of education may be elected directly by the citizens, or may represent the people indirectly when some or all of its members are appointed. In some states, these members are appointed by the legislature, but in most they are appointed by the governor. They are then well positioned to support the reforms of activist governors, thereby helping those officeholders fulfill campaign promises. By contrast, directly elected board members can pursue policies that are at odds with those of the governing political party. Elected school boards in Kansas and Texas, for example, have strayed far outside the mainstream and have generated highly publicized fights over curricula in areas such as evolution and American history. Table 12-1 shows the method of school board selection for each state. It reveals that most states keep their school boards in line with the governor's agenda by allowing him or her to appoint either all or most board members.

All states also have a **department of education,** which, like all administrative departments, implements state policies, conducts research, and makes recommendations to the governor. Within departments of education reside experts on pedagogy, finance, testing, and compliance with state and federal laws and regulations, though departments vary in their capacities to supply extensive expertise to the

Table 12-1 Methods of Selecting State School Board Members

Entire board is elected	Majority of board is elected	Majority of board is appointed	Entire board is appointed	
Alabama	Louisiana	Arizona	Alaska	Missouri
Colorado	Ohio	Idaho	Arkansas	Montana
Hawaii	Oklahoma	North Carolina	California	New Hampshire
Kansas		North Dakota	Connecticut	New Jersey
Michigan		Pennsylvania	Delaware	New York
Nebraska		Rhode Island	Florida	Oregon
Nevada		West Virginia	Georgia	South Carolina
New Mexico			Illinois	South Dakota
Washington			Indiana	Tennessee
			Iowa	Texas
			Kentucky	Utah
			Maine	Vermont
			Maryland	Virginia
			Massachusetts	Wisconsin
			Minnesota	Wyoming
			Mississippi	

SOURCE: Education Commission of the States, "State Boards of Education," http://mb2.ecs.org/reports/Report.aspx?id=167.

policymaking and policy implementation processes. Well-funded departments have the staff needed to write detailed curriculum standards, to apply for federal grants, and to support elected officials with high-quality research (Berkman and Plutzer 2010). Well-resourced departments can reflect a strong commitment to self-determination and state autonomy. Departments in less well-off states and localities can rely on national organizations such as the Education Commission of the States or the Carnegie Foundation for the Advancement of Teaching to help them find expertise, access to data, or information on what other states and school districts are doing.

From a regional or national perspective, one might view the system of state departments as inefficient because many tasks are duplicated in state after state. If New Jersey's Department of Education spends hundreds of staff hours developing proficiency benchmarks in reading, does it make sense for neighboring New York and Pennsylvania to repeat the process? Indeed, recent years have seen steps toward cooperation. For example, the relatively small education departments of Maine, New Hampshire, and Vermont have pooled resources to develop shared science standards and tests. More ambitious efforts to develop national standards are now under way; forty-two states and the District of Columbia have agreed to develop common core standards in reading and mathematics.

The eventual adoption of common national standards, however, is not assured. Their implementation will be complex and expensive, requiring changes to state and local assessment and teaching practices. Many curricular issues are contentious, public opinion on how to teach key subjects may vary considerably from state to state, and states are concerned that adopting core standards will lead them away from their own priorities. For example, support for a rigorous treatment of evolutionary biology is strongest in the Pacific, New England, and Mid-Atlantic states, but the publics of the midwestern and southern states are far less supportive. Differences on this and other subjects place limits on efficiencies that might be gained by interstate cooperation.

THE AUTHORITY DELEGATED TO LOCAL SCHOOL BOARDS

All states except Hawaii have delegated substantial powers to local school districts; in the Aloha State education is administered by the state board of education. **Local school boards** are governing institutions with power to tax, spend funds, hire teachers, and administer auxiliary services such as transportation, food, and athletics. Most school districts have a governing structure that was heavily influenced by the Progressive movement. The Progressives placed great stock in ordinary citizens' ability to participate, saw party politics as corrupt and antithetical to good public policy, and were enamored of professional management. Therefore, most Progressive districts share four characteristics: (1) they cover a small geographic area; (2) they are governed by a school board composed of local citizens; (3) school board members are elected in nonpartisan elections; and (4) each school board hires a professional manager—the superintendent—to administer the school system on a day-to-day basis.

The role of the superintendent is especially important in the smaller independent school districts because school board members rarely have extensive expertise in public policy, public administration, or education. Superintendents' expertise typically gives them considerable power to set the school board's agenda and to persuade the board to adopt their policy recommendations. Thus even though the superintendent formally serves at the pleasure of the school board, it is common to see the board take cues from their professional administrator rather than the other way around.

To protect school boards from the corruption Progressives associated with political parties, these districts have two characteristics. First, they are legally independent of larger city or county governments, even though they may lie completely within their boundaries. Second, elections are often held on days *other than* the general election in November, and in many states candidates do not identify their political party. In many of these districts, any tax and spending increase must be approved by voters in a referendum.

These Progressive-inspired districts are also diverse. Some elect their members at large; in others the board members represent smaller wards. They also vary in size. At one extreme, the Mohawk Valley School District in Arizona serves only 254 students in one school building encompassing kindergarten through the eighth grade. At the other extreme is the Los Angeles Unified School District (LAUSD), which is the largest independent school district in the nation, serving over 700,000 students. There are more students in the LAUSD than people of all ages in Wyoming, or Vermont, or North Dakota, or Alaska.

A different model is common in many of the nation's largest cities, especially in the eastern and midwestern states. The so-called dependent school district is simply a part of the local municipal or county government. Governed directly by the elected city council or indirectly via an appointed school board, these districts are controlled by partisan, professional politicians. Perhaps most important, these districts are funded through the general city budget and must compete for funds with other city services such as the fire, police, and transportation departments. In some cities, the mayoral takeover of city schools has been used as a reform strategy to help school districts that appear to be failing under their own governance (Wong et al. 2007). More generally, in the larger dependent school districts, the mayor and other elected officials play an active role in setting educational priorities, with the superintendent having less independence than is typical in the independent districts.

Finally, in New England the remnants of town meeting governance continue to thrive. Many (though not all) school districts in New England are dependent districts that are authorized by their municipalities but have their own school budget meeting once each year. Although the ultimate authority lies with the town's citizens (at least those who attend the town meeting), day-to-day governance is handled by a superintendent, just as in the Progressive-inspired districts.

Consolidation, State Sovereignty, and Racial Segregation

Three key trends have influenced the character of today's school districts and their freedom to operate with relative autonomy: consolidation, the increasingly frequent takeover of failing districts, and the resegregation of schools in metropolitan areas.

There were over 110,000 school districts in 1939, and the average district served a population of about 230 students. Districts were rapidly consolidated and merged, however, during the first half of the twentieth century, so that today there are roughly 14,000 school districts, of which about 10,000 are serving the full range of K–12 students. Of these, the one hundred largest districts serve about 22 percent of all students, and their school boards represent an average of about 600,000 citizens. The remaining districts each serve a community of roughly 20,000 residents. Thus even with consolidation, most districts are small and, some say, inefficient governments. This situation has led to further calls for consolidation. For example, in 2009 Pennsylvania governor Edward Rendell called for a commission to study further consolidation from over five hundred to just one hundred districts. New York governor Andrew Cuomo's 2011 budget proposal called for the consolidation of New York's two hundred smallest districts. It would seem, then, that as states seek to find ways to reduce education expenditures, consolidation of districts is an attractive option for state officials, but they may meet with fierce resistance from communities that wish to retain their own school systems. And yet William A. Fischel (2009) argues that consolidation is desired by the residents of school districts themselves.

The second trend in recent years is for states to invoke their constitutional supremacy in education by taking over the governance of individual schools and even whole districts. At one time, state takeovers were conducted principally in response to financial disarray or malfeasance, but today they occur most often when districts or schools are deemed to be failing their students (Wong and Shen 2003). This is one way in which states can hold school districts or individual schools accountable. Thirty states currently have laws that establish specific objectives in terms of student success and advancement. Schools not meeting these expectations—often labeled "low performing"—are subject to sanctions or corrective measures (Table 12-2). These sanctions and measures include **reconstitution**—that is, closing a school that is later reopened with a new principal and new staff (authorized in twenty-eight states), turning the school over to private management (seventeen states), and allowing a state agency to take over a school (twenty-one states). The most drastic sanction is a complete state takeover of an entire school district (authorized in twenty-nine states), in which the school board is stripped of its authority and all fiscal and

Table 12-2   State-Authorized Sanctions for Low-Performing Schools and School Districts

	State sanctions include reconstitution	State sanctions include turning school management over to state agency	State sanctions include turning schools over to private management	State sanctions include school closure	Number of authorized sanctions	Can state take over entire school districts?
District of Columbia	No	No	No	No	0	No
Kansas	No	No	No	No	0	No
Minnesota	No	No	No	No	0	No
Montana	No	No	No	No	0	No
Nebraska	No	No	No	No	0	No
New Hampshire	No	No	No	No	0	No
North Dakota	No	No	No	No	0	No
Oregon	No	No	No	No	0	No
South Dakota	No	No	No	No	0	No
Utah	No	No	No	No	0	No
Washington	No	No	No	No	0	No
Wisconsin	No	No	No	No	0	No
Alaska	No	No	No	No	0	Yes
Connecticut	No	No	No	No	0	Yes
Iowa	No	No	No	No	0	Yes
Kentucky	No	No	No	No	0	Yes
Maine	No	No	No	No	0	Yes
Missouri	No	No	No	No	0	Yes
Nevada	No	No	No	No	0	Yes
New Jersey	No	No	No	No	0	Yes
Pennsylvania	No	No	No	No	0	Yes
Florida	Yes	No	No	No	1	No
Hawaii	No	Yes	No	No	1	No
Wyoming	Yes	No	No	No	1	No
Massachusetts	Yes	No	No	No	1	Yes
Georgia	Yes	No	Yes	No	2	No
Vermont	No	Yes	No	Yes	2	No
Virginia	Yes	No	No	Yes	2	No
Delaware	Yes	No	Yes	No	2	Yes
Mississippi	Yes	Yes	No	No	2	Yes
New York	Yes	No	No	Yes	2	Yes
North Carolina	Yes	No	Yes	No	2	Yes
South Carolina	Yes	Yes	No	No	2	Yes
West Virginia	Yes	Yes	No	No	2	Yes
Arizona	Yes	Yes	Yes	No	3	No
Colorado	Yes	No	Yes	Yes	3	No
Louisiana	Yes	Yes	Yes	No	3	No
Alabama	Yes	Yes	Yes	No	3	Yes
Idaho	Yes	Yes	Yes	No	3	Yes
Michigan	Yes	Yes	No	Yes	3	Yes
New Mexico	Yes	Yes	No	Yes	3	Yes
Ohio	Yes	Yes	Yes	No	3	Yes
Rhode Island	Yes	Yes	No	Yes	3	Yes
Tennessee	Yes	Yes	Yes	No	3	Yes
Indiana	Yes	Yes	Yes	Yes	4	No
Arkansas	Yes	Yes	Yes	Yes	4	Yes
California	Yes	Yes	Yes	Yes	4	Yes
Illinois	Yes	Yes	Yes	Yes	4	Yes
Maryland	Yes	Yes	Yes	Yes	4	Yes
Oklahoma	Yes	Yes	Yes	Yes	4	Yes
Texas	Yes	Yes	Yes	Yes	4	Yes
Number of states with policy	28	21	17	14		29

SOURCES: School sanction data, 2010: Education Counts Research Center, www.edcounts.org/createtable/; district takeover data: Education Commission for the States, "Policy Briefs: Takeovers," 2004, www.ecs.org/clearinghouse/51/67/5167.htm.

academic authority is exercised by the state government or, in some cases, the mayor.

In some states, the takeover authorization is a blanket one, encompassing all school districts. But more commonly, troubled districts are singled out and the authorization becomes a warning to districts that are not meeting their fiscal responsibilities or are not achieving academic benchmarks. For example, the School District of Philadelphia was taken over by the state of Pennsylvania as a result of both low academic performance and the district's inability to raise sufficient funds solely through property taxes and state allocations. This was the largest of many big city school districts to lose local control; others included districts in Detroit, Michigan; Oakland, California; and Newark, New Jersey. Many smaller districts have been taken over as well, including multiple districts in California that accepted state money to forestall bankruptcy.

State takeovers illustrate clearly that states have the ultimate responsibility and authority in primary and secondary education, with school districts subordinate to the states. In most cases, the state legislature, governor, state school board, and state department of education are all involved in the decision to take over a district or school. The role of the department of education is generally to collect and analyze data and to thoroughly document any academic or administrative problems that might justify a takeover. In some states, such as Massachusetts and Louisiana, the state school board then considers these recommendations from the education department. Legislatures and governors, of course, must pass the laws granting takeover authority in the first place. Often, as in Tennessee, the legislature and governor offer a broad grant of discretion to the department of education and school board; other legislatures may themselves target a specific district. Philadelphia's state takeover, for example, was authorized under a law applying only to districts with populations exceeding 1 million residents, and Philadelphia was alone in meeting that criterion.

School Segregation and Resegregation

A third trend in local school districts is the resegregation of racial minorities from white students. Prior to the Supreme Court's ruling in *Brown v. Board of Education*, 347 U.S. 483 (1954), decisions about whether black and white students attended the same schools were made by the states and local school districts. The schools in seventeen southern and border states, as well as the nation's capital, had laws that mandated segregation or allowed school districts to designate some schools as black only or white only (Orfield, Frankenberg, and Lee 2002). This policy was known as **de jure segregation**, or segregation by law.

The *Brown* case arose because Kansas was one of the states that explicitly allowed segregation in certain districts, including Topeka, where a network of segregated elementary schools fed students into an integrated high school. This law was unconstitutional, the Court held, because "separate educational facilities are inherently unequal." This decision denied school districts and states the right to decide for themselves whether schools would include both black and white students.

Although *Brown* ended segregation in theory, it did not in practice. Fifteen years later, in the Charlotte, North Carolina, school district that encompassed the city of Charlotte as well as its suburbs, more than 80 percent of black students attended all-black schools. Under pressure from the federal courts, the school board finally attempted to desegregate its schools by closing some and busing black students from the city to largely white schools in the suburbs. This type of intradistrict busing was found constitutional by the Supreme Court in *Swann v. Charlotte-Mecklenburg*, 402 U.S. 1 (1971), and the remedy would be used elsewhere to address segregation.

In many northern cities, segregation resulted not from governmental decree but from patterns of residential segregation that produced segregated neighborhood schools (Orfield and Eaton 2003, 6). Known as **de facto segregation,** it arose from reasons other than laws that explicitly mandated or permitted segregation. Unlike those in the South, many busing plans in the northern states had to cross district lines, a practice that was often fiercely resisted by white parents and was soon challenged in court. In *Milliken v. Bradley*, 418 U.S. 717 (1974), the Supreme Court considered a desegregation plan that involved busing students from Detroit to districts in its largely white suburbs. The Court concluded that white suburban districts had no responsibility to help desegregate urban schools. It therefore invalidated the busing plan and banned states from developing new desegregation remedies that crossed from city to suburban districts.

A series of federal court decisions in the 1990s further hindered efforts to combat segregation (Frankenberg and Lee 2002). Indeed, by 1999 the courts had vacated the *Swann* decision, thereby allowing the Charlotte school board to end busing. Charlotte's schools promptly became resegregated. Indeed, the acceleration of de facto segregation is a nationwide phenomenon. In 2000 nearly 40 percent of black students were attending schools that were 90–100 percent black, while the average Latino student attended a school that was 70 percent minority (Orfield and Eaton 2003). Now, more than a decade later, the country's rapidly growing Latino and black populations are more segregated than at any time since the 1960s, despite the increasing *diversity* of the population at large and the fact that more and more African Americans are moving to the suburbs (Reardon and Yun 2001). This trend is likely to continue in light of Court decisions in 2007 that effectively ruled out nearly all local efforts to address segregation (Orfield and Lee 2007).

MONEY: ADEQUACY, EQUITY, AND THE POLITICS OF FUNDING

In *Brown*, the Supreme Court ruled that segregated schools created a discriminatory environment in which black schools offered inherently inferior educational opportunities compared with white schools. Resegregation has led to similar charges today. Arguing that minority schools are often segregated by poverty as well as race and language, Orfield and Lee (2007, 5) conclude that segregated minority schools are inferior in terms of teacher qualifications, curriculum, level of competition, test scores, and graduation rates.

In showing that minority schools lag far behind in financial resources, Orfield and Lee raise some of the most controversial and important questions that districts face about money. Can higher salaries, supported by a wealthier population, enable a district to hire the most qualified and effective teachers? Do students learn better when class sizes are smaller, when laboratories and libraries are modern and well stocked? Do overflowing toilets, a crumbling infrastructure, and unreliable heating create an environment in which it is difficult for students to excel?

Most Americans think that the answer to all these questions is "yes." Opinion polls show that most Americans think the country is spending too little on its public schools (Berkman and Plutzer 2005) and that affluent families with young children are paying a substantial premium to live in suburbs with well-resourced schools (Fischel 2005). In light of these beliefs, financial inequality across school districts raises questions about fairness. To research his book *Savage Inequalities,* educator and activist Jonathan Kozol travelled the country and compared affluent school districts with those in places such as east St. Louis, where a physics teacher showed Kozol his students' lab and lamented that "it would be great if we had water" (Kozol 1991, 27). Fourteen years later, Kozol (2005) would describe American education as the "restoration of apartheid in America."

The connection between funding and the quality of education is not universally accepted, however. Some affluent Americans think extra spending will have a positive impact in their own districts, but they are skeptical that spending more on inner-city schools would really help (Kozol 1991, 169–171). The connection between resources and educational outcomes has been studied extensively, but the research remains inconclusive (Burtless 1996). Some research shows little direct correlation between spending levels and student achievement (Klick 2000). Other research, however, finds that greater resources give schools access to better teachers (Elliott 1998) or in other ways positively affect student achievement (Hedges, Laine, and Greenwald 1994).

Amid this uncertainty—and perhaps because of it—the politics of school finance is contentious. Locally, cities and communities must set spending and revenue levels each year. Meanwhile, state legislatures must decide how much school spending should come from state revenues, and then determine how evenly to distribute the funds across the state—to rich and poor communities alike or to give preference to the least-affluent communities.

The Property Tax

States and local school districts determine simultaneously both the spending levels in each school district and the degree of inequality across districts. An illustration might be helpful. Imagine two communities in a state that provides no direct aid to its local school districts (see Table 12-3 for a description of these hypo-thetical communities).The communities have identical numbers of adults and chil-dren, and both wish to spend about $13,500 per student in their respective school districts (roughly the current average for all instructional, capital, and service expenses), but they differ in their abilities to pay. Struggling Town is primarily working class and has a per capita income of $20,000—somewhat below the national average of $26,000. Thriving Town, by contrast, is more middle class and has a per capita income of $35,000. Its families earn on average about 33 percent more than the typical family in the United States. According to Table 12-3, each school district would need to raise $135 million in order to spend at roughly the national norm. The challenge lies in how to raise these funds.

In practice, nearly all school districts raise revenues for their schools through a property tax, where the value of each parcel of property is assessed and its owner is then taxed at a rate determined by the school board or through a referendum. The rate of taxation is called **millage.** Certain communities have more valuable prop-erty to tax than others. Some communities may have single-family homes on large lots, which means there is more highly valued property to tax and fewer children to support in schools. By contrast, not only do most urban areas have denser housing, but many properties are not even taxable because they are used by universities, parks, civic buildings, or churches.

Ignoring these complexities, one can simply assume that incomes in Struggling Town are about 40 percent lower than in Thriving Town, and property values are about 40 percent lower as well. Table 12-3 shows that when expenditures are appor-tioned evenly across all adults, supporting the schools will consume 14 percent of all the income earned in Struggling Town, but only 8 percent of the income earned in Thriving Town. Indeed, Thriving Town can easily increase expenditures to reduce class sizes, build outstanding athletic and arts facilities, and so on—and *still* have a lower tax rate than their neighbors who live in Struggling Town.

Table 12-3   Illustration of the Tax Efforts Needed in Two Hypothetical Communities

	Struggling town	Thriving town
Town characteristics		
Number of children	10,000	10,000
Number of adults	50,000	50,000
Per capita income	$20,000	$35,000
Education spending		
Spending per pupil goal (national average)	$13,500	$13,500
Spending for all pupils	$135,000,000	$135,000,000
Tax burden		
Tax burden per adult	$2,700	$2,700
Tax burden as a percentage of income	14%	8%

SOURCE: The authors.

A tax burden representing 14 percent of all income earned—whether raised by property, income, or sales tax—would be difficult to sustain for an affluent community. For a working-class town, where a greater percentage of income goes to necessities such as food, health care, housing, and clothing, it is virtually impossible. The only real recourse is to spend less on their schools. As much as they would like to pay teachers the average salary for their state, it will become difficult: older school buses must stay in service longer; maintenance on buildings may have to be deferred; extracurricular activities such as the drama club, band, or school newspaper will be cut.

More pernicious, residents in Struggling Town who can afford to do so will have an incentive to "vote with their feet" and move to Thriving Town, where their taxes will go down (the rate will fall from 14 percent to 8 percent) and the schools will be better. But if the most affluent residents of Struggling Town leave, the average income will fall and the tax rates for everyone else will have to rise, undoing the savings from having lowered expenditures.

For state governments, this vicious cycle raises a critical question: Does the state have a responsibility to subsidize Struggling Town? A subsidy might allow the school district to pay market-level salaries to teachers and avoid the kinds of cuts that drive away middle-class citizens. But doing so necessarily means redistributing resources from more affluent taxpayers to poorer districts.

In short, state governments must decide whether equity in school spending is an appropriate goal. If the answer is yes, then state governments must also determine the minimum level of support that each district needs to educate its children. This is a question of adequacy—how much is enough? In practice, most states have developed **foundation programs.** Under these programs, states set a target level of resources that each district needs to provide a no-frills, adequate education. This foundation level is adjusted and modified to compensate for serving special populations, such as English language learners or special education students. A uniform property tax rate is then applied in each district to raise the necessary revenues, and the state allocates the revenues to enable all districts to reach the foundation level by allocating more revenues to poorer districts. In this way, each school district, no matter how poor, is guaranteed an adequate foundation on which to build. Traditionally, local districts could then raise taxes above and beyond the foundation to meet the expectations and preferences of its citizens.

Although this approach seems simple enough, the politics can be vigorous. In some cases, in fact, foundation levels were considered so low that citizens in poorer districts sued the state for violating the right to a public education enshrined in their state constitutions. The seminal case involved a parent, John Serrano, who filed a class action suit questioning the fairness and constitutionality of the wide differences in spending on students' education across California. Serrano's district, Baldwin Park, spent $577 on each student in 1968–1969, while the

Pasadena Unified School District spent $840 per student and wealthy Beverly Hills spent over $1,200 per child.

In its decision in *Serrano v. Priest*, 5 Cal.3d 584 (1971), the California Supreme Court placed the blame for these disparities squarely on the local property tax, which raised over 55 percent of all public school funds in California. Because the amount of per pupil spending varied so much, it violated guarantees of equal protection under California's constitution. The court wrote: "Affluent districts can have their cake and eat it too; they can provide a high quality education for their children while paying lower taxes. Poor districts, by contrast, have no cake at all."

Serrano was decided on equity considerations because the court agreed that the financing system was too unequal across districts. However, over the next two decades the courts would increasingly decide cases on the basis of adequacy, concluding that students in some districts were not receiving an "adequate" level of educational services (Odden and Picus 2004; *Rose v. Council*, 790 S.W.2d 186, 60 Ed. Law Rep. 1289 [1989]). As recently as 2010, Washington State's superior court ruled that the "state aid system is 'not currently correlated to what it actually costs to operate this State's public schools' and that the system, therefore, is unconstitutional" (*McLeary v. Washington*, No. 07–2-02323–2 SEA [2010]).

By 2011 forty-five states were subject to court rulings on the equity or adequacy of how education funds were raised and distributed. In twenty-five states, the funding systems were completely or partially overturned. In response, most states assumed more responsibility for funding schools, bringing state politics increasingly into play on school funding issues. In some states, there has been a series of court cases and legislative responses, as the states try to find an acceptable balance between state and local control. Texas, for example, was first sued in 1989 (*Edgewood v. Kirby*, 777 S.W.2d 391). Since then, there have been numerous lawsuits, with the legislature responding to each by tinkering with its formulas for distributing aid and raising revenues. As one observer of Texas politics writes, "Texas has a history of making its education funding reforms through lawsuits and litigation. It takes people in black robes to get lawmakers worried" (Rapoport 2011).

Today's debates over state funding are increasingly caught up in the challenges of confronting falling property values, lower tax revenues, and cuts to education spending, all of which pose challenges for states seeking to provide an adequate education equitably across the state. In February 2011, Texas state representative Mike Villarreal spoke directly to these concerns. "If the state's going to decrease its contribution by almost a quarter," he asked in response to the governor's 2011 budget proposal, "doesn't that have an implication on the constitutionality of our school finance system?" (Rapoport 2011). As states reduce their contributions to local education, additional litigation that questions the constitutionality of deep education cuts will emerge.

The Role of Unions

So far, this discussion has centered on many of the key actors that determine school finance levels in terms of both adequacy and equity: the local, state, and federal governments that make policies; the courts that rule on their constitutionality, the citizens who vote, and the parents who "vote with their feet." But there is one additional important actor: teachers' unions.

Before 1955, few states permitted public employees to form trade unions. Without collective bargaining rights, each teacher essentially negotiated his or her own salary, benefits, and conditions of employment. But state laws giving public employees the right to organize and bargain collectively for district-wide contracts led to the emergence of two strong teachers' unions. The National Education Association (NEA) and the American Federation of Teachers (AFT) are formidable voices in American education. Through unions, teachers can select representatives to bargain on their behalf, giving them significant clout in dealings with local school boards and state governments. According to estimates based on the U.S. Department of Education's School and Staffing Survey, by 2000, 79 percent of all public school teachers were members of teachers' unions. In the northeastern states, nearly 100 percent of all teachers were unionized, followed by those in the Midwest (88 percent) and West (84 percent), with only 62 percent in the southern states.

Unions are generally considered either the most or second most influential interest in state governments (see Chapter 4 on interest groups). They have helped teachers gain higher pay, better working conditions, and significant protections against arbitrary sanctions or dismissal. Moreover, some union goals related to compensation (such as a higher salary for earning advanced degrees) and working conditions (more notably, smaller class sizes) may advance goals shared more widely by citizens and parents in teachers' districts. Nevertheless, teachers' unions are not universally popular. Terry Moe contends that union objectives "are often incompatible with what is best for children, schools, society" (2001).

Unions can influence the outcome of elections by donating to and campaigning for candidates they support. In 2010, according to the nonpartisan National Institute on Money in State Politics (www.followthemoney.org), the two major teachers' unions gave over $34 million to state-level political candidates. The unions also become involved in local elections, which means they can help select the people sitting across the bargaining table from them. According to some observers, this situation leads to overly generous contracts (Moe 2001). Furthermore, teachers' unions have been accused of bargaining for work conditions that make it difficult to dismiss ineffective teachers and otherwise make school systems highly resistant to innovation.

Teachers' rights to collective bargaining were central to political battles in 2011 over state fiscal problems. Republican Chris Christie's successful 2010 run for the governorship of New Jersey featured strong criticism of unions. In 2011 Wisconsin's

Republican governor, Scott Walker, signed a law that sharply curtailed collective bargaining rights for teachers and other public employees. It is not lost on these Republican governors that teachers' unions are not only the largest contributors to state government elections, but that nearly all the money from the teachers' unions goes to Democratic candidates. As states have struggled through persistent very difficult economic conditions brought about by the 2007–2009 recession, teachers' unions have become a popular target of attack, although many residents have also rallied around their neighborhood teachers.

State Limits on Local Taxes

Earlier, we noted that foundation funding programs allow middle- and upper-class school districts to raise funds to add to their basic foundation. But state governments can and have restricted this local freedom to raise revenue, beginning with California's "tax revolt" of 1978. A combination of rising affluence and inflation had caused a sharp rise in housing values, leading to higher assessed property values. The higher assessments led in turn to higher property taxes, even when millage rates remained unchanged. In this environment, California voters approved **Proposition 13,** a state constitutional amendment that severely curtailed the ability of local governments to raise revenues. Not only was a two-thirds vote required to increase tax rates, but even if the real values of homes were rising, assessed value could not increase by more than 2 percent a year and all assessments were reduced to 1975 values (three years earlier). The result was a sharp reduction in overall spending on education in California, which ranks among the ten most affluent states in the nation, but now ranks only twenty-sixth in per pupil spending for its public schools.

A large number of other states have adopted policies that restrict the abilities of local communities to make their own financial choices. Many of these policies are called taxpayer bills of rights (TABOR), which are popular among antitax and anti-government conservatives. The first **TABOR law**, passed by Colorado in 1992, imposed strict limits on tax increases on the state government, municipalities, and school districts. Like Proposition 13 in California, the TABOR law had a dramatic effect on education funding, and Colorado declined from thirty-fifth to forty-ninth in the nation in K–12 spending (Center on Budget and Policy Priorities 2008). Between 2004 and 2008, serious efforts were made to enact TABOR laws in twenty states, and in 2010–2011 ten states imposed or called for new limits on the abilities of local governments to raise their own revenues (Center on Budget and Policy Priorities 2008; Lieb and Dudar 2011).

Currently, several more state legislatures and mostly Republican governors are trying to limit local taxing abilities. A 2006 Pennsylvania law, for example, requires any increase in property taxes over the rate of inflation in a school district to be approved by a vote of the district residents. In 2011 Wisconsin governor Walker proposed a state budget that would not only reduce the state's allocation to schools by 8 percent but also would prevent local school districts from compensating for the shortfall with their own local funds. And New Jersey recently passed legislation that prevents localities from raising local property taxes by more than 2 percent. In this fight, public schools have come a long way from the one-room schoolhouses of the previous century. Once completely independent, local school systems are now ensnared in larger national debates about the appropriate size of government and the desire of many citizens to reduce all taxes substantially.

Spending within and across the Fifty States

In the end, all these actors, working within the institutional arrangements dictated by state law, determine actual funding levels. Every state has its Struggling Towns and Thriving Towns, and the particular pattern differs from state to state. Typically, however, rural and urban schools with declining enrollments compete against suburban school districts whose populations are growing. Table 12-4 shows the most recent expenditure data for the fifty states. In addition to the average amount spent per pupil in each state, it also shows the amount spent in a low-income district (one poorer than 90 percent of all districts in the state) and the amount spent in an affluent district (one wealthier than 90 percent of all districts in the state).

The so-called 90:10 ratio in the last column of Table 12-4 shows how much more the district in the ninetieth percentile spends than the district in the tenth percentile. This ratio is an indication of **horizontal equity**, or the extent to which school districts across the states spend equally. The table is sorted so that the states with the least horizontal equity appear at the top. Equity increases as one reads down the table, but all states have at least some degree of horizontal inequality (note that the District of Columbia and Hawaii, with a single district, have no interdistrict inequality). This inequality persists despite legislative efforts and court orders to equalize spending.

Funding Regimes. States pursue different strategies in deciding how to divide the cost of education between state government and local school districts. The extreme example of a centralized funding regime is Hawaii, where a single school district serves the entire state. But even states with local school districts, such as New Mexico, can be relatively state-centralized, with the typical district receiving two-thirds of its funding from state revenues (Table 12-5). The last two columns of Table 12-5 show that even though New Mexico is relatively centralized, 10 percent of its districts (generally the wealthier ones) rely almost exclusively on local funds, whereas 10 percent of districts receive 84 percent or more of their funds from the state. Not surprisingly, according to Table 12-4 New Mexico has a high degree of inequality, and so a heavy state funding presence does not ensure equality of spending across districts. As the ongoing struggles in Texas and other states reveal, efforts to

Table 12-4   Mean, Tenth Percentile, and Ninetieth Percentile per Pupil Spending, 2008 (sorted from most to least unequal spending within each state)

	Per pupil educational spending by school districts			
	State mean	*10th percentile*	*90th percentile*	*90:10 ratio*
Alaska	26,974	13,813	49,388	3.6
Utah	11,223	6,858	22,738	3.3
Montana	14,584	8,194	23,451	2.9
New Hampshire	18,074	11,582	28,533	2.5
Arizona	12,700	7,784	18,656	2.4
Vermont	22,910	14,096	33,668	2.4
North Dakota	14,279	9,086	21,340	2.3
New Mexico	16,173	10,122	23,564	2.3
Texas	13,391	8,616	19,258	2.2
Oregon	14,034	9,031	19,794	2.2
Colorado	12,383	8,519	18,670	2.2
Wyoming	21,444	14,278	31,010	2.2
Idaho	9,900	6,609	14,181	2.1
Washington	13,220	8,978	19,152	2.1
California	12,382	8,629	17,419	2.0
Illinois	11,108	8,116	15,314	1.9
Maine	14,455	10,545	19,673	1.9
New York	20,916	14,533	26,891	1.9
New Jersey	19,784	14,515	26,517	1.8
Ohio	10,776	8,340	15,001	1.8
Nebraska	12,697	9,568	16,792	1.8
Nevada	12,458	9,439	16,508	1.7
Missouri	10,663	8,069	14,056	1.7
Massachusetts	15,836	11,910	20,676	1.7
Oklahoma	9,400	7,085	12,130	1.7
South Dakota	10,546	8,369	14,167	1.7
Pennsylvania	13,380	10,396	17,461	1.7
Connecticut	16,828	12,991	21,755	1.7
Delaware	15,215	12,125	20,140	1.7
Iowa	11,274	8,814	14,550	1.7
Michigan	10,276	8,175	13,257	1.6
Virginia	11,782	9,479	15,282	1.6
Louisiana	11,679	8,794	14,014	1.6
Mississippi	9,384	7,471	11,848	1.6
Tennessee	8,968	7,318	11,415	1.6
Rhode Island	15,834	12,490	19,472	1.6
South Carolina	11,249	8,873	13,693	1.5
Georgia	11,645	9,448	14,567	1.5
Kansas	12,547	9,627	14,789	1.5
Minnesota	12,371	9,545	14,646	1.5
Kentucky	10,282	8,643	12,914	1.5
Florida	11,590	9,614	14,162	1.5
Arkansas	9,579	7,980	11,451	1.4
Alabama	10,435	8,877	12,370	1.4
Wisconsin	12,368	10,611	14,724	1.4
Indiana	9,939	8,562	11,820	1.4
North Carolina	9,946	8,408	11,598	1.4
West Virginia	10,880	9,503	12,761	1.3
Maryland	14,558	12,773	17,109	1.3
District of Columbia	21,048	21,048	21,048	1.0
Hawaii	12,465	12,465	12,465	1.0
Mean	13,487	10,014	18,193	1.8

SOURCE: National Center for Educational Statistics, "Local Education Agency Finance Survey Data for 2008," http://nces.ed.gov/ccd/f33agency.asp.

NOTE: The 90:10 ratio is the ratio of spending in the ninetieth percentile school district and the tenth percentile school district within the state.

Table 12-5 School District Reliance on State, Local, and Federal Revenues, by State, 2008 (sorted by state share of revenue)

	Reliance on state funding			Reliance on local funds, district mean	Reliance on federal funds, district mean
	Mean	10th percentile	90th percentile		
Hawaii	85	85	85	3	12
Vermont	83	19	99	15	2
Arkansas	75	69	82	13	12
Idaho	71	57	80	18	11
Alaska	67	51	86	15	18
Washington	66	55	79	24	10
Delaware	66	51	78	27	6
New Mexico	66	12	84	23	11
Michigan	65	38	89	28	6
Kentucky	64	52	74	24	11
North Carolina	63	52	73	26	10
Alabama	63	51	72	28	10
Kansas	62	42	77	31	7
West Virginia	61	52	71	28	12
Oregon	58	39	74	33	9
Minnesota	57	12	77	34	10
Oklahoma	56	39	68	31	13
Mississippi	56	44	66	27	17
Utah	56	40	68	36	8
Wyoming	54	15	79	39	7
California	53	21	75	39	8
Georgia	52	37	65	36	11
Montana	52	37	67	36	13
South Carolina	50	28	63	40	10
Louisiana	50	29	63	35	15
Tennessee	50	30	66	37	13
Texas	49	23	70	42	9
Missouri	49	36	58	42	9
New York	48	17	72	48	4
Indiana	48	35	61	45	7
Colorado	47	18	70	45	8
Florida	47	21	68	44	9
Wisconsin	46	16	63	49	5
Arizona	46	16	70	41	13
Maryland	45	23	62	49	6
Iowa	44	35	52	51	5
Ohio	43	23	65	49	7
Pennsylvania	40	16	64	55	5
Massachusetts	39	21	61	57	4
Virginia	38	4	64	47	15
Illinois	38	12	64	54	8
New Hampshire	38	26	50	58	4
Maine	36	7	63	57	7
Connecticut	34	12	59	63	3
South Dakota	33	16	46	54	13
North Dakota	33	19	45	56	11
Rhode Island	31	12	57	63	6
New Jersey	31	13	55	66	3
Nevada	31	12	57	60	9
Nebraska	29	12	45	64	7

SOURCE: National Center for Education Statistics, "Local Education Agency (School District) Finance Survey (F-33)," http://nces .ed.gov/ccd/f33agency.asp.

equalize spending meet with substantial political opposition and inequities persist despite state involvement.

Sources of Spending Differences. Wealth and property values explain almost half of the variation in per pupil spending (Hoxby 1998), but districts do not vary solely based on the ability to afford higher taxes. Spending varies for political reasons as well. Strong unions, for example, can lead to higher per pupil spending at both the state and local levels, although the relationship is a complex one (Berkman and Plutzer 2005).

Generational and racial politics also play major roles. Most school districts rely on property taxes rather than on income or sales taxes, and these property taxes impose a greater burden on those who live on fixed incomes—such as older retirees—than on others. It is not hard to see why. Property owners on a fixed income will be especially affected by increases in property taxes if the value of their property increases while their income does not change. People who are working, by contrast, are more likely to see increases in *both* the value of their property and their income. Nevertheless, not all communities with a large number of seniors have a hard time raising funds (Berkman and Plutzer 2005). One reason is that many retirees remain loyal to the school district that may have educated their children and grandchildren.

However, seniors who have moved to new communities to retire have no particular loyalty to their new school district or its students. Moreover, the largely white baby boomer generation is retiring when newcomers to school districts are likely to be diverse in terms of race and ethnicity (Myers 2007). The effects of this transition are already appearing; school budget referenda failed "in the four New York districts where the majority of registered voters are white and nonwhite students make up the majority of the school population" (Roberts 2010).

But budgets can be defeated for many reasons. Voters in 58 percent of New Jersey's school districts defeated budgets in 2010 in large part because Governor Christie had urged them to hold the line on local taxes. Citizens in some districts may be zealous supporters of their local schools and happy to impose relatively stiff taxes on themselves, whereas support for public education spending may be more tepid when citizens do not think the schools are that important relative to other priorities. Whatever the reasons, it is clear that public opinion matters, though some governmental arrangements are better at translating public opinion into policy than others (Berkman and Plutzer 2005).

The Increasing Importance of Parental Choice

Parents influence education politics by "voting with their feet." Those with the financial means can move their families to different school districts, enroll their children in private schools, or exit formal schooling altogether. The percentage of school-age children who are homeschooled, for example, increased from 1.7 percent to 2.2 percent between 1999 and 2003, with the rates of homeschooling somewhat higher (2.8 percent) in the southern states (Princiotta and Bielick 2006). By choosing some schools and rejecting others (or all public schools), parents indicate their support or opposition to what the schools are doing and their approach to education, generating competition among schools and school districts to attract students in the process.

In recent years, this type of market-oriented philosophy has become more influential in education politics. Meanwhile, state governments are increasingly encouraging parental choice, including homeschooling. In 2011, for example, Indiana governor Mitch Daniels asked state lawmakers to give parents more opportunities for their "children to attend the school of their choice." Indiana already allowed students to attend schools outside their prescribed district, but Daniels asked for more choices. He argued that students who can complete school in eleven years be able to spend the money that would have been spent on their senior year on any other kind of educational institution. And he proposed an extensive program of **school vouchers**—a government certificate that can be used to pay for tuition at any school that admits the student. Daniels said that vouchers would benefit parents who are dissatisfied with public schools and who are not wealthy enough to be able to move to another district.

Daniels also urged an increase in the number of charter schools—alternative schools within a school district run by either the district or an outside organization. According to the National Center for Education Statistics,[1] the number of charter schools in the United States increased from nearly 1,500 in 1999–2000 to nearly 4,300 in 2007–2008. By 2008, 2.6 percent of all public school students (1.3 million) were enrolled in charter schools. However, Indiana lagged behind other states; only about 1 percent of its students were in the state's forty charter schools by 2008. Thus Daniels proposed making it easier for charters to open.

Proponents of school choice predict that parental decisions to abandon weaker schools will ultimately either strengthen them or close them. By exercising their choice, this reasoning goes, parents create competitive market pressures that will lead schools to improve as they compete for students and the tax dollars that will follow them or to close because they are uncompetitive.

Critics of voucher programs note, however, that these programs often do not provide enough to cover the entire cost of sending children to private schools. As a result, upper-middle-class students use vouchers as a subsidy, while poorer families cannot fully take advantage of the choices that are theoretically available. Furthermore, vouchers remove both tax dollars and highly involved parents from a school district, and private schools may refuse admittance to anyone they want, a prerogative not available to public schools. Public schools would then be left with a disproportionate number of students with learning disabilities, those whose parents' native language is not English, and students who otherwise have had difficulties in

1. http://nces.ed.gov/programs/coe/2010/section4/table-cht-3.asp, table A-32-3.

learning. This turn of events would, of course, have important implications for accountability, because it would mean that the public schools are left with more and more students who are less likely to do well, making some schools appear to be doing worse in terms of learning outcomes than schools that recruit already high-achieving students.

In short, efforts to introduce market incentives vary. Nearly all states offer at least a limited opportunity for students to attend schools other than the one they were assigned, either within the district or in another district. Most states also offer parents the additional choice of having their children attend a charter school. States can also offer homeschooling regulations that make it easier for families who desire to exit the public schools and educate their children themselves. For example, ten states do not require parents who are homeschooling their children to initiate any contact with the state or to have their students' progress evaluated by education professionals.

As more and more families take advantage of these programs, future research will shed light on whether these reforms have actually improved the equity and adequacy of education available to the nation's poorest families and reversed trends in the resegregation of public schools. Gary Orfield writes in a report by his colleagues at the UCLA Civil Rights Project that "the charter school movement has been a major political success, but it has been a civil rights failure" (Frankenberg, Siegel-Hawley, and Wang 2010, 1). If vouchers do succeed in reversing racial segregation, it will be quite ironic because private schools were rarely found in the South prior to *Brown v. Board of Education* and subsequent court-ordered desegregation plans throughout the region. Parents' refusals to send their children to newly integrated schools resulted in the rapid expansion of predominantly white private schools and religious academies. Even today, the pattern of private school enrollments in the South is segregated, although residential segregation has declined (Reardon and Yun 2001). If vouchers and other choice mechanisms are widely implemented, their impacts on racial segregation will be among the outcomes most closely watched.

The National Government and Fiscal Federalism

Traditionally, education was solely a state and local concern. But as in many areas of public policy, the federal government began to play an important role after the end of the World War II. President Harry S. Truman signed the National School Lunch Act in 1946, and the 1965 Elementary and Secondary Education Act (ESEA) further promoted national priorities such as racial integration, education of the handicapped, and eradication of inequities that "arise primarily from class, status and racial differences" (Wong 1999, 18). At about the same time, the federal government stepped in to help local schools address perceived needs in general literacy and in math and science education in particular. Spurred by the Soviet Union's leap ahead in the space race with the launching of the satellite *Sputnik* in 1957, and then again by the highly critical report *A Nation at Risk* (National Commission on Excellence in Education 1983), the federal government instituted a variety of grant programs and small subsidies to encourage state and local education systems to improve instruction.

As in many instances of fiscal federalism, the actual dollar amounts were very small. The federal portion of all public school spending has never exceeded 10 percent. Still, for a struggling school district or a state government trying to balance its budget, a small influx of funds can be a lifesaver, and few are willing to forgo federal assistance. And for some states the amount can be quite significant (see Table 12-5). As a consequence, the federal rules and regulations that specify conditions for receiving these funds can have major influence. President George W. Bush's flagship domestic program, **No Child Left Behind (NCLB),** is a good illustration of such influence. NCLB significantly expanded the federal government's role in the education decision making of both state and local governments (Manna 2006; Wong and Sunderman 2007). NCLB tied federal funds to the performance of schools within a state as well as to the quality of the teacher workforce. This link required local school districts to be accountable not only to state governments but to the federal government as well.

No Child Left Behind has been quite controversial. States have pushed back against its constraints on their autonomy in a variety of ways and venues, including filing lawsuits (Wong and Sunderman 2007). Even Diane Ravitch, the assistant secretary of education in the Bush administration and one of NCLB's strongest supporters, concluded that, as implemented, NCLB has taken classroom time away from science, social studies, history, geography, foreign languages, art, and music (Ravitch 2010). Attacked by conservatives and liberals alike, NCLB expired in 2007 and was not reauthorized, although it has held on through annual short-term extensions.

Meanwhile, President Barack Obama has begun a new program called **Race to the Top.** Like NCLB, the program is built around accountability. Federal money is linked to school performance, but in this case funds are awarded to states that win an annual competition, while schools that continue to produce students with low test scores will be closed, turned into charter schools, or handed over to private management. In Race to the Top, states submit applications to the federal Department of Education and are awarded points based on the extent to which their proposals meet program objectives. For example, a state would receive seventy of a possible five hundred points for developing high-quality standards and assessment tools as well as for adopting the common standards; 138 points could be earned for the quality of the state's plan to ensure great teachers and leaders. In the first round of competition, twelve states each won a share of more than $4 billion. Florida, New York, and Tennessee, for example, were each awarded more than $500 million in Race to the Top awards. It is too soon to know whether these awards have had the intended effects.

WHAT SHOULD STUDENTS LEARN?

Both the No Child Left Behind and Race to the Top programs are important—not only because of the money they provide to fiscally needy school districts, but also because of what they say about who should decide about what children should learn. A century ago, school systems were considered successful if a majority of students learned to read, write, and master the four key mathematical operations. Only a tiny fraction went to college, and so preparing for higher education was not a major goal for most districts. Indeed, until the 1940s most Americans did not even graduate from high school.

Today, expectations are higher, very specific, and heavily influenced by state and national governments. Should students learn to organize data into arrays, display the data in bar graphs, and be able to describe the arrays in terms of statistics such as the mean or mode? And if so, should students master this by the tenth grade? Sixth grade? Or even earlier? This example illustrates one of literally hundreds of learning goals that states now specify for students. But what should those goals be? Should goals differ from district to district? And who should decide?

In some disciplines, the question of what students should learn is noncontroversial and so is left largely to the experts. For example, the experts have generally agreed that it is best for geometry to come before trigonometry, and so there have been few debates about this aspect of the math curriculum. Likewise, there is a growing consensus among the experts that the basic concepts of statistics and probability will be at least as valuable to citizens as mastering calculus. So without any public debate or controversy, statistics have played a more prominent role in K–12 math education.

Other issues are much more controversial, and the experts' advice is overridden by ideological or majoritarian considerations. Should students learn to read through phonics or whole language instruction? How should the history curriculum strike a balance between diversity and the perspectives of the nation's founders? Should a health class teach comprehensive sex education or abstinence-only? Should evolution be taught, and if so, should parents be able to remove their children from this segment of tenth grade biology?

State Content Standards

Curricular standards enumerate, in varying levels of detail, what students should learn in each subject area in each year in school. State school boards and education departments spend considerable time and effort writing and periodically revising these standards. In addition, they assess achievements of these standards and hold school districts and individual schools accountable with statewide exams. Even before NCLB, many states used tests and standards to hold districts accountable, but NCLB moved this effort to a whole new level by making districts accountable to the federal government as well as to the states. In reading and mathematics, state examinations were now required by NCLB, which used them to determine whether schools were doing "well" or were "failing." But in science and other subjects not covered by NCLB, some states chose to write and administer exams anyway to better hold teachers accountable to content standards.

Content standards frequently generate controversy and become major news stories because the outcomes matter to teachers, parents, interest groups, and ordinary citizens. For example, some members of the Texas Board of Education wanted the state social studies curriculum to include more emphasis on the role of Christianity in the nation's formation. These recommendations were adopted despite opposition from six of the nine expert members—including historians—who were selected to evaluate the proposal (Mangan 2011).

There have also been conflicts in many states over expectations about what students should learn about evolution in their biology classes. Here, the experts are solidly in agreement that evolution is a central concept to biology, and several national scientific organizations have issued sample standards that reflect the scientific experts' consensus. But many Americans are uneasy about evolution and have tried to dissuade states from issuing standards in line with scientists' recommendations. As a result, standards on biology now vary widely. New York and North Carolina, for example, make evolution central to the biology curriculum and expect students to learn the varied evidence for the common ancestry of species on view today. By contrast, evolution is not mentioned at all in Iowa's generally vague science standards (although the silence of standards on evolution or any other topic does not mean that teachers do not ignore it in class).

Even though most curricula are guided by state standards approved by state boards of education, state legislatures periodically wade into instructional policy as well. A good example is sex education and education on sexually transmitted diseases (STDs). As of 2011, twenty states and the District of Columbia required that students receive sex education and instruction about HIV (human immunodeficiency virus) and STDs; twelve additional states mandate only instruction on HIV and STDs. Some states leave the precise content up to their local school districts, but twenty-seven states require that abstinence be stressed if and when sex education is taught. On the other hand, twenty states require local school districts that do offer HIV education to cover information about contraception (Guttmacher Institute 2011).

A recent controversy developed in Arizona when the state legislature and governor enacted a law banning ethnic studies, such as classes designed primarily for students of a particular race or classes that advocate ethnic solidarity or "promote resentment toward a certain ethnic group." From the perspective of the Tucson school district, which created the classes, such a curriculum made sense because of the large number of Hispanic children served by the district. To a majority of state legislators, however, the program promoted racial resentment toward whites and separatism, and therefore failed to promote the full Americanization of Mexican immigrants. In early 2011, the district defied the state law by continuing its ethnic studies program, putting at risk nearly $15 million, or 10 percent of its annual state funding (MyFoxPheonix.com 2011).

Teachers and Parents

Ultimately, the extent to which standards actually affect classroom instruction depends on teachers. The term **street-level bureaucrats** refers to government employees who implement state policies through their daily interaction with clients. Teachers fit this description because they make multiple decisions throughout the day that affect how well the standards are actually implemented. Teachers' implementation of standards depends on their own training, knowledge, and values (Cohen and Ball 1990). Moreover, teachers with substantial seniority have the least incentive to embrace new reforms and are more likely to implement only those standards and programs that fit their current agenda (Spillane, Reiser, and Reimer 2002). Berkman and Plutzer (2010) find that younger teachers are more likely to implement biology standards than are more experienced teachers. They also find that teachers' own values on the controversial topic of evolution strongly drive how much they teach it, often in defiance of standard expectations. This finding is not surprising; Brehm and Gates (1997, 20) argue that personal and professional values are a powerful influence on street-level bureaucrats' decisions in all parts of government.

But teachers are not operating in a vacuum, and the community at large influences what they teach as well. So even though parents and other citizens are probably relatively unengaged in noncontroversial issues, they may become involved in more controversial topics. This parental involvement can influence teachers' decisions about what is taught through something as obvious as pressure and questions at a back-to-school night or more subtly as school districts hire teachers unlikely to challenge the prevailing community sentiment. Of course, parents can also vote with their feet by exiting public schools and enrolling their children in private schools that might share their values—either values of nonviolence such as found at a local Quaker Friends school or conservative religious values at a Pentacostal school. Some parents may even remove their children from schools altogether in favor of homeschooling.

CONCLUSION

School politics is a complex web of intergovernmental relations. Decisions about how much to spend on education and about what students should learn are shaped by a legal framework that gives authority to political actors at the local, state, and national levels. Local school boards, state governments, and the federal government try to influence decisions in a variety of ways; as elected bodies, they often reflect the preferences of their constituents, but also the political ambitions of their members. When the goals of local, state, and federal governments differ, each seeks to influence the others. And when their policies infringe on citizens' civil rights or civil liberties, the courts play an important role in adjudicating the resulting conflicts. Along with these formal political actors, teachers, parents, and taxpayers are also highly engaged in education politics. The formal lines of authority give teachers significant discretion in the classroom, and their political power gives them the ability to influence the formulation of policy. Parents also exercise considerable power, even though they operate outside the formal lines of authority, by voting with their feet—either by moving from one school district to another or by exiting the public system altogether. The introduction of more market mechanisms into school governance and financing enhances the power of parents.

Going forward, school districts and states will confront difficult and vexing budgetary situations while the federal government continues to try to shape school reform by tying federal money to programmatic reforms. Just as states must adapt to the changing financial incentives proffered by the federal government, local districts must react to the changes in their state's appropriations and regulations. Increasingly, states are not only reducing levels of funding to local school districts, but simultaneously restricting the authority of communities to make up the difference with their own tax increases. These restrictions are intended to reduce the overall size of government and to prevent districts from agreeing to wage and benefit proposals advanced by teachers' unions.

This strategy is perhaps most apparent in New Jersey, where in 2011 Governor Christie combined deep cuts in state aid to local school districts with a new cap on local real-estate tax increases. Thus local school districts, facing shortfalls from the state, will be forced to cut their education budgets—most likely by cutting teachers' benefits and salaries, which in turn may lead to larger class sizes and the exit of some teachers from the profession. This outcome may also undercut the ability of unions to meet the goals of their members, perhaps leading to a loss of support. Unions are under more direct attack in Wisconsin, where the state legislature in early 2011 passed Governor Walker's controversial proposal to severely limit the bargaining power of public employee unions.

Although it is difficult to predict the course of education politics in the future, we are certain that education policy will continue to be an arena characterized by lively politics, with state governments playing the central role, albeit in a complicated web of entanglement with the federal and local governments. The situation is all the more complex because of the unprecedented opportunities for parents to make choices among communities and among schools, or to exit the system entirely.

All this takes Americans even further from the one-room schoolhouse. Local control of public schools may still be an important ideal in American political thought, but in reality localities have steadily lost control over school curricula and funding. The coming decade will be crucial in shaping the character of public schools, the quality of the education they are able to provide, and whether all children will have equal access to the most effective schools and teachers.

KEY TERMS

accountability, 377

de facto segregation, 384

de jure segregation, 383

department of education, 378

foundation program, 387

horizontal equity, 391

local school board, 379

millage, 386

No Child Left Behind (NCLB), 397

political responsiveness, 376

Proposition 13, 390

Race to the Top, 397

reconstitution, 381

school vouchers, 395

street-level bureaucrats, 400

TABOR (Taxpayer Bill of Rights)
law, 390

REFERENCES

Berkman, Michael, and Eric Plutzer. 2005. *Ten Thousand Democracies: Politics and Public Opinion in America's School Districts.* Washington, D.C.: Georgetown University Press.

———. 2010. *Evolution, Creationism, and the Battle to Control America's Classrooms.* New York: Cambridge University Press.

Brehm, John, and Scott Gates. 1997. *Working, Shirking, and Sabotage: Bureaucratic Response to a Democratic Public.* Ann Arbor: University of Michigan Press.

Burtless, Gary, ed. 1996. *Does Money Matter? The Effects of School Resources on Student Achievement and Adult Success.* Washington, D.C.: Brookings.

Center on Budget and Policy Priorities. 2008. "Policy Basics: Taxpayer Bill of Rights (TABOR)." www.cbpp.org/files/policybasics-tabor.pdf.

Cohen, David K., and Deborah Loewenberg Ball. 1990. "Relations between Policy and Practice: A Commentary." *Educational Evaluation and Policy Analysis* 12: 331–338.

Education Week. 2004. "Accountability." September 10. www.edweek.org/ew/issues/accountability.

Elliott, Martha. 1998. "School Finance and Opportunities to Learn: Does Money Well Spent Enhance Students' Achievement?" *Sociology of Education* 71: 223–245.

Fischel, William A. 2005. *The Homevoter Hypothesis: How Home Values Influence Local Government Taxation, School Finance, and Land-Use Policies.* Cambridge, Mass.: Harvard University Press.

———. 2009. *Making the Grade: The Economic Evolution of America's School Districts.* Chicago: University of Chicago Press.

Frankenberg, Erica, and Chungmei Lee. 2002. "Race in American Public Schools: Rapidly Resegregating School Districts." Cambridge, Mass.: The Civil Rights Project at Harvard University.

Frankenberg, Erica, Genevieve Siegel-Hawley, and Jia Wang. 2010. *Choice without Equity: Charter School Segregation and the Need for Civil Rights Standards.* Los Angeles: The Civil Rights Project/Proyecto Derechos Civiles at UCLA.

Guttmacher Institute. 2011. "State Policies in Brief: Sex and HIV Education, as of May 1, 2011." www.guttmacher.org/statecenter/spibs/spib_SE.pdf.

Hedges, Larry V., Richard D. Laine, and Rob Greenwald. 1994. "An Exchange: Part I: Does Money Matter? A Meta-Analysis of Studies of the Effects of Differential School Inputs on Student Outcomes." *Educational Researcher* 23: 5–14.

Hoxby, Caroline. 1998. "How Much Does School Spending Depend on Family Income? The Historical Origins of the Current School Finance Dilemma." *AEA Papers and Proceedings* 88: 309–314.

Klick, Jonathan. 2000. "Do Dollars Make a Difference? The Relationship between Expenditures and Test Scores in Pennsylvania's Public Schools." *American Economist* 44: 81–87.

Kozol, Jonathan. 1991. *Savage Inequalities: Children in America's Schools.* New York: Crown Publishers.

———. 2005. *The Shame of the Nation: The Restoration of Apartheid Schooling in America.* New York: Crown Publishers.

Lieb, David A., and Hasan Dudar. 2011. "Tax Caps Creating New Hurdles for Towns, Schools." Associated Press, April 6. http://abcnews.go.com/US/wireStory?id=13311007.

Madison, James. 1961. "Federalist #10." In *The Federalist Papers,* ed. Clinton Rossiter. New York: New American Library.

Mangan, Katherine. 2010. "Ignoring Experts' Pleas, Texas Board Approves Controversial Curriculum Standards." *Chronicle of Higher Education,* May 23.

Manna, Paul. 2006. *School's In: Federalism and the National Education Agenda.* Washington, D.C.: Georgetown University Press.

Moe, Terry M. 2001. "Teachers Unions and the Public Schools." In *A Primer on America's Schools,* ed. Terry Moe, 151–184. Stanford, Calif.: Hoover Press.

Myers, Dowell. 2007. *Immigrants and Boomers: Forging a New Social Contract for the Future of America.* New York: Russell Sage Foundation.

MyFOXPhoenix.com. 2011. "Horne: Tucson District Violates Ethnic Studies Ban." January 3. www.myFoxpheonix.com/dpp/news/education/arizona-ethnic-studies-ban-1-3-2010.

National Commission on Excellence in Education. 1983. *A Nation at Risk: The Imperative for Educational Reform.* Washington, D.C.: Government Printing Office.

Odden, Allan R., and Lawrence O. Picus. 2004. *School Finance: A Policy Perspective,* 3d ed. Boston: McGraw-Hill.

Orfield, Gary, and Susan Eaton. 2003. "Back to Segregation." *The Nation,* March 3.

Orfield, Gary, and Chungmei Lee. 2007. *Historic Reversals, Accelerating Resegregation, and the Need for New Integration Strategies.* Los Angeles: The Civil Rights Project/Proyecto Derechos Civiles at UCLA.

Orfield, Gary, Erica D. Frankenberg, and Chungmei Lee. 2002. "The Resurgence of School Segregation." *Educational Leadership* 60: 16.

Orfield, Gary, Erica Frankenberg, and Genevieve Siegel-Hawley. 2010. "Integrated Schools: Finding a New Path." *Educational Leadership* 68: 22–27.

Princiotta, D., and S. Bielick. 2006. "Homeschooling in the United States: 2003." NCES 2006–042. National Center for Education Statistics, U.S. Department of Education, Washington, D.C.

Rapoport, Abby. 2011. "Will Proposed Education Cuts Lead to Lawsuits?" *Texas Observer,* February 10. www.texasobserver.org/floor-play/will-proposed-education-cuts-lead-to-lawsuits.

Ravitch, Diane. 2010. *The Death and Life of the Great American School System: How Testing and Choice Are Undermining Education.* New York: Basic Books.

Reardon, Sean, and John Yun. 2001. "Suburban Racial Change and Suburban School Segregation, 1987–95: A Magazine of Theory and Practice." *Sociology of Education* 74: 79–101.

Roberts, Sam. 2010. "Racial Patterns Are Found in Recent School Budget Elections." *New York Times,* August 24.

Spillane, James, Brian Reiser, and Todd Reimer. 2002. "Policy Implementation and Cognition: Reframing and Refocusing Implementation Research." *Review of Educational Research* 72: 387–431.

Wong, Kenneth K. 1999. *Funding Public Schools: Politics and Policies.* Lawrence: University Press of Kansas.

Wong, Kenneth K., and Francis X. Shen. 2003. "Measuring the Effectiveness of City and State Takeover as a School Reform Strategy." *Peabody Journal of Education* 78: 89–119.

Wong, Kenneth K., Francis X. Shen, Dorothea Anagnostopoulos, and Stacey Rutledge. 2007. *The Education Mayor: Improving America's Schools.* Washington, D.C.: Georgetown University Press.

Wong, Kenneth K., and Gail L. Sunderman. 2007. "Education Accountability as a Presidential Priority: No Child Left Behind and the Bush Presidency." *Publius: The Journal of Federalism* 37: 333–350.

SUGGESTED READINGS

Print

Berkman, Michael, and Eric Plutzer. *Ten Thousand Democracies: Politics and Public Opinion in America's School Districts.* Washington, D.C.: Georgetown University Press, 2005. A look at how educational spending in America's 10,000 unified school districts is influenced by public opinion, labor unions, and demography and at how different characteristics of school boards and financing rules hinder or enhance responsiveness.

Chubb, John E., and Terry M. Moe. *Politics, Markets, and America's Schools.* Washington, D.C.: Brookings, 1990. The authors argue that public schools are run according to the principles of democratic governance while private schools are run according to the markets. This book explains how politics and markets are different, and how these differences affect education and the potential success of educational reforms.

Myers, Dowell. *Immigrants and Boomers: Forging a New Social Contract for the Future of America.* New York: Russell Sage Foundation, 2007. The author observes that in many communities residents are aging, and that the new immigrants to these communities differ from these older residents in race or ethnicity. He discusses the implications and suggests a new way of defining Americans' responsibilities for educating their children.

Odden, Allan, Lawrence O. Picus, and Allan Odden. *School Finance: A Policy Perspective,* 4th ed. New York: McGraw-Hill, 2007. The best textbook for students interested in understanding how education is financed and administered in a federal system.

Ravitch, Diane. *The Death and Life of the Great American School System: How Testing and Choice Are Undermining Education.* New York: Basic Books, 2010. A revealing look at why many of the reforms the author herself worked on in the George W. Bush administration, in particular those relying on testing and school choice, have been detrimental to public schools and education.

Internet

Columbia University's Teachers College National Access Network. www.schoolfunding.info. Excellent site for up-to-date state-by-state information about school financing and litigation related to financing.

Common Core State Standards Initiative. www.corestandards.org/. Comprehensive information about the common core standards, including state-by-state adoption of the standards.

Education Commission of the States. www.ecs.org/. All kinds of news and information about education policy in the American states.

National Center for Education Statistics. http://nces.ed.gov. Primary site for federal dissemination of education data at the state and school district levels. Includes very useful tools to build custom tables.

National Institute on Money in State Politics. www.followthemoney.org. Tracks campaign donations in the states.

CHAPTER 13

The Politics of Higher Education

ROBERT C. LOWRY AND
ALISA HICKLIN FRYAR

Colleges and universities have a major influence on private and public life in the United States. They educate the country's youth, train its workforce, make consistent gains in science and technology, and receive a large portion of discretionary state appropriations. And yet few political scientists pay much attention to institutions of higher learning. Indeed, ten years ago essentially no political science research was being conducted on higher education, and only a small amount is currently under way.

Today, however, concern is growing about the state of higher education in the United States, and controversy is swirling around several issues. For one thing, the traditional model of the four-year bachelor's degree earned on a campus with real classrooms and live instructors is being questioned. Tuition and fees are rising faster than the rate of inflation, and concern is also rising about the number of students who begin but do not complete a degree at all, let alone in four years. Many people nevertheless feel compelled to attend college in order to compete in an information- and service-based economy. But this attitude in turn directs attention to the fact that access to higher education is not at all equal throughout the population. And in another development, recent research implies that many undergraduates do not actually improve their thinking or writing skills while they are in college (Arum and Roksa 2011).

We begin this chapter by describing the complicated market for higher education, including brief descriptions of the private nonprofit and private for-profit sectors. We then address the finances of public higher education. Nationwide, spending and tuition and fees per student have been rising faster than inflation for three decades, while appropriations per student have roughly kept up with inflation, at least until 2007. A number of features of higher education as a political issue may explain why appropriations have not kept up with spending, not the least of which is that enrollments have continued to increase in spite of higher tuition and fees. We then move to a discussion of the administrative structures adopted by states to govern public higher education. The level of oversight and regulation by states determines whether public colleges and universities pursue missions dominated by traditional academic values or the goals of state politicians.

We also discuss issues of student access to higher education as they pertain to minorities, low-income students, and students who entered the country illegally as children. All of these students are affected by both federal and state court decisions and legislation. This discussion is followed by a review of attempts to make public colleges and universities more accountable for student success and learning and the use of public research universities as instruments of state economic policy. We conclude that the relationship between public colleges and universities and state governments that prevailed throughout much of the twentieth century may require modification, if not replacement, although a new model has yet to emerge.

THE COMPLICATED MARKET FOR HIGHER EDUCATION

The market for higher (or postsecondary) education features a diversity of institutions, ranging from online and commuter schools providing purely vocational training to massive public universities with upward of 50,000 students, world-famous research institutions, and elite private liberal arts colleges, with many other variations and gradations. Individual institutions may be publicly owned, private nonprofit, or private for-profit. They are subject to varying degrees of control and regulation by state governments and private **accreditation agencies**. Although the federal government does not directly regulate postsecondary institutions, it can exert influence through the conditions it attaches to eligibility for federal student financial aid and research funding (Lowry 2009b). In this chapter, we focus primarily on public universities and community colleges, but we begin with a brief description of the size and nature of all three higher education subsectors.

Public Institutions

Figure 13-1 shows total fall enrollment in degree-granting institutions by type for the years 1980–2009. Public institutions dominate the higher education market when measured by enrollments, as they have since the mid-1950s (National Center for Education Statistics 2010). In 2009, about 14.8 million of the 20.4 million students at degree-granting postsecondary institutions (73 percent) were enrolled in public colleges and universities. Of these, about 7.7 million were at four-year public universities, and about 7.1 million were at two-year community colleges.

Figure 13-1   Total Fall Enrollment in Degree-Granting Institutions of Higher Education, 1980–2009

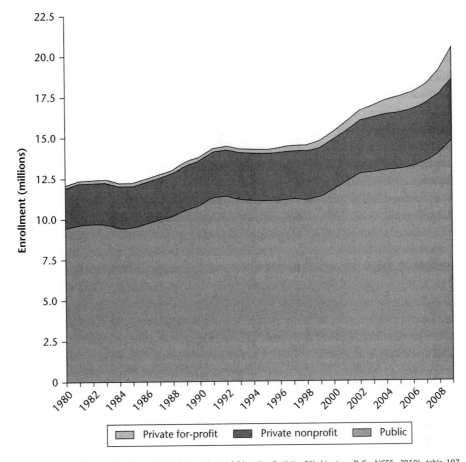

SOURCE: National Center for Education Statistics, *Digest of Education Statistics* (Washington, D.C.: NCES, 2010), table 197, http://nces.ed.gov/programs/digest/.

The oldest public university in the United States is the University of North Carolina at Chapel Hill, chartered in 1789. Many of the colleges founded before then were neither clearly public nor clearly private; instead they were governed and funded by a mixture of public, private, and religious authorities (Rudolph [1962] 1990). State-controlled universities became common in the nineteenth century, particularly in the Midwest and plains states, but state governments typically provided little or no financial support for operations (Brubacher and Rudy 1976). The earliest large-scale public support came in the form of the **Morrill Act of 1862**, which made grants of federal public land to the states for the purpose of establishing colleges that specialized in practical training in the "agricultural and mechanical" arts (Rudolph [1962] 1990; Goldin and Katz 1999). Today, these "land-grant" universities continue to receive federal funds for certain designated programs in areas, such as agriculture and engineering.

By the turn of the twentieth century, state government financial support was well established, and many states had one or two "flagship" campuses that resembled modern research universities. Most other public institutions were two-year colleges established primarily for the purpose of training primary and secondary school teachers (Goldin and Katz 1999). The big explosion in public higher education occurred in the years following World War II, when the GI Bill made it possible for millions of returning military personnel to afford a college education. Later in the 1950s, federal funding for research increased dramatically in response to the launching of the *Sputnik* satellite by the Soviet Union (Rudolph [1962] 1990). Total enrollment in public institutions tripled between 1947 and 1964, and many of the two-year teachers' colleges became four-year colleges with aspirations of becoming research universities. This development led to a desire for greater coordination and the creation of the state governance structures discussed shortly.

Public higher education enrollments continued to grow dramatically during the late 1960s and 1970s as the baby boom generation finished high school, with the most rapid growth occurring in two-year community colleges. In some states, community colleges are funded primarily by local property taxes, while in others they receive state appropriations similar to four-year institutions. The nationwide share of total public sector enrollment in community colleges has held steady at slightly less than half since 1980, but there is significant variation across states. In the fall of 2008, it ranged from a high of 71 percent in California and 65 percent in Wyoming to a low of just 3 percent in Alaska and 12 percent in Nevada (National Center for Education Statistics 2010).

Private Nonprofit Institutions

The oldest institution of higher education in the United States is Harvard College, founded in 1636. Other well-known institutions that predate the American Revolution are Yale, Princeton (formerly known as the College of New Jersey), and the College of William and Mary (now a public university). As just noted, these early institutions were often governed by a mixture of public and private authorities. It was not until 1819 that the legal autonomy of private nonprofit corporations was clearly established by the U.S. Supreme Court in *Dartmouth College v. Woodward*, 17 U.S. 518 (1819) (Rudolph [1962] 1990).

In some cases, the line between public and private nonprofit institutions can still be quite thin. A good example of this is Western Governors University (WGU), which was created following a 1995 meeting of the Western Governors Association. Many western states faced the problem of rapidly growing populations, widely dispersed population centers, and limited public funds for education. The governors decided to promote a university that would make maximum use of distance learning technology. WGU was chartered as a private nonprofit university and began accepting students in 1999. Its classes are offered entirely online, and degrees are awarded on the basis of demonstrated competencies rather than credit hours completed. Enrollment in its four colleges of business, teaching, health, and information technology grew from 5,525 in June 2006 to 19,400 in June 2010, an annual growth rate of 37 percent (Western Governors University 2010).

Today, there are more than twice as many private nonprofit four-year colleges and universities as public, although their total enrollment is less than half as large (National Center for Education Statistics 2010). The share of students enrolled in the private nonprofit sector varies substantially by region; it is highest in New England and the Mid-Atlantic states. Private institutions include research universities, "comprehensive" universities that have some graduate and professional programs, liberal arts colleges that specialize in undergraduate education, and institutions that specialize in particular areas such as business or the fine arts. Many of these institutions have religious affiliations that affect the composition of the faculty and student body, as well as the content of the curriculum at smaller liberal arts colleges. There is also a handful of private nonprofit two-year colleges.

Each private nonprofit institution is governed by a board of directors in accordance with its own charter. Nevertheless, colleges and universities need to be accredited in order to qualify for state and federal financial aid and so that their courses and degrees will be recognized by other colleges and universities. The most important accreditation agencies are the seven regional agencies that periodically review an institution's overall curriculum and finances. In addition, numerous organizations accredit specific degree programs, primarily those that offer professional training. All seven regional agencies and many of the programmatic accrediting organizations are recognized in turn by the Council for Higher Education Accreditation (2011), whose membership includes some 3,000 degree-granting colleges and universities. The process of accreditation thus amounts to a form of industry self-regulation.

State governments also have some policies directed at private nonprofit institutions. Some states provide funds directly to private institutions. These funds are distinct from appropriations to public institutions because they typically are limited to certain degree programs and awarded on the basis of degrees completed rather than enrollment or some other metric. Also, some states include private institutions in their overall planning and coordination activities, whereas others do not. Finally, states may have student financial aid programs that place no restrictions on where the aid can be spent (Zumeta 1992).

For-Profit Institutions

The smallest but fastest-growing segment of the higher education industry is private for-profit institutions. Enrollment in degree-granting for-profit institutions in fall 2009 was over 1.8 million, or 9.1 percent of total enrollment, compared with just over 400,000 a decade earlier. In addition, in fall 2008 over 300,000 students were enrolled in non-degree-granting for-profit institutions participating in federal financial aid programs (National Center for Education Statistics 2010). Until recently, for-profit institutions mostly focused on vocational training. Now, however, institutions such as the University of Phoenix and Kaplan University are offering four-year undergraduate and some graduate degree programs and are growing rapidly. Still, most for-profit institutions compete with public two-year community colleges for students. The competition has grown rather heated, to the point where one for-profit college in Florida sued Florida State College in Jacksonville for conducting a "destructive media campaign" (Vasquez 2010).

As the for-profit higher education sector becomes more prominent, it is receiving more attention from government agencies. Non-degree-granting for-profit institutions are licensed by the state in which they are located, although this function may be assigned to a consumer protection agency rather than the department of education, and actual enforcement is contingent on having adequate resources (Lesser and Smith 2011). Degree-granting for-profit institutions need to be accredited by the relevant accrediting agencies for the same reasons as public and nonprofit institutions. The U.S. Department of Education recently issued new regulations that would limit practices used by for-profit institutions to recruit students and would increase state oversight of distance education. The Association of Private Sector Colleges and Universities promptly sued to have the regulations declared invalid (Blumenstyk 2011).

Higher Education Markets in California and Texas

Table 13-1 summarizes the organization of the higher education markets in California and Texas. It lists the numbers of institutions or branches and total enrollment in various subsectors, and the notes indicate the specific missions of four-year public universities and selected private institutions. Missions are defined largely by the amount of emphasis placed on graduate programs and funded research using a classification system developed by the Carnegie Foundation for the Advancement of Teaching (2011).

California and Texas have larger total enrollments than any other state, but their systems of public higher education are organized quite differently. California has three centrally governed systems that are strictly separated along hierarchical lines. The University of California (UC) system has nine academic campuses and one health sciences center, all of which are designated as "research universities" except for UC Merced, which was just founded in 2005. The California State University system has twenty-three universities and is less selective in admitting students than the University of California. The California Community College system is limited to two-year institutions. Not only is the number of students enrolled in community colleges in California greater than total higher education enrollment in any other

Table 13-1 Higher Education Markets in California and Texas

Subsector	Size in 2008	Description/examples
California		
Public four-year	35 institutions and branches 658,000 students	University of California system (**9/1**)[a, e] California State University system (**23**)[c, g]
Public two-year	112 institutions and branches 1,582,000 students	California Community Colleges system[g]
Private nonprofit	146 institutions and branches (139 four-year) 268,000 students	California Institute of Technology[a] Pepperdine University[b] Claremont McKenna College[d] Mills College[c] Stanford University[a] University of Southern California[a]
Private for-profit	143 institutions and branches (80 two-year) 144,000 students	
Texas		
Public four-year	45 institutions and branches 570,000 students	Stephen F. Austin State University[c] Texas A&M University system (**11/1**)[a, e, f, g] Texas Southern University[b, f] Texas State University system (**8**)[b, g] Texas Tech University system (**2/1**)[a, b] Texas Woman's University[b] University of Houston system (**4**)[a, g] University of North Texas system (**2/1**)[a, g] University of Texas system (**9/6**)[a, g]
Public two-year	64 institutions and branches 593,000 students	50 public community college districts represented by the Texas Association of Community Colleges[g]
Private nonprofit	57 institutions and branches (53 four-year) 127,000 students	Austin College[d] Baylor University[a] Rice University[a] Southern Methodist University[a] Southwestern University[d] Texas Christian University[b] Trinity University[c]
Private for-profit	74 institutions and branches (55 two-year) 37,000 students	

SOURCES: Numbers of institutions and enrollments are from the National Center for Education Statistics (2009, 2010). Institutional missions are from the Carnegie Foundation for the Advancement of Teaching (2011) and from official institution Web sites.

NOTE: Enrollments are rounded to the nearest thousand. Boldface numbers in parentheses indicate the number of (**universities/health science institutes**) in a system.

a. One or more research universities.

b. One or more doctoral/research universities.

c. Master's universities.

d. Liberal arts colleges.

e. One or more campuses designated as land-grant institutions.

f. One campus designated as Historically Black College or University.

g. One or more campuses designated as Hispanic-Serving College or University.

state, but these students constitute the largest share of public higher education enrollment: 71 percent. California also has a large private higher education sector, including several well-known research universities, several liberal arts colleges, and a for-profit subsector with over 140,000 students in 2008.

The organization of public higher education in Texas is more typical of other states, except that Texas has more institutions and more students. The state has six public university systems and three stand-alone four-year universities. Four of the systems have a single "flagship" institution with one or more satellite campuses. However, the University of Texas (UT) system has UT Austin, four other research universities, four master's universities, and six health science centers that concentrate on medical training and research. The Texas State system has multiple doctoral/research universities but no flagship institution. To some extent, systems tend to occupy niches based on geography: the University of Houston system is (obviously) in and around Houston; several (but not all) UT institutions are in large urban areas; Texas A&M institutions tend to be in more rural areas; the Texas State system is concentrated in the southern part of Texas; and so forth.

Texas has roughly equal numbers of students enrolled in two- and four-year public institutions, a ratio that is close to the national average. Whereas the California Community College system has a chancellor appointed by the governor, the Texas Association of Community Colleges is more of a trade association that represents community colleges' interests before state government. Although Texas has several private institutions that meet the Carnegie criteria for research universities, only Rice University really has a national reputation for its research and graduate programs. Many private four-year institutions in Texas have religious affiliations that remain an important part of their missions. Finally, enrollment at private for-profit institutions in Texas is less than 3 percent of the total higher education enrollment, which is well below the national average.

The rapid development of for-profit and online programs is making the higher education market even more complicated than it was before. Nevertheless, public colleges and universities still account for almost three-fourths of total enrollment. Moreover, public colleges and universities are created, governed, and to a significant degree financed by the states. The rest of this chapter will therefore concentrate primarily on this subsector, beginning with the issue of finances.

PUBLIC HIGHER EDUCATION FINANCES

We begin this section by discussing trends in tuition, appropriations, and spending at public colleges and universities. We then address the politics of state support for public higher education, noting that certain aspects of public higher education make it particularly vulnerable to state government budget pressures. Statistical analyses of the variation in state funding are difficult to compare because of differences in measurement and units of analysis, but there are some robust findings.

Trends in Costs, Appropriations, and Tuition

Figures 13-2 and 13-3 present trends in revenues and spending per full-time-equivalent (FTE) student at all degree-granting public institutions of higher education for the years 1979–2008, drawn from the National Center for Education Statistics (various years). Figure 13-2 shows trends for gross tuition and fees, and state and local appropriations for operations. These make up nearly all of the unrestricted revenues at public institutions. Figure 13-3 shows **"educational and general" spending** less research and public service, because the latter are usually financed by grants and contracts restricted to these purposes. It also shows spending on instruction alone, which is a part of educational and general spending. All of the dollar amounts are national averages for all four- and two-year public institutions. The comparable levels for any given university, or for two- or four-year institutions in any given state, may differ considerably, although the general trends over time should be similar.

Figure 13-2 shows that tuition and fees have been rising faster than inflation for nearly three decades. Real tuition and fee revenue per student increased 129 percent between 1979 and 2008. Although the data shown are for gross tuition and fees before any financial aid, institutional financial aid was about 20 percent of the

Figure 13-2 Revenue per Full-Time-Equivalent Student at All U.S. Public Colleges and Universities, 1979–2008

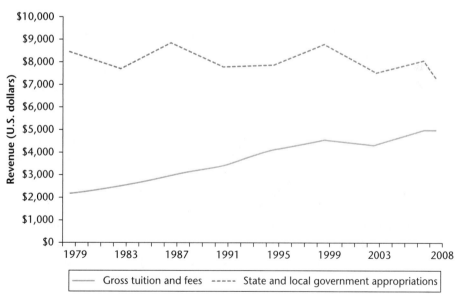

SOURCE: Authors' calculations using data from National Center for Education Statistics (various years) for fiscal years beginning in the fall of the year shown, adjusted using the consumer price index. Amounts are in 2008 dollars. Full-time-equivalent enrollment is estimated as full-time students plus 0.4 times part-time students.

Figure 13-3 Educational and General Spending per Full-Time-Equivalent Student at All U.S. Public Colleges and Universities, 1979–2008

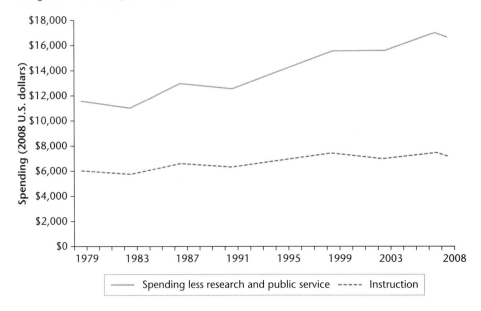

SOURCE: Authors' calculations using data from National Center for Education Statistics (various years) for fiscal years beginning in the fall of the year shown, adjusted using the consumer price index. Amounts are in 2008 dollars. Full-time-equivalent enrollment is estimated as full-time students plus 0.4 times part-time students.

"sticker price" in both 1979 and 2008. By contrast, state and local government appropriations per student hovered around the same inflation-adjusted level, with the real level in 2007 about 4 percent less than in 1979. Then in 2008, nationwide appropriations per FTE student dropped an additional 10 percent as the effects of the recession were felt.

What is driving the increase in tuition and fees? The data plotted in Figure 13-3 show that real spending per student on instruction increased 21 percent from 1979 through 2008. This spending includes faculty salaries, as well as that for information technology used in instruction and other costs that are not budgeted separately. Unlike some other industries, higher education has not become more efficient as a result of the revolution in computers and information technology. The data also reveal that educational and general spending less research and public service has increased at a faster rate than spending on instruction alone—44 percent from 1979 to 2008. Other categories included in educational and general spending are academic support, student services, general administration, and the like. The fact that these categories are growing faster than instruction reflects the increased demand for specialized services, information, and technology management, which has led to what Arum and Roksa (2011, 12) call the "nonacademic professionalization of higher education." This spending growth has not been constrained by the market, because universities and colleges tend to compete with each other on the basis of services and reputation more than price (Lyall and Sell 2006).

Although the increase in tuition and fees is certainly painful for many students, tuition and fee revenues per student are still (as of 2008) less than appropriations per student, less than spending on instruction per student, and far less than total educational and general spending per student. In other words, higher education at public colleges and universities continues to be heavily subsidized, even after three decades of price increases. Moreover, enrollments have continued to increase along with prices, reflecting both the widely held belief that a college education remains a good investment in the future and the ability of most prospective students to secure the necessary funds.

The Politics of State Financial Support

State financial support for public higher education takes several forms: funds appropriated directly to institutions to be spent on educational and general operations, capital appropriations to be spent on new buildings and other infrastructure, grants and contracts for specific projects or deliverables, and financial aid to students. In 2007–2008, state governments provided $68.4 billion in appropriations for operations, $9.7 billion in grants and contracts, and $10.0 billion in all forms of student financial aid; capital appropriations from all levels of government were $7.6 billion (NASSGAP 2007–2008; National Center for Education Statistics 2009). One reason for the heavy reliance on appropriations may be to enhance state policymakers' leverage over the recipient institutions even if there is no specific regulation or policy in place (Goldin and Katz 1999; Lowry 2009a). Capital appropriations also provide an opportunity for legislators to steer funds toward campuses in their home districts, which helps their prospects for reelection.

Some particular aspects of higher education help explain why it is relatively easy for state governments to reduce appropriations during bad times and not so easy to raise them during good times. First, most obvious is the fact that colleges and universities can compensate for a loss of state funds by raising tuition. Alternatively, some public universities can compensate by admitting more nonresident students who pay higher tuition rates, although this tactic can become a politically sensitive issue if it reduces the slots available to state residents (Marklein 2006).

Second, some other areas of state spending such as Medicaid are paid for with matching federal funds, so a cut in state spending on these programs is amplified by the loss of matching funds. Not only does higher education lack matching federal funds, but the effect on students of an increase in tuition may be partially offset by the availability of federal financial aid (Kane, Orszag, and Apostolov 2005). As noted later, however, both the form and amount of federal financial aid have shifted so that there is less help for students from low-income families.

Third, comparatively few organized interest groups are dedicated to the support of public higher education. By contrast, primary and secondary school teachers are well organized and represented by unions that are politically active and powerful in many states (see Chapter 12 in this volume). Although about 38 percent of full-time faculty members at public higher education institutions were covered by collective bargaining agreements as of 1995 (Ehrenberg et al. 2004), the bulk of these were at two-year institutions, and there is no evidence that political activity by faculty unions has an effect on appropriations. Public higher education administrators certainly advocate for state support, but they cannot engage in partisan political activities. Their primary allies among private lobbying groups appear to be local chambers of commerce in the communities in which colleges and universities are located and some business interests that depend on universities for research and employees with specialized training.

Figure 13-4 shows appropriations for operations per FTE student by all state and local governments in 2008–2009. National aggregate data reveal that virtually all local government appropriations go to two-year institutions. However, in some states, local governments make no appropriations, and all support for both two- and four-year public higher education institutions comes from the state. Differences in appropriations per FTE student reflect several factors, including the percentage of adults in the state attending public colleges and universities and the shares of students attending two- or four-year public institutions, as well as state and local government resources.

Figure 13-4 State and Local Government Appropriations for Operations to Public Colleges and Universities per Full-Time-Equivalent Student, 2008–2009

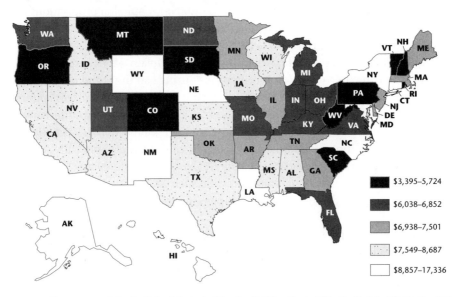

SOURCE: All states except Colorado: National Center for Education Statistics, *Digest of Education Statistics* (Washington, D.C.: NCES, 2010), http://nces.ed.gov/programs/digest; Colorado: State Higher Education Executive Officers, *State Higher Education Finance FY 2009* (Boulder, Colo.: State Higher Education Executive Officers, 2010).

A number of studies have analyzed the variation in state appropriations or spending on higher education across states and, to a lesser degree, across time. However, these studies are somewhat difficult to compare because different studies use different variables. Some examine dollars appropriated per student as the dependent variable; some use dollars as the dependent variable with enrollment as an explanatory variable; others use dollars per capita, appropriations as a percentage of state personal income, or appropriations as a percentage of state spending as the dependent variable. Lowry (2001a) investigates appropriations to individual four-year institutions in 1994–1995, and the other studies all analyze state aggregates, typically over a number of years.

Nevertheless, some robust results emerge. Appropriations are greater in states with more resources as measured by income, gross state product, or tax revenues. They tend to be lower in states in which a larger percentage of the population is sixty-five or older. Most studies do not include the partisanship of state officeholders, but McLendon, Hearn, and Mokher (2009), Tandberg (2008, 2010), and Archibald and Feldman (2006) find that states with Democratic governors and legislatures tend to spend more on public higher education, at least in recent years. Similarly, most studies do not try to measure interest group influence, but McLendon, Hearn, and Mokher (2009) and Tandberg (2008, 2010) find that the ratio of the number of four-year public higher education institutions to all registered lobbying organizations in a state is positively associated with state support.

Finally, two studies identify changes affecting many states in recent decades that have a negative effect on higher education appropriations. Archibald and Feldman (2006) find that appropriations relative to personal income are lower in states that adopted tax and expenditure limits or supermajority voting requirements for tax increases. Thus higher education appropriations are affected by institutional constraints adopted to limit state government taxes and spending in general (see Chapter 10). Kane, Orszag, and Apostolov (2005) focus on the business cycle and the relationship between spending on higher education and Medicaid. They find clear evidence of a trade-off, implying that higher Medicaid expenditures crowded out state higher education expenditures beginning in the 1990s (see Chapter 11).

STATE GOVERNANCE OF PUBLIC INSTITUTIONS

Today, public colleges and universities in almost every state are subject to oversight by some sort of centralized board or coordinating agency, but there is no consensus approach. One analyst categorized the different governance structures and came up with nineteen different models, none of which is used by more than eight states (McGuinness 2003). Nevertheless, it is possible to make some observations about which models imply more oversight, and several studies suggest that state policymakers have somewhat different priorities than do university administrators and faculty. In recent years, some public universities have sought greater freedom from state oversight as the share of their total revenues attributable to state support continues to shrink.

Evolution and Variation in Governance Structures

Before World War II, most states had little in the way of centralized oversight for their public higher education system. After the war, however, public university enrollments grew rapidly, and many campuses added new degree programs. Many states that did not already have an agency responsible for statewide oversight created one in order to promote a rational allocation of resources, plan for future growth, and ensure that policies adopted by the legislature were implemented (Lewis and Maruna 1996; McGuinness 1997).

Today, each public college or university campus has a **governing board** with direct responsibility for operations. Most governing board members are appointed by the governor, although some are elected or appointed by the legislature, and a handful (mostly at universities that began as private institutions) are selected by alumni associations. As of 2007, twenty-one states had a single consolidated governing board with authority over all four-year campuses. Most other states have multiple governing boards (which may be responsible for one or several campuses) and a central **"coordinating board"** that does not have direct responsibility for campus operations. Four states have multiple governing boards and a "planning agency." Michigan and Vermont do not even have planning agencies. In Michigan, the Department of Education performs some planning functions; Vermont has a voluntary commission. Further variations depend on whether two-year community and technical colleges have a separate governance structure, or there is one integrated structure (Education Commission of the States 2007).

Overall, the number of governing boards for four-year institutions ranges from one (twenty-one states) to fourteen (Virginia). The number of four-year campuses ranges from one (Wyoming) to forty-five (Texas), and the number of two-year campuses ranges from one (Nevada and Rhode Island) to 112 (California). Further complicating matters is the fact that individual universities may be included in the state constitution as coequal to the legislature and executive. Examples include the University of California system, the University of Michigan, Michigan State University and Wayne State University in Michigan, and the University of Minnesota (Eykamp 1995).

Despite these complications, some attempts have been made to measure the degree of oversight of four-year public institutions. Lowry (2001b) argues that states with fewer governing boards are able to have more oversight by policymakers because the costs of oversight are lower, and that in states with coordinating boards, oversight is greater for a given number of governing boards because their institutional capacity is greater. Knott and Payne (2004) propose that all consolidated governing board states be classified as highly regulated; states with multiple governing boards and no coordinating board are treated as minimally regulated. The degree of regulation in states with coordinating boards depends on the specific powers of the board.

The overall trend in recent years seems to be in the direction of greater coordination and oversight, with some important exceptions. Knott and Payne (2004) coded fourteen changes in regulatory authority between 1990 and 1997, eleven of which were in the direction of greater regulation. A more recent trend has been to integrate planning for postsecondary education with primary and secondary education through the creation of so-called **P–16 councils**.

P–16 councils are often created to address issues of coordination between public secondary schools and public colleges and universities. State policymakers regularly voice concerns about the unclear path from high school to college, and from community college to four-year institutions. As of 2008, thirty-three states had formed such councils, and twenty-eight of these councils were formed in 1998 or later (Mokher 2010). Many of these councils focus on issues related to curriculum and often lead to policies that establish which classes a "college-ready" student must take in high school. Other councils work to clarify to high schools (and individual students) the expectations faced by incoming students, and design a system in which the transition from high school to community college to four-year institution is smoother. Some councils deal with more programmatic issues, such as common course numbering to aid in transferring credits, the content for certain basic courses that often serve as prerequisites, or "articulation agreements" between individual institutions (National Center for Public Policy and Higher Education 2010).

Mokher (2010) argues that these councils are most likely to be formed in states in which governors have made education a key part their agendas. Aside from Mokher's study, little is known about why different states have adopted different governance structures. One reason for the apparent lack of a standard governance structure or easy explanations may be that public university systems in many states were relatively well developed before any statewide governance structure was created. The resulting structure thus may depend on the specific history of higher education in that state and details such as rivalries that may have developed between individual universities with well-placed alumni.

The Effects of Centralized Oversight

Although little systematic research has been done on the politics of higher education governance structures, some studies have sought to assess the consequences of more or less centralized control. In general, public universities in states with less centralized control generate more total revenue and more tuition revenue per student (Toma 1990; Lowry 2001b; Nicholson-Crotty and Meier 2003; Knott and Payne 2004). They also tend to spend more per student on instruction and related support functions (Lowry 2001b) and have lower student-faculty ratios (Toma 1990). "Flagship" campuses in these states generate more research funding and more faculty publications (Knott and Payne 2004). Finally, comparative case studies of governance structures in seven states conclude that universities in less centralized systems give less weight to the interests of the nonacademic public relative to the professional interests of academics (Bowen et al. 1997).

All of these results are consistent with the claim that typical state policymakers have different priorities for higher education than typical university administrators and faculty (Lowry 2009a). State government officials prefer to emphasize affordable access to undergraduate education, particularly for state residents, whereas academics prefer more selective admissions, higher revenues, and a greater emphasis on research. In states in which there is greater centralized control, the actual prices, spending, and outputs tend to be closer to the first vision.

Of course, it can be argued that high-quality research universities are in the long-term economic interest of the entire state (see the discussion of state economic policy in Chapter 16), and it might be possible to have it both ways by giving different degrees of autonomy to different institutions in the same state. Granting constitutional autonomy to certain research campuses may be one way to accomplish this (Eykamp 1995), but it would be very difficult to amend a state constitution to create additional autonomy for universities that already exist. The next section discusses recent proposals and developments that may provide alternative models.

Pressures for Decentralization

The tendency of public university administrators and faculty to prefer less centralized oversight has been reinforced by recent financial trends in which state government appropriations are declining as a share of total institutional revenues. State appropriations now constitute less than a third of the total revenues at many flagship universities and less than 10 percent at some (Lyall and Sell 2006). Public university leaders might reasonably ask themselves, "If the state is only going to provide 10 or 20 percent of our revenue, why should it have so much control over our mission and policies?"

Although it cannot be said that there is a general movement in the direction of decentralized governance—if anything, the opposite may be true—some proposals have emerged and some experiments undertaken. Lyall and Sell (2006) propose that seats on institutional governing boards be allocated to different stakeholders roughly in proportion to the revenues they provide. No state has adopted this suggestion, and it does not seem likely that a state would surrender majority control of public university governing boards regardless of the share of revenue it provides.

Virginia adopted reforms in 2005 that created three different levels of autonomy for university processes and decisions. Individual universities can apply for each level. In exchange, universities must commit to meeting certain performance objectives designed to further the interests of the state, which depend on the level of autonomy. Universities that meet performance objectives are eligible for financial incentives. The University of Virginia, the College of William and Mary, and

Virginia Polytechnic Institute and State University (Virginia Tech) all opted for the highest level of autonomy (Couturier 2006).

Other states have given public universities more flexibility to generate revenue from nonstate sources. In some states in which the legislature used to set tuitions directly, public universities are now allowed to set their own tuitions in exchange for a commitment to maintain access for low-income students. The University of Colorado system was exempted from a provision in Colorado's Taxpayer Bill of Rights limiting fees that can be charged by public enterprises. These kinds of reforms are examples of a state government trading increased flexibility for reduced expectations of financial support (Lyall and Sell 2006). Meanwhile, universities and colleges will likely press for more autonomy as state support declines, but state policymakers ultimately have the upper hand in that significant changes to governance require statutory or constitutional amendments.

STUDENT ACCESS TO PUBLIC HIGHER EDUCATION

Political and bureaucratic oversight in higher education most often focuses on ensuring that public universities are meeting the needs of the state. Until recently, governmental oversight of public higher education largely focused on issues of access. Early on, most higher education institutions served only privileged white males, which led to the promulgation of historical inequities with respect to race, gender, and class. Because institutions of higher education were regarded as a key vehicle for social mobility, excluding certain groups from attaining a college education was viewed as shutting the door to progress.

A number of shifts led to institutions serving a more diverse population. The Morrill Act of 1862 created institutions that were designed to educate rural populations, usually with a focus on agriculture and education, which expanded geographic access to higher education. In addition, the many institutions set up to train school teachers provided many of the earliest opportunities for women to attend colleges and universities. Much later, the GI Bill of 1944 provided a large number of veterans with the financial support needed to attend college; many came from low-income backgrounds. Despite some gains in broadening access to higher education, the higher education community continues to grapple with how to design appropriate and effective ways to ensure equal opportunities in higher education.

University Responses to Court Decisions and Ballot Initiatives

Historically, most of the debates and policy discussions related to access in higher education have centered on access for African Americans. The second Morrill Act, enacted in 1890, provided federal money to set up all-black colleges in states that restricted black students from attending the state land-grant institutions established with money from the first Morrill Act (American Public and Land-Grant Universities 2011). Although segregated and often grossly underfunded and staffed, these **Historically Black Colleges and Universities** opened doors of opportunity for many African Americans. A few of these black colleges developed into highly prestigious institutions, but most were substantially inferior options. In practice, then, the "separate but equal" doctrine of *Plessy v. Ferguson,* 163 U.S. 537 (1896), rarely paid much attention to the equality of education in segregated public schools.

The *Brown v. Board of Education,* 347 U.S. 483 (1954), decision that struck down the "separate but equal" doctrine is familiar to many people, but few are familiar with the *Sweatt v. Painter,* 339 U.S. 629 (1950), ruling that laid the groundwork for *Brown.* Herman Marion Sweatt was denied admission to the University of Texas Law School because he was black. At that time, there was no black law school in Texas, which meant that Sweatt should have been admitted even under the existing law. To avoid admitting Sweatt, the University of Texas hurriedly set up an all-black law school in Houston. Sweatt sued the university, and the case made it to the Supreme Court. The Court ruled in favor of Sweatt, finding that the all-black law school was unequal on all objective measures and, most important, that the separation of black legal students from the majority of legal students (white students) alone would result in an inherently unequal educational experience.

Today's battles over access in higher education are much different than those of sixty years ago. Many universities recruit African American and Latino students and strive to increase minority student representation on college campuses. However, these efforts are also contentious. Studies have shown that biases in standardized testing disadvantage minority students (Schmitt and Dorans 1990; Hedges and Nowell 1999; Walton and Spencer 2009), and a long list of studies has shown that minority students are much more likely to attend high schools that fail to prepare them for college (Summers and Wolfe 1977; Fletcher and Tienda 2010). There are no easy answers or quick fixes to deal with these problems, and many elite universities have chosen to compensate for these inequities by using some form of affirmative action in admissions decisions.

The decision to employ racial preferences in admissions decisions has sparked a number of legal battles. Currently, the courts permit universities to consider race in admissions decisions as long as it is used only as a "plus" when considering an individual's application—that is, status as a racial or ethnic minority would not guarantee admission in situations in which white applicants with similar profiles would be rejected (*Grutter v. Bollinger,* 539 U.S. 306 [2003]). However, many states have adopted laws that totally ban the use of racial preferences, mostly through ballot initiatives such as California's Proposition 209 and the Michigan Civil Rights Initiative. Some states have adopted policies to increase minority access to universities without using racial preferences. The policy that has gained the most attention has been the **Texas Top 10% Law**. The impetus for this law was a court case that also took root at the University of Texas Law School. In 1992 a white woman, Cheryl Hopwood, was denied admission to the law school, and she sued, arguing that she was better qualified than some of the minority students who were admitted (through an admissions process that considered race). Although the case did not make it to the Supreme Court, in 1996, the U.S. Fifth Circuit Court of Appeals ruled in favor of Hopwood, arguing that racial preference in admissions was unconstitutional. This decision raised concerns about how the state of Texas could ensure that its large and growing minority population would have access to the elite institutions in the state.

The state of Texas responded with the Top Ten Percent plan. This policy guaranteed that all students who graduated in the top 10 percent of their high school class, regardless of race or ethnicity, would be automatically admitted to any (and every) public university in the state. This policy would ensure some level of minority representation at universities, in part because of the *de facto* segregation among Texas high schools. However, most of the research on the Texas Top Ten Percent plan has found that, even with this policy, the number of minority students at the flagship universities in Texas dropped dramatically (Long and Tienda 2008).

The issue of race and higher education will continue to be a salient one in state legislatures and the courts. Minority populations continue to grow, but there are still large gaps in college attainment among racial groups (Ward 2006). Concerns over workforce development and inequities in college preparation at the K–12 level will only become more important in the future. With no easy answers in sight, states will continue to grapple with how to deal with such a complex, but perennially important, issue.

Low-Income Students and State Financial Aid

Another controversial debate in higher education stems from questions about the purpose of financial aid. Historically, Americans have considered a college education to be a good investment for everyone; after all, that is how public universities came into being. Because both the federal and state governments believed that college should be open to more people than the wealthy elite, they appropriated government funds to establish and operate public universities. For decades, students paid very little of their own money in tuition and fees, and the state picked up the tab for most of their education—that is, the states were heavily involved in providing financial aid to students, but mostly through appropriations to universities, not giving money directly to the students.

The federal government also participated in efforts to expand college access through financial aid. In 1972, it began supporting students directly through what are now known as **Pell Grants**. These grants are awarded to students based on financial need, as determined from information provided in a FAFSA (Free Application for Federal Student Aid) form. Until recently, the Pell Grant program has enjoyed considerable support from citizens and lawmakers, but current budget shortfalls have led to proposals to cut the maximum amount available ($5,550 as of 2010). In 1997 Congress passed the Taxpayer Relief Act, which included tuition tax credits through the Hope Tax Credit and the Lifelong Learning Tax Credit. These credits are targeted to the middle class, with many low-income families unable to financially benefit (Callan 2003). Some observers have voiced concerns about the decisions made by the federal government that would benefit middle-class families more than low-income families, because they believe this approach will further limit access for students from low-income families.

Much like the various financial aid efforts at the federal level, states also crafted financial aid programs that distributed money directly to students (in addition to the money appropriated to public institutions). These programs were also designed to increase college access for low-income students. However, in the early 1990s, many states began to shift financial aid policies from need-based policies (contingent on income) to merit-based policies (often tied to grades or standardized test scores). From 1998–1999 to 2008–2009, state need-based grants increased 51 percent in constant 2008–2009 dollars, from $3.97 billion to $6.01 billion, while non-need-based grants increased 158 percent, from $900 million to $2.32 billion (NASSGAP 2008). The eligibility criteria for these non-need-based grants vary substantially (Ness 2008), which has a significant effect on the programs' inclusion of low-income students (Ness and Nolan 2007).

Figure 13-5 shows the percentage of financial aid grant dollars based on need in each state in 2008–2009 (NASSGAP 2008–2009). Several large states, including California, Illinois, New York, Pennsylvania, and Texas, still awarded more than

Figure 13-5 Percentage of Financial Aid Grant Dollars Based on Need, 2008–2009

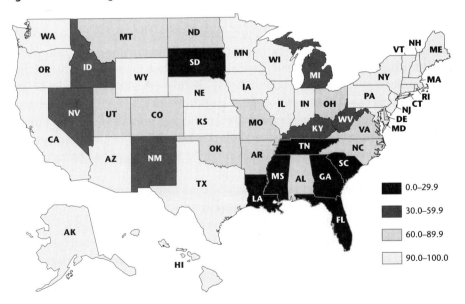

SOURCE: NASSGAP, *Annual Survey Report on State-Sponsored Student Financial Aid* (Washington, D.C.: NASSGAP, various years).

90 percent of their financial aid grants on the basis of need. However, other states, including Florida, Louisiana, Tennessee, and South Carolina, awarded less than 30 percent of their grant money based on need, and 99.7 percent of Georgia's grant aid was awarded on the basis of academic merit.

These changes have resulted in a shift in the way that some states think about financial aid. Instead of looking at financial aid as a tool to increase access to higher education for underrepresented groups, financial aid is viewed as something students earn through their intellect and good grades. Many critics of merit-based aid argue that these shifts will lead to a more inequitable society and reduce the nation's pool of educated workers. Proponents of merit-based aid argue that these programs induce a state's "best and brightest" to stay in their home state for college. Scholars have documented the effects of merit-based aid on enrollment patterns, with some finding evidence of inequities (Cornwell, Mustard, and Sridhar 2006; Heller 2006). However, there is also evidence that these programs induce students to do better in high school (Henry and Rubenstein 2002) and stay in-state for college (Orsuwan and Heck 2009). Although there are still many unanswered questions about the actual effects of the shift in financial aid policies and access for low-income students, it may be the normative debate that is most important for the future of access for low-income students.

Illegal Immigrants and In-State Tuition

Issues of broadening access to higher education have long been the subject of debate. More recently, attention has shifted to whether states should subsidize a college education for students who are residing in the United States without citizenship status or the proper documentation. The issue of whether illegal immigrants should be able to attend public universities as in-state students and have access to financial aid is very controversial, largely because there are strong arguments on both sides of the debate, as Reich and Mendoza (2008) show in the case of Kansas. As of 2010, only ten states allowed undocumented students who met certain qualifications to attend public universities in that state and pay the in-state tuition rate: California, Illinois, Kansas, Nebraska, New Mexico, New York, Texas, Utah, Washington, and Wisconsin (National Immigration Law Center 2010). As of 2009, nineteen other states had introduced similar bills, but they were voted down (Hicklin et al. 2009).

Members of Congress have introduced a similar bill at the national level. Most versions of the DREAM (Development, Relief, and Education for Alien Minors) Act, if passed, would allow an illegal immigrant student to be considered state residents for the purposes of higher education if he or she meets certain requirements: has lived in the state for five years, was younger than sixteen when migrating to the United States, is under thirty years old, is of good moral character, has been admitted to an institution of higher education, has no major criminal convictions, and has earned a high school diploma or GED (U.S. Congress 2010). The **DREAM Act** was first introduced in 2001 and has been reintroduced many times, but it still has not passed.

Recent scholarship has examined what state-level factors influence the adoption of such policies. McLendon, Mokher, and Flores (2011) hypothesize that these policies are more likely to be adopted in states that have certain characteristics. Some of these characteristics are relative to the legislature (more Latino state legislators, more Democrats, a more professional legislature); others are more about the state's residents (more immigrants, more liberal citizens, larger overall population, more unemployed workers); and some are specific to higher education in the state (such as having a consolidated governing board). They find that states that have more Latino legislators and Democratic control of the legislature are more likely to adopt policies that allow illegal students to qualify for in-state tuition, as does having more immigrants, more liberal citizens, and more unemployed workers.

STUDENT PERFORMANCE AND ACCOUNTABILITY

After decades of efforts to increase access to higher education, the nation has seen gains in the number of students going to college. However, the purpose of these efforts to expand access was not just to get more people into college, but ideally to increase the number of people—and a more diverse group of people—with college degrees. And yet the majority of students who go to college do not earn a bachelor's degree in a timely manner. Complete College America, an organization dedicated to encouraging state policymakers to focus on college graduation rates, paints a grim picture. On average, of one hundred ninth graders, only sixty-nine will graduate from high school. Of those sixty-nine, only twenty-seven will enroll in a four-year university. Of those twenty-seven, only nine will graduate within four years (Complete College America 2011).

Public Concern about Graduation and Retention Rates

Graduation rates have been a cause for concern for some time, but issues of completion have received even more attention recently because of various political and social forces. First, many scholars have documented what is often called the "wave of accountability." Worldwide, government officials have become increasingly interested in more closely monitoring the actions and outcomes of public organizations (McLendon, Hearn, and Deaton 2006). In education, the United States saw a major shift in federal oversight of education with the passing of the No Child Left Behind Act (NCLB). As the K–12 system endured greater oversight, it was only a matter of time before higher education received more scrutiny as well. Second, as tuition and fees increased and university administrators continued to ask for higher appropriations from state governments, many politicians began asking questions about where this money was going (Zumeta 2001). Third, the federal government's ability to track data has become much more sophisticated, and the U.S. Department of Education has begun tracking and releasing institutional graduation rates that are comparable across states and institutions. Finally, high-profile leaders, such as President Barack Obama and Microsoft founder Bill Gates, and advocacy organizations have begun to speak publicly about their concerns about graduation rates.

The diversity in graduation rates across public universities and across states is surprising. According to data from the U.S. Department of Education, the average graduation rate for U.S. public four-year universities is 43.5 percent, which by the federal government's definition means that of all students who began as first-time, full-time freshmen, only 43.5 percent received a bachelor's degree within six years. This finding masks important differences, however. The University of Virginia has an average graduation rate of about 92 percent, and the University of Iowa's graduation rate averages about 66 percent—considerable variation for flagship universities but both fairly good. However, the numbers are much worse at less selective schools—schools that serve low-income and high-minority populations. For example, one university that serves mostly low-income students graduates only 7.8–19.4 percent of its students. Similarly, one-fourth of all public four-year universities consistently graduate *less than a third* of their students within six years.

Other Accountability Issues

Other accountability issues have surfaced in addition to the concerns about completion of degrees, many of them related to the mission of a public university. For most policymakers, a public university's primary mission is to educate its state's students so that they can be strong additions to the workforce. However, a recent and widely noted study concluded that most college graduates learn very little during their years in college (Arum and Roksa 2011). In view of the current limitations in the ability to appropriately assess student learning, the higher education community is left in a difficult position when trying to defend the cognitive gains made by students on their campuses.

Universities routinely pay special attention to where their students come from and where they go after graduation. States usually want some of their universities to be prestigious and nationally competitive, but as these universities gain national recognition, they also draw students from out of state. Financially, out-of-state students pay more in tuition and so can be quite valuable to universities. However, if state legislators began to perceive that the best university in the state is using state appropriations to educate other states' students, they become concerned. This worry about migration extends to a university's graduates as well. Most state legislators want to see public universities taking care of the state first by educating in-state students and graduating top students in underserved fields who will stay in the state and contribute to the local economy. These interests have often led to policies that are aimed at retaining students, such as loan forgiveness in exchange for working in the state for a number of years or special internship programs funded by the state.

Performance-Based Appropriations

Concerns about accountability have led many states to consider ways in which they can induce university administrators to pursue their state's goals. Many policymakers believe that universities care more about raising endowments and starting new doctoral programs than they do about educating the state's future workforce. In an effort to compel universities to place a greater priority on the issues that policymakers care about most, states have begun to link appropriations to some measures of performance.

Joseph Burke and his colleagues have studied these policies for many years, documenting the differences in design and duration (Burke 2005). Other scholars have sought to understand what influences the adoption of these policies. Interestingly, there is little evidence that these policies are adopted in states with lower levels of educational attainment. Instead, the evidence suggests that adoption can be linked to certain political factors: more Republicans in the legislature, centralized governing boards, and the activities of policy entrepreneurs (McLendon, Hearn, and Deaton 2006; Dougherty et al. 2010). These accountability efforts are often introduced in the form of additional money for institutions that respond to incentives (Dougherty et al. 2010), and thus they are often abandoned when states are under financial stress (Dougherty, Natow, and Vega forthcoming).

Despite the concerns about the adoption and abandonment of these policies, most of the research shows that they usually do not improve performance. In fact, two national studies found no significant effect of **performance-based accountability policies** on graduation rates (Shin and Milton 2004; Volkwein and Tandberg 2008; Fryar 2011). Even when looking at what many consider to be the best of these policies—in Tennessee—there is very little evidence that the policy seems to be making much of a difference (Sanford and Hunter 2010). Budget shortfalls have led many states to abandon these policies or lose interest in adopting new ones.

PUBLIC RESEARCH UNIVERSITIES AS INSTRUMENTS OF STATE ECONOMIC POLICY

In recent years, research universities have been in the spotlight as the key players in the "knowledge economy," both in the United States and around the world (Lyall and Sell 2006; Mintrom 2009). Promoting the growth of research universities fits into the entrepreneurial approach to economic development that many states have adopted (see Chapter 16). Research universities contribute to the growth of local and regional economies in several ways. First, evidence indicates that there are spillover effects such that an increase in patents granted to university researchers leads to an increase in patents granted to corporate researchers in the surrounding area (Jaffe 1989). Second, studies of urban and regional economic growth have identified the importance of "agglomeration effects," in which highly educated individuals tend to migrate to metropolitan areas that have one or more research universities in order to take advantage of their network effects and because of the amenities available (Shapiro 2006; Glaeser and Gottlieb 2009). This migration leads in turn to more economic growth. One study finds that an increase in the percentage of college graduates in a city is associated with higher wages for high school graduates and even high school dropouts, although the causal mechanisms are not clear (Moretti 2004).

From a political standpoint, a strategy of promoting research universities can be complicated in a state in which there are several public research universities, or several public four-year institutions that might become research universities. Multiple institutions likely will compete for special attention, and elected representatives from the districts in which they are located will want their campus to be the next one chosen. The result could be gridlock. Although centralized governing boards and coordinating boards were created in part for the purpose of developing "rational" strategies for managing growth (Lewis and Maruna 1996; McGuinness 1997), this approach did not solve the fundamental political problem; it simply relocated the problem from the legislature to an administrative body.

Texas recently adopted an innovative approach to this problem through its "Tier One" initiative. Currently, the University of Texas at Austin and Texas A&M University are the state's only public, nationally prominent research institutions. (Another is Rice University, which is private.) Several other public universities aspire to this status, but the state government lacks the resources to support all of them at the level that would be required. The solution chosen was to identify seven "emerging research" universities and create two pots of money for which they can compete. One pot distributes state funds to match private gifts and scholarships that support research activities; a second pot makes money available to universities that reach certain objective benchmarks such as the number of PhDs awarded and amount of funded research (Hacker 2009). The result is a competition based on performance incentives that can have more than one winner. It remains to be seen how well this initiative will survive the current fiscal crisis, and whether it is a model that might be adopted by other states.

CONCLUSION: A NEW MODEL?

Before the mid-twentieth century, a relatively small proportion of the American population ever attended college, and it was not a severe fiscal burden for states to provide public colleges and universities with generous appropriations per student. Although there were disputes between state politicians and academics in the nineteenth century about the appropriate role of public universities (Brubacher and Rudy 1976; Rudolph [1962] 1990), during much of the twentieth century an equilibrium seemed to prevail in which both state officials and academics knew what was expected of them and were satisfied enough with the arrangement that no one was willing to bear the cost of advocating for significant change.

Recently, however, this equilibrium seems to have been disrupted, and several areas have become controversial and are likely to be contested in the foreseeable future. Many of the issues described in this chapter raise what is perhaps the fundamental political question: To what extent should public colleges and universities be treated as state agencies, such as the department of transportation, and to what extent should they be state-assisted but largely autonomous institutions of higher education, research, and public service? This question is receiving greater attention from politicians, academics, and taxpayers.

Numerous policymakers, administrators, scholars, and journalists have voiced their concerns about whether public higher education, as Americans know it, can survive today's volatile budgetary and policy environments. Will public universities regain the wide support and trust of citizens and politicians that they once enjoyed? Will escalating costs and tuition finally be too much? How will these policy changes affect institutions and their students? We can say, with confidence, that higher education is in a period of turmoil, but it is too early to know whether these tumultuous times mark a definitive turning point for higher education, or if things will restabilize, with only small changes in the policy environment. Either way, the importance of the relationship between state governments and institutions of higher education will endure.

KEY TERMS

accreditation agency, 406

coordinating board, 418

DREAM Act, 425

educational and general spending, 413

governing board, 418

Historically Black Colleges and Universities, 422

Morrill Act of 1862, 407

P-16 council, 419

Pell Grants, 423

performance-based accountability policies, 428

Texas Top 10% Law (or Top Ten Percent plan), 422

REFERENCES

Archibald, Robert B., and David H. Feldman. 2006. "State Higher Education Spending and the Tax Revolt." *Journal of Higher Education* 77: 618–644.

American Public and Land-Grant Universities. 2011. "Profile of 1890 Institutions." www.aplu .org.

Arum, Richard, and Josipa Roksa. 2011. *Academically Adrift: Limited Learning on College Campuses.* Chicago: University of Chicago Press.

Blumenstyk, Goldie. 2011. "With Lawsuit, For-Profit Colleges Step Up Fight against New Regulations." *Chronicle of Higher Education*, January 23. http://chronicle.com/article/With-Lawsuit-For-Profit/126042/.

Bowen, Frank M., Kathy Reeves Bracco, Patrick M. Callan, Joni E. Finney, Richard Richardson Jr., and William Trombley. 1997. *State Structures for the Governance of Higher Education.* San Jose: California Higher Education Policy Center.

Brubacher, John S., and Willis Rudy. 1976. *Higher Education in Transition: A History of American Colleges and Universities, 1636–1976.* 3d ed. New York: Harper and Row.

Burke, Joseph C. 2005. *Achieving Accountability in Higher Education: Balancing Public, Academic, and Market Demands.* San Francisco: Jossey-Bass.

Callan, Patrick M. 2003. "Reframing Access and Opportunity: Problematic State and Federal Higher Education Policy in the 1990s." In *The States and Public Higher Education Policy: Affordability, Access, and Accountability,* ed. D. E. Heller, 83–99. Baltimore: Johns Hopkins University Press.

Carnegie Foundation for the Advancement of Teaching. 2011. "The Carnegie Classification of Institutions of Higher Education™." http://classifications.carnegiefoundation.org/.

Complete College America. 2011. "National Data." http://completecollege.org.

Cornwell, Christopher, David Mustard, and Deepa J. Sridhar. 2006. "The Enrollment Effects of Merit-Based Financial Aid: Evidence from Georgia's HOPE Program." *Journal of Labor Economics* 24: 761–786.

Council for Higher Education Accreditation. 2011. "Informing the Public about Accreditation." www.chea.org/public_info/index.asp.

Couturier, Lara K. 2006. "Checks and Balances at Work: The Restructuring of Virginia's Public Higher Education System." National Center Report #06–3, National Center for Public Policy and Higher Education, San Jose, Calif.

Dougherty, Kevin, Rebecca Natow, Rachel Hare, and Blanca Vega. 2010. "The Political Origins of State Level Performance Funding for Higher Education." CCRC Working Paper No. 22, Community College Research Center, New York. http://ccrc.tc.columbia.edu.

Dougherty, Kevin, Rebecca Natow, and Blanca Vega. Forthcoming. "Popular but Unstable: Explaining Why State Performance Funding Systems in the United States Often Do Not Persist." *Teachers College Record.*

Education Commission of the States. 2007. "Postsecondary Governance Online Database." www .ecs.org/html/educationIssues/Governance/GovPSDB_intro.asp.

Ehrenberg, Ronald G., Daniel B. Klaff, Adam T. Kezsbom, and Matthew P. Nagowski. 2004. "Collective Bargaining in American Higher Education." In *Governing Academia: Who Is in Charge at the Modern University?* ed. Ronald G. Ehrenberg, 209–232. Ithaca, N.Y.: Cornell University Press.

Eykamp, Paul W. 1995. "Political Control of State Research Universities: The Effect of the Structure of Political Control on University Quality and Budget." PhD dissertation, University of California, San Diego.

Fletcher, Jason, and Marta Tienda. 2010. "Race and Ethnic Differences in College Achievement: Does High School Attended Matter?" *ANNALS of the American Academy of Political and Social Science* 627: 144–167.

Fryar, Alisa Hicklin. 2011. "The Disparate Impacts of Accountability: Searching for Causal Mechanisms." Paper presented at the Public Management Research Association Conference, Syracuse, N.Y., June.

Glaeser, Edward L., and Joshua D. Gottlieb. 2009. "The Wealth of Cities: Agglomeration Effects and Spatial Equilibrium in the United States." *Journal of Economic Literature* 47: 983–1028.

Goldin, Claudia, and Lawrence F. Katz. 1999. "The Shaping of Higher Education: The Formative Years in the United States, 1890 to 1940." *Journal of Economic Perspectives* 13: 37–62.

Hacker, Holly K. 2009. "Tier One Bill's Signing Has Unifying Force." *Dallas Morning News,* June 18, 11B.

Hedges, Larry V., and Amy Nowell. 1999. "Changes in the Black-White Gap in Achievement Test Scores." *Sociology of Education* 72: 111–135.

Heller, Donald E. 2006. "Merit Aid and College Access." Paper prepared for the Symposium on the Consequences of Merit-based Student Aid, Wisconsin Center for the Advancement of Postsecondary Education.

Henry, Gary T., and Ross Rubenstein. 2002. "Paying for Grades: Impact of Merit-Based Financial Aid on Educational Quality." *Journal of Policy Analysis and Management* 21: 93–109.

Hicklin, Alisa, Sarah Trousset, Alyssa Hellman, and Sara Rafferty. 2009. "Undocumented Students and In-State Tuition: Examining Bill Introduction in State Legislatures." Paper presented at the Southwest Political Science Association Conference. Denver, March.

Jaffe, Adam B. 1989. "Real Effects of Academic Research." *American Economic Review* 79: 957–970.

Kane, Thomas J., Peter R. Orszag, and Emil Apostolov. 2005. "Higher Education Appropriations and Public Universities: The Role of Medicaid and the Business Cycle." *Brookings-Wharton Papers on Urban Affairs, 2005* 1: 99–127.

Knott, Jack H., and A. Abigail Payne. 2004. "The Impact of State Governance Structures on Management and Performance of Public Organizations: A Study of Higher Education Institutions." *Journal of Policy Analysis and Management* 23: 13–20.

Lesser, Benjamin, and Greg B. Smith. 2011. "As Complaints Mount, Anemic State Agency Overwhelmed by Job of Policing For-Profit Schools." *New York Daily News*, January 18. www.nydailynews.com/ny_local/2011/01/18/.

Lewis, Dan A., and Shadd Maruna. 1996. "The Politics of Education." In *Politics in the American States: A Comparative Analysis,* 6th ed., ed. Virginia Gray and Herbert Jacob, 438–477. Washington, D.C.: CQ Press.

Long, Mark, and Marta Tienda. 2008. "Winners and Losers: Changes in Texas University Admissions Post-Hopwood." *Education Analysis and Policy* 30: 255–280.

Lowry, Robert C. 2001a. "The Effects of State Political Interests and Campus Outputs on Public University Revenues." *Economics of Education Review* 20: 105–119.

———. 2001b. "Governmental Structure, Trustee Selection, and Public University Prices and Spending: Multiple Means to Similar Ends." *American Journal of Political Science* 45: 845–861.

———. 2009a. "Incomplete Contracts and the Political Economy of the Privatized Public University." In *Privatizing the Public University: Perspectives from Across the Academy,* ed. Christopher C. Morphew and Peter D. Eckel, 33–59. Baltimore: Johns Hopkins University Press.

———. 2009b. "Reauthorization of the Federal Higher Education Act and Accountability for Student Learning: The Dog That Didn't Bark." *Publius: The Journal of Federalism* 39: 506–526.

Lyall, Katharine C., and Kathleen R. Sell. 2006. *The True Genius of America at Risk: Are We Losing Our Public Universities to de Facto Privatization?* Westport, Conn.: Praeger.

Marklein, Mary. 2006. "Are Out-of-State Students Crowding Out In-Staters?" *USA Today,* August 31, 1A.

McGuinness, Aims C., Jr. 1997. "The Functions and Evolution of State Coordination and Governance in Postsecondary Education." In *State Postsecondary Education Structures Sourcebook,* 1–48. Denver: Education Commission of the States.

———. 2003. "Models of Postsecondary Education Coordination and Governance in the States." Education Commission of the States, Boulder, Colo. www.ecs.org/clearinghouse/34/23/3423.pdf.

McLendon, Michael K., James C. Hearn, and Russ Deaton. 2006. "Called to Account: Analyzing the Origins and Spread of State Performance-Accountability Policies for Higher Education." *Educational Evaluation and Policy Analysis* 28: 1–24.

McLendon, Michael K., James C. Hearn, and Christine G. Mokher. 2009. "Partisans, Professionals, and Power: The Role of Political Factors in State Higher Education Funding." *Journal of Higher Education* 80: 686–713.

McLendon, Michael K., Christine G. Mokher, and Stella M. Flores. 2011. "Legislative Adoption of In-State Resident Tuition Policies: Immigration, Representation, and Educational Access." *American Journal of Education* 117: 563–602.

Mintrom, Michael. 2009. "Universities in the Knowledge Economy: A Comparative Analysis of Nested Institutions." *Journal of Comparative Policy Analysis* 11: 327–353.

Mokher, Christine G. 2010. "Do 'Education Governors' Matter? The Case of Statewide P-16 Education Councils." *Educational Evaluation and Policy Analysis* 32: 476–497.

Moretti, Enrico. 2004. "Estimating the Social Return to Higher Education: Evidence from Longitudinal and Repeated Cross-sectional Data." *Journal of Econometrics* 121: 175–212.

NASSGAP (National Association of State Student Grant and Aid Programs). Various. *Annual Survey Report on State-Sponsored Student Financial Aid.* Washington, D.C.: NASSGAP.

National Center for Education Statistics. Various. *Digest of Education Statistics.* Washington, D.C.: National Center for Education Statistics. http://nces.ed.gov/programs/digest/.

National Center for Public Policy and Higher Education. 2010. "Beyond the Rhetoric: Improving College Readiness through Coherent State Policy," Special Report for the National Center for Public Policy in Higher Education and the Southern Regional Education Board. San Jose, Calif., June. www.highereducation.org.

National Immigration Law Center. 2010. "Basic Facts about In-State Tuition for Undocumented Immigrant Students," March. www.nilc.org.

Ness, Erik C. 2008. *Merit Aid and the Politics of Education.* New York: Routledge.

Ness, Erik C., and Brian E. Nolan. 2007. "Targeted Merit Aid: Implications of the Tennessee Lottery Scholarship Program." *Journal of Student Financial Aid* 37: 7–17.

Nicholson-Crotty, Jill, and Kenneth J. Meier. 2003. "Politics, Structure, and Public Policy: The Case of Higher Education." *Educational Policy* 17: 80–97.

Orsuwan, Meechai, and Ronald H. Heck. 2009. "Merit-Based Student Aid and Freshman Interstate College Migration: Testing a Dynamic Model of Policy Change." *Research in Higher Education* 50: 24–51.

Reich, Gary, and Alvar Ayala Mendoza. 2008. " 'Educating Kids' versus 'Coddling Criminals': Framing the Debate over In-State Tuition for Undocumented Students in Kansas." *State Politics and Policy Quarterly* 8: 177–197.

Rudolph, Frederick. [1962] 1990. *The American College and University: A History.* Athens, Ga.: University of Georgia Press.

Sanford, Thomas, and James M. Hunter. 2010. "Impact of Performance Funding on Retention and Graduation Rates." Paper presented at the 2010 Association for the Study of Higher Education Conference, Indianapolis.

Schmitt, Alicia P., and Neil J. Dorans. 1990. "Differential Item Functioning for Minority Examinees on the SAT." *Journal of Educational Measurement* 27: 67–81.

Shapiro, Jesse M. 2006. "Smart Cities: Quality of Life, Productivity, and the Growth Effects of Human Capital." *Review of Economics and Statistics* 88: 324–335.

Shin, Jung-Cheol, and Sande Milton. 2004. "The Effects of Performance Budgeting and Funding Programs on Graduation Rate in Public Four-year Colleges and Universities." *Education Policy Analysis Archives* 12: 1–26.

State Higher Education Executive Officers. 2010. *State Higher Education Finance FY 2009.* Boulder, Colo.: State Higher Education Executive Officers.

Summers, Anita A., and Barbara L. Wolfe. 1977. "Do Schools Make a Difference?" *American Economic Review* 67: 639–652.

Tandberg, David A. 2008. "The Politics of State Higher Education Funding." *Higher Education in Review* 5: 1–36.

———. 2010. "Politics, Interest Groups, and State Funding of Public Higher Education." *Research on Higher Education* 51: 416–450.

Toma, Eugenia Froedge. 1990. "Boards of Trustees, Agency Problems, and University Output." *Public Choice* 67: 1–9.

U.S. Congress, Senate. 2010. "Development, Relief, and Education for Alien Minors Act of 2010." S. Doc. 3992, 111th Cong., 2d sess., December 1.

Vasquez, Michael. 2010. "For-Profit Colleges Slam State Schools." *Miami Herald*, October 12, A1.

Volkwein, J. Fredericks, and David Tandberg. 2008. "Measuring Up: Examining the Connections among State Structural Characteristics, Regulatory Practices, and Performance." *Research in Higher Education* 49: 180–197.

Walton, Gregory M., and Steven J. Spencer. 2009. "Latent Ability: Grades and Test Scores Systematically Underestimate the Intellectual Ability of Negatively Stereotyped Students." *Psychological Science* 20: 1132–1148.

Ward, Nadia L. 2006. "Improving Equity and Access for Low-Income and Minority Youth into Institutions of Higher Education." *Urban Education* 41: 50–70.

Western Governors University. 2010. *Annual Report.* Salt Lake City, Utah: WGU.

———. 2011. "The WGU Story." www.wgu.edu/about_WGU/WGU_story.

Zumeta, William. 1992. "State Policies and Private Higher Education: Policies, Correlates, and Linkages." *Journal of Higher Education* 63: 363–417.

———. 2001. "Public Policy and Accountability in Higher Education: Lessons from the Past and Present for the New Millennium." In *The States and Public Higher Education Policy,* ed. Donald E. Heller. Baltimore: Johns Hopkins University Press.

SUGGESTED READINGS

Print

Ehrenberg, Ronald G., ed. *What's Happening to Public Higher Education? The Shifting Financial Burden.* Baltimore: Johns Hopkins University Press, 2007. A discussion of the change in the financial support for and overall costs of higher education.

Heller, Donald E., ed. *The States and Public Higher Education Policy: Affordability, Access, and Accountability.* Baltimore: Johns Hopkins University Press, 2001. Although somewhat dated, an excellent discussion of state politics and higher education across a range of issues.

Lyall, Katharine C., and Kathleen R. Sell. *The True Genius of America at Risk: Are We Losing Our Public Universities to de Facto Privatization?* Westport, Conn.: Praeger, 2006. A discussion of the changes in higher education linked to privatization and their potential effect on public universities.

Morphew, Christopher C., and Peter D. Eckel, eds. *Privatizing the Public University: Perspectives from Across the Academy.* Baltimore: Johns Hopkins University Press, 2009. An edited volume that brings together a broad range of scholars and encompasses much of the diversity of the privatization discussion and more general changes in the higher education environment.

Richardson, Richard Jr., and Mario Martinez. *Policy and Performance in American Higher Education.* Baltimore: Johns Hopkins University Press, 2009. A set of state case studies that discuss how policies affect higher education outcomes.

Internet

Education Commission of the States. www.ecs.org. A resource for research and data on education issues (including K–12 and higher education) in the states.

National Center for Education Statistics. http://nces.ed.gov. The national clearinghouse for data on education collected by the federal government.

National Center for Higher Education Management Systems. www.nchems.org. A nonprofit organization that provides policy reports, research, and data aimed at improving state policy in higher education.

National Center for Public Policy and Higher Education. www.highereducation.org. A nonprofit organization engaged in both research and advocacy on higher education policy issues.

State Higher Education Executive Officers. www.sheeo.org. The national organization of state higher education governing boards, offering data and policy research on state issues.

CHAPTER 14

Public Opinion and Morality

JUSTIN H. PHILLIPS

Issues of representation are particularly relevant to the study of state politics. As noted throughout this volume, state governments play a key role in shaping some of the nation's most important domestic policy decisions, including those related to education, criminal justice, health care, and minority rights. These decisions not only affect the daily lives of most Americans, but also are important statements about society's values. As such, they ought to be shaped, at least in part, by the opinions of voters. Indeed, the responsiveness of elected officials to the preferences of their constituents is one way in which scholars can evaluate the quality of democracy.

It is not surprising, then, that a central question in the state politics literature is the degree to which state governments are effective at translating public sentiment into government action. This chapter presents an overview of scholars' efforts to study the relationship between public opinion and state policy. To evaluate government responsiveness, researchers must first know something about what voters want. I therefore begin by describing the various approaches that teams of scholars have employed to measure voter preferences. These approaches use different types of data to capture distinct and essential components of **public opinion**. I discuss these approaches in turn, highlighting the substantive lessons they yield about the opinions of voters across states and over time. From there, I consider the general relationship between estimates of state-level opinion and public policy. Scholars have investigated the opinion–policy linkage across a large and growing number of issue areas. Collectively, these efforts reveal a great deal about the extent to which elected officials incorporate the preferences of voters in policymaking. I then discuss the findings of this literature, emphasizing its important insights about the conditions (institutional and otherwise) that are likely to strengthen or weaken the effects of public opinion.

Finally, I consider the effects of public opinion in the area of "morality policy," focusing on two particularly salient and controversial policy areas: abortion and gay rights. Battles over where life begins and the legal status of same-sex relationships have been at the core of America's "culture wars," playing a central role in political conflict at both the national and state levels. Because of the salience of these issues, it might be particularly important for states to deliver the policies that voters want. However, the abilities of lawmakers to match policy to voter preferences in these areas can be constrained by courts and by protections written into constitutions. This situation has led to charges that abortion and gay rights policies do not ultimately reflect the public will.

MEASURING PUBLIC OPINION

Typically, political scientists measure and study public opinion using scientific polling. The beauty of a well-constructed and properly administered poll is that it will usually provide a reasonably accurate snapshot of opinion. Since its emergence in the 1930s, scientific polling has grown into a large industry, fueled by a seemingly insatiable demand for information about the public's view of politics. The advent of telephone (and, more recently, automated voice and Internet) polling has made it easier for pollsters to meet that demand. As a result, the media, elected officials, political campaigns, and researchers now have access to a wealth of invaluable data on the American voter.

Most polls, however, are conducted by national survey organizations and are only designed to measure public opinion at the national level. These polls rarely sample enough respondents from each state to make meaningful cross-state comparisons possible. Indeed, an average-sized national survey is likely to include just a few people from smaller-population states such as New Hampshire, Vermont, and Wyoming. Constructing a single poll with a representative sample from each of the fifty states is prohibitively expensive for all but the most specialized surveys.

Despite the dominance of national surveys, some organizations have a long, rich tradition of opinion polling at the state level. The oldest of these is the Iowa Poll, started by the *Des Moines Register* in 1943 (Lazarsfeld and Rosenberg 1949). A recent effort to document and publicize state opinion surveys unearthed fifty-four ongoing polls in thirty-five states (Parry, Kisida, and Langley 2008). Many of these efforts were launched in the 1970s or 1980s and are university-affiliated. There are now organizations, most notably the National Network of State Polls housed at the University of Kentucky, that promote the collection and use of state survey data.

The twenty-first century has also witnessed an explosion in nonacademic state polling by local media, candidates for public office, and political parties.

Unfortunately, finding comparable state polls can be challenging. Similar questions are rarely asked in surveys across all (or even many) states. When they are, differences in timing, question wording, survey techniques, and response categories make comparisons difficult.[1] Nonacademic polling is largely of the horse race variety, focusing almost exclusively on races for state elected office. Data from these polls are proprietary and rarely made available for scholarly study (Parry, Kisida, and Langley 2008).

Even though confronted with these limitations, some researchers have been able to effectively use state polls. For example, Beyle, Niemi, and Sigelman (2002), using a variety of public records, compiled an impressive data set of gubernatorial approval ratings. These data, though inconsistently available and missing for many governors, have helped researchers better understand the causes and effects of the approval ratings of state officials. Lupia et al. (2010) use state polls to study the adoption of constitutional same-sex marriage bans. In general, however, state polls are not a dependable source of public opinion data, and their absence is a source of much frustration for researchers engaged in the comparative study of state politics.

To compensate for the dearth of state polling, researchers have developed several measures of public sentiment. These draw on a variety of data sources and statistical techniques available to social scientists. Each measure captures a different component of public opinion and has helped further the study of politics. As is the case with nearly all social science data, however, each is imperfect and has its limitations.

Demographics as a Surrogate for Public Opinion

Early empirical research used demographic data, such as state wealth, urbanism, and racial composition, as surrogates for more direct measures of the preferences of state electorates (Elazar 1966; Jacob and Lipsky 1968; Hayes and Stonecash 1981). Demographic data were, and remain, readily available through the U.S. Census Bureau and a variety of other sources. The intuitive appeal of this approach is that demographic characteristics are known to shape opinions. The groups to which individuals belong structure their life experiences and possibly their future opportunities. Group memberships also shape the political attitudes and beliefs to which a person is exposed on an ongoing basis.

Research has demonstrated over and over again that a wide range of demographic characteristics, including income, race, education, gender, and religion,

---

1. The polling firm Survey USA has conducted many parallel state polls and makes their results available at www.surveyusa.com/index.php/surveyusa-poll-results/. To conduct their polls, however, Survey USA relies on automated voice technology, which typically leads to a much lower response rate than polls administered by telephone interviews. In addition, these polls ask a very limited set of questions.

are correlated with individuals' political opinions. Among these characteristics, race and income are particularly powerful predictors. Political scientists have shown that socioeconomic class is the principal factor dividing voters into Republicans and Democrats, with lower-income citizens more likely to support the Democratic Party and higher levels of government spending. In fact, the rich and poor continue to grow further apart politically, even as cultural issues such as abortion and gay rights have become increasingly important. Likewise, black voters are several times more likely than white voters to be Democrats (Erikson and Tedin 2011).

The underlying assumption of this approach—that people of the same demographic category think alike—has proven to be too strong for many researchers, particularly in view of the blunt demographic variables that have been employed.[2] For example, although most black survey respondents may oppose same-sex marriage, many will support it. In addition, demographic variables that are important for predicting attitudes in one area may have little predictive power in another. For example, income is an important predictor of fiscal conservatism—higher income earners are more likely to oppose progressive taxation and redistribution—but it is a fairly weak predictor of attitudes on social issues.

Demography does often shape opinion, but other factors matter as well. After controlling for demographic influences, the state and region of the country in which people live are important predictors of their core political attitudes as well as their opinions on a variety of policy debates. Erikson, Wright, and McIver (1993), for example, discovered that the effect of state residency on ideology can be as large as the effect of income. Other scholars have uncovered important interactions between demographics and geography. Gelman et al. (2008) find that the relationship between wealth and voting patterns is not as straightforward as most surveys suggest. In particular, they show that wealthy voters in the poorer states such as Mississippi and Alabama consistently support Republican candidates for elected office, while their counterparts in the more well-to-do states such as Connecticut and California regularly back Democrats.

Why does geography matter? The most common answer is that opinions are shaped by unique state and regional political cultures, which may owe their origins to the differing immigration patterns and social and economic histories of places. Scholars of American politics have long noted and documented the existence of such differences (Key 1949; Elazar 1966). It is likely that exposure to the predominant political culture of their state influences citizens to hold political views that they otherwise would not given their demographic characteristics.

---

2. For some, it has been unclear whether aggregate demographics such as urbanism and education measure public sentiment, even indirectly. In his influential studies of state policy adoption, Dye (1966, 1984) argued that these variables simply reflect the stages of economic development through which states evolve.

Mass Partisanship and Ideology

These limitations of using demographics as a surrogate for opinion led scholars to search for more direct approaches to measuring public sentiment. The ability to measure and study state public opinion took an enormous leap forward with the publication of the ground-breaking book *Statehouse Democracy* (Erikson, Wright, and McIver 1993). The authors, building on the prior work of Robert Erikson (1976), constructed state-level estimates of two key components of public sentiment: voter ideology and partisanship. Both are intended to capture the ways in which state voters view and understand politics.

A voter's **ideology** is generally thought to summarize his or her core political values or principles. In American politics, ideological labels are commonly reduced to a left–right continuum, with "liberal" on one end and "conservative" on the other. The precise meanings of these labels can be hard to pin down, and they change over time. In contemporary American politics, though, conservatives generally prefer a smaller government than liberals, often opposing redistributive programs, regulation, and efforts to use government power to champion the rights of racial, gender, and sexual minorities. Conservatives also tend to be moralistic and liberals more permissive. For researchers, ideology is a convenient classification because it contains a considerable amount of useful information. For many people, especially those who are politically knowledgeable, ideology is closely linked to the decisions they make in the voting booth and the positions they hold across a variety of issues. Among those who are less sophisticated, however, ideology may have little relevance to the way in which they respond to the political world.

Partisanship measures the disposition of individuals toward the Democratic and Republican Parties. Even more than ideology, this is the attitude that most structures the political opinions of Americans. Self-identified Republicans and Democrats have different opinions across a range of issues and usually vote for different candidates. Partisanship, unlike ideology, is relevant for individuals across nearly all levels of political sophistication and knowledge. Voters can know very little about politics but still possess and act on a partisan preference. Even though ideology and partisanship are strongly correlated, they are not the same thing. Republicans are generally more conservative than Democrats, but a fairly large (though shrinking) number of voters—liberal Republicans or conservative Democrats—do not fit neatly into this categorization (Erikson and Tedin 2011).

To estimate the ideology and partisanship of state voters, Erikson, Wright, and McIver (1993) pooled (that is, combined) 122 national CBS/*New York Times* surveys conducted between 1976 and 1988. In total, these surveys provided over 150,000 respondents. By pooling the surveys, the authors were able to obtain a large sample of respondents in each state, all of whom were asked whether they were a Democrat, Republican, or independent and also whether they were liberal, conservative, or moderate. Because the CBS/*New York Times* polls were conducted using random-digit dialing, these pooled state samples were likely to be representative of the state population, almost as if a separate poll had been conducted in each state.

Table 14-1 presents updated (as of 2008) estimates of state ideology and partisanship. These estimates say a great deal about the opinion landscape across the states. First, they show that state electorates tend to be ideologically conservative, though the balance between the share of liberals and conservatives varies. In all but six states the share of self-identified conservatives outnumbers the share of liberals. The size of the conservative advantage is greatest in the South, where it averages over 26 percent, and smallest in New England, the only region of the country in which most (but not all) state electorates tilt in the liberal direction.

Second, despite being ideologically conservative, state electorates tend be more Democratic. In thirty-three states, self-identified Democrats outnumber Republicans. This Democratic advantage is largest in Massachusetts (25 percent) and smallest in Utah (–34 percent). The Democratic advantage persists even in some states that are quite ideologically conservative such as West Virginia, Kentucky, and Arkansas. As a result, partisanship does not have the same stark geographic pattern as ideology. Meanwhile, neither the Democratic nor Republican Party reaches 50 percent identification in any state, indicating that independent voters are crucial for shaping the partisan balance of power in state capitals.

How have state ideology and partisanship changed over time? Recent work by Erikson, Wright, and McIver provides important insights (Erikson, Wright, and McIver 2007). First, ideology is quite stable. Over the last twenty-five years, relative state-level ideology has changed very little. The most liberal states in the 1970s and 1980s remain the most liberal states today. There has, however, been a shift in the partisanship of state electorates toward the Republicans. These gains have occurred largely, though not exclusively, in the South. Over time, southern states have abandoned their traditional alliance to the Democratic Party and transitioned to more competitive two-party systems. In fact, several southern electorates, including those of Alabama, Mississippi, and Texas, now have more self-identified Republicans than Democrats. This change, however, has been a gradual process—states do not experience sudden shifts in partisanship or ideology.

A second and equally noteworthy change is the higher correlation between state-level partisanship and ideology. In the 1970s and 1980s, there was almost no relationship between the two measures. Liberal states were, on average, no more likely to have Democratic electorates than were their more conservative counterparts. Over time, however, the correlation has become stronger. Now the most liberal states tend to be the most Democratic (with a few exceptions) and the most conservative states are the most Republican. Evidence indicates that this change emerged because voters have been slowly shifting their partisan identification so that they are consistent with their ideology. Liberal Republicans and conservative Democrats are becoming less common. A consequence of this

Table 14-1 State Ideology and Partisanship (in percentages)

State	Ideological identification			Partisan identification		
	Liberal	Moderate	Conservative	Democrat	Independent	Republican
Alabama	20.6%	28.1%	51.3%	33.2%	26.1%	39.0%
Arizona	25.3	32.3	42.5	30.5	30.5	36.7
Arkansas	19.1	32.1	48.8	38.3	32.8	26.9
California	35.0	30.7	34.3	41.5	26.2	29.1
Colorado	30.2	31.8	37.9	31.3	34.3	31.4
Connecticut	34.7	33.0	32.3	35.2	41.1	21.2
Delaware	32.0	35.2	32.8	38.5	30.0	30.4
Florida	26.2	33.5	40.3	35.0	28.9	33.6
Georgia	22.2	30.7	47.1	33.0	29.2	34.0
Idaho	20.8	27.6	51.5	26.6	31.3	38.1
Illinois	29.7	34.8	35.6	39.8	32.6	25.6
Indiana	24.8	30.3	44.9	30.7	33.4	33.4
Iowa	25.3	33.3	41.4	34.9	35.2	27.9
Kansas	22.8	31.4	45.8	29.1	27.4	40.6
Kentucky	24.4	31.0	44.6	44.8	24.5	29.0
Louisiana	16.7	32.9	50.3	36.7	26.0	34.5
Maine	30.8	35.4	33.8	30.0	43.0	25.1
Maryland	31.1	33.5	35.4	46.1	26.2	25.6
Massachusetts	38.6	34.3	27.0	36.6	49.4	11.8
Michigan	26.2	32.5	41.2	34.1	34.7	27.8
Minnesota	30.9	31.5	37.6	36.5	33.9	27.2
Mississippi	14.4	29.0	56.6	30.0	26.4	41.5
Missouri	25.1	31.2	43.6	34.8	32.1	30.1
Montana	25.8	31.8	42.3	30.7	36.2	28.9
Nebraska	19.6	35.5	44.9	28.2	29.0	41.1
Nevada	26.1	32.7	41.2	40.0	25.8	33.0
New Hampshire	27.6	36.8	35.7	19.5	54.5	23.6
New Jersey	30.3	36.7	33.0	37.9	34.6	25.1
New Mexico	33.7	30.1	36.2	41.1	27.5	28.4
New York	35.1	33.3	31.6	42.8	29.3	23.9
North Carolina	24.0	32.5	43.5	38.0	27.8	31.8
North Dakota	18.3	33.3	48.4	27.0	38.4	33.2
Ohio	24.8	35.9	39.3	37.4	30.2	30.1
Oklahoma	18.7	33.7	47.6	39.3	20.7	38.2
Oregon	33.4	30.9	35.7	38.1	28.5	29.9
Pennsylvania	27.4	35.3	37.3	41.5	24.0	32.2
Rhode Island	29.1	42.5	28.3	27.8	58.3	12.7
South Carolina	21.7	31.0	47.4	31.7	29.9	35.6
South Dakota	27.3	31.6	41.1	34.3	23.5	41.0
Tennessee	20.4	31.4	48.2	32.1	32.2	33.1
Texas	22.9	30.7	46.3	33.0	30.1	34.5
Utah	16.7	26.9	56.5	15.4	31.8	49.3
Vermont	42.7	28.6	28.6	30.4	47.8	18.6
Virginia	25.5	34.2	40.2	31.6	34.7	30.6
Washington	33.3	31.1	35.6	37.5	35.2	24.6
West Virginia	21.5	35.6	42.9	48.4	24.4	25.6
Wisconsin	28.9	32.5	38.6	34.3	36.0	26.9
Wyoming	16.1	30.9	53.0	23.3	27.3	47.3
Mean	26.2	32.5	41.3	34.3	32.4	30.8

SOURCE: National Annenberg Election Survey.

NOTE: This table reports self-identified ideology and partisanship by state as of 2008. These estimates were obtained by pooling the telephone and Internet components of the 2008 National Annenberg Election Survey (NAES). The NAES is a very large national survey with over 86,000 respondents. Because of its unusually large size, pooling surveys across multiple years is unnecessary. Alaska and Hawaii are excluded because voters from these states were not surveyed.

change is that state political parties are become more ideologically polarized—that is, state Democratic Parties are becoming more liberal and state Republican Parties more conservative.

The pooling technique pioneered by Erikson, Wright, and McIver (1993) has become the standard approach for estimating public sentiment at the state level.[3] However, it has important practical limitations. In order to obtain sufficiently large state samples, researchers typically must combine dozens of surveys over many years (often a decade or longer). Thus the technique can be used only for questions that consistently appear in surveys. Such questions are typically those that deal with core political attitudes such as ideology and partisanship. Questions about a timely policy debate, however, are likely to appear in just a few polls, soon to be replaced by the next newsworthy concern. Furthermore, pooling surveys should be done only for opinions that are stable. Although ideology and partisanship may be slow to change, other attitudes, such as voters' approval of the president or their support for same-sex marriage, can and do change over a short time span.

Notable exceptions to this obstacle, however, are large academic polling projects such as the National Annenberg Election Survey (NAES) and the Cooperative Congressional Election Study (CCES). These polls are very large (typically well over 30,000 respondents) and aim to provide representative samples in all or most states. However, the emergence of these polls is a relatively recent development, and they are usually conducted only during election years. Researchers may be able to use these polls without pooling or can combine them with other national surveys conducted during the same time period. Like most polls, these tend to focus primarily on issues of importance to national politics, asking a limited number of questions about state politics and policy.

Policy Mood

Public sentiment at the state level is also measured using indicators of policy mood. **Policy mood,** a concept first introduced in studies of opinion at the national level (Stimson 1991), refers to the public's general disposition toward government. According to Stimson (1991, 20), mood "connotes shared feelings that move over time and circumstance." Unlike partisanship and ideology, policy mood is not a long-standing decision or part of a voter's identity. Instead, it is a response to the ever-changing context of politics.

Mood reacts to the policy proposals and enactments of elected officials, fluctuating between preferences for more and less government. In general, the overall policy orientation of the public is moderate. However, when elected officials push policy too far to the right for the average voter, policy mood becomes more liberal; when officials push policy too far to the left, it becomes more conservative. Voters

---

3. The reliability of pooling has been confirmed by numerous scholars (Jones and Norrander 1996; Norrander 2001; Brace et al. 2002; Carsey and Harden 2010).

respond to changes in their mood by changing the identity of policymakers, often replacing incumbent officials with members of the opposition party. In this way, public mood works to correct policies that have drifted too far in a particular ideological direction. At the national level, the strong swing toward the right and support of Republican candidates in the 2010 congressional elections—a clear voter response to President Barack Obama's successes in passing liberal legislation such as health care reform—is an example of this dynamic. Shifts in electoral outcomes brought about by changes in the public mood do not necessarily represent shifts in aggregate voter ideology or even partisanship, both of which change much more slowly than mood.

Nationally, mood is measured using a series of survey questions that ask respondents about their policy preferences, including their support for gun control, labor unions, government efforts to help minorities, and current levels of government spending. For the reasons discussed earlier, state-level measures of mood cannot be constructed in this fashion, at least not over an extended period of time.[4] In the late 1990s, however, Berry et al. (1998) succeeded in creating a surrogate measure of state policy mood that does not rely on survey data. Instead, they use state election results and federal-level data on the liberalness of the roll call votes cast by members of Congress. Even though this measure only indirectly captures voters' policy preferences, it compares favorably to national survey-based measures (Berry et al. 2007). By using election results and interest group scores— data that are readily available—Berry et al. create yearly estimates of policy mood for all fifty states.[5]

The top graph in Figure 14-1 plots the average mood (across all states) from 1961 through 2007, with higher values on the y-axis indicating increased liberalness. The figure clearly demonstrates the cyclical nature of mood. Although the annual national average does not stray too far from the center of the y-axis (indicating a general moderate policy orientation), it regularly moves from periods of increasing liberalness to periods of increasing conservativeness. Nationally, mood seems to move in the opposite direction of the party in power. For example, the public became more conservative in the 1960s following the adoption of President Lyndon B. Johnson's Great Society programs that greatly expanded the reach of the federal government. More recently, the mood became much more liberal in the years following the reelection of George W. Bush as president in 2004. This increase was driven in part by the growing unpopularity of the war in Iraq.

---

4. Carsey and Harden (2010) have created measures of state policy mood using survey data. Specifically, they use data from the 2004 National Annenberg Election Survey and the 2006 Cooperative Congressional Election Study. Their measure, however, only captures state-level policy mood at a single point in time.

5. The measure created by Berry et al. (1998) was originally proposed as an indicator of voter ideology and has been used as such in many empirical analyses in the state politics literature. However, subsequent work (see Berry et al. 2007) suggests that the measure better captures policy mood.

Figure 14-1 Policy Mood, 1961–2007

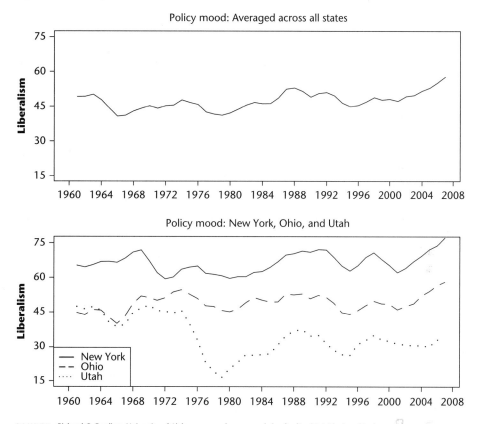

SOURCE: Richard C. Fording, University of Alabama, www.bama.ua.edu/~rcfording/stateideology.html.

NOTE: The top panel shows policy mood averaged across all states; the bottom panel shows policy mood for the states of New York, Ohio, and Utah. Three-year moving averages are reported. Higher values indicate a more liberal mood (that is, preferences for more government).

Not surprisingly, there are important differences in policy mood across states. These differences are illustrated in the bottom panel of Figure 14-1, which plots policy mood over time for three states: New York, Ohio, and Utah. Since the 1970s, these states have exhibited very different baseline or average policy orientations. New York has consistently been the most liberal, Ohio the most moderate, and Utah the most conservative. There are also important differences across the states in terms of the fluctuations in mood. For example, even though mood became more liberal in each of these states following 2004, the increase in liberalness was much larger in New York and Ohio than it was in Utah. Although voters in Ohio, Utah, and much of the rest of the nation became more conservative in the mid- to late 1960s, the mood of voters in New York remained fairly constant. Cross-state differences such as these are not surprising considering that mood reacts to state (as well as federal) policymaking. Moreover, voters in different states may have different responses to events at the national level.

Specific Opinion

In addition to global measures of opinion such as partisanship, ideology, and policy mood, researchers are often interested in **specific opinions**. Are state voters pro-choice when it comes to abortion or are they pro-life? Do a majority of state voters favor education reforms such as charter schools or voucher programs? Global preference measures will not necessarily reveal how voters feel on specific issues like these. In general, Americans cannot be described as having issue opinions that are tightly constrained by ideology or even by partisanship.

Fortunately, survey pooling can sometimes be used to estimate opinion on specific issues. For example, Norrander (2001) combines the American National Election Study's survey of Senate races in 1988, 1990, and 1992 to generate opinion on abortion, the death penalty, and affirmative action. Like the large national surveys discussed earlier, these surveys were large and included representative samples from each of the fifty states. Others have estimated specific opinion by pooling surveys over a much longer period of time (Arceneaux 2002; Brace et al. 2002; Matsusaka 2010). In doing so, however, researchers must be careful because specific opinion, unlike ideology or even partisanship, may not be particularly stable.

An alternative to pooling is simulating state opinion using survey, demographic, and geographic data.[6] Simulation works in two stages. In the first stage, individual survey responses and regression analysis are used to estimate the opinions of different types of people. Opinions are treated as being a function of individuals' demographic and geographic characteristics. From these estimates, a measure of state opinion is created by determining how many of each type live in the state. Simulation, if it works properly, requires many fewer surveys than pooling, allowing researchers to estimate state opinion on an issue without having that issue appear in several polls. This approach greatly expands the number and types of opinions that can be estimated.

Simulation as a way to study state public opinion originally gained popularity in the 1960s and 1970s (Pool, Abelson, and Popkin 1965; Weber et al. 1972). However, these early efforts were criticized for not incorporating geography as a determinant of opinion (Erikson, Wright, and McIver 1993). They also included only a fairly narrow set of voter types because of limitations in computing power and in the available statistical tools. Recent work, however, has overcome these limitations by employing more advanced statistical techniques (Park, Gelman, and Bafumi 2006). These techniques have been validated by comparing the accuracy of opinion estimates generated via simulation to the results of actual state polls and

---

6. Contemporary implementations of simulation are referred to as multilevel regression and post-stratification (MRP).

to the estimates of public opinion obtained by pooling many national surveys (Lax and Phillips 2009a). These comparisons demonstrate that simulation performs quite well and that it can be used to generate opinion estimates, sometimes employing as little as a single averaged-sized national poll.

Not surprisingly, these new techniques have resulted in a revival of simulation in studies of state opinion and have been used to estimate state-level measures of opinion across a large number of issues. With a single poll, simulation can be used to provide a snapshot of opinion across the fifty states, but by using surveys conducted over many years one can estimate more dynamic measures of specific opinion (Pacheco 2011).

Like ideology and partisanship, specific opinion is shaped in part by a person's demographic and geographic characteristics. Indeed, these factors are what enable specific opinion to be simulated in the first place. The particular characteristics that matter depend on the issue of interest. Although age is a very strong predictor of attitudes on gay and lesbian rights, it is much less important when predicting opinion on abortion.

Studies show that state-level measures of ideology and partisanship are indeed not always successful surrogates for specific opinion, regardless of whether opinion is estimated using pooling or simulation. For example, attitudes on abortion, gay and lesbian rights, and government spending on the environment are all highly correlated to a person's self-identified ideology. Opinions on a host of education policies and political reforms, such as the adoption of term limits and restrictions on campaign contributions, are not (Norrander 2001; Lax and Phillips forthcoming). Thus in some issue areas ideology may be a reasonable (if imperfect) substitute for specific opinion, but in others using ideology does not adequately represent voters' preferences. Interestingly, state partisanship tends to have fewer clear relationships to specific opinion than does ideology (Norrander 2001). Ultimately, voters often hold specific opinions that are inconsistent with their stated global preferences. For example, although the Democratic Party typically supports the continuing legalization of abortion, many self-identified Democratic voters tell pollsters that they are pro-life.

At the same time, most people are not very knowledgeable about politics or public policy. As a result, they may not have strong or well-formed preferences on a wide range of issues. This is particularly likely for issues that are complex or that have not received much media attention. The lack of an informed or considered opinion does not, however, always prevent people from answering survey questions when asked to do so by a pollster. Furthermore, survey responses can be manipulated through question wording and placement. Studies show, for example, that support for civil unions for same-sex couples jumps by eight to eleven points when the civil unions question is asked *after* a question about marriage rights (Pew Research Center for the People and the Press 2003; McCabe and Heerwig 2010). Opinion is also negatively affected if surveys ask about "homosexual marriage" instead of "gay marriage." Because of these concerns, some caution must be used when measuring specific opinion.

Public Opinion and Democratic Performance

Elections, at least in theory, link government policy to voter preferences. In elections, citizens have the opportunity to choose from a set of candidates with differing ideological and policy positions. This opportunity allows voters to populate the legislative, executive, and sometimes even the judicial branches of state government with officials who generally share their preferences. Once in office, officials' own ambitions—their desire to win reelection—give them the incentive to legislate in a way that is consistent with what their constituents want. Officials who offer policies that prove unpopular can be replaced at the next election by other politicians who offer something different.

Of course, many obstacles stand in the way of the democratic ideal. Most people pay little attention to politics. As a result, electoral choices are often made on the basis of partisan attachments or the idiosyncratic features of a candidate, such as personality traits, rather than the candidate's issue positions or prior performance in office. Incumbent lawmakers also enjoy resources that give them electoral advantages over most challengers, making them difficult to unseat even if they are unresponsive. Incumbents, for example, have higher name recognition, easier access to publicity, and easier access to the money needed to run a political campaign. The security of lawmakers is reflected in their high rates of reelection—nearly 90 percent for state legislators in many years (Jewell and Breaux 1988).

That said, lawmakers are aware that inconsistencies between their record in office and public opinion, if properly exploited by a future opponent, may lead to their defeat. Research at the national level shows that members of Congress lose votes when they take extreme policy positions (Erikson and Wright 2009). Similarly, a recent investigation of state legislative elections finds some evidence that incumbent lawmakers whose voting records place them far away from the preferences of the average voter are more likely to face a well-funded challenger in the next election (Hogan 2008).

How Do Elected Officials Gauge Public Opinion?

To be responsive, elected officials need to be able to gauge public opinion. But this is not always easy. State officials can only rarely rely on opinion polls to tell them how their constituents feel about a particular issue. Polls may be conducted for some high-profile or controversial issues, but these sorts of issues represent a very small portion of the bills lawmakers must vote on in a given legislative session. Furthermore, surveys measure statewide opinion, potentially providing little guidance to those legislators whose constituents may be very different from the average state voter. However, when polls exist, legislators report that they are an important source of information (Rosenthal 2009).

As an alternative to polling, elected officials rely on opinions expressed directly to them by constituents or by organized interest groups representing their constituents. Officials hear from voters via mail, e-mail, and telephone calls and when they travel around their districts. In a fifty-state survey with over 19,000 respondents, 7 percent of people reported contacting their state representative and 5 percent contacting their state senator over a twelve-month period. About 3–5 percent said they were expressing an opinion on a bill or policy issue (Niemi and Powell 2001). Legislators hear from organized interests and paid lobbyists throughout the legislative session.

The amount of contact depends on the nature of the issue and the extent to which grassroots support or opposition is mobilized. Though valuable for officials, contacts from voters or interest groups are not particularly representative of overall opinion. It is the individuals directly affected by a particular bill who are most likely to contact lawmakers. As for organized interest groups, not all citizens are equally represented. In particular, groups working on behalf of business and other well-heeled interests have proliferated, hiring the most lobbyists and contributing the most to political campaigns. Ultimately, though, there are many issues about which elected officials hear little to nothing from their constituents (Rosenthal 2009).

Even if officials do not know how their constituents feel on a particular issue, they are likely to be aware of their general ideological orientation. Knowing whether their constituents tend to be liberal, conservative, or moderate can be an important guide for lawmakers as they formulate policy or decide how to vote on a particular bill. Furthermore, officials may have a good understanding of public sentiment in their district simply by looking at their own values and opinions. Most have lived in their district for a long time and are likely to share many of the same core attitudes, policy positions, and political identities as the people they represent (Norrander 2007).

The Opinion–Policy Linkage

The importance of public opinion to policymaking can be gauged by determining whether the policy preferences of state electorates are related to actual state policies. To gain leverage on this question, researchers have considered two features of the opinion–policy linkage: responsiveness and congruence. Tests for responsiveness consider whether there is a positive correlation between opinion and policy. In a responsive political system, as support for a particular policy increases, so should the likelihood of policy adoption. Tests for congruence consider whether state policy matches majority opinion—that is, if a majority of voters want a state lottery, how likely is it that their state will adopt one? Although responsiveness and congruence are related concepts, they are not the same thing. It is possible for policy to be generally responsive but still remain incongruent with majority opinion in many states.

The most influential work on responsiveness is that of Erikson, Wright, and McIver (1993). They compare a state-level measure of global preferences—voter ideology—to a measure of the ideological tone of state policy, which they refer to as a state's "policy liberalism." They find a very strong relationship between voter ideology and policy liberalism, concluding that "state political structures appear to do a good job of delivering more liberal policies to more liberal states and more conservative policies to more conservative states" (p. 95). This study was the first to demonstrate a relationship between voter sentiment and government action at the state level, overturning the long-standing view that the public had little influence over state policy.[7]

Other studies have tested the opinion–policy linkage by examining the relationship between specific opinion and state policymaking on that topic. These studies have focused on a wide range of issues, including abortion rights (Norrander and Wilcox 1999), capital punishment (Mooney and Lee 2000), environmental policy (Johnson, Brace, and Arceneaux 2005), and gay and lesbian rights (Haider-Markel and Kaufman 2006; Lax and Phillips 2009b). Studies find that specific opinion matters, though its correlation to policy ranges from modest to very strong, depending on the policy area. Lax and Phillips (forthcoming) present one of the most comprehensive investigations, examining the correlation between specific opinion and government action across a variety of issue areas. They find that specific opinion is, on average, the strongest predictor of policy adoption, even after taking into account other potential influences, including the partisanship of elected officials. Lax and Phillips find that policy is responsive to both global and specific opinion.

Although policy is generally responsive to public sentiment, a great deal of incongruence remains—that is, policy is often inconsistent with the preferences of a majority of voters. State policies, at least when it comes to contested issues, match majority opinion only about half the time (Matsusaka 2010; Lax and Phillips forthcoming). While some incongruence might be expected given that neither researchers nor elected officials can measure opinion perfectly, large amounts of incongruence exist even when opinion majorities are quite sizable. For example, Lax and Phillips (forthcoming) find that when public opinion exceeds 70 percent, only about 60 percent of policies are congruent. Matsusaka (2010) uncovers an even more startling figure—when public support exceeds 90 percent, nearly one in five policies remains incongruent.

Although no one would reasonably expect opinion majorities to exercise complete control over state policy on every issue, 50 percent congruence could be

---

7. The strongest test of responsiveness would be an analysis of opinion and policy over time. If policy change follows opinion change, it would suggest a strong opinion–policy linkage and provide the most convincing evidence of responsiveness. The absence of time-varying measures of opinion by state makes this difficult, however. Instead, political scientists rely on cross-sectional analyses, looking to see whether states with higher levels of public support for a policy are more likely to have the policy.

achieved even if policy were decided by tossing a coin. In general, states fail to do much better than this toss, except when opinion majorities are large. Lax and Phillips (forthcoming) refer to the frequent mismatch between majority opinion and policy as the **"democratic deficit."** This deficit does not appear to be a short-run phenomenon. Policies that have been on state agendas for a decade or longer are only somewhat more likely to be congruent than policies that have more recently become relevant.

The amount of incongruence varies in meaningful ways across states, as can be seen in Table 14-2, which reports results from the study by Lax and Phillips (forthcoming). They consider congruence in all fifty states across thirty-nine different policies in eight issue areas, ranging from education policy to gay and lesbian rights. The states that do the best job matching policy to majority opinion are California and Louisiana, both of which do so 69 percent of the time. The states that score the poorest in their study are New Hampshire, Pennsylvania, West Virginia, and Wyoming. In each of these states, only 33 percent of the policies studied are consistent with majority opinion.

The second column of Table 14-2 reports the ideological direction of incongruence. It can occur when policy is liberal and the opinion majority is conservative or vice versa. On this measure, a score greater than 50 percent means that most of a state's incongruence is in the liberal direction—that is, when a state sets policy

Table 14-2 Democratic Deficit by State (in percentages)

State	Congruence	Liberal incongruence
California	69%	58%
Louisiana	69	33
Kansas	62	47
Massachusetts	62	53
Oklahoma	59	25
Texas	59	31
Arkansas	56	29
Arizona	56	29
Indiana	56	35
Michigan	56	35
Utah	56	41
Wisconsin	56	47
Georgia	54	33
Idaho	54	33
Missouri	54	33
Washington	54	61
Colorado	51	53
Minnesota	51	42
South Carolina	51	37
Tennessee	51	42
Connecticut	49	60
Florida	49	25
Illinois	49	60
Maryland	49	55
North Carolina	49	40
New Jersey	49	65
Ohio	49	30
South Dakota	49	40
Alabama	46	38
Mississippi	46	38
Nebraska	46	43
New Mexico	46	48
New York	46	57
Rhode Island	46	48
Virginia	46	33
Iowa	44	59
Maine	44	50
North Dakota	44	45
Kentucky	41	52
Montana	41	48
Nevada	41	48
Hawaii	38	54
Alaska	36	48
Delaware	36	40
Oregon	36	52
Vermont	36	56
New Hampshire	33	50
Pennsylvania	33	38
West Virginia	33	42
Wyoming	33	42
Mean	48	44

SOURCE: Jeffrey Lax and Justin Phillips, "The Democratic Deficit in State Policymaking," *American Journal of Political Science*, forthcoming.

NOTE: The first column is the percentage of policies that are congruent with opinion majorities (out of thirty-nine total policies). The second column is the percentage of incongruence that is in the liberal direction.

that differs from the preferences of a majority of voters it usually does so by adopting policies that are more liberal than voters prefer. A score below 50 percent indicates that incongruence is usually in the conservative direction. New Jersey "errs" more in the liberal direction than any other state: 65 percent of its incongruence is liberal. When Oklahoma and Florida "err," they only do so in the liberal direction 25 percent of the time; their incongruent policies tend to be conservative. This tendency is typical of most states. Thirty-four states have more conservative than liberal incongruence, suggesting a possible conservative bias in lawmaking, at least when it comes to particularly controversial issues.

The ideological direction of a state's incongruence is strongly correlated to the ideology of its voters. Liberal states tend to go "too far" in adopting liberal policies and conservative states tend to go "too far" in adopting conservative ones. In other words, elected officials sometimes appear to be responding more to the ideology of voters rather than their specific opinions. But ideology does not always predict the issue positions of voters. Sometimes, self-identified liberals hold issue positions that are typically associated with conservatives, and many self-identified conservatives hold some opinions that are more traditionally liberal.[8]

The consequence of responsiveness to ideology (at the expense of specific opinion) is shown in the histograms in Figure 14-2. The top histogram is the distribution of states in terms of the number of liberal opinion majorities in each, while the second is a count of the number of liberal policies. When it comes to liberal opinion majorities, most states are grouped together near the center of the scale. All but two states have between fifteen and twenty-five liberal opinion majorities (out of a possible thirty-nine). This indicates that voters in most states hold a mix of liberal and conservative policy preferences. The distribution of the number of actual liberal policies by the state, however, is bimodal and more spread out. This is readily apparent when the two histograms are overlaid. In total, twenty-nine states have liberal policy counts outside the central region of the figure (the region that contains the count of liberal opinion majorities). To put it simply, policy is polarized relative to specific opinion. This pattern is more consistent with a world in which states implement either a largely liberal or largely conservative slate of policies, rather than a world in which they select a slate of policies mixing and matching as preferred by opinion majorities.

Accounting for Differences in Responsiveness and Congruence

Research has exhaustively demonstrated that a strong correlation exists between both global and specific preferences and state policy. Few would argue (as they once did) that public opinion is not a key determinant of government action. Now, much scholarly work is aimed at accounting for observed differences in responsiveness

8. Incongruence may also result from lawmakers following their own preferences over those of their constituents. Recent advances in estimating the ideal points of state legislators may make evaluating this possibility easier in future research (see Shor, Berry, and McCarty 2010).

Figure 14-2 Distribution of Liberal Opinion Majorities and Liberal Policies

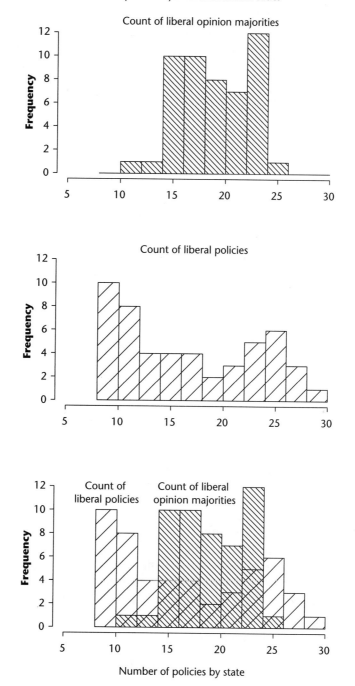

S O U R C E : Jeffrey Lax and Justin Phillips, "The Democratic Deficit in State Policymaking," *American Journal of Political Science,* forthcoming.

N O T E : Each panel shows histograms of the relevant count by state. Note the polarization of policy relative to opinion majorities.

and congruence across issue areas and states. These efforts have uncovered several factors that shape the opinion–policy linkage, though agreement among scholars about the effects of each is far from universal.

The first of these factors is the **salience** of a particular issue or policy—as the salience increases so does the opinion–policy linkage (Haider-Markel and Meier 1996; Lax and Phillips 2009b). Salient issues are those that are "widely visible to the public, particularly in the mass media, or felt directly by people and their families and friends" (Glynn et al. 2004, 356). For salient policies, citizens are more likely to hold strong opinions, to convey those opinions to their representatives, and to hold their representatives accountable. The incentive for officials to acquiesce to opinion on such issues is particularly powerful, even if doing so runs counter to their personal or partisan interests. When salience is low, however, officials may be unaware of their constituents' preferences. Alternatively, their constituents may not have particularly well-developed or strong opinions, thereby freeing lawmakers to pursue their own policy goals, repay interest groups for past or future support, or satisfy core (more extreme) constituents. Indeed, by giving constituents what they want on salient issues, lawmakers may be giving themselves additional freedom to go their own way on less salient concerns. Alternatively, lawmakers who want to be responsive to public sentiment but do not know their constituents' opinions on the particular issue may rely on voter partisanship or ideology. To measure the salience of an issue, researchers typically turn to media coverage of politics, often counting the number of times a particular policy is mentioned in newspapers.

Interest groups also have nuanced effects on the opinion–policy linkage. These groups are often vital in giving voice to citizen demands and helping citizens obtain access to elected officials. As a result, they can increase responsiveness by assisting opinion majorities in the potentially long and difficult process of translating their preferences into policy. In their study of the fiscal priorities of state governments, Schneider and Jacoby (2006) found that opinion has its greatest impact through its effect on the composition of the state interest group population. They discovered that state spending on collective goods is strongly correlated to the number of groups that support such expenditures and that the number of these groups is shaped by the ideology and partisanship of state voters. According to Lax and Phillips (forthcoming), interest groups do not consistently have a positive or negative effect on the opinion–policy linkage. They find that powerful interest groups enhance responsiveness when the policy objectives of these groups line up with majority opinion. However, when a powerful group is opposed to the majority opinion, this group can have a dampening effect on the link between opinion and policy.

Numerous studies have also considered the effect of institutions on the opinion–policy relationship. In general, two features of institutions have been shown to condition this relationship. The first is an enhanced *capacity* to assess and respond to public opinion. Such institutions include professional legislatures (Maestas 2000; Lax and Phillips forthcoming). In these bodies, awareness of public opinion is likely to be higher because lawmakers have the staff resources needed to find out what the public wants and because outside employment is less likely to constrain a legislator's attention to constituent interest. Furthermore, longer sessions allow more issues to be considered, including those of relatively lower salience.

The second feature of institutions that has been shown to matter is *majoritarianism*. It has long been hypothesized that institutions that empower electoral majorities increase the effect of public opinion on policy. Two such institutions are the election (as opposed to the appointment) of judges and access to the citizen initiative. Elected judges, because they can be held accountable to voters, may be less likely to overrule the popular actions of legislatures and less likely to issue unpopular decisions on contentious social issues such as gay rights, the death penalty, and abortion. Access to the citizen initiative allows voters to circumvent unresponsive legislatures and set policies themselves, or at least threaten to do so as a means of spurring legislative action.

A growing body of evidence indicates that elected judges are generally more responsive to voters (Huber and Gordon 2004). Indeed, a recent study finds that congruence for some issues is 11–13 percent higher in states where judges must stand for reelection (Matsusaka 2010). Evidence about the citizen initiative is more mixed. Studies have found increased responsiveness in certain policy areas, including abortion (Gerber 1999; Arceneaux 2002), capital punishment (Gerber 1996), fiscal policy (Matsusaka 2005), and gay and lesbian rights (Lupia et al. 2010). Matsusaka (2010), in a study of ten policies across various issue areas, finds that policies are 18–19 percent more congruent in states that allow the initiative. Other studies, however, have found weak or no evidence that the initiative strengthens the opinion–policy relationship (see Lascher, Hagen, and Rochlin 1996; Lax and Phillips 2009b, forthcoming).

Whose Opinions Matter?

An issue raised in the opinion literature is that the preferences of different groups of voters may not count equally. If true, this poses an important normative challenge to the quality of American democracy. Of particular concern is whether officials are more responsive to the opinions of the rich than those of the poor. This concern is compounded by the nation's growing economic inequality. Political scientists have long known that well-to-do voters have numerous advantages over their poorer counterparts. They are better informed, more politically active, have a greater sense of efficacy, and can afford to contribute money to political campaigns. In other words, they have the skills and resources to navigate the complexities of the American political system. Because politicians tend to be more affluent than the average voter, it makes sense that they might be particularly sympathetic to the interests of the wealthy.

Measuring the responsiveness of elected officials to different income groups is challenging, in part because the opinions of the wealthy and poor are often similar or at least move in tandem. That said, research has begun to uncover evidence of differential responsiveness. Both Bartels (2008) and Gilens (2010) find that the national government is more responsive to the preferences of the rich than to those of the poor. Rigby and Wright (2010) have uncovered similar effects at the state level for both social and economic policy. Moreover, they find that unequal representation is greatest in poor states. They report that this phenomenon cannot be explained simply by differences in the distribution of opinion across income groups in these types of states. Instead, their findings suggest distinct patterns of representation in wealthy versus poor states.

Elected officials may also care more about the opinions of their partisan base than the opinions of the average voter. Party activists and their organizations provide many of the resources and services that are essential for winning elections, including endorsements, campaign contributions, and staff assistance. They also represent a disproportionate share of voters in primary elections, which are typically low-turnout affairs. Because these activists tend to have ideologically extreme preferences, increased responsiveness to their wishes may drive officials away from the relatively moderate ideological and issue positions of the average voter. Although little research has been directed at evaluating this possibility at the state level, high levels of responsiveness to party activists could help account for the polarized distribution of policy shown in Figure 14-2. Furthermore, when asked, lawmakers report that they listen most to the core supporters, even more than their own staff, interest groups, and opinion polls (Rosenthal 2009).

PUBLIC OPINION AND MORALITY POLICY

Scholars who study responsiveness are often particularly interested in whether voters get what they want when it comes to issues of morality policy. **Morality policies** are defined by debates over basic values in which at least one side portrays the issue as involving morality or sin (Mooney 2001). These debates are fundamentally clashes over right and wrong, and they have their origins in differences in individuals' core values. Usually, these sorts of disagreements cannot be resolved by argument or compromise (Black 1974). In the end, the government must support one set of values at the expense of another, with the choice helping to define the morality of the polity (Mooney 2001). Examples of morality policies are abortion, capital punishment, gay and lesbian rights, physician-assisted suicide, and sex education. Concerns about these policies have been at the heart of the "culture wars" in contemporary American politics. Because morality policies are often set by state governments, some of the most intense battles over these issues have been fought in state legislatures, courtrooms, and direct democracy campaigns.

Three characteristics of morality policy suggest that public opinion plays an important role in shaping government action. First, morality policy tends to be technically simple. Unlike debates over the particulars of insurance regulation or tax policy, one does not need a lot of information to participate (Mooney 1999). Unlike other types of policy debates, debates over morality policy are not about whether a proposal will "work," but about whether it is morally the right or wrong thing to do. Thus the arguments are simpler. This finding is demonstrated repeatedly in survey data. When asked about morality policy issues, very few people are unable to express an opinion. For example, in the 1996 American National Election Study only five survey respondents (0.3 percent) did not express an opinion when asked about abortion (Norrander and Wilcox 1999). Moreover, these opinions, because they are based on an individual's fundamental values, are usually very slow to change.

Second, morality policy issues tend to be highly salient. These issues, when they are on the agenda, receive a great deal of media attention. Voters often care more about whether their state should allow abortion or same-sex marriages than they do tax policy (Mooney 1999). Indeed, people frequently appear to vote against their economic self-interests in order to support candidates and political parties who hold similar views on morality policy issues. In fact, large shares of people tell pollsters that they would not vote for a candidate who disagrees with them on the morality politics issues of the day. In 2009 *Newsweek* conducted a poll asking respondents whether they would be willing to vote for a president, governor, or senator who disagreed with them on abortion or same-sex marriage. A very sizable share of respondents—48 percent—indicated that they would not.[9]

Third, morality politics is characterized by high levels of political participation. When a morality policy issue is placed on the agenda, often by a policy entrepreneur or court decision, those citizens whose basic values are being challenged have an incentive to mobilize. According to Christopher Mooney, "With little technical information needed to participate and high salience, citizen involvement will be increased in all phases, from their paying attention to the debate, to having informed opinions, to actually speaking out and participating actively in the policymaking process" (2001, 8). Citizens are especially likely to be mobilized by advocacy organizations. Since the 1980s, conservative religious organizations have been particularly adept at mobilizing their supporters on issues that challenge their faith.

At times, obstacles may prevent lawmakers from matching policy to the preferences of their constituents. Paramount among these is litigation—morality policies are heavily litigated, with the judiciary sometimes defining which types of policies are and are not permissible. Capital punishment is an excellent example. In the case of *Furman v. Georgia*, 408 U.S. 238 (1972), the Supreme Court ruled that death sentences are handed down arbitrarily, violating the Eighth Amendment

9. Princeton Survey Research Associates International/*Newsweek* Poll, January 2009. Retrieved March 28, 2011, from the iPOLL Databank, Roper Center for Public Opinion Research, University of Connecticut, www.ropercenter.uconn.edu/data_access/ipoll/ipoll.html.

prohibition against "cruel and unusual punishment." This decision vacated state death penalty statutes, leading to a de facto moratorium on capital punishment in the thirty-five states that permitted it, despite high levels of public support for the death penalty in many states. Four years later, the Supreme Court reversed itself and states were allowed to reestablish the death penalty, but under a model of guided discretion in which the Supreme Court imposed numerous restrictions on the use of capital punishment. State courts also have been heavily involved in determining what is and is not permissible when it comes to capital punishment. In 2004, for example, the New York Court of Appeals ruled that the state's death penalty statute was unconstitutional. New York has been without the death penalty since the court's decision.

Overall, however, there is a very strong relationship between public opinion and government action when it comes to morality policy. Indeed, research consistently shows that policymakers are more responsive to public preferences and values on issues of morality than they are on other types of issues (Haider-Markel and Meier 1996; Mooney and Lee 1995, 2000; Lax and Phillips forthcoming). This is not surprising in view of the strong incentives that lawmakers have to follow constituent opinion on issues that are salient and where political participation is high. Nevertheless, despite a high level of responsiveness, policy does not always match opinion on these issues.

Abortion

Like capital punishment, the flexibility of states to set their own policies on abortion has been shaped by a series of very high-profile Supreme Court decisions. These decisions began in 1973 with *Roe v. Wade*, 410 U.S. 113 (1973), in which the Court held that a state could not limit a woman's right to an abortion on demand in the first trimester of pregnancy. The Court's decision was based on an earlier finding that the Bill of Rights implied a right to privacy.[10] In the years before the *Roe* decision, a number of states had begun to loosen their abortion regulations, primarily by allowing legal access to the procedure when a woman's life or health was at stake. The *Roe* decision went dramatically beyond these reforms and repealed most existing state restrictions on abortion. The decision came as a surprise to advocates on both sides of the issue and kick-started the political organization of abortion opponents.

In the years immediately following *Roe*, states were highly constrained in the laws they could pass regulating access to abortion. Over time, however, the Supreme Court has granted more latitude. In *Webster v. Reproductive Health Services*, 492 U.S. 490 (1989), and *Planned Parenthood v. Casey*, 505 U.S. 833 (1992), the Court gave states the latitude to enact restrictions so long as those restrictions did not impose an "undue burden" on a woman's right to an abortion. These rulings opened the door to state experimentation with abortion regulation, and many

---

10. *Griswold v. Connecticut*, 381 U.S. 479 (1965).

states have responded. The restrictiveness of abortion regulation now varies substantially across states. Examples of state restrictions are waiting periods, mandatory counseling sessions, parental consent, and bans on a procedure sometimes referred to as a "partial-birth" abortion.

Scholars have studied the effect of public opinion in this policy area by considering the relationship between voter preferences and the types of abortion restrictions adopted by a state. Research has found evidence of a strong opinion–policy linkage, as seen in Table 14-3. Column (1) of the table is the share of survey respondents by state who, when presented with several statements about abortion, answered the following question affirmatively: "Do you think that abortion should be available to anyone who wants it?" The share of respondents answering "yes" ranges from a high of 50 percent in Vermont to a low of almost 14 percent in Mississippi. Column (2) is an index of the restrictiveness of state abortion policy, ranging from 0 to 7 (with higher numbers representing increased restrictiveness).[11] The correlation between liberal opinion and the restrictiveness of a state's abortion laws is very high—0.80. Among states that score a 6 or 7 on the index, the share of respondents who report that abortion should always be available is a fairly low 24 percent. Among states scoring a 1 or 2, this figure rises significantly, to 43 percent.

However, responsiveness to public sentiment is far from perfect. For example, columns (3) and (4) show public support for a parental consent law and a ban on partial-birth abortions. Support for both of these types of restrictions is quite high, averaging 75 percent and 72 percent, respectively, with large majorities supporting such laws in all fifty states. However, only twenty-three states currently have a parental consent law in effect, and only sixteen have a ban on partial-birth abortions. For these particular regulations, the correlation between opinion and government action is only 0.5. The result is a fair amount of incongruence; public support for specific abortion restrictions does not necessarily translate into the corresponding public policy. This incongruence tends to be in the liberal direction—that is, state policy on abortion tends to be more liberal than voters would prefer.

Why does this discrepancy exist? One reason is that some states, either through legislative action or a ballot measure, have adopted the desired restriction only to have it struck down by the courts. These states are identified by the "+" sign next to their opinion estimates. In each of these instances, court action was countermajoritarian. Alternatively, the absence of voters' preferred policies might be explained by the partisanship of elected officials or features of the state's interest group environment. In their study of abortion policymaking, Norrander and Wilcox (1999) find that states with legislatures controlled by Democrats are much less likely to adopt

---

11. The policies included are parental notification or consent, pre-abortion counseling, pre-abortion waiting periods, bans on partial-birth abortion, requirements that all abortions be reported to a state authority, bans on the use of state funds for abortions, and the absence of laws protecting access to abortion clinics.

Table 14-3 Abortion Opinion and Policy

State	Should abortion always be available? (percent) (1)	Restrictiveness index (2)	Require parental consent (percent) (3)	Ban partial-birth abortion (percent) (4)
Alabama	19.1%	6	82.8%✓	79.1%+
Alaska	45.2	4	71.4	77.6+
Arizona	36.7	4	69.7✓	72.7+
Arkansas	18.5	7	83.2✓	75.0✓
California	44.4	1	61.6+	65.2
Colorado	39.2	3	66.9	69.6
Connecticut	44.8	3	70.2	65.4
Delaware	33.1	4	72.1	67.0
Florida	35.6	5	72.3	70.0+
Georgia	28.2	7	81.1	74.2✓
Hawaii	46.5	2	67.0	66.2
Idaho	30.6	6	75.5✓	81.1+
Illinois	35.6	2	76.3	63.0 +
Indiana	23.7	7	80.8✓	75.8✓
Iowa	28.2	4	78.7	68.9+
Kansas	25.5	6	77.9	77.6✓
Kentucky	20.1	5	80.1✓	77.7+
Louisiana	18.3	7	78.8✓	75.0✓
Maine	39.9	3	72.0	66.6
Maryland	41.4	1	71.6	65.2
Massachusetts	49.3	2	67.6✓	59.4
Michigan	31.6	5	77.8✓	70.5+
Minnesota	33.0	4	76.7	68.4
Mississippi	13.8	7	81.0✓	76.9✓
Missouri	26.1	5	80.3✓	73.5+
Montana	33.2	2	71.3	76.0✓
Nebraska	26.0	6	81.3	80.6+
Nevada	42.5	3	70.5	70.0
New Hampshire	41.6	2	71.6	68.7
New Jersey	42.7	1	69.9	65.8+
New Mexico	39.5	3	68.8+	70.5✓
New York	43.8	1	69.2	65.6
North Carolina	27.5	3	77.4✓	73.1
North Dakota	26.9	7	79.4✓	78.3✓
Ohio	29.2	7	79.7✓	73.1✓
Oklahoma	21.2	7	82.2✓	79.0✓
Oregon	45.0	1	66.7	64.8
Pennsylvania	30.9	6	74.9✓	67.6
Rhode Island	42.1	5	70.1✓	62.5+
South Carolina	24.8	7	79.9✓	76.0✓
South Dakota	27.5	7	79.4	76.5✓
Tennessee	21.7	6	82.5✓	76.0✓
Texas	26.9	6	76.9✓	73.4
Utah	18.4	7	84.4✓	85.3✓
Vermont	50.0	2	68.8	63.3
Virginia	31.8	7	76.7✓	70.4✓
Washington	43.7	1	68.1	66.8
West Virginia	19.3	5	75.8	75.1+
Wisconsin	29.5	5	79.9✓	73.9+
Wyoming	27.8	4	74.3✓	81.1

SOURCES: Column (1): 2008 National Annenberg Election Survey; columns (3) and (4): Jeffrey Lax and Justin Phillips, "The Democratic Deficit in State Policymaking," *American Journal of Political Science,* forthcoming.

NOTE: Column (1) reports the share of survey respondents who believe that "abortion should be available to anyone who wants it." Column (2) is an index measuring the restrictiveness of a state's abortion policies. The policies are parental notification or consent, pre-abortion counseling, pre-abortion waiting periods, bans on partial-birth abortion, requirements that all abortions be reported to a state authority, bans on the use of state funds for abortions, and the absence of laws protecting access to abortion clinics. The index ranges from 0 to 7, higher values indicating a more restrictive (conservative) set of policies. Columns (3) and (4) report public support for laws requiring parental consent and banning partial-birth abortion. States with a ✓ next to the opinion estimate have adopted the corresponding policy. Those with a + have also adopted the policy, but enforcement of the policy is blocked by the courts.

restrictive abortion policies and more likely to provide for public funding of abortions. As for interest groups, Norrander and Wilcox show that the balance between liberal (pro-choice) groups and conservative (pro-life) groups matters. If pro-life groups have more contributors than pro-choice groups do, then the state's abortion laws are likely to be more restrictive.

Gay and Lesbian Rights

Like abortion policy, the movement for gay and lesbian rights has been on state legislative agendas for several decades. The specific policy goals of this movement have changed over time. During the 1980s, much effort went into securing legal protections and health care services for victims of AIDS. Since then, efforts have focused on including sexual orientation in employment nondiscrimination and hate crime laws, allowing gays and lesbians to serve openly in the military, and, more recently, winning legal recognition for same-sex marriages. Many of these proposed policy changes challenge traditional values and, not surprisingly, have met with strong opposition from social conservatives and the organizations that represent their interests.

The result of decades of activism on gay rights issues is a complex policy mosaic. Some states have adopted numerous pro-gay policies; others have adopted few or none. This complexity is captured by the index of policy liberalness shown in column (2) of Table 14-4. This index is a count of the number of pro-gay policies adopted by a state, with possible scores ranging from 0 to 9.[12] The average score on the index is nearly 3.5. However, twelve states have not adopted any pro-gay policies, and five have adopted all of the policies included. Even a casual glance at the index reveals that the more ideologically liberal states (and states with higher levels of pro-gay opinion) receive higher scores. Rigorous analyses consistently show that opinion matters a great deal, even after controlling for other potential influences (Haider-Markel and Kaufman 2006; Lax and Phillips 2009b; Lupia et al. 2010).

As with abortion policy, however, the fit between specific opinion and policy is imperfect. Take, for example, same-sex marriage. In 1993 the Hawaii State Supreme Court ruled that limiting marriage only to heterosexual couples was a form of sex discrimination and therefore a violation of the state's constitution. This ruling was a call to action for gay rights activists, who demanded that other states follow Hawaii's lead, and for social conservatives, who called for state constitutional amendments defining a marriage as a union between one man and one woman. In the years after the Hawaii decision, twenty-nine states (including Hawaii) took the conservative position of amending their state constitutions, whereas five states, either through legislative action or a court decision, decided to allow same-sex marriage. These divergent outcomes are correlated with public

---

12. The policies are same-sex marriage, civil unions, employment nondiscrimination, housing nondiscrimination, hate crimes, joint adoption, second parent adoption, hospital visitation rights, and anti-bullying laws. Allowing same-sex marriage counts as two points; all others count as one point.

Table 14-4   Gay Rights Opinion and Policy

State	Liberalness index (1)	Same-sex marriage (percent) (2)	Civil unions (percent) (3)	Employment protections (percent) (4)	Hate crimes law (percent) (5)
Alabama	1	26.4%	38.6%	57.9%	67.0%
Alaska	1	44.5	57.4	65.6	70.5
Arizona	1	47.7	61.4	68.3	75.4✓
Arkansas	0	29.0	39.7	56.8	71.0
California	8	56.1	66.0✓	73.3✓	81.7✓
Colorado	8	52.0	64.1✓	69.9✓	77.6✓
Connecticut	9	56.6✓	70.3	73.8✓	81.3✓
Delaware	4	50.1	62.0	73.2✓	80.8✓
Florida	2	41.5	59.8	68.8	76.0✓
Georgia	0	34.2	49.3	65.1	72.7
Hawaii	6	54.4	65.4✓	69.9✓	80.2✓
Idaho	0	33.3	46.5	57.4	63.8
Illinois	8	48.2	62.0✓	72.1✓	81.7✓
Indiana	2	37.3	52.0	64.9	70.9
Iowa	9	44.1✓	58.9	67.7✓	77.1✓
Kansas	1	36.7	52.8	65.0	70.0✓
Kentucky	2	31.5	44.8	58.6	68.6✓
Louisiana	1	35.6	47.0	66.9	73.0✓
Maine	7	54.9	67.1✓	71.3✓	79.8✓
Maryland	6	50.7	63.1	74.3✓	82.4✓
Massachusetts	9	61.6✓	76.1	75.0✓	84.8✓
Michigan	1	45.6	56.7	70.2	78.9✓
Minnesota	7	46.7	59.6	69.3✓	79.4✓
Mississippi	0	27.2	39.7	60.3	69.2
Missouri	1	36.7	51.3	63.8	74.6✓
Montana	0	44.6	59.7	65.0	71.0
Nebraska	2	34.8	49.4	64.1	67.5✓
Nevada	6	50.3	63.0✓	69.4✓	77.1✓
New Hampshire	9	55.3✓	68.4	71.8✓	79.2✓
New Jersey	8	55.1	69.1✓	74.1✓	80.7✓
New Mexico	4	49.1	61.8	70.4✓	77.6✓
New York	7	57.7	72.2	75.3✓	82.9✓
North Carolina	2	36.2	46.5	65.0	73.8
North Dakota	0	37.9	51.4	65.9	69.4
Ohio	0	44.5	54.2	69.1	76.8
Oklahoma	0	26.3	40.9	55.1	65.0
Oregon	8	51.9	64.5✓	68.5✓	78.9✓
Pennsylvania	1	51.4	60.2	70.9	77.9
Rhode Island	4	59.7	72.0	74.2✓	83.2✓
South Carolina	0	32.2	47.9	63.7	70.8
South Dakota	0	37.6	51.2	64.6	70.2
Tennessee	1	31.2	41.0	59.3	71.1✓
Texas	2	34.7	49.8	65.6	71.1✓
Utah	0	21.6	35.0	44.3	59.5
Vermont	9	59.5✓	70.3	73.3✓	83.1✓
Virginia	1	41.6	51.8	68.4	75.9
Washington	8	54.2	65.7✓	70.0✓	80.3✓
West Virginia	1	41.1	51.8	66.1	72.0
Wisconsin	6	44.3	57.1✓	68.1✓	77.7✓
Wyoming	0	37.5	51.0	61.4	63.8

SOURCES: Opinion estimates: Andrew Gelman, Jeffrey L. Lax, and Justin H. Phillips, "Over Time, a Gay Marriage Groundswell," *New York Times*, August 22, 2010, WK3; Jeffrey Lax and Justin Phillips, "The Democratic Deficit in State Policymaking," *American Journal of Political Science*, forthcoming.

NOTE: Column (1) is an index counting the number of pro-gay policies adopted by a state. The policies are same-sex marriage, civil unions, employment nondiscrimination, housing nondiscrimination, hate crimes, joint adoption, second parent adoption, hospital visitation rights, and anti-bullying laws. Allowing same-sex marriage counts as two points; all others count as one point. The remaining four columns present public support for particular gay rights policies—legalizing same-sex marriage, allowing civil unions, including sexual orientation in employment nondiscrimination laws, and including sexual orientation in hate crime protections. States with a ✓ next to the opinion estimate have adopted the corresponding policy.

opinion—see column (2) of Table 14-4. In general, public support for same-sex marriage laws is much higher in states that allow same-sex marriage (55 percent) than it is in states that do not (42 percent). On average, support is lowest (39 percent) in those states that have adopted a constitutional ban. However, in some states policy does not match majority opinion. With only one exception (Iowa), the opinion majority in incongruent states favors same-sex marriage, but these marriages are prohibited by state statutory or constitutional law. The fact that policy is slow to respond to increasingly pro-gay public opinion may suggest a conservative bias in this area of policymaking.

A similar pattern exists for other policies that regulate gay and lesbian rights—public opinion shapes policy, but there are frequent mismatches between majority opinion and government action. As with same-sex marriage (and unlike abortion policies), this incongruence tends to be in the conservative direction. For example, as Lax and Phillips (2009b) show, public support is quite high for including sexual orientation in existing employment nondiscrimination laws. Support for doing so averages 67 percent across the states and represents the position of a majority of the public in forty-nine states. And yet only twenty-one states have adopted the policy.

Again, opinion is not all that matters when it comes to shaping morality policy. Research shows that the adoption of laws regulating gay and lesbian rights is influenced by the preferences and partisanship of elected officials and sometimes by state political institutions. Lupia et al. (2010) demonstrate the importance of these factors in their study of state constitutional bans on gay marriage. They find that majority opposition to same-sex marriage has been easier to translate into constitutional change in states in which voters can propose and adopt constitutional amendments themselves via the citizen initiative.[13] Where constitutional amendments must first pass the legislature, however, translating majority opinion into policy has been more difficult. This is especially true in states in which liberal or moderate Democrats control a sufficient number of legislative seats to block or defeat such efforts. Finally, the share of religious conservatives in the state population has been found to shape policymaking (Haider-Markel and Kaufman 2006; Lax and Phillips 2009b). Social conservatives are able to mobilize their resources and constituents in a way that shapes outcomes above and beyond their impact on state public opinion.

CONCLUSION

Two decades ago, many scholars believed that the public had little influence over policymaking at the state level. In an influential review of the state policy literature published in the 1980s, Jack Treadway (1985, 47) argued that voters' lack of

---

13. In addition to Lupia et al., numerous scholars have shown that gay and lesbian rights tend to suffer in states and cities that allow direct democracy (Gamble 1997; Donovan and Bowler 1998; Haider-Markel, Querze, and Lindaman 2007).

knowledge and interest in state politics leads to an incongruence between policy and public opinion. Advances in measuring opinion at the state level have fundamentally altered scholars' understanding of the link between voter preferences and government action. They can now safely conclude that public opinion matters and that it does so across a wide range of issue areas. As Erikson, Wright, and McIver note, "State political structures appear to do a good job in delivering more liberal policies to more liberal states and more conservative policies to more conservative states" (1993, 95). This is particularly true for those policies that are highly salient to voters, including abortion and gay and lesbian rights. Indeed, studies consistently find that public opinion, when compared with other potential determinants of outcomes, has the largest substantive impact on policymaking.

But the opinion–policy link is complicated. New research is uncovering evidence of a surprisingly large "democratic deficit." On average, policy matches majority opinion only about half the time. The deficit is present (though smaller) even when opinion majorities are quite large and issue salience is high. The size of the democratic deficit varies widely across states as a function of political institutions and other features of the state political environment.

Although the existing research provides important and growing insights into the relationship between public preferences and government action, important normative questions remain that are much more difficult to answer. In particular, how much consideration should elected officials give to public opinion? Does the existing literature find "too little" responsiveness, or does it find "too much" responsiveness? Any answer to these questions evokes a basic tension in democratic theory. Functioning democracy clearly requires some minimal matching of government choice to citizen preferences. However, normative concerns quickly arise. Too little responsiveness calls democracy into question, whereas complete popular sovereignty raises the specter of the "tyranny of the majority." This is particularly true for civil rights issues because minorities might be unable to rectify grievances through electoral processes. A strong relationship between public opinion and policy may suggest successful representative democracy, but still be troubling if it leads to fewer protections of or rights for minorities. Alternatively, it could be troubling if a high degree of responsiveness leads to policies that are incoherent or that produce undesirable outcomes for society. Ultimately, of course, voters have a great deal of influence over the degree of responsiveness in state political systems.

KEY TERMS

democratic deficit, 451

ideology, 440

morality policy, 456

partisanship, 440

policy mood, 443

public opinion, 436

salience, 454

specific opinion, 446

REFERENCES

Arceneaux, Kevin. 2002. "Direct Democracy and the Link between Public Opinion and State Abortion Policy." *State Politics and Policy Quarterly* 2: 372–388.

Bartels, Larry. 2008. *Unequal Democracy.* Princeton, N.J.: Princeton University Press.

Berry, William D., Evan J. Ringquist, Richard C. Fording, and Russell L. Hanson. 1998. "Measuring Citizen and Government Ideology in the American States, 1960–93." *American Journal of Political Science* 42: 327–348.

———. 2007. "The Measurement and Stability of Citizen Ideology." *State Politics and Policy Quarterly* 7: 111–132.

Beyle, Thad, Richard G. Niemi, and Lee Sigelman. 2002. "Gubernatorial, Senatorial, and State-Level Presidential Job Approval: The U.S. Officials Job Approval Ratings (JAR) Collection." *State Politics and Policy Quarterly* 2: 215–229.

Black, Charles L., Jr. 1974. *Capital Punishment: The Inevitability of Caprice and Mistake.* New York: Norton.

Brace, Paul, Kellie Sims-Butler, Kevin Arceneaux, and Martin Johnson. 2002. "Public Opinion in the American States: New Perspectives Using National Survey Data." *American Journal of Political Science* 46: 173–189.

Carsey, Thomas M., and Jeffrey Harden. 2010. "New Measures of Partisanship, Ideology, and Policy Mood in the American States." *State Politics and Policy Quarterly* 10: 136–156.

Cohen, Jeffrey E., ed. 2006. *Public Opinion in State Politics.* Stanford, Calif.: Stanford University Press.

Donovan, Todd, and Shaun Bowler. 1998. "Direct Democracy and Minority Rights: An Extension." *American Journal of Political* Science 45: 1020–1024.

Dye, Thomas R. 1966. *Politics, Economics, and the Public: Political Outcomes in the American States.* Chicago: Rand McNally.

———. 1984. "Party and Policy in the States." *Journal of Politics* 46: 1097–1116.

Elazar, Daniel. 1966. *American Federalism: A View from the South.* New York: Crowell.

Erikson, Robert S. 1976. "The Relationship between Public Opinion and State Policy: A New Look Based on Some Forgotten Data." *American Journal of Political Science* 20: 25–36.

Erikson, Robert S., and Kent L. Tedin. 2011. *American Public Opinion: Its Origins, Content, and Impact,* 8th ed. New York: Longman.

Erikson, Robert S., and Gerald C. Wright. 2009. "Voters, Candidates, and Issues in Congressional Elections." In *Congress Reconsidered,* 9th ed., ed. Lawrence C. Dodd and Bruce I. Oppenheimer. Washington, D.C.: CQ Press.

Erikson, Robert S., Gerald C. Wright, and John P. McIver. 1993. *Statehouse Democracy: Public Opinion and Policy in the American States.* Cambridge, U.K.: Cambridge University Press.

———. 2007. "Measuring the Public's Ideological Preferences in the 50 States: Survey Responses versus Roll Call Data." *State Politics and Policy Quarterly* 7: 141–151.

Gamble, Barbara. 1997. "Putting Civil Rights to a Popular Vote." *American Journal of Political Science* 41: 245–269.

Gelman, Andrew, Jeffrey L. Lax, and Justin H. Phillips. 2010. "Over Time, a Gay Marriage Groundswell," *New York Times,* August 22, WK3.

Gelman, Andrew, David Park, Boris Shor, Joseph Bafumi, and Jeronimo Cortina. 2008. *Red State, Blue State, Rich State, Poor State: Why Americans Vote the Way They Do.* Princeton, N.J.: Princeton University Press.

Gerber, Elisabeth R. 1999. *The Populist Paradox: Interest Group Influence and the Promise of Direct Legislation.* Princeton, N.J.: Princeton University Press.

Gilens, Martin. 2010. "Income Inequality and Democratic Responsiveness." In *Who Gets Represented?* ed. Peter Enns and Christopher Weleziew. New York: Russell Sage Foundation.

Glynn, Carroll J., Susan Herbst, Garrett O'Keefe, Robert Y. Shapiro, and Mark Lindeman. 2004. "Public Opinion and Democratic Competence." In *Public Opinion,* 2d ed. Boulder, Colo.: Westview Press.

Haider-Markel, Donald P., and Matthew S. Kaufman, with Clyde Wilcox. 2006. "Public Opinion and the Culture Wars: Is There a Connection between Opinion and State Policy on Gay and Lesbian Issues?" In *Public Opinion in State Politics*, ed. Jeffrey E. Cohen. Stanford, Calif.: Stanford University Press.

Haider-Markel, Donald P., and Kenneth J. Meier. 1996. "The Politics of Gay and Lesbian Rights: Expanding the Scope of the Conflict." *Journal of Politics* 58: 332–349.

Haider-Markel, Donald P., Alana Querze, and Kara Lindaman. 2007. "Lose, Win, or Draw? A Reexamination of Direct Democracy and Minority Rights." *Political Research Quarterly* 60: 304–314.

Hayes, Susan W., and Jeff Stonecash. 1981. "The Sources of Public Policy: Welfare Policy in the American States." *Policy Studies Journal* 9: 681–698.

Hogan, Robert E. 2008. "Policy Responsiveness and Incumbent Reelection in State Legislatures." *American Journal of Political Science* 42: 858–873.

Huber, Gregory A., and Sanford C. Gordon. 2004. "Accountability and Coercion: Is Justice Blind When It Runs for Office?" *American Journal of Political Science* 48: 247–263.

Jacob, Herbert, and Michael Lipsky. 1968. "Outputs, Structure, and Power: An Assessment of Changes in the Study of State and Local Politics." *Journal of Politics* 30: 510–538.

Jewell, Malcolm, and David Breaux. 1988. "The Effect of Incumbency on State Legislative Elections." *Legislative Studies Quarterly* 13: 495–514.

Johnson, Martin, Paul Brace, and Kevin Arceneaux. 2005. "Public Opinion and Dynamic Representation in the States: The Case of Environmental Attitudes." *Social Science Quarterly* 86: 87–108.

Jones, Bradford S., and Barbara Norrander. 1996. "The Reliability of Aggregated Public Opinion Measures." *American Journal of Political Science* 40: 295–309.

Key, V. O., Jr. 1949. *Southern Politics in State and Nation.* New York: Knopf.

Lascher, Edward L., Jr., Michael G. Hagen, and Steven A. Rochlin. 1996. "Gun behind the Door: Ballot Initiatives, State Policies, and Public Opinion." *Journal of Politics* 58: 760–775.

Lax, Jeffrey, and Justin Phillips. 2009a. "How Should We Estimate Public Opinion in the States?" *American Journal of Political Science* 53: 107–121.

———. 2009b. "Public Opinion and Policy Responsiveness: Gay Rights in the States." *American Political Science Review* 103: 367–385.

———. Forthcoming. "The Democratic Deficit in State Policymaking." *American Journal of Political Science.*

Lazarsfeld, Paul F., and Morris Rosenberg. 1949. "The Contribution of the Regional Poll to Political Understanding." *Public Opinion Quarterly* 13: 569–586.

Lupia, Arthur, Yanna Krupnikov, Adam Seth Levine, Spencer Piston, and Alexander Von Hagen-Jamar. 2010. "Why State Constitutions Differ in their Treatment of Same-Sex Marriage." *Journal of Politics* 72: 1222–1235.

Maestas, Cherie. 2000. "Professional Legislatures and Ambitious Politicians: Policy Responsiveness of State Institutions." *Legislative Studies Quarterly* 25: 663–690.

Matsusaka, John G. 2005. *For the Many or the Few: The Initiative, Public Policy, and American Democracy.* Chicago: University of Chicago Press.

———. 2010. "Popular Control of Public Policy: A Quantitative Approach." *Quarterly Journal of Political Science* 5: 133–167.

McCabe, Brian J., and Jennifer A. Heerwig. 2010. "Framing and Context Effects in Support for Same-Sex Marriage and Civil Unions." Working paper, New York University.

Mooney, Christopher Z., ed. 2001. *The Public Clash of Private Values: The Politics of Morality Policy.* New York: Chatham House.

Mooney, Christopher Z., and Mei-Hsein Lee. 1995. "Legislating Morality in the American States: The Case of Pre-*Roe* Abortion Regulation Reform." *American Journal of Political Science* 39: 599–627.

———. 2000. "The Influence of Values on Consensus and Contentious Morality Policy: U.S. Death Penalty Reform, 1956–1982." *Journal of Politics* 62: 223–239.

Niemi, Richard C., and Lynda W. Powell. 2001. "United Citizenship? Knowing and Contacting Legislators after Term Limits." In *The Test of Time: Coping with Legislative Term Limits*, ed. Rick Farmer, John David Rausch Jr., and John C. Green. Lanham, Md.: Lexington Books.

Norrander, Barbara. 2001. "Measuring State Public Opinion with the Senate National Election Study." *State Politics and Policy Quarterly* 1: 111–125.

———. 2007. "Choosing among Indicators of State Public Opinion." *State Politics and Policy Quarterly* 7: 152–159.

Norrander, Barbara, and Clyde Wilcox. 1999. "Public Opinion and Policymaking in the States: The Case of Post-*Roe* Abortion Policy." *Policy Studies Journal* 27: 707–722.

Pacheco, Julianna. 2011. "Measuring State Public Opinion over Time Using National Surveys: A Guideline for Scholars." *State Politics and Policy Quarterly* 11: 415–439.

Park, David K., Andrew Gelman, and Joseph Bafumi. 2006. "State Level Opinions from National Surveys: Poststratification Using Multilevel Logistic Regression." In *Public Opinion in State Politics*, ed. Jeffrey E. Cohen. Stanford, Calif.: Stanford University Press.

Parry, Janine A., Brian Kisida, and Ronald E. Langley. 2008. "The State of State Polls: Old Challenges, New Opportunities." *State Politics and Policy Quarterly* 8: 198–216.

Pew Research Center for the People and the Press. 2003. "Republicans Unified, Democrats Split on Gay Marriage: Religious Beliefs Underpin Opposition to Homosexuality." Washington, D.C.

Pool, Ithiel de Sola, Robert Abelson, and Samuel L. Popkin. 1965. *Candidates, Issues, and Strategies*. Cambridge, Mass.: MIT Press.

Rigby, Elisabeth, and Gerald C. Wright. 2010. "Whose Statehouse Democracy? How State Policy Choices Align with the Preferences of the Poor, Middle-Income, and Wealthy Segments of the Electorate." In *Who Gets Represented*, ed. Peter Enns and Christopher Weleziew. New York: Russell Sage Foundation.

Rosenthal, Alan. 2009. *Engines of Democracy: Politics and Policymaking in State Legislatures*. Washington, D.C.: CQ Press.

Schneider, Saundra K., and William G. Jacoby. 2006. "Citizen Influence on State Policy Priorities: The Interplay of Public Opinion and Interest Groups." In *Public Opinion in State Politics*, ed. Jeffrey E. Cohen. Stanford, Calif.: Stanford University Press.

Shor, Boris, Christopher Berry, and Nolan McCarty. 2010. "A Bridge to Somewhere: Mapping State and Congressional Ideology on a Cross-Institutional Common Space." *Legislative Studies Quarterly* 35: 417–448.

Stimson, James. 1991. *Public Opinion in America: Moods, Cycles, and Swings*. Boulder, Colo.: Westview Press.

Treadway, Jack M. 1985. *Public Policymaking in the States*. New York: Praeger.

Weber, Ronald E., Anne H. Hopkins, Michael L. Mezey, and Frank J. Munger. 1972. "Computer Simulation of State Electorates." *Public Opinion Quarterly* 36: 549–565.

SUGGESTED READINGS

Print

Cohen, Jeffrey E., ed. *Public Opinion in State Politics*. Stanford, Calif.: Stanford University Press, 2006. Discusses approaches to estimating public opinion and explores the relationship between various measures of public preferences and state policy.

Erikson, Robert S., Gerald C. Wright, and John P. McIver. *Statehouse Democracy: Public Opinion and Policy in the American States*. Cambridge, U.K.: Cambridge University Press, 1993. Documents the strong link between mass ideology and the liberalness of state policy.

Lax, Jeffrey, and Justin Phillips. "The Democratic Deficit in State Policymaking." *American Journal of Political Science.* Forthcoming. Provides an in-depth analysis of the responsiveness of state governments to policy-specific public opinion and documents the existence of a "democratic deficit."

Parry, Janine A., Brian Kisida, and Ronald E. Langley. "The State of State Polls: Old Challenges, New Opportunities." *State Politics and Policy Quarterly* 8 (2008): 198–216. Describes ongoing efforts to conduct state-level opinion polls.

Internet

Field Poll. www.field.com/fieldpollonline/. Nonpartisan organization that conducts opinion polls on political and social issues in California.

iPOLL Databank. www.ropercenter.uconn.edu/data_access/ipoll/ipoll.htm. Comprehensive, up-to-dateresource for U.S. public opinion data.

National Network of State Polls. http://survey.rgs.uky.edu/nnsp/. Archive of state opinion polls.

Quinnipiac University Polling Institute. www.quinnipiac.edu/x271.xml. Conducts state polls of many eastern states, including Connecticut, Florida, New Jersey, New York, Ohio, and Pennsylvania.

CHAPTER 15

Environmental Policy

DAVID M. KONISKY AND NEAL D. WOODS

On April 2, 2007, the U.S. Supreme Court issued its opinion in the case of *Massachusetts v. Environmental Protection Agency*. The state of Massachusetts, along with eleven other states, a handful of local governments, and thirteen environmental advocacy organizations, sued the U.S. Environmental Protection Agency (EPA) for its failure to regulate the emissions of greenhouse gases, most notably carbon dioxide, from new motor vehicles. The impetus for the case was the EPA's denial of a 1999 petition brought by the International Center for Technology Assessment and other organizations requesting that the agency regulate these emissions under the federal Clean Air Act. Massachusetts claimed that human-induced climate change was causing harmful effects to the state's coastal areas because of sea level rise and that the EPA had authority under the Clean Air Act to take action to address greenhouse gas emissions from motor vehicles, which were in part causing these adverse effects.[1] The Supreme Court agreed, voting 5–4 that the EPA did in fact have jurisdiction under the statute, and that it could not refuse to pursue regulation unless it provided a scientific basis for that decision.

1. Although *Massachusetts v. Environmental Protection Agency*, 549 U.S. 497 (2007), is the most prominent of cases brought by states to compel the federal government to take action to regulate greenhouse gases, it is by no means the only case. California, for example, has filed numerous rulemaking petitions under the Clean Air Act in an effort to spur the EPA to regulate emissions from a variety of sources (Engel 2010).

A clear motivating factor behind the legal efforts of Massachusetts and the other eleven states (California, Connecticut, Illinois, Maine, New Jersey, New Mexico, New York, Oregon, Rhode Island, Vermont, and Washington) participating in the case was growing frustration with the federal government's policy inaction on climate change. Despite decades of the issue being on the federal government's agenda, no policies were in place to directly curtail greenhouse gases. The intransigence of the George W. Bush administration in particular was met with dissatisfaction. Meanwhile, many state governments had begun to adopt their own initiatives, including the development of regional cap-and-trade programs for carbon dioxide and the creation of state renewable portfolio standards to encourage the use of renewable energy sources in electricity generation (Rabe 2004, 2008). *Massachusetts v. Environmental Protection Agency* represented an effort by a coalition of states to push federal policy forward.

The *Massachusetts v. Environmental Protection Agency* decision has had important implications for the direction of U.S. climate change policy. The decision provided the EPA with statutory authority to pursue limits to carbon dioxide emissions through the federal rulemaking process, an authority it has chosen to utilize in part because of the failure of Congress to enact legislation to regulate greenhouse gases.[2] The EPA did not issue any such rules during the Bush administration, but during the Obama administration it promulgated, or was actively pursuing, regulations requiring firm-level reporting of carbon dioxide emissions, inclusion of emissions limits in permits for large new and modified stationary sources of carbon dioxide, new emissions limits on cars and trucks, and emissions limits for fossil fuel–run power plants and oil refineries.[3]

Although this action was prompted by a coalition of states pushing the federal government to take action, these regulations have by no means been welcomed by all states. In response to the EPA's greenhouse gas–permitting regulation, states wishing to continue to administer permits to large stationary sources of carbon dioxide had to modify their State Implementation Plans under the federal Clean Air Act. All states but Texas indicated that they would do so. Texas, led by Gov. Rick Perry and Attorney General Gregg Abbott, rejected the EPA's authority to regulate greenhouse gas emissions, and when the state refused to implement the new permitting requirements, the EPA decided the agency itself would issue the permits to

---

2. The House of Representatives passed climate change legislation, best known as Waxman-Markey, by a slim 219–212 margin in June 2009. The legislation included a cap-and-trade system to limit emissions of carbon dioxide. The Senate considered, but failed to pass, similar legislation.

3. A necessary precondition for the new regulation was the EPA's "endangerment finding," which was the formal decision that carbon dioxide and five other greenhouse gases in the atmosphere "may reasonably be anticipated both to endanger public health and to endanger public welfare" (*Federal Register*, December 15, 2009). The endangerment finding itself is the subject of a lawsuit, with states participating both in support of and opposition to it. In addition, the U.S. House of Representatives passed a bill in April 2011 that overturned the EPA's endangerment finding and eliminated the EPA's authority to regulate greenhouse gases. A similar bill failed to pass the Senate in the same month.

facilities. Texas filed suit to stop the EPA, but the U.S. Circuit Court of Appeals for the District of Columbia ruled in favor of the agency on January 12, 2011.

The dispute between Texas and the EPA, juxtaposed with the *Massachusetts v. Environmental Protection Agency* case, illustrates the diversity of preferences across the U.S. states when it comes to environmental protection. This variation reflects differences in baseline environmental conditions as well as the preferences of citizen and elected officials. Although some states, such as California and New York, have established themselves as environmental policy leaders, others, such as Louisiana and Texas, have been characterized as environmental policy laggards (Lester 1995). How do environmental problems vary by state? What is the role of state government in addressing these environmental problems, and what is the interplay of state efforts with those of the federal government? What are the determinants of state environmental policy leadership and innovation? These are the questions we address in this chapter.

STATE ENVIRONMENTAL CONDITIONS

The United States is a large country with immense topographic, economic, political, and cultural diversity. For these and other reasons, environmental conditions across the states vary tremendously. There is no single measure at the state (or any jurisdictional) level that fully encapsulates its environmental quality. For example, the ambient air quality in a given state could be quite good, but the same state could suffer from serious water quality problems. For this reason, it is useful to consider multiple metrics of environmental conditions.

The data in Table 15-1 present information commonly used to characterize environmental conditions in the U.S. states. Researchers in political science, economics, and public health use these data to measure the severity of environmental problems at the state level; government officials use them to track progress and to inform their environmental protection strategies; and environmental organizations use them to advocate for improvements.

The data in columns (1) and (2) of Table 15-1 capture for 2009 the total emissions of toxic substances—first in absolute and then in per capita terms—for each state. The source of this information is the **Toxics Release Inventory (TRI)**, which is compiled annually by the EPA. The TRI program gathers information on toxic chemical releases from particular industries and federal facilities and then provides citizens with information about the environmental conditions in their community. The EPA receives these data directly from individual facilities, and then aggregates them to various levels. Several patterns should be noted in the state-level data. First, many of the states with the most releases in absolute terms are geographically large and populous states in which sizable parts of their economies consist of industries such as chemical manufacturing and metal works and their electricity is generated in large quantities from coal-fired power plants. Examples are states in the "Rust Belt"—Illinois, Indiana, Michigan, Ohio, and Pennsylvania—and in the

Table 15-1 State Environmental Conditions

State	Toxic emissions, 2009 Total releases (pounds) (1)	Total releases per capita (2)	Ambient air quality, 2010 Nonattainment % counties (3)	% state population (4)	Water quality, 2008 % rivers and streams impaired (5)	% lakes, reservoirs, and ponds impaired (6)
Alabama	91,075,650	19.34	6%	21%	25%	21%
Alaska	695,927,854	996.36	11	60	80	58
Arizona	60,899,299	9.23	40	85	37	15
Arkansas	34,009,523	11.77	0	—	44	54
California	36,718,326	0.99	64	94	93	93
Colorado	20,169,013	4.01	14	67	14	46
Connecticut	3,314,913	0.94	100	100	42	23
Delaware	8,085,313	9.13	100	100	100	97
Florida	84,941,381	4.58	0	—	0	0
Georgia	79,824,749	8.12	17	60	59	38
Hawaii	2,947,264	2.28	0	—	100	100
Idaho	47,871,236	30.97	11	10	57	99
Illinois	95,068,572	7.36	13	71	58	96
Indiana	132,074,361	20.56	19	43	58	96
Iowa	46,477,055	15.45	0	—	69	57
Kansas	21,123,404	7.49	0	—	88	91
Kentucky	142,607,547	33.06	6	29	61	40
Louisiana	119,527,406	26.61	8	16	78	88
Maine	8,463,681	6.42	0	—	4	8
Maryland	35,759,311	6.27	50	79	60	75
Massachusetts	5,375,009	0.82	100	100	69	88
Michigan	70,746,325	7.10	8	48	76	36
Minnesota	22,229,740	4.22	0	—	79	97
Mississippi	54,116,796	18.33	0	—	56	25
Missouri	75,727,384	12.65	4	28	20	7
Montana	41,169,093	42.23	16	52	85	86
Nebraska	29,562,754	16.45	0	—	57	66
Nevada	183,371,163	69.38	12	88	51	68
New Hampshire	2,899,274	2.19	40	74	100	100
New Jersey	12,944,597	1.49	100	100	88	95
New Mexico	15,297,901	7.61	3	10	56	86
New York	23,279,524	1.19	48	86	14	61
North Carolina	63,582,646	6.78	10	28	51	55
North Dakota	21,204,560	32.78	0	—	5	70
Ohio	158,508,558	13.73	31	67	96	100
Oklahoma	29,553,945	8.02	0	—	84	96
Oregon	17,263,571	4.51	6	11	67	97
Pennsylvania	120,400,308	9.55	36	74	48	53
Rhode Island	395,231	0.38	100	100	45	53
South Carolina	49,401,851	10.83	2	5	64	24
South Dakota	4,589,642	5.65	0	—	47	48
Tennessee	89,101,753	14.15	10	20	38	32
Texas	189,779,393	7.66	7	36	39	37
Utah	147,373,378	52.92	24	84	28	32
Vermont	262,030	0.42	0	—	7	86
Virginia	56,035,192	7.11	7	28	66	84
Washington	15,629,587	2.35	3	12	80	68

Table 15-1   *(Continued)*

| State | Toxic emissions, 2009 | | Ambient air quality, 2010 | | Water quality, 2008 | |
| | Total releases (pounds) (1) | Total releases per capita (2) | Nonattainment | | % rivers and streams impaired (5) | % lakes, reservoirs, and ponds impaired (6) |
			% counties (3)	% state population (4)		
West Virginia	42,942,705	23.60	20.0	39.1	56	71
Wisconsin	32,934,598	5.82	9.7	37.7	61	72
Wyoming	24,960,729	45.86	4.4	5.4	16	94

SOURCES: Toxic emissions: U.S. Environmental Protection Agency, Toxics Release Inventory, 2009, www.epa.gov/tri/; air quality: U.S. Environmental Protection Agency, "Greenbook, 2010," www.epa.gov/oaqps001/greenbk/; water quality: U.S. Environmental Protection Agency, ATTAINS database. Data for Florida, Maryland, and Pennsylvania are from 2002; for California from 2004; and for Delaware, Hawaii, Illinois, Louisiana, Massachusetts, Nevada, North Carolina, Oregon, Utah, and Wisconsin from 2006, www.epa.gov/waters/ir/.

Southeast—Alabama, Florida, Georgia, Kentucky, and Tennessee. Second, the states with the most emissions per capita are among the least populous. In these states, which include Alaska, Idaho, Montana, Nevada, North Dakota, Utah, and Wyoming, the releases are predominantly the result of the extraction of natural resources, particularly metal mining. In many cases, the releases are predominantly from one or two very large sources. For example, the Red Dog Operations mine in northwestern Alaska accounted for over 90 percent of the state's total toxic releases in 2009, mostly in the form of lead and zinc compounds.

The TRI data do not capture all air, water, and land pollution emissions—just those pollutants deemed toxic and reportable by the EPA. For this reason, we need to turn to other measures to examine variation in environmental conditions across the states. In terms of ambient air quality, the primary pollutants whose emissions are controlled through the federal Clean Air Act are carbon monoxide, lead, nitrogen dioxide, ozone, particulate matter, and sulfur dioxide. By statute, the EPA is required to establish **National Ambient Air Quality Standards (NAAQS)** for each of these criteria air pollutants, which govern the allowable pollution concentrations in the air people breathe. These standards are periodically updated to reflect advances in understanding the linkages between pollution and public health outcomes. Each year, the EPA uses air monitoring information to designate each county in the United States as either in "attainment" or "nonattainment" with the national standards.

A common way to characterize air quality in a state is to consider the percentage of its counties that are in **nonattainment** for at least one of these air pollutants (Konisky 2009b; Konisky and Woods 2010). Residents living in areas that are not meeting air quality standards for these pollutants face elevated risks of adverse health outcomes such as asthma and other respiratory problems, some of which are causes of premature mortality. Columns (3) and (4) in Table 15-1 present the percentage of counties in a state that were in nonattainment in 2010, as well as the percentage of the state population that resided in one of these areas. The average percentage of nonattainment counties in each state was about 8 percent, but clearly there is great variation across the country. In thirteen states, no counties failed to meet the NAAQS in 2010, and in many others just one or two counties had not achieved national standards. In many other states, however, air quality remains a significant challenge. Nearly two-thirds of counties in California were in nonattainment for at least one major air pollutant, and four of the most populous counties in southern California were in nonattainment for four such pollutants. The data presented in Table 15-1 on the percentage of the populations living in nonattainment areas further attest to the extent of air quality problems in some states. In nineteen states, at least half of the population in 2010 lived in a county that did not meet all the NAAQS (overall, about 150 million Americans).

Columns (5) and (6) in Table 15-1 contain information on water quality. Every two years, the states report to the EPA the results of an assessment of whether their water bodies are meeting their designated uses (such as being swimmable or fishable) under the federal Clean Water Act. Because of inconsistencies in evaluation procedures, one needs to be cautious in using these data to compare states or to track trends in state water quality. Nevertheless, they do illustrate that across the country the conditions of rivers and streams and lakes, reservoirs, and ponds remain a serious concern even now, nearly forty years after enactment of the Clean Water Act. On average, more than half of the assessed rivers and streams across the states were determined to be impaired, whereas almost two-thirds of assessed lakes, reservoirs, and ponds were deemed impaired.

What explains environmental conditions in the states? Obviously, pollution levels are directly related to the structure of state economies. States with large industrial bases, particularly in sectors such as manufacturing, chemical processing, and oil refining, have more pollution-intensive economies. Similarly, states that rely on coal, and to a lesser extent natural gas, for electricity generation, and states with large resource extraction industries tend to produce more pollution than do states with more service-based economies. Air and water quality are not just a function of total emissions but also how pollution is affected by topographic features and the natural attributes of airsheds and waterways.

State policies matter, too, but establishing a direct link between a state's policies—its laws, regulations, and the practices of its administrative agencies—and the environmental conditions within the state is complicated. State environmental outcomes are affected by a combination of federal, state, and local policies, making it difficult to isolate the direct consequences (positive, negative, or no effect) of any single policy. There is, however, some evidence suggesting that states that have adopted more protective policies do have better environmental conditions. Specifically, studies have found that states with stronger state air quality programs have achieved greater reductions in the emissions of environmental pollutants (Ringquist 1993) and greater improvements in ambient air quality (Ringquist 1995) than states with weaker programs. Moreover, states with stronger overall environmental programs (as measured both by state spending on environmental protection and by an index aggregating many state environmental policies) evidence lower overall levels of pollution and better public health outcomes (Woods, Konisky, and Bowman 2009).

State environmental conditions also may be affected by the environmental policies of other states. One of the challenges of managing air pollution is that many pollutants are subject to long-range transport. When pollution emitted in one jurisdiction affects the environmental conditions in another, it is called a **spillover effect**. The most vivid example is the pollutants from midwestern coal-fired power plants. The sulfur dioxide and nitrogen oxide emissions from these plants not only contribute to localized air quality problems (particularly smog), but also are transported in the upper atmosphere to the eastern part of the country. One particular problem, acid rain, occurs when these pollutants react with water molecules in the atmosphere and then are deposited hundreds of miles away through rainfall. Acid rain was a major environmental issue during the 1980s, leading to the imposition of an emissions cap-and-trade program for sulfur dioxide as part of the 1990 amendments to the Clean Air Act (Ellerman et al. 2000).

Amid growing frustration with the effects of out-of-state pollution on their states' air quality, Attorneys General Eric Schneiderman of New York and Roy Cooper of North Carolina wrote a letter in March 2011 to EPA administrator Lisa Jackson requesting that the agency speed up consideration of new rules that would govern interstate pollution. In releasing the letter, Schneiderman noted: "Every day, pollution from upwind states blows into New York, spoiling our environment, contaminating the air we breathe, and harming our health. Cutting the amount of air pollution that crosses state lines would avoid hundreds of thousands of illnesses and produce benefits worth hundreds of billions of dollars annually nationwide" (New York Office of the Attorney General 2011). Over the years, the EPA has considered various policies to address these types of interstate air pollution problems. In 2005 the Bush administration put in place the Clean Air Interstate Rule, but it was vacated and remanded back to the EPA as part of a July 2008 decision by the U.S. Court of Appeals for the D.C. Circuit. In July 2011, the Obama administration finalized its replacement, the Cross-State Rule, which applies to power plants in twenty-seven states with emissions of sulfur dioxide and nitrogen oxides that cross state borders.

States also frequently accuse each other of deliberately exporting their air pollution to other states. These types of disputes date as far back as a 1907 U.S. Supreme Court case, *Georgia v. Tennessee Copper Co.*, 206 U.S. 230, in which Georgia claimed that sulfur dioxide emissions from Tennessee-based copper smelters were despoiling forests and orchards and creating health problems for residents of bordering counties in Georgia. The Court agreed with Georgia under public nuisance law. In more recent years, there has been a series of cases in which state regulators have been accused of giving preferential treatment to polluters located on or near a state border. In 2006, for example, New Jersey sued the EPA, claiming it had failed to control the emissions of the Portland Generating Station, a Pennsylvania coal-fired power plant located just across the Delaware River (Delli Santi 2006). The long-running dispute over this particular power plant was recently addressed by the EPA. In March 2011, the EPA indicated that it would grant a petition by the New Jersey Department of Environmental Protection to require that the Portland Generating Station reduce its emissions by 81 percent over three years (Applebaum 2011).

Although some observers (such as Revesz 1992, 1997) have expressed concerns about interstate pollution spillovers, there has been little systematic investigation into how significant this problem actually is. Recent research on this topic suggests that air pollution emissions are indeed higher in counties bordering other states (Helland and Whitford 2003), although at present there is little evidence that these higher levels are the result of state government policy (Konisky and Woods 2010).

The balance of this chapter examines state environmental policy from a variety of perspectives, first by placing state actions in the context of the U.S. system of federalism, and then by considering and explaining the variation in state environmental protection efforts across the fifty states.

FEDERALISM AND THE STATES' ROLE IN ENVIRONMENTAL POLICY

Environmental protection in the United States, particularly pollution control, was decidedly a state and local issue through the 1960s, with the federal government reluctant to assume more than a supportive role by providing some technical and financial assistance. By 1970, however, there was a growing consensus that state governments were not making sufficient progress (Davies 1970; Lowry 1992). The federal government responded by establishing the EPA and enacting major pieces of legislation such as the Clean Air Act (1970), the Clean Water Act (1972), the Endangered Species Act (1973), and the Resource Conservation and Recovery Act (1976), which shifted the balance of power from the states to the federal government. Despite this federal assertion of authority, states remain deeply involved in environmental policy.

Partial Preemption and the Devolution of Environmental Policy

With the exception of the Endangered Species Act, each of the statutes just mentioned is implemented by state governments, utilizing an institutional framework that allows the federal government to devolve program responsibility to the states while retaining the ultimate authority to decide on the adequacy of state actions. This process, termed **partial preemption**, gives states an opportunity to design and implement their own regulations, as long as they are consistent with national goals and meet federal guidelines (see the discussion in Chapter 2). If a state elects not to participate or is unable to secure national approval for its programs, the EPA assumes responsibility for enforcing federal regulations within that state's boundaries. Once a state obtains approval for its programs, implementation is carried out through the EPA and the relevant state environmental agency concurrently, though the state is given primary administrative responsibility, or **primacy**, within its borders. This practice largely delegates the authority for developing and enforcing regulatory standards to state agencies, although the EPA sets a floor below which standards may not fall. States are free to rescind their assumption of program authority at any time. The EPA is likewise empowered to revoke its grant of primacy at any time it determines that the state is no longer in compliance with federal mandates. In April 2011, for example, EPA regulators were threatening to take over part of Utah's air quality program unless it changed its "unavoidable breakdown" rule. When a cement plant, refinery, or other regulated facility suffers a breakdown that causes a sudden release of air pollution in excess of allowable amounts, the EPA requires that it be treated as a violation of the law. Because Utah regulators were assuming that a breakdown was not a violation unless proven otherwise, the EPA was threatening to remove Utah's authority to administer part of its clean air program at the time this chapter was being written (Fahys 2011).

When partially preemptive environmental statutes were initially being implemented in the 1970s, the role that states played was severely constrained by the EPA, with policy delivery extensively structured by federal regulations and inducements (Crotty 1987, 1988). Later, the federal government pushed environmental policy responsibilities down to the states as part of a broader pattern of **devolution**. This was particularly evident during the presidency of Ronald Reagan, whose "New Federalism" dramatically realigned the balance between the federal government and the states in environmental policy. One lasting impact has been the return of program authority to the states in a wide variety of federal program areas (Lester 1986; Davis and Lester 1987). Responding to pressure from the Reagan administration, the EPA delegated implementation authority for many environmental programs at an accelerated rate early in the Reagan presidency. In 1981 and 1982, for example, states were delegated responsibility for the enforcement of a large majority of hazardous air pollutant standards, as well as **New Source Performance Standards** governing air pollution emissions from stationary sources (Levinson 2003). Over time, states continued to assume greater authority to implement and enforce federal environmental laws. By one recent estimate, states now operate some 96 percent of the federal programs that are delegable to them (Environmental Council of the States 2010).[4] Some states, however, have opted not to assume program

4. States and the EPA sometimes form an intergovernmental partnership in areas that are not partial preemption programs. For example, states often play an important role in cleaning up hazardous waste sites in conjunction with the federal Superfund program (Cline 2003).

authority for some major environmental laws. As of early 2012, for example, Alaska, Idaho, Massachusetts, New Hampshire, and New Mexico still had not assumed authority to implement the base permit program under the Clean Water Act (the National Pollution Discharge Elimination System), and Alaska and Iowa had not assumed base hazardous waste program authority.

When states assume primacy, they take responsibility for enforcing federal environmental laws, writing permits for industrial polluters, and setting environmental standards, although these standards must meet or exceed federal minimums. Some states have developed standards in a variety of areas that exceed the federal government's minimum standards. In a study of state air quality regulation, for example, Potoski (2001) notes that by the late 1990s eleven states had chosen to exceed EPA minimum National Ambient Air Quality Standards for at least one criteria air pollutant, eight states had stricter New Source Performance Standards than federal minimums, and twenty-five states had exceeded the EPA minimum requirements for ambient air monitoring stations.

After receiving primacy from the EPA, some states in turn further devolve authority to city, county, or regional substate government agencies, a process called **second-order devolution**. Thirty-three states have devolved clean air policy implementation to these local agencies. The number of local agencies ranges from one in several states to thirty-five in California (which is the only state to have devolved all of its clean air authority to local agencies). Only a couple of states have given local agencies the authority to set air pollution standards, whereas in thirteen states local agencies operate the majority of the ambient air monitoring stations, and in six states they conduct the majority of the inspections and enforcement actions (Woods and Potoski 2010).

What prompts states to assume authority to implement federal environmental laws? Some of the literature finds at least modest evidence that the more environmentally oriented states are more likely to assume primacy (Sigman 2003), although other studies do not (Woods 2006b). However, states may be assuming primacy for different purposes. This is the conclusion that Patricia Crotty (1987) comes to in an influential early work on the subject. She claims that some states pursue authority to implement their own programs in order to pursue pro-environment policies; others do so to weaken environmental regulations as part of a strategy to compete for industry.

Environmental Regulatory Competition

Concerns about whether states are assuming primacy in order to weaken environmental regulation reflect a larger debate about the role that federalism plays in U.S. environmental policy. Although some observers have argued that decentralizing environmental policy promotes public participation and responsiveness to local environmental concerns (Revesz 1992), others question whether the EPA should devolve authority to state and local governments. Critics argue that states and localities lack the institutional capacity to effectively make and implement policy, are hostile to innovation, and are unwilling to rigorously regulate important economic constituencies (Rabe 1997). Moreover, as discussed earlier, some pollution prevention programs may not be well suited to subnational implementation because of spillover effects, which inhibit the development of geographically self-contained policies.

One of the most significant criticisms of decentralized environmental policy is that economic competition for industry among states and localities may motivate political officials to reduce regulatory stringency to gain a competitive advantage over their neighbors. If states follow this strategy, it would cause an aggregate movement toward the lowest common denominator of environmental protection, otherwise known as an environmental **race to the bottom**.

Some observers, however, have argued that states do not respond to changes in the regulatory behavior of their neighbors (Revesz 1992, 1997), or that interstate competition might actually lead to an overall ratcheting up of environmental regulation, or a **race to the top** (Vogel 1995, and see our discussion of the "California effect" below). Studies that directly assess government behavior suggest that states do respond strategically to the level of environmental regulation in surrounding states, although the pattern of this interaction is not exactly clear. Although some studies find evidence consistent with the notion of a race to the bottom (Woods 2006a), others find evidence consistent with a race to the top (Fredriksson and Millimet 2002), or that both processes, in fact, may be in operation (Konisky 2007, 2009a).

Concerns about the effects of interstate economic competition on environmental protection reflect a more general tendency among many elected officials to view job creation and environmental protection as conflicting policy goals. Although some scholars view such notions as a false trade-off (Feiock and Stream 2001), this tension is often apparent in national politics. One recent example involved the efforts in April 2011 by the U.S. Congress to prohibit the EPA from regulating greenhouse gas emissions because of claims that such regulations would negatively affect the economy. These types of concerns have also motivated recent retrenchment in some state environmental protection efforts. For example, shortly after taking office in January 2011, Maine governor Paul LePage announced a sixty-three-part plan to cut environmental regulations in the state. He defended his proposal, highlighting the importance of jobs and economic development: "Maine's working families and small businesses are endangered. It is time we start defending the interests of those who want to work and invest in Maine with the same vigor that we defend tree frogs and Canadian lynx" (quoted in Kaufman 2011).

Although the prospect of interstate economic competition has received a lot of attention from observers of environmental policy, it should not be overlooked that states act cooperatively as well. Recognizing the interstate nature of many pollution problems, states are increasingly banding together to solve them, turning to regional interstate compacts or other interstate agreements to deal with issues such as climate change and water resource management. These agreements are one form of state innovation in environmental policy. The section that follows discusses state environmental policy leadership and innovation in a variety of areas.

STATE ENVIRONMENTAL POLICY INNOVATION AND VARIATION

The U.S. federal system of government creates many opportunities for states to determine their own paths when it comes to environmental protection. The policies imposed by the federal government—either statutorily by Congress or through the regulatory decision making of the EPA—set a floor or baseline, but states have the discretion to pursue their own policies as well. One consequence is tremendous variation in state policy. Some states have become policy laboratories, experimenting with ideas and programs to address their specific environmental challenges. Other states have opted to do the bare minimum. In this section, we describe the variation in environmentalism across the states and present several measures of policy performance. We then discuss several areas of state-level policy innovation to demonstrate state experimentation and leadership, followed by a brief discussion of state environmental policy "laggards." We conclude by summarizing the political science literature that seeks to understand the determinants of state environmental policy.

State Environmentalism

Scholars of environmental politics and policy have long recognized that the U.S. states vary in their environmental orientations. Measuring a state's overall environmentalism is challenging, however, because most public opinion surveys about government and public policy target the country as a whole. For this reason, no high-quality measure is available of a *state's* overall environmentalism in terms of citizen attitudes. Although new techniques that rely on sophisticated statistical analysis are being developed for just this type of task (Lax and Phillips 2009), we rely on nonattitudinal measures to characterize and illustrate variation in environmentalism across the U.S. states.

One way to think about state environmentalism is in terms of the positions taken by elected officials. Political scientists commonly use congressional voting scores in many areas of policy to characterize the positions of members of Congress on issues. The League of Conservation Voters (LCV) has been compiling such scores on environmental issues since 1971 at the national level,[5] and these scores are often used to measure a state's environmentalism following the logic that members' voting patterns reflect the preferences of their constituents (Wood 1992; Ringquist 1993; Davis and Davis 1999; Konisky 2007).

---

5. Similar voting scores are collected by some state chapters of the LCV for state legislatures, but on a much less consistent basis.

Figure 15-1   Sierra Club Membership and League of Conservation Voters (LCV) Scores

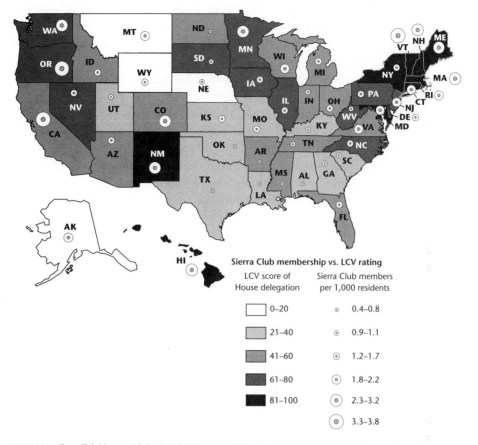

Sierra Club membership vs. LCV rating

LCV score of House delegation	Sierra Club members per 1,000 residents
0–20	0.4–0.8
21–40	0.9–1.1
41–60	1.2–1.7
61–80	1.8–2.2
81–100	2.3–3.2
	3.3–3.8

SOURCES: Sierra Club (data provided to Konisky February 1, 2011) and League of Conservation Voters, www.lcv.org/scorecard.

The map in Figure 15-1 presents the average LCV score for a state's delegation to the U.S. House of Representatives for 2010. Higher percentages reflect a more "pro-environmental" delegation (percentages reflect the proportion of votes in which members of the House voted the environmental position according to the LCV). There is clearly regional clustering in environmental voting in Congress. Members from states in the Northeast, upper Midwest, and West have stronger environmental voting records than do those representing states in the South and Upper Plains.

Another approach used by political scientists to measure a state's environmentalism looks at citizen interest and behavior on environmental issues, as measured by the percentage of a state's population that is active in environmental advocacy organizations. These types of measures have been included as part of state indices measuring state environmental policy (Hall and Kerr 1991). Superimposed on top of the map of LCV scores in Figure 15-1 are data on Sierra Club membership, measured as the number of state members of this organization per 1,000 persons. The

Sierra Club is one of the oldest and largest membership-based environmental organizations in the country. Most notable in this map is that there appears to be a close relationship between Sierra Club membership and LCV scores—members of the Sierra Club tend to live in states where U.S. House delegations are more likely to have a good environmental voting record (the correlation is 0.57).

A final way to measure a state's environmentalism is to look at government behavior directly. Doing so requires collecting across states comparable data that reasonably capture their efforts to address environmental challenges. We discuss two types of data commonly used for this purpose: state environmental spending and state enforcement actions.

Columns (1) and (2) of Table 15-2 present state environmental expenditures in 2008,[6] first in total and then per capita, from data periodically compiled by the Environmental Council of the States (2008). The states with the most total environmental expenditures are, perhaps not surprisingly, states with large overall budgets, led by California, Illinois, Florida, New York, and Pennsylvania. Per capita expenditures show a much different rank ordering. In terms of dollars spent on environmental protection per citizen, the states at the top of the list are Hawaii, West Virginia, Delaware, New Hampshire, and Wyoming. In per capita environmental expenditures, these states are spending well over $100 per citizen compared with the states at the bottom of the rankings—Ohio, Colorado, Alabama, Georgia, and Oklahoma—each of which is spending less than $20 per citizen.

A second direct measure of state environmental behavior captures the enforcement activity of state administrative agencies responsible for implementing major federal environmental legislation. As noted in the previous section of this chapter, states play a central role in environmental enforcement, and have enormous discretion to determine their own enforcement strategies. The data presented in columns (3) and (4) of Table 15-2 show the annual number of inspections per state facility regulated as major air polluters under the federal Clean Air Act or major water polluters under the Clean Water Act. An inspection rate value of 1 indicates that, on average, each facility in the state was inspected once a year over the 2006–2010 time period. Similar to the expenditures data, the extent of variation in inspection activity across the country is noteworthy. At the top end of the spectrum on air pollution are Arkansas, Hawaii, Kansas, North Carolina, and Pennsylvania, although only facilities in Kansas received on average one inspection annually. In ten states, the facilities of air polluters were on average inspected only once every two years, and in Texas (where facilities are inspected the least), the average inspection rate for major air polluters was just once every three years.

6. The Environmental Council of the States attempts to collect data that are comparable across states, but this is difficult because of budgetary vagaries and uncertainties about exactly what is included in each budgetary category.

Table 15-2 State Environmental Policy Measures

| State | Environmental expenditures, 2008 | | Clean Air Act inspections, 2006–2010 | Clean Water Act inspections, 2006–2010 |
	Total (1)	Per capita (2)	Rate per facility (3)	Rate per facility (4)
Alabama	$58,750,977	$12.56	0.77	0.93
Alaska	75,832,900	110.20	0.56	0.45
Arizona	191,425,100	29.45	0.64	0.90
Arkansas	105,485,578	36.78	0.92	1.74
California	2,080,591,000	56.88	0.89	1.34
Colorado	57,647,863	11.68	0.64	0.76
Connecticut	145,583,654	41.56	0.55	1.31
Delaware	137,456,200	156.88	0.62	4.98
Florida	1,072,843,657	58.23	0.78	1.69
Georgia	135,600,000	13.98	0.87	0.98
Hawaii	263,891,754	204.97	0.91	0.84
Idaho	60,850,400	39.84	0.51	0.69
Illinois	1,299,243,700	101.16	0.57	3.86
Indiana	303,755,276	47.55	0.76	1.09
Iowa	118,793,356	39.68	0.54	0.88
Kansas	72,772,922	26.01	1.09	1.17
Kentucky	113,571,900	26.49	0.64	1.39
Louisiana	163,402,497	36.71	0.38	0.77
Maine	80,567,231	61.05	0.43	0.81
Maryland	110,245,525	19.48	0.53	2.34
Massachusetts	133,800,626	20.45	0.43	0.81
Michigan	370,964,400	37.09	0.53	0.69
Minnesota	190,729,802	36.46	0.50	0.92
Mississippi	138,969,055	47.26	0.50	1.11
Missouri	325,564,220	54.66	0.90	0.63
Montana	80,730,441	83.40	0.51	0.88
Nebraska	85,947,670	48.23	0.64	0.94
Nevada	177,887,759	68.01	0.74	0.98
New Hampshire	153,427,724	116.07	0.50	1.16
New Jersey	338,858,000	39.11	0.53	1.81
New Mexico	NA	NA	0.49	0.78
New York	743,792,550	38.21	0.67	1.75
North Carolina	379,750,557	41.07	0.95	1.69
North Dakota	23,425,243	36.52	0.54	1.76
Ohio	86,314,093	7.49	0.51	1.25
Oklahoma	56,700,966	15.56	0.52	1.22
Oregon	148,999,972	39.39	0.50	0.70
Pennsylvania	717,292,000	57.08	0.92	1.90
Rhode Island	86,314,093	81.93	0.49	2.21
South Carolina	149,387,711	33.17	0.72	1.64
South Dakota	85,915,799	106.79	0.79	0.70
Tennessee	190,946,400	30.60	0.83	1.01
Texas	548,898,921	22.58	0.33	0.65
Utah	86,167,124	31.59	0.84	1.71
Vermont	38,167,969	61.46	0.47	0.79
Virginia	189,640,074	24.33	0.55	1.57
Washington	235,646,000	35.89	0.75	0.38
West Virginia	305,989,209	168.60	0.54	1.24
Wisconsin	237,466,091	42.20	0.48	0.97
Wyoming	61,168,228	114.77	0.47	1.33

SOURCES: Expenditures: compiled from Environmental Council of the States, "March 2008 Green Report," www.ecos.org (all data are either projected or are actual expenditures for fiscal year 2008, except for New York, which are expenditures from fiscal year 2006); Clean Air Act and Clean Water Act inspections: U.S. Environmental Protection Service, ECHO database, 2010, www.epa-echo.gov/echo/.

NOTE: NA = not available.

Facility inspection rates for major water polluters were generally much higher (about double) across the states. In about half of the states, facilities were inspected, on average, at least once a year during 2006–2010. Among the states conducting the most inspections were Delaware, Illinois, Maryland, and Rhode Island, where facilities were inspected at least twice annually. The lowest performers on this measure were Washington and Alaska, where water pollution facilities were inspected on average less than once every two years.[7] The rank orderings of the states in inspection activity depend on the program and do not always coincide with state environmental expenditures. This finding is one more sign that one needs to be cautious in characterizing a state's environmental policy by any single indicator.

States as Policy Laboratories

In many areas of environmental policy, state governments have taken actions at their own initiative. State experimentation can be an important force in a federal system of government, because the lessons learned (positive and negative) can be shared not just with other states (horizontal diffusion), but also with higher (federal) and lower (local) levels of government (vertical diffusion). In this section, to illustrate the ways in which states innovate we describe four policy areas in which states have been particularly active: vehicle fuel economy standards, climate change, renewable energy, and environmental justice.

Motor Vehicle Emissions Standards. Historically, perhaps the most notable example of state environmental policy innovation is the imposition of limits on the emissions of pollutants from cars. In 1970 Congress wrote emissions standards for motor vehicles directly into the statutory language of the Clean Air Act, limiting emissions of pollutants such as carbon monoxide, nitrogen oxides, and hydrocarbons. California, however, already had more stringent standards in place. In 1966 the state's Motor Vehicle Pollution Control Board put in place tailpipe emission standards for hydrocarbons and carbon monoxide, largely in an effort to combat smog and other localized air quality issues in the Los Angeles basin. In order not to preempt the more stringent standards in California, the 1970 Clean Air Act statutorily granted California a waiver whereby it was permitted to have more stringent standards.

The California waiver continues to be very important. Because of the size of California's economy (if it were a country, California would have the world's seventh-largest economy), the market for automobiles in the state is large. Because of the expense of manufacturing automobiles with different pollution control technologies, auto companies have generally produced and marketed cars meeting the California standards in the rest of the country as well. Many states, in fact, have formally adopted California's standards, something that was made permissible under

7. The Clean Water Act is enforced by the EPA in Alaska because the state has not been delegated authority to implement the main permitting program of the act. The other states in which the EPA enforces the Clean Water Act are Idaho, Massachusetts, New Hampshire, and New Mexico.

the 1977 amendments to the Clean Air Act. As of 2005, fifteen states had adopted at least one California standard, and the federal government itself has often elevated national standards to keep pace with those being set in California (Environment America 2005). As discussed earlier, this movement of standards upward, in a follow-the-leader type of dynamic, is often referred to as a race to the top. Because the vehicle fuel economy case is one of the best illustrations of a race to the top, some have referred to this dynamic as the **"California effect"** (Vogel 1995).

California's penchant for being out in front in vehicle emissions standards has recently taken on even more significance in the area of carbon dioxide emissions. In 2002 the California State Assembly enacted legislation requiring limits to greenhouse gas emissions from light-duty vehicles, and it authorized the California Air Resources Board to issue new standards. Several other states then decided to follow California's lead. As of 2010, seventeen other states had decided to adopt California's standards (Pew Center on Global Climate Change 2011b).

After the *Massachusetts v. Environmental Protection Agency* decision and the EPA's subsequent endangerment finding, the agency was required to regulate carbon dioxide emissions from motor vehicles. In April 2010, the EPA, along with the Department of Transportation's National Highway Traffic Safety Administration, issued such regulations as part of updated corporate average fuel economy standards for cars, light-duty trucks, and medium-duty passenger vehicles. In an agreement with California and automakers, the EPA permitted California to have a waiver under the federal Clean Air Act in order to enforce its own standards for 2009–2011 and to establish its own standards after 2016. In exchange, California agreed to adopt the new federal standards for 2012–2016, which included increasing fuel economy standards for cars and trucks to 35.5 miles per gallon by 2016. For their part, automakers agreed to drop pending litigation with California over their standards.

Climate Change. California is not the only state that has been at the forefront of efforts to address climate change. In the absence of strong federal policy activity in this area, many states have adopted measures to either directly or indirectly reduce greenhouse gas emissions. Barry Rabe (2004, 2008) has identified five reasons that explain state policy innovation on climate change. First, many states view such policy as contributing to their economic development goals, particularly in fostering new technology and "home-grown" businesses in the areas of renewable energy and energy conservation. Second, some states have concluded that they are already experiencing the detrimental effects of climate change such as sea level rise, violent storms, and severe droughts. Third, some states have adopted climate change policies in an effort to project themselves as policy entrepreneurs, often to either push national policy forward or to encourage neighboring states to join their efforts. Fourth, in many states policy networks or advocacy coalitions in state capitals have formed to promote greenhouse gas mitigation policies. And fifth, in some states action has been triggered by direct democracy or litigation.

What policies have states put in place to address climate change? The short answer is that they range considerably. Most states have established some type of climate change action plan to coordinate state policy, but these plans vary enormously in detail and ambition. More significantly, twenty-two states have adopted a greenhouse gas emissions target by which they have committed to a goal of reducing carbon dioxide emissions by a certain amount by a certain date (Pew Center on Global Climate Change 2011b). Most of these states are in the Northeast, Midwest, and West (Florida is the exception). Because these greenhouse gas emissions targets are largely nonbinding (California is the only exception), there remain questions about states' commitment to achieving them.

Another area of climate change policy innovation is the development of regional initiatives, some of which include coordination with Canadian provinces.[8] These regional initiatives—the Regional Greenhouse Gas Initiative (RGGI), the Western Climate Initiative (WCI), and the Midwestern Greenhouse Gas Reduction Accord (MGGRA)—represent cap-and-trade regimes, loosely modeled on the federal cap-and-trade program for sulfur dioxide. The specifics of these programs vary (Raymond 2010), but they reflect state-led efforts to coordinate activities in an effort to reduce greenhouse gas emissions in an economically efficient manner. The map in Figure 15-2 shows the states involved in the regional initiatives.

Ten northeastern states currently participate in the RGGI: Connecticut, Delaware, Maine, Maryland, Massachusetts, New Hampshire, New Jersey, New York, Rhode Island, and Vermont (Pennsylvania and the District of Columbia are observers). Under the RGGI, a cap is set on carbon dioxide emissions from large power plants at 2009 levels through 2014, and then the cap falls by 2.5 percent annually through 2019 (for a 10 percent total in emissions reductions). The first auction of carbon allowances occurred in September 2008. The proceeds from the carbon allowance auctions have netted the ten participating states about $750 million to share. Some of the states have used the revenue to fund energy efficiency and other programs to further reduce greenhouse gas emissions (Buntin 2010). The WCI includes seven states—Arizona, California, Montana, New Mexico, Oregon, Utah, and Washington—and four Canadian provinces—British Columbia, Manitoba, Ontario, and Quebec (Alaska, Colorado, Idaho, Kansas, Nevada, and Wyoming are observers). Although the RGGI is limited to power plants, the WCI envisions economy-wide emissions reductions and has set an emissions cap at 15 percent below 2005 levels by the year 2020. It applies to five greenhouse gases—methane, nitrous oxide, hydrofluorocarbons, perfluorocarbons, and sulfur hexafluoride—in addition to carbon dioxide. Emissions trading was scheduled to begin for the WCI in early 2012. The MGGRA is a regional plan supported by six midwestern states—Illinois, Iowa, Kansas, Michigan, Minnesota, and Wisconsin—and one Canadian province—Manitoba

8. Much like the United States, Canada is a federal system of government, and individual Canadian provinces have a long history of taking autonomous action to address environmental problems (Harrison 1996, 2006).

Figure 15-2   Regional Climate Initiatives

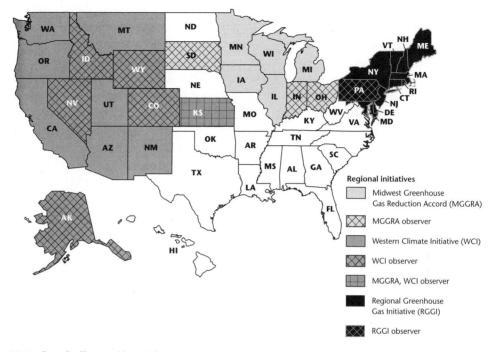

SOURCE: Center for Climate and Energy Solutions, http://www.c2es.org/what_s_being_done/in_the_states/regional_initiatives.cfm.

(Indiana, Ohio, and South Dakota are observers). The MGGRA has not advanced as far in planning as the RGGI and the WCI, but it also intends to use a cap and an emissions trading system to achieve its greenhouse gas reduction targets (Raymond 2010; Pew Center on Global Climate Change 2011b).

Are these regional efforts sustainable? Among the central questions facing these initiatives and other climate change policies more generally is their durability in the face of changing political and economic conditions within the states. For example, Arizona was a founding member of the WCI, but has since curbed its involvement. Just two weeks after Republican Janice Brewer became governor of Arizona in January 2009, she issued an executive order declaring that the state would not implement the WCI's regional carbon market because of the economic downturn it was facing. With the ascension of a large number of Republican governors and state legislators in the November 2010 elections, many of whom are overtly skeptical about the urgency (or even the existence) of climate change, other states may follow suit. Gov. Chris Christie of New Jersey pulled the state out of the RGGI in May 2011, and the legislature in New Hampshire voted in March 2011 to repeal the state's participation. More policy retrenchment on climate change may occur in the coming years.

Renewable Energy. Many states have advanced policies to encourage the development and use of renewable energy technologies for electricity generation such as wind, solar, and geothermal power. The primary policy tool employed by states to accomplish this goal has been the **renewable portfolio standard (RPS),** which mandates that electricity providers in a state obtain some minimum amount of their power from renewable sources by a particular date. As of April 2011, thirty-eight states had in place some type of renewable or alternative standard (Pew Center on Global Climate Change 2011a). In seven of these states, the RPS is voluntary, but in the rest it represents a binding commitment that some portion of electricity delivered in the state will come from renewable or alternative energy sources. These states are shown in the map in Figure 15-3. One obvious pattern in the map is that states in the southeastern United States have generally not adopted renewable energy mandates (Florida is the exception).

Three-fourths of state RPSs have been adopted in the last decade (and seventeen alone since 2005), mostly through legislation. However, two were adopted through regulatory action—Arizona and New York—and three through the ballot initiative process—Colorado, Missouri, and Washington (Pew Center on Global Climate Change 2011a). Some states, however, have experimented with these types of renewable energy mandates for much longer. Iowa created the first such mandate

Figure 15-3   State Renewable and Alternative Energy Portfolio Policies

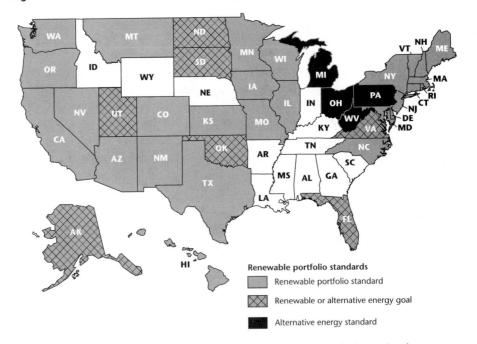

Renewable portfolio standards

▨ Renewable portfolio standard

▨ Renewable or alternative energy goal

■ Alternative energy standard

SOURCE: Center for Climate and Energy Solutions, http://www.c2es.org/what_s_being_done/in_the_states/rps.cfm.

in 1983 as part of its Iowa Alternative Energy Production law. For ten years, this program stood alone in this area. It reflects Iowa's tendency toward environmental progressivism, as evidenced by the state's activities in other policy areas such as its efforts to manage water pollution from agricultural sources (Lowry 1992; John 1994). Several other states, primarily in New England and the Southwest, adopted RPSs in the mid- to late 1990s. Recent research has revealed mixed findings about why states adopt RPSs. Some studies have found that intrastate factors such as citizen demand, political ideology, renewable energy potential, and interest group strength matter most (Matisoff 2008; Lyon and Yin 2010), whereas other studies point to the role of policy diffusion from geographic neighbors (Chandler 2009, and see our discussion of diffusion in the upcoming section on the determinants of state environmental policy).

State RPSs vary considerably along several important dimensions, including the amount of required renewable energy making up the target and the date of expected achievement. Hawaii has set the most ambitious goal: 40 percent of its electricity from renewable sources by 2030. Other states with ambitious mandates are California (33 percent by 2020); Connecticut (27 percent by 2020); and Illinois, Minnesota, Nevada, Ohio, Oregon, and West Virginia (25 percent by 2025). Most of the rest of the states are aiming for about 10–20 percent of their electricity to come from renewable sources, to be achieved in fifteen to twenty years from the time the mandate was put in place. State RPSs also tend to reward the in-state generation of renewable energy sources, and in many states electricity providers are given incentives to purchase the renewable energy they need to meet the targets from home-grown sources. The primary rationale for these incentives is to encourage the development of these new technologies, and elected officials have explicitly hailed the economic development merits of these laws as much as the environmental benefits (Rabe 2004). Finally, it is worth noting that state RPSs also differ in what counts as renewable energy. Although all of the standards include wind and solar power, some have broader definitions of renewable sources than others (for example, many count energy efficiency gains). In addition, several of the RPSs require some portion of the electricity to come from specific sources. For example, the Illinois RPS specifies that 75 percent come from wind power, and the Nevada RPS requires that 6 percent come from solar power (Pew Center on Global Climate Change 2011a).

The proliferation of renewable energy standards at the state level has, in part, prompted the federal government to consider a national standard. In 2009 a bipartisan group of U.S. senators introduced a federal renewable electricity standard that would have required that 15 percent of the nation's electricity come from renewable sources by 2021 (4 percent of which would be from improvements in energy efficiency). The bill, however, did not reach the floor of the Senate for a vote.

Environmental Justice. Another area in which some states have been at the forefront of environmental policy is in addressing inequities in the distribution of environmental risks. Concerns about the distribution of risks across the population first appeared on the environmental policy agenda during the 1980s, following widely publicized protests in places such as Warren County, North Carolina, where a predominantly black community mobilized in large numbers to fight the siting of a hazardous waste landfill. Mounting evidence that minority and low-income groups were more likely to live close to hazardous waste disposal facilities and other unwanted land uses prompted government at all levels in the 1990s to consider actions to remedy such inequities. The federal government in particular initiated several efforts to address environmental disparities, including creating the Office of Environmental Justice within the EPA in 1992, forming the National Environmental Justice Advisory Council in 1993, and integrating environmental justice concerns into federal agency decision making by means of Executive Order 12898, signed by President Bill Clinton in 1994.

After this initial flurry of federal activity during the 1990s, environmental equity concerns largely receded from the federal government's agenda (although the issue was revived by EPA administrator Lisa Jackson in 2009). Meanwhile, many state governments chose to fill this void by advancing initiatives aimed at remedying racial and class inequities in the distribution of environmental hazards. Many of states' earliest activities focused on conducting their own studies of the burdens confronting minority and poor populations in their states (Ringquist and Clark 1999). In this way, states sought to identify the extent of the problem in their own backyard. Following up on these exploratory studies, several states then took policy action. According to the most recent survey of state environmental justice initiatives, thirty-two states have enacted legislation that either explicitly references environmental justice or promotes environmental justice objectives (Bonorris 2007). Many states have also pursued actions through executive orders from governors, and institutionally through the creation of advisory commissions and enhancements of administrative capacity (Ringquist and Clark 1999; Bonorris 2007). Other states have elected not to pursue policy in this area, once again illustrating the diversity of preferences across the country.

Among the more notable actions taken by a state was the Arkansas Environmental Equity Act, enacted in 1993. This legislation was among the earliest statutes passed to address inequities in the siting of solid waste disposal facilities. The intent of the law according to the statute was to "prevent communities from becoming involuntary hosts to a proliferation of high impact solid waste management facilities." Included in the statute was a "rebuttal provision" to prevent the concentration of solid waste disposal facilities in particular communities. The law creates a presumption against siting a solid waste management facility within twelve miles of any existing facility. Several other southern states have adopted similar anticoncentration policies, including Alabama, Georgia, and Mississippi (Bonorris 2007).

State Environmental Policy Laggards

Some of the policy innovations produced by states pursuing environmental protection goals became models for other states and, in the case of motor vehicle emissions standards, for the federal government as well. Yet many states have opted not to pursue such policies. Moreover, as indicated by the data on state environmental expenditures and enforcement activity in Table 15-2, some states are clearly devoting fewer financial and human resources to environmental protection in their states than others. This reflects the fact that states vary in the degree to which they pursue environmental protection, with some serving as policy leaders and others as policy laggards. In this subsection we focus on the laggards.

Over the years, political scientists have developed typologies of states in an effort to identify leaders and laggards. James Lester (1995) placed states in four categories—progressives, strugglers, delayers, and regressives—based on their institutional capacities and commitment levels to environmental protection. Institutional capacity refers to the professionalization of the legislature and the organizational capability of the environmental bureaucracy (which we discuss in greater detail in the section on the determinants of environmental policy later in this chapter). Commitment reflects the state's history of pursuing solutions to environmental problems. The states Lester identified as lacking in both capacity and commitment—states he characterized as the "regressives"—were Arizona, Indiana, Kansas, Kentucky, Mississippi, Nebraska, New Mexico, South Dakota, Utah, and Wyoming.

Another indicator of state environmental policy reticence is that some states have decided to do only what is required of them by federal law. As of the mid-1990s (the last time such information was compiled), twenty-four states had enacted legislation that specifically forbade their environmental agencies from adopting standards more stringent than federal standards. In addition, several governors have adopted such prohibitions through executive orders (Environmental Law Institute 1996). These restrictions range from broad limitations on state standard setting such as those in Kentucky and Virginia, to more specific limitations on particular programs such as those in New Mexico, where the state legislature enacted legislation forbidding its environmental agency from developing standards more stringent than those in the Clean Air Act (Organ 1995; Patton 1996).

Concerns about economic competition tend to motivate these types of laws and policies (Organ 1995). When attempting to ease the regulatory costs for industries subject to pollution control regulations, states have several options. First, many states streamline their environmental permitting processes (Rabe 1999), which is an important factor in industry siting decisions. Second, states employ various financial incentives designed to reduce the cost of complying with environmental regulations, such as tax-free financing of pollution abatement equipment. Third, many state environmental agencies have compliance assistance programs in place, in which agency personnel work with regulated firms to help them meet regulatory standards. Fourth, many states have adopted **environmental audit privilege and immunity** legislation. An environmental audit is a voluntary assessment of a facility generally used to determine its compliance with environmental regulations. Audit privilege protects information collected during an audit from disclosure or use in an administrative or judicial hearing; audit immunity shields facilities from penalties for violations discovered during an audit as long as the facility returns to compliance (Stafford 2006). Critics of these types of policies and practices argue that they amount to little more than a free pass to firms violating pollution control laws, and thereby reflect an unwillingness among state governments to take adequate measures to protect the environment.

Next, we turn to the question of why some states are environmental policy leaders and others are environmental policy laggards. In doing so, one must consider both the dynamics and conditions operating within states and the influences from outside states.

Determinants of State Environmental Policy

A well-developed body of political science research has sought to explain why some states adopt relatively pro-environment policies. These studies parallel research on state policy liberalism more generally (see the discussion in Chapter 1). From this literature, one can identify three broad classes of explanations for the strength of state environmental programs: problem severity, institutional and fiscal capacity, and politics (Lester 1995).

As discussed earlier in this chapter, states show tremendous variation in their environmental conditions. Severe environmental problems put pressure on state officials to generate policy responses. When states generate policies to deal with specific environmental problems, it is referred to as **policy matching**. The extent to which states successfully match environmental policies to pollution problems tends to vary across states (Lowry 1992), but research often shows a relationship between the severity of an environmental problem and the stringency of the state's policy response. It is not surprising, for example, that states faced with toxic releases, hazardous waste sites, or groundwater contamination adopt stringent, innovative hazardous waste policies (Sapat 2004; Daley and Garand 2005), or that states experiencing poor air or water quality adopt strong air or water pollution programs (Lowry 1992).

States also differ in their capacities to effectively make and implement environmental policies. One element of capacity is a state's *fiscal* status: wealthier states have the financial resources needed to produce effective policy, and thus often have stronger environmental programs than the poorer states (Bacot and Dawes 1997; Daley and Garand 2005; Woods 2008).[9] Wealthier states also tend to have substan-

---

9. Greater wealth also tends to increase citizens' demands for environmental protection (Yandle, Bhattarai, and Vijayaraghavan 2004).

tially better environmental conditions, especially in the area of air quality (List and McHone 2000).

Capacity may also be *institutional*, residing in either the legislative or executive branch. State legislatures vary significantly in their capacities to effectively make and oversee policy. More professionalized legislatures have larger and more professional staffs and sit for longer sessions, giving them a greater capacity to generate legislative responses to public problems (see the discussion of state legislatures in Chapter 6). Some studies have shown that states with more professional legislatures produce stronger environmental policies (Hays, Esler, and Hays 1996; Woods 2008). The task of implementing policies falls on administrative agencies, which also vary in their organizational capacities to effectively accomplish these tasks. Organizational effectiveness in environmental policy implementation is associated with larger budgets and more abundant personnel resources (Lester 1995; Sapat 2004). One study suggests that it is also associated with the adoption of "best practices" management systems that provide agencies with greater capital, human resources, financial, information technology, and result-based management capability (Jennings and Woods 2007).

The strength of state environmental programs also reflects the political context within the state. A more pro-environment citizenry is likely to press for stronger environmental programs, and states whose citizens are more supportive of environmental policy or are more liberal generally tend to have stronger environmental programs (Hays, Esler, and Hays 1996; Daley and Garand 2005; Woods 2008). The interplay of organized interests also plays a role. Several studies have found that environmental policy is responsive to the strength of environmental and manufacturing interests in a state (Ringquist 1993; Hays, Esler, and Hays 1996; Bacot and Dawes 1997; Davis and Davis 1999; Daley and Garand 2005).

A final important aspect of a state's political context is the political control of state government. It is generally assumed that states with Democratic governors and state legislatures are more likely to favor strong environmental protection efforts, whereas states under Republican control will be more inclined to sacrifice environmental protection for economic growth. Some of the empirical evidence in the political science literature supports this basic pattern (Wood 1992; Woods 2008). However, one can certainly find high-profile exceptions. For example, while governor of California, Republican Arnold Schwarzenegger (2003–2011) was a staunch advocate of addressing climate change, signing into law the Global Warming Solutions Act of 2006, which represents the most far-reaching state-level effort to limit greenhouse gas emissions. Other Republican governors also have had distinguished records on the environment. For example, Gov. George Pataki of New York (1995–2006) made substantial efforts to protect wilderness areas, helping to set aside 900,000 acres of open space (Cooper 2005). Some Democratic governors have also exhibited fewer proclivities to support stringent environmental protection policies, particularly in southern states. A quote from Louisiana governor Edwin Edwards (1972–1980, 1984–1988, 1992–1996) illustrates:

> We have . . . taken the position that the need for . . . stimulation to our economy justified . . . serious tradeoffs, where the environment became either totally or partially damaged. None of us . . . in positions of authority in the state apologize for that. We did what we thought was best for the people and the economy of Louisiana. We accommodated industry where we thought we could in order to get the jobs and the development, and in some instances we knowingly and advisedly accepted environmental tradeoffs. (Quoted in Levinson 1996.)

The effects of these influences may vary across the types of activity being performed. In a study of state air quality regulation, for example, Potoski and Woods (2002) found evidence that different factors drive state decisions within each of three policy dimensions: allocating resources, gathering information, and enforcement. Policy activities within the resource allocation dimension (such as setting clean air standards) tend to be driven largely by politics; bureaucratic capacity has the greatest impact on policy activities within the information dimension (such as monitoring air quality); and task factors related to the environmental problem itself are the most important determinants of activities that fall along the implementation dimension (such as regulatory enforcement).

The internal determinants of environmental policy are accompanied by some important external factors as well. As the discussion in the preceding sections suggests, state behavior in many areas of environmental policy is greatly shaped and constrained by the actions of the federal government. The EPA therefore plays a large role in influencing the actions of state environmental agencies. In fact, some of the differences observed in state environmental behavior may reflect differences in how the EPA's regional offices administer federal programs (Crotty 1988; Church and Nakamura 1993). In addition, states often adopt innovative environmental policies that have already been adopted by their neighbors (Daley and Garand 2005; Chandler 2009). This process, referred to as **policy diffusion**, may occur either through policy learning (as states emulate programs perceived to be successful in other states), competition (as states try to avoid being disadvantaged in the pursuit of capital relative to their neighbors), or internal political pressure from citizens to adopt policies from other states (Berry and Berry 1999). For environmental policies, there is also some evidence that the EPA plays a role in facilitating the diffusion of environmental policies, possibly through its regional offices (Daley and Garand 2005; Stoutenborough and Beverlin 2008).

Lowry (1992) provides a framework that integrates the horizontal and vertical dimensions of state environmental policy. His model uses the amount of federal involvement and interstate competition as dimensions of federalism that affect state environmental policy. His theory suggests that the higher the level of interstate competition in the policy area, the less likely it is that states will regulate environmental pollution aggressively because they will be seeking to recruit and maintain industry by keeping regulation light. Along the other dimension, the greater the degree of federal involvement in a policy area, the more rapidly state environmental policy innovations will be diffused across the states. Thus in a policy area characterized by high vertical involvement and low horizontal competition (such as mobile source air pollution regulation), there should be a high degree of policy matching between an environmental problem and a state's policy response. In these instances, states receive relatively strong direction from the EPA, and there is little countervailing economic incentive to reduce environmental regulations. The converse should occur in instances of low vertical involvement and high horizontal competition (such as stationary source air pollution regulation). In issue areas in which both dimensions are high or low, the relationship between severity and response will depend on other factors. Lowry's analyses of four pollution control policies generally support this argument.

CONCLUSION

States play an enormous role in U.S. environmental policy. In 2008 states were spending about $12.7 billion annually to protect the environment (Environmental Council of the States 2008). Although states vary significantly in the degree of emphasis that they place on environmental protection, several have developed innovative, rigorous policies that outstrip efforts by the federal government in important areas such as encouraging renewable energy use and cutting greenhouse gas emissions. States also take the lead in implementing and enforcing most major federal pieces of environmental regulation, including the Clean Air and Clean Water Acts. Meanwhile, states are increasingly forming partnerships to deal with a variety of pollution problems that cross state lines.

The cloudy fiscal future poses a significant challenge to state pollution control efforts. The fiscal crisis that began the fall of 2007 has left a deep hole in state budgets—one that promises to have ramifications for the foreseeable future. As states scramble to cut budgets, spending on environmental protection, like many other policy areas, is likely to be on the chopping block. Moreover, because environmental protection is a deeply intergovernmental policy area, cutbacks in federal support for environmental protection will be felt in the states as well. Even before the fiscal crisis, the EPA was imposing additional responsibilities on the states without providing commensurate funding to cover costs (Rabe 2007). In their 2009 budgets, states were able to count on fiscal stimulus money to offset some of these state and federal funding cuts. But a recent survey of sixteen state environmental agencies suggests that despite the additional funds, state environmental budgets fell from fiscal year 2009 through fiscal year 2011 (Economic Council of the States 2010). In the absence of federal stimulus money, state environmental agencies face the challenge of continuing their environmental protection efforts with significantly fewer resources.

The stalemate at the national level on many important environmental issues, notably climate change, makes the state role even more important. Because of the

Republican ascendency in Congress after the 2010 midterm elections, it is likely that this stalemate will continue, at least in the short term. As a consequence, we can expect some (but certainly not all) states to continue to lead in addressing climate change and other environmental problems.

KEY TERMS

"California effect," 485

devolution, 477

environmental audit privilege and immunity, 492

National Ambient Air Quality Standards (NAAQS), 473

New Source Performance Standards, 477

nonattainment, 473

partial preemption, 476

policy diffusion, 494

policy matching, 492

primacy, 477

race to the bottom, 479

race to the top, 479

renewable portfolio standard (RPS), 488

second-order devolution, 478

spillover effect, 475

Toxics Release Inventory (TRI), 471

REFERENCES

Applebaum, Aliza. 2011. "EPA to Require Coal Plant to Cut Emissions Affecting Air Quality in Warren, Morris, Hunterdon, Sussex." *Star-Ledger*, March 31.

Bacot, A. Hunter, and Roy A. Dawes. 1997. "State Expenditures and Policy Outcomes in Environmental Program Management." *Policy Studies Journal* 25: 355–370.

Berry, Francis Stokes, and William D. Berry. 1999. "Innovation and Diffusion Models in Policy Research." In *Theories of the Policy Process*, ed. Paul A. Sabatier. Boulder, Colo.: Westview Press.

Bonorris, Steven. 2007. *Environmental Justice for All: A Fifty State Survey of Legislation, Policies, and Cases.* San Francisco: Hastings College of Law.

Buntin, John. 2010. "A Cap-and-Trade Program That Works." *Governing.* December.

Chandler, Jess. 2009. "Trendy Solutions: Why Do States Adopt Sustainable Energy Portfolio Standards?" *Energy Policy* 37: 3274–3281.

Church, Thomas W., and Robert T. Nakamura. 1993. *Cleaning Up the Mess: Implementation Strategies in Superfund.* Washington, D.C.: Brookings.

Cline, Kurt D. 2003. "Influences on Intergovernmental Implementation: The States and the Superfund." *State Politics and Policy Quarterly* 3: 66–83.

Cooper, Michael. 2005. "The Shadow of His Predecessor Dominates the Pataki Legacy." *New York Times,* July 29.

Crotty, Patricia M. 1987. "The New Federalism Game: Primacy Implementation of Environmental Policy." *Publius: The Journal of Federalism* 17: 57–63.

———. 1988. "Assessing the Role of Federal Administrative Agencies: An Exploratory Analysis." *Public Administration Review* 48: 642–648.

Daley, Dorothy, and James C. Garand. 2005. "Horizontal Diffusion, Vertical Diffusion, and Internal Pressure in State Environmental Policymaking, 1989–1998." *American Politics Research* 37: 615–644.

Davies, J. Clarence, III. 1970. *The Politics of Pollution.* New York: Pegasus.

Davis, Charles, and Sandra K. Davis. 1999. "State Enforcement of the Federal Hazardous Waste Program." *Polity* 31: 450–468.

Davis, Charles E., and James P. Lester. 1987. "Decentralizing Federal Environmental Policy: A Research Note." *Western Political Quarterly* 40: 555–565.

Delli Santi, Angela. 2006. "State Reveals Plan to Sue EPA over Pollution from Pa. Plant." Associated Press, December 8.

Ellerman, A. Denny, Paul L. Joskow, Juan-Pablo Montero, Richard Schmalensee, Elizabeth M. Bailey, and Paul L. Joskow. 2000. *Markets for Clean Air: The U.S. Acid Rain Program.* Cambridge, U.K.: Cambridge University Press.

Engel, Kirsten H. 2010. "Courts and Climate Policy: Now and in the Future." In *Greenhouse Governance: Addressing Climate Change in America*, ed. Barry G. Rabe, 229–259. Washington, D.C.: Brookings.

Environment America. 2005. *Power to Protect: The Critical Role States Play in Cleaning Up Pollution from Mobile Sources.* Report 2005-06-15, Washington, D.C.

Environmental Council of the States. 2008. "March 2008 Green Report Appendix." www.ecos.org/files/3058_file_March_2008_ECOS_Green_Report_Appendix.pdf.

———. 2010. "August 2010 Green Report." www.ecos.org/files/4157_file_August_2010_Green_Report.pdf.

Environmental Law Institute. 1996. *Federal Regulations and State Flexibility in Environmental Standard Setting.* Washington, D.C.: Environmental Law Institute.

Fahys, Judy. 2011. "EPA Threatens to Take Over Part of Utah's Clean-Air Regulation." *Salt Lake Tribune*, April 15, 2011.

Feiock, Richard C., and Christopher Stream. 2001. "Environmental Protection Versus Economic Development: A False Trade Off?" *Public Administration Review* 61: 313–321.

Fredriksson, Per G., and Daniel L. Millimet. 2002. "Strategic Interaction and the Determinants of Environmental Policy across U.S. States." *Journal of Urban Economics* 51: 101–122.

Hall, Bruce, and Mary Lee Kerr. 1991. *1991–92 Green Index: A State-by-State Guide to the Nation's Environmental Health.* Washington, D.C.: Island Press.

Harrison, Kathryn. 1996. *Passing the Buck: Federalism and Canadian Environmental Policy.* Vancouver: UBC Press.

———. 2006. *Racing to the Bottom? Provincial Interdependence in the Canadian Federation.* Vancouver: UBC Press.

Hays, Scott P., Michael Esler, and Carol F. Hays. 1996. "Environmental Commitment among the States: Integrating Alternative Approaches to State Environmental Policy." *Publius: The Journal of Federalism* 26: 41–58.

Helland, Eric, and Andrew B. Whitford. 2003. "Pollution Incidence and Political Jurisdiction: Evidence from TRI." *Journal of Environmental Economics and Management* 46: 403–424.

Jennings, Edward T., and Neal D. Woods. 2007. "Does Management *Really* Matter? Management Quality and State Environmental Performance." Paper presented at the 2007 biannual meeting of the Public Management Research Association.

John, DeWitt. 1994. *Civic Environmentalism: Alternatives to Regulation in States and Communities.* Washington, D.C.: CQ Press.

Kaufman, Leslie. 2011. "G.O.P. Push in States to Deregulate Environment." *New York Times,* April 15, 2011.

Konisky, David M. 2007. "Regulatory Competition and Environmental Enforcement: Is There a Race to the Bottom?" *American Journal of Political Science* 51: 853–872.

———. 2009a. "Assessing U.S. State Susceptibility to Environmental Regulatory Competition." *State Politics and Policy Quarterly* 9: 404–428.

———. 2009b. "Inequities in Enforcement? Environmental Justice and Government Performance." *Journal of Policy Analysis and Management* 28: 102–121.

Konisky, David M., and Neal D. Woods. 2010. "Exporting Air Pollution? Regulatory Enforcement and Environmental Free Riding in the United States." *Political Research Quarterly* 63: 771–782.

Lax, Jeffrey R., and Justin H. Phillips. 2009. "How Should We Estimate Public Opinion in the States?" *American Journal of Political Science* 53: 107–121.

Lester, James. 1986. "New Federalism and Environmental Policy." *Publius: The Journal of Federalism* 16: 149–165.

———. 1995. "Federalism and State Environmental Policy." In *Environmental Politics and Policy: Theories and Evidence*, ed. James P. Lester. Durham, N.C.: Duke University Press.

Levinson, Arik. 1996. "Environmental Regulations and Industry Location: International and Domestic Evidence." In *Fair Trade and Harmonization: Prerequisites for Free Trade?* ed. Jagdish N. Bhagwati and Robert E. Hudec. Cambridge, Mass.: MIT Press.

———. 2003. "Environmental Regulatory Competition: A Status Report and Some New Evidence." *National Tax Journal* 56: 91–106.

List, John A., and W. Warren McHone. 2000. "Ranking State Environmental Outputs: Evidence from Panel Data." *Growth and Change* 31: 23–39.

Lowry, William R. 1992. *The Dimensions of Federalism: State Governments and Pollution Control Policies*. Durham, N.C.: Duke University Press.

Lyon, Thomas P., and Haitao Yin. 2010. "Why Do States Adopt Renewable Portfolio Standards? An Empirical Investigation." *Energy Journal* 31: 133–157.

Matisoff, Daniel C. 2008. "The Adoption of State Climate Change Policies and Renewable Portfolio Standards: Regional Diffusion or Internal Determinants?" *Review of Policy Research* 25: 527–546.

New York Office of the Attorney General. 2011. "A.G. Schneiderman Presses EPA to Implement Key Measures to Protect New York from Out-of-State Air Pollution" (press release). www.ag.ny.gov/media_center/2011/mar/mar21a_11.html.

Organ, Jerome M. 1995. "Limitations on State Agency Authority to Adopt Environmental Standards More Stringent than Federal Standards: Policy Considerations and Interpretive Problems." *Maryland Law Review* 54: 1373–1434.

Patton, Vickie L. 1996. "A Balanced Partnership." *Environmental Forum* (May/June): 16–22.

Pew Center on Global Climate Change. 2011a. "Detailed Table of State Policies." www.pewclimate.org/docUploads/09–09–01-state-rps-aeps-details.xls.

———. 2011b. U.S. Climate Maps. www.pewclimate.org/what_s_being_done/in_the_states/state_action_maps.cfm.

Potoski, Matthew. 2001. "Clean Air Federalism: Do States Race to the Bottom?" *Public Administration Review* 61: 335–342.

Potoski, Matthew, and Neal D. Woods. 2002. "Dimensions of State Environmental Policies: Air Pollution Regulation in the United States." *Policy Studies Journal* 30: 208–227.

Rabe, Barry G. 1997. "Power to the States: The Promise and Pitfalls of Decentralization." In *Environmental Policy in the 1990s*, 3d ed., ed. Norman J. Vig and Michael Kraft. Washington, D.C.: CQ Press.

———. 1999. "Federalism and Entrepreneurship: Explaining American and Canadian Innovation in Pollution Prevention and Regulatory Integration." *Policy Studies Journal* 27: 288–306.

———. 2004. *Statehouse and Greenhouse: The Emerging Politics of American Climate Change Policy*. Washington, D.C.: Brookings.

———. 2007. "Environmental Policy and the Bush Era: The Collision between the Administrative Presidency and State Experimentation." *Publius: The Journal of Federalism* 37: 413–431.

———. 2008. "States on Steroids: The Intergovernmental Odyssey of American Climate Change Policy." *Review of Policy Research* 25: 105–128.

Raymond, Leigh. 2010. "The Emerging Revolution in Emissions Trading Policy." In *Greenhouse Governance: Addressing Climate Change in America*, ed. Barry G. Rabe. Washington, D.C.: Brookings.

Revesz, Richard L. 1992. "Rehabilitating Interstate Competition: Rethinking the 'Race-to-the-Bottom' Rationale for Federal Environmental Regulation." *New York University Law Review* 67: 1210.

————. 1997. "Federalism and Environmental Regulation: A Normative Critique." In *The New Federalism: Can the States Be Trusted?* ed. John Ferejohn and Barry R. Weingast. Stanford, Calif.: Hoover Institution Press.

Ringquist, Evan J. 1993. *Environmental Protection at the State Level.* Armonk, N.Y.: M. E. Sharpe.

————. 1995. "Is Effective Regulation Always Oxymoronic? The States and Ambient Air Quality." *Social Science Quarterly* 76: 69–87.

Ringquist, Evan J., and David H. Clark. 1999. "Local Risks, States' Rights, and Federal Mandates: Remedying Environmental Inequities in the U.S. Federalist System." *Publius: The Journal of Federalism* 29: 73–93.

Sapat, Alka. 2004. "Devolution and Innovation: The Adoption of State Environmental Policy Innovations by Administrative Agencies." *Public Administration Review* 64: 141–151.

Sigman, Hilary. 2003. "Letting States Do the Dirty Work: State Responsibility for Federal Environmental Regulation." *National Tax Journal* 56: 107–122.

Stafford, Sarah. 2006. "State Adoption of Environmental Audit Initiatives." *Contemporary Economic Policy* 24: 172–187.

Stoutenborough, James W., and Matthew Beverlin. 2008. "Encouraging Pollution-Free Energy: The Diffusion of State Net Metering Policies." *Social Science Quarterly* 89: 1230–1251.

Vogel, David. 1995. *Trading Up: Consumer and Environmental Regulation in a Global Economy.* Cambridge, Mass.: Harvard University Press.

Wood, B. Dan. 1992. "Modeling Federal Implementation as a System: The Clean Air Case." *American Journal of Political Science* 36: 40–67.

Woods, Neal D. 2006a. "Interstate Competition and Environmental Regulation: A Test of the Race to the Bottom Thesis." *Social Science Quarterly* 87: 174–189.

————. 2006b. "Primacy Implementation of Environmental Policy in the U.S. States." *Publius: The Journal of Federalism* 36: 259–276.

————. 2008. "The Policy Consequences of Political Corruption: Evidence from State Environmental Programs." *Social Science Quarterly* 89: 258–271.

Woods, Neal D., and Matthew Potoski. 2010. "Environmental Federalism Revisited: Second-Order Devolution in Air Quality Regulation." *Review of Policy Research* 27: 721–739.

Woods, Neal D., David M. Konisky, and Ann O'M Bowman. 2009. "You Get What You Pay For: Environmental Policy and Public Health." *Publius: The Journal of Federalism* 39: 95–116.

Yandle, Bruce, Madhusudan Bhattarai, and Maya Vijayaraghavan. 2004. *Environmental Kuznets Curves: A Review of Findings, Methods, and Policy Implications.* Property and Environment Research Center Research Study 02–1, Bozeman, Montana.

SUGGESTED READINGS

Print

Rabe, Barry G. *Statehouse and Greenhouse: The Emerging Politics of American Climate Change Policy.* Washington, D.C.: Brookings, 2004. A look at the surprisingly vigorous efforts of state governments to address the issue of global climate change.

Rechtschaffen, Clifford, and David L. Markell. *Reinventing Environmental Enforcement and the State/Federal Relationship.* Washington, D.C.: Environmental Law Institute, 2003. An examination of the allocation of authority between the states and the U.S. Environmental Protection Agency in enforcing federal environmental programs.

Ringquist, Evan J. *Environmental Protection at the State Level.* Armonk, N.Y.: M. E. Sharpe, 1993. A comprehensive look at state air and water pollution policies. Ringquist empirically examines why some states develop stronger pollution control programs than others and assesses the effects these programs have on environmental quality.

Scheberle, Denise. *Federalism and Environmental Policy: Trust and the Politics of Implementation,* 2d ed. Washington, D.C.: Georgetown University Press, 2004. An investigation of the working relationships between federal and state agency officials in a variety of environmental programs.

Vig, Norman J., and Michael E. Kraft, eds. *Environmental Policy: New Directions for the 21st Century,* 7th ed. Washington, D.C.: CQ Press, 2010. An edited volume that features chapters from experts on a wide range of current environmental policy issues.

Internet

Environmental Council of the States. www.ecos.org/. The national nonprofit association of state environmental agency leaders whose Web site contains a host of information and analysis related to a variety of state environmental policy areas.

Pew Center on Global Climate Change. www.pewclimate.org/states-regions. An updated list of state policy actions related to climate change for all fifty states.

State Environmental Agencies. www.epa.gov/epahome/state.htm. A page on the U.S. Environmental Protection Agency Web site that provides a link to the Web site of each state's environmental agency.

State Environmental Leadership Program. www.selp.org/. A network of independent environmental activist organizations that focuses on state environmental policy.

Stateline.org. www.stateline.org/live/issues/Environment. Updated daily, provides links to state environmental news stories from around the nation.

CHAPTER 16

Economic Development and Infrastructure Policy

MARTIN SAIZ AND SUSAN E. CLARKE

Recession. Climate change. Globalization. Not typical state economic development concerns. But states are confronting complex problems stemming from just such events, problems that affect state economies in significant ways and highlight the tensions between state and national authority. Where problems are so complex and interdependent that states cannot solve them on their own, federal intervention seems a logical response.

State governments have few policy tools with which to fight a recession and must rely on federal use of monetary and fiscal policy. Climate change caused by greenhouse emissions also exemplifies this dilemma: states seem to be in a weak position to address this issue because each state fears driving investment to other states if they consider environmental regulations that might add to the costs of doing business (Rabe 2004; also see Chapter 15). Similarly, globalization poses for state officials the problem of heightened competition for investment and trade—and often immigration issues that bring both benefits and costs to individual states. Certainly, the magnitude, scope, and complexity of a recession, climate change, and globalization seem to indicate that national initiatives should be given urgent priority. These factors also underscore the need for states to integrate their traditional development priorities with a capacity for resilience in the face of crisis, change, and competitiveness in a global economy.

RESILIENCE AND COMPETITIVENESS CONCERNS SHAPE STATE ECONOMIC DEVELOPMENT AGENDAS

In past years, a capacity for resilience was deemed crucial in responding to security threats and natural disasters. It still is. But the resilience of American states is now sorely tested by the economic crisis and recession that began to unfold in 2007. As the ripples spread throughout the American economy, states saw their tax revenues shrink while expenditure demands continued to go up. Meanwhile, the unemployment rates in several states escalated to historic highs, and many states faced budget deficits. Congress passed the American Recovery and Reinvestment Act (ARRA) in 2009, thereby allocating $787 billion for "shovel-ready" projects in states and communities. In the form of contracts, grants, and loans, these funds went to a wide range of recipients such as school districts, state and local governments, construction companies, Boys and Girls Clubs, transportation projects, and energy retrofitters—all aimed at stimulating the economy through jobs, services, and projects. In ARRA's first year, the president's Council of Economic Advisers found that every federal ARRA dollar leveraged "roughly three dollars of investment by state or local governments or the private sector" (Peirce 2010). By the end of 2010, 586,340 jobs had been funded through ARRA projects. But ARRA was a one-shot national response to fiscal crisis. As ARRA funds are spent out, states again confront weakened economic conditions.

Globalization seems to be a particularly complex problem. Not long ago, national borders protected state and local economies from the effects of global capitalism. Today, with the help of free trade agreements and advanced by a revolution in worldwide communications, global competition is transforming the economy of the United States. Industries that were thought of as state or national assets commonly migrate across borders and oceans. Parts suppliers and production subcontractors are often located in faraway lands. So each year state and local governments spend billions of dollars on economic development programs designed to grow, attract, and retain businesses and jobs that will integrate their states with the global economy and the vibrant sectors of the new economy.

As we demonstrate here, the economic development tools used vary among states and over time. Historically, they have often involved public policies that cut the costs of doing business—such as lowering taxes or targeted tax incentives, providing land or subsidies to firms, and building needed infrastructure. States also target growth processes, regions, and economic sectors rather than individual firms. They do so in many ways: participating in public-private partnerships, establishing venture capital funds and foreign trade offices, offering seed money for new ventures, encouraging collaboration and networking among clusters of firms, and devising other innovative strategies. After we began tracking these trends in the 1980s, state policy efforts to stimulate economic growth processes by fostering innovation and entrepreneurism appeared to characterize new thinking on state economic development strategies (Saiz and Clarke 2004, 2008; Hall 2007, 2009).

More recently however, state policy orientations appear to diverge along regional lines. The growth in entrepreneurial approaches has slowed, and more traditional policies designed to attract business investment by reducing the business costs in a particular location have experienced a comeback. Specifically, the Mid-Atlantic and midwestern states have continued to move in an entrepreneurial direction, while the southern and Mountain states have chosen a more traditional approach.

All these diverse goals and initiatives fall under the broad label of **state economic development** programs. Still, there is little agreement among scholars that economic development programs actually work—in other words, that they change the quality and quantity of economic activity in a state. Although it is not clear that economic development policies work as planned, it is also not clear whether such expenditures are a complete waste of money. More than economic calculations are at stake: these policy issues create a dilemma for public officials. Because of the potential political benefits of claiming to protect jobs and businesses, public officials tend to support these programs even in the absence of solid evidence that they accomplish the intended goals.

The political and economic uncertainties surrounding economic development decisions, particularly in the face of global competition, contribute to a distinctive climate for state economic development policymakers. Four dimensions merit special attention in this chapter: (1) the significance of federalism and globalization in shaping state economic development options; (2) the changing definitions of the problems and consequently the strategies states use to induce business investment; (3) the periodic shifts in policy orientation between conventional cost reduction, **smokestack-chasing strategies**, and more entrepreneurial policy approaches; and (4) the enduring debate about the effectiveness of state economic development policies in influencing state growth and development.

FEDERALISM, GLOBALIZATION, AND STATE ECONOMIC DEVELOPMENT POLICY

The objective of a state's economic development policy is to bring about more economic activity in the state. Unlike national governments, however, state governments are limited in the policy tools they can use to control their economies. States cannot control the movement of raw materials, capital, or workers across their borders, although several states are experimenting with legislation aimed at checking unauthorized immigration. They cannot affect the supply of money or the rate of interest on borrowed funds. Most important, state governments cannot command business to invest; they can only hope to induce investment by offering or creating incentives to promote the desired economic activity. It is hoped that these incentives will stimulate new investment that would otherwise not be made in that location.

That said, states offer low-interest loans, loan guarantees, special tax breaks, and outright grants of cash and land to attract, retain, and stimulate private businesses in the state. If a company's site needs improvement, some state governments will prepare the ground for development, bring utility lines to the site, or link it to the transportation system by building roads and laying new railroad tracks. If labor is a problem, they will train workers for individual firms or reimburse the firms for the costs of customized job training. The states can use their power of eminent domain, among other tools, on behalf of industries to consolidate multiple land parcels into developable units. States link businesses to university research, underwrite vocational education to upgrade the skills of the local labor force, and develop industrial parks to compensate for perceived shortages of industrial land. Almost every state offers programs that help businesses export their products to foreign markets, and governors commonly embark on overseas trade missions to promote their state's firms. More indirectly, states induce investment by granting tax incentives to businesses in general or some industries in particular. Or they may reduce personal taxes to entice corporate managers and entrepreneurs to come to (or remain in) the state. States do these and many other things all with the aim of creating jobs and stimulating business investment in the state. Indeed, in what follows we analyze the array of state economic development policies by classifying them in terms of strategies aimed at building infrastructure, influencing locational decisions, or facilitating entrepreneurial growth processes, and we include more than thirty examples of programs that have worked or have gone awry.

Federalism and State Policy Choices

The decentralized American federal system places many responsibilities on state and local governments, but it provides few fiscal resources to help meet these burdens. As a result, the states compete with each other for private investment that brings them jobs and tax revenues. Paul Peterson (1981) argues that businesses and residents are attracted to locations with the most favorable ratio of taxes paid to services received. Thus states have a common interest in policies that promote economic activity that generates tax revenues, especially if such activity also creates jobs. If successful, these policies improve the state's economic position (relative to that of other states) because it can now offer more and higher-quality services without having to raise taxes. But implicit in this analysis is the inevitability of competition that encourages observers to see states in a race for economic investment, often using incentives to attract businesses rather than diagnosing their core economic problems (Markusen and Glasmeier 2008, 116).

And yet when states offer incentives to retain and attract companies, they often are acting without sufficient information. They are uncertain of the deals being offered by other states as well as the needs of the firms they are trying to attract or keep from leaving. Because most state governments pursue this strategy and few dare disengage from the competition, they often promise more than is wise or necessary to secure the deal, frequently with no guarantee that the benefits will outweigh the costs. State incentive packages ratchet upward because only the firm knows what it really needs and states do not want to submit a bid that is too low to attract the firm (Jones and Bachelor 1986). As a result of this **interjurisdictional competition,** businesses can play states off each other to get the best deal. Governments take part in this process because there are political advantages to winning the investment competition with other states (Wolman and Spitzley 1996).

This competitive environment of bidding up incentives across states sometimes resembles the spiral of decisions in an arms race (Hanson 1993; Hansen 2006). William Fulton, a planner and the mayor of Ventura, California, writes of watching governors of seven states begging General Motors to build their new Saturn plant in their state: "It was, to put it bluntly, a pretty pathetic excuse for an economic development campaign" (Fulton 2010). In one of the most infamous races, more than thirty-five states competed in 1993 to be the site for Mercedes-Benz's new sport utility vehicle plant. With Mercedes-Benz in the "auctioneer's" seat, states presented custom-tailored incentive packages to entice the company to locate in their state. Alabama's $300 million winning package included tax breaks, promises to buy the vehicles for the state fleet, payments to workers while in training, commitments to develop the new site, and construction of a welcome center for visitors to the plant as well as the more traditional infrastructure development (Mahtesian 1994).

These giant incentive packages are not limited to automobile manufacturers. Computer maker Dell got several states to bid for their jobs and ended up with a package worth more than $242 million in grants and corporate tax credits from North Carolina (Martinez 2005). Dell then initiated a bidding war between counties within the state, and Forsyth County came up with an additional $37 million in incentives in the form of land, cash, and infrastructure. In addition to the financial incentives, Dell would also be exempted from minimum wage laws, allowing the company to reduce its average annual pay from $31,000 to $28,000 and pay only 50 percent of the cost of health insurance for its employees (Speizer 2005). And yet less than five years after capturing these subsidies, Dell closed down its North Carolina plant. Such policies imply a beggar-thy-neighbor outcome in which one state seeks to gain at the expense of the others. Such a practice has led many observers to conclude that traditional state economic development policies merely shift economic activity from one location to another and do not really create new wealth or distribute it more equitably (Peters and Fisher 2004).

Some states, however, take an entrepreneurial approach to economic development, fostering the creation of new firms, new products (and the markets they create), or perhaps even new industries. Eisinger (1988) characterizes these policies as entrepreneurial because of their attention to higher-risk investments and their reliance on market-based solutions to produce indigenous growth. To Plosila (2004), these programs emphasize risk by focusing on nontraditional methods of financing, but they also increase awareness of the importance of entrepreneurs, recognize technology as an important component of assistance, and often bring higher education to the table as a partner in the economic development process. Using this approach, states can construct a new economic role for themselves that avoids the bidding wars and zero-sum consequences of interstate economic competition. Within this general orientation, subsequent "waves" of economic development policy orientations have been identified by various scholars (Clarke and Gaile 1992). Third-wave orientations emphasize leadership roles, strategic planning, and public-private partnerships to focus on strategic advantages for growth in particular sectors or areas (Bradshaw and Blakely 1999). Fourth-wave orientations center on the problems of global warming and environmental sustainability by attempting to capitalize future markets for a "green economy" (Campbell 1996).

Globalization and State Policy Choices

Although the federal structure is constant, globalization trends change the conditions under which states make economic development policy choices. Growth no longer can be captured within politically bounded and relatively closed economies. Investment flows and decision makers are international rather than local or national. The most salient features of globalization are the greater mobility of capital, a new international division of labor with many production jobs moving outside the United States, the elimination of national trade barriers, new information and transportation technologies, and global competition increasingly driven by innovation rather than by the costs of land, labor, and capital (Reich 1991; Hall 2007). These features alter the investment priorities of firms and the policy options of states.

With globalization, the competitive forces between established and emerging market countries appear to be, as Thomas Friedman (2005) puts it, "flattening" the world into a single competitive landscape. Today, the inexpensive personal digital technologies carried by a global fiber-optic network have turned individuals into the main ingredients of globalization. Thus workers in a country such as China become part of the global supply chain for manufacturing, while countries such as India, with its highly educated, English-speaking citizens, are part of the global supply chain for the service industry in areas such as telemarketing, accounting, and computer programming (Friedman 2005).

But critics of Friedman's "flat world" thesis argue that the impacts of globalization are uneven and often harmful to vulnerable groups and regions, and they generate widely different policy responses. Indeed, Hansen (2006) argues that globalization is often an "excuse" for political choices to suppress workers' wages, benefits, and job security in the name of competition with international labor forces. At a minimum, globalization means that state policymakers are faced with the need to make their communities competitive in a global arena. The traditional interjurisdictional competition for investment takes on a new dimension when the costs of production are lower outside the United States and all states are potential losers. In the absence of a national industrial policy, states have been compelled to craft their own responses to the diverse effects of globalization trends.

CHANGING ECONOMIC POLICY PROBLEMS AND DEFINITIONS

The American states are not newcomers to the practice of economic development; they have been promoting economic growth since the earliest days of the Republic. The current array of economic development policies is only the latest stage in a continuing, albeit wavering, process of state intervention in economic activities.

States as Economic Policy Activists

Originally, states built **infrastructure** (ports, roads, bridges, and so forth) as economic development projects to facilitate the movement of goods to the coast and then to other eastern cities or overseas. As competition among eastern seaports developed, the states rushed to build canals. Cumberland (1971) estimates public investment in canal building at $432 million, of which $300 million was paid by the states and $125 million by local governments.

The economic role of the states did not end with financing harbors and canals. The states contributed 48 million of the 179 million acres allocated to railroads for development of rail systems (North, Anderson, and Hill 1983). After the railroads came highways with automobiles, then air transportation, all of which involved state government financing. State economic development policy as an activity separate from transportation policy became a formal function of state government in Alabama, Florida, Maine, and North Carolina in the 1920s. In other states, economic development planning was adopted as an aspect of participation in the New Deal economic recovery programs in the 1930s and 1940s or as a way to coordinate industrial production in World War II. But, except for a few states in the South, all states had phased out their economic development agencies by the 1950s (Eisinger 1988). Since the mid-1970s, however, economic development has been a perennial issue at the state level. Throughout the 1980s and continuing through the 1990s and into the twenty-first century, governors have ranked economic development with education, highways, corrections, welfare, and health care as enduring state policy issues. Today, every state recognizes economic development as an integral part of state government.

States Define the Problems Differently

Citizens and public officials in each state understand their economic development problems differently; thus their policy solutions differ as well. Policymaking for state economic development is especially intriguing because of competing definitions of the problem. Policymakers draw on various theories of economic growth in defining and diagnosing state development problems—these theories help policymakers pinpoint what causes these problems and what the appropriate solutions might be (Rochefort and Cobb 1994). The traditional locational strategies, for example, reflect a theory of economic growth that emphasizes the importance of low costs for basic production factors—land, labor, raw materials, and capital—in attracting investment to a particular location. In the past, these efforts were often referred to as "smokestack-chasing" strategies as officials tried to persuade an industrial factory to move to their state by promising tax breaks, free land, job training programs, and other incentives to lower the cost of doing business. Today, "chip-chasing" strategies are more likely as states use similar cost-reduction incentives to attract high-tech firms to their states.

In response to global competition, a different economic model has emerged. According to this theory, state development problems stem not from high production costs but from environments not receptive to new and innovative technologies and business activities. From the perspective of this theory, the problems of economic development are not loss of investment but the possibility of relegation to the status of global backwater as innovation centers grow elsewhere. State officials persuaded by this perspective are experimenting with entrepreneurial strategies. These strategies emphasize flexibility, risk-taking, and market structuring on the part of state government to minimize barriers to innovation (Clarke and Gaile 1998).

The sheer diversity of state policy responses to these problem diagnoses is impressive. According to the *Directory of Incentives* (Miles Friedman and Partners 2006), in 2006 the states offered 1,193 separate economic development programs.[1] Some programs, such as industrial revenue bonds and tax incentives for the purchase of industrial machinery, are offered by almost all states. Most states also offer direct financial assistance to firms through direct loans, grants, loan guarantees, or other interest subsidies. Other programs are more targeted at new businesses, often entrepreneurial start-ups. For example, the New Hampshire Capital Consortium (NHCC) is a venture capital partnership organized to fund new business formations with high growth potential. Nebraska's Microenterprise Partnership Fund

---

1. Not including programs funded primarily by the federal government; basic state taxes such as income, sales, and property taxes; and subsidies offered to induce compliance with environmental regulations. Our state program data are drawn from the 2006 edition of the *Directory of Incentives*, produced by Miles Friedman, former director of the National Association of State Development Agencies (NASDA), and available online (www.milesfriedman.com/id12.html). Previous versions of this chapter used the same directory produced by NASDA in 1983, 1986, 1994, 1998, and 2002. The directory presents the state programs in a searchable format that includes a description of the incentive and its terms, conditions, and eligibility criteria. The program information is self-reported by the state economic development agencies in a standardized format. Another frequently used data source, the *Industrial Development and Site Selection Handbook* (the "Conway data"), is also based on self-reporting, but is more oriented toward industrial recruitment strategies. It slights entrepreneurial programs and reports merely the presence or absence of programs rather than providing the narrative detail included in the *Directory of Incentives*. State economic development policy efforts continue to expand. The State Business Finance and Incentives Resource Center also maintains a database at www.stateincentives.org/index.asp and claims 1,700 programs, but the data are available only to members. Finally, the *Incentives for Business: 50 State Handbook* is available for downloading from the State Capital Group at www.statecapitalgroup.org/newspublications/IncentivesforBusinesses.pdf. This source is prepared by the member law firms working to secure tax incentives and overcome regulatory hurdles.

(NMPF), in business since 1995, is one of the few statewide programs for developing and supporting "micro" loans to business start-ups and training for entrepreneurs (Nebraska Enterprise Fund, www.nebbiz.org/index.php).

ALTERNATIVE STRATEGIES FOR ECONOMIC DEVELOPMENT

To make sense of this array of state economic development policies, we classify strategies according to the three major policy strategies that characterize state economic development agendas: infrastructure strategies, locational strategies, and entrepreneurial strategies. Briefly, **infrastructure strategies** emphasize the construction and maintenance of physical infrastructure such as roads and highways to encourage and support development. **Locational strategies** seek to reduce the costs of doing business relative to other locations; they may be aimed at attracting businesses that wish to relocate, retaining those tempted by other states to relocate, or encouraging existing businesses to expand in place. By contrast, **entrepreneurial strategies** emphasize facilitating growth processes rather than influencing particular firms in their choice of location.

Each of these policy paths implies distinctive initiatives that reflect different understandings of the logic underlying economic development processes. That said, policymakers must also be pragmatists and choose orientations that are in line with the political dispositions of state voters. Although these investment and promotional strategies do not entail mutually exclusive choices, each state nevertheless presents a distinctive economic development policy profile. We compare these state policy profiles by developing a standardized index of policy attributes for each of the three policy orientations: the infrastructure investment approach, the locational incentive approach, and the entrepreneurial approach.[2]

The Infrastructure Investment Approach

Although a traditional infrastructure strategy centers on the provision of seemingly prosaic fixed assets such as highways, sewers, and waste treatment plants, the very term itself is subject to debate. Perry (1994) traces the evolving taxonomy from a focus on internal improvements in the early nineteenth century to a more inclusive and systemic view of infrastructure systems over time. In contrast with a specific focus on bridges or roads, the term *infrastructure* now signifies a concern with both the technical systems of physical facilities and the roles, particularly the economic role, these assets play in future growth and development. This link between infrastructure and development became prominent in the 1970s, when economic development needs displaced historical concerns with health, safety, and environmental needs as the primary justification for infrastructure investment

2. To construct our indexes, we coded the 5,023 program descriptions from the 1983, 1986, 1991, 1994, 1998, 2002, and 2006 editions of the *Directory of Incentives* (Friedman 2006). Our standardized index scores are the ratio of attributes to programs for each state for the infrastructure, locational, and entrepreneurial approaches. For full details on index construction and tests of validity, see Saiz (2001b).

(Felbinger 1994). In the absence of national infrastructure policy initiatives, however, there is concern that there will be continued underinvestment in public infrastructure, with potentially negative effects on development.

Federalism and Infrastructure Investment. Federal participation in infrastructure provision has been erratic and reluctant. Indeed, a recent "report card" compiled by the American Society of Civil Engineers (2009) gave the nation's infrastructure a grade of D, with drinking water, inland waterways and levees, and roads receiving a D–. But the leaders of the national government perceive most public works projects as having primarily local impacts and thus have been averse to taxing or borrowing for such purposes (Rivlin 1995). Federal capital spending for the nation's infrastructure peaked in the 1980s. Since then, there has been a precipitous decline in federal support for state and local infrastructure, with federal attention directed increasingly to highways (supported by a national fuel tax) and aviation. State and local governments now account for more than 75 percent of all public infrastructure spending, with a growing share of those expenditures by special-purpose governments such as public authorities and special districts (U.S. Congressional Budget Office 2010).

In the past, this aversion to federal action was only overcome by framing local infrastructure issues as national problems: politicians justified the 1956 National Highway Act by pointing out its defense purposes and claimed the Water Pollution Control Act of 1972 would ensure national standards for water quality. After the terrorist attacks on the United States on September 11, 2001, state governments and national policymakers began to assess state and local infrastructures in terms of their interdependencies and vulnerability to attack. Framing infrastructure issues in terms of security problems redirects attention to "critical infrastructures" rather than infrastructure systems as a whole or to only public facilities.[3] The concern about improving the condition of the nation's infrastructure is now overshadowed by a concern about its protection.

Even with these recent threats, the federal government's responsibilities in financing and regulating the development of infrastructure continue to be in question. One important exception to this stalemate was the passage of the Intermodal Surface Transportation Efficiency Act of 1991 (ISTEA), authorizing expenditures for intermodal transit—highways, mass transit, and safety and research programs—as well as nonroadway enhancements such as greenways, bike paths, and historic preservation (U.S. Department of Transportation 1993). ISTEA gave the states a prominent and flexible policy role in exchange for providing 20 percent of funding, and it brought new interests into the transportation policy arena by requiring states to share planning for new transportation

---

3. Critical infrastructure includes information, telecommunications, transportation, energy, water, health care, and financial services and the information systems that support them, with a special emphasis on emergency preparedness communications.

projects with metropolitan planning organizations (Kincaid 1992). In 2005 Congress passed SAFETEA-LU (Safe, Accountable, Flexible, Efficient, Transportation Equity Act—A Legacy for Users) and provided $286.4 billion for transportation spending, and recently this legislation was extended through the end of fiscal year 2011. SAFETEA-LU continues many earlier initiatives, but also gives states expanded tax-exempt bonding authority and encourages state infrastructure banks that provide infrastructure revolving funds using federal transportation funds to leverage additional nonfederal public and private investment. In the face of the anti-earmark movement, Congress proposes to transform some megaproject funding, such as "projects of national and regional significance," from targeted projects perceived as rife with earmarks to funds distributed to all states.

ARRA stimulus funds appear to provide another exception to the usual federal inattention. Discretionary funds allocated to the Department of Transportation led to a new competitive grant initiative potentially linking transportation and sustainability. The $75 Million Transit Investments in Greenhouse Gas and Energy Reduction (TIGGER) program targets funds to capital investments in programs that will reduce energy consumption and greenhouse gases in public transportation systems. In 2011 the second round of TIGGER awards included Chicago's plan to purchase all-electric, battery-powered buses as well as the Alaska Railroad Corporation's plan to upgrade locomotives to reduce diesel emissions. But however inventive, the $97 billion spent on infrastructure in the $787 billion ARRA budget is considered only a small down payment on the actual infrastructure needs across the country.

State Infrastructure Policy Agendas. Infrastructure investment is the most traditional state investment and development tool and a good gauge of state involvement in economic development. The traditional state agenda centers on financing infrastructure, but in recent years public investments in information highways and cultural facilities have become salient issues in addition to concerns about critical infrastructure.

State and local governments rarely debate whether infrastructure investment and maintenance are needed; rather, the central issue is how to provide and pay for them. Even when the national government pays significant infrastructure construction costs, as in the highways programs, states and localities are responsible for their maintenance. This stewardship is expensive, and it is tempting to defer maintenance. Indeed, until recently the incentives of federal capital grants for replacement and renewal activities perversely encouraged delays on maintenance until deteriorating structures became eligible for federal funds (Perry 1994).

Historically, taxes and bond financing supported most state public works activities, but the financing has become increasingly complex. Pennsylvania's governor Ed Rendell, for example, worked long and hard to rent the Pennsylvania Turnpike for seventy-five years to a group of investors for up-front cash that the state could have used to pay for other state infrastructure projects (Barnsted 2008). But the proposal ran into political opposition from state legislators, commuters, truckers, the U.S. Congress, and the Pennsylvania Turnpike Commission, which would have been disbanded under the proposed lease agreement (Barnes 2007). More recently, Ohio governor John Kasich proposed a similar idea for the Ohio Turnpike. The proposal has already generated concerns from the Northeast Ohio Areawide Coordinating Agency, whose analysis argues that the proposal would create a conflict between the contractor's profit motive and the requirement for road maintenance (Bischoff 2011).

Although transportation remains a core infrastructure issue, changes in information technology continue to reshape state infrastructure agendas. States took the lead in developing innovative information infrastructure. In 1995 North Carolina formed a public-private partnership with twenty-eight state telephone firms to build the North Carolina Information Highway, the first statewide broadband network, as part of the state's economic development strategy. Now the use of information technology for e-government is widespread, with nearly every state offering its citizens some kind of online services. Utah, a top-ranked digital state in 2010, uses online technologies for everything from issuing hunting and fishing licenses to streamlining criminal justice proceedings (Center for Digital Government 2010).

Culture is now an infrastructure issue as well. Similar to the fevered competition over professional sports teams and stadiums, there is a growing conviction that cultural facilities are essential infrastructure for the "new economy." Constructing new art museums, libraries, performing arts centers, and other specialized cultural amenities that would appeal to and attract the educated and cosmopolitan workers in a knowledge-based economy seems a sure economic development bet, even surer because of the provocative argument by Richard Florida (2002, 2005) for the "3 Ts of economic growth—technology, talent, and tolerance." Florida identified a "creative class" of professionals, artisans, computer experts, and others—mostly young, skilled and educated, highly mobile, often single, some gay, potentially entrepreneurial creative workers associated with high-growth cities. Although Florida presented a story of linkages rather than causal relations, many policymakers rushed to create incentives and amenities to attract these creative types as a means of promoting growth and increasing innovative capacities. However, as even Florida pointed out, it is not clear that policymakers can "build in" creativity, innovation, growth, and entrepreneurism by attracting certain types of workers.

But Florida's work highlighted an important new dimension of economic competition: competing for tourists, media attention, and key workers in the cultural economy. In this new competition, quality of life becomes a locational asset as important as business climate (Markusen and Gadwa 2010). Investments in cultural infrastructure could increase an area's appeal to mobile professional workers, attract new cultural industries, and have broader spillover effects on growth as well. As a result, there is an astonishing boom in the construction of stunning new buildings such as the Denver Art Museum (2006). But as state budgets dwindle, state-designated cultural districts are emerging as a new strategy. Maryland, for example, is designating arts and entertainment districts throughout the state that are eligible for tax incentives. Rhode Island has gone one step further with its tax-free arts districts: artists who live and work in designated districts are not charged sales tax on their work and do not pay state income tax.

To gain a more precise sense of state infrastructure policy agendas, we examined state programs that have offered tax breaks to companies for transportation and communication equipment or incentives to communities to develop infrastructure. In 1983 no state offered an infrastructure assistance program, but by 1991 there were twenty-five programs. By 2002 the states were collectively offering eighty infrastructure programs, and by 2006 six more programs had been added. Some states link transportation funding to other policy goals—for example, New York's Transportation Capital Assistance Program provides working capital loans to small business enterprises and New York State–certified minority and women-owned programs that have transportation-related construction contracts or subcontracts with the State's Department of Transportation. Maryland ties infrastructure funding to the state's overall planning strategy through "One Maryland"—the state's Smart Growth Economic Development Infrastructure Fund. The program is designed to preserve natural resources and reduce infrastructure costs by targeting funding to established communities and locally designated growth areas. The program provides incentives for targeted distressed communities to develop collaborative plans that encourage compact building and community design that will foster walkable communities and preserve open space, farmland, and critical environmental areas (Maryland Department of Business and Economic Development 2004).

Our index of state infrastructure programs (Table 16-1) measures the commitment of states to infrastructure policies in relation to their overall economic development policy effort—the higher the score, the greater a state's commitment to infrastructure relative to its other economic development programs. In 2006 there was a slight decrease in infrastructure programs as a share of overall economic development effort. Some states such as Indiana, New Jersey, and Texas increased their efforts in this area, while a few others such as Montana, South Carolina, Tennessee, and West Virginia decreased their offerings relative to other economic development programs. The magnitude of the index scores has remained steady since 1983, because even though the number of programs for transportation or infrastructure incentives adopted by the states continues to increase, the number remains small in relation to the total number of economic development programs the states offer.

The Locational Incentive Approach

Locational economic development strategies aim at improving a community's ability to compete with other locations for industry, jobs, and economic growth.

Table 16-1 Infrastructure Economic Development Policy Indexes, Selected Years, 1983–2006

State	1983	1986	1991	1994	1998	2002	2006
Alabama	0.00	0.00	0.08	0.12	0.30	0.24	0.19
Alaska	0.00	0.00	0.00	0.00	0.11	0.11	0.15
Arizona	0.00	0.00	0.00	0.00	0.00	0.10	0.10
Arkansas	0.00	0.00	0.00	0.04	0.05	0.00	0.00
California	0.22	0.20	0.25	0.25	0.18	0.06	0.06
Colorado	0.11	0.14	0.08	0.08	0.10	0.10	0.11
Connecticut	0.00	0.00	0.00	0.00	0.00	0.00	0.00
Delaware	0.00	0.00	0.00	0.00	0.00	0.00	0.00
Florida	0.00	0.00	0.11	0.05	0.13	0.22	0.24
Georgia	0.00	0.00	0.00	0.04	0.00	0.00	0.19
Hawaii	0.08	0.07	0.07	0.14	0.10	0.00	0.00
Idaho	0.00	0.00	0.00	0.00	0.00	0.00	0.00
Illinois	0.00	0.00	0.08	0.04	0.14	0.14	0.14
Indiana	0.19	0.15	0.16	0.16	0.08	0.05	0.10
Iowa	0.00	0.00	0.00	0.00	0.05	0.05	0.05
Kansas	0.00	0.00	0.08	0.12	0.08	0.08	0.07
Kentucky	0.20	0.33	0.27	0.27	0.16	0.09	0.10
Louisiana	0.00	0.00	0.00	0.00	0.04	0.03	0.02
Maine	0.00	0.00	0.00	0.13	0.09	0.18	0.09
Maryland	0.00	0.00	0.00	0.00	0.00	0.04	0.04
Massachusetts	0.00	0.00	0.00	0.00	0.00	0.00	0.00
Michigan	0.07	0.06	0.13	0.20	0.27	0.27	0.20
Minnesota	0.15	0.06	0.10	0.10	0.22	0.22	0.14
Mississippi	0.00	0.00	0.08	0.12	0.12	0.19	0.19
Missouri	0.00	0.17	0.13	0.07	0.06	0.10	0.10
Montana	0.13	0.05	0.05	0.00	0.14	0.47	0.17
Nebraska	0.00	0.00	0.00	0.00	0.00	0.00	0.00
Nevada	0.00	0.00	0.00	0.00	0.00	0.00	0.00
New Hampshire	0.29	0.14	0.40	0.11	0.18	0.09	0.09
New Jersey	0.27	0.13	0.14	0.09	0.11	0.09	0.12
New Mexico	0.00	0.00	0.11	0.08	0.17	0.16	0.16
New York	0.06	0.06	0.08	0.12	0.06	0.05	0.05
North Carolina	0.00	0.00	0.00	0.00	0.00	0.05	0.05
North Dakota	0.00	0.00	0.00	0.00	0.00	0.00	0.00
Ohio	0.00	0.00	0.00	0.14	0.14	0.15	0.15
Oklahoma	0.00	0.00	0.00	0.00	0.00	0.00	0.05
Oregon	0.43	0.33	0.27	0.00	0.17	0.25	0.26
Pennsylvania	0.17	0.23	0.27	0.32	0.33	0.17	0.18
Rhode Island	0.10	0.07	0.08	0.08	0.04	0.07	0.07
South Carolina	0.13	0.09	0.06	0.30	0.33	0.13	0.06
South Dakota	0.00	0.00	0.00	0.00	0.00	0.00	0.00
Tennessee	0.30	0.33	0.40	0.36	0.29	0.53	0.27
Texas	0.40	0.40	0.08	0.14	0.19	0.10	0.13
Utah	0.33	0.25	0.11	0.00	0.00	0.10	0.10
Vermont	0.33	0.00	0.00	0.00	0.00	0.00	0.00
Virginia	0.00	0.00	0.05	0.00	0.00	0.00	0.00
Washington	0.20	0.20	0.20	0.11	0.24	0.22	0.22
West Virginia	0.00	0.00	0.00	0.00	0.13	0.12	0.05
Wisconsin	0.14	0.11	0.07	0.08	0.09	0.08	0.08
Wyoming	0.00	0.00	0.00	0.00	0.00	0.00	0.25
U.S. mean	0.09	0.07	0.08	0.08	0.10	0.10	0.10

SOURCES: Computed from program descriptions in National Association of State Development Agencies, *Directory of Incentives for Business Investment and Development in the United States: A State-by-State Guide* (Washington, D.C.: NASDA, 1983, 1986, 1991, 1994, 1998, and 2002), and Miles Friedman and Partners LLC, *Directory of Incentives* (2006), www.milesfriedman.com/id12.html.

NOTE: The method of computing the policy indexes is described in Martin Saiz, "Using Program Attributes to Measure and Evaluate State Economic Development Activism," *Economic Development Quarterly* 15 (2001): 45–57.

This policy orientation is grounded in economic location theory, which suggests that, other things being equal, firms will seek those locations where the combined costs of land, labor, capital, energy, and transportation are minimal (Weber 1984). Thus the state seeking a competitive advantage over other states must create an advantageous price structure for these "production factors," thereby creating a comparative locational advantage.

Tools commonly used in making locations more attractive to investors include low-interest financing (frequently offered in the form of industrial revenue bonds), tax credits, abatements, deferments and exemptions, subsidized employee training, and assistance with site selection and preparation (Fosler 1988). The rubric of locational economic development policy also includes the notion of creating a "positive business climate" or a pro-business atmosphere. These are vague concepts, but the associated policies often include low taxes and regulatory policies—such as right-to-work laws and relaxed environmental legislation—designed to keep production costs low (Plaut and Pluta 1983).

The Boeing Company's many megadeals exemplify how firms can play states against each other over locational incentives. When Boeing announced in 2001 that it was considering relocating its headquarters from Seattle to Chicago, Dallas, or Denver, state and local boosters put together incentive packages to lure Boeing's five hundred employees. Chicago and Illinois won the competition with a $63 million offer that included $41 million in state tax credits; ten years of income tax grants for Boeing's employees; $20 million in job training, technology, and capital improvements; and $2 million in property tax abatements and improvements to Midway Airport's hangars. The deal illustrates a classic zero-sum game: 80 percent of the jobs were transfers, few new jobs were created, and Chicago gained at Seattle's expense (Lyne 2002). Boeing repeated this strategy in 2003 by starting a bidding war between twenty-two states when it launched the production of its 7E7 Dreamliner. In exchange for Boeing's jobs, the winning bidder would furnish the company with cheap land, low taxes, quality schools, workers with low absentee rates, and "local community and government support for manufacturing business" (Frank 2004, 87). The "winner" was the Kansas state legislature, which extended $500 million in loans to refurbish Boeing's Wichita facility. Other states had bid more, but Kansas allowed the company to pay the interest on its bonds by diverting the payroll taxes paid by its *existing* workers (Frank 2004, 87). One of the "losers" in the 7E7 competition, South Carolina, recently offered an incentive package to Boeing worth more than $900 million. According to an analysis by the Charleston *Post and Courier*, for every dollar Boeing promises to invest, the state is promising more than $1.25 in cash or future tax breaks (Stech and Slade 2010). If there is any doubt about the primary purpose of these policies, even the Boeing Company's CEO said, "We consider it nothing more than lowering the cost of doing business" (Wallace 2004).

Another corporate giant, Wal-Mart, is the beneficiary of over a billion dollars in state and local subsidies; as a matter of practice, the company requests subsidies for a third of its stores and distribution centers, in amounts reaching more than $40 million per project (Mattera and Purinton 2004). The green economy can also make expensive demands: Skypoint Solar, a start-up firm making solar power cells in Vermont, eventually persuaded the state to provide subsidies and loans covering over half the $50 million needed for the project (www.goodjobsfirst.org/states/ vermont). And even the film and television entertainment industries are increasingly deciding on filming locations in terms of which states offer them the biggest tax breaks (Christopherson and Rightor 2010).

Attributes of Locational Policy Orientations. We have developed an index for assessing the degree to which states pursue a locational economic development approach by measuring the extent to which their policies reflect key attributes of the locational orientation. We created our index by identifying program characteristics aimed at reducing direct costs by offering financial subsidies to business or indirectly reducing costs to business by offering tax relief or accelerated depreciation on capital expenditures. Such policies are administratively simple to operate, and because they represent forgone revenues, they do not require legislators to appropriate current funds to provide benefits to business. We did not include programs that target specific areas or economic sectors (other than manufacturing)— only nontargeted, administratively passive programs that require little initiative on the part of a government agency to implement. Thus the attributes of locational economic development policies show an acceptance of the prevailing economic forces. Other than attempting to lower costs within the state, the economic role of state governments remains subordinate to private sector decisions (Eisinger 1988; Fosler 1988).

Changes in Locational Orientations. The locational policy index just described measures the degree to which state governments have adopted policies with locational attributes in relation to their state's overall economic development policy effort. Thus states with higher index scores (as shown in Table 16-2) demonstrate a greater commitment to a locational policy orientation than do states with lower scores. The average locational index score (produced with data going back to 1983) has declined consistently since we began calculating the index. However, the most recent average score, calculated from programs adopted between 2002 and 2006, has increased, indicating a mild resurgence of policies aimed at reducing costs to business. South Carolina and Idaho consistently emphasize locational policy orientations, whereas Georgia, Kentucky, and Nevada have emerged in the last few years as states that give priority to locational strategies.

In past years, the less densely populated, less urbanized southern and border states with a history of adopting locational policies were the most prominent users of this strategy. Since 2002, however, a distinctive regional pattern of locational policy orientations has been evident, featuring the south-central states of Alabama, Arkansas, Kentucky, Louisiana, Mississippi, Oklahoma, Tennessee, and Texas (see Figure 16-1). And yet these strategies may not be the smokestack-chasing efforts of

Table 16-2 Locational Economic Development Policy Indexes, Selected Years, 1983–2006

State	1983	1986	1991	1994	1998	2002	2006
Alabama	2.40	2.40	2.15	1.82	1.40	1.36	1.43
Alaska	2.25	2.75	1.36	1.11	0.84	1.16	1.05
Arizona	2.50	2.67	2.67	2.00	1.64	1.20	1.80
Arkansas	2.50	2.33	1.56	1.19	1.58	1.56	1.62
California	1.67	1.70	1.58	1.58	1.00	1.12	1.19
Colorado	2.56	2.43	1.92	1.83	1.90	1.40	1.56
Connecticut	2.00	1.88	1.65	1.37	1.66	1.58	1.69
Delaware	2.00	2.13	1.46	2.09	1.56	1.53	1.35
Florida	2.27	2.10	1.47	1.05	1.08	1.09	1.14
Georgia	2.33	1.29	1.29	1.50	1.82	2.00	1.61
Hawaii	2.17	2.14	1.93	1.79	1.60	1.67	1.73
Idaho	2.50	2.43	2.43	2.22	2.00	1.57	2.08
Illinois	2.30	1.89	1.31	1.38	0.81	0.76	0.80
Indiana	1.88	1.80	1.79	1.74	1.04	0.85	0.90
Iowa	2.10	2.00	1.56	1.45	1.10	1.05	1.10
Kansas	2.50	1.91	1.25	1.64	1.31	1.52	1.60
Kentucky	1.60	2.00	1.91	2.00	1.53	1.96	1.86
Louisiana	1.83	1.93	1.53	1.67	1.58	1.71	1.55
Maine	1.85	1.71	1.92	1.63	1.68	1.68	1.68
Maryland	1.57	1.63	1.42	1.20	1.26	1.00	0.96
Massachusetts	1.77	1.79	1.38	1.45	1.29	1.07	1.07
Michigan	2.21	1.56	1.33	1.65	1.33	1.09	1.30
Minnesota	1.46	1.76	0.90	0.85	0.56	0.89	0.64
Mississippi	1.83	1.83	1.92	1.77	1.38	1.37	1.56
Missouri	2.00	1.54	1.40	1.46	1.23	1.03	1.03
Montana	2.25	1.53	1.60	1.39	1.36	1.67	1.67
Nebraska	2.00	1.63	1.73	1.73	1.85	1.79	1.57
Nevada	2.50	1.17	1.17	1.22	1.89	1.75	1.75
New Hampshire	2.43	2.43	2.60	1.21	0.55	0.82	0.82
New Jersey	1.91	1.63	1.36	1.30	0.89	0.76	0.79
New Mexico	1.80	2.20	2.00	1.38	1.71	1.40	1.56
New York	2.13	1.72	1.19	1.12	1.19	1.28	1.32
North Carolina	2.20	1.22	1.50	1.36	1.56	1.50	1.58
North Dakota	1.91	2.00	1.69	1.56	0.90	0.95	1.63
Ohio	1.69	1.50	1.46	1.71	1.33	1.24	1.32
Oklahoma	2.29	2.22	2.10	1.92	1.71	1.71	1.87
Oregon	1.86	1.44	1.36	1.35	1.28	1.10	1.05
Pennsylvania	1.67	1.27	1.05	1.32	1.21	1.00	0.98
Rhode Island	2.10	1.79	2.00	2.00	1.61	1.55	1.68
South Carolina	2.13	2.09	2.39	2.09	2.60	2.31	2.28
South Dakota	2.75	2.20	2.13	1.89	2.00	1.45	0.67
Tennessee	2.10	2.33	2.30	2.36	1.53	1.47	1.47
Texas	1.60	1.60	1.83	1.24	0.94	1.30	1.13
Utah	2.67	2.75	1.67	1.78	1.42	0.90	0.90
Vermont	2.00	1.75	1.71	1.71	1.58	1.25	1.08
Virginia	2.13	1.79	1.60	1.57	1.28	1.41	1.33
Washington	2.40	2.40	1.80	1.68	1.10	1.13	1.13
West Virginia	2.00	2.00	2.06	1.54	1.60	1.35	1.48
Wisconsin	1.86	1.44	1.27	1.08	0.78	0.77	0.77
Wyoming	2.75	1.83	2.00	1.67	1.33	1.00	1.00
U.S. mean	2.10	1.91	1.69	1.57	1.39	1.32	1.34

SOURCES: Computed from program descriptions in National Association of State Development Agencies, *Directory of Incentives for Business Investment and Development in the United States: A State-by-State Guide* (Washington, D.C.: NASDA, 1983, 1986, 1991, 1994, 1998, and 2002), and Miles Friedman and Partners LLC, *Directory of Incentives* (2006), www.milesfriedman.com/id12.html.

NOTE: The method of computing the policy indexes is described in Martin Saiz, "Using Program Attributes to Measure and Evaluate State Economic Development Activism," *Economic Development Quarterly* 15 (2001): 45–57.

Figure 16-1   2006 Locational Economic Development Policy Index

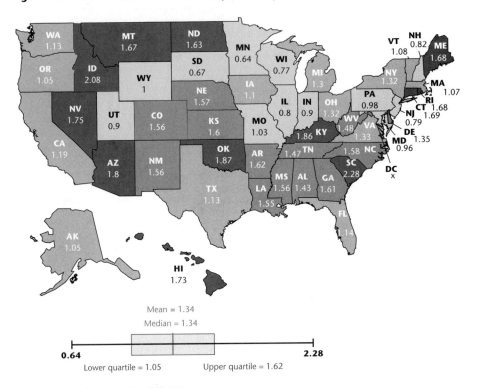

SOURCE: Authors' calculations from Table 16.2.

the past. For example, the North Carolina/Dell Computer tax subsidy described earlier narrowly targeted a growing computer industry; North Carolina had resisted the incentives game for years and only resumed bidding for business after it appeared to be losing jobs to neighboring states.

Entrepreneurial Economic Development Policy Approaches

Entrepreneurial policies are grounded in a theoretical model of economic development processes that emphasizes the wealth-generating capacities of innovative activities. Rather than attempting to influence business locational decisions, state policymakers use public resources and authority to encourage new markets and economic ventures. This process sometimes requires public officials to act like business entrepreneurs by taking risks and creating opportunities in the hope of generating a more vibrant state economy (Eisinger 1988; Clarke and Gaile 1998).

These entrepreneurial policies are fairly recent additions to the states' economic development policy arsenal, most having been adopted during and after the recession of the early 1980s (Sherman, Wallace, and Pitney 1995). The 2008 recession similarly creates an incentive to not just restart but transform state economies by both budget cutting and investing (Brookings Institution 2011). This entrepreneurial approach generates new roles for state governments, particularly a more central role in efforts to create jobs and facilitate growth processes (Osborne 1988, 249). Leadership, information, strategic planning, public-private partnerships, university-industry partnerships, and policy brokering become the new tools of state economic development (Bradshaw and Blakely 1999). Three examples illustrate this policy orientation:

- E Ink, a Cambridge, Massachusetts–based developer of the electronic paper displays in Amazon's Kindle and the Sony Reader, received a $1 million loan from the state's Emerging Technology Fund (ETF) to expand its manufacturing facility and purchase new equipment. This project is typical of those initiated by the fund in that it consists of loans and loan guarantees—over $37 million to twenty-two firms by June 2010—to leverage private debt for firms specializing in research and development (MassDevelopment 2010).
- The Kansas Economic Growth Act (KEGA), adopted in 2004, provides over $500 million over a period of 10–12 years for investments in bioscience. The funds are from tax increments generated by additional employment in bioscience and research institutions. A new Kansas Bioscience Authority uses incentives to encourage university-industry bioscience collaboration, including a national Collaborative Biosecurity Research Initiative (Mayer 2010).
- The Energy Policy Division of the Indiana Department of Commerce offers grants to businesses and other institutions to acquire alternative fuel vehicles and to make use of alternative transportation fuels, especially biofuels derived from agricultural products and by-products. On the supply side, the state makes grants through its Alternative Power and Energy Grant program to the state's public, nonprofit, commercial, industrial, and agricultural sectors for the purchase and installation of alternative energy systems.

Although economic development processes are driven primarily by private sector decisions, state government initiatives provide critical support. Creating an entrepreneurial "climate" in a state can promote new economic activity, often through strategic clustering and targeting of existing programs (Goetz and Freshwater 2001; Atkinson and Andes 2010). Policy also may be guided by new public-private institutions. These new organizations, generally outside the governmental arena and staffed by development professionals, provide a means of coordinating investment decisions. They often have independent financing authority and can leverage private sector investments with public funds in ways not available to state agencies. For example, quasi-public state organizations may supply seed money to stimulate new business formation or to fund the research needed to bring technological innovations to the market. These state organizational innovations allow state governments to be more flexible and versatile than bureaucratic structures normally permit.

Attributes of Entrepreneurial Economic Development Orientations. Several core attributes of entrepreneurial economic development programs distinguish them from more conventional locational economic development approaches. First are the programmatic features that target entrepreneurs by limiting incentives to high-technology and small businesses or to firms at the high-risk (start-up, new product, technology transfer, and basic research) stages of development. Second are programs that target growth-producing economic sectors, identified by Sternberg (1987, 159) as banking, education, and communications. Third, based on observations by Bowman (1987), are attributes of programs that attempt to improve the capacity of a firm or individual to take advantage of, or adjust to, new production processes. Customized job training, technical or entrepreneurial assistance for individual firms, business incubators, and programs aimed at the rehabilitation of plants (or the provision of new infrastructure) to take advantage of new technologies, for example, reflect these attributes. And fourth are features of programs that work through public-private partnerships, such as local or state development (and credit) corporations, that expand financial opportunities by leveraging private capital with public dollars, thereby increasing the pool of local investment funds (Saiz 2001b).

Changes in Entrepreneurial Orientations. The index score reflects the degree to which state governments have adopted policies with entrepreneurial attributes in relation to their overall economic development policy effort. Again, the higher the index value, the greater is the state's reliance on this approach. As shown in Table 16-3, the trend toward adoption of policies with more entrepreneurial attributes has continued since 2002. Between 1983 and 2006, the average index score increased considerably, and yet the rate of increase has slowed in recent years. Still, Florida,[4] Massachusetts, Minnesota, New Hampshire, New Jersey, New York, and Wisconsin are placing the greatest emphasis on entrepreneurial approaches (see Figure 16-2). These states ranked high in our previous analyses and maintained their positions by consistently adding programs with these characteristics. But North Carolina, Ohio, and Pennsylvania—entrepreneurial policy leaders in the 1980s and 1990s—seem to be moderating their approaches. Although our previous analysis of entrepreneurial policy scores showed no regional pattern, one has emerged since 2002. The Mid-Atlantic states of New Jersey, New York, and Pennsylvania, and the midwestern states of Illinois, Indiana, Michigan, Minnesota, and Wisconsin are clusters of states with more or less clear entrepreneurial orientations.

4. Florida also ranked high on the infrastructure policy index, indicating that the three policy indexes measure policy orientation across three orientations rather than along a single dimension. Thus Florida can emphasize entrepreneurial policies relative to other states and still rank high on infrastructure policies.

Table 16-3 Entrepreneurial Economic Development Policy Indexes, Selected Years, 1983–2006

State	1983	1986	1991	1994	1998	2002	2006
Alabama	0.30	0.30	0.62	0.65	1.15	1.52	1.52
Alaska	1.00	1.25	1.57	1.56	1.37	1.63	1.60
Arizona	0.00	0.00	0.00	0.45	1.00	1.20	1.20
Arkansas	0.30	0.33	1.88	2.65	1.53	1.76	1.57
California	0.56	0.50	0.58	0.58	1.29	1.53	1.63
Colorado	0.11	0.14	0.50	0.42	0.60	0.90	0.67
Connecticut	0.93	0.76	0.90	1.05	1.50	1.53	1.66
Delaware	0.40	0.50	1.08	0.45	1.17	1.67	1.50
Florida	0.64	0.80	1.42	2.14	1.92	2.35	2.38
Georgia	0.50	1.86	1.59	1.31	1.12	1.32	1.19
Hawaii	0.25	0.21	0.50	0.71	1.10	1.40	1.40
Idaho	0.38	0.14	0.14	0.22	1.00	1.71	1.15
Illinois	0.50	0.61	1.08	1.08	1.75	2.04	2.00
Indiana	0.56	0.70	0.89	0.84	1.92	1.79	1.83
Iowa	0.30	0.50	0.78	0.75	1.48	1.75	1.95
Kansas	0.38	0.45	1.33	1.24	1.31	1.68	1.19
Kentucky	1.10	1.33	1.18	1.27	1.32	1.48	1.48
Louisiana	0.50	0.53	0.68	1.00	1.46	1.74	1.75
Maine	0.77	0.86	0.77	0.81	1.23	1.18	1.18
Maryland	1.14	1.00	0.96	1.24	1.33	1.92	2.12
Massachusetts	1.31	1.36	1.76	2.00	1.71	2.20	2.20
Michigan	0.71	1.00	1.17	1.25	1.13	1.55	1.50
Minnesota	1.00	0.65	1.95	2.05	1.56	2.22	2.29
Mississippi	0.08	0.50	0.58	0.62	1.15	1.15	1.26
Missouri	0.58	1.33	1.60	1.54	1.81	2.06	2.13
Montana	0.38	1.05	1.20	1.43	1.86	1.60	1.67
Nebraska	0.38	0.63	1.00	1.00	1.00	1.14	3.00
Nevada	0.00	0.92	0.92	0.78	1.33	1.50	2.63
New Hampshire	0.57	0.57	0.40	2.05	2.18	3.00	3.00
New Jersey	0.73	0.81	1.73	1.76	2.00	2.47	2.59
New Mexico	0.60	0.40	0.22	0.85	1.00	1.52	1.52
New York	0.69	1.17	1.89	1.79	2.19	2.15	2.20
North Carolina	0.40	2.44	2.20	2.09	1.44	1.70	1.37
North Dakota	0.82	0.83	1.13	1.06	2.15	2.55	2.21
Ohio	1.19	1.50	1.54	1.21	1.57	1.62	1.65
Oklahoma	0.29	0.33	0.30	0.92	1.33	1.57	1.65
Oregon	1.00	1.44	1.55	1.59	1.78	1.70	1.74
Pennsylvania	0.92	1.91	1.91	1.36	1.63	1.77	2.04
Rhode Island	0.30	0.93	0.69	0.69	1.25	1.28	1.21
South Carolina	0.38	0.64	0.56	0.57	0.73	0.69	1.03
South Dakota	0.25	0.40	0.38	0.56	0.78	1.36	2.00
Tennessee	0.80	0.44	0.40	0.36	1.71	1.80	1.80
Texas	0.60	0.60	0.58	0.95	1.69	1.85	1.93
Utah	0.67	0.25	1.11	1.11	1.67	2.00	2.00
Vermont	1.00	1.08	1.29	1.36	1.58	1.67	1.67
Virginia	0.63	0.79	0.75	1.17	0.89	1.91	1.93
Washington	0.20	0.40	0.70	1.53	1.76	2.00	2.09
West Virginia	0.63	0.73	0.82	1.46	1.60	1.94	2.14
Wisconsin	1.00	1.22	1.20	1.44	1.61	2.21	2.26
Wyoming	0.00	0.83	0.50	1.00	2.00	1.33	1.25
U.S. mean	0.57	0.80	1.01	1.16	1.45	1.71	1.78

SOURCES: Computed from program descriptions in National Association of State Development Agencies, *Directory of Incentives for Business Investment and Development in the United States: A State-by-State Guide* (Washington, D.C.: NASDA, 1983, 1986, 1991, 1994, 1998, and 2002), and Miles Friedman and Partners LLC, *Directory of Incentives* (2006), www.milesfriedman.com/id12.html.

NOTE: The method of computing policy indexes is described in Martin Saiz, "Using Program Attributes to Measure and Evaluate State Economic Development Activism," *Economic Development Quarterly* 15 (2001): 45–57.

Figure 16-2   2006 Entrepreneurial Economic Development Policy

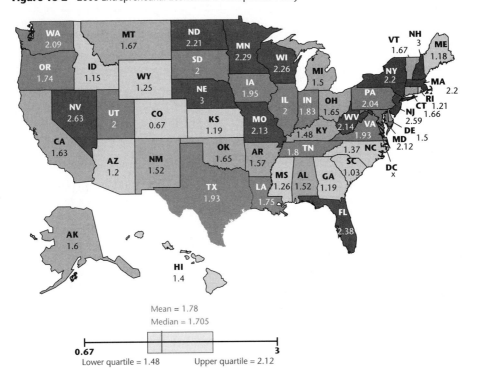

Mean = 1.78
Median = 1.705

0.67   3
Lower quartile = 1.48   Upper quartile = 2.12

SOURCE: Authors' calculations from Table 16.3.

WHY DO STATES ADOPT DIFFERENT STRATEGIES?

The rising levels of state economic development activism make sense, especially in view of the incentives embedded in decentralized federalism structures, but the reasons why states favor one orientation rather than another are less clear. The logic of competitive federalism may be sufficient for explaining conventional cost-reduction strategies; the use of state authority to shape market structures, create public-private partnerships, or pursue strategies involving higher-risk and longer-term investments is less explicable.

Saiz (2001a) used the indexes just described as indicators in a pooled time series analysis to predict the adoption of state economic development strategies between 1983 and 1994. His analysis supports the hypothesis that a state's choice of state economic development policies is largely determined by the degree to which its neighbors pursue locational approaches, other factors held constant.[5] Perhaps

5. The effect of the policy adopted by a state's neighbor is large and robust: a one-unit increase in the average locational score of a state's neighbors increases the state's locational strategy score by 0.91—a considerable impact given that the average locational score for all states over the ten-year period is only 1.75.

more notable is the negative relationship between the locational scores of a state's neighbors and the state's efforts to pursue an entrepreneurial strategy.[6] Here, the data suggest that not only does the adoption of locational strategies increase the likelihood that one's neighbors will pursue a locational approach (recall the North Carolina case), but also such policy behavior decreases the likelihood that bordering states will seek entrepreneurial strategies. Thus the decline of policies with locational, cost-reduction attributes throughout the Mid-Atlantic and midwestern regions and the emergence of entrepreneurial orientations over the last twenty years created a relatively safe haven for such policies.

Other factors also appear to encourage the adoption of entrepreneurial policies: strong governors, professional legislatures, robust labor and business organizations, competitive political environments, and historical policy legacies that created enduring administrative capacities (Jenkins, Leicht, and Wendt 2006). The implication is that to generate new wealth, states need strong organizational and administrative capabilities and an environment conducive to policy innovation. At the same time, the resurgence of locational policies aimed at luring jobs by reducing business costs relative to other states is consistent with reports of a resurgence of the southern "Moonlight and Magnolias" strategy of economic development on the heels of the Republican governorships (Kilgore 2011).

THE POLICY EFFECTIVENESS DEBATE

But do state economic development policies make a difference? This simple **policy effectiveness** question is a hard one to answer because experts disagree on what success should look like, how to measure it, and how to sort out the effects of public policies from other changes also affecting state economic development. Many studies conclude that state and local incentives are still too small to matter much. Contrary to what public officials believe, scholars find that, at best, "incentives work about 10 percent of the time and are simply a waste of money the other 90 percent" (Peters and Fisher 2004, 32). After reviewing 122 studies published in academic journals between 1962 and 2003, Lynch (2004) concludes that there is not much basis to support either tax cuts or other policy incentives as the best means to increase jobs or economic growth. Even economic development officials admit they see only a weak relation between their efforts and economic improvement. Because of the political context and uncertainty about the effectiveness of their tools, policymakers are tempted, in Rubin's words (1988), to "shoot anything that flies; claim anything that falls."

Do tax breaks matter? It seems almost self-evident that lower taxes should stimulate an economy, but how taxes matter is not always clear. Lynch (2004) finds that state and local taxes are not typically a significant cost of doing business.

6. In this case, a one-unit increase in the average locational scores of a state's neighbors decreases the state's entrepreneurial policy efforts by 0.82.

Until recently, survey work showed that surprisingly few employers mentioned taxes or other inducements as the primary reasons for choosing to invest (Bridges 1965). Answering this basic question is complicated because corporate managers have every reason to overstate the importance of economic development incentives in order to encourage officials to sweeten the deal (Donahue 1997). The importance of tax incentives probably varies by sector: for example, in relatively technology-intensive sectors, they appear to be an increasingly important cost factor (Atkinson 2007).

Is it possible to measure the effects of policy strategies? Here is where it becomes clear that little consensus exists on what a successful economic development policy means. Are investigators looking for changes in general aggregate indicators such as employment, income, and capital investment, or should they seek particular measures such as the movement, expansion, or creation of firms and jobs? If the latter, many environmentalists, for example, question the use of job growth as a measure of economic well-being because it is accompanied by more congestion and pollution. It is better to focus on increased per capita income as an indicator, they would argue, as does the National Governors Association (Atkinson and Andes 2010). And in a knowledge economy, should the focus actually be on innovation processes that contribute to economic development (Hall 2007; Atkinson and Andes 2010)?

Are some types of policies more effective than others? Even if scholars could agree on what a successful economic development policy should do, it is very difficult to determine whether the effects are actually caused by the policy adopted or some other factors affecting the state economy independent of the policy strategy. And, as we demonstrated earlier, states combine several economic development approaches in making policy. Some approaches may be more effective than others, but the combined effect obscures the contribution of any particular policy.

Here again, the dominant view is that the use of public funds to attract large industrial facilities is not effective (Peirce 1994; Lee 2004). And although they are politically popular—forty-five states have them—there is little evidence that job creation tax credits generate new jobs effectively and efficiently (Atkinson and Andes 2010). So far, there are no adequate state-level measures of the development impacts of some of the most vital factors shaping state economies—such as tourism, gambling, and lotteries (but see Chapter 10). States subsidizing film and television production media in a bid to enhance their "creative economy" regularly invest two to five times more in tax credits for those industries than in their own statewide arts programs. But there is scant evidence that the returns on these incentives cover the costs, much less generate new creative economies (Christopherson and Rightor 2010).

But some policies do seem to make a difference. Investments in state telecommunication infrastructure appear to have a positive impact on service sector productivity, although it depends on how efficient that infrastructure is (Yilmaz and Dinc 2002). An analysis by Saiz (2001b) shows a statistically significant relationship between the adoption of entrepreneurial economic development strategies and higher manufacturing employment. A further boost for entrepreneurial approaches is Langer's finding (2001) that states adopting more entrepreneurial policies have more equitable distributions of income than states pursuing the more traditional subsidy strategies. Although equally difficult to measure (Hall 2009), investment in innovation makes a difference. When states provide R&D tax credits to promote innovation, Wu (2005, 2008) finds that every dollar in tax credit given generates a dollar in private R&D investment as well as increases in high-tech sector establishments in a state.

Sometimes, it seems that the sheer levels of economic development policy activity or expenditures make a difference. Higher general investment in economic development programs, for example, seems to boost manufacturing employment growth (de Bartolome and Speigel 1995; Koropeckyj 1997). By contrast, in his study of economic development policy activism in four states, Brace (1993) shows a negative relationship between high policy usage and income growth. These divergent findings are useful reminders that what scholars decide to measure influences their assessments. It is also true that quick benefits are unlikely and that the potential beneficiaries of these policies must be taken into account in any assessment.

Does evidence matter? Even in the absence of compelling evidence of policy effectiveness, state policymakers—probably responding to political rather than economic logic—continue to support economic development agencies and programs (Brace 2002). Agency budgets climbed rapidly in the 1980s, displaying a near fivefold increase in constant dollars by 1990. During this time, real expenditure growth averaged more than 50 percent a year. The rate of growth slowed in the early 1990s, but growth had returned robustly by the end of the decade. Steady budget increases since 1992, with only a slight dip since the 2008 recession, signal the durability of economic development appropriations even in the face of widespread state budget reductions.

THE NEW POLITICS OF STATE ECONOMIC DEVELOPMENT POLICIES

In a paradoxical turn of events, states and regions are the new arenas for global competition. As firms scan the globe for the locations best fitting their needs, their menu of possible locations is less likely to be defined by national boundaries and more likely to reflect specific configurations of features and amenities sought by each firm. California's strongest competitors for investment, for example, may be provinces or regions in Europe or Latin America rather than other states in the United States. Although states now compete beyond state or national boundaries, they are increasingly thinking in regional terms. It was a strikingly consistent theme among the new crop of governors taking office in 2011 in the face of fiscal crisis and political turmoil. In Michigan, Rick Snyder began his first term in office by declaring the state's regions the drivers of state economic development policy. One of Colorado governor John W. Hickenlooper's first acts was to launch a bottom-up initiative in which all sixty-four counties would develop economic development plans that would then be "rolled up" into fourteen regional plans comprising the state's new economic development strategy. Also championing a bottom-up strategy, New York's Andrew Cuomo established ten regional economic development councils shortly after taking office. Although the nation's decentralized federal structure historically encouraged arms race–type bidding wars among and within the states, states now seek regional cooperation in order to compete globally.

Many states continue to emphasize the need to be competitive with other states in attracting firms and investment with locational incentives. Given the decentralized federal system, it is hard to imagine this interstate competition disappearing completely. Even in the face of recession, few states seem willing to curb business tax subsidy programs to recoup lost tax revenues, and fewer still are willing to raise taxes to improve their budget picture (Maynard 2010). But it is also true that the changing nature of global competition and the demands of the new economy are prompting more attention to state incentives that support innovation and growth processes rather than subsidies for specific firms. Oregon's Innovate Collaborate Oregon program (http://icoregon.net/) exemplifies fledgling state efforts to harvest and link innovative technologies throughout state higher education (Mayer 2010). By 2009 twenty states—with Montana in the lead—had adopted at least two of the four policy strategies (codified microenterprise priority, sufficient funding, stable funding, and training) considered essential for strong state support of microenterprises (Corporation for Enterprise Development 2010). In addition to microenterprise loans, Nebraska also provides a $10,000 lifetime tax credit to microbusiness owners located in distressed geographic areas that make a "new investment or employment in the microbusiness." In contrast to the high-tech view of innovation, 76 percent of businesses that received the credit (as of 2007) were in the agricultural industry, and only 2 percent were in the service industry (Corporation for Enterprise Development 2010). Thus new types of entrepreneurial approaches continue to emerge, even as some states turn again to the more traditional locational strategies.

In an era in which technological changes radically alter the costs of production as well as the costs of overcoming distance, states remain responsible for infrastructure investments. In contrast with the segmented infrastructure programs of the past, new state policies emphasize integration of infrastructure systems, information technologies, competition rather than regulation, and complex financing arrangements. Since the events of September 11, 2001, these issues are framed in terms of the security of critical infrastructure. Meanwhile, states are struggling to balance these security needs with their economic development agendas.

Over time, these strategy shifts and different mixes of policy orientations may be in response to changing state political conditions or to the waxing and waning of state commitments to activist, expensive economic development initiatives

(Eisinger 1995; Hart 2008). It is also possible that they reflect an intentional, evolutionary effort to adapt state economic development strategies to a fluid and uncertain context. In particular, the escalating costs of industrial recruitment—the megadeals—are fueling an increasingly critical view of the use of business incentives. Thomas (2000) conservatively estimated total state and local economic development expenditures at $48.8 billion in 1996. "Using a variety of methods and using a conservative definition of economic development," Peters and Fisher (2004, 28) estimated in their 2002 study the "likely top-end annual state and local" cost at about $50 billion. Critics claim that such expenditures create windfalls for business, fail to create net job increases, promote inequities among firms and industries within a state, and reduce the opportunities for state action on other programs—such as education and transportation—important for economic growth (National Conference of State Legislatures 2006).

Although it seems to be an uphill battle, groups opposed to the use of incentives to lure businesses sometimes pursue legal action to block that route. And now more than ever, states are being asked to justify program dollars. Performance standards and accountability measures are providing more transparency in budget processes, and this is a first step in determining who benefits from tax incentives and subsidies and how productive these investments are in reality. Estimates of economic development subsidies are difficult to calculate because many states fail to disclose their true costs. That said, Good Jobs First, a Washington, D.C.–based policy research center, reports that thirty-seven states are providing recipient disclosure for at least one key subsidy program, several states have enacted legislation mandating recipient reporting, and four states are providing reporting for all key programs examined (www.goodjobsfirst.org). Zelio (2009) confirms the trend toward more "sunshine"—greater transparency about state economic development goals, costs, and results, particularly as budget shortfalls sharpen the focus on all expenditures and subsidies. And several states now are using performance-based incentives, whereby the companies assisted must reach agreed-on employment and revenue goals if they are to enjoy the full value of incentives. Louisiana, Ohio, and Texas pioneered the use of "clawbacks" for reclaiming some of the value of incentives when job goals are not achieved or a company leaves the state prematurely.

Meanwhile, states continue to face an imperative to compete, but now on a global scale. But their abilities to compete are hampered by recessions and other events beyond their control. In response, states are drawing on an ever-shifting mix of policy strategies to encourage economic development, with greater attention to regional identities, innovation processes, and more policy transparency. New institutional arrangements allow state officials to think "outside the box" and to circumvent established interests and outdated ideas in considering policy options. Whether these new arrangements also will represent the voices of those often adversely affected by globalization trends or will encourage state officials to address their needs remains to be seen.

KEY TERMS

REFERENCES

American Society of Civil Engineers. 2009. *Report Card for America's Infrastructure.* www.infra structurereportcard.org/.

Atkinson, Robert. 2007. *The 2007 State New Economy Index: Benchmarking Economic Transformation in the States.* Washington, D.C.: National Governors Association.

Atkinson, Robert, and Scott Andes. 2010. *The 2010 State New Economy Index: Benchmarking Economic Transformation in the States.* Washington, D.C.: Information Technology and Innovation Foundation.

Barnes, Tom. 2007. "Angry Rendell Revises Turnpike Lease." *Pittsburgh Post-Gazette,* July 26. www.post-gazette.com/pg/07207/804588–147.stm.

Barnsted, Brad. 2008. "Rendell to Revise Turnpike Lease in '09." *State Capitol Reporter* (Pittsburgh), September 26. www.pittsburghlive.com/x/pittsburghtrib/news/cityregion/s_590203 .html.

Bischoff, Laura. 2011. "Kasich Considers Leasing Turnpike to Make Money ODOT Report Says." *Dayton Daily News,* March 11. www.daytondailynews.com/news/dayton-news/kasich-considers-leasing-turnpike-to-make-money-odot-report-says-1103945.html.

Bowman, Ann O'M. 1987. "Tools and Targets: The Mechanics of City Economic Development." A Research Report of the National League of Cities. Washington, D.C.: National League of Cities.

Brace, Paul. 1993. *State Government and Economic Performance.* Baltimore: Johns Hopkins University Press.

———. 2002. "Mapping Economic Development Policy Change in the American States." *Review of Policy Research* 19: 161–178.

Bradshaw, Ted K., and Edward J. Blakely. 1999. "What Are 'Third-Wave' State Economic Development Efforts? From Incentives to Industrial Policy." *Economic Development Quarterly* 13: 229–244.

Bridges, Benjamin. 1965. "State and Local Inducements for Industry, Part II." *National Tax Journal* 18: 1–14.

Brookings Institution. 2011. "The Hamilton Project." www.brookings.edu/PROJECTS/HAMIL TONPROJECT.ASPX.

Campbell, Scott. 1996. "Green Cities, Growing Jobs, Just Cities? Urban Planning and the Contradictions of Sustainable Development." *Journal of the American Planning Association* 62: 296–312.

Center for Digital Government. 2010. *Digital States Survey.* Folsom, Calif.: Center for Digital Government. www.centerdigitalgov.com.

Christopherson, Susan, and Ned Rightor. 2010. "The Creative Economy as 'Big Business': Evaluating State Strategies to Lure Filmmakers." *Journal of Planning Education and Research* 29: 336–352.

Clarke, Susan E., and Gary L. Gaile. 1992. "The Next Wave: Local Economic Development Strategies in the Post-Federal Era." *Economic Development Quarterly* 6: 187–198.

———. 1998. *The Work of Cities.* Minneapolis: University of Minnesota Press.

Corporation for Enterprise Development. 2010. "2009–2010 Assets and Opportunities Scorecard." Washington, D.C. http://scorecard.cfed.org/.

Cumberland, John H. 1971. *Regional Development Experiences and Prospects in the United States of America.* The Hague: Mouton.

de Bartolome, Charles A. M., and Mark M. Spiegel. 1995. "Regional Competition for Domestic and Foreign Investment: Evidence from State Development Expenditures." *Journal of Urban Economics* 37: 239–259.

Donahue, John D. 1997. *Disunited States.* New York: Basic Books.

Eisinger, Peter. 1988. *The Rise of the Entrepreneurial State: State and Local Economic Development Policy in the United States.* Madison: University of Wisconsin Press.

———. 1995. "State Economic Development in the 1990s." *Economic Development Quarterly* 9: 146–158.

Felbinger, Claire F. 1994. "Conditions of Confusion and Conflict: Rethinking the Infrastructure-Economic Development Linkage." In *Urban Affairs Annual Review,* vol. 43, *Building the Public City: Politics, Governance, and Finance of Public Infrastructure,* ed. David C. Perry. Newbury Park, Calif.: Sage.

Florida, Richard. 2002. *The Rise of the Creative Class, and How It's Transforming Work, Leisure, Community, and Everyday Life.* New York: Basic Books.

———. 2005. *Flight of the Creative Class.* New York: HarperBusiness.

Fosler, R. Scott, ed. 1988. *The New Economic Role of American States.* New York: Oxford University Press.

Frank, Thomas. 2004. *What's the Matter with Kansas?* New York: Metropolitan Books.

Friedman, Miles, and Partners LLC. 2006. *Directory of Incentives.* www.milesfriedman.com/id12 .html.

Friedman, Thomas. 2005. *The World Is Flat.* New York: Farrar, Straus, and Giroux.

Fulton, William. 2010. *Romancing the Smokestack: How Cities and States Pursue Prosperity.* Ventura, Calif.: Solimar Books.

Goetz, Stephan J., and David Freshwater. 2001. "State-level Determinants of Entrepreneurship and a Preliminary Measure of Entrepreneurial Climate." *Economic Development Quarterly* 15: 58–70.

Good Jobs First. 2005. "Examples of Clawback Provisions in State Subsidy Programs." www .goodjobsfirst.org/sites/default/files/docs/pdf/clawbacks_chart.pdf.

Hall, Jeremy L. 2007. "Informing State Economic Development Policy in the New Economy: A Theoretical Foundation and Empirical Examination of State Innovation in the United States." *Public Administration Review* 67: 630–645.

———. 2009. "Adding Meaning to Measurement: Evaluating Trends and Differences in Innovation Capacity among the States." *Economic Development Quarterly* 23: 3–12.

Hansen, Susan B. 2006. *Globalization and the Politics of Pay: Policy Choices in the American States.* Washington, D.C.: Georgetown University Press.

Hanson, Russell L. 1993. "Bidding for Business: A Second War between the States?" *Economic Development Quarterly* 7: 183–198.

Hart, David M. 2008. "The Politics of 'Entrepreneurial' Economic Development Policy of States in the U.S." *Review of Policy Research* 25: 149–168.

Jenkins, J. Craig, Kevin T. Leicht, and Heather Wendt. 2006. "Class Forces, Political Institutions, and State Intervention: Subnational Economic Development Policy in the United States, 1971–1990." *American Journal of Sociology* 111: 1122–1180.

Jones, Bryan, and Lynn Bachelor. 1986. *The Sustaining Hand.* Lawrence: University Press of Kansas.

Kilgore, Ed. 2011. "Dixie Madison, Republicans Want Wisconsin to Become Just Like the South." *New Republic,* February 28. www.tnr.com/article/politics/84170/republicans-wisconsin-labor-unions-south.

Kincaid, John. 1992. "Developments in Federal-State Relations, 1990–91." In *The Book of the States, 1992–93.* Lexington, Ky.: Council of State Governments.

Koropeckyj, Sophia. 1997. "Do Economic Development Incentives Matter?" Regional Financial Associates, West Chester, Pa.

Langer, L. 2001. "The Consequences of State Economic Development Strategies on Income Distribution in the American States." *American Politics Research* 29: 392–415.

Lee, Yoonsoo. 2004. "Geographic Redistribution of U.S. Manufacturing and the Role of State Development Policy." Working paper 04–15, Federal Reserve Bank of Cleveland.

Lynch, Robert G. 2004. *Rethinking Growth Strategies: How State and Local Taxes and Services Affect Economic Development.* Washington, D.C.: Economic Policy Institute.

Lyne, Jack. 2002. "New York's $500M Incentive Package Aims to Retain Lower Manhattan Firms." www.conway.com/ssinsider.

Mahtesian, Charles. 1994. "Romancing the Smokestack." *Governing,* November, 36–40.

Markusen, Ann, and Anne Gadwa. 2010. "Arts and Culture in Urban/Regional Planning: A Review and Research Agenda." *Journal of Planning Education and Research* 29: 379–391.

Markusen, Ann, and Amy Glasmeier. 2008. "History, Leadership, Place Prosperity, Rationales, Competitiveness, Outcomes. A Response to Drabenstott, Finkle, John, and Singerman." *Economic Development Quarterly* 22: 115–118.

Martinez, Amy. 2005. "Motion Challenges Dell Incentives," *News and Observer* (Raleigh, N.C.), June 24.

Maryland Department of Business and Economic Development. 2004. "Smart Growth Economic Development Infrastructure Fund." www.choosemaryland.org/aboutdbed/Documents/ProgramReports/2005/06-OneMarylandAnnual%20Report.pdf.

MassDevelopment. 2010. "Emerging Technology Fund Quarterly Report to the Legislature and Summary for FY 2010." www.massdevelopment.com/wp-content/uploads/2010/12/ETF_annual report_10.pdf.

Mattera, Philip, Thomas Cafcas, Leigh McIlvaine, Caitlin Lacy, Elizabeth Williams, and Sarah Gutschow. 2010. *Show Us the Subsidies: An Evaluation of State Government Online Disclosure of Economic Development Subsidies.* Washington, D.C.: Good Jobs First.

Mattera, Philip, and Anna Purinton. 2004. *Shopping for Subsidies: How Wal-Mart Uses Tax-Payer Money to Finance Its Never-Ending Growth.* Washington, D.C.: Good Jobs First.

Mayer, Heike. 2010. "Catching Up: The Role of State Science and Technology Policy in Open Innovation." *Economic Development Quarterly* 24: 195–209.

Maynard, Melissa. 2010. "As States Slash Budgets Tax Breaks Survive." *Stateline,* July 6. www.stateline.org/live/details/story?contentId=496158.

National Association of State Development Agencies. 1983, 1986, 1991, 1994, 1998, 2002. *Directory of Incentives for Business Investment and Development in the United States: A State-by-State Guide.* Washington, D.C.: National Association of State Development Agencies.

National Conference of State Legislatures. 2006. "Economic and Tourism Development." www.ncsl.org/programs/econ/.

North, Douglas C., Terry Anderson, and Peter Hill. 1983. *Growth and Welfare in the American Past.* Englewood Cliffs, N.J.: Prentice-Hall.

Osborne, David. 1988. *Laboratories of Democracy.* Boston: Harvard Business School Press.

Peirce, Neal R. 1994. "The When, How, and Why of Wooing." *National Journal,* February 26, 488.

———. 2010. "Infrastructure Bank Proposal: Ignore at Our Peril." *Washington Post,* September 19.

Perry, David C. 1994. "Introduction: Building the Public City." In *Urban Affairs Annual Review,* vol. 43, *Building the Public City,* ed. David C. Perry. Newbury Park, Calif.: Sage.

Peters, Alan, and Peter Fisher. 2004. "Commentary: The Failures of Economic Development Incentives." *Journal of the American Planning Association* 70: 27–37.

Peterson, Paul E. 1981. *City Limits.* Chicago: University of Chicago Press.

Plaut, Thomas, and Joseph Pluta. 1983. "Business Climate Taxes and Expenditures, and State Industrial Growth in the United States." *Southern Economic Journal* 50: 99–119.

Plosila, Walter H. 2004. "State Science- and Technology-Based Economic Development Policy: History, Trends and Developments, and Future Directions." *Economic Development Quarterly* 18: 113–126.

Rabe, Barry G. 2004. *Statehouse and Greenhouse: The Emerging Politics of American Climate Change Policy.* Washington, D.C.: Brookings.

Reich, Robert. 1991. *The Work of Nations.* New York: Knopf.

Rivlin, Alice. 1995. *Reviving the American Dream.* Washington, D.C.: Brookings.

Rochefort, David A., and Roger W. Cobb. 1994. "Problem Definition: An Emerging Perspective." In *The Politics of Problem Definition,* ed. David A. Rochefort and Roger W. Cobb. Lawrence: University Press of Kansas.

Rubin, Herbert J. 1988. "Shoot Anything That Flies; Claim Anything That Falls: Conversations with Economic Development Practitioners." *Economic Development Quarterly* 2: 236–251.

Saiz, Martin. 2001a. "Politics and Economic Development: Why Governments Adopt Different Strategies to Achieve Similar Goals." *Policy Studies Journal* 29: 203–214.

———. 2001b. "Using Program Attributes to Measure and Evaluate State Economic Development Activism." *Economic Development Quarterly* 15: 45–57.

Saiz, Martin, and Susan E. Clarke. 2004. "The Politics of Economic Development and Transportation." In *Politics in the American States: A Comparative Analysis,* 8th ed., ed. Virginia Gray and Russell L. Hanson. Washington, D.C.: CQ Press.

———. 2008. "The Politics of Economic Development and Transportation." In *Politics in the American States: A Comparative Analysis,* 9th ed., ed. Virginia Gray and Russell L. Hanson. Washington, D.C.: CQ Press.

Sherman, Don Grant, II, Michael Wallace, and William D. Pitney. 1995. "Measuring State-Level Economic Development Programs, 1970–1992." *Economic Development Quarterly* 9: 134–145.

Speizer, Irwin. 2005. "Dell Pickle." *Business North Carolina* 25: 46.

Stech, Katy, and David Slade. 2010. "Boeing's Whopping Incentives," *Post and Courier* (Charleston, N.C.), January 17. www.postandcourier.com/news/2010/jan/17/boeings-whopping-incentives/.

Sternberg, Ernest. 1987. "A Practitioner's Classification of Economic Development Policy Instruments, with Some Inspiration from Political Economy." *Economic Development Quarterly* 1: 149–161.

Thomas, Kenneth. 2000. *Competing for Capital: Europe and North America in a Global Era.* Washington, D.C.: Georgetown University Press.

U.S. Congressional Budget Office. 2010. *Public Spending on Transportation and Water Infrastructure.* Washington, D.C.: Congressional Budget Office.

U.S. Department of Transportation, Federal Highway Administration. 1993. *Intermodal Surface Transportation Efficiency Act of 1991: Selected Fact Sheets.* Washington, D.C.: Government Printing Office.

Wallace, James. 2004. "Boeing: Tax Breaks No Bargaining Chip," *Seattle Post-Intelligencer,* October 28. www.seattlepi.com/business/197093_subsidy28.html.

Weber, Melvin. 1984. *Industrial Location.* Beverly Hills, Calif.: Sage.

Wolman, Harold, and David Spitzley. 1996. "The Politics of Local Economic Development." *Economic Development Quarterly* 10: 115–150.

Wu, Yonghong. 2005. "The Effects of State R&D Tax Credits in Stimulating Private R&D Expenditure: A Cross-State Empirical Analysis." *Journal of Policy Analysis and Management* 24: 785.

———. 2008. "State R&D Tax Credits and High-Technology Establishments." *Economic Development Quarterly* 22: 136–148.

Yilmaz, Serdar, and Mustafa Dinc. 2002. "Telecommunications and Regional Development: Evidence from the U.S. States." *Economic Development Quarterly* 16: 211–228.

Zelio, Judy. 2009. *Taking the Measure of State Economic Development.* Denver: National Conference of State Legislatures.

SUGGESTED READINGS

Print

Blakely, Edward J., and Nancey Green Leigh. *Planning Local Economic Development: Theory and Practice,* 4th ed. Thousand Oaks, Calif.: Sage, 2009. Revised edition of a classic volume that addresses the nuts and bolts of economic development policymaking, including the planning process, high-technology economic development strategies, sustainable development, and implementation of local economic development initiatives.

Fulton, William. *Romancing the Smokestack: How Cities and States Pursue Prosperity.* Ventura, Calif.: Solimar Books, 2010. A collection of columns from *Governing* magazine about the practice of economic development by state and local governments in the United States.

Hansen, Susan B. *Globalization and the Politics of Pay: Policy Choices in the American States.* Washington, D.C.: Georgetown University Press, 2006. The author finds that as state governments compete for jobs, business investment, and factory locations, they exaggerate the declining wages caused by globalization. Such policy behavior has adverse social consequences, including family instability, high crime rates, poverty, and low voter turnouts.

Markusen, Ann, ed. *Reining in the Competition for Capital.* Kalamazoo, Mich.: W. E. Upjohn Institute for Employment Research, 2007. An edited collection of critical essays on state economic development incentive systems, clawback policies, negotiating subsidies, determinants of incentive competition, and other basic elements of interstate economic competition.

Internet

Corporation for Enterprise Development. http://cfed.org. Offers balanced analyses of different development strategies and provides annual "report cards" assessing and ranking each state's economic performance, business vitality, and development capacity.

Council of Development Finance Agencies. www.cdfa.net/. A national association of public, private, and nonprofit organizations involved in financing economic development activities. The Web site includes data on state programs as well as a database of articles, legislation, and documents relevant to state programs.

Good Jobs First. www.goodjobsfirst.org/. This Web site provides critical analyses of economic development subsidies. It includes a Subsidy Tracker, a search engine for state economic development subsidies; state profiles detailing the programs, subsidies, and controversial deals in all fifty states; a Corporate Subsidy Watch; as well as analyses of green jobs initiatives. The site also identifies best-practice strategies that encourage smart growth and accountable development and provides links to many other data sources.

Pew Center on the States. www.pewcenteronthestates.org/. Nonprofit nonpartisan organization that collects state data and analyzes state initiatives in a wide range of policy areas. The center focuses on helping states develop more effective, efficient, and evidence-based state policy strategies. Many analyses and updates are available through the center's online newsletter at www.stateline.org/live/.

2010 State New Economy Index. www.itif.org/files/2010-state-new-economy-index.pdf. Uses twenty-six indicators to track state transformations from smokestack-chasing strategies to policies focusing on innovation processes. Builds on four previous reports to show which states are leading and lagging in developing knowledge-based, globalized, entrepreneurial, information technology–driven, and innovation-based economies.

Glossary of Key Terms

"527" (or "501c4") organizations   Political committees organized under Section 527 (or 501c) of the U.S. tax code that are not required to file reports with the Federal Election Commission or state election agencies, and are not allowed (unlike political action committees) to make political contributions to federal candidates but may use soft money to influence the election of candidates through political advertising and voter mobilization. (Chapter 3)

accountability   The idea of holding schools, districts, educators, and students responsible for results, most typically by the use of high-stakes examinations to demonstrate student learning. (Chapter 12)

accreditation agency   Private agency that periodically reviews and certifies a college's or university's curriculum, faculty qualifications, and facilities. Accreditation is needed for acceptance of courses and degrees by other colleges and universities, and for an institution to be eligible for many financial aid programs. (Chapter 13)

administrative oversight   Process by which a legislature monitors the actions and behavior of other political bodies to ensure that the implementation of public policy is consistent with legislative intent. (Chapter 6)

affirmative gerrymandering   Form of redistricting in which electoral districts or constituency boundaries are manipulated in a manner to achieve an electoral advantage for a particular racial, linguistic, religious, or political group. (Chapter 6)

appropriations   Statutory authorization to spend a specific amount of money for a stated purpose. (Chapter 6)

associations   Organizational interests that are composed not of individuals but of organizations such as businesses or labor unions. (Chapter 4)

balanced-budget law   Statutory or constitutional provision requiring that either projected or actual government spending be less than or equal to revenues over a specified time period. (Chapter 10)

Bipartisan Campaign Reform Act (BCRA)   Federal campaign finance law passed in 2002, also known as the McCain-Feingold Act, that features a ban on soft money to political parties and a prohibition on interest group advertising with soft money thirty days before a primary election and sixty days before a general election. (Chapter 3)

body mass index (BMI)   The relationship between weight and height that is associated with body fat. The higher a person's BMI, the greater are that person's health risks (a BMI of over twenty-five is considered overweight). (Chapter 11)

"California effect"   Other states' adoption of California's tougher environmental standards, such as automobile emissions standards. (Chapter 15)

capital budget   Document specifying planned spending on buildings and other long-term projects. The planning horizon ranges from three to ten years, but five years is the most common. (Chapter 10)

capitated   A term used to describe a health care program in which the medical provider is allotted a set fee per patient, regardless of how much medical care each patient needs. (Chapter 11)

casework   Assistance provided by an elected official on behalf of a constituent when dealing with another political body. (Chapter 6)

categorically needy   Individuals, typically those in low-income families with dependent children, the elderly, or the disabled, who automatically qualify for Medicaid benefits under federal law. The states are required to provide Medicaid benefits to the categorically needy. (Chapter 11)

communications theory of lobbying   Theory of lobbying that posits that lobbyists help legislators achieve their goals by providing them with political, policy-analytical, and career-relevant information. (Chapter 4)

confederal   Relation of constitutional equals, which may take the form of interactions, formal associations, or constitutional agreements. (Chapter 2)

constituency service   Assistance performed or information provided to a constituent by an elected official, the official's staff, or both. (Chapter 6)

constitutional initiative   Initiatives that seek to amend or otherwise change the constitution. (Chapter 5)

coordinated campaigns   Electoral strategy that combines the resources of candidates, parties, and interest groups to pursue campaign activities jointly, especially to mobilize voters. (Chapter 3)

coordinating board   A state-level agency that collects information and coordinates the development of public universities, but does not have direct responsibility for governing individual campuses. (Chapter 13)

correctional classification   Procedures for determining the needs of offenders and their risks to the safety of others, enabling their placement into the most appropriate correctional facility environments. (Chapter 9)

correctional facility   Facility for the long-term confinement of convicted criminals, most often those convicted of felony crimes. In the past, correctional facilities were referred to more commonly as prisons and penitentiaries. (Chapter 9)

corrections policy Procedures related to the processing and treatment of convicted criminals, particularly the types of appropriate punishments and how those punishments are implemented. (Chapter 9)

countermajoritarian The process by which the courts undermine legislative or other popular majorities by invalidating statutes, ordinances, executive orders, and ballot initiatives. (Chapter 8)

courts of last resort The states' highest courts, with appellate jurisdiction (usually discretionary) largely over the intermediate appellate courts and with original jurisdiction in some limited types of cases defined by law. Decisions of these courts can be appealed only to the Supreme Court of the United States and only if there is a federal question involved. Oklahoma and Texas each have two courts of last resort—one court to hear criminal cases and one to hear civil cases. (Chapter 8)

de facto segregation School segregation that resulted not from government decree but from patterns of residential segregation that produced segregated neighborhood schools. (Chapter 12)

de jure segregation School segregation resulting from laws that mandated segregation or allowed school districts to designate some schools as blacks-only or whites-only. (Chapter 12)

democratic deficit The mismatch between majority opinion and government policy. (Chapter 14)

department of corrections A state agency charged with overseeing state prison operations, guiding prison administration, and developing and refining correctional policies; most of these forty-three agencies are also responsible for overseeing community corrections. (Chapter 9)

department of education A part of the executive branch of each state government that implements state education policies, conducts research in education, and makes recommendations to the governor on education policy. (Chapter 12)

devolution Delegation of policy responsibilities to a state. (Chapter 15)

Dillon's Rule Legal holding that local governments only possess powers expressly granted to them by their state government, or fairly implied in an express delegation of power or necessary to its exercise. (Chapter 2)

direct democracy Processes that give voters a direct vote on a policy matter, usually by means of an initiative, referendum, or recall. (Chapter 5)

direct initiative A measure that is put directly to voters after its submission by a petition (under the indirect initiative, a measure is first referred to the legislature and put to a popular vote only if the legislature does not pass the measure). (Chapter 5)

direct primary election Election in which voters choose the party nominee for the general election, in contrast with a party convention or caucus, in which party activists select the nominee. (Chapter 3)

direct techniques   Lobbying techniques that involve direct contact with government officials. (Chapter 4)

district magnitude   Number of seats to be elected from an electoral district or constituency. (Chapter 6)

DREAM Act   The Development, Relief, and Education for Alien Minors Act. A proposed federal statute that would allow illegal immigrant students to be considered state residents for higher education purposes if they meet certain requirements. (Chapter 13)

dual federalism   A legal doctrine holding that federal and state governments have distinct spheres of responsibility, and that each is sovereign within its sphere. (Chapter 2)

educational and general spending   Spending by colleges and universities on academic functions, including instruction, research, public service, and related administration and support services. (Chapter 13)

energy-stability-area (ESA) model   A model created by Virginia Gray and David Lowery to explain variation in group numbers across states. (Chapter 4)

entrepreneurial strategy   A policy or plan of economic development that focuses on the creation of new firms and products as well as on the markets, jobs, and revenues they create. (Chapter 16)

environmental audit privilege and immunity   Audit privilege protects information collected during an audit from disclosure or use in an administrative or judicial hearing; audit immunity shields facilities from penalties for violations discovered during an audit, as long as the facility returns to compliance. (Chapter 15)

executive budget   A budget document prepared by the governor's office, often with the help of other executive branch officials. It gives governors an opportunity to present a unified statement of their spending priorities. State legislatures typically have nearly unlimited power to alter the budget once they receive it. (Chapter 7)

federal benefit standard   The size of the cash payments provided by the federal government to individuals qualifying for the Supplemental Security Income program. (Chapter 11)

federalism   A division of political labor in which powers are allocated to different levels of government according to whether their responsibilities are national or regional in scope, as determined by the collective decisions of units constituting this system of governance. (Chapter 2)

fee-for-service program   A medical program in which the medical provider is reimbursed for each service administered to a patient. (Chapter 11)

felon disenfranchisement   Laws in most states limit the voting rights of convicted felons, usually while they are under state supervision, although some states impose longer or even permanent restrictions. (Chapter 3)

fiscal initiative　A measure that relates to fiscal matters (government spending and taxation). The most famous fiscal initiative may be California's Proposition 13. (Chapter 5)

fiscal year　The twelve-month period used for budgeting purposes. The fiscal year in most states begins July 1. (Chapter 10)

folded Ranney index　Index that measures how close a state's level of interparty competition is to "perfect" competition on the Ranney index. It is calculated as $1 - |(0.5 - \text{Ranney})|$, with high values indicating greater competition. (Chapter 3)

formal power　*See* institutional power. (Chapter 7)

foundation program　A program under which a state sets a target level of resources that each school district needs to provide no-frills, adequate education. (Chapter 12)

general jurisdiction trial courts　Courts of first instance that hear major civil and criminal disputes (including felonies). (Chapter 8)

general obligation debt　Borrowed money that is backed by the "full faith and credit" of a state government and may be repaid with any revenues from taxes and fees. (Chapter 10)

general revenue (or general spending)　Total state government revenue (or spending) minus amounts for state-owned liquor stores, public utilities, and insurance trusts. (Chapter 10)

get-tough movement　Period from the 1980s to the present characterized by a growing political interest in harsher punishments for convicted criminals. (Chapter 9)

globalization of capitalism　Increasing integration of world markets for capital, goods, and services. (Chapter 1)

governance policy　A policy aimed at changing the structure of state political institutions. (Chapter 5)

governing board　The body of individuals responsible for governing a public university, usually appointed by the governor or state legislature or chosen by popular election. Governing boards may be responsible for one or several campuses. (Chapter 13)

gross state product　The value added in production by the labor and property located in a state. Thus the GSP corresponds to the nation's gross domestic product (GDP). (Chapter 1)

group system power　Overall influence of interest groups in a state relative to that of political parties and other political institutions and actors. (Chapter 4)

gubernatorial power　*See* institutional power. (Chapter 7)

Historically Black Colleges and Universities　Colleges and universities established by the second Morrill Act, enacted in 1890, to serve black students in states in which public universities practiced discrimination based on race. (Chapter 13)

home rule   A charter from state government granting broad powers of self-determination to a county or municipal government in that state. (Chapter 2)

horizontal equity   The extent to which school districts across the states spend equally. (Chapter 12)

ideology   A person's core political values or principles. In American politics, ideological labels are commonly reduced to a left–right continuum, with liberal on one end and conservative on the other end. (Chapter 14)

indirect initiative   An initiative that must first pass through the legislature (if the legislature approves the measure it does not go to the ballot; if the legislature rejects the measure it goes to the ballot). (Chapter 5)

indirect techniques   Lobbying techniques that target citizens rather than government officials. (Chapter 4)

individualist political culture   Subculture that emphasizes the marketplace, views bureaucracy negatively, and limits government intervention to a minimum. (Chapter 1)

infrastructure   A set of public works elements that provides physical support and capacity for commercial activity. Includes roads, bridges, and mass transit systems as well as utilities such as electric, sewer, and water systems. Also includes the physical channels of communication such as the telephone, Internet, airwave, and microwave systems. (Chapter 16)

infrastructure strategy   A policy or plan of economic development that focuses on the creation of public infrastructure that provides the support and capacity needed for commercial activity. (Chapter 16)

inmates' rights movement   Era during the 1960s and 1970s when both federal and state courts began to look into conditions of confinement in prisons. The movement focused primarily on humane treatment and living conditions, the right to medical services, freedom of religion, and freedom of expression and speech; it also established the substantive rights of prison inmates. (Chapter 9)

institutional interests   Nonmembership interest groups such as business firms, local governments, hospitals, state and federal agencies, think tanks, and universities and colleges. (Chapter 4)

institutional power   Power that is inherent in the governorship itself. Sometimes called a formal power or gubernatorial power. (Chapter 7)

interest group   Association of individuals or organizations or a public or private institution that attempts to influence government decisions. (Chapter 4)

interest group power   An assessment of how much influence interests have over decision making and public policies in a state. (Chapter 4)

intergovernmental relations   Legal, political, and financial interactions between agencies from different levels of government, as well as different governments at the same level, within the same system of governance. (Chapter 2)

interjurisdictional competition   A rivalry among governments whereby each is trying to draw resources, such as tax revenues, to their areas or push costs, such as pollution or low-income residents, to other jurisdictions. Much of this competition is a consequence of the public services offered in different jurisdictions, which creates a market for public goods. (Chapter 16)

intermediate appellate courts Courts with mandatory appellate jurisdiction over the trial courts. (Chapter 8)

interstate compact A congressionally approved agreement between two or more states for jointly addressing common problems. (Chapter 2)

legislative referendum A measure put on the ballot by the legislature. (Chapter 5)

limited jurisdiction trial courts Courts of first instance that hear minor civil and criminal disputes, including misdemeanors (usually traffic violations) and small claims (typically cases involving claims of less than $10,000). (Chapter 8)

lobbying Interaction of an individual, interest group, or interest with government decision makers, either directly or indirectly, for the purpose of influencing current government decisions or creating a relationship conducive to shaping future government decisions for the benefit of that individual, group, or interest. (Chapter 4)

lobbyist Person who represents an interest group in an effort to influence government decisions. (Chapter 4)

local school board When independent of other local governments, the governing institution with the power to tax, spend funds, hire teachers, and administer auxiliary services such as transportation, food, and athletics. Some local school boards, especially in large cities, are dependent on municipal or county governments that have the ultimate power to set policy. (Chapter 12)

locational strategy A policy or plan of economic development that focuses on reducing the costs of doing business in a particular location in order to attract business investment to that location. (Chapter 16)

managed care program A health care arrangement in which some organization acts as intermediary between the patient and the medical provider, typically with the goal of controlling costs. (Chapter 11)

mandate Obligation imposed upon one government by a constitutionally supreme government or as a condition for receiving financial or other assistance. (Chapter 2)

means-tested program A program in which eligibility for benefits is based on income or assets. (Chapter 11)

mechanical jurisprudence A normative account of judicial decision making in which the act of judging consists of the objective, straightforward application of existing and readily knowable laws to the established facts of the cases, without subjectivity or discretion. (Chapter 8)

Medicaid waiver Request made by a state to obtain federal Medicaid matching funds for special populations or services. Waiver requests must be approved by the federal Centers for Medicare and Medicaid Services. (Chapter 11)

medically needy Individuals who qualify for Medicaid benefits under state laws because they have extensive medical problems but have too much income to qualify as categorically needy. (Chapter 11)

merit system Method of filling offices in the executive branch on the basis of skills and credentials rather than political connections. Often referred to as the civil service plan, the merit system replaced the spoils system that awarded government jobs as patronage (political rewards). (Chapter 7)

millage Rate of taxation imposed on property. (Chapter 12)

Missouri Plan A method for selecting judges that combines initial appointment with subsequent retention elections. (Chapter 8)

moralist political culture Subculture that emphasizes the commonwealth in which government's role is to advance the public interest and in which politics tends to revolve around issues. (Chapter 1)

morality policy Policy that is defined by debates over basic values, where at least one side portrays the issue as involving morality or sin. These debates are fundamentally clashes over right and wrong, and they have their origins in differences in people's core values. (Chapter 14)

Morrill Act of 1862 A federal statute that transferred federally owned lands to the states for the purpose of establishing colleges that specialized in practical training in the "agricultural and mechanical" arts. (Chapter 13)

National Ambient Air Quality Standards (NAAQS) Guidelines established by the U.S. Environmental Protection Agency to govern the allowable concentrations in the air of the pollutants carbon monoxide, lead, nitrogen dioxide, ozone, particulate matter, and sulfur dioxide. (Chapter 15)

National Voter Registration Act (NVRA) of 1993 Act of Congress that required states to offer voter registration forms at driver's license renewal offices, public assistance agencies, and by mail. (Chapter 3)

New Source Performance Standards U.S. Environmental Protection Agency standards governing air pollution emissions from new or substantially modified stationary sources. (Chapter 15)

No Child Left Behind (NCLB) The flagship domestic program of President George W. Bush that tied federal funds to the performance of schools within a state as well as to the quality of the teacher workforce. (Chapter 12)

nonattainment area An area that does not meet air quality standards set by the U.S. Environmental Protection Agency for key pollutants. (Chapter 15)

P–16 council A state agency that conducts integrated planning of public education from preschool through postsecondary education. (Chapter 13)

partial preemption An institutional framework that allows the federal government to devolve program responsibility to the states while retaining the ultimate authority to decide on the adequacy of state actions. The process gives states an opportunity to design and implement their own regulations, as long as they are consistent with national goals and meet federal guidelines. (Chapter 15)

partisanship A person's disposition toward the Democratic and Republican Parties. (Chapter 14)

Pell Grants   A federal program that makes financial aid grants to college students on the basis of financial need. (Chapter 13)

per capita personal income   Personal income is the income received by persons from their participation in production, from both government and business transfer payments, and from government interest. Per capita personal income is the personal income received by the residents in the state divided by the state's population. (Chapter 1)

performance-based accountability policies   Policies that tie some portion of appropriations for public universities to performance measures such as graduation rates. (Chapter 13)

personal power   Attributes of governors that can be turned into either a strength or a weakness. Can include an electoral mandate, position on the state political ambition ladder, personal future, and performance ratings. (Chapter 7)

plenary power   Full or complete authority assigned to a single government entity and exercised over a specific policy area. (Chapter 2)

plurality   Candidate who wins the most votes wins a plurality of votes, even if the candidate does not win a majority. (Chapter 3)

polarization   A situation in which each political party becomes more internally cohesive while the ideological space between the two parties grows greater. (Chapter 6)

policy diffusion   When a state adopts innovative policies that have already been adopted by its neighbors. (Chapter 15)

policy effectiveness   A policy is effective if it accomplishes what it sets out to do. An economic development policy is effective if it creates jobs, generates tax revenues, or generally increases the economic well-being of the jurisdiction. (Chapter 16)

policy matching   When states generate policies to deal with specific environmental problems. (Chapter 15)

policy mood   The public's disposition toward government. Mood reacts to the policy proposals and enactments of elected officials, fluctuating between preferences for more or less government. (Chapter 14)

political responsiveness   The degree to which governing bodies adhere closely to majority preferences. (Chapter 12)

popular referendum   If enough citizens sign a petition, putting an existing law or policy to a popular vote (depending on the version of popular referendum being used, voters may be able to veto legislation passed by a legislature). (Chapter 5)

Populists   Popular early twentieth-century political party and reformers who sought change in the political structure of the time; allies of the Progressives. (Chapter 5)

post-designate   Form of multimember district electoral system in which the candidate must declare the particular seat that the candidate is attempting to win. (Chapter 6)

preemption   Limits or prohibitions imposed upon the actions of one government by a government that is constitutionally supreme in a particular policy area. (Chapter 2)

primacy   Primary administrative responsibility for implementing a government program. (Chapter 15)

privatization The handling of various aspects of prison construction, management, and programming by nongovernment or private enterprises. Use of privatization varies by state. (Chapter 9)

professionalism   The degree to which a legislature has the resources and incentives to act as an independent body. Generally, these resources and incentives involve time in session, size of legislative staff, and compensation for members of the legislature. (Chapter 6)

Progressives   Largely middle-class and professional early twentieth-century reformers—and allies of the Populists—who sought reform in political structures. (Chapter 5)

progressive tax   A tax in which people with high incomes pay a larger percentage of their income than people with low incomes. (Chapter 10)

Proposition 13   A 1978 state constitutional amendment in California that severely curtailed the abilities of local governments to raise revenues. (Chapter 12)

public opinion   The aggregate of individual attitudes or beliefs held by the adult population. It is most accurately measured using scientific polling. (Chapter 14)

public policies   Means to governmental ends. (Chapter 1)

race to the bottom   A criticism of decentralized environmental policy that argues that economic competition for industry among states and localities may motivate political officials to reduce regulatory stringency to gain a competitive advantage over their neighbors, causing an aggregate movement toward the lowest common denominator of environmental protection. (Chapter 15)

Race to the Top   Education reform program announced by President Barack Obama in 2009 that, like No Child Left Behind, is built around accountability. (Chapter 12)

race to the top   A follow-the-leader trend in which interstate competition in the area of environmental regulation leads to an overall ratcheting up of environmental standards. (Chapter 15)

rainy day funds   Money set aside by a state government to be used in future years when revenues fall short of spending. (Chapter 10)

Ranney index   Measure of party control of state government (the state legislature and governorship) with theoretical limits of 0 (absolute Republican control) and 1 (absolute Democratic control). (Chapter 3)

reapportionment   Process of altering the number of seats allocated in the legislature based on the relative size of a state's population. (Chapter 6)

reconstitution   The closing by the state of low-performing schools, which are later reopened with new principals and new staff. (Chapter 12)

redistricting   Process by which state legislatures redraw state legislative and congressional district boundaries every ten years following the U.S. Census. (Chapter 6)

regressive tax   A tax in which people with high incomes pay a smaller percentage of their income than people with low incomes. (Chapter 10)

renewable portfolio standards (RPSs)   Primary policy tool employed by states to encourage the development and use of renewable energy technologies for electricity generation, such as wind, solar, and geothermal power. RPSs are mandates that electricity providers in a state obtain some minimum amount of their power from renewable sources by a particular date. (Chapter 15)

reorganization   A process of rearranging divisions of the bureaucracy, usually into fewer agencies so that the governor has greater power to manage the bureaucracy. (Chapter 7)

salience   The importance and visibility of an issue to the public; its prominence in public discourse. (Chapter 14)

school vouchers   Government certificates that can be used to pay for some or all of a student's tuition to any school that admits the student. (Chapter 12)

second-order devolution   The further delegation of policy authority by a state to city, county, or regional substate governments. (Chapter 15)

sentencing philosophies   Goals sought by the government when punishing offenders. The primary philosophies include retribution (punishment inflicted to pay back the offender for the harm inflicted on society), deterrence (punishment as a means of persuading the offender or others not to engage in future crimes), incapacitation (preventing crime by removing the offender from society), and rehabilitation (reforming the offender). (Chapter 9)

sentencing schemes   Procedures and considerations for determining the appropriate sanctions for offenders based on sentencing philosophies. Indeterminate schemes allow judges more discretion in sentencing decisions and offer broader ranges for prison terms relative to determinate schemes. (Chapter 9)

severance tax   Tax imposed on the extraction of nonrenewable natural resources such as oil and gas. (Chapter 1)

sin tax   Tax applied to goods or activities that are often associated with undesirable behavior and that may impose costs on the rest of the population. The most common examples are tobacco, alcohol, and gambling. (Chapter 10)

smokestack-chasing strategy   A policy or plan of economic development that focuses on offering incentives to existing businesses, prompting them to relocate to one's home location. (Chapter 16)

soft money   Campaign funds that are exempt from limits and source restrictions under federal campaign finance law because they are not used to support specific candidates for federal office. (Chapter 3)

sovereign immunity   A constitutional doctrine that precludes civil suits or criminal proceedings against units of government without their consent. (Chapter 2)

special-purpose governments   Units of local government with specific responsibilities, limited powers, and singular jurisdictions, such as public school districts. (Chapter 2)

specific opinion   Public opinion on a particular policy. This is in contrast to measures of ideology, partisanship, or mood. (Chapter 14)

spillover effect   When pollution emitted in one jurisdiction affects the environmental conditions in another. (Chapter 15)

state disenfranchisement law   Law that prohibits inmates, parolees, or felony probationers from voting. (Chapter 9)

state economic development   Policies designed to encourage business investment and growth in order to produce jobs and tax revenues for the state. (Chapter 16)

state interest group system   Array of groups and organizations, both formal and informal, and the lobbyists who represent them working to affect government decisions within a state. (Chapter 4)

statutory initiative   A proposal that changes state law as opposed to one that changes the state constitution. (Chapter 5)

street-level bureaucrats   Government employees who implement state policies through their daily interaction with clients. (Chapter 12)

supermajority   A requirement that, in order to pass, a proposal must gain more than 50 percent plus one of the votes cast (an example of a supermajority is the requirement for a two-thirds vote). (Chapter 5)

supermax prison   Facility designed to manage the most dangerous offenders. The purpose of the prison is control via separate cells, twenty-three-hour lockdown, limited access to staff, and no access to other inmates; no treatment programming is available to inmates. (Chapter 9)

TABOR (Taxpayer Bill of Rights) law   Popular among antitax and antigovernment conservatives, laws that impose strict limits on tax increases on the state government, municipalities, and school districts. (Chapter 12)

tax and expenditure limits (TELs)   Statutory or constitutional provisions that limit the growth in state government spending or revenues relative to the state's population and economy. (Chapter 10)

tax base   The total economic value of all activities subject to taxation in a given jurisdiction. (Chapter 10)

term limits   Institutional arrangement within a legislature designed to limit the maximum number of terms an elected official can serve in a particular office. (Chapter 6)

Texas Top 10% Law (or Top Ten Percent plan)   Plan adopted by Texas that guarantees admission to any and every public university to any Texas student who finishes in the top 10 percent of his or her high school graduating class. (Chapter 13)

tort case   Civil dispute involving injury, negligence, or misconduct. (Chapter 8)

Toxics Release Inventory (TRI)   Data compiled annually by the U.S. Environmental Protection Agency on toxic chemical releases from particular industries and federal facilities. Intended to provide citizens with information about the environmental conditions in their community. (Chapter 15)

traditional membership group   Group made up of individuals promoting economic, social, or political concerns (or some combination thereof) such as senior citizens, environmentalists, schoolteachers, farmers, students, and antitax advocates. (Chapter 4)

traditionalist political culture   Subculture that is rooted in an ambivalent attitude toward the marketplace and the commonwealth and in which government's purpose is to maintain the existing social and economic hierarchy. (Chapter 1)

unitary   Hierarchical relation subordinating local units of government to a constitutionally supreme state or national government. (Chapter 2)

venue shop   The practice of political actors searching for the arena in which they have the best chance of success—that is, they try to pass a proposal directly rather than lobby one through the legislature, or vice versa, if that is where it is easier to get it passed. (Chapter 5)

vertical coalitions   Geographically dispersed organizations united in purpose and allied to influence state or national policy in an area of common interest. (Chapter 2)

veto   The ability of a governor to reject legislation presented by the legislature. In some states, the governor must accept or reject an entire piece of legislation; in others, governors have the ability to reject portions of a bill while accepting the rest. (Chapter 7)

welfare magnet   A state believed to be attractive to the poor because of its relatively generous social benefits. (Chapter 11)

Name Index

Footnotes are indicated with an n following the page number.

Subject Index

Boxes, figures, and tables are indicated with b, f, and t, respectively, following the page number.